COMPUTER VISION FOR VISUAL EFFECTS

Modern blockbuster movies seamlessly introduce impossible characters and action into real-world settings using digital visual effects. These effects are made possible by research from the field of computer vision, the study of how to automatically understand images. *Computer Vision for Visual Effects* will educate students, engineers, and researchers about the fundamental computer vision principles and state-of-the-art algorithms used to create cutting-edge visual effects for movies and television.

The author describes classical computer vision algorithms used on a regular basis in Hollywood (such as blue screen matting, structure from motion, optical flow, and feature tracking) and exciting recent developments that form the basis for future effects (such as natural image matting, multi-image compositing, image retargeting, and view synthesis). He also discusses the technologies behind motion capture and three-dimensional data acquisition. More than 200 original images demonstrating principles, algorithms, and results, along with in-depth interviews with Hollywood visual effects artists, tie the mathematical concepts to real-world filmmaking.

Richard J. Radke is an Associate Professor in the Department of Electrical, Computer, and Systems Engineering at Rensselaer Polytechnic Institute. His current research interests include computer vision problems related to modeling 3D environments with visual and range imagery, calibration and tracking problems in large camera networks, and machine learning problems for radiotherapy applications. Radke is affiliated with the NSF Engineering Research Center for Subsurface Sensing and Imaging Systems; the DHS Center of Excellence on Explosives Detection, Mitigation and Response (ALERT); and Rensselaer's Experimental Media and Performing Arts Center. He received an NSF CAREER award in March 2003 and was a member of the 2007 DARPA Computer Science Study Group. Dr. Radke is a senior member of the IEEE and an associate editor of *IEEE Transactions on Image Processing*.

Computer Vision for Visual Effects

RICHARD J. RADKE

Rensselaer Polytechnic Institute

CAMBRIDGE
UNIVERSITY PRESS

CAMBRIDGE
UNIVERSITY PRESS

Shaftesbury Road, Cambridge CB2 8EA, United Kingdom

One Liberty Plaza, 20th Floor, New York, NY 10006, USA

477 Williamstown Road, Port Melbourne, VIC 3207, Australia

314–321, 3rd Floor, Plot 3, Splendor Forum, Jasola District Centre, New Delhi – 110025, India

103 Penang Road, #05–06/07, Visioncrest Commercial, Singapore 238467

www.cambridge.org
Information on this title: www.cambridge.org/9780521766876

First published 2013 (version 2, May 2023)

Printed in Great Britain by CPI Group (UK) Ltd, Croydon CR0 4YY

A catalog record for this publication is available from the British Library.

Library of Congress Cataloging in Publication Data
Radke, Richard J., 1974–
    Computer vision for visual effects / Richard J. Radke.
       pages cm
    Includes bibliographical references and index.
    ISBN 978-0-521-76687-6
    1. Cinematography–Special effects–Data processing. 2. Computer vision. I. Title.
    TR858.R33 2013
    621.39′93–dc23   2012017763

ISBN 978-0-521-76687-6 Hardback

You're here because we want the best and you are it.
So, who is ready to make some science?

– Cave Johnson

Contents

1 Introduction

43 of the top 50 films of all time are visual effects driven. Today, visual effects are the "movie stars" of studio tent-pole pictures — that is, visual effects make contemporary movies box office hits in the same way that big name actors ensured the success of films in the past. It is very difficult to imagine a modern feature film or TV program without visual effects.

The Visual Effects Society, 2011

Neo fends off dozens of Agent Smith clones in a city park. Kevin Flynn confronts a thirty-years-younger avatar of himself in the Grid. Captain America's sidekick rolls under a speeding truck in the nick of time to plant a bomb. Nightcrawler "bamfs" in and out of rooms, leaving behind a puff of smoke. James Bond skydives at high speed out of a burning airplane. Harry Potter grapples with Nagini in a ramshackle cottage. Robert Neville stalks a deer in an overgrown, abandoned Times Square. Autobots and Decepticons battle it out in the streets of Chicago. Today's blockbuster movies so seamlessly introduce impossible characters and action into real-world settings that it's easy for the audience to suspend its disbelief. These compelling action scenes are made possible by modern visual effects.

Visual effects, the manipulation and fusion of live and synthetic images, have been a part of moviemaking since the first short films were made in the 1900s. For example, beginning in the 1920s, fantastic sets and environments were created using huge, detailed paintings on panes of glass placed between the camera and the actors. Miniature buildings or monsters were combined with footage of live actors using forced perspective to create photo-realistic composites. Superheroes flew across the screen using rear-projection and blue-screen replacement technology.

These days, almost all visual effects involve the manipulation of digital and computer-generated images instead of in-camera, practical effects. Filmgoers over the past forty years have experienced the transition from the mostly analog effects of movies like *The Empire Strikes Back* to the early days of computer-generated imagery in movies like *Terminator 2: Judgment Day* to the almost entirely digital effects of movies like *Avatar*. While they're often associated with action and science fiction movies, visual effects are now so common that they're imperceptibly incorporated into virtually all TV series and movies — even medical shows like *Grey's Anatomy* and period dramas like *Changeling*.

1

Like all forms of creative expression, visual effects have both an artistic side and a technological side. On the artistic side are visual effects artists: extremely talented (and often underappreciated) professionals who expertly manipulate software packages to create scenes that support a director's vision. They're attuned to the filmmaking aspects of a shot such as its composition, lighting, and mood. In the middle are the creators of the software packages: artistically minded engineers at companies like The Foundry, Autodesk, and Adobe who create tools like *Nuke*, *Maya*, and *After Effects* that the artists use every day. On the technological side are researchers, mostly in academia, who conceive, prototype, and publish new algorithms, some of which eventually get incorporated into the software packages. Many of these algorithms are from the field of computer vision, the main subject of this book.

Computer vision broadly involves the research and development of algorithms for automatically understanding images. For example, we may want to design an algorithm to automatically outline people in a photograph, a job that's easy for a human but that can be very difficult for a computer. In the past forty years, computer vision has made great advances. Today, consumer digital cameras can automatically identify whether all the people in an image are facing forward and smiling, and smartphone camera apps can read bar codes, translate images of street signs and menus, and identify tourist landmarks. Computer vision also plays a major role in image analysis problems in medical, surveillance, and defense applications. However, the application in which the average person most frequently comes into contact with the results of computer vision — whether he or she knows it or not — is the generation of visual effects in film and television production.

To understand the types of computer vision problems that are "under the hood" of the software packages that visual effects artists commonly use, let's consider a scene of a human actor fighting a computer-generated creature (for example, Rick O'Connell vs. Imhotep, Jack Sparrow vs. Davy Jones, or Kate Austen vs. The Smoke Monster). First, the hero actor is filmed on a partially built set interacting with a stunt performer who plays the role of the enemy. The built set must be digitally extended to a larger environment, with props and furniture added and removed after the fact. The computer-generated enemy's actions may be created with the help of the motion-captured performance of a second stunt performer in a separate location. Next, the on-set stunt performer is removed from the scene and replaced by the digital character. This process requires several steps: the background pixels behind the stunt performer need to be recreated, the camera's motion needs to be estimated so that the digital character appears in the right place, and parts of the real actor's body need to appropriately pass in front of and behind the digital character as they fight. Finally, the fight sequence may be artificially slowed down or sped up for dramatic effect. All of the elements in the final shot must seamlessly blend so they appear to "live" in the same frame, without any noticeable visual artifacts. This book describes many of the algorithms critical for each of these steps and the principles behind them.

1.1   COMPUTER VISION FOR VISUAL EFFECTS

This book, *Computer Vision for Visual Effects*, explores the technological side of visual effects, and has several goals:

- To mathematically describe a large set of computer vision principles and algorithms that underlie the tools used on a daily basis by visual effects artists.
- To collect and organize many exciting recent developments in computer vision research related to visual effects. Most of these algorithms have only appeared in academic conference and journal papers.
- To connect and contrast traditional computer vision research with the real-world terminology, practice, and constraints of modern visual effects.
- To provide a compact and unified reference for a university-level course on this material.

This book is aimed at early-career graduate students and advanced, motivated undergraduate students who have a background in electrical or computer engineering, computer science, or applied mathematics. Engineers and developers of visual effects software will also find the book useful as a reference on algorithms, an introduction to academic computer vision research, and a source of ideas for future tools and features. This book is meant to be a comprehensive resource for both the front-end artists and back-end researchers who share a common passion for visual effects.

This book goes into the details of many algorithms that form the basis of commercial visual effects software. For example, to create the fight scene we just described, we need to estimate the 3D location and orientation of a camera as it moves through a scene. This used to be a laborious process solved mostly through trial and error by an expert visual effects artist. However, such problems can now be solved quickly, almost automatically, using visual effects software tools like *boujou*, which build upon structure from motion algorithms developed over many years by the computer vision community.

On the other hand, this book also discusses many very recent algorithms that aren't yet commonplace in visual effects production. An algorithm may start out as a university graduate student's idea that takes months to conceive and prototype. If the algorithm is promising, its description and a few preliminary results are published in the proceedings of an academic conference. If the results gain the attention of a commercial software developer, the algorithm may eventually be incorporated into a new plug-in or menu option in a software package used regularly by an artist in a visual effects studio. The time it takes for the whole process — from initial basic research to common use in industry — can be long.

Part of the problem is that it's difficult for real-world practitioners to identify which academic research is useful. Thousands of new computer vision papers are published each year, and academic jargon often doesn't correspond to the vocabulary used to describe problems in the visual effects industry. This book ties these worlds together, "separating the wheat from the chaff" and clarifying the research keywords relevant to important visual effects problems. Our guiding approach is to describe the theoretical principles underlying a visual effects problem and the logical steps to its solution, independent of any particular software package.

This book discusses several more advanced, forward-looking algorithms that aren't currently feasible for movie-scale visual effects production. However, computers are constantly getting more powerful, enabling algorithms that were entirely impractical a few years ago to run at interactive rates on modern workstations.

Finally, while this book uses Hollywood movies as its motivation, not every visual effects practitioner is working on a blockbuster film with a looming release date and a rigid production pipeline. It's easier than ever for regular people to acquire and manipulate their own high-quality digital images and video. For example, an amateur filmmaker can now buy a simple green screen kit for a few hundred dollars, download free programs for image manipulation (e.g., GIMP or IrfanView) and numerical computation (e.g., Python or Octave), and use the algorithms described in this book to create compelling effects at home on a desktop computer.

1.2   THIS BOOK'S ORGANIZATION

Each chapter in this book covers a major topic in visual effects. In many cases, we can deal with a video sequence as a series of "flat" 2D images, without reference to the three-dimensional environment that produced them. However, some problems require a more precise knowledge of where the elements in an image are located in a 3D environment. The book begins with the topics for which 2D image processing is sufficient, and moves to topics that require 3D understanding.

We begin with the pervasive problem of **image matting** — that is, the separation of a foreground element from its background (Chapter 2). The background could be a blue or green screen, or it could be a real-world natural scene, which makes the problem much harder. A visual effects artist may semiautomatically extract the foreground from an image sequence using an algorithm for combining its color channels, or the artist may have to manually outline the foreground element frame by frame. In either case, we need to produce an **alpha matte** for the foreground element that indicates the amount of transparency in challenging regions containing wisps of hair or motion blur.

Next, we discuss many problems involving **image compositing and editing**, which refer to the manipulation of a single image or the combination of multiple images (Chapter 3). In almost every frame of a movie, elements from several different sources need to be merged seamlessly into the same final shot. Wires and rigging that support stunt performers must be removed without leaving perceptible artifacts. Removing a very large object may require the visual effects artist to create complex, realistic texture that was never observed by any camera, but that moves undetectably along with the real background. The aspect ratio or size of an image may also need to be changed for some shots (for example, to view a wide-aspect ratio film on an HDTV or mobile device).

We then turn our attention to the detection, description, and matching of **image features**, which visual effects artists use to associate the same point in different views of a scene (Chapter 4). These features are usually corners or blobs of different sizes. Our strategy for reliably finding and describing features depends on whether the images are closely separated in space and time (such as adjacent frames of video spaced a fraction of a second apart) or widely separated (such as "witness" cameras that observe a set from different perspectives). Visual effects artists on a movie set also commonly insert artificial markers into the environment that can be easily recognized in post-production.

We next describe the estimation of **dense correspondence** between a pair of images, and the applications of this correspondence (Chapter 5). In general, this problem is called **optical flow** and is used in visual effects for retiming shots and creating interesting image transitions. When two cameras simultaneously film the same scene from slightly different perspectives, such as for a live-action 3D movie, the correspondence problem is called **stereo**. Once the dense correspondence is estimated for a pair of images, it can be used for visual effects including video matching, image morphing, and view synthesis.

The second part of the book moves into three dimensions, a necessity for realistically merging computer-generated imagery with live-action plates. We describe the problem of camera tracking or **matchmoving**, the estimation of the location and orientation of a moving camera from the image sequence it produces (Chapter 6). We also discuss the problems of estimating the lens distortion of a camera, calibrating a camera with respect to known 3D geometry, and calibrating a stereo rig for 3D filming.

Next, we discuss the acquisition and processing of **motion capture** data, which is increasingly used in films and video games to help in the realistic animation of computer-generated characters (Chapter 7). We discuss technology for capturing full-body and facial motion capture data, as well as algorithms for cleaning up and post-processing the motion capture marker trajectories. We also overview more recent, purely vision-based techniques for markerless motion capture.

Finally, we overview the main methods for the direct acquisition of **three-dimensional data** (Chapter 8). Visual effects personnel routinely scan the 3D geometry of filming locations to be able to properly insert 3D computer-generated elements afterward, and also scan in actors' bodies and movie props to create convincing digital doubles. We describe laser range-finding technology such as LiDAR for large-scale 3D acquisition, structured-light techniques for closer-range scanning, and more recent multi-view stereo techniques. We also discuss key algorithms for dealing with 3D data, including feature detection, scan registration, and multi-scan fusion.

Of course, there are many exciting technologies behind the generation of computer-generated imagery for visual effects applications not discussed in this book. A short list of interesting topics includes the photorealistic generation of water, fire, fur, and cloth; the physically accurate (or visually convincing) simulation of how objects crumble or break; and the modeling, animation, and rendering of entirely computer-generated characters. However, these are all topics better characterized as **computer graphics** than computer vision, in the sense that computer vision always starts from real images or video of the natural world, while computer graphics can be created entirely without reference to real-world imagery.

Each chapter includes a short **Industry Perspectives** section containing interviews with experts from top Hollywood visual effects companies including Digital Domain, Rhythm & Hues, LOOK Effects, and Gentle Giant Studios. These sections relate the chapter topics to real-world practice, and illuminate which techniques are commonplace and which are rare in the visual effects industry. These interviews should make interesting reading for academic researchers who don't know much about filmmaking.

Each chapter also includes several homework problems. The goal of each problem is to verify understanding of a basic concept, to understand and apply a formula, or to fill in a derivation skipped in the main text. Most of these problems involve simple linear algebra and calculus as a means to exercise these important muscles in the service of a real computer vision scenario. Often, the derivations, or at least a start on them, are found in one of the papers referenced in the chapter. On the other hand, this book doesn't have any problems like "implement algorithm X," although it should be easy for an instructor to specify programming assignments based on the material in the main text. The emphasis here is on thoroughly understanding the underlying mathematics, from which writing good code should (hopefully) follow.

As a companion to the book, the website `cvfxbook.com` will be continually updated with links and commentary on new visual effects algorithms from academia and industry, examples from behind the scenes of television and films, and demo reels from visual effects artists and companies.

1.3 BACKGROUND AND PREREQUISITES

This book assumes the reader has a basic understanding of linear algebra, such as setting up a system of equations as a matrix-vector product and solving systems of overdetermined equations using linear least-squares. These key concepts occur repeatedly throughout the book. Less frequently, we refer to the eigenvalues and eigenvectors of a square matrix, the singular value decomposition, and matrix properties like positive definiteness. Strang's classic book [469] is an excellent linear algebra reference.

We also make extensive use of vector calculus, such as forming a Taylor series and taking the partial derivatives of a function with respect to a vector of parameters and setting them equal to zero to obtain an optimum. We occasionally mention continuous partial differential equations, most of the time en route to a specific discrete approximation. We also use basic concepts from probability and statistics such as mean, covariance, and Bayes' rule.

Finally, the reader should have working knowledge of standard image processing concepts such as viewing images as grids of pixels, computing image gradients, creating filters for edge detection, and finding the boundary of a binary set of pixels.

On the other hand, this book doesn't assume a lot of prior knowledge about computer vision. In fact, visual effects applications form a great backdrop for learning about computer vision for the first time. The book introduces computer vision concepts and algorithms naturally as needed. The appendixes include details on the implementation of several algorithms common to many visual effects problems, including dynamic programming, graph-cut optimization, belief propagation, and numerical optimization. Most of the time, the sketches of the algorithms should enable the reader to create a working prototype. However, not every nitty-gritty implementation detail is provided, so many references are given to the original research papers.

1.4 ACKNOWLEDGMENTS

I wrote most of this book during the 2010-11 academic year while on sabbatical from the Department of Electrical, Computer, and Systems Engineering at Rensselaer Polytechnic Institute. Thanks to Kim Boyer, David Rosowsky, and Robert Palazzo for their support. Thanks to my graduate students at the time — Eric Ameres, Siqi Chen, David Doria, Linda Rivera, and Ziyan Wu — for putting up with an out-of-the-office advisor for a year.

Many thanks to the visual effects artists and practitioners who generously shared their time and expertise with me during my trip to Los Angeles in June 2011. At LOOK Effects, Michael Capton, Christian Cardona, Jenny Foster, David Geoghegan, Buddy Gheen, Daniel Molina, and Gabriel Sanchez. At Rhythm & Hues, Shish Aikat, Peter Huang, and Marty Ryan. At Cinesite, Shankar Chatterjee. At Digital Domain, Nick Apostoloff, Thad Beier, Paul Lambert, Rich Marsh, Som Shankar, Blake Sloan, and Geoff Wedig. In particular, thanks to Doug Roble at Digital Domain for taking so much time to discuss his experiences and structure my visit. Special thanks to Pam Hogarth at LOOK Effects and Tim Enstice at Digital Domain for organizing my trip. Extra special thanks to Steve Chapman at Gentle Giant Studios for his hospitality during my visit, detailed comments on Chapter 8, and many behind-the-scenes images of 3D scanning.

This book contains many behind-the-scenes images from movies, which wouldn't have been possible without the cooperation and permission of several people. Thanks to Andy Bandit at Twentieth Century Fox, Eduardo Casals and Shirley Manusiwa at adidas International Marketing, Steve Chapman at Gentle Giant Studios, Erika Denton at Marvel Studios, Tim Enstice at Digital Domain, Alexandre Lafortune at Oblique FX, Roni Lubliner at NBC/Universal, Larry McCallister and Ashelyn Valdez at Paramount Pictures, Regan Pederson at Summit Entertainment, Don Shay at Cinefex, and Howard Schwartz at Muhammad Ali Enterprises. Thanks also to Laila Ali, Muhammad Ali, Russell Crowe, Jake Gyllenhaal, Tom Hiddleston, Ken Jeong, Darren Kendrick, Shia LaBeouf, Isabel Lucas, Michelle Monaghan, and Andy Serkis for approving the use of their likenesses.

At RPI, thanks to Jon Matthis for his time and assistance with my trip to the motion capture studio, and to Noah Schnapp for his character rig. Many thanks to the students in my fall 2011 class "Computer Vision for Visual Effects" for commenting on the manuscript, finding errors, and doing all of the homework problems: Nimit Dhulekar, David Doria, Tian Gao, Rana Hanocka, Camilo Jimenez Cruz, Daniel Kruse, Russell Lenahan, Yang Li, Harish Raviprakash, Jason Rock, Chandroutie Sankar, Evan Sullivan, and Ziyan Wu.

Thanks to Lauren Cowles, David Jou, and Joshua Penney at Cambridge University Press and Bindu Vinod at Newgen Publishing and Data Services for their support and assistance over the course of this book's conception and publication. Thanks to Alice Soloway for designing the book cover.

Special thanks to Aaron Hertzmann for many years of friendship and advice, detailed comments on the manuscript, and for kindling my interest in this area. Thanks also to Bristol-Myers Squibb for developing Excedrin, without which this book would not have been possible.

During the course of writing this book, I have enjoyed interactions with Sterling Archer, Pierre Chang, Phil Dunphy, Lester Freamon, Tony Harrison, Abed Nadir, Kim Pine, Amelia Pond, Tim Riggins, Ron Swanson, and Malcolm Tucker.

Thanks to my parents for instilling in me interests in both language and engineering (but also an unhealthy perfectionism). Above all, thanks to Sibel, my partner in science, for her constant support, patience, and love over the year and a half that this book took over my life and all the flat surfaces in our house. This book is dedicated to her.

RJR, March 2012

2 Image Matting

Separating a foreground element of an image from its background for later compositing into a new scene is one of the most basic and common tasks in visual effects production. This problem is typically called **matting** or **pulling a matte** when applied to film, or **keying** when applied to video.[1] At its humblest level, local news stations insert weather maps behind meteorologists who are in fact standing in front of a green screen. At its most difficult, an actor with curly or wispy hair filmed in a complex real-world environment may need to be digitally removed from every frame of a long sequence.

Image matting is probably the oldest visual effects problem in filmmaking, and the search for a reliable automatic matting system has been ongoing since the early 1900s [393]. In fact, the main goal of Lucasfilm's original Computer Division (part of which later spun off to become Pixar) was to create a general-purpose image processing computer that natively understood mattes and facilitated complex compositing [375]. A major research milestone was a family of effective techniques for matting against a blue background developed in the Hollywood effects industry throughout the 1960s and 1970s. Such techniques have matured to the point that blue- and green-screen matting is involved in almost every mass-market TV show or movie, even hospital shows and period dramas.

On the other hand, putting an actor in front of a green screen to achieve an effect isn't always practical or compelling, and situations abound in which the foreground must be separated from the background in a natural image. For example, movie credits are often inserted into real scenes so that actors and foreground objects seem to pass in front of them, a combination of image matting, compositing, and matchmoving. The computer vision and computer graphics communities have only recently proposed methods for semi-automatic matting with complex foregrounds and real-world backgrounds. This chapter focuses mainly on these kinds of algorithms for still-image matting, which are still not a major part of the commercial visual effects pipeline since effectively applying them to video is difficult. Unfortunately, video matting today requires a large amount of human intervention. Entire teams of rotoscoping artists at visual effects companies still require hours of tedious work to produce the high-quality mattes used in modern movies.

---

[1] The computer vision and graphics communities typically refer to the problem as matting, even though the input is always digital video.

We begin by introducing matting terminology and the basic mathematical problem (Section 2.1). We then give a brief introduction to the theory and practice of blue-screen, green-screen, and difference matting, all commonly used in the effects industry today (Section 2.2). The remaining sections introduce different approaches to the **natural image matting** problem where a special background isn't required. In particular, we discuss the major innovations of Bayesian matting (Section 2.3), closed-form matting (Section 2.4), Markov Random Fields for matting (Section 2.5), random-walk matting (Section 2.6), and Poisson matting (Section 2.7). While high-quality mattes need to have soft edges, we discuss how image segmentation algorithms that produce a hard edge can be "softened" to give a matte (Section 2.8). Finally, we discuss the key issue of matting for video sequences, a very difficult problem (Section 2.9).

2.1   MATTING TERMINOLOGY

Throughout this book, we assume that a color image I is represented by a 3D discrete array of pixels, where $I(x,y)$ is a 3-vector of (red, green, blue) values, usually in the range $[0,1]$. The matting problem is to separate a given color image I into a **foreground** image F and a **background** image B. Our fundamental assumption is that the three images are related by the **matting** (or **compositing**) **equation**:

$$I(x,y) = \alpha(x,y)F(x,y) + (1 - \alpha(x,y))B(x,y) \tag{2.1}$$

where $\alpha(x,y)$ is a number in $[0,1]$. That is, the color at (x,y) in I is a mix between the colors at the same position in F and B, where $\alpha(x,y)$ specifies the relative proportion of foreground versus background. If $\alpha(x,y)$ is close to 0, the pixel gets almost all of its color from the background, while if $\alpha(x,y)$ is close to 1, the pixel gets almost all of its color from the foreground. Figure 2.1 illustrates the idea. We frequently abbreviate Equation (2.1) to

$$I = \alpha F + (1 - \alpha)B \tag{2.2}$$

with the understanding that all the variables depend on the pixel location (x,y). Since α is a function of (x,y), we can think of it like a grayscale image, which is often called a **matte**, **alpha matte**, or **alpha channel**. Therefore, in the matting problem, we are given the image I and want to obtain the images F, B, and α.

At first, it may seem like $\alpha(x,y)$ should always be either 0 (that is, the pixel is entirely background) or 1 (that is, the pixel is entirely foreground). However, this isn't the case for real images, especially around the edges of foreground objects. The main reason is that the color of a pixel in a digital image comes from the total light intensity falling on a finite area of a sensor; that is, each pixel contains contributions from many real-world optical rays. In lower resolution images, it's likely that some scene elements project to regions smaller than a pixel on the image sensor. Therefore, the sensor area receives some light rays from the foreground object and some from the background. Even high resolution digital images (i.e., ones in which a pixel corresponds to a very small sensor area) contain fractional combinations of foreground and background in regions like wisps of hair. Fractional values of α are also generated by motion of the camera or foreground object, focal blur induced by the camera aperture, or transparency or translucency in parts of the foreground. Thus, every image, no matter how high resolution, has fractional alpha values.

Matting is closely related to a computer vision problem called **image segmentation**, but they are not the same. In segmentation, the goal is to separate an image into hard-edged pieces that snap together to reconstitute the whole, which is the same as creating a binary alpha matte for each object. On the other hand, for matting we expect that the foreground "piece" should have soft edges, so that pixels at the boundary contain a combination of foreground and background colors. As illustrated in Figure 2.2, clipping a hard-segmented object out of one image and placing it in another generally results in visual artifacts that would be unacceptable in a production environment, while a continuous-valued alpha matte produces a much better result. Nonetheless, we discuss a few hard segmentation algorithms in Section 2.8 and discuss how they can be upgraded to a continuous matte.

Unfortunately, the matting problem for a given image can't be uniquely solved, since there are many possible foreground/background explanations for the observed colors. We can see this from Equation (2.2) directly, since it represents three equations

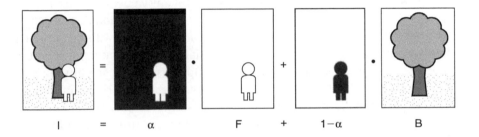

Figure 2.1. An illustration of the matting equation $I = \alpha F + (1 - \alpha)B$. When α is 0, the image pixel color comes from the background, and when α is 1, the image pixel color comes from the foreground.

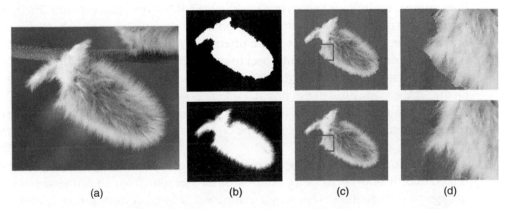

Figure 2.2. Image segmentation is not the same as image matting. (a) An original image, in which the foreground object has fuzzy boundaries. (b) (top) binary and (bottom) continuous alpha mattes for the foreground object. (c) Composites of the foreground onto a different background using the mattes. The hard-segmented result looks bad due to incorrect pixel mixing at the soft edges of the object, while using the continuous alpha matte results in an image with fewer visual artifacts. (d) Details of the composites in (c).

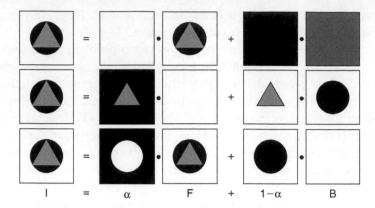

Figure 2.3. The matting problem can't be uniquely solved. The three (alpha, foreground, background) combinations at right are all mathematically consistent with the image at left. The bottom combination is most similar to what a human would consider a natural matte.

in seven unknowns at each pixel (the RGB values of F and B as well as the mixing proportion α). One result of this ambiguity is that for any values of I and a user-specified value of F, we can find values for B and α that satisfy Equation (2.2), as illustrated in Figure 2.3. Clearly, we need to supply a matting algorithm with additional assumptions or guides in order to recover mattes that agree with human perception about how a scene should be separated. For example, as we will see in the next section, the assumption that the background is known (e.g., it is a constant blue or green), removes some of the ambiguity. However, this chapter focuses on methods in which the background is complex and unknown and there is little external information other than a few guides specified by the user.

In modern matting algorithms, these additional guides frequently take one of two forms. The first is a **trimap**, defined as a coarse segmentation of the input image into regions that are definitely foreground ($\mathcal{F}$), definitely background ($\mathcal{B}$), or unknown ($\mathcal{U}$). This segmentation can be visualized as an image with white foreground, black background, and gray unknown regions (Figure 2.4b). An extreme example of a trimap is a **garbage matte**, a roughly drawn region that only specifies certain background $\mathcal{B}$ and assumes the rest of the pixels are unknown. An alternative is a set of **scribbles**, which can be quickly sketched by a user to specify pixels that are definitely foreground and definitely background (Figure 2.4c). Scribbles are generally easier for a user to create, since every pixel of the original image doesn't need to explicitly labeled. On the other hand, the matting algorithm must determine α for a much larger number of pixels. Both trimaps and scribbles can be created using a painting program like GIMP or Adobe Photoshop.

As mentioned earlier, matting usually precedes **compositing**, in which an estimated matte is used to place a foreground element from one image onto the background of another. That is, we estimate α, F, and B from image I, and want to place F on top of a new background image $\hat{B}$ to produce the composite $\hat{I}$. The corresponding compositing equation is:

$$\hat{I} = \alpha F + (1-\alpha)\hat{B} \qquad (2.3)$$

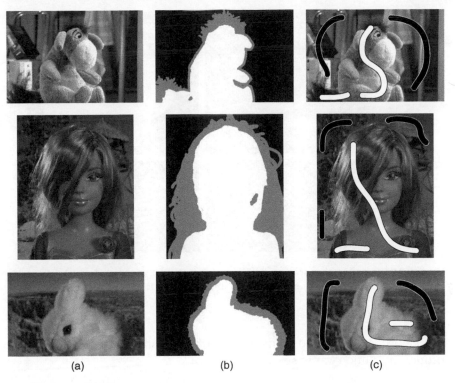

Figure 2.4. Several examples of natural images, user-drawn trimaps, and user-drawn scribbles. (a) The original images. (b) Trimaps, in which black pixels represent certain background, white pixels represent certain foreground, and gray pixels represent the unknown region for which fractional α values need to be estimated. (c) Scribbles, in which black scribbles denote background pixels, and white scribbles denote foreground regions. α must be estimated for the rest of the image pixels.

No matter what the new background image is, the foreground element F always appears in Equation (2.3) in the form αF. Therefore, the foreground image and estimated α matte are often stored together in the **pre-multiplied** form $(\alpha F_r, \alpha F_g, \alpha F_b, \alpha)$, to save multiplications in later compositing operations [373]. We'll talk more about the compositing process in the context of image editing in Chapter 3.

2.2 BLUE-SCREEN, GREEN-SCREEN, AND DIFFERENCE MATTING

The most important special case of matting is the placement of a blue or green screen behind the foreground to be extracted, which is known as **chromakey**. The shades of blue and green are selected to have little overlap with human skin tones, since in filmmaking the foreground usually contains actors. Knowing the background color also reduces the number of degrees of freedom in Equation (2.2), so we only have four unknowns to determine at each pixel instead of seven.

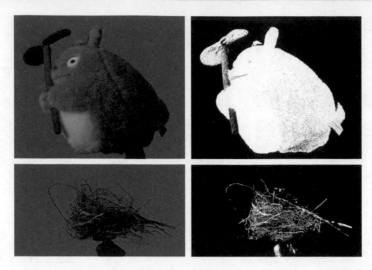

Figure 2.5. Blue-screen matting using Equation (2.4) with $a_1 = \frac{1}{2}$ and $a_2 = 1$. We can see several errors in the estimated mattes, including in the interiors of foreground objects and the boundaries of fine structures.

Vlahos [518] proposed many of the early heuristics for blue-screen matting; one proposed solution was to set

$$\alpha = 1 - a_1(I_b - a_2 I_g) \tag{2.4}$$

where I_b and I_g are the blue and green channels of the image normalized to the range $[0, 1]$, and a_1 and a_2 are user-specified tuning parameters. The resulting α values are clipped to $[0, 1]$. The general idea is that when a pixel has much more blue than green, α should be close to 0 (e.g., a pure blue pixel is very likely to be background but a pure white pixel isn't). However, this approach only works well for foreground pixels with certain colors and doesn't have a strong mathematical basis. For example, we can see in Figure 2.5 that applying Equation (2.4) results in a matte with several visual artifacts that would need to be cleaned up by hand.

In general, when the background is known, Equation (2.2) corresponds to three equations at each pixel (one for each color channel) in four unknowns (the foreground color F and the α value). If we had at least one more consistent equation, we could solve the equations for the unknowns exactly. Smith and Blinn [458] suggested several special cases that correspond to further constraints — for example, that the foreground is known to contain no blue or to be a shade of gray — and showed how these special cases resulted in formulae for α similar to Equation (2.4). However, the special cases are still fairly restrictive.

Blue-screen and green-screen matting are related to a common image processing technique called **background subtraction** or **change detection** [379]. In the visual effects world, the idea is called **difference matting** and is a common approach when a blue or green screen is not practical or available. We first take a picture of the empty background (sometimes known as a **clean plate**) B, perhaps before a scene is filmed. We then compare the clean plate to the composite image I given by Equation (2.2). It seems reasonable that pixels of I whose color differs substantially from B can be classified as parts of the foreground. Figure 2.6 shows an example in which pixels with $I - B$ greater than a threshold are labeled as foreground pixels with $\alpha = 1$. However,

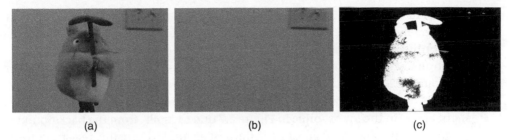

(a)   (b)   (c)

Figure 2.6. Difference matting. The difference between the image with foreground (a) and clean plate (b) can be thresholded to get a hard segmentation (c). Even prior to further estimation of fractional α values, the rough matte has many tiny errors in places where the foreground and background have similar colors.

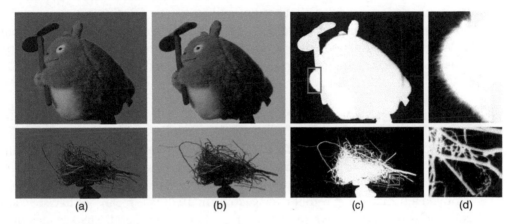

(a)   (b)   (c)   (d)

Figure 2.7. (a),(b) Static objects are photographed in front of two backgrounds that differ in color at every pixel (here, two solid-color backgrounds). (c) Triangulation produces a high-quality matte. (d) Detail of matte.

since there are still three equations in four unknowns, the matte and foreground image can't be determined unambiguously. In particular, since the clean plate may contain colors similar to the foreground, mattes created in this way are likely to contain more errors than mattes created using blue or green screens.

Smith and Blinn observed that if the foreground F was photographed in front of two different backgrounds B_1 and B_2, producing images I_1 and I_2, we would have six equations in four unknowns:

$$I_1 = \alpha F + (1 - \alpha)B_1$$
$$I_2 = \alpha F + (1 - \alpha)B_2$$

$$(2.5)$$

As long as $B_1 \neq B_2$, we can solve Equation (2.5) for α as

$$\alpha = 1 - \frac{(I_1 - I_2) \cdot (B_1 - B_2)}{(B_1 - B_2) \cdot (B_1 - B_2)}$$

$$(2.6)$$

Then F can be recovered from the matting equation or by solving the overdetermined system in Equation (2.5). Smith and Blinn called this approach **triangulation**, and it can be used for generating high-quality ground-truth mattes, as illustrated in Figure 2.7. However, triangulation is difficult to use in practice since four separate, precisely aligned images must be obtained (i.e., B_1, I_1, B_2, and I_2). It can be difficult to obtain exact knowledge of each background image, to ensure that these don't change, and to ensure that F is exactly the same (both in terms of intensity and position) in front of both backgrounds. Therefore, triangulation is typically limited to extremely controlled circumstances (for example, a static object in a lab setting). If Equation (2.5) does not hold exactly due to differences in F and α between backgrounds or incorrect values of B, the results will be poor. For example, we can see slight errors in the toy example in Figure 2.7 due to "spill" from the background onto the foreground, and slight ghosting in the nest example due to tiny registration errors.

Blue-screen, green-screen, and difference matting are pervasive in film and TV production. A huge part of creating a compelling visual effects shot is the creation of a matte for each element, which is often a manual process that involves heuristic combinations and manipulations of color channels, as described in Section 2.11. These heuristics vary from shot to shot and even vary for different regions of the same element. For more discussion on these issues, a good place to start is the book by Wright [553]. The book by Foster [151] gives a thorough discussion of practical considerations for setting up a green-screen environment.

2.3   BAYESIAN MATTING

In the rest of this chapter, we'll focus on methods where only one image is obtained and no knowledge of the clean plate is assumed. This problem is called **natural image matting**. The earliest natural image matting algorithms assumed that the user supplied a trimap along with the image to be matted. This means we have two large collections of pixels known to be background and foreground. The key idea of the algorithms in this section is to build probability density functions (pdfs) from these labeled sets, which are used to estimate the α, F, and B values of the set of unknown pixels in the region $\mathcal{U}$.

2.3.1   The Basic Idea

Chuang et al. [99] were the first to pose the matting problem in a probabilistic framework called **Bayesian matting**. At each pixel, we want to find the foreground color, background color, and alpha value that maximize the probability of observing the given image color. That is, we compute

$$\arg\max_{F,B,\alpha} \ P(F,B,\alpha|I) \tag{2.7}$$

We'll show how to solve this problem using a simple iterative method that results from making some assumptions about the form of this probability. First, by Bayes' rule, Equation (2.7) is equal to

$$\arg\max_{F,B,\alpha} \ \frac{1}{P(I)}P(I|F,B,\alpha)P(F,B,\alpha) \tag{2.8}$$

We can disregard $P(I)$ since it doesn't depend on the parameters to be estimated, and we can assume that F, B, and α are independent of each other. This reduces Equation (2.8) to:

$$\arg\max_{F,B,\alpha} \ P(I|F,B,\alpha)P(F)P(B)P(\alpha) \tag{2.9}$$

Taking the log gives an expression in terms of log likelihoods:

$$\arg\max_{F,B,\alpha} \ \log P(I|F,B,\alpha) + \log P(F) + \log P(B) + \log P(\alpha) \qquad (2.10)$$

The first term in Equation (2.10) is a **data term** that reflects how likely the image color is given values for F, B, and α. Since for a good solution the matting equation (2.2) should hold, the first term can be modeled as:

$$P(I|F,B,\alpha) \propto \exp\left(-\frac{1}{\sigma_d^2}\|I - (\alpha F + (1-\alpha)B)\|_2^2\right) \qquad (2.11)$$

where σ_d is a tunable parameter that reflects the expected deviation from the matting assumption. Thus,

$$\log P(I|F,B,\alpha) = -\frac{1}{\sigma_d^2}\|I - (\alpha F + (1-\alpha)B)\|_2^2 \qquad (2.12)$$

The other terms in Equation (2.10) are **prior probabilities** on the foreground, background, and α distributions. This is where the trimap comes in. Figure 2.8 illustrates an example of a user-created trimap and scatterplots of pixel colors in RGB space corresponding to the background and foreground. In this example, since the background colors are very similar to each other and the foreground mostly contains shades of gray, we can fit Gaussian distributions to each collection of intensities.

That is, for a color B, we estimate a pdf for the background given by:

$$f_{\mathcal{B}}(B) = \frac{1}{(2\pi)^{3/2}|\Sigma_B|^{1/2}} \exp\left(-\frac{1}{2}(B-\mu_B)^\top \Sigma_B^{-1}(B-\mu_B)\right) \qquad (2.13)$$

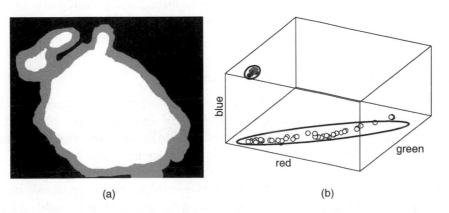

(a)   (b)

Figure 2.8. (a) A user-created trimap corresponding to the upper left image in Figure 2.5, and (b) a scatterplot of the colors in the labeled foreground and background regions. Black dots represent background and white dots represent foreground. Since the image was taken against a blue screen, the background colors are tightly clustered in one corner of RGB space. Both the foreground and background color distributions are well approximated by Gaussians (ellipses).

The mean μ_B and covariance matrix Σ_B can can computed from the collection of N_B background sample locations $\{B_i\}$ in $\mathcal{B}$ using:

$$\mu_B = \frac{1}{N_B} \sum_{i=1}^{N_B} I(B_i)$$

$$\Sigma_B = \frac{1}{N_B} \sum_{i=1}^{N_B} (I(B_i) - \mu_B)(I(B_i) - \mu_B)^\top \tag{2.14}$$

We can do the same thing for the foreground pixels in the trimap. Therefore, we can obtain estimates for the prior distributions in Equation (2.10) as:

$$\log P(B) \approx -(B - \mu_B)^\top \Sigma_B^{-1} (B - \mu_B)$$

$$\log P(F) \approx -(F - \mu_F)^\top \Sigma_F^{-1} (F - \mu_F) \tag{2.15}$$

where we've omitted constants that don't affect the optimization. For the moment, let's also assume $P(\alpha)$ is constant (we'll relax this assumption shortly). Then substituting Equation (2.12) and Equation (2.15) into Equation (2.10) and setting the derivatives with respect to F, B, and α equal to zero, we obtain the following simultaneous equations:

$$\begin{bmatrix} \Sigma_F^{-1} + \alpha^2/\sigma_d^2 \, \mathbf{I}_{3\times3} & \alpha(1-\alpha)/\sigma_d^2 \, \mathbf{I}_{3\times3} \\ \alpha(1-\alpha)/\sigma_d^2 \, \mathbf{I}_{3\times3} & \Sigma_B^{-1} + (1-\alpha)^2/\sigma_d^2 \, \mathbf{I}_{3\times3} \end{bmatrix} \begin{bmatrix} F \\ B \end{bmatrix}$$

$$= \begin{bmatrix} \Sigma_F^{-1} \mu_F + \alpha/\sigma_d^2 \, I \\ \Sigma_B^{-1} \mu_B + (1-\alpha)/\sigma_d^2 \, I \end{bmatrix} \tag{2.16}$$

$$\alpha = \frac{(I - B) \cdot (F - B)}{(F - B) \cdot (F - B)} \tag{2.17}$$

Equation (2.16) is a 6×6 linear system for determining the optimal F and B for a given α; $\mathbf{I}_{3\times3}$ denotes the 3×3 identity matrix. Equation (2.17) is a direct solution for the optimal α given F and B. This suggests a simple strategy for solving the Bayesian matting problem. First, we make a guess for α at each pixel (for example, using the input trimap). Then, we alternate between solving Equation (2.16) and Equation (2.17) until the estimates for F, B, and α converge.

2.3.2   Refinements and Extensions

In typical natural image matting problems, it's difficult to accurately model the foreground and background distributions with a simple pdf. Furthermore, these distributions may have significant local variation in different regions of the image. For example, Figure 2.9a illustrates the sample foreground and background distributions for a natural image. We can see that the color distributions are complex, so using a simple function (such as a single Gaussian distribution) to create pdfs for the foreground and background is a poor model. Instead, we can fit multiple Gaussians to each sample distribution to get a better representation. These Gaussian Mixture Models (GMMs) can be learned using the Expectation-Maximization (EM) algorithm [45] or using vector quantization [356]. Figure 2.9b shows an example of multiple Gaussians fit to the same sample distributions as in Figure 2.9a. The overlap between

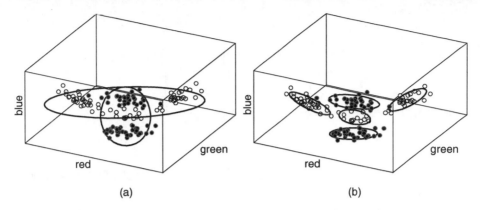

(a)   (b)

Figure 2.9. (a) A tougher example of a scatterplot of the colors in labeled foreground and background regions. Black dots represent background and white dots represent foreground. In this case, the foreground and background densities are neither well separated nor well represented by a single Gaussian. (b) Gaussian mixture models fit to the foreground and background samples do a better job of separating the distributions.

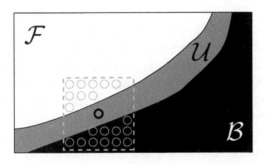

Figure 2.10. The local foreground and background samples in a window around each pixel can be used to compute the distributions for Bayesian matting.

distributions remains, but the Gaussian mixture components are better separated and model the data more tightly.

In the multiple-Gaussian case, solving Equation (2.10) directly is no longer straightforward, but Chuang et al. [99] suggested a simple approach. We consider each possible pair of (foreground, background) Gaussians independently, and solve for the best F, B, and α by alternating Equations (2.16)–(2.17). Then we compute the log likelihood given by the argument of Equation (2.10) for each result. We need to include the determinants of Σ_F and Σ_B when evaluating $\log P(F)$ and $\log P(B)$ for each pair, since they are not all the same — these factors were ignored in Equation (2.15). Finally, we choose the estimates for F, B, and α that produce the largest value of Equation (2.10).

For complicated foregrounds and backgrounds, it makes sense to determine the foreground and background distributions in Equation (2.15) locally at a pixel, rather than globally across the whole image. This can be accomplished by creating a small (relative to the image size) window around the pixel of interest and using the colors of $\mathcal{F}$ and $\mathcal{B}$ inside the window to build the local pdfs (Figure 2.10). As F, B, and α for pixels inside both the window and the unknown region are estimated, they can supplement the samples. Generally, the estimation begins at the edges of the unknown area and

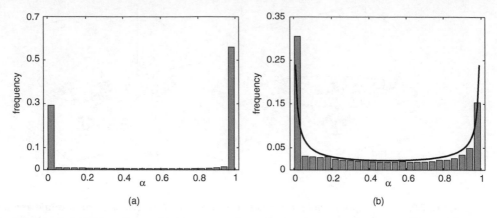

Figure 2.11. (a) The normalized histogram of α values for the ground-truth matte for the middle example in Figure 2.4. (b) The normalized histogram of α values just over the trimap's unknown region, superimposed by a beta distribution with $\eta = \tau = \frac{1}{4}$.

proceeds toward its center. We'll say more about the issue of local pixel sampling in Section 2.6.1.

While the original Bayesian matting algorithm treated the prior term $P(\alpha)$ as a constant, later researchers observed that $P(\alpha)$ is definitely not a uniform distribution. This stands to reason, since there are a relatively large number of pixels that are conclusively foreground ($\alpha = 1$) or background ($\alpha = 0$) compared to mixed pixels, which typically occur along object boundaries. Figure 2.11 illustrates the distributions of α for a real image; the left panel shows that over the whole image the distribution is highly nonuniform, and the right panel shows that even over the trimap's uncertain region, the distribution is biased toward α values close to 0 and 1. Wexler et al. [544] and Apostoloff and Fitzgibbon [16] suggested modeling this behavior with a beta distribution of the form

$$P(\alpha) = \frac{\Gamma(\eta + \tau)}{\Gamma(\eta)\Gamma(\tau)} \alpha^{\eta-1}(1-\alpha)^{\tau-1} \tag{2.18}$$

A sketch of a beta distribution with $\eta = \tau = \frac{1}{4}$ is superimposed on Figure 2.11b to give a sense of the fit. Unfortunately, incorporating a more complex prior for α makes Equation (2.10) harder to solve.

It's also important to remember that the pixels in the α image are highly correlated, so we should be able to do a much better job by enforcing that the α values of adjacent pixels be similar (the same type of correlation holds, though more weakly, for the background and foreground images). We will discuss algorithms that exploit this coherence in the rest of this chapter.

2.4   CLOSED-FORM MATTING

In Bayesian Matting, we assumed that the foreground and background distributions were Gaussians (i.e., that the samples formed ellipsoidal clusters in color space). However, it turns out that in many natural images, the foreground and background distributions look more like lines or skinny cigar shapes [355]. In fact, this is visible in Figures 2.8 and 2.9 — the fitted Gaussians are generally long and skinny. Levin et al. [271] exploited this observation in an elegant algorithm called **closed-form matting**.

2.4.1   The Color Line Assumption

Let's assume that within a small window w_j around each pixel j, the sets of foreground and background intensities each lie on a straight line in RGB space. That is, for each pixel i in w_j,

$$F_i = \beta_i F_1 + (1 - \beta_i) F_2$$
$$B_i = \gamma_i B_1 + (1 - \gamma_i) B_2 \tag{2.19}$$

Here, F_1 and F_2 are two points on the line of foreground colors, and β_i represents the fraction of the way a given foreground color F_i is between these two points. The same idea applies to the background colors. This idea, called the **color line assumption**, is illustrated in Figure 2.12.

Levin et al.'s first observation was that under the color line assumption, the α value for every pixel in the window was simply related to the intensity by

$$\alpha_i = a^\top I_i + b \tag{2.20}$$

where a is a 3×1 vector, b is a scalar, and the same a and b apply to every pixel in the window. That is, we can compute α for each pixel in the window as a linear combination of the RGB values at that pixel, plus an offset. While this may not be intuitive, let's show why Equation (2.20) is algebraically true.

First we plug Equation (2.19) into the matting equation (2.2) to obtain:

$$I_i = \alpha_i(\beta_i F_1 + (1 - \beta_i)F_2) + (1 - \alpha_i)(\gamma_i B_1 + (1 - \gamma_i)B_2) \tag{2.21}$$

If we rearrange the terms in this equation, we get a 3×3 system of linear equations:

$$[F_2 - B_2 \quad F_1 - F_2 \quad B_1 - B_2]\begin{bmatrix} \alpha_i \\ \alpha_i \beta_i \\ (1 - \alpha_i)\gamma_i \end{bmatrix} = I_i - B_2 \tag{2.22}$$

Note that the 3×3 matrix on the left-hand side only depends on F_1, F_2, B_1, and B_2, which we assumed were constant in the window. We multiply by the inverse of this

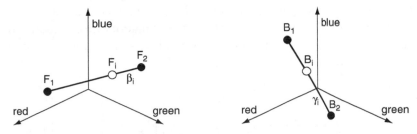

Figure 2.12. The color line assumption says that each pixel I_i in a small window of the image is a mix of a foreground color F_i and a background color B_i, where each of these colors lies on a straight line in RGB space.

matrix on both sides, and denote the rows of this inverse by r's:

$$
\begin{bmatrix} \alpha_i \\ \alpha_i \beta_i \\ (1-\alpha_i)\gamma_i \end{bmatrix} = [F_2 - B_2 \quad F_1 - F_2 \quad B_1 - B_2]^{-1}(I_i - B_2)
$$

$$
= \begin{bmatrix} r_1^\top \\ r_2^\top \\ r_3^\top \end{bmatrix}(I_i - B_2)
$$

(2.23)

Taking just the first element of the vector on both sides, we see that

$$
\alpha_i = r_1^\top I_i - r_1^\top B_2
$$

(2.24)

which corresponds to Equation (2.20) with $a = r_1$ and $b = -r_1^\top B_2$.

2.4.2   The Matting Laplacian

The assumption that the α values and colors inside a window are related by Equation (2.20) leads to a natural cost function for the matting problem:

$$
J(\{\alpha_i, a_i, b_i, i=1,\dots,N\}) = \sum_{j=1}^{N} \sum_{i \in w_j} (\alpha_i - (a_j^\top I_i + b_j))^2
$$

(2.25)

This cost function expresses the total error of the linearity assumption in Equation (2.20) over each window. We want to minimize J to find α_i at each pixel as well as the coefficients a_i and b_i for every window w_i around pixel i. For brevity, we'll write the left-hand side as $J(\alpha, \mathbf{a}, \mathbf{b})$, where α is an $N \times 1$ vector that collects all the α values in the image, and $\mathbf{a}$ and $\mathbf{b}$ represent the collections of affine coefficients for each window. Since the windows between adjacent pixels overlap, the α estimates at each pixel are not independent. We also add a **regularization term** to Equation (2.25):

$$
J(\alpha, \mathbf{a}, \mathbf{b}) = \sum_{j=1}^{N} \left(\sum_{i \in w_j} (\alpha_i - (a_j^\top I_i + b_j))^2 \right) + \varepsilon \|a_j\|_2^2
$$

(2.26)

This term acts to bias the mattes toward being constant, since if $a = 0$, $\alpha_i = b_i$ within the whole window w_i. Usually ε is chosen to be on the order of 10^{-7} if each color channel is in the range $[0, 1]$.

On first glance, this formulation doesn't seem to help us solve the matting problem, since we still have many more equations than unknowns (i.e., the five values of α, a, and b at each pixel). However, by a clever manipulation, we can reduce the number of unknowns to exactly the number of pixels. First, we rearrange Equation (2.26) as a matrix equation:

$$
J(\alpha, \mathbf{a}, \mathbf{b}) = \sum_{j=1}^{N} \left\| \begin{bmatrix} I_1^{j\top} & 1 \\ \vdots & \vdots \\ I_W^{j\top} & 1 \\ \sqrt{\varepsilon}\mathbf{I}_{3\times 3} & 0 \end{bmatrix} \begin{bmatrix} a_j \\ b_j \end{bmatrix} - \begin{bmatrix} \alpha_1^j \\ \vdots \\ \alpha_W^j \\ \mathbf{0}_{3\times 1} \end{bmatrix} \right\|^2
$$

(2.27)

where W is the number of pixels in the window and $\{I_1^j, \ldots, I_W^j\}$ and $\{\alpha_1^j, \ldots, \alpha_W^j\}$ represent the ordered list of image colors and α values inside window j. More compactly, we can write Equation (2.27) as

$$J(\boldsymbol{\alpha}, \mathbf{a}, \mathbf{b}) = \sum_{j=1}^{N} \left\| G_j \begin{bmatrix} a_j \\ b_j \end{bmatrix} - \bar{\alpha}_j \right\|^2 \tag{2.28}$$

where $\bar{\alpha}_j$ is a $(W+3) \times 1$ vector containing the α's in window j followed by three 0's. If we suppose that the matte is known, then this vector is constant and we can minimize Equation (2.27) for the individual $\{a_j, b_j\}$ as a standard linear system:

$$\begin{bmatrix} a_j^* \\ b_j^* \end{bmatrix} = (G_j^\top G_j)^{-1} G_j^\top \bar{\alpha}_j \tag{2.29}$$

That is, the optimal a and b in each window for a given matte α are linear functions of the α values. This means we can substitute Equation (2.29) into Equation (2.26) to get

$$J(\boldsymbol{\alpha}) = \min_{\mathbf{a}, \mathbf{b}} J(\boldsymbol{\alpha}, \mathbf{a}, \mathbf{b}) \tag{2.30}$$

$$= \min_{\mathbf{a}, \mathbf{b}} \sum_{j=1}^{N} \left\| G_j \begin{bmatrix} a_j \\ b_j \end{bmatrix} - \bar{\alpha}_j \right\|^2 \tag{2.31}$$

$$= \sum_{j=1}^{N} \left\| G_j \begin{bmatrix} a_j^* \\ b_j^* \end{bmatrix} - \bar{\alpha}_j \right\|^2 \tag{2.32}$$

$$= \sum_{j=1}^{N} \left\| G_j (G_j^\top G_j)^{-1} G_j^\top \bar{\alpha}_j - \bar{\alpha}_j \right\|^2 \tag{2.33}$$

$$= \sum_{j=1}^{N} \bar{\alpha}_j^\top \left[\mathbf{I}_{(W+3) \times (W+3)} - G_j (G_j^\top G_j)^{-1} G_j^\top \right] \bar{\alpha}_j \tag{2.34}$$

$$= \boldsymbol{\alpha}^\top L \boldsymbol{\alpha} \tag{2.35}$$

In the last equation, we've collected all of the equations for the windows into a single matrix equation for the $N \times 1$ vector $\boldsymbol{\alpha}$. The $N \times N$ matrix L is called the **matting Laplacian**. It is symmetric, positive semidefinite, and quite sparse if the window size is small. This matrix plays a key role in the rest of the chapter.

Working out the algebra in Equation (2.34), one can compute the elements of the matting Laplacian as:

$$L(i,j) = \sum_{k|(i,j) \in w_k} \left[\delta_{ij} - \frac{1}{W} \left(1 + (I_i - \mu_k)^\top \left(\Sigma_k + \frac{\varepsilon}{W} \mathbf{I}_{3 \times 3} \right)^{-1} (I_j - \mu_k) \right) \right] \tag{2.36}$$

where μ_k and Σ_k are the mean and covariance matrix of the colors in window k and δ_{ij} is the Kronecker delta. Frequently, the windows are taken to be 3×3, so $W = 9$. The notation $k|(i,j) \in w_k$ in Equation (2.36) means that we only sum over the windows k that contain both pixels i and j; depending on the configuration of the pixels, there could be from 0 to 6 windows in the sum (see Problem 2.11).

Alternately, we can write

$$L(i,j) = \begin{cases} \sum_k A(i,k) & \text{if } i = j \\ -A(i,j) & \text{if } i \neq j \end{cases} \tag{2.37}$$

where

$$A(i,j) = \sum_{k|(i,j) \in w_k} \frac{1}{W}\left[1 + (I_i - \mu_k)^\top \left(\Sigma_k + \frac{\varepsilon}{W}\mathbf{I}_{3\times3}\right)^{-1}(I_j - \mu_k)\right] \tag{2.38}$$

The matrix A specified by Equation (2.38) is sometimes called the **matting affinity**.

From Equation (2.35) we can see that minimizing $J(\alpha)$ corresponds to solving the linear system $L\alpha = 0$. That is, we must simply find a vector in the nullspace of L.

2.4.3   Constraining the Matte

However, so far we haven't taken into account any user-supplied knowledge of where the matte values are known; without this knowledge, the solution is ambiguous; for example, it turns out that any constant α matte is in the nullspace of L. In fact, the dimension of the nullspace is large (e.g., each of the matrices in the sum of Equation (2.34) has nullspace of dimension four [454]). Therefore, we rely on user scribbles to denote known foreground and background pixels and constrain the solution. That is, the problem becomes:

$$\begin{aligned}\min \quad & \alpha^\top L\alpha \\ s.t. \quad & \alpha_i = 1 \quad i \in \mathcal{F} \\ & \alpha_i = 0 \quad i \in \mathcal{B}\end{aligned} \tag{2.39}$$

Another way to phrase this is:

$$\min \alpha^\top L\alpha + \lambda(\alpha - \alpha_K)^\top D(\alpha - \alpha_K) \tag{2.40}$$

where α_K is an $N \times 1$ vector equal to 1 at known foreground pixels and 0 everywhere else, and D is a diagonal matrix whose diagonal elements are equal to 1 when a user has specified a $\mathcal{F}$ or $\mathcal{B}$ scribble at that pixel and 0 elsewhere. λ is set to be a very large number (e.g., 100) so that the solution is forced to agree closely with the user's scribbles. Setting the derivative of Equation (2.40) to 0 results in the sparse linear system:

$$(L + \lambda D)\alpha = \lambda\alpha_K \tag{2.41}$$

Levin et al. showed that if:

- the color line model was satisfied exactly in every pixel window,
- the image was formed by exactly applying the matting equation to some foreground and background images,
- the user scribbles were consistent with the ground-truth matte, and
- $\varepsilon = 0$ in Equation (2.26),

then the ground-truth matte will solve Equation (2.41). However, it's important to realize that the user might need to experiment with scribble quantity and placement to ensure that the solution of Equation (2.41) is acceptable, since the nullspace of the left-hand side may be non-trivial (see more in Section 2.4.5). Figure 2.13 illustrates an example of using closed-form matting using only a few scribbles on a natural image.

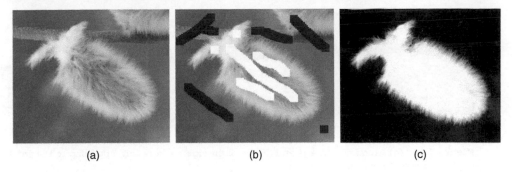

(a)   (b)   (c)

Figure 2.13. (a) An image with (b) foreground and background scribbles. (c) The α matte computed using closed-form matting, showing that good estimates are produced in fine detail regions.

Choosing the right window size for closed-form matting can be a tricky problem depending on the resolution of the image and the fuzziness of the foreground object (which may not be the same in all parts of the image). He et al. [192] considered this issue, and showed how the linear system in Equation (2.41) could be efficiently solved by using relatively large windows whose sizes depend on the local width of the uncertain region $\mathcal{U}$ in the trimap. The advantage of using large windows is that many distant pixels are related to each other, and the iterative methods typically used to solve large systems like Equation (2.41) converge more quickly.

2.4.4   Recovering F and B from α

After solving the linear system in Equation (2.41) we obtain α values but not estimates of F and B. One way to get these estimates is to treat α and I as constant in the matting equation and solve it for F and B. Since this problem is still underconstrained, Levin et al. suggested incorporating the expectation that F and B vary smoothly (i.e., have small derivatives), especially in places where the matte has edges. The corresponding problem is:

$$\min_{F_i,B_i} \sum_{i=1}^{N} \|I_i - (\alpha_i F_i + (1-\alpha_i)B_i)\|^2$$

$$+ |\nabla_x \alpha_i| \left(\|\nabla_x F_i\|^2 + \|\nabla_x B_i\|^2 \right) + |\nabla_y \alpha_i| \left(\|\nabla_y F_i\|^2 + \|\nabla_y B_i\|^2 \right)$$

$$(2.42)$$

where the notation $\nabla_x I$ represents the gradient of image I in the x direction, which is a scalar for a grayscale image and a 3-vector for a color image. Solving Equation (2.42) results in a sparse linear system instead of a problem solved independently at every pixel, since the gradients force interdependence between the pixels (see Problem 2.18).

2.4.5   The Matting Laplacian's Eigenvectors

Levin et al. observed that even before the user imposes any scribbles on the image to be matted, the eigenvectors of the matting Laplacian corresponding to the smallest eigenvalues reveal a surprising amount of information about potentially good mattes. For example, Figure 2.14 illustrates the eight eigenvectors corresponding to the

(a)   (b)

Figure 2.14. (a) An original image and (b) the eight eigenvectors corresponding to the smallest eigenvalues of its matting Laplacian.

smallest eigenvalues of an input image. We can see that these eigenvector images tend to be locally constant in large regions of the image and seem to follow the contours of the foreground object. Any single eigenvector is generally unsuitable as a matte, because mattes should be mostly binary (i.e., solid white in the foreground and solid black in the background). On the other hand, since any linear combination of null vectors is also a null vector, we can try to find combinations that are as binary as possible in the hopes of creating "pieces" useful for matting.

Levin et al. [272] subsequently proposed an algorithm based on this natural idea called **spectral matting**. We begin by computing the matting Laplacian L and its eigenvectors $E = [e_1, ..., e_K]$ corresponding to the K smallest eigenvalues (since the matrix is positive semidefinite, none of the eigenvalues are negative). Each e_i thus roughly satisfies $e_i^\top L e_i = 0$ and thus roughly minimizes Equation (2.30), despite being a poor matte. We then try to find K linear combinations of these eigenvectors called **matting components** that are as binary as possible by solving the constrained optimization problem

$$\min_{y^k \in \mathbb{R}^K, k=1,...,K} \sum_{k=1}^{K} \sum_{i=1}^{N} |\alpha_i^k|^\rho + |1 - \alpha_i^k|^\rho \tag{2.43}$$

$$s.t. \qquad \alpha^k = Ey^k \tag{2.44}$$

$$\sum_{k=1}^{K} \alpha_i^k = 1, \quad i = 1, ..., N \tag{2.45}$$

That is, Equation (2.44) says that each matting component must be a linear combination of the eigenvectors, while Equation (2.45) says that the matting components must sum to 1 at each pixel. Figure 2.15 illustrates the score function in Equation (2.43) with $\rho = 0.9$; we can see that it's lowest when α is either 0 or 1.

The result of applying this process to the eigenvectors in Figure 2.14 is illustrated in Figure 2.16a. At this point, the user can simply view a set of matting components and select the ones that combine to create the desired foreground (this step takes the place of the conventional trimap or scribbles). For example, selecting the highlighted components in Figure 2.16a results in the good initial matte in Figure 2.16b. User scribbles can be used to further refine the matte by forcing certain components to contribute to the foreground or the background.

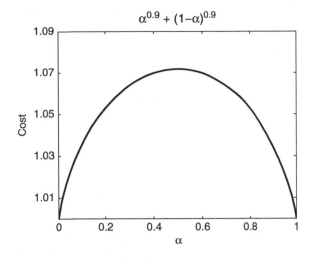

$$\alpha^{0.9} + (1-\alpha)^{0.9}$$

Figure 2.15. The cost function in Equation (2.43) as a function of α, with $\rho = 0.9$.

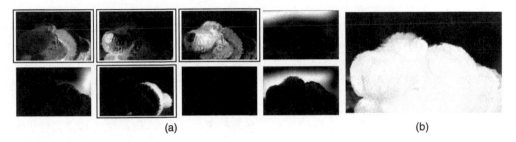

(a)   (b)

Figure 2.16. (a) The eight nearly binary matting components computed using spectral matting for the image in Figure 2.14a. (b) The four selected matting components are summed to give an estimate of the full matte.

2.4.6   Learning-Based Matting

Zheng and Kambhamettu [579] described a generalization to the color line model described previously that enables what they called **learning-based matting**. Suppose we revisit the assumption about how the α values and image colors are related in a window, that is, that

$$\alpha_i = a^\top I_i + b \tag{2.46}$$

In closed-form matting, we eliminated a and b from the estimation problem entirely; that is, we never directly estimated or recovered these values. On the other hand, suppose that we knew α and I within a window w_j of pixel j; we could compute a and b directly:

$$\underset{a,b}{\arg\min} \sum_{i \in w_j} (\alpha_i - (a^\top I_i + b))^2 \tag{2.47}$$

If we write this as a matrix equation and add a regularization term to give a preference to smaller values of a and b, we obtain:

$$\operatorname*{arg\,min}_{a,b} \left\| \boldsymbol{\alpha}_j - X_j \begin{bmatrix} a \\ b \end{bmatrix} \right\|^2 + \varepsilon(\|a\|^2 + b^2) \tag{2.48}$$

where $\boldsymbol{\alpha}_j$ collects all of the α values in w_j into a vector, and X_j is a $W \times 4$ matrix containing image colors in the window. As we have seen, the solution to Equation (2.48) is

$$\begin{bmatrix} a^* \\ b^* \end{bmatrix} = (X_j^\top X_j + \varepsilon \mathbf{I}_{4 \times 4}) X_j^\top \boldsymbol{\alpha}_j \tag{2.49}$$

which, plugging back into Equation (2.46), gives a mutual relationship between the α at the center of the window and all the α's in the window by way of the colors in X_i:

$$\alpha_i = [I_i^\top \ \ 1]^\top (X_i^\top X_i + \varepsilon \mathbf{I}_{4 \times 4}) X_i^\top \boldsymbol{\alpha}_i \tag{2.50}$$

That is, Equation (2.50) says that the α in the center of the window can be linearly predicted by its neighbors in the window; the term multiplying $\boldsymbol{\alpha}_i$ can be thought of as a $1 \times W$ vector of linear coefficients. If we compute this vector for every window, we get a large, sparse linear system mutually relating all the α's in the entire image; that is,

$$\boldsymbol{\alpha} = F^\top \boldsymbol{\alpha} \tag{2.51}$$

where as before, $\boldsymbol{\alpha}$ is an $N \times 1$ vector of all the α's. Just like in closed-form matting, we want to determine α's that satisfy this relationship while also satisfying user constraints specified by foreground and background scribbles. This leads to the natural optimization problem

$$\min \boldsymbol{\alpha}^\top (\mathbf{I}_{N \times N} - F)(\mathbf{I}_{N \times N} - F)^\top \boldsymbol{\alpha} + \lambda(\boldsymbol{\alpha} - \boldsymbol{\alpha}_K)^\top D(\boldsymbol{\alpha} - \boldsymbol{\alpha}_K) \tag{2.52}$$

where $\boldsymbol{\alpha}_K$, D, and λ have the same interpretations as in the closed-form matting cost function in Equation (2.40). In fact, Equation (2.52) is in exactly the same form as Equation (2.40). The only difference is that the matting Laplacian L has been replaced by the matrix $(\mathbf{I}_{N \times N} - F)(\mathbf{I}_{N \times N} - F)^\top$. Solving Equation (2.52) results in a sparse linear system of the same form as Equation (2.41).

Zheng and Kambhamettu noted that the relationship in Equation (2.46) could be further generalized to a nonlinear relationship using a **kernel**; that is, we model

$$\alpha_i = a^\top \Phi(I_i) + b \tag{2.53}$$

where Φ is a nonlinear map from three color dimensions to a larger number of features (say, p) and a becomes a $p \times 1$ vector. The I_i and X_i entries in Equation (2.50) are replaced by kernel functions between image colors (e.g., Gaussian kernels) that reflect the relationship in high-dimensional space.

2.5   MARKOV RANDOM FIELDS FOR MATTING

Many matting algorithms use the basic structure of a **Markov Random Field (MRF)** to measure the quality of an alpha matte, based on two premises: (1) the estimated alpha, foreground, and background values should agree with the matting equation, and (2) alpha values at adjacent pixels should be similar. These assumptions result in an energy function of the form

$$E(\boldsymbol{\alpha}) = \sum_{i \in \mathcal{V}} E_{\text{data}}(\alpha_i) + \sum_{(i,j) \in \mathcal{E}} E_{\text{smoothness}}(\alpha_i, \alpha_j) \tag{2.54}$$

Here, $\mathcal{V}$ is the set of pixels in the image and $\mathcal{E}$ is the set of all adjacent pixels (for example, 4-neighbors). This formulation is also known as a **Gibbs energy**. We want to minimize E to find an optimal $\boldsymbol{\alpha}$ given the user-specified information (i.e., scribbles or trimap).

If we knew the foreground and background pixel values at i, then a natural choice for the **data energy** E_{data} is a function like the one we used for the data term in Bayesian matting (2.11):

$$E_{\text{data}}(\alpha_i) = 1 - e^{-\frac{1}{\sigma_d^2} \|I_i - (\alpha_i F_i + (1-\alpha_i) B_i)\|_2^2} \tag{2.55}$$

Note that we negated the term from Equation (2.11) since we want the E_{data} term to be small when the fit to the data is good. Along the same lines, a natural choice for the **smoothness energy** $E_{\text{smoothness}}$ is

$$E_{\text{smoothness}}(\alpha_i, \alpha_j) = 1 - e^{-\frac{1}{\sigma_s^2}(\alpha_i - \alpha_j)^2} \tag{2.56}$$

Again, the term is small when the two α values agree.

Wang and Cohen [531] proposed an algorithm that minimizes an energy in this form. The basic idea is that the user supplies information to constrain the matte in the form of foreground and background scribbles. These known labeled pixels form a set $\mathcal{K} = \mathcal{F} \bigcup \mathcal{B}$, while the rest of the image pixels form a set $\mathcal{U}$. Each pixel is also assigned an initial α value and uncertainty u between 0 and 1; for pixels in $\mathcal{K}$ the α value is specified by the scribble and the uncertainty is 0, and for pixels in $\mathcal{U}$ the α value is set to 0.5 with uncertainty 1.

The algorithm proceeds by moving pixels from $\mathcal{U}$ that are within a certain radius of a $\mathcal{K}$ pixel to $\mathcal{K}$ (this is like a "rind" of the unlabeled region). Then values for F, B, α, and u are estimated for each pixel in $\mathcal{K}$. The process iterates until $\mathcal{U}$ is empty and the uncertainties in $\mathcal{K}$ stop decreasing.

At each iteration, the goal is to minimize a function of the form of Equation (2.54), where $\mathcal{V}$ is the set of pixels currently in $\mathcal{K}$. This minimization is accomplished with an algorithm called **loopy belief propagation** (LBP) [341], which is described further in Section 5.5.3 and Appendix A.2. The LBP algorithm assumes that α can take on one of K discrete states between 0 and 1. The $E_{\text{smoothness}}$ term is the same as Equation (2.56) (with suggested variance $\sigma_s = 0.2$), but the E_{data} term requires a little more explanation.

Recall that in Bayesian matting (Section 2.3), samples of the known $\mathcal{F}$ and $\mathcal{B}$ pixels in the local neighborhood of an unknown pixel were used to build Gaussian mixture models for the foreground and background. Instead, Wang and Cohen proposed a non-parametric approach similar to a kernel density estimate. The basic idea is to determine a set of candidate foreground $\{F_1, \ldots, F_C\}$ and background $\{B_1, \ldots, B_C\}$ samples for each pixel, which could be either original scribbles or estimates filled in on a previous iteration. Then we compute a likelihood that pixel i has α value α_k as

$$L_k(i) = \frac{1}{C^2} \sum_{m=1}^{C} \sum_{n=1}^{C} w_m^F w_n^B e^{-\frac{1}{\sigma_d^2} \|I_i - (\alpha_k F_m + (1-\alpha_k) B_n)\|_2^2} \qquad (2.57)$$

Here, the weights w of each foreground and background sample are related to the spatial distance from the sample to the pixel under consideration and the uncertainty of the sample, and the covariance σ_d^2 is related to the variances of the foreground and background samples. Then the final formula for the E_{data} term is

$$E_{\text{data}}(\alpha_i^k) = 1 - \frac{L_k(i)}{\sum_{k=1}^{K} L_k(i)} \qquad (2.58)$$

After minimizing Equation (2.54), we obtain α values but not estimates of F and B. We discussed one method for getting such estimates in Section 2.4.4. Wang and Cohen proposed a slightly similar approach based on the foreground samples $\{F_m\}$ and background samples $\{B_n\}$ generated at pixel i during the creation of the data energy. The idea is simply to estimate the foreground and background values as:

$$\{F_i^*, B_i^*\} = \arg \min_{\{F_m\}, \{B_n\}} \|I_i - (\alpha_i F_m + (1-\alpha_i) B_n)\|^2 \qquad (2.59)$$

That is, we select the pair of foreground and background samples that gives the best fit to the matting equation for the given α_i and I_i. The uncertainty of the pixel is updated based on the weights w of the selected pair $\{F_i^*, B_i^*\}$.

Guan et al. [182] proposed an algorithm called **easy matting** that uses the same MRF model with a few differences. They create E_{data} and $E_{\text{smoothness}}$ using log likelihoods instead of the exponential forms in Equations (2.55)–(2.56). The smoothness term $E_{\text{smoothness}}$ is also modulated by the image gradient; that is,

$$E_{\text{smoothness}}(\alpha_i, \alpha_j) = \frac{(\alpha_i - \alpha_j)^2}{\|I_i - I_j\|} \qquad (2.60)$$

The balance between E_{data} and $E_{\text{smoothness}}$ is updated dynamically, so that the smoothness term is weighted less as the iterations proceed. Finally, instead of using belief propagation to solve for the matte, the minimization of Equation (2.54) with respect to the user scribble constraints is posed as a variational problem that can be solved directly as a linear system.

2.6   RANDOM-WALK METHODS

A family of successful matting algorithms is based on the concept of **random walks** for image segmentation as proposed by Grady [176]. As in a Markov Random Field, we form a graph in which the set of vertices $\mathcal{V}$ contains all the image pixel locations

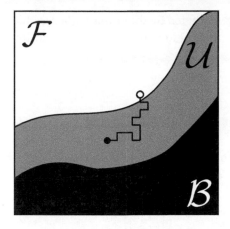

Figure 2.17. Random-walk matting methods are based on estimating the probability that a random walk starting at a pixel in the unknown region (black pixel) ends up in the foreground region. The illustrated instance of the random walk ends up in the foreground (white pixel).

and the set of undirected edges $\mathcal{E}$ represents connections between pixels (typically, 4-neighbor adjacency). Each edge $e_{ij} \in \mathcal{E}$ is associated with a nonnegative weight w_{ij}.

As discussed later, different random-walk-based algorithms use different formulations for the weights w_{ij}, but the common intuition is that w_{ij} should be large for pixels that are "similar" and near zero for pixels that are dissimilar. As in the algorithms shown earlier, the user provides prior information about foreground and background regions in the form of a trimap or scribbles. Random walk algorithms estimate α_i at a pixel i in the unknown region as the probability that a random walker starting at i and choosing edges according to the weights w_{ij} will first encounter a foreground pixel rather than a background pixel, as illustrated in Figure 2.17.

While this approach lacks the mathematical model for how intensities and α's are related through the matting equation that underlies Bayesian and closed-form matting, it turns out to work well in practice and be computationally efficient. It additionally matches our intuition; if there exists a path containing similar intensities between an unknown pixel i to the labeled foreground region $\mathcal{F}$, while paths from i to the background region $\mathcal{B}$ need to cross dissimilar pixels, pixel i is more likely to be foreground. However, we should note that the random-walk algorithm isn't evaluating the shortest or most likely path, it's evaluating the probability over all possible paths the random walker may take. It may seem that this probability is intractable to estimate; however, Grady showed how it could be computed using a similar linear system.

Let the degree d_i of node i be the sum of edge weights coming into it, that is:

$$d_i = \sum_{j | e_{ij} \in \mathcal{E}} w_{ij} \tag{2.61}$$

The **graph Laplacian** matrix is defined as

$$L_{ij} = \begin{cases} d_i & \text{if } i = j \\ -w_{ij} & \text{if } e_{ij} \in \mathcal{E} \\ 0 & \text{otherwise} \end{cases} \tag{2.62}$$

Since some pixels in the image have been labeled by the trimap or a scribble, we can re-index the pixels into a known set $\mathcal{K}$ and an unknown set $\mathcal{U}$ and partition the graph Laplacian as

$$L = \begin{bmatrix} L_\mathcal{K} & R \\ R^\top & L_\mathcal{U} \end{bmatrix} \tag{2.63}$$

where the $L_\mathcal{K}$ block corresponds to the set of known pixels and the $L_\mathcal{U}$ block to the unknown set.

Grady showed that the desired random walker probabilities described earlier correspond to minimizing the functional

$$\alpha^\top L \alpha = [\alpha_k^\top \; \alpha_u^\top] \begin{bmatrix} L_\mathcal{K} & R \\ R^\top & L_\mathcal{U} \end{bmatrix} \begin{bmatrix} \alpha_k \\ \alpha_u \end{bmatrix} \tag{2.64}$$

using results from combinatorial graph theory. Taking the gradient of Equation (2.64) with respect to the unknown values α_u and setting it equal to 0 leads to the linear system

$$L_\mathcal{U} \alpha_u = -R^\top \alpha_k \tag{2.65}$$

This is generally an extremely sparse system; for example, if 4-neighbors are used for adjacency there are only five nonzero elements per row. As a bonus, all elements of the solution of Equation (2.65) are guaranteed to be in the range [0,1] by the maximum modulus principle (i.e., the interpolated harmonic function must take its minimum and maximum values on its boundary, which are 0 and 1 respectively from the trimap/scribbles).

The key issue is thus how to choose the weights for random-walk matting. Grady [176] originally proposed to simply use

$$w_{ij} = e^{-\beta \|I_i - I_j\|^2} \tag{2.66}$$

with $\beta = 900$ assuming the images are normalized so $\|I_i - I_j\|^2 \in [0, 1]$, and later proposed a more general weight

$$w_{ij} = e^{-\beta(I_i - I_j)^\top Q^\top Q(I_i - I_j)} \tag{2.67}$$

where Q is a linear transformation of RGB space defined by the locality-preserving projections algorithm [178, 193].

Note that the derivation of closed-form matting based on the matting equation and color line assumption leads to a minimization in exactly the same form as Equation (2.64), except that the weights that form L arise from the matting Laplacian in Equation (2.36) instead; that is, for closed form matting we would use

$$w_{ij} = \sum_{k|(i,j)\in w_k} \frac{1}{W} \left[1 + (I_i - \mu_k)^\top \left(\Sigma_k + \frac{\varepsilon}{W} \mathbf{I}_{3\times3} \right)^{-1} (I_j - \mu_k) \right] \tag{2.68}$$

where μ_k and Σ_k are the mean and covariance matrix of the colors in the window w_k centered around pixel k. These are exactly the values of the matting affinity in Equation (2.38).

2.6.1   Robust Matting

Wang and Cohen proposed a well-known algorithm called **robust matting** [532] that used the same random-walk approach to solve for α's. They used the weights defined by the matting Laplacian in Equation (2.68), but also added two extra nodes $\mathbb{F}$ and $\mathbb{B}$ to $\mathcal{V}$ that represent foreground and background "terminals." Every pixel is connected to both terminals by an edge. Thus, in addition to encountering a pixel labeled $\mathcal{F}$ or $\mathcal{B}$ by the user, the random walker can also immediately take a step to one of the terminals at any time. The pixel-to-terminal weight can be interpreted as a confidence that the pixel is foreground or background, respectively. Similar to Bayesian matting or belief propagation matting, these priors are formed based on samples of the known foreground and background, but unlike these algorithms, the samples are allowed to come from much further away from the unknown pixel and are distributed along the boundary of the known regions in a trimap, as illustrated in Figure 2.18.

If a particular pair of foreground and background samples for pixel i are fixed, we can compute an estimate $\hat{\alpha}_i$ at this pixel from Equation (2.17), that is:

$$\hat{\alpha}_i = \frac{(I_i - B_i) \cdot (F_i - B_i)}{\|F_i - B_i\|^2} \tag{2.69}$$

We can also compute a confidence c_i for how much we trust the estimate $\hat{\alpha}_i$ based on several factors. First, the quality of fit based on the matting equation should be high. Also, Wang and Cohen argued that the selected foreground and background samples should be widely spread in color space, so that the denominator of Equation (2.69) is not close to zero (this could result in a sensitive estimate of α). This results in what they called the **distance ratio**

$$\frac{\|I_i - (\hat{\alpha}_i F_i + (1 - \hat{\alpha}_i) B_i)\|}{\|F_i - B_i\|} \tag{2.70}$$

The distance ratio, combined with terms that measure how similar the foreground and background samples are to I_i, is used to form a confidence c_i that measures how certain we are of the $\hat{\alpha}_i$ estimate, and these quantities are combined to produce two weights $w_{\mathbb{F}}(i)$ and $w_{\mathbb{B}}(i)$ for connecting each pixel to the foreground and background terminals.

Figure 2.18. The sampling strategy in robust matting spreads the potential foreground and samples along the boundaries of the known regions, compared to the nearest-neighbors approach from Bayesian matting (Figure 2.10).

Ultimately, robust matting is equivalent to a random walk problem in which we minimize

$$
\begin{bmatrix} \boldsymbol{\alpha} \\ 1 \\ 0 \end{bmatrix}^{\top} M \begin{bmatrix} \boldsymbol{\alpha} \\ 1 \\ 0 \end{bmatrix} \tag{2.71}
$$

with

$$
M = \begin{bmatrix} L + \mathrm{diag}(w_{\mathbb{F}}) + \mathrm{diag}(w_{\mathbb{B}}) & -w_{\mathbb{F}} & -w_{\mathbb{B}} \\ -w_{\mathbb{F}}^{\top} & \sum w_{\mathbb{F}} & 0 \\ -w_{\mathbb{B}}^{\top} & 0 & \sum w_{\mathbb{B}} \end{bmatrix} \tag{2.72}
$$

where L is the standard matting Laplacian and $w_{\mathbb{F}}$ and $w_{\mathbb{B}}$ are $N \times 1$ vectors of terminal weights. Expanding Equation (2.71) results in the equivalent objective function

$$
\boldsymbol{\alpha}^{\top} L \boldsymbol{\alpha} + (\boldsymbol{\alpha} - \mathbf{1}_{N \times 1})^{\top} W_{\mathbb{F}} (\boldsymbol{\alpha} - \mathbf{1}_{N \times 1}) + \boldsymbol{\alpha}^{\top} W_{\mathbb{B}} \boldsymbol{\alpha} \tag{2.73}
$$

where $W_{\mathbb{F}}$ and $W_{\mathbb{B}}$ are $N \times N$ diagonal matrices with the vectors $w_{\mathbb{F}}$ and $w_{\mathbb{B}}$ on the diagonals, respectively. This objective function is quadratic in $\boldsymbol{\alpha}$ and thus results in a slightly modified linear system from the one used in closed-form matting.

Rhemann et al. [389] suggested a modification to the objective function that more explicitly involves the estimates $\hat{\alpha}_i$ and confidences c_i:

$$
\min \boldsymbol{\alpha}^{\top} L \boldsymbol{\alpha} + \lambda (\boldsymbol{\alpha} - \hat{\boldsymbol{\alpha}})^{\top} D (\boldsymbol{\alpha} - \hat{\boldsymbol{\alpha}}) \tag{2.74}
$$

where $\hat{\boldsymbol{\alpha}}$ is an $N \times 1$ vector that acts as a prior estimate of $\boldsymbol{\alpha}$ at every pixel in the matte, λ is a tunable parameter, and D is a diagonal matrix with the confidences c_i on the diagonal. In this way, it's clear that when the confidence in the $\hat{\alpha}_i$ estimate is high, the objective function puts a higher weight on the prior that $\alpha_i = \hat{\alpha}_i$, and when the confidence is low, the usual neighborhood constraints from the matting Laplacian have a stronger effect.[2]

Robust matting was later refined into an algorithm called **soft scissors** [529] that solves the matting problem incrementally based on real-time user input. That is, a local trimap is generated on the fly as a user paints a wide stroke near the boundary of a foreground object. The pixels on either edge of the stroke are used to build local foreground and background models, and the stroke automatically adjusts its width based on the local image properties. The pixels interior to the stroke are treated as unknown and their α's are estimated with the robust matting algorithm. Since this region is relatively small, the drawing and matte estimation can proceed at interactive rates.

Rhemann et al. [391] also extended robust matting by incorporating a sparsity prior on α that presumes the observed α is created from an underlying sharp-edged (nearly binary) matte with a constant point-spread function (PSF) induced by the camera. The underlying matte and PSF are iteratively estimated and used to bias the matting result to be less blurry. They later extended their technique to allow the PSF to spatially vary [390].

---

[2] Rhemann et al. [389] also defined the $\hat{\alpha}_i$ estimates and confidence terms slightly differently from robust matting, and generated the foreground samples based on a geodesic-distance approach instead of a Euclidean-distance one.

Gastal and Oliviera [163] proposed an objective function of the same form as Equation (2.74), with yet another approach toward computing the foreground/background samples, $\hat{\alpha}_i$ estimates, and confidences. The key observation is that nearby pixels are likely to have very similar F, B, and α values, and thus that the sets of foreground and background samples considered for nearby pixels are likely to have many common elements. Much unnecessary computation can be avoided by creating disjoint sample sets for each pair of adjacent pixels and then asking adjacent pixels to share their choices for the best samples to come up with estimates for F_i and B_i. This method for computing $\hat{\alpha}_i$ is extremely efficient, and the $\hat{\alpha}_i$'s are already quite good even without minimizing Equation (2.74), potentially leading to a real-time video matting algorithm.

2.6.2   Geodesic Matting

The random walk technique considers all possible paths from an unknown pixel to a labeled foreground or background region, which is somewhat hard to visualize. A natural alternative is to consider the weighted *shortest* paths (i.e., geodesics) from the unknown pixel to $\mathcal{F}$ and $\mathcal{B}$ and determine α based on these path lengths. Bai and Sapiro [25] proposed a similar idea as follows. First, foreground and background probability densities $f_{\mathcal{F}}(I)$ and $f_{\mathcal{B}}(I)$ are computed from user scribbles using kernel density estimates. Then the usual graph on image pixels is built, with the weight for an edge connecting adjacent pixels defined as

$$w_{ij} = \left| L_{\mathcal{F}}(I_i) - L_{\mathcal{F}}(I_j) \right| \tag{2.75}$$

where the likelihood $L_{\mathcal{F}}$ is defined as

$$L_{\mathcal{F}}(I) = \frac{f_{\mathcal{F}}(I)}{f_{\mathcal{F}}(I) + f_{\mathcal{B}}(I)} \tag{2.76}$$

In this case, the weight is small if the two pixels have similar foreground likelihoods (or equivalently, similar background likelihoods). The weighted shortest paths between an unknown pixel i and both the foreground and background scribbles are computed using a fast marching algorithm [565]; let these distances be $D_{\mathcal{F}}(i)$ and $D_{\mathcal{B}}(i)$. Then Bai and Sapiro proposed to estimate α as

$$\alpha_i = \frac{D_{\mathcal{F}}(i)^{-r} L_{\mathcal{F}}(I_i)}{D_{\mathcal{B}}(i)^{-r}(1 - L_{\mathcal{F}}(I_i))} \tag{2.77}$$

where r is an adjustable parameter between 0 and 2.

2.7   POISSON MATTING

Finally, we mention Poisson matting [478], one form of gradient-based image editing. We will discuss similar methods more extensively in Chapter 3. The user begins by specifying a trimap. We first take the spatial gradient of the matting equation on both sides:

$$\nabla I = (F - B)\nabla \alpha + \alpha \nabla F + (1 - \alpha)\nabla B \tag{2.78}$$

This gradient is typically taken in the intensity channel of the image. If the foreground and background are relatively smooth compared to α, then the first term dominates the other two and we can make the approximation

$$\nabla\alpha \approx \frac{1}{F-B}\nabla I \tag{2.79}$$

That is, the matte gradient is proportional to the image gradient. Interpreted as a continuous problem, this gives a differential equation for α inside the unknown region $\mathcal{U}$ with boundary conditions on $\partial\mathcal{U}$ given by the known values of α in the foreground and background regions. That is, we want to minimize

$$\iint_{(x,y)\in\mathcal{U}} \left\| \nabla\alpha(x,y) - \frac{\nabla I(x,y)}{F(x,y)-B(x,y)} \right\|^2 dx\,dy \tag{2.80}$$

subject to the constraint

$$\alpha(x,y) \text{ on } \partial\mathcal{U} = \begin{cases} 1 & (x,y)\in\mathcal{F} \\ 0 & (x,y)\in\mathcal{B} \end{cases} \tag{2.81}$$

As we'll discuss in Section 3.2, minimizing Equation (2.80) turns out to be the same as solving the **Poisson equation** with the same boundary conditions, i.e.,

$$\nabla^2\alpha = \text{div}\,\frac{\nabla I}{F-B} \tag{2.82}$$

The Poisson equation can be solved quickly and uniquely, if we know $F-B$ at the pixel. In practice, this quantity is estimated using the nearest labeled foreground and background pixels and smoothed before solving the equation. After α has been computed, $F-B$ can be refined using pixels that have been estimated to have very high and very low α, and the process iterated.

This process works reasonably well when the foreground and background are both smooth, justifying the approximation in Equation (2.79). If the matte fails in a region where the foreground and/or background image has locally strong gradients, then the user can try to apply further constraints and relax Equation (2.79) in just this subregion.

2.8   HARD-SEGMENTATION-BASED MATTING

It's important to understand the relationship between the matting problem and **image segmentation**. The key difference is that the goal of segmentation is to decompose an image into disjoint pieces that fit together to form a whole. In traditional segmentation, the edges of the pieces are hard, not fuzzy, and a segmentation can be defined by an integer label for every pixel in the image. In the case where only two pieces are desired, that is, foreground and background, we can label the pieces by 1 and 0 respectively and think of a segmentation as a coarse matting problem with no fractional α values. These hard-edged pieces are unlikely to be acceptable for generating visual effects, but several researchers have proposed methods for turning a hard segmentation into a "soft" segmentation or matte. The most well-known of these methods, called GrabCut, is a highly competitive user-guided matting algorithm.

2.8.1   Graph Cut Segmentation

Many of the leading hard segmentation algorithms are based on Boykov and Jolly's pioneering work on **graph cuts** [59]. The setup is similar to the graphs from belief-propagation and random-walk methods, but the graph problem solved is quite different. We create a set of nodes $\mathcal{V}$ that contains all the pixels of the image, as well as two special **terminal nodes** that we call $\mathbb{F}$ and $\mathbb{B}$ for foreground and background. We also create a set of edges $\mathcal{E}$ between nodes, typically based on 4-adjacency in the image. Each node is also connected to both $\mathbb{F}$ and $\mathbb{B}$ by an edge. An example graph is shown in Figure 2.19a. Finally, we put a nonnegative weight w_{ij} on each edge e_{ij} so that w_{ij} is large if the nodes are similar (i.e., we have evidence that they should be assigned to the same region) and small otherwise.

A **cut** is a subset of edges $\mathcal{C}$ such that if we remove these edges from $\mathcal{E}$, there is no path from $\mathbb{F}$ to $\mathbb{B}$ in the resulting subgraph; that is, the terminals are separated (Figure 2.19b). A cut induces a segmentation in the sense that all the nodes connected to $\mathbb{F}$ constitute the foreground and all the nodes connected to $\mathbb{B}$ constitute the background. Our goal is to find the **minimum cut**, that is, the one that minimizes the cost:

$$|\mathcal{C}| = \sum_{(i,j) \in \mathcal{C}} w_{ij} \qquad (2.83)$$

Boykov and colleagues showed that the globally optimal minimum cut could quickly be computed in low-order polynomial time [60], leading to an explosion of interest in graph-cut methods in the computer vision community. Appendix A.3 gives more details on the basic algorithm. GPU-based [515] and multi-core [296] algorithms have been proposed to further accelerate finding the minimum cut.

As with scribble-based matting, the user designates certain pixels to belong to the foreground $\mathcal{F}$ and others to the background $\mathcal{B}$. For a labeled foreground pixel i, the weight on edge $(i, \mathbb{B})$ is set to 0 and the weight on edge $(i, \mathbb{F})$ is set to infinity (or a very large number) to force the minimum cut to assign i to the foreground. The reverse is true for labeled background pixels. The scribbles also serve to generate weights for connecting the rest of the nodes to the terminals. Boykov and Jolly originally

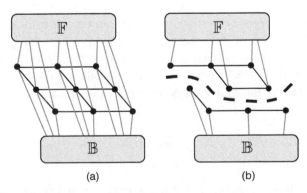

(a)   (b)

Figure 2.19. (a) The configuration of nodes and edges for graph-cut-based segmentation. Each pixel is connected to its neighbors as well as to two special foreground and background terminals. (b) A cut (dotted line) removes edges so that there is no path from the foreground terminal to the background terminal.

(a)   (b)

Figure 2.20. (a) An original image with foreground/background scribbles. (b) A hard segmentation produced with graph cuts.

proposed to compute the histograms of the labeled pixels to approximate probability density functions $f_{\mathcal{F}}(I)$ and $f_{\mathcal{B}}(I)$, and to let

$$w_{i,\mathbb{F}} = -\lambda \log f_{\mathcal{B}}(I_i)$$
$$w_{i,\mathbb{B}} = -\lambda \log f_{\mathcal{F}}(I_i)$$

(2.84)

For example, if $f_{\mathcal{B}}(I_i)$ is very low, then $w_{i,\mathbb{F}}$ will be very high, making it much more likely that the edge between i and $\mathbb{B}$ is cut. The inter-node weights are computed using a simple similarity measure

$$w_{ij} = \frac{1}{\mathrm{dist}(i,j)} \exp\left(-\frac{\|I_i - I_j\|^2}{2\sigma^2}\right)$$

(2.85)

Blake et al. [49] showed how the parameter σ could be estimated based on the local contrast of an image sample. Figure 2.20 illustrates a segmentation of an image from scribbles with this original graph-cut formulation. If the segmentation is incorrect in a subregion, new foreground/background scribbles can be added and the solution quickly updated without recomputing the minimum cut from scratch.

Finding the minimum cut is actually the same as minimizing a Gibbs energy of the form of Equation (2.54) when $\boldsymbol{\alpha}$ is restricted to be binary (i.e., 0 for background and 1 for foreground). The edge weights between pixels and the foreground/background terminals make up the data energy term E_{data} and the inter-node weights make up the smoothness energy $E_{\mathrm{smoothness}}$. That is,

$$
\begin{array}{lll}
E_{\mathrm{data}}(\alpha_i = 0) = 0 & E_{\mathrm{data}}(\alpha_i = 1) = \infty & i \in \mathcal{B} \\[4pt]
E_{\mathrm{data}}(\alpha_i = 0) = \infty & E_{\mathrm{data}}(\alpha_i = 1) = 0 & i \in \mathcal{F} \\[4pt]
E_{\mathrm{data}}(\alpha_i = 0) = -\lambda \log f_{\mathcal{B}}(I_i) & E_{\mathrm{data}}(\alpha_i = 1) = -\lambda \log f_{\mathcal{F}}(I_i) & \text{otherwise}
\end{array}
$$

(2.86)

$$E_{\mathrm{smoothness}}(\alpha_i, \alpha_j) = |\alpha_i - \alpha_j| \cdot \frac{1}{\mathrm{dist}(i,j)} \exp\left(-\frac{\|I_i - I_j\|^2}{2\sigma^2}\right)$$

(2.87)

Li et al. [280] proposed an algorithm called **lazy snapping** that speeds up the graph-cut segmentation algorithm by operating on **superpixels** instead of pixels. That is, the image pixels are clustered into small, roughly constant color regions using the watershed algorithm [514]. These regions then become the nodes of the graph-cut problem, since it's assumed that all pixels within a superpixel have the same label. Since there are typically about ten to twenty times fewer nodes and edges in the superpixel problem, the cut can be computed at interactive rates. Liu et al. [296] proposed an interactive algorithm called **paint selection** that uses an efficient multi-core graph cut algorithm to progressively hard segment an image as the user drags the mouse around an object boundary.

2.8.2   GrabCut

Rother et al. [405] were the first to extend graph-cut segmentation to the matting problem. The basic idea of their **GrabCut** algorithm is to first compute a hard segmentation using graph cuts (Figure 2.21a), and then to dilate the border around the hard edge to effectively create a trimap (Figure 2.21b). Inside the unknown region of the trimap, an α profile that transitions smoothly from 0 to 1 is fit (Figure 2.21c).

The process begins with user input in the form of a simple bounding box around the foreground (i.e., a garbage matte). Everything outside the box is assumed to be background with $\alpha = 0$, and everything inside the box is assumed to be unknown, with an initial estimate of $\alpha = 1$. As in Bayesian matting, initial Gaussian mixture models are fit to the foreground and background intensities inside and outside the box. The GrabCut algorithm iterates three steps until the binary α labels have converged:

1. Each pixel is assigned to one of the foreground (if $\alpha_i = 1$) or background (if $\alpha_i = 0$) Gaussian mixture components.
2. The parameters of each Gaussian mixture component are re-estimated based on pixel memberships. This results in updated terms like Equation (2.84) for the pixel-to-terminal weights.
3. The graph cut algorithm is used to update the hard segmentation.

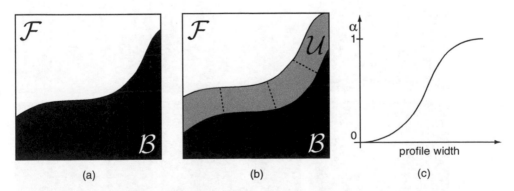

(a)   (b)   (c)

Figure 2.21. (a) A hard segmentation. (b) A trimap is created by dilating the foreground-background boundary. (c) Parameters of a smooth transition of α between 0 and 1 are fit inside profiles of the unknown region (dotted lines).

A fixed-width ribbon of pixels around the segmentation boundary is then computed; inside this region α is allowed to be fractional. For each line through the ribbon perpendicular to the boundary, a sigmoid-like profile that smoothly ranges from 0 to 1 is estimated, so that the profiles at adjacent lines are similar. We note that this approach of using a fixed-width ribbon is likely to fail for objects with large wispy regions, such as the image in the second row of Figure 2.4.

2.9   VIDEO MATTING

So far, this chapter has focused on the problem of natural image matting from a single image. Of course, for visual effects, we must compute mattes that last several seconds, resulting in hundreds of frames (Figure 2.22). The result is sometimes called a **traveling matte**. Certainly, any of the methods outlined earlier may be applied frame by frame, but the process would be extremely time-consuming, and it would impractical to expect a user to provide a trimap or scribbles in each frame. Furthermore, there is no guarantee that the results from adjacent frames will vary smoothly, which could lead to visually unacceptable "jitter." In this section, we overview techniques for **video matting**, which exploit the temporal coherence of the input video and desired output mattes.

Just as single-image matting is related to image segmentation, video matting is related to the well-known problem of **visual tracking**. The goal of visual tracking is to estimate the location of one or more objects in a video sequence, preferably ensuring that the estimated locations vary smoothly and that tracking is not lost in the presence of occlusions or object crossings. However, despite the huge amount of research and substantial advances in the field of tracking, most such methods are not immediately applicable to video matting for the same reason that many segmentation results are not immediately applicable to single-image matting. That is, the output of a typical tracking algorithm is a bounding rectangle or ellipse for each object, which is much too coarse to use for high-quality matting and composition. Even if the estimated foreground pixels in each frame form a relatively tight fit around the object, we still

Figure 2.22. Video matting requires many similar matting problems to be solved over a large number of frames.

have the same problems as hard segmentation in the presence of wispy or semi-transparent foreground objects. Nonetheless, many video matting algorithms begin with the extraction of temporally consistent, hard-edged foreground pieces in each frame of video.

Generally, video matting algorithms depend on the **optical flow** estimated from the image sequence, which is defined as the dense correspondence field corresponding to the apparent motion of brightness patterns. That is, we compute a vector at pixel (x, y) at time t of the video sequence that points at the apparent location of that pixel at time $t + 1$. This vector field can then be used to propagate the matte estimated from time t to time $t + 1$. Section 5.3 discusses the optical flow problem in detail.

Layered motion techniques represented an early approach to the video matting problem. For example, Wang and Adelson [528] proposed to cluster the pixels of a video sequence into multiple layers by fitting multiple affine motions to its optical flow field, while Ayer and Sawhney [23] proposed an expectation-maximization algorithm to estimate such affine motions based on the change in pixels' appearance and a minimum-description-length formulation for finding the number of layers. Ke and Kanade [234] observed that if the layers arise from planar patches in the scene, the corresponding affine transformations lie in a low-dimensional subspace, which acts as a strong constraint for robust layer extraction.

Several video matting methods are somewhat direct extensions of single-image matting algorithms to video, incorporating a temporal consistency prior to produce smoothly varying, non-jittery α mattes. For example, Chuang et al. [96] built upon Bayesian matting by combining it with optical flow. That is, the trimap at time t is estimated by "flowing" user-generated trimaps from keyframes on either side using the estimated optical flow fields. The trimaps are modified to ensure the foreground and background regions are reliable before being input to the standard Bayesian matting algorithm. If the background is roughly planar, projective transformations can be estimated as the camera moves to build a background mosaic that acts as a clean plate, which significantly helps the speed and quality of pulling the matte. Wexler et al. [544] and Apostoloff and Fitzgibbon [16] proposed a related Bayesian approach, using a similar mosaicing method to obtain the background before estimating the matte, and modeling the prior distribution for α with a beta distribution as mentioned in Section 2.3.2. They also incorporated a spatiotemporal consistency prior on α, using learned relationships between the gradients of α and the original image. The observation was similar to the basic assumption of Poisson matting: that the matte gradient is roughly proportional to the image gradient.

Another family of approaches is based on extending the graph-cut methods of Section 2.8 to hard foreground/background segmentation in video. These approaches can be viewed as methods for **rotoscoping**, or manually outlining contours of foreground objects in each of many frames of film. Agarwala et al. [8] proposed a well-known method for semi-automatic rotoscoping based on joint optimization of contours over a full video sequence, using manually traced keyframes and incremental user edits as hard constraints and image edges as soft constraints. While in this work, contours were represented as splines, graph-cut algorithms would allow the segmentation in each frame to be much more detailed, that is, an arbitrary binary matte. The human-assisted motion annotation algorithm of Liu et al. [288] discussed in Section 5.3.6 also can be viewed as an interactive rotoscoping tool.

Figure 2.23. Images with shadows don't obey the assumptions of the matting equation and pose challenges for the algorithms described so far.

Li et al. [279] proposed a natural generalization of the Lazy Snapping work from Section 2.8.1 to video. The Gibbs energy formulation is similar to the methods in Section 2.8, but the nodes in the graph (here, image superpixels) are connected both in space and time, with inter-frame edge weights estimated similarly to intra-frame edge weights. Criminisi et al. [107] also posed video segmentation as a conditional random field energy minimized with graph cuts, but added an explicit learned prior on the foreground likelihood at a pixel based on its label in the previous two frames. Non-binary α values in these techniques are typically obtained independently per frame by applying a "border matting" algorithm similar to GrabCut (Figure 2.21b-c). Wang et al. [530] also proposed a graph-cut-based video segmentation method, but extended the superpixel formation, user stroking, and border matting algorithms to operate natively in the space-time "video volume" formed by stacking the frames at each time instant. Finally, Bai et al. [26] proposed to propagate and update local classifiers applied at points distributed around the foreground boundary of the previous frame to generate constraints for the graph cut at the current frame. This was followed by a space-time version of robust matting (Section 2.6.1) that rewards consistency with the α values from the previous frame.

2.10   MATTING EXTENSIONS

2.10.1   Violations of the Matting Equation

When a matte of an object needs to be created from an image containing strong directional lighting, the shadow of the object should intuitively be part of the foreground instead of part of the background. However, shadows don't obey the matting equation, since they arise from a different method of image formation. That is, shadows come from the occlusion of light by a physical object, not by the translucent mixture of a gray foreground object with the background (Figure 2.23).

Chuang et al. [97] proposed an algorithm for pulling **shadow mattes** based on a shadow compositing equation similar to Equation (2.2). This approach relied on a video sequence from a fixed camera with fixed background and a moving foreground object, so that a "clean plate" background image without the shadow can be created. Finlayson et al. [141] proposed methods for removing shadows from images (e.g., the unwanted shadow of a photographer) based on finding the edges of the shadow, estimating shadow-free illumination-invariant images, and solving a Poisson equation. Wu et al. [555] addressed a similar problem of shadow removal using a generalized trimap (actually with four regions) in which the user specifies definitely-shadowed, definitely-unshadowed, unknown, and shadow/object boundary regions. The algorithm minimizes a Gibbs-like energy function built from the statistics of the regions. Regardless of how a shadow is extracted, when composited into a new image it must deform realistically with respect to the new background; some 3D information about the scene is necessarily required for high-quality results (see Chapter 8).

Hillman [199] observed that in natural images, the subject is often illuminated from behind, causing a highlight of bright pixels around the foreground boundary. Like shadow pixels, these highlight pixels do not obey the matting equation's assumption and could be estimated by assuming a mixture of three colors (foreground, background, highlight) rather than two.

Most of the algorithms in this chapter make the underlying assumption that the foreground object is opaque, and that fractional α values arise from sub-pixel-sized fine features combined with blur from the camera's optics or motion. In this context, it makes the most sense to interpret α as a measure of coverage by the foreground. However, most of the methods in this chapter will fail in the presence of "optically active" objects that are transparent, reflective, or refractive, such as a glass of water (Figure 2.24). In this case, even though a pixel may be squarely in the foreground, its color may arise from a distorted surface on the background. Pulling a coverage-based matte of the foreground and compositing it on a new background will look awful, since the foreground should be expected to distort the new background and contain no elements of the old background. To address this issue, Zongker et al. [582] proposed **environment matting**, a system that not only captures a coverage-based matte of an optically active object but also captures a description of the way the object reflects and refracts light. The method requires the object to be imaged in the presence of different lighting patterns from multiple directions using a special acquisition stage. The method was refined by Chuang et al. [98] and extended to work in real-world environments by Wexler et al. [545].

2.10.2 Matting with Custom Hardware

Finally, we note that additional, customized hardware can greatly improve the ease and quality of pulling a matte. Such methods have the advantage of not requiring user input like a trimap or scribbles, but have disadvantages in terms of generalizability, expense, and calibration effort.

For example, early work on matting in Hollywood used sodium lighting to create a yellowish background of a frequency that could be filtered from color film and used to expose a registered strip of matte film, removing the need to unmix colors [393, 517]. More recently, Debevec et al. [116] built a stage containing infrared light sources and an infrared camera for difference matting, combined with a sphere of many color LEDs that could surround an actor and produce realistic light distributions for subsequent compositing. Grundhöfer and Bimber [181] proposed an alternate approach using active lighting; a high-frame-rate system records a scene illuminated by LED lights during even frames, and a background illuminated by a bright video projector during odd frames. The odd frames can be chromakeyed to produce mattes that are interpolated for the even frames.

McGuire et al. [319] constructed a customized system using three pixel-aligned cameras with different focal lengths and depths of field for what they termed **defocus matting**. One large-aperture camera is tightly focused on the foreground, so the background appears very blurry, and another such camera is focused on the background, so the foreground appears very blurry. The third camera has a small aperture and produces typical pinhole images focused on the foreground. By reasoning about which pixels are sharp in the three images, a trimap can be automatically created for the pinhole image. The defocus matting problem is over-constrained (nine equations in the seven unknowns of the matting equation) and the matte can be computed using the approximate depth of the foreground and the three cameras' optical parameters. The system was extended by Joshi et al. [227] so that one camera could have a different center of projection from the others. McGuire et al. [320] also designed a system comprising a dual-imager camera (i.e., a camera with two imaging sensors that share the same optical axis) and a special diffuse-gray screen. The two sensors identically capture the foreground pixels but differ on the background pixels, thus satisfying Smith and Blinn's condition for ideally recovering mattes using triangulation (Section 2.2). Finally, Joshi et al. [226] proposed a matting method that used a linear array of synchronized video cameras to estimate the α matte for the central camera. The foregrounds in all cameras are aligned, but due to parallax, the backgrounds are all different. Trimaps and mattes can be estimated by exploiting the observation that the variance of background pixels should be high and the variance of foreground pixels should be low.

Sun et al. [479] proposed **flash matting**, which is based on the observation that images of the same scene taken with and without a flash tend to have similar colors at background pixels but very different colors at foreground pixels (Figure 2.25). By

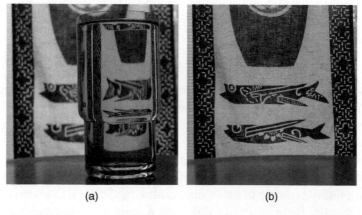

(a)   (b)

Figure 2.24. It's challenging to pull mattes of foreground objects that are transparent, reflective, or refractive; environment matting algorithms were designed for this purpose. (a) Image with foreground, (b) clean plate.

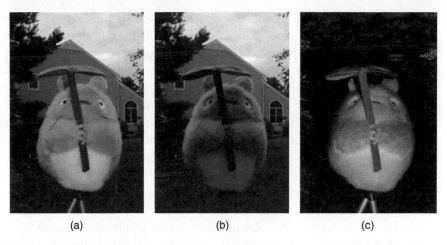

(a)   (b)   (c)

Figure 2.25. Two images of the same scene taken (a) with a flash and (b) without a flash. (c) The difference of the flash and no-flash images results in a mostly-foreground image.

subtracting the without-flash image from the flash image, a "flash-only" image is created that contains mostly foreground pixels and that can be used to generate a good trimap. An extension of Bayesian matting is then used to generate the matte. In a sense, flash matting reverses Smith and Blinn's triangulation assumption: instead of observing the same foreground in front of two different-color backgrounds, we observe two different-color foregrounds in front of the same background. In practice, it may be difficult to ensure that the foreground and background remain exactly the same and that the flash doesn't create strong shadows.

If an estimate of the depth at each pixel is available in addition to a color image, it forms a valuable prior on whether pixels should be classified as foreground or background, and can help disambiguate situations where the foreground and background have nearly the same color. We'll discuss many methods for directly acquiring or indirectly estimating scene depth in Chapter 8. In the context of this chapter, methods for estimating depth to aid in creating digital mattes include using a color-filtered aperture to slightly offset the color channels [28] or a time-of-flight sensor to directly acquire depth [580].

2.11   INDUSTRY PERSPECTIVES

Nick Apostoloff, senior software engineer, Paul Lambert, compositing supervisor, and Blake Sloan, software engineer from Digital Domain in Venice, California, and David Geoghegan, Flame operator from LOOK Effects in Los Angeles, California, discuss the process of image and video matting in feature filmmaking.

RJR: How does academic work in matting compare with how it's done in the visual effects world?

Apostoloff: I came from an academic background — but academic matting is very different than what you see in the film industry. It's primarily because in industry, things have to be very robust and give very predictable results almost all the time, so they'd much rather have something that requires a little bit of user interaction but gets you eighty to ninety percent of the way there all the time. In academia, it's often all about minimizing user interaction, giving you fantastic results for a subset of the images you'd experience in reality. You look at many of these matting papers and you see very similar types of test images. Thankfully academic research is coming around to the point of view that interactive user input is considered to be good, such as adding incremental foreground and background scribbles to refine a matte. My experience was that academic papers sometimes used very complicated models that tend to work very well for some datasets and extremely poorly on other datasets, whereas the film industry tends to split the difference and go for something that works reliably most of the time.

Another big issue with the film industry is that you're always working on video. A lot of these single-image techniques work really well given user input, but getting something to work well on video is incredibly hard because you need that temporal consistency. On the other hand, most algorithms that have temporal consistency built into them are amazingly slow and will only work on very small, very short image sequences. It's hard to get the best of both worlds. As far as I understand, everything's very manual in the film industry when it comes to things like matting. People will still roto (rotoscope) out stuff by hand if they don't have a blue screen shot instead of using some of the more advanced computer vision techniques. That's disappointing since I'd like to see some of the progress that's made on the academic side come back to the film industry — but getting that reliability is hard.

RJR: Can you describe how an artist does blue-screen or green-screen matting in practice?

Lambert: Say I'm assigned a shot that has a green-screen background and I have to pull a key to put over a particular new background. My keying program will have several built-in algorithms to try: Ultimatte, Primatte, Knockout, channel differencing, and so on. Each of these corresponds to a rule for processing the RGB colors of each pixel to produce a matte. For example, you may subtract weighted combinations of the red and blue from the green channel to make the alpha, changing the weights of the red and green channels depending on the subject matter. Often as part of the process you click around on the green screen to find a background color that will produce a good matte. From experience, you know that if you pick a brighter color, you'll pick up a certain amount of foreground detail, and if you go with a darker color, you'll pick up another kind of detail.

I invented one algorithm called the IBK keyer that's part of a software package called Nuke. It generates a background model on a per-pixel basis, so rather than just feeding the keyer one background green color you actually feed it a whole varying-green image. In essence, you're expanding the green-screen colors into the foreground to make a clean green-screen plate that has a nice color gradient.

When I was first trying to work all of this stuff out, I was obsessed with finding a perfect way to do keying, but over time you realize that you never pull a key without

Figure 2.26. (a) Blue-screen and green-screen matting is pervasive in modern visual effects. This shot from *Source Code* illustrates a matting problem with a wide range of non-binary alpha values due to blowing, wispy hair. (b) This shot from *Iron Man 2* illustrates a difficult natural image matting problem. For example, the globe in the foreground contains many intricate, thin structures that must be outlined to be able to composite it convincingly onto a different background. *Source Code* courtesy of Summit Entertainment, LLC. *Iron Man 2* images appear courtesy of Marvel Studios, TM & ©2010 Marvel and Subs. www.marvel.com.

knowing what the final background will be. You can make temporary mattes for people to use in between, but for a fully finished professional look to an edge in a composite, you have to create the matte with the background in mind. The best case is when the background has a similar luminance to the original plate. If I'm compositing the foreground onto a darker background, I know there are going to be certain problems around the edges. If I'm compositing onto a brighter background, like a a flaring light or bright explosion, I know the background will show through the foreground where the alphas aren't exactly 1, and that I'm going to have to do extra work to actually get the matte. So from just a single image you're never going to be able to pull a perfect key.

It's also important for the overall pipeline to do things procedurally as opposed to painting alphas in by hand, since if something else changes in the composite, your paintstrokes may not be valid anymore. When you know you're the very final step and it's got to go out because the client's waiting to take the shot away on a hard drive, then yes. If it's the first comp and I know there are going to be fifty iterations of the background with camera moves and changes in color correction, then I'm going to do it procedurally because in the long run it'll save me time.

Geoghegan: The matte could be a combination of whatever keying algorithms come with the software package, or it could be rewiring red, green, and blue channels, or crunching or clamping them down — theoretically anything can be a key. If a certain keyer gets me part of the way on one foreground character, I'll keep that part and try another approach somewhere else. It's like the matte is its own composite, and the sooner you start seeing it that way, the better off you're going to be. It really takes a lot of time and practice to be efficient and develop an eye for what approach to use in each part of a plate. For example, I may say, for this guy's hair, I know this keyer works really well for me, so I'll do a garbage matte just to affect the hair; then on the left side of his face I can key off the red channel and the luminance, and the other side it'll be easiest if I roto it by hand, and so on.

When it comes to keying, denoising is probably the most vital part of it. If you just cycle through the channels in video taken from a digital movie camera, you can often see the simulated grain. This is added to make digital video look more like film. Our eyes love grain when we're watching movies; it's great, but if you pull a key on a plate with film grain, you're going to end up with "chewing" and "chatter" in the matte. You should start off with a very nice denoised plate where you're not sacrificing detail, and generate the key using the best starting point possible.

On the other hand, you probably won't use the denoised foreground in compositing because you'll notice something's off if everything in the background is grained and the foreground isn't. In general, you have to process the foreground after extracting it. For example, some characters in the foreground may be a little further back from the main camera than others, and you may want to sharpen up their faces. Or the skin color of an actor may be off due to a combination of makeup and lighting, so you may do a gentle hue shift to bring it back to a good flesh tone. You may need to do a lot of things to really make the foreground live in the new environment; it's never as easy as an "A over B comp."

RJR: What about the workflow when you need to pull a matte on a non green-screen, natural background?

Lambert: A really good example was a movie set during World War II called *Flags of Our Fathers*. The production made a conscious decision that they weren't going to put green or blue screens anywhere. We took on the show knowing that it was going to be a bunch of roto — people running around, motion blur, and so on. If it's a locked-off shot, that is, the camera isn't moving, you may be able to get some of the matte with a difference matte, if you have a clean plate — but that will only get you to a certain point. The only way to really extract it correctly is to roto it — actually draw Bezier splines around the foreground. For example, if I had to roto a person off of a natural background, I'd be drawing separate shapes for the person's head, their arm, their body, and so on for a bunch of keyframes spread across the sequence. I might put keyframes every three frames — so go three frames, adjust the splines, three frames, adjust, play it back and see if it's actually matching, and then apply extra keyframes just to make it a bit better. Then you can generate the alpha by adding a softer edge to the roto curves or looking at their direction and speed of motion, and you may need to animate that softer edge on a per-frame basis. It's a very time-consuming process! You would hope that if the production knows in advance that they'll need to extract a person with flowing hair from a plate that they'll put a green screen behind them, since to extract them otherwise it'll be very labor-intensive and cost half a million dollars.

Scribble-based kinds of approaches tend to work really well on a still frame, but it's when you go to video imagery where it's changing frame to frame and you have film grain structure to it, you find that those kind of algorithms jump and around and flicker.

Sloan: Very often they'll end up having to use a clean plate that is either generated or captured on set. But sometimes there will be people whose job it is to matte every wisp of hair that has gotten outside of the blue screen area or for whatever reason can't be extracted very well. You typically go to a roto artist and they bring everything they have to bear on the problem — which is typically patience and skill at drawing those outlines. I have a feeling that whenever people say "we used our proprietary software to solve this tough matting problem," that means a bunch of hard-working roto artists! Sometimes you end up having to make entirely computer-generated versions of natural foreground elements that for some reason you didn't get properly in camera and you have to generate from scratch instead of trying to matte.

The natural matting problem is a huge issue for 3D conversion of movies filmed with a single camera. They basically have to rotoscope everything, pulling out all the foreground objects and assigning them different depths for the two eyes. Colorization of old black-and-white movies is a similar problem. Often the heart of 3D conversion algorithms is a planar tracker that allows you to interactively create and push forward very precise roto shapes on each frame. The software package called *mocha* is one very popular example of that kind of planar tracker. The output of it is something similar to a trimap that the artist can use to synthesize motion blur or some kind of fall-off to get the final alpha. The holy grail for 3D conversion is "decompositing" — to take any foreground object, however nebulous or wispy or fragmented, and extract only it from the scene.

Again, there are some academic matting algorithms that work wonders on still photographs, but the minute you have a video with wispy hair blowing in front of a forest, you can get a solution but it's not natural. It's critical that the alphas have that spatial softness and temporal continuity that you need for believability — you can't have the big thick line around Godzilla that everyone tolerated in the '60s! A third-party vendor may come out with a software plug-in for natural image matting, but unless it really nails every problem you throw at it, it's not going to become a standard.

2.12   NOTES AND EXTENSIONS

Matting for Hollywood movies was pioneered by Petro Vlahos and his son, Paul Vlahos, who patented many techniques related to blue-screen and green-screen matting and compositing from the late 1960s to the early 2000s. They won several Oscars for their contributions and founded the Ultimatte Corporation, which produces an industry-standard product for blue- and green-screen matte extraction.

Originally, mattes were strips of monochrome film that were exposed (i.e., transparent) in regions corresponding to the foreground and opaque (i.e., black) elsewhere — an analogue of the alpha channel discussed in this chapter. For early special effects, different elements and mattes were laboriously segmented, aligned and sandwiched together to produce a final composite for such films as *Mary Poppins*, *Superman*, and the original *Clash of the Titans*. For more on the early history of matting in film, see the book by Rickitt [393].

While Chuang et al. were the first to put the matting problem in the Bayesian context, Ruzon and Tomasi [412] had previously proposed a related algorithm that involved mixtures of isotropic Gaussian distributions (i.e., diagonal Σ_i) to model the foreground and background. This is viewed as one of the first principled natural matting algorithms from the computer vision/graphics community.

Singaraju et al. [454] showed that when the foreground or background intensities of a window around a pixel are less general than the color line assumption (i.e., either or both is of constant color), then the closed-form matting equations permit more degrees of freedom than necessary. They showed how to analyze the rank of image patches to create an adaptive matting Laplacian that outperforms closed-form matting in these situations.

We note that while most of the algorithms described here represented colors using the usual RGB values, and measured similarity using Euclidean distance in this space, some authors have recommended using a different color space that better reflects when two colors are perceptually similar. For example, Ruzon and Tomasi [412], Bai and Sapiro [25], and others proposed to use the CIE Lab color space for matting operations, while Grady [178] used the linear transform of RGB defined by the locality-preserving projections algorithm [193]. For Poisson matting, Sun et al. [478] recommended a linear transform of RGB that is computed to minimize the variance between the background samples. Another possibility would be to use a higher-dimensional set of filter responses (e.g., a Gabor filter bank applied to luminance as in [377]) which might be more sensitive to local texture in an image.

We focused in this chapter on the basic mathematical formulations for natural image matting. However, it's important to note that a key aspect of matting is real-time user interactivity, and that much research has gone into semiautomatically creating trimaps [391], quickly updating matte estimates based on additional scribbles, and compositing the matte on its new desired background simultaneously with estimation [533]. Several usability studies have been conducted on different methods for segmentation and matting, such as [280].

Given the large number of matting algorithms proposed and the variety of approaches to the problem, it can be difficult to know how to choose a good algorithm. Unfortunately, there is no single best algorithm, and the results of different algorithms are difficult to numerically compare in a way that matches what a human thinks will look "good." For this purpose, Rhemann et al. [392] created a carefully ground-truthed dataset for the impartial evaluation of matting algorithms, and maintain the website alphamatting.com with ranked results from state-of-the-art algorithms. This site is an excellent resource for comparing, choosing, and developing matting algorithms. They also proposed several new perceptually motivated error functions for quantifying matting performance, noting that common metrics like mean-squared error don't always correlate with visual quality.

Image segmentation is one of the major problems in computer vision; here, we only discussed algorithms used as a starting point for matting. While graph-cut and normalized-cut [441]- based methods have dominated the recent literature, other approaches to interactive image segmentation include "intelligent scissors" [339] and particle filtering [363].

In this chapter, we focused on extracting mattes from natural images, but in practice, the ultimate goal is to place the matte on a new background to create a composite image. We'll discuss the process of combining elements from multiple images more generally in Chapter 3. Several books discuss practical aspects of compositing for film and video, notably Wright [553] and Brinkmann [68].

2.13 HOMEWORK PROBLEMS

Note: in the homework problems we often assume that image color channels and intensities are in the range [0, 255] rather than [0, 1] for more direct compatibility with image manipulation tools like GIMP and Matlab.

2.1 Take or find a photograph for which hard segmentation of the foreground is likely to fail for high-quality compositing.

2.2 Suppose it was observed that the RGB values at pixel i were $I_i = [200, 100, 40]^\top$. Determine B_i and α_i that are consistent with the hypotheses that F_i = pure red, pure green, and pure blue, respectively. None of your α's should be 0 or 1.

2.3 Suppose we obtain the clean plate B given in Figure 2.27, and observe the given image I. Determine two different values for the images F and α that are consistent with the matting equation: one that conforms to human intuition and one that is mathematically correct but is perceptually unusual. Assume that the intensity of the middle circle is 128.

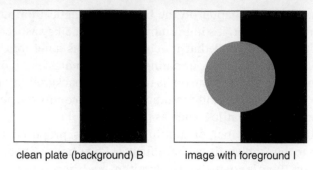

clean plate (background) B   image with foreground I

Figure 2.27. A clean plate and an image containing a foreground element.

2.4   Consider α as a function of I_b and I_g in Vlahos's equation (2.4), where both color channels are in $[0, 1]$. Plot this surface for $a_1 = \frac{1}{2}$ and $a_2 = 1$. What happens as a_1 is increased for fixed a_2? What happens as a_2 is increased for fixed a_1? Interpret your results.

2.5   The color $I_i = [40, 50, 150]^\top$ was observed in front of a pure blue background. Compute two possibilities for (α_i, F_i), keeping in mind both values must stay in a valid range.

2.6   Derive the triangulation formula for α; that is, prove that the solution of Equation (2.5) is given by Equation (2.6).

2.7   A pixel is observed to have intensity $[150, 100, 200]^\top$ in front of a pure blue background, and intensity $[140, 180, 40]^\top$ in front of a pure green background. Compute α using triangulation.

2.8   Prove that Equation (2.16) and Equation (2.17) minimize the Bayesian matting objective function.

2.9   Suppose that the foreground and background pdfs in a matting problem are modeled as Gaussian distributions with

$$\mu_F = \begin{bmatrix} 150 \\ 150 \\ 150 \end{bmatrix} \quad \Sigma_F = \begin{bmatrix} 20 & 5 & 5 \\ 5 & 30 & 8 \\ 5 & 8 & 25 \end{bmatrix} \tag{2.88}$$

$$\mu_B = \begin{bmatrix} 50 \\ 50 \\ 200 \end{bmatrix} \quad \Sigma_B = \begin{bmatrix} 5 & 0 & 0 \\ 0 & 5 & 0 \\ 0 & 0 & 15 \end{bmatrix} \tag{2.89}$$

If the observed pixel color is $[120, 125, 170]^\top$, compute F, B, and α by alternating Equation (2.16) and Equation (2.17), assuming $\sigma_d = 2$. Repeat the experiment with $\sigma_d = 10$ and interpret the difference.

2.10   Continuing Problem 2.9, suppose the foreground is modeled with a mixture of two Gaussian distributions: the one from Equation (2.88) and one given by

$$\mu_{F_2} = \begin{bmatrix} 130 \\ 150 \\ 180 \end{bmatrix} \quad \Sigma_{F_2} = \begin{bmatrix} 10 & 0 & 0 \\ 0 & 10 & 0 \\ 0 & 0 & 10 \end{bmatrix} \tag{2.90}$$

Assuming $\sigma_d = 2$, what is the Bayesian matting solution for the best F, B, and α using the strategy discussed on p. 19?

2.11 Sketch configurations for pixels i and j such that there are 0, 1, 2, 3, 4, or 6 windows k in the sum for the matting Laplacian element $L(i,j)$ in Equation (2.36).

2.12 a) Verify that Equation (2.34) follows from Equation (2.33).
      b) If G_j is defined by Equations (2.27)–(2.28), show that $G_j^\top G_j$ can be written as a function of μ_j and Σ_j, the mean and covariance matrix of the colors in window j.

2.13 Prove that, in the absence of any scribbles or user constraints, any constant matte minimizes the closed-form matting objective function.

2.14 Consider one of the matrices that makes up the matting Laplacian in Equation (2.34), i.e.,

$$M_j = \mathbf{I}_{(W+3)\times(W+3)} - G_j(G_j^\top G_j)^{-1}G_j^\top \tag{2.91}$$

Show that M_j has a nullspace of at least dimension 4. (Hint: what is $M_j G_j$?)

2.15 Suppose we compute the matting affinity A in Equation (2.38) using 3×3 windows. Determine the values in the ith row of A if pixel i is at the center of a 5×5 region of constant intensity. How many nonzero values are there?

2.16 Show that the closed-form matting minimization problem in Equation (2.40) leads to the linear system in Equation (2.41).

2.17 We know that a constant matte (i.e., $\alpha = 1$) is a null vector of the matting Laplacian. Suppose the matte that has $\alpha = \frac{3}{4}$ on its left-hand side and $\alpha = \frac{1}{4}$ on its right-hand side is also a null vector. Compute a linear combination of these two matting components that is as binary as possible (but is not constant).

2.18 a) Show how the term $\|\nabla_x F_i\|^2$ in Equation (2.42) for a particular pixel i can be written in the form $F^\top D_x F$ where F is a vector of all the foreground values and D_x is a diagonal matrix with only two nonzero entries.
      b) Hence, determine the linear system corresponding to Equation (2.42) for computing F and B images from given α and I images.

2.19 Show that solving Equation (2.51) in learning-based matting leads to Equation (2.52).

2.20 Plot the smoothness energy in Equation (2.56) for belief-propagation-based matting as a surface over the (α_1, α_2) plane, where $\sigma_s = 0.1$.

2.21 Suppose for a given pixel in belief-propagation-based matting, we gathered the foreground samples and background samples given by

$$F_1 = \begin{bmatrix} 95 \\ 120 \\ 100 \end{bmatrix} \qquad F_2 = \begin{bmatrix} 105 \\ 80 \\ 70 \end{bmatrix} \qquad (2.92)$$

$$B_1 = \begin{bmatrix} 105 \\ 160 \\ 100 \end{bmatrix} \qquad B_2 = \begin{bmatrix} 95 \\ 180 \\ 170 \end{bmatrix} \qquad (2.93)$$

Suppose we observed $I_i = [100, 140, 110]^\top$ and had estimated that $\alpha_i = 0.5$. Estimate the optimal samples (F_i^*, B_i^*) according to Equation (2.59). How would the answer change if we instead used the distance ratio criterion in Equation (2.70) from robust matting?

2.22 Show that minimizing the random walk objective function in Equation (2.64) leads to the linear system in Equation (2.65).

2.23 Show that Equation (2.71) and Equation (2.73) have the same minimum with respect to α (that is, the objective functions differ by a constant term).

2.24 A typical sigmoid function for border matting resembles Figure 2.21c and can be parameterized using the profile

$$p(w) = \frac{1}{1 + e^{-a(w-b)}} \qquad (2.94)$$

where w ranges from 0 to 1. If we observe the samples $\{(w_i, p_i), i = 1, \ldots, s\}$, what would be good initial estimates for the values of a and b?

3 Image Compositing and Editing

In this chapter, we discuss **image compositing and editing**, the manipulation of a single image or the combination of elements from multiple sources to make a convincing final image. Like image matting, image compositing and editing are pervasive in modern TV and filmmaking. Virtually every frame of a blockbuster movie is a combination of multiple elements. We can think of compositing as the inverse of matting: putting images together instead of pulling them apart. Consequently, the problems we consider are generally easier to solve and require less human intervention.

In the simplest case, we may just want to place a foreground object extracted by matting onto a different background image. As we saw in Chapter 2, obtaining high-quality mattes is possible using a variety of algorithms, and new images made using the compositing equation (2.3) generally look very good. On the other hand, a fair amount of user interaction is often required to obtain these mattes — for example, heuristically combining different color channels, painting an intricate trimap, or scribbling and rescribbling to refine a matte. The algorithms in the first half of this chapter take a different approach: the user roughly outlines an object in a source image to be removed and recomposited into a target image, and the algorithm automatically estimates a good blend between the object and its new background without explicitly requiring a matte. These "drag-and-drop"-style algorithms could potentially save a lot of manual effort.

The second half of the chapter addresses image editing problems that can't be solved by simple applications of the matting equation. We first discuss **image inpainting**, an extremely common visual effects problem. In inpainting, we want to remove unwanted elements from a shot, such as wires or rigging from special effects, and construct plausible new pixels in regions the original camera didn't see. We may also want to **recomposite** or **reshuffle** an image or video by moving its elements around after the fact or combining elements from different takes. Finally, in post-production we may want to resize or **retarget** a shot so it looks good at different aspect ratios or on different devices.

In the terminology of image manipulation software like GIMP or Adobe Photoshop, some image editing problems are often referred to as **cloning** — for example, when we want to cut and paste multiple copies of an object into a scene (here, the object is "cloned") or when we want to replace an unwanted object with realistic-looking background (here, the background is "cloned"). Software tools with names like the clone stamp, clone brush, or healing brush are all examples of the algorithms discussed in this chapter. The algorithms in this chapter also form the basis for the wide array of image retouching that occurs in the world of commercial photography — to the extent that it is now very difficult to judge whether a digital image represents the true recording of an actual real-world scene.

We first discuss classical methods for blending image intensities across a hard boundary or seam (Section 3.1). We then introduce gradient-domain blending methods based on solving the Poisson equation, which typically produce a more natural-looking transition (Section 3.2). We also consider an alternate approach based on graph cuts: instead of fractionally weighting the source and target contributions near the seam, we try to find a seam such that a hard transition is imperceptible (Section 3.3). We then address the problem of image inpainting — filling in "holes" specified by the user with realistic texture (Section 3.4). We next introduce the concept of image retargeting — changing the size, aspect ratio, or composition of an image (Section 3.5). Finally, we discuss extensions of the various methods from still images to video (Section 3.6).

3.1   COMPOSITING HARD-EDGED PIECES

As we mentioned earlier, high-quality mattes are essential for most visual effects compositing problems, but these take substantial effort to create. It would be much easier for the user to roughly outline the object to be extracted from one image and placed in another, without interactively struggling to create a good matte. In this and the following sections, we investigate methods for pasting a hard-edged foreground region into a new background image, letting the algorithms do the work of creating a pleasing (and hopefully imperceptible) blend.

Mathematically, we pose the problem as follows. We are given a source image $S(x,y)$, a binary mask image $M(x,y) \in \{0,1\}$ specifying the general outline of an object or region in the source image, and a target image $T(x,y)$. Our goal is to create a convincing composite $I(x,y)$ in which the source region is rendered on top of the target image with minimal visible artifacts. This is sometimes called the "over" operation for compositing two images [373]. We assume the two images are already aligned, so that (x,y) corresponds to the same location in all the images.

Clearly, the matting equation (2.1) from the previous chapter encapsulates the simplest way to composite the two images:

$$I(x,y) = M(x,y)S(x,y) + (1 - M(x,y))T(x,y)$$

$$= \begin{cases} S(x,y) & \text{if } M(x,y) = 1 \\ T(x,y) & \text{if } M(x,y) = 0 \end{cases} \qquad (3.1)$$

where the binary image M plays the role of the α matte. If we were to directly superimpose the source region on the target image using Equation (3.1) without any blending, we would see a visible boundary — also known as a **seam** or **matte line** — between the source and target (Figure 3.1).

In the early days of visual effects, this type of compositing was often used to insert a special effects shot (e.g., a model spaceship) into a live-action plate. Similar techniques are used to combine two videos of the same actor from multiple camera passes

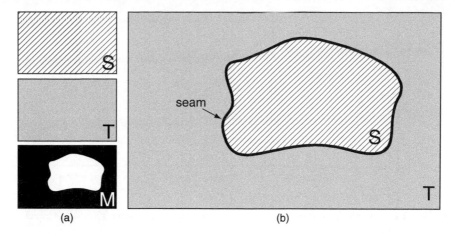

Figure 3.1. The compositing problem with hard-edged pieces. (a) Source, target, and mask images. (b) In the composite image, regions from the source and target images are separated by a seam. We want to make the transition between source and target as imperceptible as possible.

for "twinning" effects, such as in *Friends*, *Back to the Future II*, or *Moon*. For example, an actor is filmed interacting with him/herself twice: once on the left side of the screen and once on the right. In early versions of this effect, the seam between the two shots was either very visible (e.g., a line down the middle of the screen) or hidden by an obvious foreground object (e.g., a fence or tree). In this case, the problem is to fuse two images I_1 and I_2 along a given seam, where neither image is naturally the foreground or background and both are of equal importance.

Why were seams so visible using the simple technique of Equation (3.1)? Even if the camera was locked down with identical location and exposure to take both the source and target shots, lighting conditions between shots are extremely difficult to match exactly, and the human visual system is extremely sensitive to the presence of edges, especially in constant-intensity, low-frequency regions (see Figure 3.3a). The situation only becomes worse if one image is taken at a different time or under different conditions than the other (for example, an actor shot on a studio set is to be composited into an outdoor scene). Much of this chapter is about the problem of *hiding seams* — both by choosing clever, non-straight-line paths for the seams to take, and by more intelligently blending intensities across the seam.

3.1.1 Weighted Transition Regions

An obvious approach to making the seam less noticeable is to blend the pixel intensities across the seam with a parametric weighting function. That is, in the neighborhood of the seam, the composite pixel color is a weighted average of the source and target colors, depending on how close the pixel is to the source. For an object that's not too complex, this weighted average looks like Figure 3.2 on a profile perpendicular to the source boundary. This approach is similar to border matting

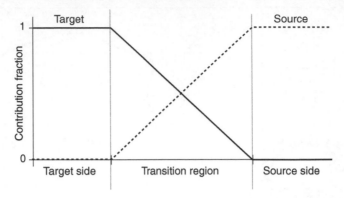

Figure 3.2. The composite contains a weighted average of source and target pixels across the transition region.

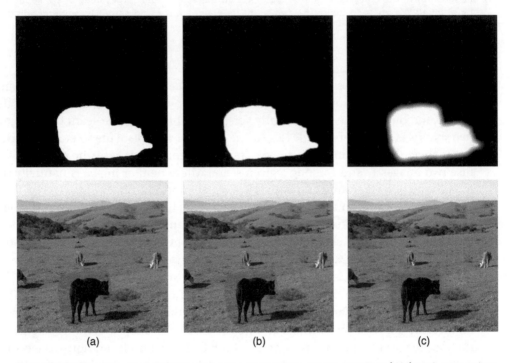

Figure 3.3. Possible compositing strategies illustrating source weights (top) and composites (bottom). (a) A hard seam produces a visible, distracting edge. (b) A narrow, linearly-weighted transition region still creates a visible seam. (c) A wider, linearly-weighted transition region can result in low-detail regions around the boundary where the two images are averaged, resulting in a diffuse "halo."

from Section 2.8.2, since we're effectively creating a non-binary alpha matte for the source based on a hard foreground segmentation.

However, deciding on the width of the transition region (that is, the region in which pixels are a mix between source and target) is difficult. If the region is too narrow, the seam will still be visible, but if the region is too wide, the averaging in the transition region will remove details, as illustrated in Figure 3.3b-c.

3.1.2   Multiresolution Blending with a Laplacian Pyramid

Burt and Adelson [78] made a key observation about blending across a seam, rooted in a *frequency-domain* interpretation of the images to be combined. The idea is simple: low-frequency components (i.e., smooth, gradual intensity variations) should be blended across wide transition regions, while high-frequency components (i.e., edges and regions with fine detail) should be blended across narrow transition regions. These goals can be easily, simultaneously accomplished using a **Laplacian pyramid**, a common multiresolution representation for images. In this section, we assume that the images are grayscale, and that for color images each channel is processed independently and recombined.

For a given image I, the first step is to blur it at different scales, by successively filtering it with a Gaussian (or more generally, low-pass) kernel. At each step, the resolution of the image is halved in both dimensions, so that successive images appear as smaller, blurrier versions of the original. The top row of Figure 3.4 illustrates several steps of this process, which is called a **Gaussian pyramid**. That is, we create a hierarchy of images given by

$$G_i = (K * G_{i-1})_{\downarrow 2}, \quad i = 1, \ldots, N \tag{3.2}$$

where $*$ indicates two-dimensional convolution, $\downarrow 2$ indicates downsampling by 2 in both dimensions, and $G_0 = I$, the original image. K is an approximate Gaussian kernel, or a low-pass filter whose elements sum to 1, such as

$$K = [-0.05, \ 0.25, \ 0.6, \ 0.25, \ -0.05]^\top \ [-0.05, \ 0.25, \ 0.6, \ 0.25, \ -0.05] \tag{3.3}$$

For compositing, we're interested in the edges that are significant at every scale, which can be obtained by taking the **difference of Gaussians** at each scale:

$$L_i = G_i - (K * G_i), \quad i = 0, \ldots, N-1 \tag{3.4}$$

The images L_i form what is called a **Laplacian pyramid,** since the shape of the two-dimensional Laplacian operator (also known as the "Mexican hat" function) is similar to a difference of Gaussians at different scales (we'll discuss this property more in Section 4.1.4). As illustrated in the bottom row of Figure 3.4, each image in the Laplacian pyramid can be viewed as a bandpass image at a different scale. The smallest image L_N in the pyramid is defined to be a small, highly blurred version of the original image, given by G_N, while the other images contain edges prevalent at different image scales (for example, L_0 contains the finest-detail edges). Therefore, we can write the original image as the sum of the images of the pyramid:

$$I = \sum_{i=0}^{N} L_{i\uparrow} \tag{3.5}$$

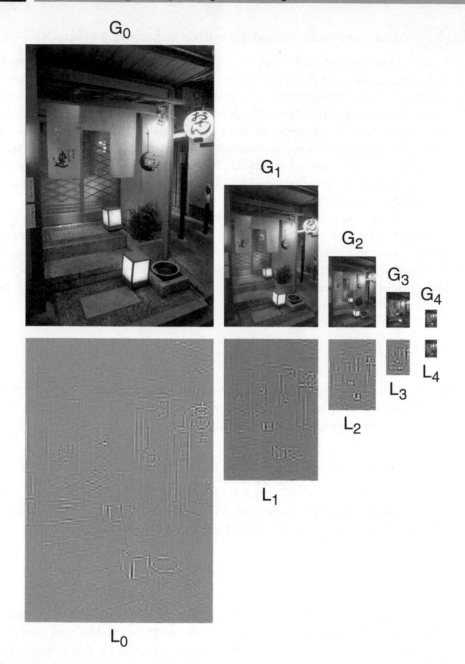

Figure 3.4. The top row illustrates the Gaussian pyramid of an image $I = G_0$, generated by filtering with the matrix in Equation (3.3) and downsampling by 2 at each step. Each image is a smaller, blurrier version of its predecessor. The bottom row illustrates the Laplacian pyramid for the image I, generated by successive differencing of the images in the top row according to Equation (3.4). Each Laplacian image contains the edges at successively coarser scales.

where $\uparrow$ indicates the images have been upsampled and interpolated to the original image resolution before summing them.

To compose a source image S onto a target image T using Burt and Adelson's approach, we first compute the Laplacian pyramids L^S and L^T for both images. We also assume we have a binary mask M specifying the desired boundary, so that pixels inside S have $M = 1$ and pixels inside T have $M = 0$, and compute a Gaussian pyramid G for this mask. Then we compute a Laplacian pyramid $\{L^I\}$ for the composite image as follows:

$$L_i^I(x,y) = G_i(x,y)L_i^S(x,y) + (1 - G_i(x,y))L_i^T(x,y), \quad i = 0,\dots,N \qquad (3.6)$$

We sum the Laplacian components according to Equation (3.5) to get the new image. Effectively, the transition region is wider at lower spatial frequencies and narrower at high spatial frequencies, producing a more natural transition between the source and target. Figure 3.5 illustrates the process for the same images as in Figure 3.3; note the higher quality of the composite and the relative lack of artifacts.

The general approach of a multiresolution filter-bank decomposition applies to other operators besides the Laplacian. For example, a **steerable pyramid** [453] further decomposes each bandpass image into the sum of orientation bands, which can be used to selectively enhance or de-emphasize components at different orientations. Another important alternative is a **discrete wavelet transform** (e.g., [277, 278]), which also represents images at different scales and can be computed very efficiently.

Figure 3.5. Laplacian Image Compositing. (a) The target image. (b) The source image, indicating the boundary of the compositing region. (c) Several levels of the Laplacian pyramid for the target image. (d) Several levels of the Laplacian pyramid for the source image. (e) Several levels of the Gaussian pyramid for the compositing mask. (f) The combination of the source and target at each level according to Equation (3.6). (g) The final composite.

However, none of these pyramid-style methods are well suited to the situation when the source and target colors are not already well matched, as we'll see in the next section.

3.2   POISSON IMAGE EDITING

An appealing approach to compositing, pioneered by Pérez et al. [364], seamlessly merges the source region into the target image using an application of the **Poisson equation**. To understand the Poisson compositing technique, we need to define several concepts from continuous partial differential equations and vector calculus, which we then translate into the discrete world to apply to digital images.

3.2.1   The Basic Idea

In place of a binary compositing mask M, we assume that the source image S is defined over a closed region Ω; the boundary of this region is denoted as $\partial\Omega$. Figure 3.6 illustrates these terms. The target image T is assumed to be defined over some rectangular region in $\mathbb{R}^2$.

Formally, the composite image we want to construct, $I(x,y)$, exactly agrees with $T(x,y)$ outside of Ω, and should "look like" $S(x,y)$ inside Ω. The problem is that if we directly place the source region on top of T and blend across the edge, for example using the Laplacian pyramid approach, the result can be unacceptable due to color mismatches, as illustrated in Figure 3.7.

What can we do to make the interior of Ω "look like" the source, but avoid the color mismatch problem? The key idea is to transfer the *edges* of the source image into Ω, and then compute colors inside the region that are as harmonious as possible with the pixels from T surrounding Ω. That is, we want the *gradient* of the desired image, $\nabla I(x,y)$, inside Ω to be as close as possible to $\nabla S(x,y)$, subject to the constraint that the result must match the existing values of $T(x,y)$ on the boundary $\partial\Omega$. This approach is generally known as **gradient-domain compositing**. In continuous terms, this means

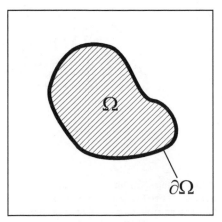

Figure 3.6. Terminology for Poisson image editing.

Source image

Figure 3.7. (a) The target image and (b) the source image, indicating the region Ω to be composited. (c) Laplacian pyramid blending fails when the source and target regions' colors differ by too much.

that we want to solve

$$\min_{I(x,y)\in\Omega} \iint_{\Omega} \|\nabla I(x,y) - \nabla S(x,y)\|^2 \, dx\, dy \tag{3.7}$$

$$s.t. \;\; I(x,y) = T(x,y) \;\; \text{on } \partial\Omega$$

If we denote the integrand as

$$F(x,y) = \|\nabla I(x,y) - \nabla S(x,y)\|^2 = \left(\frac{\partial I}{\partial x} - \frac{\partial S}{\partial x}\right)^2 + \left(\frac{\partial I}{\partial y} - \frac{\partial S}{\partial y}\right)^2 \tag{3.8}$$

then the calculus of variations implies that the $I(x,y)$ that solves Equation (3.7) is a solution of the **Euler-Lagrange equation**:

$$\frac{\partial F}{\partial I} - \frac{d}{dx}\frac{\partial F}{\partial I_x} - \frac{d}{dy}\frac{\partial F}{\partial I_y} = 0 \;\; \text{in } \Omega \tag{3.9}$$

Plugging Equation (3.8) into Equation (3.9) yields[1]

$$2\left(\frac{\partial^2 I}{\partial x^2} - \frac{\partial^2 S}{\partial x^2}\right) + 2\left(\frac{\partial^2 I}{\partial y^2} - \frac{\partial^2 S}{\partial y^2}\right) = 0 \;\; \text{in } \Omega \tag{3.10}$$

or more simply,

$$\nabla^2 I(x,y) = \nabla^2 S(x,y) \;\; \text{in } \Omega \tag{3.11}$$

$$s.t. \;\; I(x,y) = T(x,y) \;\; \text{on } \partial\Omega \tag{3.12}$$

---

[1] Note that the term $\frac{\partial F}{\partial I}$ in Equation (3.9) equates to 0 in this case, since the partial is treated with respect to the symbol I, and I doesn't appear by itself in Equation (3.8).

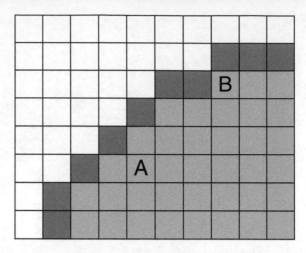

Figure 3.8. Discrete sets required for solving the Poisson equation using digital images. A small image region is shown. The lightly shaded squares comprise Ω; the darker-shaded squares comprise $\partial\Omega$.

where we have used the common notation of $\nabla^2 I = \frac{\partial^2 I}{\partial x^2} + \frac{\partial^2 I}{\partial y^2}$ for the Laplacian operator.

An equation of the form (3.11) (with a generic right-hand side) is called a **Poisson equation**, and a constraint of the form (3.12) is called a **Dirichlet boundary condition**. If the right-hand side of Equation (3.11) is zero, it is called a **Laplace equation**[2]; if the right-hand side of Equation (3.12) is zero, it is called a **Neumann boundary condition**.

Before we discuss how the Poisson equation is solved in practice, we mention an important generalization. In Equation (3.11), we assumed that the Laplacian of the new image was equal to the Laplacian of another image (i.e., the source) inside Ω. However, the technique is more powerful if we minimize the difference between the Laplacian of the new image and *some arbitrary guidance vector field* $(S_x(x,y), S_y(x,y))$ at every pixel (x,y). The distinction is that the guidance vector field need not arise by taking the gradient of some original image (in which case it is called a **non-conservative field**). The Poisson equation in Equation (3.11) slightly changes to

$$\nabla^2 I(x,y) = \mathrm{div}\left[\begin{array}{c} S_x(x,y) \\ S_y(x,y) \end{array}\right] = \frac{\partial S_x}{\partial x} + \frac{\partial S_y}{\partial y} \text{ in } \Omega \qquad (3.13)$$

where div represents the divergence of an arbitrary vector field.[3]

To solve the Poisson equation for a real-world pixellated image, we create a discrete version of Equations (3.11)–(3.12). As illustrated in Figure 3.8, Ω is a user-defined collection of pixels (i.e., the pixels where $M = 1$ in the previous section) and $\partial\Omega$ is the set of pixels not in Ω that have one of their 4-neighbors in Ω. The source image S must at least be defined on Ω plus a one-pixel-wide dilation of Ω.

---

[2] The Laplace equation is also sometimes known as the **heat equation** or **diffusion equation**.

[3] For a readable refresher on vector calculus and derivatives, see the book by Schey [427].

Each pixel $p = (x, y) \in \Omega$ generates a linear equation in the unknown values of $I(x, y)$. There are two cases, depending on the 4-neighborhood of p (denoted $\mathcal{N}(p)$):

1. $\mathcal{N}(p) \subset \Omega$. In this case — such as pixel A in Figure 3.8 — the neighborhood of the pixel is fully contained in Ω. There are no boundary conditions and we use the usual approximations of the Laplacian:

$$I(x+1, y) + I(x-1, y) + I(x, y+1) + I(x, y-1) - 4I(x, y)$$
$$= S(x+1, y) + S(x-1, y) + S(x, y+1) + S(x, y-1) - 4S(x, y) \quad (3.14)$$

2. $\mathcal{N}(p) \not\subset \Omega$. In this case — such as pixel B in Figure 3.8 — the pixel is on the edge of the source region, and the estimate of the Laplacian includes pixels from the target that are specified by the boundary condition:

$$\left(\sum_{q \in \mathcal{N}(p) \cap \Omega} I(q) \right) + \left(\sum_{q \in \mathcal{N}(p) \cap \partial\Omega} T(q) \right) - 4I(x, y)$$
$$= S(x+1, y) + S(x-1, y) + S(x, y+1) + S(x, y-1) - 4S(x, y) \quad (3.15)$$

Typically, the region Ω is well inside the target image (i.e., surrounded by a healthy border of target pixels). However, if Ω runs all the way to the image border, Equation (3.14) and Equation (3.15) need to be modified to avoid querying pixel values outside the image. For example, if the upper left-hand corner $(1, 1) \in \Omega$, we would modify Equation (3.14) to

$$I(2, 1) + I(1, 2) - 2I(1, 1) = S(2, 1) + S(1, 2) - 2S(1, 1) \quad (3.16)$$

Collecting together all the equations for each $p \in \Omega$ results in a large, sparse linear system. There are as many unknowns as pixels in Ω, but at most five nonzero elements per row, with a regular structure on where these elements occur.[4]

Solving the Poisson equation for the example images in Figure 3.7 results in the improved composite in Figure 3.9. As with the Laplacian pyramid, the Poisson equation was applied to each color channel independently. We can see that the overall colors of the target image merge naturally into the source region, while keeping the sharp detail of the source region intact.

We can obtain a slightly different interpretation of Equations (3.11)–(3.12) by defining $E(x, y) = I(x, y) - S(x, y)$ and rearranging:

$$\nabla^2 E(x, y) = 0 \text{ in } \Omega \quad (3.17)$$

$$s.t. \ E(x, y) = T(x, y) - S(x, y) \text{ on } \partial\Omega \quad (3.18)$$

That is, $E(x, y)$ is a "correction" that we add to the source pixels to get the final image pixels. We can think of $E(x, y)$ as a smooth membrane that interpolates the samples of the difference between the target and source pixels around the boundary of Ω. Now Equation (3.17) is a Laplace equation, which implies that the solution $E(x, y)$ is a **harmonic function**. Once we compute $E(x, y)$, we recover $I(x, y) = S(x, y) + E(x, y)$.

---

[4] In fact, the same kinds of systems occurred when we considered the matting problem in Sections 2.4 and 2.6.

Figure 3.9. Successful image composition using the Poisson equation.

(a)   (b)   (c)

Figure 3.10. (a) The region Ω includes some key features of the target image. (b) Poisson image compositing without modification creates unacceptable visual artifacts; the mountain's color is smudged into the source region. (c) Using mixed gradients to preserve the target edges in Ω is a big improvement.

We've assumed that the pixels from the source image entirely overwrite whatever pixels used to be in the same place in the target image. However, in some cases, it may be appropriate for the original target pixels to "show through." For example, we may want to maintain some of the texture of the target image, or give the sense that the source pixels are slightly transparent. In this case, we could use a guidance vector field given by a mixture of the source and target gradients, such as:

$$\begin{bmatrix} S_x(x,y) \\ S_y(x,y) \end{bmatrix} = \begin{cases} \nabla T(x,y) & \text{if } \|\nabla T(x,y)\| > \|\nabla S(x,y)\| \\ \nabla S(x,y) & \text{otherwise} \end{cases} \tag{3.19}$$

This would preserve whatever gradients were stronger inside Ω. This is an example of a non-conservative vector field, so we must use Equation (3.13), not Equation (3.11) (though the numerical implementation is basically the same). Figure 3.10 illustrates an example.

3.2.2 Refinements and Extensions

The numerical analysis and computer vision communities have investigated fast ways to solve Poisson and Laplace equations, which despite their sparsity can become quite time-consuming to solve when the region Ω is very large. These equations are frequently solved using **multigrid** techniques [413, 374]; the basic idea is to iterate between exactly solving the equation on a coarser grid than the original problem, and applying a correction step to approximate the solution on the finer, original grid. Other approaches include early work on orthogonal-transform-based methods [452], and more recently methods based on hierarchical basis preconditioning [484], quadtrees [6], exploiting GPUs [52, 318, 218], and fast multigrid [177, 233].

Farbman et al. [132] proposed an extremely efficient approximation to the solution of Equations (3.17)–(3.18) using **mean-value coordinates** [146] that directly produces results perceptually indistinguishable from those of the previous section without solving a large linear system. The interpolating function $E(x,y)$ is directly computed from the values of $T(x,y) - S(x,y)$ on $\partial\Omega$ as follows.

Let the closed boundary $\partial\Omega$ be specified by a sequence of points, ordered counter-clockwise and denoted $(p_1, p_2, \ldots, p_N)$. Then define

$$\lambda_i(p) = \frac{w_i(p)}{\sum_{j=1}^{N} w_j(p)}, \quad i = 1, \ldots, N \tag{3.20}$$

where

$$w_i(p) = \frac{\tan(\theta_{i-1}(p)/2) + \tan(\theta_i(p)/2)}{\|p_i - p\|}, \quad i = 1, \ldots, N \tag{3.21}$$

and $\theta_i(p)$ is the angle formed by p_i, p, and p_{i+1}, as illustrated in Figure 3.11. (For the purposes of Equation (3.21), $p_0 = p_N$.)

Then we can obtain an estimate of the harmonic function $E(p)$ at any point in Ω as a simple weighted combination of the boundary conditions:

$$E(p) = \sum_{i=1}^{N} \lambda_i(p)(T(p_i) - S(p_i)) \tag{3.22}$$

As previously, we recover $I(p) = E(p) + S(p)$. Note that we can directly evaluate $I(p)$ for any point in Ω by computing Equation (3.22), which is extremely efficient and highly parallelizable. While the values of E do not precisely solve the Laplace

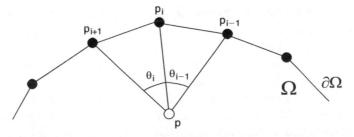

Figure 3.11. Mean-value coordinates for fast approximation of Equations (3.17)–(3.18).

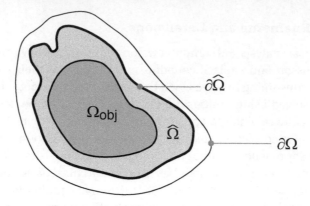

Figure 3.12. Contours for drag-and-drop pasting. The outer contour $\partial\Omega$ was roughly drawn by the user. The inner region Ω_{obj} is produced by the GrabCut algorithm. The drag-and-drop pasting algorithm estimates an intermediate contour $\partial\hat{\Omega}$.

equation, Farbman et al. showed that the differences in typical compositing problems are imperceptible, and the fast formulation allows Poisson-type problems to be solved in real time, allowing virtually instant compositing.

Jia et al. [219] proposed a variation to Poisson image editing called **drag-and-drop pasting**, making the key observation that Poisson composites may have unappealing visual artifacts due to a user's poor choice of boundary $\partial\Omega$. Since the user is not expected to provide a highly conformal outline for the source region, there is typically some space between the user-provided boundary $\partial\Omega$ and the actual object boundary, so that an intermediate contour $\partial\hat{\Omega}$ can be found to produce a more visually pleasing composite. The idea is to optimize $\partial\hat{\Omega}$. Jia et al. observed that the less variation along the boundary provided to the Laplace equation in Equations (3.17)–(3.18), the smoother (lower-energy) the correcting membrane E would be. They proposed to estimate $\partial\hat{\Omega}$ as a contour between the user-specified contour $\partial\Omega$ and the contour $\partial\Omega_{obj}$ produced by the GrabCut algorithm from Section 2.8.2 (Figure 3.12). The optimal contour $\partial\hat{\Omega}$ is estimated by alternating the following two steps, starting from the initial estimate $\partial\hat{\Omega} = \partial\Omega$:

1. Compute c as the average color of $T(x,y) - S(x,y)$ on $\partial\hat{\Omega}$.
2. Find the $\partial\hat{\Omega}$ satisfying $\Omega_{obj} \subset \hat{\Omega} \subset \Omega$ that minimizes the average value of $\|T(x,y) - S(x,y) - c\|^2$ on $\partial\hat{\Omega}$. This contour can be computed using a shortest-closed-path algorithm based on dynamic programming.

Jia et al. also proposed to incorporate the object's alpha matte into the compositing process by modifying the guidance vector field $(S_x(x,y), S_y(x,y))$, which further mitigates visible differences between the source and target.

Lalonde et al. [261] observed that in many visual effects compositing situations, the user may not care about pasting a particular source image into a scene, but instead wants to insert an object from a certain class (e.g., the job is to populate a clean plate of a street with cars and pedestrians). In this case, they proposed to leverage a library of thousands of "clip art" foreground objects, automatically providing the user with choices that fit well with the target scene in terms of estimated lighting, camera orientation, and resolution. These objects are then composited into the target image with an approach very similar to drag-and-drop pasting.

While we focused specifically on the compositing problem in this section, similar gradient-domain techniques based on the Poisson equation have been applied in several other areas of computer vision and graphics, including the removal of visible seams in panorama construction [6], high dynamic range compression [136], and locally changing color, illumination, and detail [364]. More generally, researchers have proposed optimization frameworks that operate directly on image pixels and their gradients for similar effects, such as Bhat et al.'s GradientShop [43].

3.3 GRAPH-CUT COMPOSITING

Poisson image editing works very well when the source and target images are relatively simple and smooth near the desired boundary. However, if the source or target is highly textured, it may be difficult to manually guess a good boundary around the source object that will be harmonious with the texture at the desired region in the target image. Drag-and-drop pasting offers one approach to automatically estimating a good boundary for gradient-domain compositing, but there may be no low-energy contours in a highly textured image. As another consideration, the colors of a gradient-domain composite may seem unnatural, since the original colors of the source image inside the target region are not preserved.

An alternative is to not blend the images across a boundary at all, but instead to select a region of the source image that can be directly copied to its position in the target image in the most unobtrusive way possible. The idea is to hide the compositing boundary in places where either the source and target are very similar, or there is enough texture in the target to obscure the presence of a discontinuity. This can be naturally viewed as a labeling problem: given a measure of the quality of a boundary and certain constraints, which pixels should come from the source and which from the target? This is quite similar to the graph-cut-based segmentation problem from Section 2.8.2.

Suppose the user has aligned a source image S with a target image T, as illustrated in Figure 3.13. The user designates a set of pixels S that definitely must come from the source, and another set T that definitely must come from the target. These constraints are analogous to those of the trimap and scribbles in the matting problem of

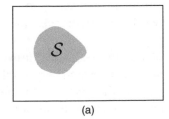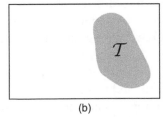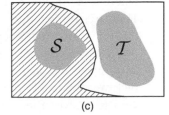

(a)   (b)   (c)

Figure 3.13. Seam-based compositing. (a) The source image with a constrained set S. (b) The target image with a constrained set T. (c) The final composite contains some pixels from the source image (striped region) and some from the target image (white region), separated by a seam.

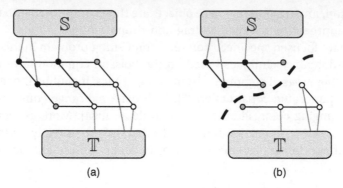

(a)   (b)

Figure 3.14. Graph formation for seam-based compositing. (a) Nodes in the set $\mathcal{S}$ (black dots) are attached to $\mathbb{S}$ with infinite weight and have no links to $\mathbb{T}$; conversely, nodes in the set $\mathcal{T}$ (white dots) are attached to $\mathbb{T}$ with infinite weight and have no links to $\mathbb{S}$. Gray nodes are uncommitted and are not directly connected to the terminals. (b) The minimum-cost cut separates the source and target terminals and defines a seam in the composite image.

Chapter 2. The remaining pixels comprise a region where the source/target boundary, or **seam**, is allowed to pass. We build a graph over the potential boundary pixels, creating an edge between each pair of 4-neighbors. An easy choice for the weight w_{ij} assigned to edge e_{ij} is:

$$w_{ij} = \|S(i) - T(i)\| + \|S(j) - T(j)\| \tag{3.23}$$

That is, the cost is low if the source and target pixels have similar colors on either side of a potential seam. We also create a pair of terminal nodes $\mathbb{S}$ and $\mathbb{T}$, and create edges $(i, \mathbb{S})$, $(j, \mathbb{T})$ with infinite weight for all $i \in \mathcal{S}$ and all $j \in \mathcal{T}$. The optimal seam is then defined as the minimum-cost cut that separates $\mathbb{S}$ from $\mathbb{T}$, as illustrated in Figure 3.14. Just like in the previous chapter, we use **graph cuts** [59] to solve the problem. Figure 3.15 illustrates an example of graph-cut-based compositing.

This approach to compositing was first proposed by Efros and Freeman [128] and Kwatra et al. [259], although their primary interest was synthesizing realistic texture (see Section 3.8). To bias the seam to go through higher-spatial-frequency regions where it will be less noticeable, Kwatra et al. suggested modifying Equation (3.23) to:

$$w_{ij} = \frac{\|S(i) - T(i)\| + \|S(j) - T(j)\|}{|d \cdot \nabla S(i)| + |d \cdot \nabla T(i)| + |d \cdot \nabla S(j)| + |d \cdot \nabla T(j)|} \tag{3.24}$$

where d is the direction of the edge (i.e., the vector pointing from pixel i to pixel j). This way, the denominator will be small and the weight will be large if the seam passes through a low-frequency (i.e., small-gradient) region.

We can generalize the graph-cut approach to deal with compositing multiple overlapping sources at the same time. For example, we may have several very similar pictures of a family portrait, and want to create a composite that contains the best view (e.g., eyes open, smiling) of each person. In this case, no single image acts as the target; instead we begin with several registered source images $S_1, \ldots, S_K$ and want to create a composite $I(x, y)$ where each pixel comes from one of the source images. We want to bias contiguous chunks to come from each image, and as before, to hide the seams in perceptually unimportant regions. Using graph cuts to make such a

Figure 3.15. An example of graph-cut compositing. (a) Target image. (b) Source image, with user strokes overlaid to indicate regions that must be included. (c) Graph-cut composite. (d) Region labels used to form the composite (black pixels are from (a), white pixels are from (b)).

multi-image **photomontage** was suggested by Agarwala et al. [7], building off Kwatra et al.'s framework.

The basic idea is to minimize a Gibbs energy of the form:

$$E(L) = \sum_{i \in \mathcal{V}} E_{\text{data}}(L(i)) + \sum_{(i,j) \in \mathcal{E}} E_{\text{smoothness}}(L(i), L(j)) \qquad (3.25)$$

Here, $\mathcal{V}$ is the set of pixels in the output image, $\mathcal{E}$ is the set of all adjacent pixels (for example, 4-neighbors), and L is a **labeling**; that is, an assignment in $\{1, \ldots, K\}$ to each pixel i. For the multi-image compositing problem, the user paints initial strokes in each source image, signifying that pixels stroked in image S_k must have label k in the final composite. Natural forms of the two energy terms are:

$$E_{\text{data}}(L(i) = k) = \begin{cases} 0 & \text{if pixel } i \text{ is stroked in } S_k \\ \infty & \text{if pixel } i \text{ is stroked in some image } S_j \neq S_k \\ 0 & \text{otherwise} \end{cases} \quad (3.26)$$

$$E_{\text{smoothness}}(L(i) = k, L(j) = l) = \|S_k(i) - S_l(i)\| + \|S_k(j) - S_l(j)\| \qquad (3.27)$$

Figure 3.16. A multi-image photomontage created with α-expansion. (a) The original images, color-coded as red, green, and blue. Each image has some unsatisfactory facial expressions. (b) A user scribbles on faces and body parts to keep from each source image, resulting in the labeling map at right. Note that in several cases, a person's head is taken from one source image and their body from another. (c) The final composite.

We can modify Equation (3.27) similarly to Equation (3.24) to bias seams to lie along existing image edges.

Unfortunately, the graph-cut algorithm cannot directly minimize a function like Equation (3.25) where we have more than two possible labels per pixel (i.e., more than two terminal nodes). Instead, we use an extension called α-**expansion** [61][5], which briefly works as follows. We cyclically iterate over the possible labels $k = 1, \ldots, K$. For a given label, we form an auxiliary minimum-cut problem in which each node will either be associated with the label it had in the previous iteration, or the new label k, which corresponds to a two-terminal graph (i.e., k or not-k). That is, at each step, the region of pixels labeled k is allowed to expand by solving a new minimum-cut problem. The algorithm stops after a cycle through all the labels fails to decrease the cost function. While we aren't guaranteed to find a global minimum of Equation (3.25) as in the two-label case, the cost of the α-expansion result will be within a factor of 2 of the global minimum. Appendix A.3 gives details on the algorithm.

Figure 3.16 illustrates a result of fusing multiple images into a composite image with this technique. Agarwala et al. [7] discussed how simple modifications to the energies in Equations (3.26)–(3.27) could be used for other visual effects, such as creating clean plates, constructing panoramas from multiple images without seams or artifacts from moving objects, and interactively relighting an object using source images taken under different lighting conditions. They also mentioned how to combine the approach with Poisson compositing to improve results for dissimilar source images. Rother et al. [404] extended the multi-image compositing approach to create collages of very different source images (for example, to summarize in a single composite the people and places contained in many different images of a vacation). Johnson et al. [225] described how realistic composite "photographs" could be easily created with graph-cut techniques based on a user's rough placement of meaningful regions on a blank canvas (e.g., "sky" above "building" above "water") and a library of labeled images.

3.4   IMAGE INPAINTING

While compositing different elements into a final scene is the backbone of visual effects production, it is often necessary to *remove* objects from a scene, such as the wires suspending a stunt performer or a gantry supporting special effects equipment. In this case, we specify a region Ω in a source image and want to replace it with pixels that realistically "fill the hole." There should be no blurring or visual artifacts that would lead a viewer to believe the resulting image was manipulated. This hole-filling problem is known as **image inpainting**. The term was introduced to the computer vision community by Bertalmio et al. [40] to describe the process of removing thin artifacts like scratches in an old photograph or an unwanted caption on a digital image. However, the term has grown to include the general filling-in problem, no matter how large the hole. This problem is also sometimes called **image completion**.

The best-case scenario is when we have a clean plate of the scene from exactly the same camera perspective and under the same lighting conditions (similar to the setup for difference matting). In this case, we can treat inpainting as a compositing problem in which the clean plate plays the role of the source image. Even if an actual clean plate is unavailable, visual effects artists can often synthesize a good approximation by stealing pixels from the unoccluded background in different frames, or by

---

[5] There is no relationship between this α and α mattes from the previous chapter.

"warping in" background texture from images taken from different perspectives (see Section 3.7). In this section, we focus on what can be done when a clean plate or an approximation to one is unavailable, and we only have the pixels in the current frame as the basis for inpainting.

Most inpainting algorithms iteratively fill in the target region Ω from its boundary inward; in this context $\partial\Omega$ is sometimes called the **fill front**. We initialize the process with

$$I_0(x,y) = \begin{cases} I(x,y) & (x,y) \notin \Omega \\ \text{black} & (x,y) \in \Omega \end{cases} \tag{3.28}$$

Then at each step we produce a new image $I_{n+1}(x,y)$ based on $I_n(x,y)$, until the hole is filled in.

Here, we discuss two basic approaches to the problem: a partial-differential-equation-based approach better suited to inpainting thin holes, and a texture-synthesis approach better suited to inpainting large missing regions.

3.4.1   Partial-Differential-Equation-Based Methods

Bertalmio et al. [40] were originally inspired by the way that professional art conservators restore damaged paintings. The basic approach is to work inward from the boundary $\partial\Omega$, propagating the image colors and structure from the surrounding pixels into the hole. In this section, we assume that each color channel is processed independently.

We need to answer two questions to make this approach more precise. First, exactly what information should be smoothly propagated into the hole? Second, in what direction should the propagation occur? Bertalmio et al. proposed to propagate the **Laplacian** of the image intensities, since this operator represents the local smoothness of the image. While it would seem natural to propagate the Laplacian in the direction normal to the hole boundary $\partial\Omega$, this can lead to counterintuitive results in the presence of strong image structure, as illustrated in Figure 3.17b. Instead, we propagate along **isophote directions** — that is, along contours where the intensity change is the smallest — producing a more natural result (Figure 3.17c). Essentially, we try to continue strong image edges into the hole.

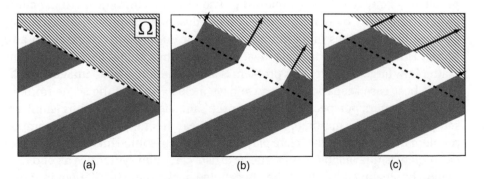

      (a)   (b)   (c)

Figure 3.17. (a) The image and inpainting region. (b) Propagating image information normal to the region boundary can produce unwanted artifacts. (c) Instead, we propagate along isophote directions to maintain visual continuity.

Since the gradient at a pixel indicates the direction of greatest change, we can locally compute the isophote direction as the unit vector perpendicular to the gradient; that is,

$$\nabla^\perp I(x,y) = \text{unit}\left(\begin{bmatrix} I(x,y) - I(x,y+1) \\ I(x+1,y) - I(x,y) \end{bmatrix}\right) \tag{3.29}$$

Putting all this together mathematically, the pixel intensities that fill the hole should satisfy the partial differential equation (PDE):

$$\nabla(\nabla^2 I) \cdot \nabla^\perp I = 0 \tag{3.30}$$

That is, the change in the Laplacian $\nabla(\nabla^2 I)$ should be zero in the direction of the isophote $\nabla^\perp I$. Ideally, we could solve Equation (3.30) by creating an image that changes as a function of time according to the following PDE:

$$\frac{\partial I}{\partial t} = \nabla(\nabla^2 I) \cdot \nabla^\perp I \tag{3.31}$$

When the image stops changing, $\frac{\partial I}{\partial t} = 0$ and thus the solution satisfies Equation (3.30). In practice, we approximate Equation (3.31) with discrete time steps, letting

$$I_{n+1}(x,y) = I_n(x,y) + (\nabla t)U_n(x,y), \quad \forall (x,y) \in \Omega \tag{3.32}$$

The update image $U_n(x,y)$ is derived from a discrete approximation of Equation (3.30), with the usual approximations of the gradient and the Laplacian. Bertalmio et al. recommended several enhancements to the implementation, including interleaved steps of **anisotropic diffusion** to smooth the intermediate images without losing edge definition. A typical result of inpainting an image with thin holes is illustrated in Figure 3.18, showing several steps of evolution.

Note that we could achieve a similar result using the Poisson compositing technique from the previous section, simply by setting the guidance vector field $(S_x, S_y) = 0$

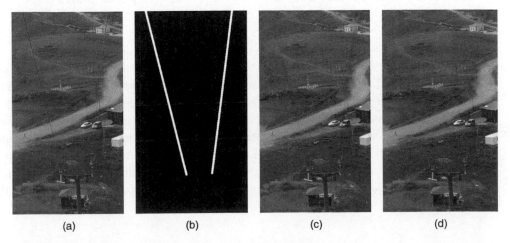

(a)   (b)   (c)   (d)

Figure 3.18. (a) The original image. (b) The inpainting mask. (c) After 4,000 iterations of PDE-based inpainting, the wire locations are still perceptible as blurry regions. (d) After 10,000 iterations of PDE-based inpainting, the wires have disappeared.

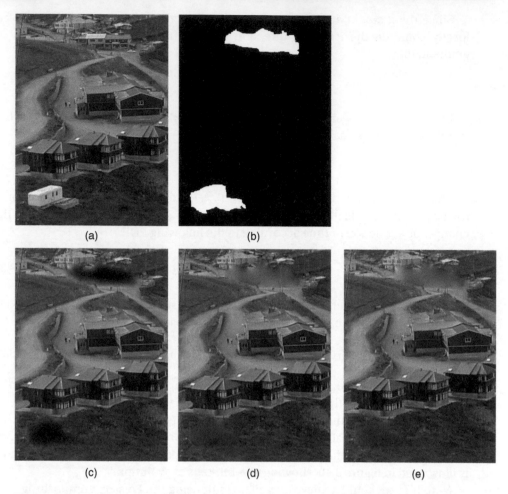

Figure 3.19. A failure case of PDE-based inpainting. (a) The original image. (b) The inpainting mask. (c) The result after 20,000 iterations of PDE-based inpainting. (d) The result after 200,000 iterations of PDE-based inpainting. The inpainting region is unacceptably blurry. (e) Poisson compositing with a guidance vector field of 0 inside the inpainting mask, giving a similar result.

inside Ω. This would result in a second-order PDE (i.e., a Laplace equation with Dirichlet boundary conditions) as opposed to the third-order PDE of Equation (3.30).[6]

PDE-based inpainting techniques are a reasonable choice for certain visual effects scenarios, such as painting out thin wires holding up a stunt performer. However, a major drawback of PDE-based techniques is that the interior of the inpainted region is inevitably smoother and blurrier than its surroundings, leading to unacceptable visual artifacts when a large hole is located inside a textured region, as illustrated in Figure 3.19. The patch-based methods we discuss next do not have this shortcoming.

---

[6] Since inpainting can take many iterations to converge, using the Poisson approach is also likely to be much faster.

3.4.2 Patch-Based Methods

A promising class of inpainting methods incrementally fills in patches of the target region Ω by copying patches from the surrounding image. That is, the region outside the hole, $\Phi = I - \Omega$, acts as a source region for the appearance of new patches inside the hole. Here, we present the algorithm proposed by Criminisi et al. [108], which is effective and easy to understand. Until the target region is completely filled in, we iterate over the following steps:

1. Determine a priority $P(p)$ for every pixel $p \in \partial\Omega$.
2. Select the pixel $\hat{p}$ with highest priority and denote the $W \times W$ patch of pixels centered around it as $\Psi_{\hat{p}}$. A typical value for W is 9.
3. Find the patch of pixels $\Psi_{\hat{q}} \subset \Phi$ that best matches $\Psi_{\hat{p}}$.
4. Overwrite the pixels in $\Psi_{\hat{p}} \cap \Omega$ with the corresponding pixels from $\Psi_{\hat{q}}$, and shrink the target region Ω accordingly.

One cycle of the process is illustrated in Figure 3.20.

The first step, computing the priorities of the pixels on the boundary of the fill front, is the most important. Criminisi et al. proposed that the priority be the product of a **confidence term** $C(p)$ and a **data term** $D(p)$. The confidence term is high when the pixel is surrounded by many pixels whose intensities are already known. For example, the point A at the end of the "peninsula" in Figure 3.21a is a good candidate for filling in since it juts out into a region of known pixels. On the other hand, the point B at the end of the "dent" in Figure 3.21a is a bad candidate for filling in since almost all the pixels in its neighborhood are unknown. Initially, we set the confidence $C(p) = 0$ for all $p \in \Omega$, and $C(p) = 1$ for all $p \notin \Omega$. Then $C(p)$ for any point on the fill

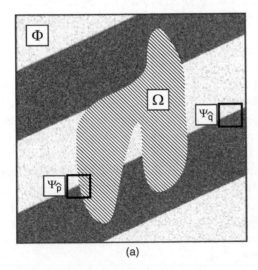 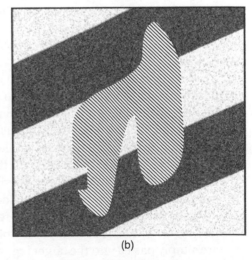

(a) (b)

Figure 3.20. One cycle of patch-based inpainting. (a) The patch of pixels $\Psi_{\hat{p}}$ centered around the pixel on the fill front with the highest priority is selected. The patch of pixels $\Psi_{\hat{q}} \subset \Phi$ that best matches $\Psi_{\hat{p}}$ is determined. (b) Pixels are copied from $\Psi_{\hat{q}}$ to shrink the target region.

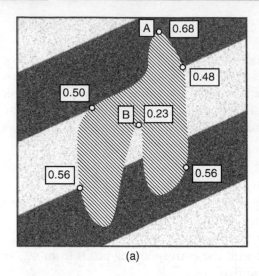
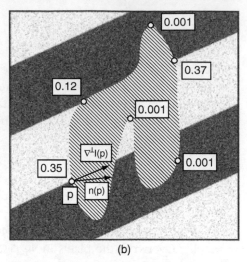

(a)   (b)

Figure 3.21. (a) The confidence term for patch-based inpainting. The term is high where $\partial\Omega$ is convex (e.g., point A), low where $\partial\Omega$ is concave (e.g., point B), and near 0.5 where $\partial\Omega$ is straight. (b) The data term for patch-based inpainting. The term is relatively high when a strong edge is nearly perpendicular to $\partial\Omega$, lower when a strong edge is nearly parallel to $\partial\Omega$, and very small in nearly-constant-intensity regions. Point p illustrates the vectors used to compute the data term.

front is computed as the average confidence of the pixels in Ψ_p:

$$C(p) = \frac{1}{W^2} \sum_{q \in \Psi_p} C(q) \tag{3.33}$$

The data term incorporates similar reasoning as the PDE-based method; we want to propagate intensities into the target region along isophote directions, starting with strong edges that should continue into Ω. We prefer strong edges that hit the boundary $\partial\Omega$ head-on (i.e., at a right angle) as opposed to a strong edge tangent to the boundary. Thus the data term for an image with intensities in [0, 1] is computed as:

$$D(p) = \|\nabla I(p)\| \left| \nabla^\perp I(p) \cdot n(p) \right| \tag{3.34}$$

where $n(p)$ is a unit vector orthogonal to $\partial\Omega$ at p and $\nabla^\perp I(p)$ is the unit vector perpendicular to the gradient defined in Equation (3.29). Thus, the data term at a pixel increases with the strength of the image gradient and with its alignment to the tangent of the fill front. Figure 3.21b illustrates the vectors in Equation (3.34) and some values of the data term for an example I and Ω.

After we compute the pixel $\hat{p}$ on the fill front with the highest priority, we form a patch around it and find its best match in the source region, defined simply as the patch with the minimum Euclidean distance (measured in color space). The distance is only computed over the region of the patch containing known pixels — i.e., $\Psi_{\hat{p}} \cap (I - \Omega)$. The corresponding pixel colors from the resulting "exemplar" patch are simply pasted into the target region $\Psi_{\hat{p}} \cap \Omega$.

Finally, the confidence values for the newly copied pixels are all assigned to be $C(\hat{p})$, so that as we work toward the interior of the target region, the confidences get lower and lower. The algorithm stops when all the target pixels have been filled in.

Figure 3.22. Results of patch-based inpainting. (a) The original image. (b) The inpainting mask. (c) The final inpainted image. The bottom row illustrates the result after (d) 200, (e) 800, and (f) 2,000 iterations. Note that strong linear structures are propagated through the inpainting region first.

Figure 3.22 illustrates an example result showing several intermediate steps; we can see that the algorithm tends to propagate strong linear structures through the target region first, leaving large flat regions until the end. While the result has several regions that look unusual (e.g., along the left crossbar and on the foreground post), several regions are very convincing (e.g., the bridges, trees, and foreground terrain). PDE-based inpainting cannot achieve a result with this level of realistic texture.

Drori et al. [126] proposed a similar inpainting method at about the same time, which used a coarse-to-fine approach and Laplacian-pyramid-based blending instead of direct copying of pixel regions. They also allowed the target patches to adaptively change size and the source patches to change in scale and orientation, permitting a wider range of possibilities at the cost of speed.

Sun et al. [481] noted that while patch-based methods try to continue strong linear features into the target region, these methods cannot guarantee that salient features like straight lines or junctions will correctly "meet up" in its interior. They proposed a belief-propagation-based algorithm to first complete salient structures drawn in the target region by the user, afterward filling in the remaining pixels with a patch-based algorithm and Poisson blending. This approach produces good results compared to Criminisi's algorithm when the target region should contain continuations of structures to which the human eye is sensitive, such as horizon lines or fences. Komodakis and Tziritas [249] took the belief-propagation approach a step further by applying it to the entire target region instead of just the linear structures specified by the user. While this method has the advantage of posing the problem globally instead of greedily selecting the best patch at each iteration, the main difficulty is managing the large space of patch labels at each target position.

Finally, Hays and Efros [191] noted that the source region need not be confined to the pixels in the image outside the target region. Instead, they proposed to use *millions* of photographs gathered from the Internet to suggest plausible completions for a large target region, filling it with a large chunk from one of these images. These plausible alternatives can vary widely, and the user is allowed to pick the best one for his or her purpose. The main problem is devising a highly parallelizable algorithm to efficiently search the huge database of images for good matches. Once each matching image is aligned to the target image, a seam-based algorithm similar to that of Section 3.3 is used to create the composite.

3.5   IMAGE RETARGETING AND RECOMPOSITING

Finally, we discuss **image retargeting** techniques for changing the size and aspect ratio of an image. While many retargeting algorithms were designed for making an image smaller (for example, to fit on a mobile device), these types of techniques could also be used to reshape high-resolution images and video — for example, to change a movie from the theater aspect ratio of 2.39:1 to the HDTV aspect ratio of 16:9. Common techniques for retargeting an image to a new aspect ratio include cropping, scaling, and letterboxing, but as Figure 3.23 illustrates, these methods can remove, distort, or shrink image features in perceptually distracting ways. However, there has recently been an explosion of interest in the computer vision and graphics communities in **content-aware image retargeting**. These methods resize an image

(a)   (b)   (c)   (d)

Figure 3.23. Resizing an original image (a). (b) Cropping can remove important details from the image (e.g., the second cow.) (c) Scaling changes the aspect ratio, causing unnatural distortions. (d) Letterboxing makes all the elements of the image small, losing detail.

by moving and removing pixels in such a way that the aspect ratios of important sub-objects (such as faces) are preserved, while omitting information in areas that are less perceptually important (such as large flat regions). Image retargeting techniques can also be used for realistic, automatic **image recompositing** or **reshuffling** — that is, the spatial rearrangement of elements of a scene.

3.5.1   Non-Uniform Warping

Initial work on retargeting simply addressed the automatic selection of a good cropping rectangle for a given image or each frame of a video sequence (e.g., [292]). However, as mentioned previously, cropping inevitably removes image content, and it may not be possible to fit all objects of interest into a single cropping rectangle. An alternative is to consider the image domain as a "rubber sheet" made up of rectangular elements. To resize the image, each element is locally deformed while maintaining connectivity with its neighbors. The idea is to maintain the original aspect ratio of rectangles containing **regions of interest** (or **ROIs**) while squishing rectangles in perceptually unimportant regions.

One of the first approaches of this type was proposed by Liu and Gleicher [291]. They used an **importance map** to determine the ROI in an image, based on an automatic estimation of salience (i.e., visual importance) at each pixel and a face detection algorithm. Given the ROI, a simple nonlinear warp is applied to create the resized image, as illustrated in Figure 3.24.

Wang et al. [536] proposed a scheme called **optimized scale-and-stretch** that deforms the image mesh at a much finer level and doesn't rely on a single ROI. As before, we begin with an importance map, in this case computed as the product of the gradient magnitude at each pixel and a saliency map. The saliency map is based on a popular algorithm proposed by Itti et al. [215] that combines pixel colors and

(a)   (b)   (c)

Figure 3.24. (a) An original image, with ROI given by the center box. (b) The ROI is uniformly scaled to avoid distortion, while the eight rectangular regions surrounding it are warped with piecewise linear transformations. (c) Final result.

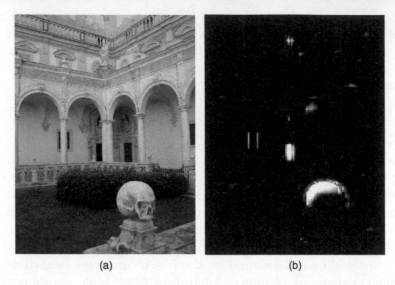

(a)   (b)

Figure 3.25. (a) An original image. (b) The saliency map obtained using Itti et al.'s algorithm.

gradient magnitudes/orientations to estimate regions in the image likely to attract visual attention; an example is illustrated in Figure 3.25.

We partition the image into a set $\mathcal{Q}$ of rectangular elements, or **quads**, which are defined by sets of vertices $\mathcal{V}$ and edges $\mathcal{E}$. Each quad q is given a weight $w(q)$ computed as the average importance of the pixels inside it. We denote the vertices of quad q as $\mathcal{V}_q$. A deformation of the quad mesh results in a new set of vertex positions $\mathcal{V}'$ with the same edges as the original mesh. For a candidate deformation $\mathcal{V}'$, we compute a cost as:

$$C(\mathcal{V}') = \sum_{q\in\mathcal{Q}} w(q) \left(\sum_{v_i,v_j\in\mathcal{V}_q} \|(v'_i - v'_j) - s_q(v_i - v_j)\|^2 \right) + \sum_{(v_i,v_j)\in\mathcal{E}} \|(v'_i - v'_j) - l_{ij}(v_i - v_j)\|^2$$

$$(3.35)$$

Here, the first term in Equation (3.35) encourages each quad q to be uniformly scaled by a factor s_q, with a higher weight on quads with higher saliency.[7] The second term in Equation (3.35) encourages the top-to-bottom and left-to-right grid lines that define the quads not to bend too much; here, $l_{ij} = \|v'_i - v'_j\|/\|v_i - v_j\|$. The basic idea is to minimize the cost function in Equation (3.35) subject to the boundary constraints that the output image be rectangular with the desired dimensions, resulting in a series of linear systems in the vertex locations. Figure 3.26 illustrates an example result of the method.

3.5.2   Seam Carving

One of the most exciting approaches for image retargeting in recent years is **seam carving**, a simple algorithm that can effectively resize and reshape images and that can also be used for inpainting. The key concept is the addition and removal of

---

[7] s_q can be determined as a function of a given $\mathcal{V}$ and $\mathcal{V}'$ and eliminated from the equation; see Problem 3.19.

(a)

(c)

(b)

(d)

Figure 3.26. (a) An original image. (b) Its importance map. (c) The optimized scale-and-stretch grid. Note that unimportant rectangles can be squished, while important rectangles retain their original aspect ratio. (d) The final result of stretching the image to be about fifty percent wider.

(a)

(b)

Figure 3.27. (a) Vertical and (b) horizontal seams in an image.

seams in an image. Unlike the seams in Section 3.3 that can have an arbitrary non-self-intersecting shape, here we consider only connected paths of pixels that start at the top edge of the image and end at the bottom edge, passing through exactly one pixel per row (or similarly, paths that go from the left to right passing through one pixel per column), as illustrated in Figure 3.27.

Clearly, removing a top-to-bottom seam and pushing the remaining pixels together will reduce the image width by one column; similarly, removing a left-to-right seam reduces the image height by one row. Avidan and Shamir [21] made a simple observation: to reduce the size of an image, we should first remove those seams that pass through perceptually uninteresting regions of the image. The notion of "interesting" is encapsulated in a **seam energy**, the simplest of which is the sum of image gradients along a given seam s:

$$E(s) = \sum_{(x,y)\in s} \left| \frac{\partial I}{\partial x}(x,y) \right| + \left| \frac{\partial I}{\partial y}(x,y) \right| = \sum_{(x,y)\in s} e_1(x,y) \tag{3.36}$$

Finding the lowest-cost top-to-bottom seam is easy using dynamic programming; we simply work from the second row to the last row, keeping track of the cumulative minimum energy path to each pixel. We then find the pixel in the bottom row with the lowest cumulative energy and backtrack to find the optimal seam (see Appendix A.1). The computation for left-to-right seams is analogous. Any energy function (such as the measures of saliency used in the previous section) can easily be substituted for the gradient sum in Equation (3.36). Seam carving can also be done in the gradient domain, using Poisson reconstruction as in Section 3.2 to recover the image.

Therefore, if we want to reduce an image's width by k columns, we perform k iterations of finding and removing the lowest-cost vertical seam. Figure 3.28 shows the results of resizing an example image with this simple technique. For interactive resizing applications, Avidan and Shamir showed how the cost-ordering of seams could be pre-computed and stored in a matrix the same size as the original image.

To enlarge an image by k columns (which may be of more practical use for visual effects), we instead *insert* pixels into the image at the k lowest-energy vertical seams, under the assumption that these are the least perceptually distracting locations to introduce new information. That is, we insert a one-pixel-wide gap at each seam location and create new colors by interpolating the image colors on either side of the seam. Figure 3.29 shows the results of expanding an example image with this technique.

For a different approach to image inpainting, we can force seams to go through a target region Ω by setting the seam energy for these pixels equal to 0. We then remove seams until all the pixels in Ω have been removed, and then expand the image by the same number of seams to regain an image with the original dimensions. Figure 3.30 illustrates an example of inpainting with this seam-based approach; this effect would be very difficult to achieve with the methods in Section 3.4. Similarly, to make sure that seams don't pass though perceptually critical regions of the image (such as faces), the energy can be made punitively high in such regions.

(a)	(b)	(c)

Figure 3.28. Reducing an image's width by successively removing the lowest-energy vertical seams. (a) The original image. (b) The lowest-energy seams. (c) The result of seam removal.

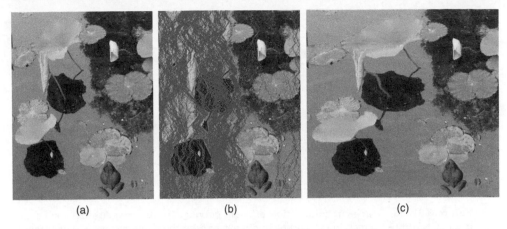

(a) (b) (c)

Figure 3.29. Increasing an image's width by adding pixels at the lowest-energy vertical seams. (a) The original image. (b) The lowest-energy seams. (c) The result of seam expansion.

(a) (b)

Figure 3.30. Inpainting with seam carving. (a) The original image. (b) An inpainted image of the same size created by removing, then adding vertical seams. Can you find the two books that have been removed, and identify other books that have been compressed/expanded to compensate?

Rubinstein et al. [408] proposed two key algorithmic refinements to the original seam carving algorithm. First, they showed how the problem of finding the optimal seam could be naturally posed as computing the minimum cut on a graph, which can be generalized more easily than dynamic programming. As usual, the vertices of the graph correspond to image pixels. However, unlike the graph-cut methods in Section 3.3 and the previous chapter, we create a **directed graph** in which each pair of 4-neighbors can be connected by two **arcs** going in different directions. Figure 3.31 illustrates the graph setup and arc weights that correspond to seam carving. For a vertical seam, we attach all the pixels on the left edge of the image to one terminal $\mathbb{S}$, and all the pixels on the right edge to another terminal $\mathbb{T}$. We seek a cut of the graph that separates the terminals; the cost of such a cut is the sum of the weights of the

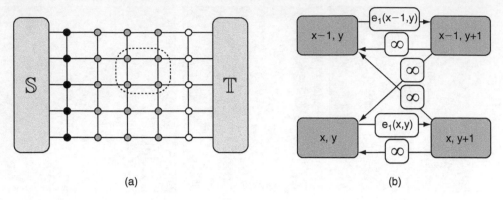

(a)   (b)

Figure 3.31. (a) Graph-cut formulation of seam carving. (b) Arc weights for a subset of the graph (the dotted region in (a)) corresponding to finding the minimal-cost vertical seam. Here, e_1 represents the sum of gradients in the summand of Equation (3.36).

directed arcs from $\mathbb{S}$ to $\mathbb{T}$. After computing the cut, we remove the pixels to the left of the seam in each row. The special configuration of infinite-weight arcs ensures that the cut forms a connected path of pixels that only intersects one pixel per row (see Problem 3.21).

Rubinstein et al. also observed that the original formulation of the seam energy in Equation (3.36) ignores energy that may be *inserted* into the image by removal of the seam, since new edges are created when previously non-neighboring pixels are pushed together. Instead, they proposed to measure the energy of a seam as the energy *introduced* by removing the seam. They called this the **forward energy** of the seam to distinguish it from the **backward energy** in Equation (3.36). As illustrated in Figure 3.32, there are three possibilities for new edges introduced for a vertical seam depending on its direction at pixel (x,y).

These three cases correspond to the forward energy cost function terms

$$C(x,y) = \begin{cases} C_{LR}(x,y) + C_{LU}(x,y) & \text{Case 1} \\ C_{LR}(x,y) & \text{Case 2} \\ C_{LR}(x,y) + C_{RU}(x,y) & \text{Case 3} \end{cases} \tag{3.37}$$

where

$$C_{LR}(x,y) = \|I(x,y+1) - I(x,y-1)\|$$
$$C_{LU}(x,y) = \|I(x-1,y) - I(x,y-1)\| \tag{3.38}$$
$$C_{RU}(x,y) = \|I(x-1,y) - I(x,y+1)\|$$

The total forward energy of a seam is thus

$$E(s) = \sum_{(x,y)\in s} C(x,y) \tag{3.39}$$

which can again be minimized using dynamic programming. To minimize the forward energy using graph cuts instead, we modify the subgraph in Figure 3.31b to have the weights in Figure 3.33a. Figure 3.33b-d illustrates an example of reducing an image's size using both the backward and forward energies, showing that using

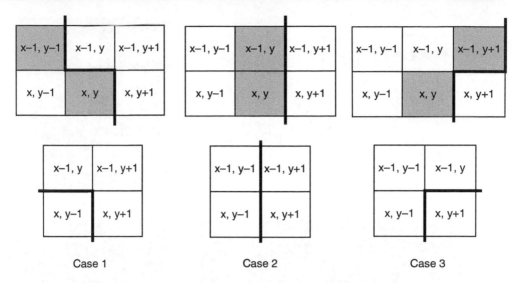

Figure 3.32. Pixel configurations introduced by seam removal. The shaded seam pixels in the top row are removed to produce the new pixel arrangements in the bottom row. New neighbors are indicated by bold lines in the bottom row. The bold lines in the top row represent the edges cut in a graph-cut formulation of the problem.

the forward energy avoids introducing visual artifacts. For this reason, the forward energy is usually preferred in implementations of seam carving.

3.5.3   Patch-Based Methods

As we saw in Section 3.4.2, patch-based methods enabled high-quality image inpainting; as we discuss here, they also enable high-quality image retargeting. Furthermore, they naturally enable image recompositing, in which elements of one or more images can be seamlessly combined, deleted, and rearranged.

The key concept of patch-based methods is called **bidirectional similarity**, proposed by Simakov et al. [451]. Suppose we want to retarget an image I into a new image I'. Simakov et al. argued that a good retargeting should have two properties. First, the new image I' should be **complete**: it should contain as much of the visual information from I as possible. Second, the new image should be **coherent**: it should not contain any visual information not present in the original image. The idea is illustrated in Figure 3.34.

If we consider each image as a collection of overlapping patches at different scales, this means that every patch of I should be present in I' (for completeness) and every patch of I' should be present in I (for coherence). This leads to a simple bidirectional similarity measure for the pair (I, I'):

$$D(I, I') = \frac{1}{N} \sum_{\Psi \subset I} \min_{\Psi' \subset I'} d(\Psi, \Psi') + \frac{1}{N'} \sum_{\Psi' \subset I'} \min_{\Psi \subset I} d(\Psi, \Psi') \tag{3.40}$$

Here, each Ψ is a patch in I and each Ψ' is a patch in I'; these patches are effectively generated at multiple scales, as described next. We assume N patches are created in I

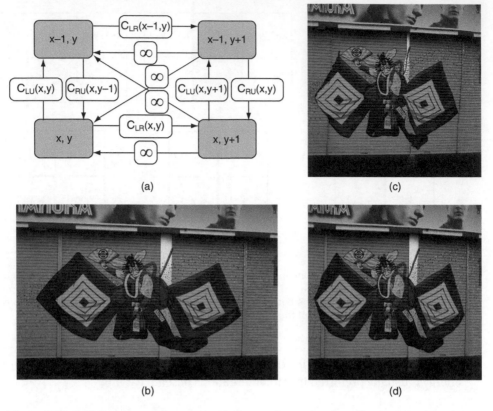

Figure 3.33. (a) The arc weights corresponding to forward energy in graph-cut-based seam carving, corresponding to finding the minimal-cost vertical seam. (b) An original image. (c) Seam carving with backward energy, showing visual artifacts (e.g., the right leg, the sword, the vertical white bar). (d) Seam carving with forward energy results in a more acceptable image with fewer introduced artifacts.

and N' patches are created in I'. The function d in the summands is the average sum-of-squared-distance between the colors of corresponding pixels in a pair of same-sized patches. The first term in Equation (3.40) captures the notion of completeness, and the second term captures the notion of coherence. The measure $D(I, I')$ is low when both properties are well satisfied.

If we specify the desired dimensions of the retargeted image, then our goal is to find the image I' that minimizes $D(I, I')$. We use an iterative update rule for this estimation problem, as follows.

Let's consider a pixel $j \in I'$ and think about how it contributes to the cost function in Equation (3.40), as illustrated in Figure 3.35. Suppose we only consider $W \times W$ patches in Equation (3.40). That means that j will be a member of W^2 patches $\{\Psi'_1, \ldots, \Psi'_{W^2}\}$ in I', which have the best matches $\{\Psi_1, \ldots, \Psi_{W^2}\}$ in I. Let the pixels in I corresponding to pixel j in each of these patches be $i_1, \ldots, i_{W^2}$. Thus, the second term in Equation (3.40) corresponding to pixel j is:

$$\frac{1}{N'} \sum_{k=1}^{W^2} \|I(i_k) - I'(j)\|^2 \tag{3.41}$$

where the norm in Equation (3.41) is the Euclidean distance in color space.

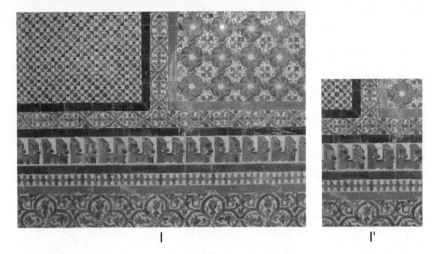

I   I'

Figure 3.34. An original image I and a proposed retargeted image I'. Most patches from I are present in I', indicating a high degree of completeness. Conversely, I' doesn't contain patches that don't appear in I, indicating a high degree of coherence. The retargeted image can remain complete and coherent while removing large chunks of repetitive texture, which is difficult to do with seam carving.

On the other hand, the contribution of j to the first term in Equation (3.40) is harder to determine, since we don't know how many patches from I (if any) include j in their best-match patches. If we assume that N_j patches in I include j in their best-match patch in I', and let the pixels in I corresponding to pixel j in each of these patches be $i'_1, \ldots, i'_{N_j}$, then the first term in Equation (3.40) corresponding to pixel j is:

$$\frac{1}{N} \sum_{k=1}^{N_j} \|I(i'_k) - I'(j)\|^2 \tag{3.42}$$

Therefore, the overall contribution from pixel j to the cost function in Equation (3.40) is the sum of Equation (3.41) and Equation (3.42). Since we want to determine the best value of the color $I'(j)$, we take the derivative of this sum and set it equal to zero, obtaining

$$I'(j) = \frac{\frac{1}{N}\sum_{k=1}^{N_j} I(i'_k) + \frac{1}{N'}\sum_{k=1}^{W^2} I(i_k)}{\frac{N_j}{N} + \frac{W^2}{N'}} \tag{3.43}$$

This suggests a simple iterative algorithm, repeated until the retargeted image stops changing:

1. For each patch Ψ' in I', find the most similar patch in I to find the pixel colors for Equation (3.41).
2. For each patch Ψ in I, find the most similar patch in I' to find the pixel colors for Equation (3.42).
3. Update the image I' using Equation (3.43).

A scaled version of the original image is a good choice for initializing the process if the retargeted dimensions are not too different than the original dimensions; otherwise, the desired dimension can be reached using several steps in which the relative

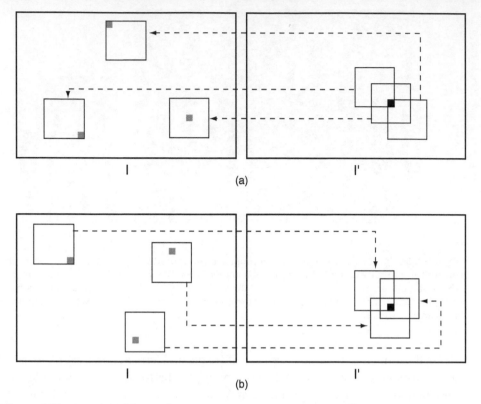

Figure 3.35. An original image I and a proposed retargeted image I'. We consider the contribution of the black pixel j in I' to the bidirectional similarity cost function. (a) For the coherence term, we consider the W^2 patches in I' that contain the black pixel j, and find their best matches in I. (b) For the completeness term, we consider the N_j patches in I whose best matches in I' contain the black pixel j, where N_j changes from pixel to pixel. The pixel color at j in the retargeted image is iteratively updated as the weighted sum of colors at the gray pixels in I involved in both terms.

change in dimension is not too large. Applying the algorithm with a coarse-to-fine approach using a Gaussian pyramid effectively creates multi-scale patches if W is the same at every level, and produces good approximations for successively finer scales. Weights can also be applied at each pixel, for example using the saliency measure from Section 3.5.1, to bias the algorithm to preserve important regions (e.g., faces), or to place zero weights on pixels to be removed from the image for inpainting.

Bidirectional similarity seems to do a better job at creating extremely small versions of images compared to seam carving (which is not really of interest for visual effects); for example, it allows repetitive textures like windows on a building to automatically be condensed. However, this approach is exciting for its ability to easily recompose or reshuffle images. For example, the user can roughly cut image features out of an image, rearrange them on the target image I', and fix these pixels' intensities. Then the iterative algorithm is applied to find the remaining pixels' intensities so that the resulting image is as complete and coherent as possible. An example of this approach is illustrated in Figure 3.36. Similarly, a realistic expansion of an original image can be created by fixing the position of the original on a larger canvas and optimizing the coherence term in Equation (3.41) only over the unknown border regions.

(a)   (b)   (c)

Figure 3.36. Reshuffling an image using bidirectional similarity. (a) An original image. (b) Constraints fixing certain pixels (note that the trays in the center are in new positions). (c) The automatically created recomposition.

The result effectively synthesizes realistic texture around the original, similar to the patch-based inpainting methods in Section 3.4.2. If two separate images are used to provide patches for I, the retargeted image I' will resemble a seamless montage of the inputs, similar to Section 3.3.

However, this algorithm has one serious drawback: it is highly computationally time-consuming, as well as memory-intensive, to search for the minimum-cost patches in Equation (3.40). The algorithm can be substantially accelerated — by factors of 20 to 100 — using an approximate nearest-neighbor algorithm proposed by Barnes et al. called **PatchMatch** [30]. The approximate algorithm is based on random sampling and exploits the coherence of natural images to find good approximate matches for the bidirectional similarity algorithm (but which could apply to any of the block-matching algorithms discussed throughout this book). Barnes et al. performed several experiments on real and synthetic data to show that PatchMatch substantially outperformed other algorithms conventionally used for approximate nearest neighbors (such as [19]), to the extent that image reshuffling can be performed at interactive rates. By restricting the search areas for the nearest neighbors, PatchMatch also allows new effects that were difficult to obtain with the other methods in this section, such as preserving long straight lines.

Cho et al. [93] proposed an algorithm for retargeting and reshuffling called the **patch transform** at the same time as Simakov et al.'s bidirectional similarity approach; the two methods share a similar philosophy and produce similar-looking results. However, the patch transform uses loopy belief propagation as its optimization engine, and explicitly constrains the output image to be composed of a disjoint set of patches from the original image, each of which is only used once.

In the extreme case where we only consider patches of size 1×1 pixel, a retargeted image can be thought of as a collection of pixels from the input image. That is, $I'(x, y)$ is defined by a label $(\delta x, \delta y)$ such that $I'(x, y) = I(x + \delta x, y + \delta y)$. From this perspective, retargeting the image can be thought of as a label assignment problem. Pritch et al. [376] proposed an algorithm called **shift-map editing** based on this concept. If L is a labeling, that is, an assignment $(\delta x, \delta y)$ at each pixel of the retargeted image, then a cost function over labelings is defined in the same way as Equation (3.25); that is, we create a data term $E_{\text{data}}(L(i))$ that encapsulates retargeting constraints, and a smoothness term $E_{\text{smoothness}}(L(i), L(j))$ that encapsulates neighborhood constraints for each pair of 4-neighbors. For example, to perform inpainting, the data term at pixel (x,y) with label $(\delta x, \delta y)$ would be ∞ if $(x+\delta x, y+\delta y)$ was inside the target region Ω. To perform reshuffling, the data term at pixel (x,y) with label $(\delta x, \delta y)$ would be 0 if the user wanted to force $I'(x,y) = I(x+\delta x, y+\delta y)$ and infinite for any other shift. The smoothness term is a typical penalty for label disagreements between neighbors based on color and gradient mismatches, similar to the discussion in Section 3.3. As before, α-expansion is used to solve the labeling problem, using a coarse-to-fine algorithm to make the problem computationally tractable.

3.5.4   Combinations of Methods

Since the explosion of interest in content-aware image retargeting techniques, several groups have investigated the problem of combining cropping, scaling, non-uniform warping, and seam carving to resize images. Dong et al. [123] considered seam carving followed by scaling, investigating the best intermediate image size at which to make the transition. Rubinstein et al. [409] considered sequences of cropping, scaling, and seam carving, viewing a candidate sequence as a path through a multidimensional resizing space. The goal is to find the best path from the original image (represented as the origin of the space) to a resized image with the desired dimensions (represented as a hyperplane in the space). Liu et al. [297] considered cropping followed by the non-uniform warping of Wolf et al. mentioned in the next section. An interesting aspect of this work was that the retargeted images were synthesized based on aesthetic guidelines generally followed by professional photographers — for example, the "rule of thirds" specifying that the main subject of a photograph should be roughly located a third of the distance from each of the horizontal/vertical edges to the other.

Rubinstein et al. [407] presented a comprehensive user study that compared the retargeting algorithms in this section for the task of reducing image size. The study suggested that users generally preferred the multi-operator retargeting approach from the previous paragraph [409], the video-motivated algorithm discussed in the next section [255], and — perhaps surprisingly — simple manual cropping. This paper also investigated image similarity metrics that correlated with user preferences from the study.

3.6   VIDEO RECOMPOSITING, INPAINTING, AND RETARGETING

Wang et al. [527] were the first to extend the Poisson gradient-domain image editing approach to video; the 3D Poisson equation and its discrete approximation are straightforward generalizations of what we discussed in Section 3.2.1. This allows dynamic elements to be composited into a video sequence, such as flickering flames or a lake with waves and ripples. Since the size of the linear system to be solved is much larger, fast numerical methods to solve the Poisson equation are critical, as discussed in Section 3.2.2.

Many algorithms for video inpainting approach the problem based on the layered motion model mentioned in Section 2.9. That is, the video is separated into a static background layer and one or more moving foreground layers. There are generally three possibilities for a pixel (x, y, t) in the region to be inpainted:

1. The pixel lies on a moving foreground object and the desired result is a static background pixel exposed in a different frame. In this case, the known background pixel can simply be pasted from this other frame after compensating for the layer motion (e.g., [243]).

2. The pixel lies on a static background object, so the desired background is static and unknown. In this case, patch-based inpainting can be generalized to fill in a plausible background.

3. The pixel should represent the continuation of some object that moves in and out of the hole as the video progresses. For example, we may want to remove a tree that people walk behind, generating plausible results of people walking through an empty field. If such regions are known to contain objects that move in a predictable, cyclical way, object-based video inpainting algorithms can exploit the consistency. For example, Venkatesh et al. [512] used background subtraction to generate a set of moving object templates that could be pasted into a video hole, and Jia et al. [220] explicitly estimated which positions in an object's motion cycle are missing at each time instant.

Wexler et al. [546] presented a general algorithm for video inpainting that was the predecessor of the bidirectional similarity approach in Section 3.5.3 and requires no object detection or segmentation. The method basically maximizes a coherence term of the form

$$C(V, V') = \prod_{\Psi' \subset V'} \max_{\Psi \subset V} \exp(-\lambda d(\Psi, \Psi')^2) \qquad (3.44)$$

Here, V is an original video sequence that is retargeted to a new sequence V', Ψ and Ψ' are 3D spatio-temporal patches in the video sequences, and d is a distance measure between patches based on their color and gradient differences. The optimization of the criterion proceeds in a coarse-to-fine manner using a similar observation about the update rule for each pixel's color in the retargeted video. On the other hand, the subsequent patch-based retargeting method of Simakov et al. [451] can be directly applied to changing the size and/or duration of a video sequence, and accelerated using PatchMatch [30]. Either technique enables complex inpainting effects to be achieved — for example, reconstructing reasonable-looking human motion that passes through an inpainting region or interpolating dropped frames of a complex input video.

Wolf et al. [552] proposed a non-uniform-warping-based algorithm for video resizing, combining a salience map, a face detection algorithm, and a motion detection algorithm into an importance map for every pixel of a video shot. Neighboring salient pixels are encouraged to maintain unit spacing from each other in the resized video, while nonsalient pixels are allowed to shrink, similar to the optimized scale-and-stretch method. Krähenbühl et al. [255] proposed a related algorithm for interactive non-uniform warping of video that incorporates similar cost function terms for preserving spatio-temporally salient regions and the sharpness and straightness of edges,

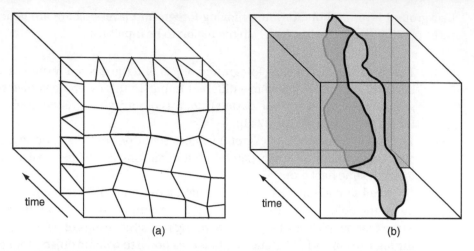

Figure 3.37. (a) Generalizing optimized scale-and-stretch to video encourages temporal coherence between the quads in each frame. (b) Generalizing seam carving to video results in a spatio-temporal seam that separates the left half of each image from the right half.

and introduced new constraints based on user keyframing of important objects and structures.

Wang et al. [534, 535] generalized the optimized scale-and-stretch algorithm of [536] to video. In [534], all the frames are first aligned to compensate for camera motion. Moving objects are detected and tracked across video frames, and constraints are imposed to ensure that the quads on these objects are resized consistently. The single-frame salience map is also replaced by a moving average across several neighboring frames. Overall, the approach avoids artifacts that would be created by retargeting each frame independently. In [535], the constraints on separating camera and object motion were relaxed, replaced by a simpler optical-flow-based method for determining a critical region in each frame that will not be removed. A cost function is proposed that penalizes the deviation of each quad transformation from a similarity transform and encourages temporal coherence in the quad transformations based on the estimated optical flow, as sketched in Figure 3.37a.

Rubinstein et al. also showed how seam carving could be applied to resize video; the generalizations of the graphs in Figures 3.31b and 3.33a to (x, y, t) pixels are straightforward. In this case, a cut on the graph defines a spatio-temporal seam that cuts through the video volume, as illustrated in Figure 3.37b. Alternately, we could make the video shorter in the temporal direction by removing seams "parallel" to the (x, y) plane. Since the number of vertices in the graph can be very large, a coarse-to-fine strategy for computing the cut may be required (e.g., [299]).

3.7   INDUSTRY PERSPECTIVES

Paul Lambert, compositing supervisor, and Blake Sloan, software engineer from Digital Domain in Venice, California, Shankar Chatterjee, software developer at Cinesite in Hollywood, and Gabriel Sanchez, 2D supervisor from LOOK Effects in Los Angeles, discuss various aspects of video editing and compositing.

RJR: In what kinds of situations do pieces of two video sequences need to be seamlessly merged, and how do you handle them?

Lambert: That kind of thing is all about slight of hand. The easiest thing is if there's an element in a shot that passes behind something like a telegraph pole. That pole is the natural place to draw the dividing line between the two pieces of footage, especially if the element isn't really where the viewer's expected to look. If there's no pole, it makes sense to pick a flat area with not a lot of detail to draw the seam.

Suppose you've got a stunt, like a guy's on a motorbike doing a big jump and there's a big explosion behind him, but the stuntman obviously doesn't look like our hero character since you don't want to put your A-list actor in danger. Nowadays you could probably do it all in CG, but years ago you could try to match a take of the actor's head onto the real footage as well as possible. But you've got this explosion going on, with light coming from behind, so ideally you'd want to shoot the actor with roughly the same color light. You'd have had to draw a roto spline and fake it in, but if done poorly it can look very fake since the lighting is very tough to match.

For both *TRON: Legacy* and *The Curious Case of Benjamin Button*, we did a lot of splicing a CG head onto a real actor's body. We'd always roto along the actual collar line and just replace the neck and head. If you have a shot where that neckline's going into shadow, into the noise floor of the camera, you'll never be able to find it and you just make it up. You take the curve and just imagine what would happen. With *TRON*, the roto of the collar was easier, since the neckline on the character's bodysuit was basically a rigid piece of plastic, so you knew it always had a certain shape. On *Benjamin Button*, it was much harder since the character wore many types of different, natural clothing — in some scenes he was wearing a flimsy shirt. In some sequences where the body double was moving around a lot, we actually had to roto the collar and warp it around. Those shots took the longest to do in roto, paint, and compositing — sometimes we'd have to make up the whole inside of the shirt because the body double was wearing a kind of blue hoodie that reflected color back into the shirt in the original plate. Plus once we put the CG head back in, there might be a gap, so sometimes we'd have to clone that piece of texture and track or warp it in; that was all done by hand. It was very intensive work.

Sanchez: Generally if you're doing a split-screen composite, you're going to have someone experienced on the camera, but sometimes the camera will slightly move between the two takes, say because someone kicked the cable. A bigger issue is that some things may change in the scene between takes. For example, say we're filming at a sports bar and you have TV monitors and tables everywhere. Now we want to combine take 1 from when the actor's in a dark shirt with take 20 when he's in a light shirt, and between all those takes a table or chair in the background moved, or somebody walks across the scene in take 1 and we've got to carry that motion through.

In my experience, when two shots need to be split-screened together, I have to analyze and a lot of times eye-loop the footage, and I just stare at it before I determine what I'm going to do. You're trying to find out, am I going to have to blend across the seam or am I going to use a hard line? Is there architecture in there that's going to help me hide what I need to do?

If it's a still background, there's no movement, and it's slightly out of focus, using a fuzzy or a soft matte line will usually help. I can use the width of blur along a vertical surface in the background as a rule of thumb for how much to blur the seam. If the background's really sharp, then you try to follow strong edges and cut though empty regions with the dividing line. In the sports bar example, I may follow the edge of a table, arbitrarily go through the blank wall since it won't matter, then follow the edge of a TV since I don't want to split the TV in half, and so on. You'll get a kind of jigsaw-puzzle pattern that will be less detectable than a straight line; you purposely want to go back and forth, grabbing a table from the A side and a monitor from the B side. But even when the background is sharp, you always want some amount of blend, even if it's just a pixel and a half.

If the cameras are moving, then you need to track or keyframe that line. A lot of it depends on how well the two videos are registered. If they're both moving quickly and at the same speed, you may be able to get away with a super-wide, soft line, because something's always moving across the screen and the blend is twenty-five percent of the image, you're not going to see where it's transferring from one side to the other. Now, if there are very detailed objects in the background, say you see a specific car go by, you may have to roto out that car frame by frame and use it only from the B side.

This kind of thing happens in TV as well as movies. Sometimes it's easy — say an actor misses his cue and walks into a room too soon. You can actually use the original footage as its own clean plate, and basically "slip" him — instead of having him come in on frame 1 you have him come in on frame 25, because the information's there to create a clean back plate. You hear a lot of "we'll just fix it in post." There are so many of those things that people don't know about — things that were not meant to obviously be an effects shot, but where effects were done.

RJR: How do you deal with inpainting problems, where you need to synthesize realistic texture inside a hole?

Lambert: The most common approach is to track and warp a piece of existing texture into the hole. These days, every shot that comes into Digital Domain gets tracked, so we know the camera motion in 3D space, and we often survey the set or environment to obtain accurate 3D geometry (see Chapters 6 and 8). Then the compositors have tools where we can project a given image of the scene onto this 3D geometry. To fill in a hole in one image, we can figure out which 3D surface lies behind the object we want to replace, project that surface onto a region in a different image where the background is visible, and fill in the pixels we couldn't see with a piece of texture that looks correct and moves in the right way. We do that kind of thing all the time for set extensions. It's like a 2D compositing tool that actually uses 3D under the hood. Achieving spatial and temporal consistency is still difficult, though; it's very noticeable if there's a slight camera shake and your texture all of a sudden swims in the opposite direction of what it's supposed to be doing.

Chatterjee: At Cinesite, I was able to apply some of the texture synthesis research from my PhD for inpainting and wire removal problems. At that time, in the mid-nineties, I was using Markov Random Field approaches to resynthesize texture; the artist would outline the areas of defects, and I would run my texture synthesis program to fill in the pixels. A common example was painting out marker balls that had been placed around a set for camera tracking.

We used to use a wire removal tool that was similar to PDE-based inpainting, but it didn't work very well; you could see that something had been done. They used to call it the "glass rod" effect because that's what the filled-in wire region kind of looked like. Later I moved on to Efros et al.'s technique, and then to Criminisi et al.'s algorithm.

The same kinds of tools apply to general problems of image restoration. For example, a frame may contain random dirt, which is very hard to automatically detect. It was also common to see scratches on frames that came from something inside the projector periodically or continuously contacting the film. It may show up as a long, unbroken vertical scratch, or intermittently recur in some parts of some frames. For historical films — for example I helped on the restoration of *To Kill a Mockingbird* — you don't want to touch a pixel unless it's absolutely essential. For very thin scratches you can use something simple like a median filter, but the artifacts you introduce can be very subtle. If you freeze a frame and look at the one before and the one after you won't notice a problem, but if you watch the moving footage, you'll be very suspicious about that area — something must have happened there but you can't put your finger on it — some subtle motion that evokes critical analysis in the viewer.

For the recent movie *Hereafter*, there was a problem with a "hair in the gate" in one scene — a hair got stuck in the film scanner and was there throughout the sequence. We used patch-based inpainting, motion compensated to pull from other frames, to remove the hair. In another scene outside the San Francisco airport, a dark cloudy scene with a taxicab, there was actually a fairly large scratch on the film — about forty pixels at its widest point. The artist created a matte painting for one frame and the software was able to track that scratch throughout the whole sequence and inpaint it from the artist's background.

RJR: How is the aspect ratio change between a widescreen cinema release and a DVD or Blu-Ray handled?

Sloan: You might hope that there's an automatic solution, but there are several reasons why it's problematic. At any step in production before the final shot is done, you run the risk of things running into each other in a way that you don't expect. So you can't do content-aware retargeting before all the content is in the scene. The more important issue is that a well-composed frame is like a visual art form. Yes, an automatic algorithm could do a nice job of preserving the content and making sure everyone's heads were in frame when it got cropped down, but every frame is kind of like a painting. It has a composition and it has spatial relationships that are probably best preserved by a human, making the decision during actual filming about what part's going to be in the frame and what part's going to be out. Skilled cinematographers do that all the time; there's this idea of an importance gradient that kind of flows out from a central rectangle that's literally marked in their

Figure 3.38. (a) In this *Impossible is Nothing* commercial for adidas, a young Muhammad Ali from archival footage fights his daughter Laila Ali in a seamless composite. (b,c) Image inpainting is used to remove blue-painted stand-in objects in these sequences from *Transformers: Dark of the Moon*. (d) To remove larger objects, like these green-suited fighters from *The Mummy: Tomb of the Dragon Emperor*, more extensive manual work is usually required. adidas, the 3-Stripes mark and the *Impossible is Nothing* mark are registered trademarks of the adidas Group used with permission. The name, image, and likeness of Muhammad Ali are provided courtesy of Muhammad Ali Enterprises LLC. *Transformers: Dark of the Moon* ©2011 Paramount Pictures. All Rights Reserved. *The Mummy: Tomb of the Dragon Emperor* courtesy of Universal Studios Licensing LLC.

camera viewfinder. They'll see the part of the frame corresponding to the aspect ratio of the movie in the theater, as well as a TV-safe area. Productions are now designed to be targeted to different types of media without any intervention, to avoid the noticeable pan-and-scans you used to see when movies were shown on TV in the eighties. It's also much better now that the 16:9 HDTV aspect ratio is closer to the movie aspect ratios than standard-definition video was, so letterboxing is less obnoxious.

Lambert: For the movie we're working on now, *Jack the Giant Killer*, they're filming it using the RED Epic camera, with 5K resolution. We're going to be taking a portion out of this huge frame, which is exciting. We can see the regions corresponding to the 2.39 cinema release, the proposed 16:9 TV release, and we have extra information on the sides of the plates that will help in the stereo conversion. We're using the extra information from the top and bottom as well, because there are giants in this movie, and when they hit the ground, the camera shakes, and we'll be able to pull in information from pixels that are out of frame instead of making it up.

This is the first time we've had this kind of oversize plate. There are so many pixels that for the TV release they may not even use the 16:9 rectangle but blow up a piece of the actual 2.39 cinema release. With a normal camera, you can get away with a blow-up up to about fifteen to twenty percent. On this show, they're shooting at 5K, 5120×2700, but actually rendering the show at half that resolution, they're actually reframing some of the shots, knowing that they can zoom into the shot because they have this exceptional resolution. I've got a plate that just came in with 170 percent blow-up, which I've never seen before, but because you have the extra resolution you can do that.

David Geoghegan, Flame operator at LOOK Effects in Los Angeles, California, discusses the compositing involved in a pair of shots from *Captain America: The First Avenger*.

Geoghegan: The setup here is that one of Captain America's team runs out of the forest to a road. He lies down in the middle of the road as an armored truck approaches, and just as it rolls over him, he places a bomb on its underside. So here, the A side is just a stationary camera in the middle of the road that the truck drives over, and the B side is a moving camera that follows the guy as he runs out of the forest, lies down in the empty road, and raises his hands up to place the bomb. Since the B side is moving, we had to get a really good camera track, which wasn't so bad because they put lots of markers on trees in the forest — but then you have to go back and paint out all the markers.

The key problem is getting the truck plate to really "live" in the other plate. Luckily, they shot both plates in the same location, but the color is very different in the two shots. I did a really tight roto of the truck from the A side so I could pull it completely off. Then before putting it into the B side, I had to color-correct it, "slip" or alter the timing, and flop it — that is, reverse it left to right. I had to recreate the shadowing under the truck to marry the two shots together. It's stuff like contact shadows that really sell the effect. If the blacks in the underside of that truck aren't exactly the same as the actor's, when the truck shadows and his shadows are in the same space, they won't match, and it'll be a dead giveaway. It won't look like that truck is really rolling over that guy. They even shot stills of the underside of that truck as it rolls over, since they wanted to see more detail; we had to track those underside stills into the plate, just by hand.

Since the guy actually hangs onto the bomb throughout the whole B side, the bomb itself was CG past a certain point and it also had to be painted out. This again is all done essentially with roto shapes hand-drawn frame by frame, which is difficult since there's a lot of motion blur as he's pulling the bomb back to his chest.

In the next shot you see the truck drive away and explode after a few moments. That explosion was another A and B situation — putting them together and painting, making truck parts fly apart. The A plate was basically the truck driving off safely, not much happening, and the B plate was a practical explosion — the two shots are totally different. The B shot looks like it's nighttime, but it's not; they just cranked down the exposure so the explosion would be exposed right. Even though it's literally only a few frames, there's just a lot of hand working to make it look good to the human eye. There are very few things that can really be automated; software gets you so far, and then it comes down to your ingenuity of actually connecting the A and B sides and making them live in the same plate.

3.8   NOTES AND EXTENSIONS

Wang and Cohen [533] studied the problem of simultaneous matting and compositing; that is, instead of treating the process as two separate steps, the matte of the foreground region is optimized to minimize visual artifacts in the resulting composite. The benefit is that the foreground matte need not be highly accurate in regions where the foreground and new background are similar. The computation of the matte is similar to the methods in Section 2.6.

Early work on image editing by manipulating gradients was proposed by Elder and colleagues (e.g., [130]). Later, McCann and Pollard [318] proposed tools for directly "painting" in the gradient domain for image manipulation and art creation. Orzan et al. [357] showed how smooth-shaded vector graphics artwork could be created by specifying the locations of curved edges and the colors on either side. Gradient-domain techniques can also be used to combine or remove artifacts in flash/no-flash pairs [10]. Sunkavalli et al. [483] observed that the results of gradient-domain compositing may exhibit a mismatch in *texture* between the source and target, even if the colors are consistent. For example, the source patch may be sharp and clear while the target image might have visible film grain and blurring. They proposed a wavelet-pyramid-based compositing framework that matches the histograms of both the image intensities and the estimated noise in the source and target images, to propagate the target texture into the pasted source region. They called this approach "image harmonization."

Lo et al. [298] proposed a compositing method for 3D stereoscopic movies, an area of increasing interest to the visual effects community (see Chapter 5). An unusual application of compositing was proposed by Chu et al. [95], whose goal was to create realistic "camouflage images" containing hidden elements, as in a child's picture book. Agarwala et al. [9] extended the ideas in Section 3.3 to build a "panoramic video texture," a seamlessly looping moving image created from a video shot by a single panning camera. Rav-Acha et al. [384] showed how to create a similar effect, as well as nonlinear temporal edits of a video, such as the manipulation of a race to create a different winner.

While the topic is outside the scope of this chapter, the patch-based approach to inpainting in Section 3.4.2 is an application of **texture synthesis**, the problem of creating a large chunk of realistic, natural texture from a small example. Major work in this area includes that of Wei and Levoy [539], Ashikhmin [20], Efros and Freeman [128], and Hertzmann et al. [197]. We also note that inpainting can be generalized to apply to non-image-based scenarios, such as filling in holes in a depth image or 3D triangle mesh [221, 124].

An early hybrid approach to retargeting was proposed by Setlur et al. [437], who used an importance map to compute ROIs, removed these from the image, and inpainted the holes to create an "empty" background image. This image is uniformly resized to the desired dimensions, and the ROIs pasted back onto the new background in roughly the same spatial relationship.

Krähenbühl et al. [255] made an interesting observation that naïve retargeting can introduce aliasing into the resulting image, manifesting as blurring of sharp edges, and proposed cost function terms to preserve the original image gradients, as well as a low-pass filter to limit the spatial frequencies in the retargeted image. Mansfield et al. [313] showed that when a user-supplied depth map was available, a seam-carving-based approach could be used to create retargeted images that respected depth ordering and could even contain realistically overlapping foreground objects. Cheng et al. [90] described reshuffling applications specifically in the context of scenes with many similar repeated elements.

Rav-Acha et al. [383] proposed an interesting approach to video editing of a foreground object that undergoes pose changes (e.g., a person's rotating head). They estimated a non-photorealistic 2D texture map for the 3D object and its mapping to each image in the video sequence. The user performs editing/compositing operations directly on the texture map, which is then warped to produce a retextured video.

This chapter should provide fairly convincing evidence that today it is very difficult to tell if a digital image resulted from an untouched photograph of a real scene or if it has been manipulated. This is great news for visual effects in movies, but somewhat unsettling for photographs in other spheres of life that we expect to be trustworthy (e.g., newspaper photographs of historic events, photographic evidence in trials). In fact, a new field of **digital forensics** has arisen to detect such tampering. Farid provided an excellent general overview [134] and technical survey [133] of techniques for detecting whether a digital image has been manipulated. Such techniques include the detection of telltale regularities in pixel correlations, or inconsistencies in JPEG quantization/blocking, camera transfer function and/or noise, lighting directions, and perspective effects. Lalonde et al. [261, 260] also noted the importance of matching lighting, camera orientation, resolution, and other cues to make a composite image look convincing.

3.9   HOMEWORK PROBLEMS

3.1   Sketch the hard composite implied by the images S, T, and M in Figure 3.39.

Figure 3.39. Source, target, and mask images for a compositing problem.

3.2   Consider the corresponding rows of a source and target image given by Figure 3.40. We want to use a weighted transition region between columns 50 and 70 so that pixels to the left of column 50 come entirely from the source, pixels to the right of column 70 come entirely from the target, and pixels in the transition region are a linearly weighted blend between the two images. Sketch the row of the composite, indicating important values on the x and y axes.

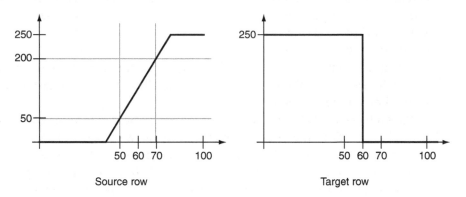

Figure 3.40. Two corresponding rows of a source and target image.

3.3   Show that the pyramid image G_i can also be obtained as

$$G_i = (K_i * I)_{\downarrow 2^i} \qquad (3.45)$$

where I is the original image, and K_i is a low-pass filter whose spatial extent increases with i.

3.4   Prove that Equation (3.5) is true — that is, that the original image can be obtained as the sum of the upsampled images of the Laplacian pyramid. Use induction; that is, show that

$$G_i = (G_{i+1})_{\uparrow 2} + L_i \qquad (3.46)$$

is true for $i = 0, \ldots, N - 1$.

3.5   Suppose we use a Laplacian pyramid to blend two images along a vertical boundary using the 5×5 kernel in Equation (3.3). If we use five levels of the pyramid, how wide is the transition band at the lowest level (with respect to the original image resolution)?

3.6   Show how Equations (3.11)–(3.12) result from Equation (3.7) based on the Euler-Lagrange equation.

3.7   Prove that when (S_x, S_y) is a conservative vector field, Equation (3.13) is the same as Equation (3.11).

3.8   Suppose the region Ω for a Poisson compositing problem is given by Figure 3.41, with the pixels labeled from 1 to 30 as shown.

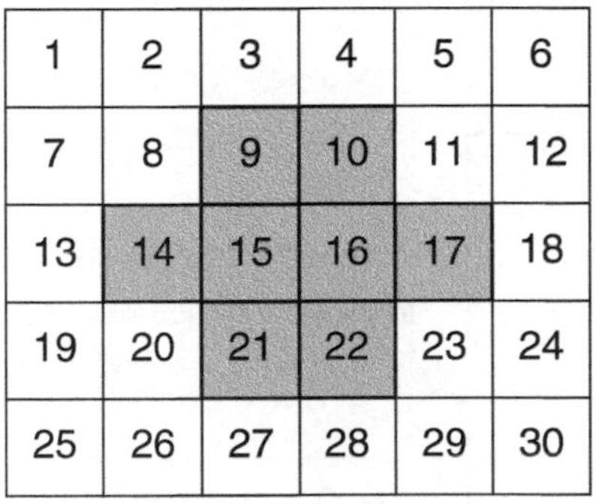

1	2	3	4	5	6
7	8	9	10	11	12
13	14	15	16	17	18
19	20	21	22	23	24
25	26	27	28	29	30

Figure 3.41. An example region Ω for a Poisson compositing problem.

a)   Which pixels make up the set Ω?

b)   Which pixels make up the set $\partial\Omega$?

c)   Explicitly determine the linear system relating the knowns (the source S and target T) and unknowns (composite pixels I) for this region. Your answer should be in the form of a linear system $Ax = b$, where x contains the unknown values of I.

3.9   Prove that the harmonic interpolant $E(x,y)$ obtained by solving Equations (3.17)–(3.18) satisfies

$$|E(x,y)| \leq \max_{(x,y) \text{ on } \partial\Omega} |S(x,y) - T(x,y)| \tag{3.47}$$

(Hint: use a concept from complex analysis.)

3.10   Compute the mean-value coefficients $\lambda_i(p)$ for the point p and $\partial\Omega$ specified by the points $\{p_1, \ldots, p_4\}$ in Figure 3.42.

3.11   Can Farbman's approach using mean-value coordinates be applied to the mixed-gradient compositing scenario of Equation (3.19)? Explain your reasoning.

3.12   Suppose we solve a compositing problem using graph cuts, where the user-specified source and target pixels are given in Figure 3.43. Prove that none of the pixels in the striped region can come from T in the composite.

3.13   Sketch a plausible series of α-expansion label changes to get from the initial labeling to the final labeling in Figure 3.44.

3.14   Compute the discrete approximation $U_n(x,y)$ in Equation (3.32) to the continuous derivative $\frac{\partial I}{\partial t}$ in Equation (3.31).

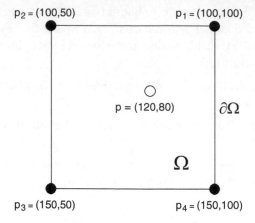

Figure 3.42. An example mean-value coordinates problem.

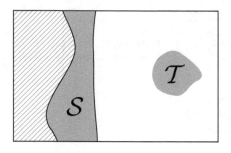

Figure 3.43. User-specified pixels $\mathcal{S}$ and $\mathcal{T}$ for a graph-cut compositing problem.

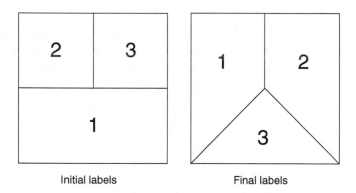

Initial labels   Final labels

Figure 3.44. Initial and final states for a series of α-expansion steps.

3.15 Consider the images and inpainting regions in Figure 3.45. Explain why, using PDE-based inpainting, the inpainted region will be identical in both cases. (For more investigation of this issue, see [273].)

3.16 Determine the white point in Figure 3.21 with the highest inpainting priority, given the labeled confidence and data values.

3.17 Determine a target region Ω such that every pixel on the fill front for patch-based inpainting has the same confidence term.

3.18 Construct an image and inpainting region for patch-based inpainting that contains both a point with a very high confidence term and a very low data term, and a point with very high data term and a very low confidence term.

Figure 3.45. Two images with inpainting regions Ω.

3.19   Consider the distortion energy for one quad q in optimized scale-and-stretch resizing, given by

$$\sum_{v_i, v_j \in \mathcal{V}_q} \| (v_i' - v_j') - s_q(v_i - v_j) \|^2 \tag{3.48}$$

Show that the optimal scaling factor s_q that minimizes Equation (3.48) is given by:

$$s_q = \frac{\sum\limits_{v_i, v_j \in \mathcal{V}_q} (v_i - v_j)^\top (v_i' - v_j')}{\sum\limits_{v_i, v_j \in \mathcal{V}_q} \| v_i - v_j \|^2} \tag{3.49}$$

3.20   Consider the image and seams in Figure 3.46. Note that the region on the left side of the image is darker than the region on the right side. Order the seams in increasing energy (assuming we use Equation (3.36)).

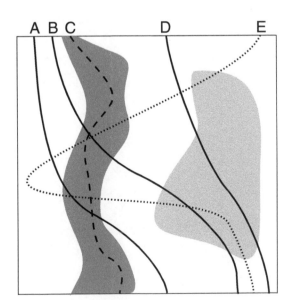

Figure 3.46. An example image with five vertical seams.

3.21   Show why the arc weights in Figure 3.31b result in a minimal cut that (a) forms a connected path of pixels that (b) only intersects one pixel per row.

3.22   Show why the three cases in Figure 3.32 and the costs in Equation (3.37) imply the arc weights in Figure 3.33a.

3.23   Verify that the bidirectional similarity update rule in Equation (3.43) is obtained from differentiating the sum of Equation (3.41) and Equation (3.42).

3.24   Construct an example pair of images such that the number of patches N_j in the bidirectional similarity completeness term is equal to 0 for some pixel, and much larger than W^2 for some other pixel.

4 Features and Matching

In many visual effects applications, we need to relate images taken from different perspectives or at different times. For example, we often want to track a point on a set as a camera moves around during a shot so that a digital creature can be later inserted at that location. In fact, finding and tracking many such points is critical for algorithms that automatically estimate the 3D path of a camera as it moves around a scene, a problem called **matchmoving** that is the subject of Chapter 6. However, not every point in the scene is a good choice for tracking, since many points look alike. In this chapter, we describe the process of automatically detecting regions of an image that can be reliably located in other images of the same scene; we call these special regions **features**. Once the features in a given image have been found, we also discuss the problems of describing, matching, and tracking them in different images of the same scene.

In addition to their core use for matchmoving, feature detection is also important for certain algorithms that estimate dense correspondence between images and video sequences (Chapter 5), as well as for both marker-based and markerless **motion capture** (Chapter 7). Outside the domain of visual effects, feature matching and tracking is commonly used for stitching images together to create panoramas [72], localizing mobile robots [432], and quickly finding objects [456] or places [424] in video databases.

Feature tracking is a subset of the more general problem of **visual tracking** from computer vision. However, there are some big differences to keep in mind. Visual tracking algorithms are usually designed to follow a particular meaningful object such as a person or car throughout a video sequence. On the other hand, features are automatically extracted from an image based purely on mathematical considerations, and usually look like individually uninteresting blobs or corners. Precise localization of features is critical for subsequent applications like matchmoving, while a general visual tracker may use a crude box or ellipse (e.g., [103]) to outline the region of interest. It's also common for general visual trackers to maintain a probabilistic representation of an object's state, for example using a Kalman filter (e.g., [58]), while this approach is fairly uncommon in feature tracking. Finally, a major area of interest in feature matching is the **wide-baseline** case in which the images under consideration were taken from cameras that were physically far apart, whereas visual tracking generally assumes the camera moves only slightly between images.

While we generally use the term **features** throughout this chapter to denote image regions of interest, several other terms are often used to describe the same concept, including **interest points**, **keypoints**, and **tie points**. We generally use the word **matching** when discussing an arbitrary pair of images of the same scene, and use the word **tracking** when the images come from a video sequence.

This chapter is split into two main sections. We first discuss the key problem of feature **detection** — that is, deciding which image regions are sufficiently distinctive (Section 4.1). We then discuss the problem of feature **description** — that is, deciding how to represent the image information inside each region for later matching (Section 4.2). We briefly describe evaluation techniques that help in deciding on a good detector/descriptor combination (Section 4.3) as well as extensions to color images (Section 4.4).

In this chapter, we generally assume that the problem is to detect and match feature points in a set of natural images, e.g., acquired from a camera on location. This is frequently the situation for matchmoving with a freely moving camera, as we'll discuss in Chapter 6. When we have more control over the environment — for example, a soundstage set — it's common to introduce artificial tracking markers (e.g., gaffer-tape crosses on the surfaces of a blue- or green-screen set) that are relatively straightforward to detect and track. We discuss the problem of designing distinctive artificial tracking markers in Section 4.5.

4.1   FEATURE DETECTORS

Initially, we'll assume that a feature is a square block of pixels centered at a certain location in an image. Our first goal is to mathematically characterize what makes a good feature. Intuitively, we want to select a block that is highly distinctive, so that in a different image of the same scene, we can find a unique match. Put another way, we want the detection to be **repeatable** — that is, given a different image of the same scene, the feature is distinctive enough that we can find it again in the correct location.

Figure 4.1 illustrates several feature candidates in an example image. Candidate A is a poor choice of feature, since this nearly-constant-intensity patch is almost identical to other nearly-constant-intensity patches in the image. Candidate B is a better feature, since the strong edge passing through it makes it more distinctive. However, there are still several blocks in the image that are almost identical to Candidate B, which can be obtained by sliding the block along the edge; this ambiguity is called the **aperture problem**. Candidates C and D are good choices for features; the image intensities at Candidate C form a **corner** and those at Candidate D form a **blob**; both blocks are locally unique. That is, each block does not resemble any other block in its local neighborhood. In the following sections, we formalize this intuition that a feature should have locally distinctive intensities, and discuss detectors or **interest operators** that automatically find such features. In this section, we'll assume that the images under consideration are grayscale, and will discuss extensions to color in Section 4.4.

4.1.1   Harris Corners

Moravec [335] was among the first to observe that the **cornerness** of a block of pixels could be quantified by comparing it to adjacent blocks in the horizontal, vertical, and

Figure 4.1. Square blocks of feature candidates in an image.

diagonal directions. If the difference is high in all directions, the block is a good candidate to be a feature. Harris and Stephens [186] are widely credited with extending this idea to create what has become known as the **Harris corner detector**,[1] which can be derived as follows.

Let $w(x,y)$ be a binary indicator function that equals 1 for pixels (x,y) inside the block under consideration and 0 otherwise. Then consider the function $E(u,v)$ that corresponds to the sum of squared differences obtained by a small shift of the block in the direction of the vector (u,v):

$$E(u,v) = \sum_{(x,y)} w(x,y)(I(x+u, y+v) - I(x,y))^2 \tag{4.1}$$

If we think of $I(x,y)$ as a continuous function and expand it in terms of a Taylor series around $(u,v) = (0,0)$, we obtain the approximation

$$
\begin{aligned}
E(u,v) &= \sum_{(x,y)} w(x,y)\left(I(x,y) + u\frac{\partial I}{\partial x}(x,y) + v\frac{\partial I}{\partial y}(x,y) - I(x,y)\right)^2 \\
&= \sum_{(x,y)} w(x,y)\left(u\frac{\partial I}{\partial x}(x,y) + v\frac{\partial I}{\partial y}(x,y)\right)^2 \\
&= \sum_{(x,y)} w(x,y)\left(u^2\left(\frac{\partial I}{\partial x}(x,y)\right)^2 + 2uv\left(\frac{\partial I}{\partial x}(x,y)\frac{\partial I}{\partial y}(x,y)\right) + v^2\left(\frac{\partial I}{\partial y}(x,y)\right)^2\right) \\
&= \left[\begin{array}{c} u \\ v \end{array}\right]^\top \left[\begin{array}{cc} \sum_{(x,y)} w(x,y)\left(\frac{\partial I}{\partial x}(x,y)\right)^2 & \sum_{(x,y)} w(x,y)\left(\frac{\partial I}{\partial x}(x,y)\frac{\partial I}{\partial y}(x,y)\right) \\ \sum_{(x,y)} w(x,y)\left(\frac{\partial I}{\partial x}(x,y)\frac{\partial I}{\partial y}(x,y)\right) & \sum_{(x,y)} w(x,y)\left(\frac{\partial I}{\partial y}(x,y)\right)^2 \end{array}\right] \left[\begin{array}{c} u \\ v \end{array}\right]
\end{aligned}
$$

$$\tag{4.2}$$

---

[1] While Harris's name is now attached to the idea, other authors proposed very similar approaches earlier, notably Förstner [150].

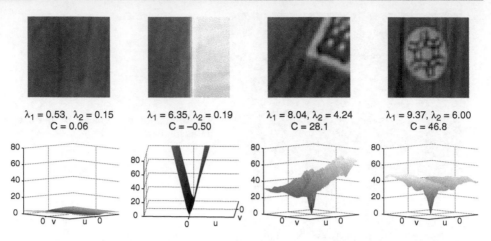

$$\lambda_1 = 0.53,\ \lambda_2 = 0.15 \qquad \lambda_1 = 6.35,\ \lambda_2 = 0.19 \qquad \lambda_1 = 8.04,\ \lambda_2 = 4.24 \qquad \lambda_1 = 9.37,\ \lambda_2 = 6.00$$
$$C = 0.06 \qquad\qquad C = -0.50 \qquad\qquad C = 28.1 \qquad\qquad C = 46.8$$

Figure 4.2. Top row: Candidate feature blocks from Figure 4.1. Middle row: Harris matrix eigenvalues and Harris quality measure C with $k = 0.04$. Bottom row: Error surfaces $E(u, v)$ around block center.

The symmetric positive definite matrix in Equation (4.2) is called the **Harris matrix**:[2]

$$H = \begin{bmatrix} \sum_{(x,y)} w(x,y) \left(\frac{\partial I}{\partial x}(x,y) \right)^2 & \sum_{(x,y)} w(x,y) \left(\frac{\partial I}{\partial x}(x,y) \frac{\partial I}{\partial y}(x,y) \right) \\ \sum_{(x,y)} w(x,y) \left(\frac{\partial I}{\partial x}(x,y) \frac{\partial I}{\partial y}(x,y) \right) & \sum_{(x,y)} w(x,y) \left(\frac{\partial I}{\partial y}(x,y) \right)^2 \end{bmatrix} \qquad (4.3)$$

The eigenvalues and eigenvectors of the Harris matrix can be analyzed to assess the cornerness of a block. Let these be (λ_1, λ_2) and (e_1, e_2) respectively, with $\lambda_1 \geq \lambda_2$.[3] Consider the following cases, illustrated in Figure 4.2:

1. The block is nearly-constant-intensity. In this case, $\frac{\partial I}{\partial x}$ and $\frac{\partial I}{\partial y}$ will both be nearly zero for all pixels in the block. The surface $E(u, v)$ will be nearly flat and thus $\lambda_1 \approx \lambda_2 \approx 0$.

2. The block straddles a linear edge. In this case, $\frac{\partial I}{\partial x}$ and $\frac{\partial I}{\partial y}$ will both be nearly zero for pixels far from the edge, and the gradient $\begin{bmatrix} \frac{\partial I}{\partial x} \\ \frac{\partial I}{\partial y} \end{bmatrix}$ will be perpendicular to the edge direction for pixels near the edge. Thus, λ_1 will be a non-negligible positive value, with e_1 normal to the edge direction, while $\lambda_2 \approx 0$ with e_2 along the edge direction. The surface $E(u, v)$ will resemble a trough in the direction of the edge.

3. The block contains a corner or blob. In this case, the surface $E(u, v)$ will resemble a bowl, since any (u, v) motion generates a block that looks different than the one in the center. Both λ_1 and λ_2 will be positive.

Consequently, we look for blocks where both eigenvalues are sufficiently large. However, to avoid explicitly computing the eigenvalues, Harris and Stephens proposed

---

[2] This is also sometimes called the **second moment matrix** and is related to the image's local autocorrelation.

[3] Note that both eigenvalues are real and non-negative since the matrix is positive semidefinite.

the quality measure

$$C = \det(H) - k\, \text{trace}(H)^2 \qquad (4.4)$$

where k is a tunable parameter (frequently set to around 0.04; the lower the value of k, the more sensitive the detector). When both eigenvalues are large, C will be a large positive number, while C will be near zero if one eigenvalue is small. Figure 4.2 illustrates the candidate blocks from Figure 4.1, along with the corresponding error surfaces $E(u, v)$, eigenvalues of H, and quality measures C. We can see that both eigenvalues are large for Candidates C and D, with correspondingly high quality measures, while the quality measures for Candidates A and B are very low.

To detect features in an image, we simply evaluate the quality measure at each block in the image, and select feature points where the quality measure is above a minimum threshold. The resulting points are called **Harris corners**. Figure 4.3 illustrates Harris corners detected in an example image; we can see that most of the features lie on actual image corners and other distinctive features, while few features are found in flat regions or along edges. Since the test only depends on the eigenvalues and not the direction of the eigenvectors, the detected feature locations are approximately rotation-invariant (meaning that we would detect roughly the same apparent features if the image were rotated).[4]

We usually apply **non-maximal suppression** to the results of Harris corner detection, since the Harris quality measure will be high for many pixels in the neighborhood of a corner. That is, to avoid multiple detections for the same underlying corner, we

Figure 4.3. Harris corners detected in an image, using 15×15 windows and a threshold of one percent of the maximum quality measure value. Non-maximal suppression is applied to avoid generating many responses for the same feature.

[4] The proper term is actually rotation-**covariant**. That is, the feature locations detected in a rotated image will be approximately the same as the rotations of the locations in the original image. However, the term "invariant" is often misused to mean "covariant" in the context of feature detection.

only retain Harris corners whose quality measure is larger than that of all the points in their $N \times N$ pixel neighborhood for some user-selected N.

4.1.1.1 Implementation Details

For a digital image, Harris and Stephens proposed to approximate the gradients in Equation (4.3) with

$$\frac{\partial I}{\partial x}(x,y) = I(x+1,y) - I(x-1,y) \qquad \frac{\partial I}{\partial y}(x,y) = I(x,y+1) - I(x,y-1) \tag{4.5}$$

An alternative that ties in more closely with techniques discussed in the rest of the chapter is to approximate the gradients by convolving them with the derivatives of a Gaussian function:

$$\frac{\partial I}{\partial x}(x,y) = I(x,y) * \frac{\partial G(x,y,\sigma_D)}{\partial x} \qquad \frac{\partial I}{\partial y}(x,y) = I(x,y) * \frac{\partial G(x,y,\sigma_D)}{\partial y} \tag{4.6}$$

where $*$ indicates convolution, and

$$G(x,y,\sigma) = \frac{1}{2\pi\sigma^2} \exp\left(-\frac{1}{2\sigma^2}(x^2+y^2)\right) \tag{4.7}$$

That is, we smooth the image to remove high frequencies before taking the derivative. Also, to make the response as a function of window location smoother, we can replace the binary function $w(x,y)$ in Equation (4.3) with a radially symmetric function that weights pixels in the center of the window more strongly, such as a Gaussian:

$$w(x,y) = \frac{1}{2\pi\sigma_I^2} \exp\left(-\frac{1}{2\sigma_I^2}((x-x_0)^2 + (y-y_0)^2)\right) \tag{4.8}$$

$$= G(x-x_0, y-y_0, \sigma_I) \tag{4.9}$$

where (x_0, y_0) is the pixel at the center of the block.

There are two Gaussian functions at work here. The first Gaussian, in Equation (4.6), uses a **derivation scale** σ_D that specifies the domain over which the image is differentiated to compute the x and y gradients and the amount of smoothing that is applied. The second Gaussian, in Equation (4.8), uses an **integration scale** σ_I that specifies the domain over which the image is integrated to determine which pixels form the "window." These two parameters play a major role in scale-space feature detection, discussed in the next section. For convenience, σ_I is usually taken to be a fixed multiple of σ_D, with the scaling factor in the range [1.0, 2.0] [326].

4.1.1.2 Good Features to Track

Shi, Tomasi, and Kanade [492, 442] observed that the same matrix in Equation (4.3) naturally results from investigating the properties of blocks of pixels that are good for tracking. That is, we consider a sequence of images obtained by a video camera and indexed by time, $I(x,y,t)$. We hypothesize that a given block of pixels at time $t+1$ is actually some block of pixels $\mathcal{W}$ at time t translated by a vector (u,v). That is,

$$I(x+u, y+v, t+1) = I(x,y,t) \quad \forall (x,y) \in \mathcal{W} \tag{4.10}$$

If we fix a block of pixels at time t and want to find its translation at time $t + 1$, we therefore minimize the cost function

$$F(u,v) = \sum_{(x,y)} w(x,y)(I(x+u, y+v, t+1) - I(x,y,t))^2 \qquad (4.11)$$

where $w(x,y)$ is 1 for pixels inside $\mathcal{W}$ and 0 otherwise. Using the same type of Taylor series approximation as we did in Equation (4.2) and setting the derivative equal to zero yields the linear system

$$\begin{bmatrix} \sum_{(x,y)} w(x,y) \left(\frac{\partial I}{\partial x}(x,y,t) \right)^2 & \sum_{(x,y)} w(x,y) \left(\frac{\partial I}{\partial x}(x,y,t) \frac{\partial I}{\partial y}(x,y,t) \right) \\ \sum_{(x,y)} w(x,y) \left(\frac{\partial I}{\partial x}(x,y,t) \frac{\partial I}{\partial y}(x,y,t) \right) & \sum_{(x,y)} w(x,y) \left(\frac{\partial I}{\partial y}(x,y,t) \right)^2 \end{bmatrix} \begin{bmatrix} u \\ v \end{bmatrix}$$

$$= - \begin{bmatrix} \sum_{(x,y)} w(x,y) \left(\frac{\partial I}{\partial x}(x,y,t) \frac{\partial I}{\partial t}(x,y,t) \right) \\ \sum_{(x,y)} w(x,y) \left(\frac{\partial I}{\partial y}(x,y,t) \frac{\partial I}{\partial t}(x,y,t) \right) \end{bmatrix} \qquad (4.12)$$

We can see that the square matrix in Equation (4.12) is exactly the Harris matrix H of Equation (4.3). Shi, Tomasi, and Kanade argued that for the linear system to be well conditioned — that is, for the feature to be reliably trackable — both eigenvalues of H should be sufficiently large, suggesting the criterion

$$\min(\lambda_1, \lambda_2) > \tau \qquad (4.13)$$

where τ is a user-defined threshold. Features discovered in this way are quite similar to Harris corners, and are sometimes called **KLT corners** since they form the basis for the well-known KLT (Kanade-Lucas-Tomasi) tracker [307, 492].

Shi and Tomasi extended their model for the motion of a feature from a translation to an affine transformation, to account for the deformation of features that typically occur over long sequences (see also Section 4.1.5). That is, the scene patch corresponding to a square feature block in the first image will eventually project to a non-square area as the camera and scene objects move, so Equation (4.10) is modified to

$$I(ax + by + u, cx + dy + v, t+1) = I(x,y,t) \quad \forall (x,y) \in \mathcal{W} \qquad (4.14)$$

where the parameters a, b, c, d allow the feature square to deform into a parallelogram. The corresponding tracker is again obtained using a Taylor expansion. We will discuss more advanced methods for affine-invariant feature detection in Section 4.1.5.

When the feature dissimilarity (e.g., the error in Equation (4.11)) gets too large, the feature is no longer reliable and should not be tracked. When many features are simultaneously matched or tracked, outlier rejection techniques can be used to dispose of bad features [494], and the underlying epipolar geometry provides a strong constraint on where the matches can occur [576]. We will discuss the latter issue further in Chapter 5. Wu et al. [554] noted that the KLT tracker could be improved by processing frames both forward and backward in time, instead of always matching the current frame to the previous one.

Jin et al. [222] extended Shi and Tomasi's affine tracker to account for local photometric changes in the image — that is, instead of assuming that the pixel intensities in the transformed block remain the same from frame to frame, we allow for a scale and shift:

$$e \cdot I(ax + by + u, cx + dy + v, t + 1) + f = I(x, y, t) \quad \forall (x, y) \in \mathcal{W} \tag{4.15}$$

When training images of the target feature under different illuminations are available, more advanced photometric models can be obtained [184].

4.1.2   Harris-Laplace

A major drawback of Harris corners is that they are only extracted for a fixed, user-defined block size. While setting this block size to a small value (e.g., 7×7 pixels) enables the extraction of many fine-detail corners, it would also be useful to extract features that take up a relatively larger portion of the image. That is, we would like to detect features at different spatial **scales**. Detecting features in **scale space** is a critical aspect of most modern feature detectors. We first describe how Harris corners can be extracted at multiple scales, and in the following sections introduce new criteria not based on the Harris matrix. Lindeberg [285, 286] pioneered the use of scale space for image feature detection, providing much of the theoretical basis for subsequent work.

The key concept of scale space is the convolution of an image with a Gaussian function:[5]

$$L(x, y, \sigma_D) = G(x, y, \sigma_D) * I(x, y) \tag{4.16}$$

where σ_D takes on a sequence of increasing values, typically a geometrically increasing sequence of scales $\{\sigma_0, k\sigma_0, k^2\sigma_0, \ldots\}$. As σ_D increases, the image gets blurrier, since the Gaussian acts as a low-pass filter. The idea is similar to the Gaussian pyramid discussed in Section 3.1.2, except that the output image is not downsampled after convolution.

Revisiting Section 4.1.1.1, we can rewrite the Harris matrix evaluated at a point (x, y) using derivation scale σ_D and integration scale σ_I as:

$$H(x, y, \sigma_D, \sigma_I) = G(x, y, \sigma_I) * \begin{bmatrix} \left(\frac{\partial L(x,y,\sigma_D)}{\partial x}\right)^2 & \frac{\partial L(x,y,\sigma_D)}{\partial x}\frac{\partial L(x,y,\sigma_D)}{\partial y} \\ \frac{\partial L(x,y,\sigma_D)}{\partial x}\frac{\partial L(x,y,\sigma_D)}{\partial y} & \left(\frac{\partial L(x,y,\sigma_D)}{\partial y}\right)^2 \end{bmatrix} \tag{4.17}$$

Note that

$$\frac{\partial L(x, y, \sigma_D)}{\partial x} = \frac{\partial G(x, y, \sigma_D)}{\partial x} * I(x, y) \tag{4.18}$$

since differentiation and convolution are commutative, which implies that we can take the derivative and smooth the image in either order.

If we compute features at different scales and look at the eigenvalues of the Harris matrix to decide which features are the most significant, we don't want larger features to outweigh smaller features just because they're computed over a larger domain. We would like to **scale-normalize** the Harris matrix so that feature quality can be directly compared across scales. Furthermore, it's sometimes desirable to detect and match features at different scales — for example, to match a large square of pixels from a zoomed-in shot with a small square of pixels from a wider angle shot. In this case, we

---

[5] The use of $L(x, y, \sigma)$ to denote this Gaussian-blurred image is conventional notation and shouldn't be confused with the Laplacian pyramid images from Chapter 3.

should make sure that the derivatives we compute in creating the Harris matrix are **scale-invariant** — that is, that we compute the same matrix regardless of the image resolution.

We can determine the correct scale normalization as follows [127]. Suppose that we have two versions of the same image: a high-resolution one $I(x,y)$ and a low-resolution one $I'(x',y')$. The coordinates of the two images are related by $x = kx'$ and $y = ky'$, where k is a scale factor greater than 1. If we consider a block centered at (x',y') with scales (σ'_D, σ'_I) in the low-resolution image, it will correspond to the block centered at (kx', ky') with scales $(k\sigma'_D, k\sigma'_I)$ in the high-resolution image. From the chain rule, we can also compute that the image gradients at corresponding points satisfy $\nabla I' = k\nabla I$. Substituting everything into Equation (4.17), we have that

$$H(x,y,k\sigma'_D,k\sigma'_I) = \frac{1}{k^2}H'(x',y',\sigma'_D,\sigma'_I) \qquad (4.19)$$

where H and H' are the scale-dependent Harris matrices computed for the high- and low-resolution images, respectively. This implies that if we compute a scale space where each derivation scale and integration scale is a multiple of a base scale σ, i.e., at $\{\sigma_0, k\sigma_0, k^2\sigma_0, \ldots\}$, then we should compute the **scale-normalized Harris matrix** as

$$\hat{H}(x,y,k\sigma_D,k\sigma_I) = k^2 H(x,y,k\sigma_D,k\sigma_I)$$

$$= k^2 G(x,y,k\sigma_I) * \begin{bmatrix} \left(\frac{\partial L(x,y,k\sigma_D)}{\partial x}\right)^2 & \frac{\partial L(x,y,k\sigma_D)}{\partial x}\frac{\partial L(x,y,k\sigma_D)}{\partial y} \\ \frac{\partial L(x,y,k\sigma_D)}{\partial x}\frac{\partial L(x,y,k\sigma_D)}{\partial y} & \left(\frac{\partial L(x,y,k\sigma_D)}{\partial y}\right)^2 \end{bmatrix}$$
$$(4.20)$$

That is, in order to directly compare the response from the Harris matrix at different scales, we must multiply Equation (4.17) by the compensation term k^2. Now we can apply the Harris criterion with the same threshold at every scale, that is:

1. Create the scale space of the image for a fixed set of scales $\sigma_D \in \{\sigma_0, k\sigma_0, k^2\sigma_0, \ldots\}$, with $\sigma_I = a\sigma_D$. Typical values are $\sigma_0 = 1.5$, $k \in [1.2, 1.4]$, and $a \in [1.0, 2.0]$ (see [325, 327]).
2. For each scale, compute the scale-normalized Harris matrix in Equation (4.20) and find all local maxima of the Harris function in Equation (4.4) that are above a certain threshold.

Features detected in this way are known as **multi-scale Harris corners**.

This new approach can detect multiple features centered at the same location (x,y) at different scales. However, we would often rather select a **characteristic scale** that defines the scale at which a given feature is most significant. Lindeberg [286] suggested using the maximum of the **normalized Laplacian** for this purpose:

$$NL(x,y,\sigma) = \left| \sigma^2 \left(\frac{\partial^2 G(x,y,\sigma)}{\partial x^2} + \frac{\partial^2 G(x,y,\sigma)}{\partial y^2} \right) * I(x,y) \right| \qquad (4.21)$$

Figure 4.4 illustrates the idea; if we fix the (x,y) value specified by the dot in each image and plot the normalized Laplacian as a function of σ, we see that the function assumes a maximum at the same apparent scale in each case (visualized as the radius

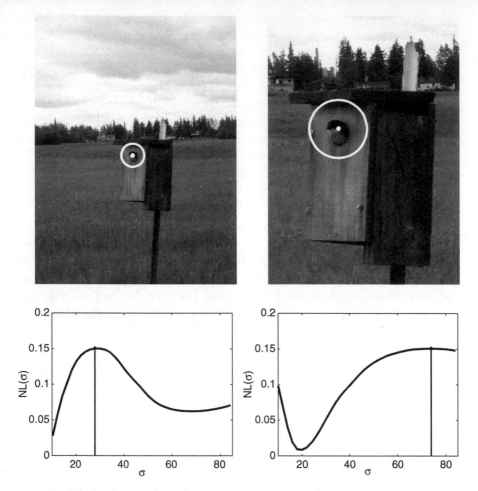

Figure 4.4. Selecting the characteristic scale of a feature using the normalized Laplacian. Top row: original images with manually-selected center locations (white dots). Bottom row: the normalized Laplacian as a function of scale. The characteristic scale σ that maximizes the normalized Laplacian is used as the radius of the corresponding circle in the top row. The ratio between the two characteristic scales is 2.64, which is almost the same as the actual underlying scale factor of 2.59 relating the images.

of the circle in the top row). We will discuss the normalized Laplacian further in the next section.

Mikolajczyk and Schmid [325] adopted this approach to compute what they called **Harris-Laplace features**. We use the same two steps as previously shown to detect Harris corners at each scale, and add the additional step[6]

3. For each detected feature (say at scale $k^n\sigma_0$), retain it only if its normalized Laplacian is above a certain threshold, and it forms a local maximum in the scale dimension, that is:

$$NL(x, y, k^n\sigma_0) > NL(x, y, k^{n-1}\sigma_0) \text{ and } NL(x, y, k^n\sigma_0) > NL(x, y, k^{n+1}\sigma_0) \quad (4.22)$$

---

[6] A slight modification that gives higher localization accuracy but has more computational cost was described in [327].

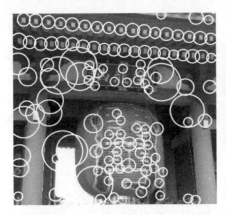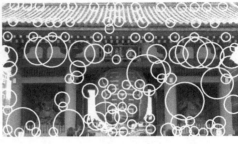

Figure 4.5. Harris-Laplace features detected in a pair of images of the same scene. The radius of each circle indicates the characteristic scale of the feature located at that circle's center. (Fairly aggressive non-maximal suppression was used so that the features don't overwhelm the image. In practice, a much larger number of features is detected.)

(Note that it's still possible to generate multiple detections at the same (x, y) location with different characteristic scales, but the scales will be somewhat separated.)

Figure 4.5 illustrates a pair of images and a subset of their detected Harris-Laplace features, using circles to indicate each feature's scale. We can see that the features center on distinctive regions of the image and that the detected scales are natural. More important, many of the same scene locations are detected at the same apparent scales, indicating the promise of Harris-Laplace features for automatic matching. This critical property is called **scale covariance**.[7]

4.1.3　Laplacian-of-Gaussian and Hessian-Laplace

In addition to proposing the Laplacian for scale selection, Lindeberg [286] also proposed a method for feature detection using the **scale-normalized Hessian matrix** of second derivatives:

$$\hat{S}(x, y, \sigma_D) = \sigma_D^2 \begin{bmatrix} \frac{\partial^2 L(x,y,\sigma_D)}{\partial x^2} & \frac{\partial^2 L(x,y,\sigma_D)}{\partial x \partial y} \\ \frac{\partial^2 L(x,y,\sigma_D)}{\partial x \partial y} & \frac{\partial^2 L(x,y,\sigma_D)}{\partial y^2} \end{bmatrix} \tag{4.23}$$

As before, $L(x, y, \sigma_D)$ is the Gaussian-filtered image at the specified scale. Note that

$$\text{trace } \hat{S}(x, y, \sigma_D) = \sigma_D^2 \left(\frac{\partial^2 L(x,y,\sigma_D)}{\partial x^2} + \frac{\partial^2 L(x,y,\sigma_D)}{\partial y^2} \right) \tag{4.24}$$

$$\det \hat{S}(x, y, \sigma_D) = \sigma_D^4 \left(\frac{\partial^2 L(x,y,\sigma_D)}{\partial x^2} \frac{\partial^2 L(x,y,\sigma_D)}{\partial y^2} - \left(\frac{\partial^2 L(x,y,\sigma_D)}{\partial x \partial y} \right)^2 \right) \tag{4.25}$$

In particular, we can see that the absolute value of the Hessian's trace is the same as the normalized Laplacian in Equation (4.21).

---

[7] As seen earlier, this property is often colloquially called **scale invariance**.

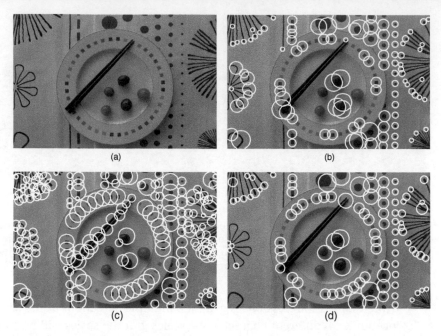

Figure 4.6. (a) An original image. (b) Harris-Laplace features. (c) Laplacian-of-Gaussian features (i.e., obtained with the trace of the Hessian). Note that the detector responds to both blobs and edges. (d) Hessian-Laplace features (i.e., obtained with the determinant of the Hessian). The detector does not respond to edges.

We can substitute the Hessian matrix and either its trace or determinant in Step 2 on p. 115 to obtain a feature detector that responds strongly to **blobs**, as illustrated in the bottom row of Figure 4.6. Using the trace, that is, the Laplacian, has a pleasing symmetry in that we can view the detector as selecting local maxima of the same function in both the spatial and scale dimensions. These features are called **Laplacian-of-Gaussian** or **LoG** features, since we're computing the Laplacian of a Gaussian-smoothed image at a given scale. That is, to detect LoG features, we compute the quantity in Equation (4.24) at every (x, y, σ_D), and find points where this function of three parameters is locally maximal.

Figures 4.6c-d illustrate that the determinant of the Hessian does a better job than the trace for rejecting long, thin structures and finding well-proportioned blobs. This approach (using the determinant of the Hessian for detection and its trace for scale selection) produces what are called **Hessian-Laplace** features. One can also require that the trace and determinant of the Hessian are simultaneously maximized [326]. All of these features are scale-covariant.

Bay et al. [33] noted that the discrete Gaussian filters used in the computation of the scale-normalized Hessian could be approximated by extremely simple box filters, as illustrated in Figure 4.7. Since box filters only involve simple sums and differences of pixels, they can be applied very quickly compared to filters with floating-point coefficients. If integral images [516] are used for the computation, the speed of applying the box filter is independent of the filter size. Bay et al. proposed to use the box filters in an approximation of the Hessian's determinant, resulting in what they called the **Fast Hessian** detector. We will discuss additional fast feature detectors in Section 4.1.6.

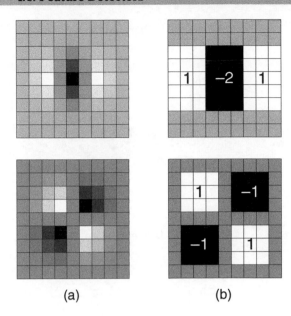

Figure 4.7. (a) Example discrete 9×9 Gaussian derivative filters used for computing the Hessian, with $\sigma = 1.2$. The top filter is $\frac{\partial^2 L(x,y,\sigma)}{\partial x^2}$ and the bottom filter is $\frac{\partial^2 L(x,y,\sigma)}{\partial x \partial y}$. Light values are positive, black values are negative, and gray values are near zero. (b) Efficient box-filter approximations of the filters at left. Gray values are 0.

(a)   (b)

4.1.4   Difference-of-Gaussians

Lowe [306] made the important observation that the Laplacian-of-Gaussian detector could be approximated by a **Difference-of-Gaussians** or **DoG** detector. Why is this the case? From the definition of the Gaussian function in Equation (4.7), we can show that

$$\frac{\partial G}{\partial \sigma} = \sigma \nabla^2 G \tag{4.26}$$

If we assume that we generate Gaussian-smoothed images where adjacent scales differ by a factor of k, then we can approximate

$$\frac{\partial G}{\partial \sigma} \approx \frac{G(x,y,k\sigma) - G(x,y,\sigma)}{k\sigma - \sigma} \tag{4.27}$$

Equating Equation (4.26) and Equation (4.27) gives that

$$(k-1)\sigma^2 \nabla^2 G \approx G(x,y,k\sigma) - G(x,y,\sigma) \tag{4.28}$$

That is, the difference of the Gaussians at adjacent scales is a good approximation to the scale-normalized Laplacian, which we used to construct LoG features in the previous section. This is highly advantageous, since to compute scale-space features we had to create these Gaussian-smoothed versions of the image anyway. Figure 4.8 compares a difference of Gaussians with the Laplacian of Gaussian, showing that the DoG is a good approximation to the LoG.

Therefore, the key quantity for DoG feature detection is the difference of adjacent Gaussians applied to the original image:

$$\begin{aligned} D(x,y,\sigma) &= (G(x,y,k\sigma) - G(x,y,\sigma)) * I(x,y) \\ &= L(x,y,k\sigma) - L(x,y,\sigma) \end{aligned} \tag{4.29}$$

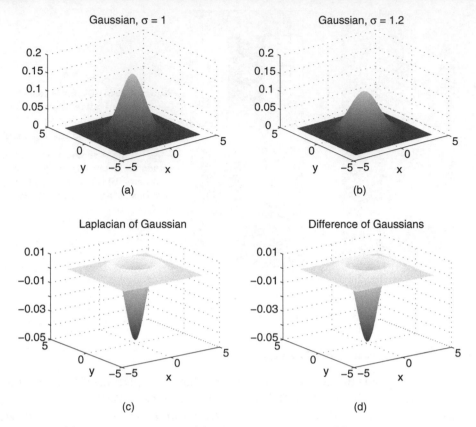

Figure 4.8. (a) A Gaussian with $\sigma = 1$. (b) A Gaussian with $\sigma = 1.2$. (c) The Laplacian of Gaussian with $\sigma = 1$. (d) The difference of the Gaussians in (b) and (a), normalized to have the same maximum value as (c). We can see that the DoG is a good approximation to the LoG.

As with LoG detection, we seek maxima in both the spatial and scale dimensions to detect features.

Lowe proposed a rearrangement of scale space to make the detection of local maxima more computationally efficient. We define an **octave** of a Gaussian scale space as a pair of images whose smoothing factors σ differ by a factor of two.[8] Lowe's idea was to define the constant factor k characterizing the scale space as $k = 2^{\frac{1}{s}}$, so that each set of $s + 1$ images results in an octave. The image beginning each octave is downsampled by a factor of 2 in both directions, but the sizes of the sequence of Gaussian filters applied at each octave remains the same. In this way, we avoid applying very large filters to original-sized images, and instead apply same-sized filters to increasingly smaller images. If we just took the first image in each octave, we would have a Gaussian pyramid, as discussed in Section 3.1.2. Figure 4.9 illustrates the idea. Lowe suggested using $s = 3$ intervals (that is, four images per octave), with a base scale of $\sigma_0 = 1.6$ applied to the first image in each octave (after downsampling).

---

[8] While the word "octave" might imply a factor of eight is involved, the term originally comes from music theory (i.e., there are eight notes in a major scale, which corresponds to a doubling of frequency).

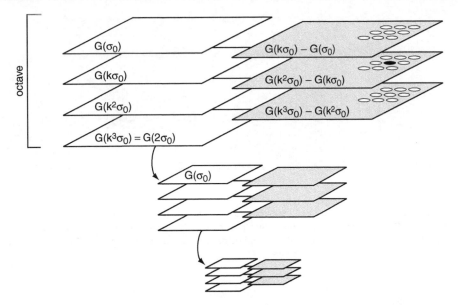

Figure 4.9. Lowe's octave structure for computing the scale-space DoG representation of an image. In this example, $s = 3$. The white images represent Gaussians with the same sequence of scales applied to octaves of images of different resolutions. The images at each octave are half the size of the ones above. The gray images represent the differences of adjacent Gaussian-filtered images. Features are detected as extrema in both the spatial and scale dimensions of the DoG function. For example, the response at the black pixel must be larger or smaller than all of its white neighbors.

The specific DoG-based detection algorithm proposed by Lowe includes several additional refinements:

1. Instead of finding a single characteristic scale for each feature, local extrema (i.e., both maxima and minima) of the DoG function in Equation (4.29) with respect to both space and scale are computed. That is, the DoG value must be larger or smaller than all twenty-six of its neighbors (see Figure 4.9). To compute the extrema at the "ends" of each octave of equally sized images, we compute an extra pair of images such that the first and last images of adjacent octaves represent the same scale. This way we don't have to directly compare images of different sizes. (These extra images aren't shown in Figure 4.9.)

2. After detecting the DoG extrema, we further localize each keypoint's position in space and scale by fitting a quadratic function to the twenty-seven values of $D(x, y, \sigma)$ at and around the detected point (x_i, y_i, σ_i). This function is given by:

$$Q(x, y, \sigma) = D(x_i, y_i, \sigma_i) + g^\top \begin{bmatrix} x \\ y \\ \sigma \end{bmatrix} + \frac{1}{2} \begin{bmatrix} x \\ y \\ \sigma \end{bmatrix}^\top \Gamma \begin{bmatrix} x \\ y \\ \sigma \end{bmatrix} \qquad (4.30)$$

where g is the 3×1 gradient and Γ is the 3×3 Hessian of the function D with respect to (x, y, σ), evaluated at (x_i, y_i, σ_i) using the usual finite-difference approximations. The updated location and scale can be shown to be

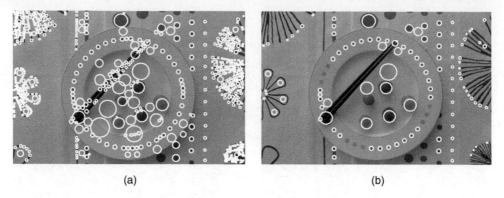

(a)   (b)

Figure 4.10. (a) A sampling of extrema of the multi-scale DoG function for the image in Figure 4.6a prior to feature rejection. The size of the circle illustrates its detected scale. (b) After feature rejection, low-contrast and edge-like features are removed. 110 of 777 original DoG extrema passed the rejection tests.

given by

$$
\begin{bmatrix} \hat{x}_i \\ \hat{y}_i \\ \hat{\sigma}_i \end{bmatrix} = -\Gamma^{-1} g \Big|_{(x_i, y_i, \sigma_i)}
\tag{4.31}
$$

Thus, features are located with sub-pixel accuracy.

3. Finally, we reject features that have poor contrast or correspond to edges rather than blobs. For the contrast issue, we simply remove features for which the function Q in Equation (4.30) is too small. To remove edge-like features, we consider the eigenvalues of the 2×2 spatial Hessian and reject features for which one eigenvalue is much larger than the other — that is, the local bowl approximation to D is too oblong. To avoid explicitly computing the eigenvalues, Lowe proposed a measure based on the trace and determinant of the Hessian, analogous to the Harris function in Equation (4.4).

Figure 4.10 illustrates DoG features detected at multiple scales using this technique. We can see that, like the LoG and Hessian-Laplace detectors, the DoG feature detector qualitatively detects blobs. As with these other feature detectors, each feature carries with it an associated scale that is used in the subsequent description and matching processes. Each feature that survives the rejection tests is also assigned a dominant orientation; we will discuss this process further in Section 4.2.3. Features detected in this way are sometimes called **SIFT features**, where SIFT stands for Scale-Invariant Feature Transform.

4.1.5   Affine-Invariant Regions

Scale-invariant features such as Hessian-Laplace, LoG, and DoG are usually adequate for dealing with images sampled close together in time and acquired by a zooming camera. However, when images to be matched are acquired using a **wide baseline** — that is, the camera undergoes substantial translational motion between acquiring the images — scale invariance alone may not be sufficient. Figure 4.11 illustrates the problem. A square centered at a point in the left-hand image contains different

(a) (b)

Figure 4.11. (a) Two images of the same scene taken from different perspectives as a result of substantial camera motion. A fixed-size square is centered on corresponding locations in both images. (b) A close-up of the two squares shows that the patches of pixels are quite different.

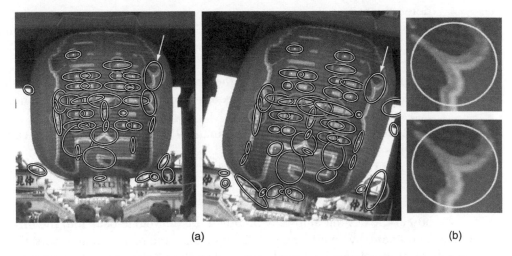

(a) (b)

Figure 4.12. (a) Hessian-Laplace (green circles) and Hessian-Affine (yellow ellipses) features detected in a pair of wide-baseline images. We can see that despite the rotation and skew, many features are repeated and the elliptical regions are roughly covariant with the transformation. (b) Affine-adapted circular regions created from the feature at the upper right corner of the lantern. We can see that the circular regions are almost identical (in general up to a rotation).

pixels than a square centered at the same point in the right-hand image. If we were to detect such a feature using a scale-invariant detector (e.g., Hessian-Laplace) and draw a circle corresponding to the scale, the circles would contain different sets of pixels. This means that descriptors based on these neighborhoods would use different information, resulting in suboptimal — and perhaps incorrect — matches.

To combat this problem, we require an **affine-invariant** way of detecting features. The basic idea is illustrated in Figure 4.12; after detecting a good spatial location for a feature, we also estimate an elliptical neighborhood that we expect to be reliably detectable in an image of the same scene patch from a different perspective. Mathematically, we want this ellipse to be **covariant** with an affine transformation of the image. That is, if $E(I)$ is an elliptical region produced by a detector in an image I and T is an affine transformation, we want

$$T(E(I)) = E(T(I)) \tag{4.32}$$

Before creating the feature descriptor, we can warp the detected affine-covariant ellipse to a circle, and be confident that the circle produced by the same feature in a different image contains the same set of pixels (up to a rotation). The fundamental theory of affine-invariant regions was first proposed by Lindeberg and Gårding [287] and applied by other researchers including Baumberg [32], Schaffalitzky and Zisserman [423], and Mikolajczyk and Schmid [327].

We can find affine-invariant elliptical regions around feature points with a straightforward iterative procedure called **affine adaptation**:

1. Detect the feature point position and its characteristic scale (e.g., using Harris-Laplace or Hessian-Laplace).

2. Compute the local second-moment matrix H at the given scale (i.e., the scale-normalized Harris matrix in Equation (4.20)). Scale H so it has unit determinant.[9]

3. Compute the **Cholesky factorization** $H = CC^\top$, where C is a lower-triangular matrix with non-negative diagonal elements.[10] C is sometimes called the **matrix square root** of H.

4. Warp the image structure around the feature point using the linear transformation C. That is, the new image coordinates are related to the old ones by $I_{\text{new}}(x_{\text{new}}) = I_{\text{old}}(Cx_{\text{old}})$.

5. Compute the local second-moment matrix H for the new image and scale H so it has unit determinant.

6. If H is sufficiently close to the identity (i.e., its eigenvalues are nearly equal), stop. Otherwise, go to Step 3.

We obtain the desired ellipse by mapping the unit circle back into the original image coordinates by inverting the chain of scalings and matrix square roots. Lindeberg and Gårding showed that under an ideal affine transformation of the image and using Harris-Laplace features, the process will indeed produce covariant elliptical regions. If we consider the same feature before and after an affine transformation, the circular regions resulting from the affine adaptation process will be identical up to a rotation. We will describe one way to account for this rotation when describing the feature in Section 4.2.4.

Mikolajczyk and Schmid [327] proposed to simultaneously detect feature point locations and corresponding affine-invariant regions using an iterative algorithm, resulting in **Harris-Affine features**. The basic idea is the same as the algorithm described earlier, except that within each iteration the location and characteristic scale of the feature point are re-estimated. They proposed the ratio of the smaller eigenvalue to the larger one in Step 6 as a measure of the local isotropy of the region, stopping when the ratio was above a threshold (e.g., 0.95). On the other hand, features can be rejected when the ratio of eigenvalues in the original image is too low, indicating a highly elliptical (i.e., edge-like) region. If we use the Hessian matrix in

---

[9] This normalization was suggested by Baumberg [32]; Lindeberg and Gårding [287] instead recommended dividing H by its smallest eigenvalue.

[10] The factorization exists since H is symmetric with non-negative eigenvalues, but it is not unique unless the eigenvalues are both positive.

place of the second-moment matrix during the feature detection stage, we obtain **Hessian-Affine features**.

4.1.6 High-Speed Feature Detection

While the detectors in the previous sections were generally derived from principled analysis of scale- and affine-invariance, they can also be somewhat computationally intensive (e.g., due to the many Gaussian convolutions and eigenvalue computations). The feature detectors in this section are designed to be much faster, rapidly processing image pixels to produce robustly repeatable corner- and blob-like features.

4.1.6.1 FAST Corners

Rosten and Drummond [400] proposed a detection algorithm for what they called **FAST Corners**, where FAST stands for Features from Accelerated Segment Test. Figure 4.13 illustrates the idea. A candidate pixel p is compared to a discretized circle of pixels around it; if all the pixels on a contiguous arc of n pixels around the circle are significantly darker or lighter than the candidate pixel, it is detected as a feature. In the original algorithm, the circle contained sixteen pixels and an arc of $n = 12$ pixels had to satisfy the brightness comparison. A series of tests can be performed to quickly reject feature candidates; for example, three of the four pixels labeled 1, 5, 9 and 13 must pass the test for a corner to exist.

Rosten and Drummond [401] later extended the FAST idea using a machine learning approach that substantially improved the detector's performance and speed. They created a ground-truth database of a large number of pixel patches labeled as corners or not-corners, and learned the structure of a decision tree based on the intensities of the sixteen surrounding pixels that was able to correctly classify all the patches in this training set. This decision tree — basically a long list of if-then-else statements — was then optimized into highly efficient code to produce an improved

(a)   (b)

Figure 4.13. (a) An original image, (b) A zoomed-in image illustrating the candidate pixel (labeled p) and the circle of pixels (labeled 1-16) used for the FAST corner test. In this example, the twelve-pixel clockwise arc from 11 to 6 is substantially darker than the center pixel, resulting in a FAST corner.

detector. On the average, fewer than three intensity comparisons need to be made to determine if a candidate pixel is a FAST corner. Both the original detector and the extended version were found to produce repeatable features while running at least an order of magnitude faster than the Harris and DoG detectors, enabling frame-rate corner detection. A later extension that investigated a neighborhood of forty-eight pixels around the candidate pixel improved the repeatability even more [402].

4.1.6.2 Maximally Stable Extremal Regions

Matas et al. [314] proposed a new type of feature called **maximally stable extremal regions** or **MSERs**. These too are extremely fast to compute, and are based on thresholding, a simple image processing operation. An extremal region is defined as a connected subset of pixels Ω such that for all $p \in \Omega$ and q adjacent to but not in Ω, the image intensities all satisfy either $I(p) < I(q)$ or $I(p) > I(q)$. That is, the pixels inside the region are either all darker or all lighter than the pixels on the boundary. An easy way to obtain an extremal region is to threshold the image at a given pixel value; in this case, each connected component of pixels above the threshold forms a bright extremal region. As we decrease the threshold, connected components grow in size, and eventually merge to cover the entire image domain. Conversely, each connected component of pixels below the threshold forms a dark extremal region, which grows as the threshold is increased. Figure 4.14 illustrates the concept on a real image.

For detecting features, we choose extremal regions that are stable; that is, as the image threshold is varied, the connected component changes little. This is desirable for repeatably finding the same regions in different views of a scene. We can find these stable extremal regions by finding local minima of the function

$$M(i) = \frac{|\Omega_{i+1} - \Omega_{i-1}|}{|\Omega_i|} \tag{4.33}$$

where $\{\Omega_i\}$ is a nested sequence of corresponding extremal regions obtained by thresholding the image at intensity i, and $|\Omega_i|$ is the area of Ω_i. Figures 4.15a and b

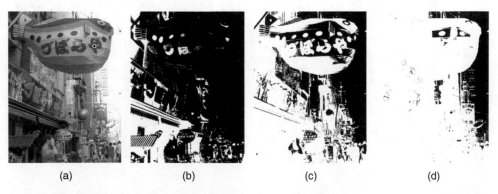

(a)   (b)   (c)   (d)

Figure 4.14. Examples of dark extremal regions obtained by thresholding an (a) original image. (b)-(d) illustrate dark extremal regions (connected components) obtained by highlighting pixels below the intensity thresholds 20, 125, and 200, respectively. Bright extremal regions are obtained by complementing these binary images.

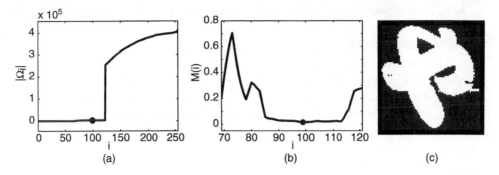

Figure 4.15. (a) The area of the dark extremal region at the location of the dot in Figure 4.14a as a function of increasing intensity threshold. (b) The measure in Equation (4.33) as a function of intensity threshold for this extremal region. The function is minimized at intensity level 99, roughly corresponding to the center of the nonzero plateau in (a). (c) The corresponding dark MSER.

illustrate the area of Ω_i and value of Equation (4.33) as a function of intensity threshold i for the component centered at the dot in Figure 4.14a. Figure 4.15c illustrates the maximally stable extremal region corresponding to the minimizer of $M(i)$; we can see that the region corresponds to a dark, irregularly shaped blob in the original image that has high contrast with the lighter background.

All the extremal regions in an image can be quickly generated using an efficient algorithm for computing **watersheds** [514], and the test for extracting the maximally stable extremal regions is fast. The overall algorithm can extract MSERs at video frame rates. Matas et al. [314] also showed that MSERs are also affine-covariant, as well as invariant to affine changes in the overall image intensity.

4.2   FEATURE DESCRIPTORS

Once a feature's location (and perhaps some additional information such as its scale or support region) has been determined, the next step is to describe the feature with a vector of numbers called a **descriptor**. To enable high-quality feature matching — especially among images taken from widely separated cameras — the descriptor must be designed so that features arising from the same 3D location in different views of the same scene result in very similar descriptor vectors. That is, we desire that $D(f) \approx D(\hat{f})$, where D is an algorithm to create a descriptor, and f and $\hat{f}$ are detected features in two different images, such that $\hat{f} = Tf$ for some geometric and photometric transformation T of the first image. Thus, while we want feature detection to be *covariant* to geometric transformations, we want feature description to be *invariant* to them. We must also specify a criterion for **matching** two descriptor vectors from different images to form **correspondences**.

The easiest descriptor is simply a vector containing the intensity values from a fixed-size block of pixels centered at the feature's location. Two such vectors can be compared simply by computing the sum of squared differences (SSD) between corresponding elements. When the change between two images is small (with respect to both geometry and intensity), as in two frames of video separated by a fraction of a second, this approach works reasonably well, and is indeed the basis for some of the earliest video tracking algorithms (e.g., [307, 442]).

However, we can see that this approach is unsuitable for description and matching of features in a general image pair. Problems arise when the images have significantly different rotations, scales, illuminations, and perspective changes, as illustrated in Figure 4.11. This section discusses descriptor designs designed to be roughly invariant to these transformations.

4.2.1   Support Regions

The first problem is determining the support region of pixels that should contribute to a feature's descriptor. We exploit the information produced by the feature detectors discussed previously. For example, scale-invariant features such as Harris-Laplace, Hessian-Laplace, and DoG are already detected at a characteristic scale. Therefore, we can draw a circle around each feature whose radius is the characteristic scale, and these circles will ideally be scale-covariant (as illustrated in Figure 4.5). Features such as MSERs or Hessian-Affine automatically produce affine-covariant regions (as illustrated in Figure 4.12). In particular, we can use the circular region produced at the end of the affine adaptation process in Section 4.1.5 as the basis for an affine-invariant descriptor. Thus, we can immediately assume that any feature detected in scale space can be associated with a scale-covariant circle or an affine-covariant ellipse. Any uniform scaling of this circle or ellipse is also covariant; we typically use a larger neighborhood of pixels to build the descriptor than just this neighborhood (see Figure 4.16d).

Many descriptor algorithms assume a square patch is given around the feature location as opposed to a circular one. This means we need to assign a reliable orientation to the feature to consistently define the "top" edge of the square. The easiest approach is to estimate the **dominant gradient orientation** of a patch. Lowe [306] suggested estimating this orientation based on a histogram of pixel gradient orientations over the support region of the scale-covariant circle. Concretely, for each pixel (x, y) in the support region, we estimate the gradient magnitude $M(x, y)$ and orientation $\theta(x, y)$. We create a histogram $h(\theta)$ of the gradient orientations, where the angles are quantized (for example, using thirty-six bins, one for each ten degrees). For each pixel (x, y), we increment the bin corresponding to $\theta(x, y)$ by the quantity $M(x, y)G(x - x_0, y - y_0, 1.5\sigma)$, where G is a Gaussian function, (x_0, y_0) is the center of the support region, and σ is the scale of the feature. That is, each pixel contributes in proportion to the strength of its gradient and its proximity to the center of the support region. After forming the orientation histogram, we detect its peak and use the maximizer θ^* as the dominant gradient orientation. If the histogram contains more than one large peak, multiple features can be generated at the same location and scale with different orientations. Figure 4.16 illustrates the process. An alternative, as discussed in Section 4.2.4, is to build a descriptor that is itself rotation-invariant, instead of explicitly estimating the orientation of the feature and rotating the support region.

After determining a scale- and rotation-normalized patch around a feature location, we resample it to have a uniform number of pixels (for example, 41×41 pixels

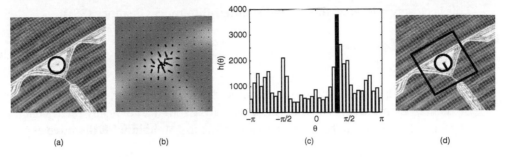

(a)   (b)   (c)   (d)

Figure 4.16. Estimating the dominant orientation of a feature. (a) A detected feature point with its scale. (b) Gradient angles of the scale-blurred image for points in the feature's neighborhood. Vector lengths are weighted by their gradient magnitude and the centered Gaussian function. (c) The gradient orientation histogram peaks at about $\pi/3$ radians. (d) The estimated orientation of the feature is indicated by the short line inside the circle, which agrees well with the perceptual gradient. A descriptor support region larger than the characteristic scale can be built using this orientation, indicated by the square.

[328]). This ensures that we use the same number of support region pixels when constructing a descriptor, regardless of its size. The final step is usually to normalize the patch to compensate for affine illumination changes. That is, we compute the mean μ and standard deviation s of the pixels in the support region, and rescale the intensities of the patch by

$$I_{\text{new}} = \frac{I_{\text{old}} - \mu}{s} \tag{4.34}$$

4.2.2   Matching Criteria

Before proceeding to the detailed algorithms for constructing descriptors, we introduce several common methods for matching descriptors and deciding whether a given match is correct. For the purposes of this section, a descriptor is simply a vector of real numbers in $\mathbb{R}^n$. Typically we independently compute a set of feature descriptors $\mathcal{A} = \{a^1, \ldots, a^{N_1}\}$ in one image and another set of descriptors $\mathcal{B} = \{b^1, \ldots, b^{N_2}\}$ in a second image, and want to generate a list of feature **correspondences** $\{(c_a^j, c_b^j), j = 1, \ldots, N_3\}$, which says that $a^{c_a^j} \in \mathcal{A}$ and $b^{c_b^j} \in \mathcal{B}$ are a match. Each descriptor should be matched to at most one descriptor in the other image, but many descriptors in both images will not be matched at all. The goal is to design a matching criterion that produces a high-quality set of correspondences, with few false matches and few missed matches.

The most frequently used descriptor distance measure is the **Euclidean distance**, also known as the 2-norm. That is, for two descriptor vectors a and b,

$$
\begin{aligned}
D_{\text{euc}}(a, b) &= \|a - b\|_2 \\
&= \left(\sum_{i=1}^{n} (a_i - b_i)^2 \right)^{1/2}
\end{aligned}
\tag{4.35}
$$

This is closely related to the sum-of-squared-differences distance (**SSD**)

$$\begin{aligned} D_{\text{ssd}}(a,b) &= \|a-b\|_2^2 \\ &= D_{\text{euc}}(a,b)^2 \end{aligned} \tag{4.36}$$

In certain cases, a training set of ground-truth matches may be available that can be used to estimate the $n \times n$ covariance matrix Σ that statistically relates each pair of descriptor values. In this case, we can define the **Mahalanobis distance** as

$$D_{\text{mahal}}(a,b) = \left((a-b)^\top \Sigma^{-1}(a-b) \right)^{1/2} \tag{4.37}$$

Given a distance function D between two descriptors, matches are typically generated using the method of **nearest neighbors**. That is, the match to a descriptor a from a set of candidates $\mathcal{B}$ is computed as

$$b^* = \arg\min_{b \in \mathcal{B}} D(a,b) \tag{4.38}$$

Typically (a,b^*) is accepted as a match only if the distance $D(a,b^*)$ is below a user-specified threshold. After all, not every feature in one image is expected to appear in another, and incorrect feature matches can severely affect the performance of subsequent algorithms that depend on matches (e.g., matchmoving in Chapter 6).

Lowe [306] proposed a rule for more precise descriptor matching based on both $D(a,b^*)$ and $D(a,b^{**})$, where b^{**} is the descriptor with the second closest distance to a. The rule is to accept (a,b^*) as a match if $D(a,b^*)/D(a,b^{**})$ is below a user-specified threshold (e.g., 0.8). This criterion is sometimes called the **nearest neighbor distance ratio**. The goal is to prevent situations where a has several very similar matches in $\mathcal{B}$, making it impossible to choose an unambiguously best match. For example, the corner of a window on the wall of a building may make an excellent feature on its own, but the wall may have several nearly identical windows that prevent the corner from being matched correctly in a second image.

Another less-often used matching criterion is the **normalized cross-correlation** given by

$$NCC(a,b) = \sum_{i=1}^{n} \frac{1}{s_a s_b}(a_i - \mu_a)(b_i - \mu_b) \tag{4.39}$$

where μ_a and s_a are the mean and standard deviation of the elements of a. Two vectors that match well should have a high NCC, near 1. The NCC is most often used for matching raw blocks of intensities as opposed to derived descriptors. If the blocks are already normalized for affine illumination changes as described in the previous section, then the NCC is simply the dot product between the two descriptor vectors (i.e., the cosine of the angle between the vectors). While the NCC is not a distance function, the same concepts of best and second-best matches can apply to detecting and filtering potential matches. The NCC can also be computed very efficiently using the Fast Fourier Transform due to its similarity to convolution.

Finally, we note that a match to a given feature in one image cannot occur at an arbitrary location in a second image; the match location is constrained by the **epipolar geometry**. That is, the match location in the second image must lie along the **epipolar line** corresponding to the feature in the first image. We can iteratively estimate the epipolar geometry and reject feature matches that pass the above tests but are inconsistent with the epipolar lines (e.g., [576]). We discuss epipolar geometry in detail in Chapter 5.

4.2.3   Histogram-Based Descriptors

Several of the most commonly-used descriptors can be characterized as histograms of pixel intensities or gradient values measured over a set of subregions superimposed on the feature's support region. In particular, the **SIFT descriptor** proposed by Lowe [306] has proven extremely popular. The input to the detector is a feature location (x, y), its estimated scale σ, and its estimated dominant orientation θ. We first create an oriented square centered at the feature location so that the top edge corresponds to the dominant orientation (Figure 4.17a). Each side of the square is a multiple of the feature's scale (e.g., 6σ).

We then rotate the square, resampling the image pixels and smoothing the intensities with the appropriate Gaussian for the feature's characteristic scale. The gradient at each resampled pixel is estimated and weighted by a Gaussian centered at the middle of the square with a standard deviation of half the square's width; the goal is to emphasize gradients closer to the center of the square.

Next, we subdivide the square into a 4×4 grid of smaller squares and create a coarsely-quantized histogram of eight gradient orientations within each grid square (Figure 4.17b). To make the descriptor more robust to small misalignments, the gradient at a given pixel contributes to multiple grid squares and multiple histogram bins based on trilinear interpolation (see Problem 4.19). We collect the eight histogram values from each of the sixteen grid squares into a 128-dimensional vector. The final descriptor is obtained by normalizing this vector to unit length, zeroing out any extremely large values (e.g., greater than 0.2), and renormalizing to unit

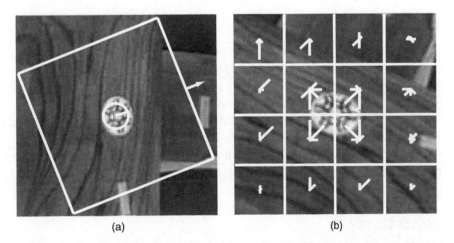

(a)   (b)

Figure 4.17. Constructing the SIFT descriptor. (a) An original detected feature, with characteristic scale and dominant orientation. The descriptor is computed from the pixels inside the indicated square, where the small arrow indicates the top edge. (b) The rotated and resampled square of pixels, with the 4×4 grid overlaid. The eight lines inside each square indicate the size of the histogram bin for each corresponding orientation. The SIFT descriptor is the concatenation of these 8×4×4 = 128 gradient magnitudes into a vector, which is then normalized.

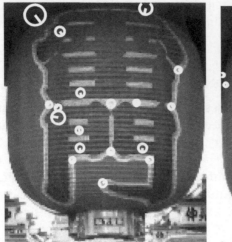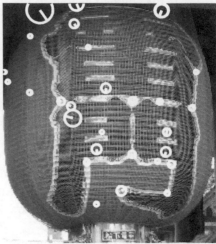

Figure 4.18. Correspondences obtained using the nearest neighbor distance ratio to match SIFT descriptors computed for images taken of the same scene under different imaging conditions. Most of the matches are correct.

length. The overall normalization makes the descriptor invariant to affine illumination changes, and the zeroing-out step prevents large gradients (which may be erroneous or viewpoint dependent) from dominating the descriptor.

Figure 4.18 illustrates the result of using the nearest neighbor distance ratio to match the SIFT descriptors between two images taken from different perspectives with different resolutions and illumination conditions. We can see that many of the correspondences are correct in terms of the matches' location, scale, and orientation; the incorrect correspondences can be removed with an outlier rejection rule based on the images' epipolar geometry, as discussed in Section 5.4.

4.2.3.1 GLOH

Mikolajczyk and Schmid [328] proposed a SIFT variant called **GLOH** (for Gradient Location and Orientation Histogram) that they claimed outperformed Lowe's original formulation. Instead of using a square grid as the domain for orientation histograms, a log-polar grid is created, as illustrated in Figure 4.19. The center region (of radius 6) is undivided, while the two outer rings (of radii 11 and 15) are divided into eight regions. The gradients in each grid region are quantized into sixteen angles (as opposed to eight for SIFT). Thus, the raw descriptor is $17 \times 16 = 272$-dimensional. Based on a training set of image patches, principal component analysis (PCA) is applied to reduce the dimensionality of the descriptor to 128.

4.2.3.2 DAISY

Winder and Brown [548] and Tola et al. [490] suggested a generalized histogram-based descriptor called DAISY.[11] Instead of specifying "hard" support regions in which to compute histograms, we specify the centers of "soft" support regions and a Gaussian

---

[11] The name DAISY comes from the petal-like appearance of the descriptor support regions.

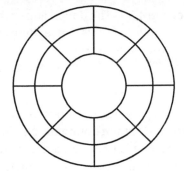

Figure 4.19. Log-polar bins used to construct the GLOH descriptor.

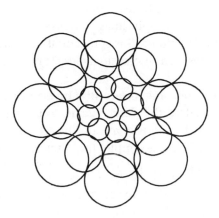

Figure 4.20. Support region centers used to construct a DAISY descriptor. The circles' radii correspond to the standard deviation of the Gaussian function at each position used to weight contributions to the orientation histogram.

function at each support region, as illustrated in Figure 4.20. Like GLOH, the support regions are arranged radially around a center point. Like the dominant orientation estimation algorithm in SIFT, the Gaussian function at each center point specifies a weighting function for the gradients in the neighborhood, so that points further from the center contribute less to the orientation histogram.

4.2.3.3 Shape Contexts

Belongie et al. [38] proposed **shape contexts** as a method for matching shapes, which were modified by Mikolajczyk and Schmid [328] for feature point description. The approach is similar to GLOH in that a log-polar location grid is constructed at the feature point location. However, instead of using the gradients of all points to construct the histograms in each subregion, only edge points detected with the Canny detector are allowed to contribute their gradient orientations. Each edge point's contribution is further weighted by its gradient magnitude. Shape contexts are also used in 3D feature detection, as discussed in Section 8.4.1.

4.2.3.4 Spin Images

Spin images were originally proposed by Johnson and Hebert [224] for describing features in range data (see Section 8.4.1). Lazebnik et al. [264] proposed modifying them to create feature descriptors for grayscale images. We simply compute a histogram of quantized intensities for each of several rings around the feature location, after the intensities have been normalized as described in Section 4.2.1. The dimension of the descriptor is the number of intensity bins times the number of rings. Since there are no angular subdivisions of the rings, the descriptor is rotation-invariant.

4.2.4 Invariant-Based Descriptors

The first step in SIFT and the similar approaches in the previous section is the rotation of a patch around the estimated feature location so that the dominant gradient orientation points in a consistent direction. An alternative is to design a descriptor that's invariant to the rotation of the patch in the first place, bypassing this estimation and explicit rotation. Such approaches are generally based on **invariant functions** of the patch pixels with respect to a class of geometric transformations — typically rotations or affine transformations. For example, the spin image discussed in the previous section is a crude rotation-invariant descriptor, but substantial discriminative information may be lost as the intensities from increasingly larger rings are aggregated into histograms.

Schmid and Mohr [430] popularized the idea of using **differential invariants** for constructing rotation-invariant descriptors. That is, the descriptor is constructed using combinations of increasingly higher-order derivatives of the Gaussian-smoothed image $L(x,y)$ given by Equation (4.16). For example, the total intensity $\sum_{(x,y)} L(x,y)$, sum of squared gradient magnitude $\sum_{(x,y)} \left(\frac{\partial L(x,y)}{\partial x} \right)^2 + \left(\frac{\partial L(x,y)}{\partial y} \right)^2$, and sum of Laplacians $\sum_{(x,y)} \frac{\partial^2 L(x,y)}{\partial x^2} + \frac{\partial^2 L(x,y)}{\partial y^2}$ are all invariant to rotation as long as the sums are taken over equivalent circular regions (such as the ones we obtain at the end of the affine adaptation process, Figure 4.12). A vector of these three quantities could be used as a descriptor. Since an image can be uniquely defined by its derivatives (e.g., consider a Taylor series), the more differential invariants we use, the more uniquely we describe the region around the feature location. For example, there are five differential invariants that use combinations of up to second derivatives, and nine differential invariants that use combinations of up to third derivatives. On the other hand, the higher-order derivatives we need, the more difficult they are to accurately estimate from an image patch, especially in the presence of noise.

Another approach is to use **moment invariants**, which are computed using both image intensities and spatial coordinates. The $(m,n)^{th}$ moment of a function defined over a region is the average value of $x^m y^n f(x,y)$. The $(0,0)$ moment is thus the average value of the function, and the $(1,0)$ and $(0,1)$ moments give the center of gravity with respect to the function. Higher-order moments represent moments of inertia and skewness. Flusser [147] derived combinations of moments that were invariant to rotations based on earlier work by Hu [205]. Van Gool et al. [510] enumerated the affine-invariant moments up to $m + n \leq 2$, which can be used to construct affine-invariant feature descriptors. Mikolajczyk and Schmid [328] suggested that moment invariants could be applied to x and y gradient images as well.

Schaffalitzky and Zisserman [423] proposed to use a bank of complex filters whose magnitude responses are invariant to rotation, indexed by two positive integers and given by the coefficients

$$K_{mn}(x,y) = (x + iy)^m (x - iy)^n G(x,y) \tag{4.40}$$

These complex filters are similar to the derivatives of a Gaussian. For example, for $m + n \leq 6$, we obtain a descriptor of length 15. Again, this approach avoids the need to explicitly estimate the dominant gradient orientation.

4.2.5   Other Approaches

Here, we briefly mention a few notable descriptors that don't fit into any of the previously outlined main categories.

4.2.5.1 Steerable Filters

Steerable filters are used to efficiently apply a desired filter (for example, the nth derivative of a Gaussian) with respect to a desired angle. Freeman and Adelson [153] showed that many such arbitrarily angled filters could be easily computed as the sum of responses to a small number of basis filters at canonical orientations. Mikolajczyk and Schmid [325] proposed to apply a filter bank of Gaussian derivatives with respect to the angle given by the dominant gradient orientation at a patch, using the vector of responses as a descriptor. The response vector is rotationally invariant assuming the estimation of the dominant gradient orientation is correct.

4.2.5.2 SURF

Bay et al. [33] proposed a simplified descriptor inspired by SIFT called **SURF** (for Speeded-Up Robust Features). As in SIFT, the oriented square at a feature's detected scale is split into a 4×4 square grid. However, instead of computing gradient orientation histograms in each subregion, Haar wavelet responses at twenty-five points in each subregion are computed. The sums of the original and absolute responses in the x and y directions are computed in each subregion, yielding a 4×4×4 = 64-dimensional descriptor. Since Haar wavelets are basically box filters, the SURF descriptor can be computed very quickly.

4.2.5.3 PCA-SIFT

The SIFT descriptor is extremely popular, and is most frequently used as Lowe originally described it, that is, a 128-dimensional vector. However, it's natural to question whether all 128 dimensions of the descriptor are necessary and should receive equal weight in matching. Ke and Sukthankar [235] partially addressed this question using a dimensionality reduction step based on principal component analysis (PCA). The technique is generally known as **PCA-SIFT**, but this is a misnomer; the principal component analysis is not performed directly on SIFT descriptor vectors, but on the raw gradients of a scale- and rotation-normalized patch. More precisely, they collected a large number of DoG keypoints and constructed 41×41 patches at the estimated scale and orientation of each keypoint. The x and y gradients at the interior pixels of each patch were collected into a $39 \times 39 \times 2 = 3042$-dimensional vector, and PCA was applied to determine a much smaller number of basis vectors (e.g., twenty or thirty-six). Thus, the high-dimensional vector of gradients for a candidate feature is represented by a low-dimensional descriptor given by its projection onto the learned basis vectors. Nearest-neighbor matching was then carried out on these lower-dimensional descriptor vectors.

4.3   EVALUATING DETECTORS AND DESCRIPTORS

Given the wide range of available detectors and descriptors discussed so far, choosing an appropriate combination for a given problem seems a daunting task. Luckily, several research groups have undertaken thorough analyses of detectors and descriptors both separately and together. We briefly summarize several findings here.

The main figure of merit for evaluating a feature detector is its **repeatability**. That is, a feature detected in one image should also be detected in the correct location in an image of the same scene under different imaging conditions. These different conditions could include changes in camera settings (such as focal length, blur, or image compression), camera viewpoint (inducing affine or more complex changes in pixel patterns), or the environment (such as global or local illumination).

Studies of detector repeatability [431, 329] first focused on images of a planar surface, like a graffiti-covered wall, taken from different perspectives. Since all points in such an image pair are related by the same projective transformation (see Section 5.1), we can immediately determine the correct location in the second image of any feature point detected in the first image, and check to see if any features were detected near this location. Figure 4.21a illustrates the idea. The **repeatability score** of a detector for a given image pair is then

$$RS = \frac{R}{\min(N_1, N_2)} \qquad (4.41)$$

where N_1 and N_2 are the numbers of features detected in each image respectively, and R is the number of repeated detections. An ideal detector has a repeatability of 1.

If the feature detector also produces an estimated support region (e.g., an affine-covariant ellipse), these regions should also transform appropriately under different

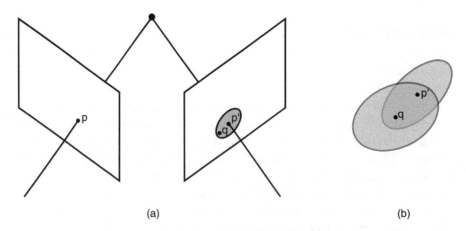

(a)   (b)

Figure 4.21. Evaluating feature detector repeatability. (a) A feature is detected at location p in the left image. If two images are related by a projective transformation, we can easily determine the location p' corresponding to the same position in the right image. If a feature q is detected within a small neighborhood of p' in the second image, we say the detection is repeated. (b) If a feature detector produces a support region, we can compare them for a more stringent test of repeatability. A detection is repeated if the ratio of the intersection of the two regions to their union is sufficiently large.

imaging conditions, and should be taken into account when determining if a detection is repeated. Figure 4.21b illustrates this more stringent test. A detection is considered repeated if the area of intersection of the two regions is sufficiently large compared to the area of their union (e.g., above sixty percent).

Mikolajczyk et al. [329] surveyed the affine-covariant feature detectors discussed in Section 4.1, and tested them with respect to viewpoint and scale change, blurring, JPEG compression, and illumination changes on a varied set of images. Their general conclusions were that the Hessian-Affine and MSER detectors had the highest repeatability under the various conditions, followed by the Harris-Affine detector. In general, Hessian-Affine and Harris-Affine produced a larger number of detected pairs than the other algorithms. They then used the SIFT descriptor as the basis for matching features from each detector, computing a **matching score** as

$$MS = \frac{M}{\min(N_1, N_2)} \qquad (4.42)$$

where M is the number of correct nearest-neighbor matches computed using Euclidean distance between the descriptors. They generally concluded that the Hessian-Affine and Harris-Affine detectors produced a large number of matches (but with a relatively high false alarm rate), while MSER produced a lower number of matches (but with a low false alarm rate).

Mikolajczyk and Schmid [328] followed up with a more comprehensive evaluation of feature descriptors, considering combinations of the Harris-Laplace/Affine and Hessian-Laplace/Affine detectors with most of the descriptors discussed in Section 4.2. They investigated the same changes in imaging conditions, computing the precision and recall of each detector/descriptor combination as functions of a changing parameter (e.g., the rotation angle between the images). Here, precision and recall are defined as

$$precision = \frac{\# \text{ correct matches}}{\# \text{ total matches}} \qquad recall = \frac{\# \text{ correct matches}}{\# \text{ true correspondences}} \qquad (4.43)$$

where the correct matches and true correspondences are determined from the repeatability score and region overlap measure defined previously. A good descriptor should have high precision — that is, few false matches — and high recall — that is, few matches that are present in the detector results but poorly represented by the descriptor. Their general conclusions, independent of the detector used, were that the GLOH and SIFT descriptors had the best performance. Shape contexts and PCA-SIFT also performed well. This study also confirmed the usefulness of the nearest neighbor distance ratio for matching SIFT descriptors.

Moreels and Perona [336] undertook a similar controlled evaluation of detector/descriptor combinations, for the specific problem of matching features in close-up images of 3D objects with respect to viewpoint and lighting changes. They found that Hessian-Affine and DoG detectors with SIFT descriptors had consistently high performance for viewpoint changes. MSER and shape contexts, which performed well on planar scenes in [328], were found to have only average performance for matching 3D objects. The Harris-Affine detector with the SIFT descriptor was found to perform the best for lighting and scale changes. In general, far fewer matches were found when comparing images of 3D objects versus images of planar scenes.

4.3.1   Learning Good Parameters

Based on the success of SIFT and GLOH, Winder, Brown, and Hua [548, 549, 71] undertook an extensive effort to learn good parameters for the general class of histogram-based descriptors. They began with a very large set of known match and non-match pairs of patches obtained from DoG interest points, and simultaneously learned the parameters and combinations of descriptor components that gave the best performance on the training set. For example, they considered the number of gradient orientation bins, grid configuration of SIFT and GLOH regions, configuration and Gaussian variance of DAISY regions, and number of basis vectors for dimensionality reduction using PCA, among many other factors. They generally recommended that a DAISY-like configuration was best, where the Gaussian variances increase with distance from the feature location. These studies differed from the testing procedure of Mikolajczyk et al. in that the training and testing data were based on ground-truth point correspondences in general images of large 3D scenes acquired by multi-view stereo techniques (see Section 8.3).

4.4   COLOR DETECTORS AND DESCRIPTORS

It's somewhat surprising that almost all research on detectors and descriptors assumes a grayscale image as input. Since distinctive color regions provide obvious cues for feature detection that are often lost or subdued by conversion to grayscale, it's worthwhile to investigate detectors and descriptors that preserve color information throughout the process. Here we mention a few such algorithms.

In terms of color detectors, Kenney et al. [237] extended the Harris matrix from Section 4.1.1 using several basic axioms for properties of a good corner detector. They showed how to generalize the Harris matrix in Equation (4.3) and Shi-Tomasi criterion in Equation (4.13) to images with multidimensional range (such as color images) and/or domain (such as 3D medical images). Unnikrishnan and Hebert [505] introduced a generalization of scale space for feature detection in color images. They proposed a family of functions involving first and second derivatives of the three color channels at a given scale, so that the output of the function at each scale is roughly invariant to linear illumination changes. Similar to Harris-Laplace, feature points are detected at local extrema in scale space. Forssén [148] described an extension of MSERs to color. The one-dimensional watershed algorithm to compute the extremal regions is replaced with an agglomerative clustering scheme to produce the nested set of connected components.

In terms of color descriptors, early work focused on invariant-based techniques. For example, grayscale moment invariants were generalized to color images by Mindru et al. [330]. That is, we compute the generalized moments

$$\sum\sum x^m y^n (I_R(x,y))^r (I_G(x,y))^g (I_B(x,y))^b \tag{4.44}$$

where the integers $m, n \geq 0$ specify the order of the moment, and the integers $r, g, b \geq 0$ specify the degree of the moment for each color channel. Mindru et al. showed various ratios of sums and products of the color moments to be invariant to both geometric (e.g., affine) and photometric transformations of an image, which can be concatenated to form a descriptor. Montesinos et al. [333] extended first-order grayscale differential invariants to form a color descriptor.

The popularity of SIFT led to various attempts to "colorize" the SIFT descriptor. An obvious approach is simply to concatenate the SIFT descriptors for a feature point location computed in three color channels (e.g., RGB or HSV) to create a $3 \times 128 =$ 384-dimensional descriptor, possibly reducing the dimensionality with PCA. van de Weijer and Schmid [509] augmented the standard 128-dimensional SIFT descriptor computed on luminance values with an additional 222 dimensions representing color measurements, including histograms of weighted hue values and photometric invariants. More straightforwardly, Abdel-Hakim and Farag [1] proposed to apply the usual SIFT detector/descriptor to a color invariant image obtained as the ratio of two linear functions of RGB. Both Burghouts and Geusebroek [77] and van de Sande et al. [508] recently presented surveys and evaluations of color descriptors, generally concluding that augmenting the SIFT descriptor with color information improved repeatability results over using luminance alone.

Even if a grayscale feature detector/descriptor scheme is dictated by the application, it may still be possible to improve performance by modifying the input to the detector. For example, Gooch et al. [174] proposed an algorithm for processing a color image into a one-channel image that differs from the traditional luminance image. Instead, adjacent pixel differences in the new image are optimized to match a function of color differences in the original image as well as possible. It may also be possible to apply an algorithm like that of Collins et al. [101] to adaptively choose the most discriminating one-dimensional space over the course of object tracking. For example, the green channel may be most discriminating for tracking a certain feature on an actor in a natural environment, but a combination of red and blue channels may be better as the actor crosses into a green-screen background.

4.5　ARTIFICIAL MARKERS

In a controlled environment such as a movie set, it's common to introduce **artificial markers** for tracking — that is, patterns designed to be robustly, unambiguously detected. Then, instead of using a generic feature detector, a customized detector can be designed for rapidly locating and identifying such features. The most common use of artificial markers today is for augmented reality as opposed to visual effects. Figure 4.22 illustrates several types of artificial markers, discussed in more detail next.

Two-dimensional bar codes used to encode information are now commonplace, for example in the context of tracking shipped packages. More recently, **QR codes**[12] (Figure 4.22a) have become popular for encoding information into a pattern of black and white squares, which can be detected and decoded quickly by mobile devices like cell phones. However, these patterns must fill a large percentage of an image to

[12] QR Code is a registered trademark of Denso Wave Incorporated, Japan.

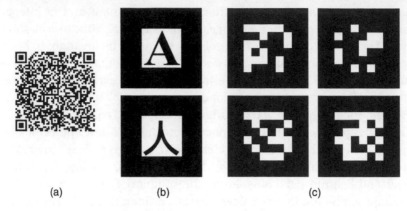

(a)   (b)   (c)

Figure 4.22. Various artificial markers. (a) A QR code. (b) ARToolKit markers. English or Japanese characters are frequently used for the interior pattern. (c) ARTag fiducial markers. The interior pattern is a 6×6 pattern designed for robust detection and identification.

be detectable and decodable, which is not useful in visual effects situations where we want to detect a large number of markers. They are also not designed for accurate localization.

ARToolKit markers [231], designed for augmented reality applications, are square patches with a thick black border and an arbitrary binary interior (Figure 4.22b). A marker is detected in an image by thresholding, finding the lines defining the black border, rectifying the pattern to be a square, and identifying the interior pattern using cross-correlation with a library of known templates. As with QR codes, robust detection of these patterns is only possible when they take up a relatively large fraction of a camera's field of view, and since the interior patterns are arbitrary, the approach is not optimized for detectability.

Fiala [140] introduced **ARTag** markers, designed to be robustly detectable at various scales in an image in the presence of perspective distortion, lighting conditions, and mild occlusion, making them a good choice for visual effects applications. Like ARToolKit markers, ARTags are delimited by a black border and contain a binary interior pattern; however, the interior patterns are grids of 6×6 binary squares designed to minimize inter-marker confusion and provide resistance to decoding errors (Figure 4.22c). Markers are found by connecting detected edges into quadrilaterals, extracting the thirty-six bits in the interior of each pattern, and applying forward error detection and correction to extract a valid ten-bit marker ID. The markers are not rotationally symmetric, so four orientations of the marker must be tested; on the other hand, detection produces a useful orientation estimate. A similar approach was taken by Wagner and Schmalstieg [524] to create **ARToolKitPlus** markers optimized for detection by mobile devices.

4.6   INDUSTRY PERSPECTIVES

Doug Roble, creative director of software, and Som Shankar, integration supervisor from Digital Domain in Venice, California discuss the role of features on a movie set.

RJR: When you need to track natural features in plates, what detection and description strategies do you use?

Roble: When we do automatic feature detection and tracking we tend to use things like Harris corners. These are important first steps for matchmoving algorithms.

However, we're often trying to specifically follow a point an artist has selected in an image. For example, the artist may know that a CGI character is going to be dancing on top of a cabinet in the scene. The rest of the points in the scene don't matter; it's

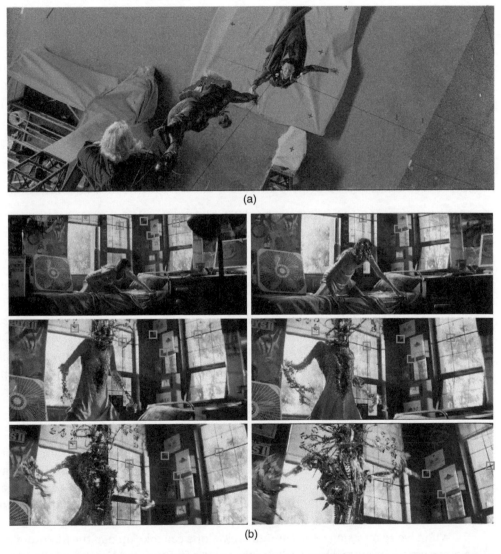

(a)

(b)

Figure 4.23. (a) In blue- or green-screen environments, artificial features are often introduced to aid camera tracking, such as the red tape marks in this frame from *Thor*. (b) In natural environments, automatically extracted image features such as Harris corners play the same role, as in this sequence from *Transformers: Revenge of the Fallen*. Scale and rotation invariance may be necessary to compensate for camera rotation and zoom. *Thor* images appear courtesy of Marvel Studios, TM & ©2011 Marvel and Subs. www.marvel.com. *Transformers: Revenge of the Fallen* ©2009 DW Studios L.L.C. and Paramount Pictures Corporation. All Rights Reserved.

that cabinet that counts. The artist will specifically choose points that are close to where the effect is going to happen, which may or may not show up in an automatic corner detector. They might be near a gradual slope or a pattern.

The artist can also draw a pattern or outline around that point and say, "track this stuff." That outline doesn't need to be a square or rectangle — for example, a rectangle might contain background pixels that you don't want to deal with. It could be an arbitrary shape, which avoids the need to do some sort of automatic outlier rejection on pixels you don't care about.

To follow the pattern through a sequence, we use a template-based method based on cross-correlation in three-channel color space. Of course, there are lots of problems with that. The object may rotate or slide around. The pattern tracker that we use solves for not just translation and rotation, but also skew, perspective, and lighting changes using an affine or nonlinear transformation as necessary. I definitely started with Shi and Tomasi's Good Features to Track, because that's the classic approach, but these days my approach is more related to a paper by J. P. Lewis that does a good job of addressing lighting changes [276]. Of course, motion blur and occlusions are always a real pain to deal with.

RJR: SIFT is incredibly popular in the computer vision community; what about in visual effects?

Roble: Right now, we don't really use SIFT all that much here. It's isn't necessary for the kind of pattern tracking through frames of a shot that we deal with all the time. Also, the SIFT descriptor contains a much different kind of information than artists are used to.

One idea I wanted to investigate using SIFT was as a pre-process before doing corner matching. The problem is occlusion: the actors on the sets walk in front of the features all the time. With a corner-matching algorithm, or something that's purely template-based, once a feature gets occluded, by the time it becomes visible again, the camera's often moved significantly, and it comes in as a whole new track. SIFT seems like it could potentially help hook those tracks back together across the gap.

RJR: What's it like to place artificial features on a movie set?

Shankar: Every set is different; it's totally free-form. This is a good example of the pragmatic side of filmmaking. It would be awesome to be able to place regularly spaced markers with coded patterns on the set and write software to automatically recognize their unique IDs, but the reality is you have to get in and out fast without interfering with the crew or the actors.

When we're on a stage, the camera crew alone can take up half the afternoon and you've got to throw up what markers you can in a few minutes. You'll see little squares of gaffer's tape on corners here and there because sometimes that's all you can get. We often use markers that consist of big orange triangles, which contrast well with blue screens. An advantage of these is that by looking at their edges they help us a bit with estimating motion blur from moving footage — but tracking through motion blur is always a hard problem.

If it's a locked-off, stationary camera we just need a couple of good markers that stay out of people's hair. If we have a moving camera I have to think about where to place these points so that we get good parallax with good visibility, where the actors aren't going to walk.

There's a tradeoff between our data integration and roto/paint departments since every marker we put up on a set, they eventually have to paint out later in production. It can be very difficult — for example if you have an actor's hair in front of a marker on a blue screen, it's murder to get rid of it. However, especially with a moving camera in front of a blue screen, we need to make sure we have enough markers to give us an accurate 3D camera track — that's the priority.

We also have what we call our "tepee"s. These are simple assemblies made of tubes and balls that look like an upside-down three-sided pyramid on top of another three-sided pyramid. We carry the pieces around in a bag and can quickly assemble and dissemble them on a set to quickly get objects in the scene that have known dimensions and geometry. For smaller-scale scenes we have the "cubee," which is just a rigid metal frame with balls on the vertices.

Roble: A lot of times, people not in the filmmaking business will say, "Why don't you try this cool new technique?" The environment on set is extraordinarily stressful. The producers are there watching how much time everything is taking; they basically have this little stopwatch that counts in units of money. The guys in the data integration group are really good about running into the scene, throwing up just enough markers to get what they need, and then running out before the director notices. A lot of careful setup is a rarity. Most of it is get what you can and go.

RJR: Any other interesting applications of features?

Roble: For *AI: Artificial Intelligence*, Steven Spielberg wanted to be able to just walk around the set, film it with a handheld camera, and see the result in real time on a kind of virtual set. They mounted a couple of little cameras on top of the camera pointed upward, and put a whole bunch of checkerboard patterns on the ceiling. The upward-facing cameras could then find the checkerboards no matter where he was on the set, and since they knew exactly where the checkerboards were in 3D they could track the camera position pretty accurately in real time. Industrial Light and Magic uses similar black-and-white patterns for their iMocap system, which lets them track the heads and bodies of performers on set who will later be replaced by CGI characters.

4.7 NOTES AND EXTENSIONS

Tuytelaars and Van Gool [503] proposed two affine-covariant-region-based feature detectors not discussed here. The first is based on the edges in an image, under the assumption that edges and their intersections can be reliably detected in views of the same scene from different perspectives. The basic idea is to detect a Harris corner and trace two roughly perpendicular Canny edges in its neighborhood until a photometric measure reaches its extremum, ultimately producing an affine-covariant parallelogram. The second method is less reliant on edges. Instead, we begin at local intensity extrema and trace many rays outward until a photometric measure reaches an extremum along each ray. An ellipse is fit to the resulting points, producing an affine-invariant region. Mikolajczyk et al. [329] found the performance of the two detectors to be reasonable, but noted that their computational cost was quite high compared to the Harris/Hessian-Laplace and MSER detectors. Kadir and Brady [229] also proposed an affine-invariant detector based on the idea that good features should be detected at patches whose intensity distributions have high entropy. However, the algorithm is extremely slow, and Mikolajczyk et al. [329] found its performance not to compare with the algorithms discussed here.

FAST corners were predated by an early approach to fast low-level corner detection called SUSAN proposed by Smith and Brady [461]. A disc is centered around a candidate point and the area of pixels in the disc with intensities similar to the center pixel is computed. A corner is detected if the area is a local minimum and below half the disc area. Another approach by Trajković and Hedley [497] uses the same concept of a circle of pixels around a candidate point, assuming that for some pair of diametrically opposite points, the intensities must substantially differ from the center point.

Tell and Carlsson proposed an affine-invariant descriptor based on the line of intensities connecting pairs of detected features [487]. However, choosing appropriate feature pairs and obtaining a sufficient number of matches for a given application can be problematic. Forssén and Lowe [149] proposed a descriptor for MSERs based on the region's shape alone, since MSER shapes can be quite distinctive. The descriptor is based on applying the SIFT descriptor to the binary patch corresponding to the MSER.

Lepetit and Fua [270] proposed a feature recognition algorithm based on randomized trees that assumes that several registered training images of the object to be detected are available. The idea is to build a library of the expected appearances of each feature from many different synthetic viewpoints, and then to build a classifier that determines the feature (if any) to which a new pixel patch corresponds. While the training phase requires some computational effort, the recognition algorithm is fast, since it only requires the traversal of a precomputed tree. Thus, feature descriptors are not explicitly formed and compared. The approach was later extended to non-hierarchical structures called ferns [358]. Stavens and Thrun [466] similarly noted that if a feature matching problem is known to arise from a certain domain (e.g., tracking shots of buildings), a machine learning algorithm could be used to tune the parameters of a detector/descriptor algorithm to obtain the best performance on domain-specific training data. These kinds of learning algorithms are worth investigation, with the understanding that performance may suffer if input from a different domain is used.

The popularity of SIFT and its validation as a high-performance descriptor has led to a variety of extensions (for example, the color versions in Section 4.4). One area of particular interest is the acceleration of the algorithm, since in its original form descriptor computation and matching was fairly slow, especially compared to template-based cross-correlation. One approach is to leverage the processing power of GPUs (e.g., [455]). Alternately, other groups have stripped out features of SIFT to make the basic idea viable on a resource-constrained platform like a mobile phone (e.g., [523]). In general, any approach that requires the matching of a high-dimensional candidate descriptor against a large library (e.g., for wide-baseline matching) should take advantage of an approximate nearest-neighbor search algorithm for computational efficiency (e.g., Beis and Lowe's best-bin-first search [36]).

4.8   HOMEWORK PROBLEMS

4.1   Show that the Harris matrix for any positive set of weights must be positive semidefinite. That is, show that $b^\top H b \geq 0$ for any $b \in \mathbb{R}^2$.

4.2   Consider the $N \times N$ patch in Figure 4.24a, where the slanted line passes through the center of the patch at an angle of $\theta°$ from the positive x axis, and the intensity is 1 above the line and 0 below the line. Estimate the eigenvectors and eigenvalues of the Harris matrix for the pixel in the center of the patch (assuming $w(x,y)$ is an ideal box filter encompassing the whole patch).

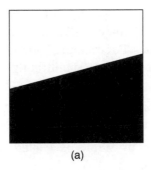 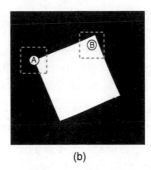

(a)   (b)

Figure 4.24. (a) A binary $N \times N$ patch. (b) A binary image, with two potential feature locations.

4.3   Consider the image in Figure 4.24b. Will the Harris measure using an ideal box filter give a higher response at point A (centered on a corner) or at point B (further inside a corner)? Think carefully about the gradients in the dotted regions.

4.4   Write the Harris measure C in Equation (4.4) as a function of the eigenvalues of H.

4.5   Show that if one eigenvalue of the Harris matrix is 0 and the other is very large, the Harris measure C is negative.

4.6   Explain why the Gaussian derivative filters in Equation (4.6) act as gradient operators on the original image.

4.7   Show that minimizing Equation (4.11) leads to Equation (4.12).

4.8   Determine the generalization of Equation (4.12) that corresponds to the affine deformation model of Equation (4.14).

4.9   Sketch a simple example of an image location that would fail the Harris corner test at a small scale but pass it at a larger scale.

4.10   Use Equation (4.21) and a real image of your choice to duplicate the result in Figure 4.4. That is, create a zoomed version of the original image, and determine the characteristic scale of the same blob-like point in both images. You should verify that the ratio of characteristic scales is approximately the same as the zoom factor.

4.11   Verify with a simple real image that the Laplacian-of-Gaussian detector responds strongly to edges, while the Hessian-Laplace detector does not.

4.12   Speculate about the form of a simple detector based on box filters (similar to the Fast Hessian detector in Figure 4.7) that approximates the normalized Laplacian in Equation (4.21).

4.13   Prove that the Gaussian function in Equation (4.7) satisfies the diffusion equation in Equation (4.26).

4.14   Show why the refined keypoint location in Equation (4.31) follows from the quadratic fit in Equation (4.30).

4.15   If C is the matrix square root of a positive semidefinite matrix H, show how the eigenvalues/eigenvectors of C and H are related.

4.16   The FAST Corner detector, which requires three of the four pixels labeled 1, 5, 9 and 13 in Figure 4.13 to be brighter or darker than the center pixel, can miss some good corner candidates. For example, show that a strong corner can exist if only two of the four pixels are significantly brighter or darker than the center pixel.

4.17   Explain the shape of the curve in Figure 4.15a — notably the low plateau, sharp increase, and subsequent slow increase.

4.18   Describe how the computation of MSERs is related to the watershed algorithm from image processing.

4.19   Explain why MSER detection is invariant to an affine change in intensity.

4.20   Show how the normalized cross-correlation between two real vectors can be computed using the Discrete Fourier Transform. (Fast Fourier Transform algorithms make this approach computationally efficient when searching for a template patch across a large image region.)

4.21   In Lowe's definition of the SIFT descriptor, the gradient at each sample location contributes to the surrounding spatial and orientation bins using trilinear interpolation. This means the descriptor will change smoothly as its center and orientation are varied. For example, the point with gradient indicated in Figure 4.25a will contribute to the eight labeled histogram bins in Figure 4.25b, with most of the weight in Bin 3. If the point lies two-thirds of the way along the line segment connecting the center of the lower left bin and the upper right bin, and the angle of the gradient from the positive vertical axis is $\pi/16$, compute the weights $w_1, \ldots w_8$ that represent the contribution of the point to each orientation bin.

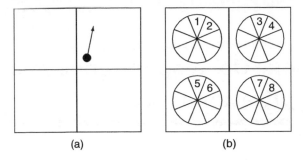

(a)   (b)

Figure 4.25. The point with the indicated gradient contributes to eight bins in the SIFT descriptor.

4.22   Show that the descriptors given by the total intensity $\sum_{(x,y)} L(x,y)$, sum of squared gradient magnitudes $\sum_{(x,y)} \left(\frac{\partial L(x,y)}{\partial x}\right)^2 + \left(\frac{\partial L(x,y)}{\partial y}\right)^2$, and sum of Laplacians $\sum_{(x,y)} \frac{\partial^2 L(x,y)}{\partial x^2} + \frac{\partial^2 L(x,y)}{\partial y^2}$ are invariant to rotation around the central point of the descriptor. Assume that the image's range and domain are continuous (so the sums become integrals) and that the aggregations are taken over equivalent circular regions.

4.23   Show that the directional derivative of a Gaussian function G (given by Equation (4.7)) at a point (x,y) in an arbitrary unit direction v is a linear combination of its x and y derivatives at (x,y). This is a simple example of a steerable filter [153].

4.24   The performance of a descriptor can be measured by plotting a curve of (1-precision) versus recall as the descriptor distance defining a match is varied. Sketch two such curves for two hypothetical descriptor algorithms, and discuss which one represents a better algorithm and why.

4.25   ARTag markers are based on the theory of error correcting codes. They include ten bits to define the marker ID, sixteen bits for a checksum, and ten bits for error correction, leading to thirty-six bits arranged in a 6×6 square. Show that $e = 10$ bits are required to correct $c = 2$ errors in the initial $n = 26$ bits, using the formula

$$e \approx c \log_2 n \tag{4.45}$$

5 Dense Correspondence and Its Applications

In the last chapter we focused on detecting and matching distinctive **features**. Typically, features are sparsely distributed — that is, not every pixel location has a feature centered at it. However, for several visual effects applications, we require a **dense correspondence** between pixels in two images, even in relatively flat or featureless areas. One of the most common applications of dense correspondence in filmmaking is for slowing down or speeding up a shot after it's been filmed for dramatic effect. To create the appropriate intermediate frames, we need to estimate the trajectory of every pixel in the video sequence over the course of a shot, not just a few pixels near features.

More mathematically, we want to compute a vector field $(u(x,y), v(x,y))$ over the pixels of the first image I_1, so that the vector at each pixel (x,y) points to a corresponding location in the second image I_2. That is, the pixels $I_1(x,y)$ and $I_2(x + u(x,y), y + v(x,y))$ correspond. We usually abbreviate the vector field as (u,v) with the understanding that both elements are functions of x and y.

Defining what constitutes a correspondence in this context can be tricky. As in feature matching, our intuition is that a correspondence implies that both pixels arise from the same point on the surface of some object in the physical world. The vector (u,v) is induced by the motion of the camera and/or the object in the interval between taking the two pictures. Thus, it is often called a **motion vector**. Unfortunately, changes in pixel intensity can occur in the absence of camera/object motion and vice versa. For example, if we move a spotlight around a static object between taking two pictures with a stationary camera, the pixel intensities are likely to be very different even though the object has not moved. On the other hand, two pictures of an ideal, matte-white rotating sphere under identical lighting conditions will look the same at different times, even though the points on the surface of the sphere have moved. In practice, we try to avoid these worst-case scenarios by assuming sufficiently textured scenes in which the interval between taking the pictures is small enough to avoid major lighting changes. This means that changes in apparent pixel brightness are for the most part caused by camera and object motion. The dense correspondence field we seek in this chapter is thus generally assumed to arise from underlying physical point correspondence, just like in the previous chapter.

Obtaining dense correspondence between images is one of the oldest and most well-studied problems in computer vision, with literally thousands of papers on the topic in several different forms. The easiest case is when the two images are assumed to be related by a global, parametric transformation, so that (u,v) is a closed-form function of (x,y). In this case, the problem is called **registration**, and we discuss estimation methods when the transformation is affine or projective (Section 5.1). The next class of methods assumes that a set of sparse feature matches is available (e.g., obtained using any of the methods in the previous chapter) and that the dense correspondence field smoothly interpolates these matches. We discuss this problem of **scattered data interpolation** in Section 5.2.

The methods in these sections implicitly assume that every point in the first image has a match in the second image, and vice versa, so that the dense correspondence is like a "rubber sheet" that warps the coordinate system of the first image to that of the second. However, these approaches do not allow for the possibility of **occlusions**, regions visible in one image but not the other, or **discontinuities**, regions where the (u,v) field does not smoothly vary, both of which are common in real-world scenes.

Most generally, we consider a pair of images of the same scene at different times taken from different perspectives, which could contain multiple moving objects. The dense correspondence field resulting from changes in apparent brightness is typically called the **optical flow field**. We discuss this well-studied problem, from early, now-classical methods to more modern approaches (Section 5.3). Initial work assumed that the different perspectives were relatively close together spatially and that there were no occlusions or discontinuities. However, robust hierarchical methods and other extensions now permit dense correspondence to be estimated when the cameras are relatively far apart.

When the images are known to be taken close together and the scene has not changed (e.g., by two synchronized cameras mounted on a rigid rig), the special case of the optical flow problem is called **stereo correspondence**. This configuration forces the correspondence of each pixel in one image to lie on a straight line in the other image, greatly reducing the search space for the motion vectors. We introduce the **epipolar geometry** for an image pair and methods for its estimation using a set of feature matches (Section 5.4). We also discuss how to **rectify** an image pair to ease the search for correspondences along pairs of epipolar lines. We then overview the stereo correspondence problem, an area of major interest in computer vision (Section 5.5). Since the motion vectors in the stereo problem are discretized to a small set of values, we can apply modern optimization tools like graph cuts and belief propagation to efficiently solve the problem.

The rest of the chapter addresses visual effects applications of a dense correspondence field once it has been obtained. We first discuss **video matching**, the problem of aligning two sequences that follow roughly the same camera trajectory but at different speeds (Section 5.6). Video matching is the central problem for effects shots in which multiple camera passes of different elements need to be composited into a final result. Next, we discuss **image morphing**, the visually compelling effect of transforming one object into another (Section 5.7). In this case, we need to create a dense correspondence field between two fundamentally *different* scenes, so scattered data interpolation methods are typically used instead of optical flow and stereo methods. Finally, we discuss the problem of **view synthesis**, where the goal is to generate physically realistic "in-between" views of a scene from different perspectives than either of the source images (Section 5.8).

This chapter focuses on the problem of dense correspondence between exactly two images. We discuss methods using more than two images in Chapter 8, in the context of multi-view stereo algorithms for estimating dense 3D depth maps.

5.1   AFFINE AND PROJECTIVE TRANSFORMATIONS

The assumption that two images are related by a simple parametric transformation is extremely common in computer vision. For example, if we denote a pair of images and their coordinate systems by $I_1(x,y)$ and $I_2(x',y')$, the two are related by an **affine transformation** if

$$x' = a_{11}x + a_{12}y + b_1 \qquad\qquad y' = a_{21}x + a_{22}y + b_2 \qquad (5.1)$$

Affine transformations are useful since they encompass rigid motions (translations and rotations), similarity transformations (rigid motions plus a uniform change in scale) and some shape-changing transformations (such as shears).

However, except under restrictive circumstances, images of the same scene from different viewpoints are rarely exactly related by affine transformations, although the approximation may be locally acceptable.[1] A more general parametric model is a **projective transformation** or **homography**, given by:

$$x' = \frac{h_{11}x + h_{12}y + h_{13}}{h_{31}x + h_{32}y + h_{33}} \qquad\qquad y' = \frac{h_{21}x + h_{22}y + h_{23}}{h_{31}x + h_{32}y + h_{33}} \qquad (5.2)$$

Images acquired using perspective projection (see Section 6.2) are exactly related by a projective transformation in two situations: either the camera undergoes pure rotation (i.e., panning, tilting, and zooming only) or the scene is entirely planar. We can see that a projective transformation with $h_{31} = h_{32} = 0$ and $h_{33} \neq 0$ reduces to an affine transformation. Also, note that multiplying all the parameters by the same scalar parameter results in the same transformation. Thus, a projective transformation has eight degrees of freedom. Figure 5.1 illustrates an image and the results of various projective transformations.

Estimating an affine or projective transformation relating an image pair typically begins by detecting and matching features, as discussed in the previous chapter. The further apart the camera viewpoints, the more likely it is that scale- or affine-covariant detectors and invariant descriptors will be necessary for generating a large number of high-quality matches. Let's denote the locations of these matches as $\{(x_1,y_1),\ldots,(x_n,y_n)\}$ in the first image plane and $\{(x'_1,y'_1),\ldots,(x'_n,y'_n)\}$ in the second image plane. Due to matching errors and image noise, the matches are unlikely to be exact, and due to deviations from the ideal assumptions of the parametric transformation, the model is unlikely to be exact. Therefore, we search for the parameters that best fit the correspondences, usually in a robust least-squares sense. This parameter estimation problem is usually referred to as **image registration**.

---

[1] For an affine transformation to exactly represent the motion of all pixels in images acquired using perspective projection (see Section 6.2), the image planes must both be parallel to each other and to the direction of camera motion. Furthermore, if the translational motion is nonzero, the scene must be a planar surface parallel to the image planes. Nonetheless, the affine assumption is often made when the scene is far from the camera and the rotation between viewpoints is very small.

(a)   (b)   (c)   (d)

Figure 5.1. An original image (a) and the results of various affine and projective transformations. (b) A similarity transformation (i.e., translation, rotation, and uniform scale). (c) A vertical shear. (d) A general projective transformation. While (b) and (c) can be written as affine transformations, (d) cannot.

It's usually convenient to represent image coordinates and transformations in **homogeneous coordinates** for parameter estimation. This means that we represent an image location (x, y) as a triple $(x, y, 1)$, and that any triple (x, y, z) can be converted back to an image coordinate by dividing by its third element to get an image location $(\frac{x}{z}, \frac{y}{z})$. In this way we can rewrite Equation (5.2) as

$$\begin{bmatrix} x' \\ y' \\ 1 \end{bmatrix} \sim \begin{bmatrix} h_{11} & h_{12} & h_{13} \\ h_{21} & h_{22} & h_{23} \\ h_{31} & h_{32} & h_{33} \end{bmatrix} \begin{bmatrix} x \\ y \\ 1 \end{bmatrix} \tag{5.3}$$

The symbol $\sim$ in Equation (5.3) means that the two vectors are equivalent up to a scalar multiple; that is, to obtain actual pixel coordinates on the left side of Equation (5.3), we need to divide the vector on the right side of Equation (5.3) by its third element.

Hartley and Zisserman [188] described how to obtain an initial estimate of the parameters of a projective transformation given a set of feature matches using the normalized **direct linear transform**, or **DLT**. The steps are as follows:

1. The input is two sets of features $\{(x_1, y_1), \dots, (x_n, y_n)\}$ in the first image plane and $\{(x'_1, y'_1), \dots, (x'_n, y'_n)\}$ in the second image plane. We normalize each set of feature matches to have zero mean and average distance from the origin $\sqrt{2}$. This can be accomplished by a pair of similarity transformations, represented as 3×3 matrices T and T' applied to the homogeneous coordinates of the points.

2. Construct a $2n \times 9$ matrix A, where each feature match generates two rows of A, that is, the 2×9 matrix

$$A_i = \begin{bmatrix} 0 & 0 & 0 & x_i & y_i & 1 & -y'_i x_i & -y'_i y_i & -y'_i \\ x_i & y_i & 1 & 0 & 0 & 0 & -x'_i x_i & -x'_i y_i & -x'_i \end{bmatrix} \tag{5.4}$$

Note that Equation (5.3) for feature match i is equivalent to

$$A_i \, [h_{11} \ h_{12} \ h_{13} \ h_{21} \ h_{22} \ h_{23} \ h_{31} \ h_{32} \ h_{33}]^\top = 0 \tag{5.5}$$

3. Compute the singular value decomposition of A, $A = UDV^\top$. D will be a 9×9 diagonal matrix with positive entries that decrease from upper left to lower right. Let h be the last column of V (a 9×1 vector).

4. Reshape h into a 3×3 matrix $\hat{H}$, filling in the elements from left to right in each row.

5. Recover the final projective transformation estimate as $H = T'^{-1}\hat{H}T$.

While the DLT is easy to implement, the resulting estimate does not minimize a symmetric, geometrically natural error. Under the assumptions that the measurement errors in each feature location are independently, identically distributed (i.i.d.) with a zero-mean Gaussian pdf, we can obtain a maximum likelihood estimate for the projective transformation by minimizing

$$\sum_{i=1}^{n} \left\| \begin{bmatrix} x_i \\ y_i \end{bmatrix} - \begin{bmatrix} \hat{x}_i \\ \hat{y}_i \end{bmatrix} \right\|_2^2 + \left\| \begin{bmatrix} x_i' \\ y_i' \end{bmatrix} - \begin{bmatrix} \hat{x}_i' \\ \hat{y}_i' \end{bmatrix} \right\|_2^2 \tag{5.6}$$

over the nine elements of H and $\{(\hat{x}_1,\hat{y}_1),\ldots,(\hat{x}_n,\hat{y}_n)\}$, which are estimates of the true feature locations exactly consistent with the projective transformation. Each $(\hat{x}_i',\hat{y}_i')$ is the transformation of the corresponding $(\hat{x}_i,\hat{y}_i)$ by H. This cost function is nonlinear and can be minimized by the Levenberg-Marquardt algorithm (Appendix A.4).

When the feature matches have errors not well modeled by an i.i.d. Gaussian distribution — for example in the case of outliers caused by incorrect matches — the RANSAC algorithm [142] should be used to obtain a robust estimate of H by repeatedly sampling sets of four correspondences, computing a candidate H, and selecting the estimate with the largest number of inliers (see Problem 5.18). Hartley and Zisserman [188] give a detailed description of these and further methods for estimating projective transformations. We will not focus heavily on parametric correspondence estimation here, since correspondence in most real-world scenes is not well modeled by a single, simple transformation.

5.2   SCATTERED DATA INTERPOLATION

A different way to think about the problem of obtaining dense correspondence from sparse feature matches is to view the matches as samples of a continuous deformation field defined over the whole image plane. That is, we seek a continuous function $f(x,y)$ defined over the first image plane so that $f(x_i,y_i) = (x_i',y_i'), i = 1,\ldots,n.$[2] This problem can be viewed as **scattered data interpolation** since the (x_i,y_i) are sparsely, unevenly distributed in the first image plane (as opposed to being regularly distributed in a grid pattern, in which case we could use a standard method like bilinear interpolation). The scattered data interpolation problem is sketched in Figure 5.2.

For all scattered data interpolation methods, it may be necessary for a user to manually add additional feature matches to further constrain the deformation field in areas where the estimated correspondence seems unnatural. We discuss this issue further in Section 5.7.

---

[2] The motion vector (u,v) at a point (x,y) is thus $(u,v) = f(x,y) - (x,y)$.

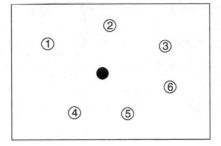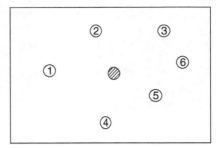

Figure 5.2. In scattered data interpolation, we're given a set of feature matches (numbered circles) unevenly distributed in each image. The goal is to generate a dense correspondence for every point in the first image plane. In this example, the match for the black point in the left image is estimated to be the striped point in the right image.

5.2.1   Thin-Plate Spline Interpolation

Bookstein [53] popularized the idea of using **thin-plate splines**[3] to compute deformation fields corresponding to scattered data samples. The idea is to write $f(x,y)$ in the following form:

$$f(x,y) = \left[\begin{array}{c} \sum_{i=1}^{n} w_{1i}\phi(r_i) + a_{11}x + a_{12}y + b_1 \\ \sum_{i=1}^{n} w_{2i}\phi(r_i) + a_{21}x + a_{22}y + b_2 \end{array} \right] \tag{5.7}$$

where $\phi(r)$ is called a **radial basis function** and

$$r_i = \left\| \left[\begin{array}{c} x \\ y \end{array} \right] - \left[\begin{array}{c} x_i \\ y_i \end{array} \right] \right\|_2 \tag{5.8}$$

The weights on the radial basis functions and the affine coefficients can be easily computed by solving a linear system:

$$\begin{bmatrix} 0 & \phi(r_{12}) & \cdots & \phi(r_{1n}) & x_1 & y_1 & 1 \\ \phi(r_{21}) & 0 & \cdots & \phi(r_{2n}) & x_2 & y_2 & 1 \\ \vdots & \vdots & \ddots & \vdots & \vdots & \vdots & \vdots \\ \phi(r_{n1}) & \phi(r_{n2}) & \cdots & 0 & x_n & y_n & 1 \\ x_1 & x_2 & \cdots & x_n & 0 & 0 & 0 \\ y_1 & y_2 & \cdots & y_n & 0 & 0 & 0 \\ 1 & 1 & \cdots & 1 & 0 & 0 & 0 \end{bmatrix} \begin{bmatrix} w_{11} & w_{21} \\ w_{12} & w_{22} \\ \vdots & \vdots \\ w_{1n} & w_{2n} \\ a_{11} & a_{21} \\ a_{12} & a_{22} \\ b_1 & b_2 \end{bmatrix} = \begin{bmatrix} x'_1 & y'_1 \\ x'_2 & y'_2 \\ \vdots & \vdots \\ x'_n & y'_n \\ 0 & 0 \\ 0 & 0 \\ 0 & 0 \end{bmatrix} \tag{5.9}$$

where

$$r_{ij} = \left\| \left[\begin{array}{c} x_i \\ y_i \end{array} \right] - \left[\begin{array}{c} x_j \\ y_j \end{array} \right] \right\|_2 \tag{5.10}$$

[3] So named because they correspond to the shape a thin metal plate would take if constrained at certain points.

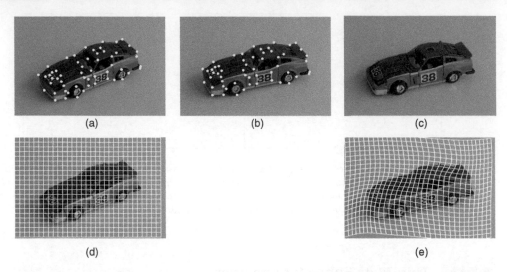

(a) (b) (c)

(d) (e)

Figure 5.3. An example of thin-plate spline interpolation between two images of the same scene. (a) Image 1 with feature locations. (b) Image 2 with feature locations. (c) Image 1 warped to Image 2's coordinates using an estimated thin-plate spline deformation. The images look virtually identical, except for minor color changes (e.g., the hubcaps). Rectilinear grid lines (d) on the coordinate system of Image 1 are transformed into non-rectilinear grid lines (e) in the coordinate system of Image 2.

Bookstein showed that the choice of ϕ given by $\phi(r) = r^2 \log r$ corresponds to a surface $f(x,y)$ that interpolates the original feature matches with the smallest bending energy.[4] That is, among the class of all functions $f(x,y)$ that exactly interpolate the data, the choice of weights and basis functions in Equation (5.9) minimizes the integral

$$\iint \left(\frac{\partial^2 f}{\partial x^2}\right)^2 + \left(\frac{\partial^2 f}{\partial x \partial y}\right)^2 + \left(\frac{\partial^2 f}{\partial y^2}\right)^2 dx\, dy \qquad (5.11)$$

The thin-plate spline results in a smooth deformation field from the coordinates of one image plane to the coordinates of the second, as illustrated in Figure 5.3. It also has the appealing property of being covariant to rigid transformations of the input data. However, the interpolating function at (x,y) explicitly depends on all the point correspondences, so adding a new correspondence requires the deformation field to be recomputed everywhere (see also Section 8.4.3).

5.2.2 B-Spline Interpolation

An attractive alternative is to create the interpolating function using a cubic **B-spline** approximation. As earlier, the function $f(x,y)$ is expressed as a combination of basis functions. These functions are now centered not at the feature point locations but at control points on a lattice overlaid on the first image plane. In the easiest case, these control points are simply the integer-valued vertices of the pixel grid. The value of the function at a point (x,y) only depends on the basis functions at the sixteen control

---

[4] Actually, there are two surfaces here; the first satisfies $f_x(x_i, y_i) = x_i'$ and the second satisfies $f_y(x_i, y_i) = y_i'$.

points in its neighborhood. This means that new control points can be added in one place without changing the interpolation far away. Thus,

$$f(x,y) = \sum_{k=0}^{3}\sum_{l=0}^{3} w_{kl}(x,y)\psi_{kl}(x,y) \qquad (5.12)$$

for appropriate basis functions ψ (usually cubic polynomials), and k and l that define which basis functions are active at pixel (x,y).

Lee et al. [267] described the details of computing the B-spline basis functions and weights for scattered data interpolation, and proposed a method for adaptively varying the resolution of the control point lattice to avoid a very large number of basis functions. Depending on the algorithm settings, the B-spline can either exactly interpolate the feature matches, or merely approximate the matches to a desired tolerance (which generally allows a coarser lattice). Further details about the B-spline interpolation process can be found in the book by Farin [135].

5.2.3 Diffeomorphisms

Joshi and Miller [228] noted that the thin-plate spline approach is not guaranteed to produce a **diffeomorphism**[5] in cases where the deformation underlying the feature matches is extreme. Figure 5.4a-b illustrates a simple example of the problem; the deformation field corresponding to the thin-plate spline causes the grid lines in the center to intersect themselves. Instead, the deformation field can be computed as the solution of a ordinary differential equation. The idea is to "flow" the first image $I_1(x,y)$ to the second image $I_2(x,y)$ over a time interval $t \in [0,1]$. This flow can be represented by an instantaneous velocity field at each point in time, $(u(x,y,t),v(x,y,t))$, where $t \in [0,1]$, and a mapping $S(x,y,t)$ that specifies the flowed location of each point (x,y) at time t. At $t=0$ we have the image I_1 and at $t=1$ we have the image I_2.

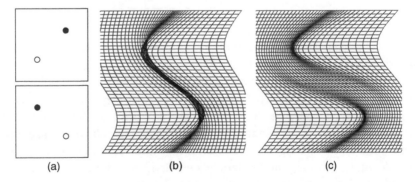

(a)   (b)   (c)

Figure 5.4. (a) Two feature correspondences in a pair of images. The black dot moves to the left while the white dot moves to the right. (b) A thin-plate spline interpolant results in a non-diffeomorphic deformation field — that is, the grid lines self-intersect. (c) Forcing the mapping to be a diffeomorphism avoids this self-intersection.

[5] That is, a one-to-one, differentiable mapping whose inverse is also differentiable.

The velocity field and the mapping are thus related by the differential equation

$$\frac{\partial S(x,y,t)}{\partial t} = \left[\begin{array}{c} u(x,y,t) \\ v(x,y,t) \end{array} \right], \ t \in [0,1] \tag{5.13}$$

with the initial condition that $S(x,y,0) = (x,y)$. The problem is to minimize a function characterizing the smoothness of the velocity field, subject to the constraint that each feature location (x_i,y_i) at $t = 0$ ends up at (x_i',y_i') at $t = 1$. Joshi and Miller specifically proposed to solve the problem

$$\min_{(u(x,y,t),v(x,y,t))} \int_{t=0}^{1} \int (-\nabla^2 u + cu)^2 + (-\nabla^2 v + cv)^2 \, dx \, dy \, dt$$

$$s.t. \ x_i' = x_i + \int_{t=0}^{1} u(S(x,y,t),t) \, dt \tag{5.14}$$

$$y_i' = y_i + \int_{t=0}^{1} v(S(x,y,t),t) \, dt$$

Here, ∇^2 is the 2D (spatial) Laplacian and c is a constant. The result is a diffeomorphism that does not suffer from the grid line self-intersection problem in Figure 5.4b, as illustrated in Figure 5.4c. This approach is commonly used to generate dense correspondences in medical imagery, as mentioned in Section 5.10.

5.2.4   As-Rigid-As-Possible Deformation

Schaefer et al. [422] proposed a simple idea to generate a dense correspondence field from a set of feature matches inspired by the concept of as-rigid-as-possible deformation. That is, the deformation field at each point should look as much like a rigid transformation (i.e., translation plus rotation) as possible, subject to the constraint that feature matches are preserved. The interpolating function is thus $f(x,y) = T_{x,y}(x,y)$, where $T_{x,y}$ is a rigid transformation defined at each point (x,y). Each $T_{x,y}$ is estimated as the transformation that minimizes

$$\sum_{i=1}^{n} \frac{\left\| T_{x,y}(x_i,y_i) - (x_i',y_i') \right\|_2^2}{\left\| (x,y) - (x_i,y_i) \right\|_2^{2\alpha}} \tag{5.15}$$

where α is a user-specified parameter (e.g., $\alpha = 1$). From Equation (5.15) we can see that the weight on each feature (x_i,y_i) decreases as (x,y) gets further away from it, and goes to infinity when (x,y) coincides with one of the feature points (which forces the function to exactly interpolate the feature matches). The rigid transformation at each point can actually be computed in closed form and the deformation field can be computed over large image domains interactively. However, as with thin-plate splines, the computed dense correspondence mapping can be non-diffeomorphic if the deformation is large, and it depends explicitly on all the input feature matches.

One problem with scattered-data-interpolation techniques is that it's difficult to control what happens between the features (e.g., to keep straight lines straight). Also, the computed deformation fields are independent of the underlying image intensities, although using this intensity information is clearly critical to estimate a high-quality deformation. Finally, significant user interaction may be required to obtain a set of feature matches that results in a high-quality deformation; matched features that come directly from an automated method like those discussed in the previous chapter will probably not be sufficient. We now turn to optical flow algorithms, which have the natural interpretation of moving pixels from the first image toward the second. Every pixel intensity in the image plays a role in the deformation.

5.3   OPTICAL FLOW

The general problem of estimating the dense correspondence field corresponding to the apparent motion of brightness patterns is called **optical flow**, one of the oldest concepts in computer vision [167]. We are given two images of the same scene at different times, possibly from different perspectives, and the goal is to estimate a motion vector (u, v) at every point (x, y) such that $I_1(x, y)$ and $I_2(x + u, y + v)$ correspond. We first introduce the classical optical flow methods of Horn-Schunck and Lucas-Kanade, and then describe more modern refinements and extensions that produce high-quality optical flow fields. Algorithms for both optical flow and stereo are typically defined over grayscale images, but can be naturally extended to color images by adding terms for each channel. As discussed in Section 5.9, optical flow is commonly used in visual effects for slowing down or speeding up shots, adding new textures onto a moving object, or creating interesting transitions between objects.

5.3.1   The Horn-Schunck Method

Horn and Schunck [203] were among the first to formalize a computational method for determining the optical flow between an image pair. First, we assume that the two images are samples of a function I of both space and time, so that $I_1(x, y) = I(x, y, t)$ and $I_2(x, y) = I(x, y, t + 1)$ for some time t. The key assumption of optical flow is that image intensities of corresponding points are preserved over time; that is,

$$I(x + u, y + v, t + 1) = I(x, y, t) \qquad (5.16)$$

This is known as the **brightness constancy assumption**. Equation (5.16) actually combines several assumptions, including that the surfaces in the scene have the same brightness regardless of viewing direction (the **Lambertian assumption**), that the illumination of the scene doesn't change, and that the image formation process is ideal (e.g., there is no **vignetting** or darkening of the image toward its edges).

If we perform a Taylor expansion of Equation (5.16) around (x, y, t) assuming that u and v are small, we obtain

$$\frac{\partial I}{\partial x} u + \frac{\partial I}{\partial y} v + \frac{\partial I}{\partial t} = 0 \qquad (5.17)$$

where all the quantities are functions evaluated at (x, y, t). Put another way, Equation (5.17) tells us that

$$\nabla I \cdot \begin{bmatrix} u \\ v \end{bmatrix} = -\frac{\partial I}{\partial t} \qquad (5.18)$$

Thus, the component of the flow vector in the direction of the gradient ∇I is given by

$$-\frac{\frac{\partial I}{\partial t}}{\|\nabla I\|_2^2} \nabla I \qquad (5.19)$$

Without any other information, this is the only part of the optical flow field that can be obtained. This makes sense because the problem is inherently underconstrained: we want to estimate two unknowns (u and v) at each pixel, but only have one equation (5.16). Therefore, we must make additional assumptions to resolve the remaining degree of freedom at each pixel.

The most natural assumption is that the optical flow field varies smoothly across the image; that is, neighboring pixels should have similar flow vectors. Horn and Schunck phrased this constraint by requiring that the gradient magnitude of the flow field, namely the quantity

$$\left(\frac{\partial u}{\partial x}\right)^2 + \left(\frac{\partial u}{\partial y}\right)^2 + \left(\frac{\partial v}{\partial x}\right)^2 + \left(\frac{\partial v}{\partial y}\right)^2 \tag{5.20}$$

should be small. Overall, this leads to an energy function to be minimized over the flow fields $u(x,y)$ and $v(x,y)$:

$$E_{\text{HS}}(u,v) = \sum_{x,y} \left(\frac{\partial I}{\partial x}u + \frac{\partial I}{\partial y}v + \frac{\partial I}{\partial t}\right)^2 + \lambda\left(\left(\frac{\partial u}{\partial x}\right)^2 + \left(\frac{\partial u}{\partial y}\right)^2 + \left(\frac{\partial v}{\partial x}\right)^2 + \left(\frac{\partial v}{\partial y}\right)^2\right) \tag{5.21}$$

$$= E_{\text{data}}(u,v) + \lambda E_{\text{smoothness}}(u,v)$$

where λ is a parameter that specifies the influence of the smoothness term, also known as a **regularization** parameter. The larger the value of λ, the smoother the optical flow field. A large weight on the regularizer (which depends on the domain and range of I) is often used to enforce a smooth flow field. As in Section 3.2.1, minimizing a function like Equation (5.21) can be accomplished by solving the Euler-Lagrange equations, which in this case are:

$$\lambda \nabla^2 u = \left(\frac{\partial I}{\partial x}\right)^2 u + \frac{\partial I}{\partial x}\frac{\partial I}{\partial y}v + \frac{\partial I}{\partial x}\frac{\partial I}{\partial t}$$
$$\lambda \nabla^2 v = \frac{\partial I}{\partial x}\frac{\partial I}{\partial y}u + \left(\frac{\partial I}{\partial y}\right)^2 v + \frac{\partial I}{\partial y}\frac{\partial I}{\partial t} \tag{5.22}$$

evaluated simultaneously for all the pixels in the image. Computationally, the solution proceeds in a similar way to the method described in Section 3.2.1. The partial derivatives of the spatiotemporal function I are approximated using finite differences between the two given images. That is, at pixel (x,y),

$$\frac{\partial I}{\partial x} \approx \frac{1}{4}\big(I_1(x+1,y) - I_1(x,y) + I_1(x+1,y+1) - I_1(x,y+1)$$
$$+ I_2(x+1,y) - I_2(x,y) + I_2(x+1,y+1) - I_2(x,y+1)\big)$$
$$\frac{\partial I}{\partial y} \approx \frac{1}{4}\big(I_1(x,y+1) - I_1(x,y) + I_1(x+1,y+1) - I_1(x+1,y)$$
$$+ I_2(x,y+1) - I_2(x,y) + I_2(x+1,y+1) - I_2(x+1,y)\big) \tag{5.23}$$
$$\frac{\partial I}{\partial t} \approx \frac{1}{4}\big(I_2(x,y) - I_1(x,y) + I_2(x+1,y) - I_1(x+1,y)$$
$$+ I_2(x,y+1) - I_1(x,y+1) + I_2(x+1,y+1) - I_1(x+1,y+1)\big)$$

One advantage of the Horn-Schunck approach is that since Equation (5.22) is fundamentally a diffusion equation, it will create good estimates of the dense correspondence field even when the local gradient is nearly zero, smoothly filling in reasonable flow vectors based on nearby locations where the flow is unambiguous. That is, we avoid the **aperture problem** discussed in Section 4.1, in which the correspondence of flat or edge-like patches could not be reliably estimated. On the other hand, the Taylor series approximation in Equation (5.17) is only valid when (u, v) is close to zero, meaning that the method can only be applied when the images I_1 and I_2 are already very similar — that is, with u and v each less than one pixel.

This issue can be addressed using a **hierarchical** or **multiresolution** approach. For example, Bergen et al. [39] recommended using a Laplacian pyramid (see Section 3.1.2) to compute optical flow.[6] First, the flow is computed as shown earlier for the coarsest level of the pyramid (i.e., a low-resolution version of the original pair). The coarsest level should be chosen so that the expected (u, v) is on the order of a pixel at that level. Now we consider the next higher level of the pyramid. We can't simply multiply the estimated (u, v) at each pixel by two and use these as initial guesses for the flow field at the next level, since the Taylor series expansion at this higher level won't be valid for vectors with these magnitudes. Instead, we **warp** the second image plane toward the first using the estimated flow, so that the flow between the first image and the warped second image is again expected to be nearly zero. We continue this process as we go up the pyramid, computing the final optical flow vectors as the sum of several small increments at each level. To summarize,

1. Create the Laplacian pyramids for I_1 and I_2, indexed from 0 to N, where N is the coarsest level of the pyramid. Initialize the working level n to N and let $\tilde{I}_1$ and $\tilde{I}_2$ be the images at the coarsest level of the pyramid, i.e., $\tilde{I}_1 = I_1^N$, $\tilde{I}_2 = I_2^N$.

2. Estimate the optical flow field $(u, v)^{(n)}$ between $\tilde{I}_1$ and $\tilde{I}_2$ at level n.

3. Construct the optical flow field $(u, v)^{\text{warp}}$ as $\sum_{k=n}^{N} 2^{k-n+1}(u, v)^{(k)}$ — that is, the sum of all the incremental motion fields so far, at the scale of level $n - 1$. Since this generates motion vector estimates only for even x and y, use bilinear interpolation to fill in motion vectors for the whole image.

4. Warp the pyramid image for I_2 at level $n - 1$ using $(u, v)^{\text{warp}}$ to create a new image $\tilde{I}_2$. That is, $\tilde{I}_2(x, y) = I_2^{n-1}(x + u^{\text{warp}}, y + v^{\text{warp}})$. Use bilinear interpolation to sample pixels from I_2^{n-1}. Let $\tilde{I}_1 = I_1^{n-1}$.

5. Let $n = n - 1$.

6. If $n \geq 0$, go to Step 2. Otherwise, the final optical flow field is $(u, v) = \sum_{k=0}^{N} 2^k (u, v)^{(k)}$.

Figure 5.5 shows an example of optical flow estimated using a hierarchical implementation of the Horn-Schunck algorithm. Note that the algorithm produces reasonable estimates even in flat regions.

Sun et al. [475] showed that applying a median filter to the incremental flow fields during the warping process, as proposed by Wedel et al. [538], significantly improved the resulting final flow field. It's also possible to apply incremental warping within each level of the pyramid image in addition to between levels.

---

[6] A Gaussian pyramid can also be used.

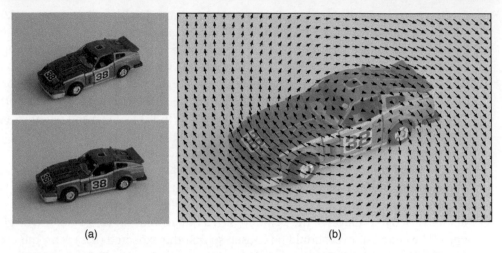

(a)   (b)

Figure 5.5. Optical flow computed using a hierarchical implementation of the Horn-Schunck algorithm. (a) Image 1 (top) and Image 2 (bottom). (b) Optical flow field overlaid on Image 1, indicated by arrows (only a sampling of arrows are illustrated for visibility). We can see that the flow field accurately captures the motion introduced by camera rotation, even in flat regions.

5.3.2   The Lucas-Kanade Method

An alternative to the Horn-Schunck algorithm is the classical Lucas-Kanade algorithm [307], which we discussed in Section 4.1.1.2 in the context of finding good features to track. Reproducing Equations (4.11)–(4.12), we recall that the optical flow vector at a point (x_0, y_0) was defined as the minimizer (u, v) of

$$E_{\text{LK}}(u, v) = \sum_{(x,y)} w(x, y)(I(x + u, y + v, t + 1) - I(x, y, t))^2 \tag{5.24}$$

where $w(x, y)$ is a window function centered at (x_0, y_0) (for example, a box filter, or a Gaussian with a given scale σ). Effectively, we're assuming that all the pixels in the window have the same motion vector. The minimizer corresponds to the solution of the linear system

$$\begin{bmatrix} \sum_{(x,y)} w(x,y) \left(\frac{\partial I}{\partial x}(x,y) \right)^2 & \sum_{(x,y)} w(x,y) \left(\frac{\partial I}{\partial x}(x,y) \frac{\partial I}{\partial y}(x,y) \right) \\ \sum_{(x,y)} w(x,y) \left(\frac{\partial I}{\partial x}(x,y) \frac{\partial I}{\partial y}(x,y) \right) & \sum_{(x,y)} w(x,y) \left(\frac{\partial I}{\partial y}(x,y) \right)^2 \end{bmatrix} \begin{bmatrix} u \\ v \end{bmatrix}$$

$$= - \begin{bmatrix} \sum_{(x,y)} w(x,y) \left(\frac{\partial I}{\partial x}(x,y) \frac{\partial I}{\partial t}(x,y) \right) \\ \sum_{(x,y)} w(x,y) \left(\frac{\partial I}{\partial y}(x,y) \frac{\partial I}{\partial t}(x,y) \right) \end{bmatrix} \tag{5.25}$$

In the last chapter, we used the eigenvalues of the matrix on the left-hand side of Equation (5.25) — the Harris matrix — as the basis for detecting good feature locations. Windows where one of the eigenvalues is small correspond to flat or edge-like regions that suffer from the aperture problem and for which a reliable optical flow vector can't be estimated. Thus, the only way to use Equation (5.25) to obtain dense correspondence across the whole image is to make the support of the window large enough (for example, to make σ large if we're using a Gaussian) to ensure both eigenvalues are far from zero. Using large windows may not do a very good job of estimating flow, since as we observed in Figure 4.11, large square windows are unlikely to remain square in the presence of camera motion.

On the other hand, the Lucas-Kanade algorithm is local, in that the flow vector can be computed at each pixel independently, while the Horn-Schunck algorithm is global, since all the flow vectors depend on each other through the differential equations (5.22). This makes the Lucas-Kanade problem computationally easier to solve. Since the linear system in Equation (5.25) also resulted from the assumption that the flow vectors (u, v) are small, a pyramidal implementation can be used in the same way as in the previous section to handle large motions [55].

5.3.3 Refinements and Extensions

Many modern optical flow algorithms modify Equation (5.21) in some way — for example, by changing the data term that measures deviation from the brightness constancy assumption, the smoothness term that measures deviation from prior expectations of realistic flow fields, or the form of the cost functions used to combine the two terms. In this section, we briefly describe common modifications; many of the best-performing algorithms combine several of these modifications.

5.3.3.1 Changes to the Data Term

The original Horn-Schunck data term encapsulates the assumption that pixel intensities don't change over time, which isn't realistic for many real-world scenes. Uras et al. [506] proposed instead the **gradient constancy assumption** that

$$\nabla I(x+u, y+v, t+1) = \nabla I(x, y, t) \tag{5.26}$$

where ∇ is the spatial gradient. This allows some local variation to illumination changes; consequently, Brox et al. [74] proposed a modified data term reflecting both brightness and gradient constancy:

$$E_{\text{data}}(u, v) = \sum_{x,y} (I_2(x+u, y+v) - I_1(x, y))^2 + \gamma \|\nabla I_2(x+u, y+v) - \nabla I_1(x, y)\|_2^2 \tag{5.27}$$

where γ weights the contribution of the terms (typically γ is around 100). Note that Equation (5.27) directly expresses the deviation from the constancy assumptions, instead of using the Taylor approximation in Equation (5.17) that is only valid for small u and v. Xu et al. [558] claimed that it was better to use either the brightness constancy or gradient constancy assumption at each pixel (but not both), and introduced a binary switch variable for this purpose. An alternate approach is to explicitly model an affine change in brightness at each pixel, as proposed by Negahdaripour [346] (in which case these parameters also need to be estimated and regularized).

Bruhn et al. [76] proposed to replace the Horn-Schunck data term with one inspired by the Lucas-Kanade algorithm, that is,

$$E_{\text{data}}(u,v) = \sum_{(x,y)} w(x,y)(I_2(x+u,y+v) - I_1(x,y))^2 \qquad (5.28)$$

where $w(x,y)$ is a Gaussian with scale σ centered at the point (x_0, y_0) at which the flow is computed. The scale σ is usually in the range of one to three pixels. This approach combines the advantages of Lucas-Kanade's local spatial smoothing, which makes the data term robust to noise, with Horn-Schunck's global regularization, which makes the flow fields smooth and dense. Bruhn et al. also extended this approach to spatiotemporal smoothing when more than two images are available.

Sun et al. [476] collected ground-truth optical flow fields to learn a more accurate model of how real images deviate from the brightness constancy assumption. The learned distribution of $I_2(x+u, y+v) - I_1(x,y)$ can be used to build a probabilistic data term (e.g., approximating the distribution by a mixture of Gaussians). The same approach can be used to learn distributions of filter responses applied to the flow field (such as the gradient proposed by Brox et al. above).

5.3.3.2 Changes to the Smoothness Term

Nagel and Enkelmann [343] were among the first to note the undesirability of applying the smoothness term uniformly across the entire image. In particular, the smoothness term should be down-weighted perpendicular to image edges, since these often correspond to depth discontinuities in the scene, where the underlying optical flow field is not actually smooth. This observation can be encapsulated by modifying the smoothness term as follows:

$$E_{\text{smoothness}}(u,v) = \text{trace}\left(\begin{bmatrix} \frac{\partial u}{\partial x} & \frac{\partial v}{\partial x} \\ \frac{\partial u}{\partial y} & \frac{\partial v}{\partial y} \end{bmatrix}^{\top} D(\nabla I_1(x,y)) \begin{bmatrix} \frac{\partial u}{\partial x} & \frac{\partial v}{\partial x} \\ \frac{\partial u}{\partial y} & \frac{\partial v}{\partial y} \end{bmatrix} \right) \qquad (5.29)$$

where $D: \mathbb{R}^2 \to \mathbb{R}^{2 \times 2}$ is the **anisotropic diffusion tensor** defined by

$$D(g) = \frac{1}{\|g\|_2^2 + 2\beta^2}\left(g^{\perp} g^{\perp\top} + \beta^2 \mathbf{I}_{2 \times 2} \right) \qquad (5.30)$$

where $g^{\perp}$ is g rotated clockwise by 90 degrees and β is a constant that controls the amount of anisotropy. That is, the flow is prevented from being smoothed across edges in I_1 where the gradient magnitude is significantly larger than β.

Figure 5.6 illustrates the shape of the diffusion tensor for an example image, showing how the smoothing neighborhood is circular (uniform) in flat regions and elliptical near edges, which prevents the smoothness term from smoothing across edges.

The smoothness term can also be viewed as a prior term on the optical flow field, since it reflects our assumptions about "good" flows. Similar to Sun et al., Roth and Black [403] collected ground-truth optical flow fields to learn a more accurate model of the distribution of optical flow vectors in real images. As seen earlier, this leads to a probabilistic smoothness term that Roth and Black modeled as a product of t-distributions applied to filtered versions of the data (also known as a Field-of-Experts model).

Figure 5.6. Neighborhoods corresponding to the anisotropic diffusion tensor with $\beta = 0.25$ at different points in an image. The major and minor axes of each ellipse are aligned with the tensor's eigenvectors and weighted by the corresponding eigenvalues. Flat neighborhoods result in nearly circular smoothing regions while edge-like neighborhoods result in ellipses that indicate smoothing along, but not across, image edges.

5.3.3.3 Robust Cost Functions

Horn and Schunck's original formulation penalized deviation from the brightness constancy and smoothness assumptions using quadratic functions in the respective terms. However, it's well known that quadratic functions are extremely sensitive to noise; for example, an incorrect estimate in one of the gradient computations can have a disproportionate effect on the optical flow field, pulling the solution far away from the correct answer.

Black and Anandan [48] were the first to propose the use of **robust estimation** methods for optical flow. The idea is to replace the quadratic function in the data term with the function

$$E_{\text{data}}(u, v) = \sum_{x,y} \rho \left(\frac{\partial I}{\partial x} u + \frac{\partial I}{\partial y} v + \frac{\partial I}{\partial t} \right) \tag{5.31}$$

where $\rho(z)$ is a general penalty function. When the error in z is normally distributed, then the optimal penalty function (i.e., the one that results in the maximum likelihood estimate of the parameters) is $\rho(z) = z^2$, which gives the original Horn-Schunck data term. However, if the values of z are expected to contain outliers (i.e., the distribution of z is heavy tailed), then we want to choose ρ to reduce the weight of these outliers. Table 5.1 defines and illustrates several robust penalty functions with this property commonly used for optical flow, including the Lorentzian, Charbonnier, and Generalized Charbonnier functions.

An appealing property satisfied by the Lorentzian penalty function is that the derivative of $\rho(z)$ is **redescending**; that is, it initially increases in magnitude from 0 as $|z|$ grows, but drops back to 0 for large $|z|$. On the other hand, the Charbonnier penalty function is nearly equal to $|z|$, but unlike $|z|$ is differentiable at 0. That is, it is a differentiable approximation to the L^1 norm.

Table 5.1: **Robust penalty functions typically used for optical flow.** β is an adjustable parameter, and ε is a very small number (e.g., 0.001) so that the Charbonnier penalty function is nearly equal to $|z|$.

Name	Definition	$\rho(z)$
Lorentzian	$\rho(z) = \log\left(1 + \frac{1}{2}\left(\frac{z}{\beta}\right)^2\right)$	
Charbonnier	$\rho(z) = \sqrt{z^2 + \varepsilon^2}$	
Generalized Charbonnier	$\rho(z) = (z^2 + \varepsilon^2)^\beta$	

In the same way, we can robustify the smoothness term in optical flow. In this case, we need to robustly compare a vector at each pixel (i.e., the four optical flow gradients) to that of its neighbors. A typical robust smoothness term has the form

$$E_{\text{smoothness}}(u, v) = \rho\left(\left\|\left[\frac{\partial u}{\partial x}, \frac{\partial u}{\partial y}, \frac{\partial v}{\partial x}, \frac{\partial v}{\partial y}\right]\right\|_2\right) \tag{5.32}$$

where ρ is again one of the robust functions in Figure 5.1 (it need not be the same penalty function used for the data term). In particular, when ρ is the (approximate) L^1 penalty function, the optical flow method is said to use a **total variation** regularization (e.g., [74, 538]). An alternative approach is to apply a different ρ to each of the four gradient terms and sum the results.

5.3.3.4 Occlusions

The techniques discussed so far implicitly assume that every pixel in I_2 corresponds to some pixel in I_1. However, this assumption is violated at **occlusions** — regions visible in one image but not the other. Occlusions are generally caused by objects close to a stationary camera that move in the interval between taking the images, or by changes in perspective due to a moving camera. In either case, background pixels formerly visible in I_1 will be hidden behind objects in I_2, and background pixels

Figure 5.7. Occlusions in optical flow occur when either the camera or objects in the scene move between taking the images. In this sketch, occlusions are introduced due to a difference in camera perspective. Point A in the left image is occluded in the right image, and Point B in the right image is occluded in the left image.

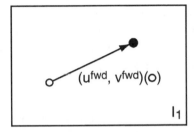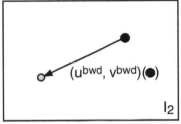

Figure 5.8. Cross-checking for detecting occlusions in optical flow. If the flow vector at the white pixel in the left image points to the black pixel, then the flow vector at the black pixel in the second image should point back at the white pixel. That is, the gray and white pixels in image I_1 should be the same. Otherwise, the correspondence is inconsistent and the pixel is probably occluded in one of the images.

formerly occluded by objects in I_1 will be revealed in I_2. Figure 5.7 illustrates a simple example.

The easiest way to detect these occluded regions[7] is by **cross-checking**, also known as **left-right checking**. That is, we compute the forward flow $(u,v)^{\text{fwd}}$ from I_1 to I_2 and the backward flow $(u,v)^{\text{bwd}}$ from I_2 to I_1. For a non-occluded pixel (x,y) in I_1, we should have that

$$(u,v)^{\text{fwd}}(x,y) = -(u,v)^{\text{bwd}}(I_2(x + u^{\text{fwd}}(x,y), y + v^{\text{fwd}}(x,y))) \tag{5.33}$$

That is, as illustrated in Figure 5.8, the optical flow vector at the location given by the forward flow in the second image should point back to the original pixel in the first image. If the two vectors are not opposites, then the pixel is likely to be occluded in one of the images. The "direction" of the occlusion can be determined by examining the value of the cost function for each of the flows.

The robust cost functions discussed in the previous section can partially mitigate the occlusion problem, but several proposed algorithms (e.g., [556]) explicitly detect

---

[7] Belhumeur [37] notes that "half-occluded" regions is more accurate, since the problematic pixels are visible in one image but not the other.

and deal with occlusions while estimating the flow. We will return to the role of occlusions in dense correspondence in Section 5.5.3.

5.3.4   Layered Flow

One way to get around a global smoothness assumption on the flow field is to split the image into regions called **layers**, and assume that the motion field within each layer is smooth. This allows substantial discontinuities of the flow at layer boundaries. We mentioned **layered motion** in Section 2.9 as a classical approach for video matting; these methods grew out of early research on video processing and optical flow. We can look at Figure 5.7 in a different way as an example of decomposing an observed image (left side) into a pair of planar layers (right side), each of which moves independently. Layered flow methods are also related to the visual effects problem of post-converting a monocular film into stereo.

Black and Anandan [48] proposed a classical layered motion approach using the robust penalty functions of Section 5.3.3.3 to estimate a dominant motion in the scene, classify inlier pixels into a solved layer, and re-apply the process to outlier pixels. This approach may not work well if there are a large number of roughly equal-support motions in the scene, and there is no way to enforce cleanly segmented layers.

Black and Jepson [47] proposed a more explicit layer-based optical flow algorithm. The scene is assumed to be composed of multiple, independently moving planar regions, so that the flow field in each region can be represented by a low-dimensional (e.g., affine or quadratic) parametric transformation. First, a coarse optical flow field is estimated for the entire image. A parametric model is then fit to the flow field in each roughly-constant-intensity image region. Finally, an additional low-magnitude local deformation field is estimated in each region to obtain the final optical flow field. Weiss [541] proposed the concept of "smoothness in layers," removing the assumption that each layer had to be well fit by a parametric model and instead requiring that the (non-parametric) flow field in each layer simply be smooth. The EM algorithm is used to alternate between estimating layer memberships and estimating the flow field in each layer.

Historically, the best-performing optical flow algorithms have not used layered motion models, instead using robust penalty functions and cross-checking to deal with discontinuities. However, Sun et al. [477] recently proposed a competitive layer-based method that builds on the previous two approaches with an advanced non-parametric Bayesian graphical model.

5.3.5   Large-Displacement Optical Flow

While the hierarchical approach to optical flow estimation can handle certain cases involving large values of (u, v), additional techniques are often necessary to deal with such **large displacements**. Brox et al. [73] noted that hierarchical differential techniques (like Horn-Schunck and its modifications) are not able to detect the flow of a structure whose size in the image is smaller than its motion vector magnitude. For example, a person's hand may appear to be a few pixels wide but may move tens of pixels between frames due to fast motion. In such cases, the small structure may be smoothed away and not detectable at the coarser levels of the pyramid where the small (u,v) assumption is valid. Thus, the correct motion never gets propagated to finer levels of the pyramid.

Techniques for large-displacement optical flow often adapt ideas from the invariant descriptor literature discussed in the last chapter to match regions that are far apart. For example, Brox et al. [73] proposed an algorithm that begins with the segmentation of each image into roughly constant-texture patches, each of which is described by a SIFT-like descriptor. The descriptors are matched to obtain several nearest-neighbor correspondences, and optical flow is estimated for each patch pair. Finally, an additional term is added to a robust Horn-Schunck-type cost function that biases the flow at (x,y) to be close to one of the (u_i, v_i) candidates at (x,y) obtained from the descriptor matching.

Liu et al. [289] proposed another option called "SIFT Flow" that replaces the brightness constancy assumption with a SIFT-descriptor constancy assumption. That is, the optical flow data term is based on $\|S_2(x+u, y+v) - S_1(x,y)\|$, where $S_1(x,y)$ and $S_2(x,y)$ are the SIFT descriptor vectors computed at (x,y) in I_1 and I_2, respectively. The descriptors are computed densely at each pixel of the images instead of at sparsely detected feature locations. However, the method is really designed to match between different scenes, and the resulting flow fields typically appear blocky compared to the method of Brox et al.

5.3.6   Human-Assisted Motion Annotation

In the context of visual effects, it's important to be able to interactively evaluate and modify optical flow fields, since the result of an automatic algorithm is unlikely to be immediately acceptable. Liu et al. [288] proposed a human-assisted motion annotation algorithm that semiautomatically creates an optical flow field for a video sequence in two steps. First, the user draws contours around foreground and background objects in one frame, which are automatically tracked across the rest of the frames. The user then employs a graphical user interface to refine the contours in each frame until they conform tightly to the desired object boundaries, and also specifies the relative depth ordering of the objects. Next, the optical flow is automatically estimated across the sequence within each labeled contour. The user interactively refines the optical flow in each layer by introducing point

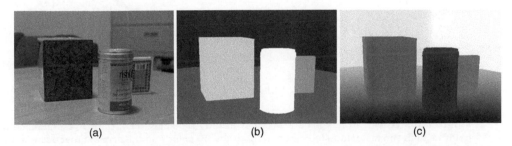

(a)   (b)   (c)

Figure 5.9. (a) One frame of an original video sequence. (b) Layers created semi-automatically based on the human-assisted motion estimation algorithm of Liu et al. [288]. (c) The u components of an optical flow field semiautomatically generated using the layers in (b). The optical flow field is very smooth within the layers.

and line correspondences, resulting in a high-quality dense correspondence field for the entire image sequence. An example result of this approach is illustrated in Figure 5.9.

5.4   EPIPOLAR GEOMETRY

We now consider a special case of the optical flow problem in which the two images I_1 and I_2 are taken at the same time instant by two cameras in different positions.[8] That is, any differences in the positions of corresponding points is entirely due to the underlying camera motion. In this special case, we don't need to search across the entire image to estimate the motion vector (u, v). In fact, there is only one degree of freedom for the possible location of a point in I_2 corresponding to a fixed point in I_1. This important constraint is described by the **epipolar geometry** relating the image pair. In this section, we introduce the epipolar geometry and the constraints it puts on feature matches. In the next section, we return to the optical flow problem in this special case, which is called **stereo correspondence**.

Figure 5.10 illustrates the situation, illustrating the image planes of the two cameras, a scene point P, and its projection (x, y) on the first image plane. Any point on the ray extending from the optical center of the first camera through P will project to the same position (x, y). This line, when viewed from the second camera, generates the **epipolar constraint** mentioned earlier. That is, the correspondence (x', y') must occur somewhere along this line (called an **epipolar line**). Similarly, any point in the second image must have its correspondence on an epipolar line in the first image.

Of course, if we don't know the positions and orientations of the cameras that took the images, it seems like we can't determine the location of the epipolar line for a

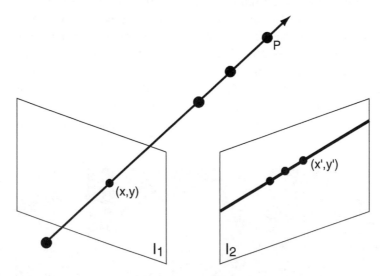

Figure 5.10. When two images are taken at exactly the same time, the correspondence of a point (x, y) in the first image (corresponding to the 3D point P in the scene) must occur along a special line in the second image (the epipolar line corresponding to (x, y)).

---

[8] Or equivalently, the same camera changes position while looking at a static scene. We assume the cameras use the perspective projection model (discussed further in Chapter 6).

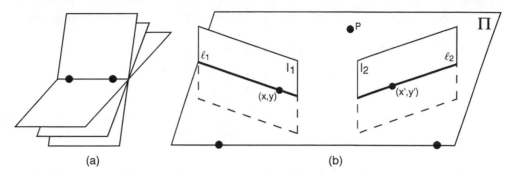

Figure 5.11. (a) A family of planes that tilts around the line connecting the two camera centers. Every point in the scene has to lie on one of these planes. (b) Fixing one plane creates a pair of conjugate epipolar lines in the two images. All of the epipolar lines in one image intersect at the epipole, the projection of the camera center of the other image.

given (x, y). However, the epipolar lines are even more constrained than Figure 5.10 suggests. Figure 5.11a illustrates a family of planes that tilts along a common "axis" — the line connecting the two camera centers. Every point in the scene has to lie on one of these planes. If we fix a plane Π, as illustrated in Figure 5.11b, it will intersect the image planes in two lines, ℓ_1 and ℓ_2. These two lines are exactly the epipolar lines mentioned previously, and now we can see that they come in **conjugate pairs**. That is, if a point on ℓ_1 in I_1 has a correspondence in I_2, it must lie on ℓ_2, and vice versa.[9] Thus, in each image we have a one-dimensional family of epipolar lines. The epipolar lines in each image all intersect at a special point called the **epipole**, which we can see from Figure 5.11b is the projection of the other camera.[10]

In stereo, we reduce the optical flow problem to a one-dimensional correspondence problem along each pair of epipolar lines. The next subsections discuss the **fundamental matrix**, which mathematically encapsulates the epipolar geometry and can be estimated from feature matches in a similar manner to how we estimated a projective transformation in Section 5.1. It's conventional to **rectify** the images before applying a stereo algorithm, which means that we transform each image with a projective transformation so that the epipolar lines coincide with rows of the resulting pair of images. Section 5.4.3 discusses that process.

5.4.1 The Fundamental Matrix

The epipolar line in one image corresponding to a point in the other image can be computed from the **fundamental matrix**, a 3×3 matrix F that concisely expresses the relationship between any two matching points. The key relationship is that any correspondence $\{(x, y) \in I_1, (x', y') \in I_2\}$ must satisfy

$$\begin{bmatrix} x' \\ y' \\ 1 \end{bmatrix}^\top F \begin{bmatrix} x \\ y \\ 1 \end{bmatrix} = 0 \tag{5.34}$$

---

[9] Not all points on ℓ_1 may have a correspondence in I_2 due to occlusions; see Figure 5.16.
[10] In many real situations, the epipole is not visible in the captured image.

The equation of the epipolar line in I_2 for a fixed $(x,y) \in I_1$ is easily obtained from Equation (5.34):

$$\begin{bmatrix} x' \\ y' \\ 1 \end{bmatrix}^\top \left(F \begin{bmatrix} x \\ y \\ 1 \end{bmatrix} \right) = 0 \tag{5.35}$$

That is, the coefficients on x', y', and 1 are given by the three values of $\left(F \begin{bmatrix} x \\ y \\ 1 \end{bmatrix} \right)$.

The equations for epipolar lines in I_1 can be similarly obtained by fixing (x',y') in Equation (5.34).

The fundamental matrix is only defined up to scale, since any scalar multiple of F also satisfies Equation (5.34). Furthermore, the 3×3 fundamental matrix only has rank 2; that is, it has one zero eigenvalue. We can see why this is true from a geometric argument. As mentioned earlier, all the epipolar lines in I_1 intersect at the epipole $e = (x_e, y_e)$. Therefore, for any $(x', y') \in I_2$, e lies on the corresponding epipolar line; that is,

$$\begin{bmatrix} x' \\ y' \\ 1 \end{bmatrix}^\top \left(F \begin{bmatrix} x_e \\ y_e \\ 1 \end{bmatrix} \right) = 0 \tag{5.36}$$

holds for every (x', y'). This means that

$$F \begin{bmatrix} x_e \\ y_e \\ 1 \end{bmatrix} = 0 \tag{5.37}$$

That is, $[x_e, y_e, 1]^\top$ is an eigenvector of F with eigenvalue 0. Similarly, $[x'_e, y'_e, 1]^\top$ is an eigenvector of $F^\top$ with eigenvalue 0. Therefore, the epipoles in both images can easily be obtained from the fundamental matrix by extracting its eigenvectors.

A useful way of representing F is a factorization based on the epipole in the second image:[11]

$$F = \begin{bmatrix} x'_e \\ y'_e \\ 1 \end{bmatrix}_\times M \tag{5.38}$$

where M is a full-rank 3×3 matrix, and we use the notation

$$[e]_\times = \begin{bmatrix} 0 & -e_3 & e_2 \\ e_3 & 0 & -e_1 \\ -e_2 & e_1 & 0 \end{bmatrix} \tag{5.39}$$

In this form, F is clearly rank-2 since the skew-symmetric matrix $[e]_\times$ is rank-2.

The fundamental matrix is not defined for an image pair that shares the same camera center; recall our assumption was that the two cameras are in different positions. In this case, the images are related by a stronger constraint: a projective transformation that directly specifies each pair of corresponding points, as discussed in Section 5.1. The same type of relationship holds when the scene contains only a

---

[11] See Problem 6.10 for a derivation of this factorization.

single plane. In general, the fundamental matrix for an image pair taken by a pair of separated cameras of a real-world scene is defined and unique (up to scale).[12]

5.4.2 Estimating the Fundamental Matrix

Just like a projective transformation, the fundamental matrix can be estimated from a set of feature matches at locations $\{(x_1, y_1), \ldots, (x_n, y_n)\}$ in the first image plane and $\{(x'_1, y'_1), \ldots, (x'_n, y'_n)\}$ in the second image plane. The simplest estimation algorithm is very similar to the DLT algorithm described in Section 5.1. Each correspondence defines a linear equation in the nine unknowns of F via Equation (5.34), namely

$$[x'_i x_i \; x'_i y_i \; x'_i \; y'_i x_i \; y'_i y_i \; y'_i \; x_i \; y_i \; 1] \, [f_{11} \; f_{12} \; f_{13} \; f_{21} \; f_{22} \; f_{23} \; f_{31} \; f_{32} \; f_{33}]^\top = 0 \qquad (5.40)$$

Collecting the linear equations for each point yields an $n \times 9$ linear system $Af = 0$, which can be solved similarly to the method we discussed for a projective transformation. The basic algorithm, also called the normalized **eight-point algorithm**[13], is:

1. The input is two sets of features $\{(x_1, y_1), \ldots, (x_n, y_n)\}$ in the first image plane and $\{(x'_1, y'_1), \ldots, (x'_n, y'_n)\}$ in the second image plane. Normalize each set of feature matches to have zero mean and average distance from the origin $\sqrt{2}$. This can be accomplished by a pair of similarity transformations, represented as 3×3 matrices T and T' applied to the homogeneous coordinates of the points.

2. Construct the $n \times 9$ matrix A, where each feature match generates a row given by Equation (5.40).

3. Compute the singular value decomposition of A, $A = UDV^\top$. D will be a 9×9 diagonal matrix with positive entries that decrease from upper left to lower right. Let f be the last column of V (a 9×1 vector).

4. Reshape f into a 3×3 matrix $\hat{F}$, filling in the elements from left to right in each row.

5. Compute the singular value decomposition of $\hat{F}$, $\hat{F} = UDV^\top$. D will be a 3×3 diagonal matrix with positive entries that decrease from upper left to lower right. Set the lower right (3,3) entry of D equal to zero to create a new diagonal matrix $\hat{D}$ and replace $\hat{F}$ with $U\hat{D}V^\top$.

6. Recover the final fundamental matrix estimate as $F = T'^\top \hat{F} T$.

The new Step 5 is required since the previous steps don't guarantee that the estimated F is rank two (a requirement for a fundamental matrix). Step 5 has the effect of replacing the $\hat{F}$ from Step 4 with the nearest rank-2 matrix.[14]

Figure 5.12 illustrates the result of estimating the fundamental matrix (and thus, the epipolar geometry) for a real image pair using the normalized eight-point algorithm. We can see that the resulting epipolar lines are well estimated — that is, the original feature matches and other corresponding points clearly lie along the estimated conjugate epipolar lines.

---

[12] For details on degenerate scene configurations where the fundamental matrix is not uniquely defined, see Maybank [317].

[13] So named since at least eight points are required to obtain a unique solution.

[14] In the sense of minimizing the Frobenius, or sum-of-squares, norm.

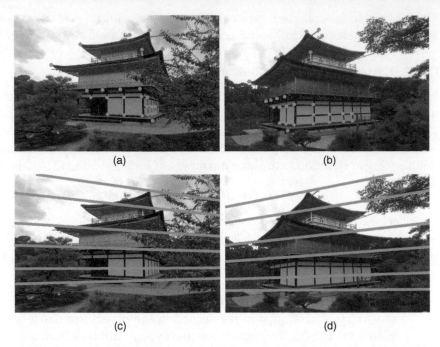

(a)   (b)

(c)   (d)

Figure 5.12. An example of estimating the epipolar geometry using the normalized eight-point algorithm. (a) and (b) Images of the same scene from different perspectives, with feature matches overlaid. (c) and (d) The green lines are epipolar lines computed from the estimated fundamental matrix. We can see that corresponding points lie on conjugate epipolar lines (for example, the corners of the roof and the brown line down the right side of the building). Note that the epipoles (where the epipolar lines in each image intersect) are not visible in this example.

Hartley and Zisserman [188] describe further extensions of the eight-point algorithm and discuss how the estimate of the fundamental matrix can be improved (e.g., to a maximum likelihood estimate under the assumptions that the measurement errors in each feature location are Gaussian). Nonlinear minimization is required to solve the problem and RANSAC can be used to detect and remove outliers in the data to obtain a robust estimate.

So far, we have avoided detailed discussion of the 3D configuration of the cameras, focusing on purely 2D considerations of the relationship between correspondences. When we discuss matchmoving in Chapter 6, these 3D relationships will be made more explicit. In particular, when each camera's location, orientation, and internal configuration are known, the fundamental matrix can be computed directly (see Section 6.4.1). Conversely, estimating the fundamental matrix is often involved in the early process of matchmoving.

5.4.3   Image Rectification

As we can see from Figure 5.12, epipolar lines are typically slanted, which can make estimating correspondences along conjugate epipolar lines complicated due to repeated image resampling operations. It's conventional to **rectify** the images before estimating stereo correspondence — that is, to apply a projective transformation to each image so that in the resulting image pair, conjugate epipolar lines coincide with aligned image rows (or **scanlines**). This means that the images are resampled only

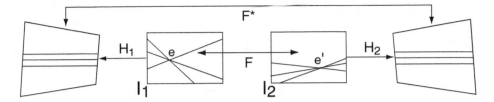

Figure 5.13. Prior to rectification, epipolar lines are slanted, which complicates computing dense correspondence. After rectification by appropriate projective transformations, epipolar lines coincide with matching image rows (scanlines), making the correspondence search easier.

once at the beginning of the process, when the rectifying projective transformations are applied, easing the search for dense correspondence.

Figure 5.13 illustrates the idea of rectification. In a rectified image pair, the epipolar lines are parallel; thus, the epipoles are said to be "at infinity," represented by the homogeneous coordinate $[1, 0, 0]$, which informally corresponds to the "point" $[\infty, 0]$ infinitely far away on the x axis. The fundamental matrix for a rectified image pair is given by

$$F^* = \begin{bmatrix} 0 & 0 & 0 \\ 0 & 0 & 1 \\ 0 & -1 & 0 \end{bmatrix} \qquad (5.41)$$

Plugging F^* into Equation (5.34) gives the simple constraint that for a correspondence in the rectified pair of images, $y' = y$, corresponding to our definition of rectification.

There are many choices for selecting a pair of rectifying projective transformations (H_1, H_2) for a given image pair.[15] For example, horizontally stretching a rectified pair by an arbitrary amount will still produce rectified images. The main consideration is that the rectified images should not be too distorted.

Here, we describe the rectification method proposed by Hartley [187], which uses a set of feature matches $\{(x_1, y_1), \ldots, (x_n, y_n)\} \in I_1$ and $\{(x_1', y_1'), \ldots, (x_n', y_n')\} \in I_2$. The idea is to estimate a projective transformation H_2 for the second image that moves the epipole to the homogeneous coordinate $[1, 0, 0]$ while resembling a rigid transformation as much as possible. Then a matching rectifying transformation is determined for the first image that minimizes the distance between the matches in the rectified images. In more detail, we apply the following algorithm:

1. Estimate the fundamental matrix F from the feature matches using the algorithm in the previous section.
2. Factor F in the form $F = [e']_\times M$, where $e' = [x_e', y_e', 1]^\top$ is the homogeneous coordinate of the epipole in the second image.
3. Choose a location (x_0', y_0') in the second image — for example, the center of the image — and determine a 3×3 homogeneous translation matrix T that moves (x_0', y_0') to the origin.
4. Determine a 3×3 homogeneous rotation matrix R that moves the epipole onto the x-axis; let its new location be $(x^*, 0)$.

---

[15] In fact, there are seven degrees of freedom in the sixteen parameters of H_1 and H_2.

5. Compute H_2 as

$$H_2 = \begin{bmatrix} 1 & 0 & 0 \\ 0 & 1 & 0 \\ -1/x^* & 0 & 1 \end{bmatrix} RT \qquad (5.42)$$

The first matrix in Equation (5.42) moves the epipole to infinity along the x-axis, while the overall transformation resembles a rigid motion in the neighborhood of (x_0', y_0').

6. Apply the projective transformation H_2M (where M was determined in Step 2) to the features in I_1 and the projective transformation H_2 to the features in I_2 to get a transformed set of feature matches $\{(\hat{x}_1, \hat{y}_1), \ldots, (\hat{x}_n, \hat{y}_n)\}$ and $\{(\hat{x}_1', \hat{y}_1'), \ldots, (\hat{x}_n', \hat{y}_n')\}$ respectively.

7. At this point, the two images are rectified, but applying H_2M to I_1 may result in an unacceptably distorted image. The next step is to find a horizontal shear and translation that bring the feature matches as close together as possible. We compute this transformation by minimizing the function

$$\sum_{i=1}^{n} (a\hat{x}_i + b\hat{y}_i + c - \hat{x}_i')^2 \qquad (5.43)$$

to obtain values for a, b, and c. This is a simple linear least-squares problem.

8. Compute H_1 as

$$H_1 = \begin{bmatrix} a & b & c \\ 0 & 1 & 0 \\ 0 & 0 & 1 \end{bmatrix} H_2M \qquad (5.44)$$

Figure 5.14 illustrates the result of applying Hartley's rectification algorithm to the real images from Figure 5.12. We can see that the new epipolar lines are horizontal and aligned, and that the inevitable warping of the two images is not too severe.

An alternate approach that does not require an initial estimate and factorization of the fundamental matrix was proposed by Isgrò and Trucco [213]. Seitz and Dyer [434] also proposed a rectification method particularly well suited to the view morphing application discussed in Section 5.8.

       (a)   (b)

Figure 5.14. Rectifying the two images from Figure 5.12 results in horizontal and aligned epipolar lines.

5.5 STEREO CORRESPONDENCE

Suppose that the two images I_1 and I_2 for which we want to compute dense correspondence are taken at the same time instant by two cameras in different positions. Thus, we can estimate the epipolar geometry and rectify the image pair, as described in the previous section. In this case, the dense correspondence problem reduces to the **stereo correspondence** problem, one of the most well-studied problems in computer vision. We can think of stereo correspondence as a special case of optical flow, with a few key differences:

- The dense correspondence field is specified by one number at each pixel, the **disparity**. The disparity is simply defined as $x - x'$ for a correspondence $\{(x, y), (x', y')\}$.[16] Note that $y' = y$ since the images are already rectified. An image $d(x, y)$ formed from estimates of the disparity d at each point $(x, y) \in I_1$ is called a **disparity map** for I_1.

- Unlike optical flow, where (u, v) takes on continuous values, the disparity values in stereo are conventionally **quantized**, most frequently into units of pixels. The physical configuration of the cameras also introduces a maximum range of possible disparity values. The set of possible disparity values being discrete and finite allows us to use powerful, efficient optimization methods based on graph cuts and belief propagation.

- **Occlusions** in the scene are often explicitly modeled in stereo algorithms as opposed to implicitly modeled as in optical flow.

- In addition to an analogue of the smoothness assumption from optical flow, stereo algorithms sometimes (but not always) introduce a **monotonicity** assumption stating that corresponding points appear in the same order along matching scanlines. This simplifies the problem even further at the risk of poorly modeling certain real-world scenes containing thin objects (see Section 5.5.1).

- Stereo algorithms sometimes (but not always) assume that additional **calibration** information is known about the cameras that acquired the images. This camera calibration results in immediate, high-quality estimates of the epipolar geometry and maximum disparity range. However, feature matches can typically be used to estimate the epipolar geometry to set up a stereo problem, as described in the previous section.

- We must always remember that stereo algorithms assume that the images are acquired **simultaneously**, which means there can be no non-rigid motion of the scene or independent motion of objects between the two images.

We now discuss the main approaches to the stereo correspondence problem, which we will see have a very different character than methods for optical flow. In their overview of optical flow algorithms, Baker et al. [27] noted that the current top

---

[16] We conventionally assume I_1 is to the left of I_2 with respect to the scene. Therefore, a point in I_1 should appear to be further to the right than its matching position in I_2 (see Figure 5.11b), and we define the disparity to be the positive number $x - x'$. Note that we're assuming a Cartesian coordinate system for pixels (i.e., the x axis is horizontal and the y axis is vertical).

stereo algorithms significantly outperform the current top optical flow algorithms, when the conditions allow either type of method to be applied. The improvement is generally attributable to the facts that (1) stereo is an easier problem (since we only need to search for correspondences along conjugate epipolar lines instead of anywhere in the images) and (2) the discrete nature of the disparity values enables sharp discontinuities to be distinguished more accurately, and allows powerful discrete global optimization methods to be applied.

We begin by briefly mentioning several early methods for estimating stereo correspondence, which are generally only locally optimal. These methods have been superceded by global optimization algorithms based on algorithms like graph cuts and belief propagation, which consistently rank highly in quantitative benchmarks for stereo [425]. For the rest of the section we assume that I_1 and I_2 have already been rectified.

5.5.1 Early Methods

The earliest stereo algorithms used extremely simple block-matching approaches to determine the disparity at each pixel. That is, we form a small block around each pixel $(x,y) \in I_1$ and find the disparity d that minimizes some cost function of a corresponding block around $(x-d,y) \in I_2$. For example, we might minimize the sum-of-squared differences between the blocks (as in Lucas-Kanade optical flow) or the normalized cross-correlation (see Section 4.2.2). In stereo, the **sum of absolute differences** is frequently used for computational efficiency, defined by

$$C_{\text{SAD}}(x_0,y_0,d) = \sum_{(x,y)\in\mathcal{W}} |I_2(x-d,y) - I_1(x,y)| \tag{5.45}$$

where $\mathcal{W}$ is a window centered at the pixel of interest (x_0,y_0).

In place of the absolute difference between each pair of corresponding pixels in Equation (5.45), Birchfield and Tomasi [46] proposed a measure that is insensitive to effects introduced by image sampling and that has consequently found widespread use in the stereo community.[17] The **Birchfield-Tomasi measure** is given by

$$C_{\text{BT}}(x_0,y_0,d) = \sum_{(x,y)\in\mathcal{W}} \min(\max(0, I_1(x,y) - I_2^{\max}(x-d,y), I_2^{\min}(x-d,y) - I_1(x,y)),$$

$$\max(0, I_2(x-d,y) - I_1^{\max}(x,y), I_1^{\min}(x,y) - I_2(x-d,y))) \tag{5.46}$$

where $I_1^{\min}(x,y)$ and $I_1^{\max}(x,y)$ are the minimum and maximum of the set

$$\left\{ \frac{1}{2}(I_1(x-1,y) + I_1(x,y)), \ I_1(x,y), \ \frac{1}{2}(I_1(x,y) + I_1(x+1,y)) \right\} \tag{5.47}$$

$I_2^{\min}(x,y)$ and $I_2^{\max}(x,y)$ are similarly defined. Effectively, we're linearly interpolating between pixels in the row of I_1 to determine the best match to a pixel in I_2 and vice versa.

---

[17] Birchfield and Tomasi actually proposed to use the measure only between pairs of pixels (i.e., 1×1 "windows"), but other researchers have aggregated the measure into larger blocks.

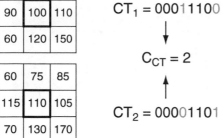

$$CT_1 = 00011100$$

$$\downarrow$$

$$C_{CT} = 2$$

$$\uparrow$$

$$CT_2 = 00001101$$

Figure 5.15. The census transform of example 3×3 blocks. The bit string is computed clockwise starting from the upper left corner, recording a 1 if the pixel is brighter than the center pixel and 0 if it is darker. The distance between blocks is computed as the Hamming distance between the corresponding bit strings (in this case, 2).

Zabih and Woodfill [567] proposed an alternate block-matching scheme based on the **census transform**, which turns a block into a binary bit string that defines whether each pixel in the block is brighter (1) or darker (0) than the pixel at the center. Figure 5.15 illustrates the idea with a 3×3 block. If $CT_i(x, y)$ denotes the census transformation of a $N \times N$ block around (x, y) in image I_i into a length $N^2 - 1$ bit string, then

$$C_{CT}(x_0, y_0, d) = \sum_{(x,y) \in \mathcal{W}} \#(CT_2(x - d, y) \neq CT_1(x, y)) \tag{5.48}$$

That is, we sum the Hamming distances between corresponding bit strings over the window to arrive at the final cost. Hirschmüller and Scharstein [200] investigated a large set of proposed stereo matching costs and concluded that methods based on the census transform performed extremely well and were robust to photometric differences between images.

Block-matching stereo methods in which each pixel independently determines its disparity — known as **winner-take-all** approaches — are clearly suboptimal compared to methods that simultaneously determine all the disparities according to some global criterion. Using overlapping blocks implicitly encourages some degree of coherence between disparities at neighboring pixels (or smoothness, in the terminology of optical flow). However, disparity maps determined in this way typically exhibit artifacts both within and across scanlines and don't produce high-quality dense correspondence. These artifacts include poor performance in flat, constant-intensity image regions where local methods have no way to determine the correct match due to the aperture problem, as well as near object boundaries where blocks overlap regions with significantly different disparities. In addition, multiple matches may occur between different pixels in I_1 and the same pixel in I_2.

A better idea is an algorithm that enforces global optimality of the estimated disparity along each pair of scanlines. One of the earliest approaches, proposed by Ohta and Kanade [352], used **dynamic programming** to find the globally optimal correspondence between a scanline pair, using detected edges in each scanline as a guide to build a piecewise-linear disparity map. Figure 5.16 illustrates the idea. The disparities $d(x, y)$ for an entire row (i.e., fixed y) are selected to minimize

$$\sum_{x=1}^{N} C(x, y, d) \tag{5.49}$$

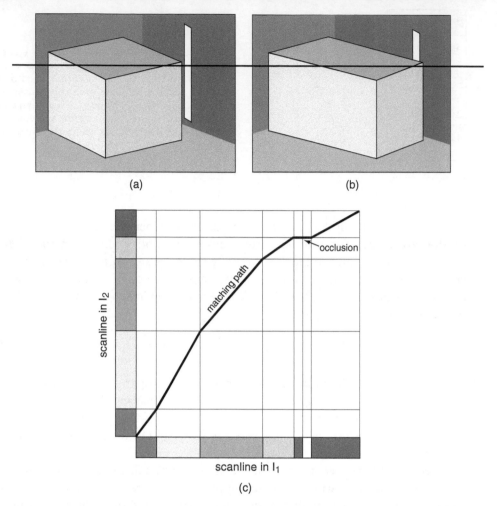

(a)   (b)

(c)

Figure 5.16. Scanline matching using dynamic programming, as described by Ohta and Kanade [352]. (a) and (b) Two rectified images of the same scene from different perspectives, with an overlaid scanline. (c) The matching path for the dynamic programming problem must go through the nodes generated by pairs of edges in each scanline. The path must proceed from the lower left corner to the upper right corner without doubling back on itself; occlusions can be modeled as horizontal or vertical lines.

where C could be any of the cost functions discussed earlier. Appendix A.1 describes how to set up and solve the dynamic programming problem. Limiting the maximum allowable disparity can greatly reduce the complexity of finding the solution.

As illustrated in Figure 5.16, occlusions in either image can be modeled as horizontal or vertical segments in the dynamic programming graph. However, note that this formulation requires **monotonicity** — that is, the property that corresponding points appear in the same order along matching scanlines. This assumption is not always justified for real images, as characterized by the **double nail illusion** illustrated in Figure 5.17.

Extensions to the basic dynamic programming approach involved determining the best cost function C in Equation (5.49), and more importantly, determining how to assign reasonable costs to occluded regions. For example, Belhumeur [37]

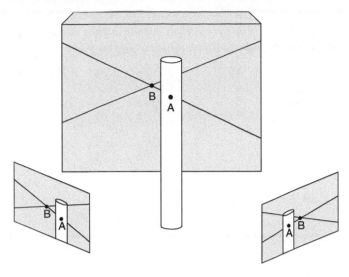

Figure 5.17. The double nail illusion. Point A (on the foreground object) and point B (on the background wall) appear in different order in the left and right images. This phenomenon typically occurs with thin vertical objects close to the cameras.

built a Bayesian model for the disparity estimation problem from first principles, with respect to multiple occluding objects that may have sharp interior depth edges (creases). This led to an explicit prior distribution on disparities that could be incorporated into a dynamic programming problem for each scanline.

Dynamic programming approaches overcome many of the limitations of winner-take-all techniques; they can deal naturally with low-contrast regions and avoid the multiple-match problem. However, a major issue is enforcing the consistency of disparities across neighboring scanlines, since dynamic programming only applies to matching two one-dimensional signals. While many authors (including [352, 37]) proposed ways of enforcing consistent disparities across scanlines, these methods inevitably produce undesirable "streaky" disparity maps that come from inconsistent estimates between adjacent rows. The global methods in the next sections operate directly in the 2D image plane, and neither suffer from these artifacts nor require the monotonicity assumption.

5.5.2 Optimization with Graph Cuts

As mentioned in Section 2.8, the work of Boykov and colleagues (e.g., [59, 61]) at the turn of the century generated an explosion of interest in graph-cut-based techniques for computer vision, including stereo correspondence. Several researchers (e.g., Ishikawa and Geiger [214] and Roy and Cox [406]) had previously proposed graph-cut formulations for global optimization applied to the stereo problem. However, their formulations only allowed a certain class of cost function whose smoothness term could not accurately model behavior at object boundaries (or **discontinuities**). Consequently, disparity maps from such algorithms still contained visible artifacts. Also, the monotonicity assumption was still required.

Boykov et al. [61] proposed a very well-known graph-cut-based stereo algorithm. The fundamental mechanism is α-**expansion**, mentioned in Section 3.3 and reviewed

Table 5.2: Discontinuity-preserving smoothness functions typically used for stereo. K and β are user-defined constant parameters.

Name	$E_{smoothness}(L(i), L(j))$
Truncated quadratic	$\beta \cdot \min(K, (L(i) - L(j))^2)$
Truncated absolute	$\beta \cdot \min(K, \|L(i) - L(j)\|$
Potts model	$\begin{cases} K & \text{if } L(i) \neq L(j) \\ 0 & \text{otherwise} \end{cases}$
Intensity-adaptive Potts model	$\begin{cases} 2K & \text{if } \|I_1(i) - I_2(j)\| \leq \beta \text{ and } L(i) \neq L(j) \\ K & \text{if } \|I_1(i) - I_2(j)\| > \beta \text{ and } L(i) \neq L(j) \\ 0 & \text{otherwise} \end{cases}$

in Appendix A.3. As in optical flow, we minimize the sum of a data term and a smoothness term; however, as in Section 3.3, the energy to be minimized is of the form:

$$E(L) = \sum_{i \in \mathcal{V}} E_{\text{data}}(L(i)) + \sum_{(i,j) \in \mathcal{E}} E_{\text{smoothness}}(L(i), L(j)) \tag{5.50}$$

Here, $\mathcal{V}$ is the set of pixels in I_1, $\mathcal{E}$ is the set of all adjacent pixels (for example, 4-neighbors), and L is a **labeling**; that is, an assignment in $\{0, \ldots, d_{\max}\}$ to each pixel i, where $d_{\max}$ is the maximum allowable value of the disparity. The data term can be formed from any of the matching cost functions defined in the previous section; for example, at a vertex i corresponding to the location (x, y), we could choose the Birchfield-Tomasi measure

$$E_{\text{data}}(L(i) = d) = C_{\text{BT}}(x, y, d) \tag{5.51}$$

Here, it makes sense for the window size to be a single pixel, since the smoothness term handles consistency between pixels.

The critical issue is choosing a smoothness term that accurately handles discontinuities. The easiest choice, the quadratic function

$$E_{\text{smoothness}}(L(i), L(j)) = (L(i) - L(j))^2 \tag{5.52}$$

encourages the disparity map to be smooth everywhere but does a poor job at object boundaries. Another option is to use a robust cost function ρ, as we discussed in Section 5.3.3.3. However, in stereo, it's more common to use one of the simpler functions given in Table 5.2.

Each of these functions avoids over-penalizing sharp changes in disparity between neighboring pixels, while generally favoring disparity maps in which regions have similar labels. In particular, the Potts model encourages regions to have constant disparity, a more extreme case of smoothness. The intensity-adaptive Potts model incorporates contextual information about the image intensities; that is, we impose a higher penalty if the intensity levels are similar but the disparity labels are different.

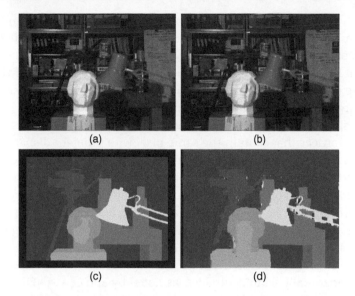

(a)   (b)

(c)   (d)

Figure 5.18. An example stereo result using graph cuts. (a), (b) An original stereo image pair. (This is the "Tsukuba" dataset frequently used for benchmarking stereo algorithms, originally created and ground-truthed by Nakamura et al. [344].) (c) The ground-truth disparity map, in which the disparity labels $\{0, 1, \ldots, 14\}$ are mapped from black to white. Objects closer to the cameras (e.g., the lamp) have higher disparities. (d) The stereo result using graph-cut optimization as described by Boykov et al. [61].

As mentioned in Section 3.3, minimizing a function like Equation (5.50) using α-expansion proceeds by cyclically iterating over the possible disparity labels $d \in \{0, \ldots, d_{\max}\}$. For a given disparity label, we form an auxiliary minimum-cut problem in which each node will either be associated with the label it had in the previous iteration, or the new label d, which corresponds to a two-terminal graph (i.e., d or not-d). That is, at each step, the region of pixels labeled d is allowed to expand by solving a new minimum-cut problem. The algorithm stops after a cycle through all the labels fails to decrease the cost function. Boykov et al. showed that while we are not guaranteed to find a global minimum of Equation (5.50), the cost of the α-expansion result will be within a factor of 2 of the global minimum if the smoothness term is given by the Potts model. Appendix A.3 gives details on the algorithm.[18]

Figure 5.18 illustrates an example stereo result using a data term based on the Birchfield-Tomasi measure and a smoothness term based on the intensity-adaptive Potts model. We can see that the result reflects many of the underlying smooth- and constant-intensity regions in the ground-truth disparity map, and contains no "streaking" artifacts.

Kolmogorov and Zabih [246] noted that despite its good performance in practice, the graph-cut formulation does not enforce **uniqueness**; that is, two pixels in the first image might be matched to the same pixel in the second image. More important, every pixel in the first image must be assigned a disparity, meaning that the method is not able to deal with occlusions. Kolmogorov and Zabih proposed a graph-cut

---

[18] Technically, the truncated quadratic can't be used in the α-expansion algorithm since it's not a metric.

approach based on α-expansion that both enforces uniqueness and properly handles occlusions. However, the set of vertices is quite different than that shown earlier. Instead, each vertex in the graph is a viable correspondence: a match $\{(x,y),(x',y')\}$ such that $x - x' \in \{0,1,\ldots,d_{max}\}$ and $y = y'$. An edge connects two vertices if they have the same disparity, with a small weight if the two pixel pairs have similar intensities and a large weight otherwise. This encourages pairs of adjacent pixels with similar intensities to have similar disparities. Edges with infinite weight are also defined between vertices that contain the same pixel with different disparities, so that cutting such an edge would violate the uniqueness property. Finally, edges are defined connecting each vertex to two terminals, so that cutting such an edge implies that the pixel is occluded in one image or the other. They constructed α-expansion steps on a series of such graphs, so that the final labeling approximately minimizes a sum of data, smoothness, and occlusion penalty terms, while maintaining uniqueness and allowing some pixels to remain unmatched.

While uniqueness seems like a desirable property, it can be problematic in the case of horizontally slanted surfaces, as noted by Sun et al. [480]. That is, a surface may extend across many pixels in one image but only a few pixels in the other image due to foreshortening. They proposed a more general **visibility** constraint that non-occluded pixels must have at least one match in the other image, while occluded pixels must have no matches; this required the estimation of an additional occlusion map (see more in the next section).

5.5.3   Optimization with Belief Propagation

An energy function in the form of Equation (5.50) can also be approximately minimized using **loopy belief propagation**, an algorithm frequently used for inference on Markov Random Fields (we discussed an application to matting in Section 2.5). The idea is to iteratively update each vertex's **belief** that it should have a certain disparity, represented as a $d_{max} + 1$-dimensional vector. In each iteration, the belief is updated based on **messages** sent from its neighbors in the graph (also $d_{max} + 1$-dimensional vectors). After some number of **message passing** iterations, the vertex chooses the maximizer of its belief vector as its final disparity. Concretely, we apply the following basic algorithm:[19]

1. Initialize $m_{ij}^0 = 0$ for all $(i,j) \in \mathcal{E}$
2. Form the $d_{max} + 1$-dimensional message vector from each $i \in \mathcal{V}$ to each of its neighbors $j | (i,j) \in \mathcal{E}$ at iteration t by:

$$m_{ij}^t(d) = \min_{d'} \left(E_{\text{data}}(L(i) = d') + E_{\text{smoothness}}(L(i) = d', L(j) = d) \right.$$

$$\left. + \sum_{k|(i,k)\in\mathcal{E}, k \neq j} m_{ki}^{t-1}(d') \right) \tag{5.53}$$

    where $d \in \{0, 1, \ldots, d_{max}\}$. Effectively, this message conveys vertex i's assessment that vertex j should have disparity d.
3. Repeat Step 2 for T iterations.

---

[19] This can be viewed as a version of the **max-product algorithm**.

4. Form the final belief vector at each $i \in \mathcal{V}$ and $d \in \{0, 1, \ldots, d_{\max}\}$ as:

$$b_i(d) = E_{\text{data}}(L(i) = d) + \sum_{j|(i,j)\in\mathcal{E}} m_{ji}^T(d) \qquad (5.54)$$

5. Assign vertex i to have the disparity label that maximizes $b_i(d)$.

Felzenszwalb and Huttenlocher [138] described several simple modifications to the basic loopy belief propagation algorithm that dramatically speed up its convergence for the graphs and cost functions typically encountered in computer vision applications like stereo. Consequently, we can put any of the data/smoothness term combinations that would work with α-expansion into a belief-propagation framework. Even though there are no guarantees that the result of loopy belief propagation achieves the global minimum of the cost function, in practice its performance is very good. Appendix A.2 gives more details on belief propagation.

Szeliski et al. [485] concluded that the stereo results obtained by minimizing an energy function using graph cuts were generally better than those obtained by minimizing the same function using belief propagation. However, many of the currently-top-performing stereo algorithms use some type of belief propagation, possibly because it more naturally results from a probabilistic interpretation of the data and smoothness terms and is amenable to parallelization.

Sun et al. [482] proposed a early belief-propagation-based algorithm for stereo, using a Birchfield-Tomasi data term and a smoothness term related to the truncated absolute function in Table 5.2. A key innovation was the introduction of a separate **occlusion map**. Ideally, this is a binary map $\mathcal{O}$ defined over the vertices that equals 0 at visible pixels and 1 at occluded pixels; then the cost function becomes

$$E(L) = \sum_{i\in\mathcal{V},i\notin\mathcal{O}} E_{\text{data}}(L(i)) + \sum_{i\in\mathcal{V},i\in\mathcal{O}} E_{\text{occlusion}} + \sum_{(i,j)\in\mathcal{E}} E_{\text{smoothness}}(L(i), L(j)) \qquad (5.55)$$

That is, we only compute disparities for unoccluded pixels, and add a constant penalty $E_{\text{occlusion}}$ for each occluded pixel. In practice, the computation is simplified by allowing the values in the occlusion map to range continuously between 0 and 1, resulting in a soft combination of the data and occlusion terms in the cost function. Sun et al. also proposed a binary **discontinuity map** defined over the edges, which explicitly encodes the presence or absence of a discontinuity. Similar to how Equation (5.55) differs from Equation (5.50), the smoothness term is decomposed into a term for edges along continuous surfaces and a penalty for discontinuities. Sun et al. [480] later refined the approach to a symmetric stereo model, where consistent disparities, occlusions, and discontinuities for the left and right images are computed simultaneously (instead of just computing these quantities for the left image). Xu and Jia [557] took a similar approach, using a data term inspired by robust matting ([532], Section 2.6.1).

5.5.4   Incorporating Segmentation

Top-performing stereo algorithms usually involve some type of reasoning about groups of pixels with similar colors. A common assumption is that the disparity inside a similar-colored region is well modeled by a planar patch; that is, $d(x,y) \approx ax + by + c$, where a, b, and c can be estimated with robust methods [486]. In this case, we can add a **segmentation-based** regularization term to the data term of a stereo cost function, such as

$$\sum_{i \in \mathcal{V}} E_{\text{segment}}(L(i) - (a_i x(i) + b_i y(i) + c_i)) \tag{5.56}$$

where a_i, b_i, and c_i are the estimated plane parameters for the segment containing pixel i, and $E_{\text{segment}}(x)$ could be based on one of the robust cost functions in Tables 5.1 and 5.2. Of course, now we must perform an extra step of segmenting the image into roughly constant-intensity pieces, which is commonly solved using the mean-shift algorithm [102]. If necessary, initial estimates of the disparity map within each segment can be obtained by an algorithm like Lucas-Kanade. High-performing stereo algorithms that use a segmentation approach include Sun et al. [480], Klaus et al. [242], Wang and Zheng [537], and Yang et al. [563]. Bleyer et al. [50] extended the approach to incorporate a term based on minimum description length to penalize the number of segments and to allow higher-order disparity surfaces such as B-splines.

Yang et al. [563] also noted that quadratic interpolation could be used to enhance the quantized disparity estimates from a stereo algorithm, recovering a sub-pixel disparity image. This step would likely be critical for obtaining good results for the applications of dense correspondence we discuss in the next three sections.

5.6   VIDEO MATCHING

We can extend the two-frame dense correspondence problem in several ways. One possibility is to consider simultaneous correspondences between additional synchronized cameras at different locations in the scene; this problem is called **multi-view stereo** and will be discussed in detail in Section 8.3. Another possibility is to extend the dense correspondence problem to video sequences, generalizing optical flow in the case of a single camera and stereo in the case of a rigidly mounted pair of cameras. These cases can generally be handled by adding a temporal regularization term to the cost function that encourages the flow values (u, v) or disparity labels L to be similar to those of the previous frame. For example, for stereo video this term might look like

$$\sum_{i \in \mathcal{V}} E_{\text{temporal}}(L^t(i) - L^{t-1}(i)) \tag{5.57}$$

where the superscript t indicates the time index in the video. Alternately (or in addition), the flow field/disparity map from the previous frame can be used as an initial estimate for the current frame. Sawhney et al. [421] described an algorithm for high-resolution dense correspondence for stereo video in this vein.

A third situation arises when we consider a pair of video cameras that move through a scene at different times and different velocities. This is related to the visual effects problem of **motion control** — that is, the synchronization of multiple camera passes over the same scene. Motion control for an effects-quality shot typically requires a computer-controlled rig that moves through an environment along a pre-programmed path with extremely high precision. In this way, an environment can be set up multiple times so that different elements can be independently filmed (e.g.,

separate passes for live action, dangerous elements, lighting, models and miniatures[20], and so on). The different elements are then matted and composited together
to create the final shot, as discussed in Chapters 2 and 3.

While motion control rigs are highly precise, they are also extremely large and
expensive. In this section, we generalize optical flow techniques to achieve a motion-
control effect in situations where it would be infeasible to use a professional rig.
We call this problem **video matching**. Formally, we consider two video sequences
$I_1(x, y, t)$ and $I_2(x, y, t)$. The problem is to estimate a flow field and time offset at each
frame according to a generalized brightness constancy assumption:

$$I_2(x + u, y + v, t + \delta) = I_1(x, y, t) \tag{5.58}$$

Caspi and Irani [84] addressed a simplified version of the video matching problem
for a rigidly mounted pair of cameras, assuming the two video sequences were related
by a spatial projective transformation and a constant temporal offset. Sand and Teller
[420] addressed the more general video matching problem, illustrated in Figure 5.19;
we summarize the approach here.

Consider a candidate pair of images, one from each video sequence. We estimate
a set of feature matches between the pair, for example, by detecting and matching
Harris corners. Each match is assigned a confidence based on the similarity of the
local neighborhoods around the pair of feature locations. These confidence-weighted
feature matches are used to build a dense correspondence field between the image
pair, using a locally weighted regression to estimate a smooth optical flow field. The
input and the output of the algorithm are the same as the scattered data interpolation
methods described in Section 5.2; like these methods, the resulting dense correspondence field cannot represent discontinuities. By comparing the actual second image
with the warped first image predicted by the motion field, we identify regions of

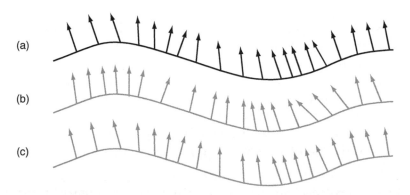

Figure 5.19. The video matching problem. We begin with two video sequences (a) and (b) that
follow roughly the same trajectory in space (curved line). The arrows indicate viewpoints at
equally spaced points in time, showing that the video sequences have different fields of view and
velocities. After video matching in (c), frames of the second sequence are aligned both spatially
and temporally with the first sequence, for subsequent use in applications like compositing.

---

[20] For models and miniatures, the camera motion and software must compensate for the different
scale with respect to live action. For more information on motion control, see Rickitt [393].

high- and low-probability correspondence; low-probability regions are caused by areas that have changed between the two video sequences.

Finally, we can compute a matching score for the candidate frame pair $I_1(t), I_2(t + \delta)$ based on the estimated dense correspondence field (u, v). This score is computed as a weighted average as follows:

$$\lambda \left(\sum_{(x_i, y_i) \in I_1(t)} \sum_{(x_j, y_j) \in I_1(t)} \left\| \begin{bmatrix} x_i \\ y_i \end{bmatrix} - \begin{bmatrix} x_j \\ y_j \end{bmatrix} \right\|_2 - \left\| \begin{bmatrix} x_i + u(x_i, y_i) \\ y_i + v(x_i, y_i) \end{bmatrix} - \begin{bmatrix} x_j + u(x_j, y_j) \\ y_j + v(x_j, y_j) \end{bmatrix} \right\|_2 \right)^2$$

$$+ \left(\sum_{(x, y) \in I_1(t)} \left\| \begin{bmatrix} u(x, y) \\ v(x, y) \end{bmatrix} \right\|_2 \right)^2 \quad (5.59)$$

The first term in Equation (5.59) is based on the **parallax** between a pair of matches — that is, the difference between their distance in the first image and their distance in the second image. The parallax is invariant to image rotation and translation. Here, we compute the average parallax over all correspondences introduced by the optical flow field, as a measure of the introduced image distortion. The second term in Equation (5.59) is the average optical flow vector magnitude, which is small when the overlap between the two images is large. Sand and Teller used $\lambda = 5$ to emphasize the importance of parallax.

Now we can use the pairwise matching cost between pairs of frames in the first and second video sequences to build a set of frame-to-frame correspondences. The user initializes the process by selecting the first pair of corresponding frames $(I_1(t_0), I_2(t_0 + \delta_0))$. Then we iteratively determine the frame-to-frame correspondences with the following procedure:

1. Set $k = 0$.
2. Set the initial guess for the offset δ_{k+1} as a weighted average of the five previous offsets, where the weight decreases as we move back in time.
3. Compute the matching cost between $I_1(t_{k+1})$ and the set of frames $I_2(t_k + \delta_{k+1})$, $I_2(t_k + \delta_{k+1} + 1)$, $I_2(t_k + \delta_{k+1} - 1)$, $I_2(t_k + \delta_{k+1} + 5)$, and $I_2(t_k + \delta_{k+1} - 5)$.
4. Fit a quadratic function to these costs as illustrated in Figure 5.20. Determine the minimizer δ^* of the quadratic function.
5. If $\delta^* = \delta_{k+1}$ — that is, the minimizer stays in the same place — set $k = k + 1$ and go to Step 2. Otherwise, set $\delta_{k+1} = \delta^*$ and go to Step 3.

Once the two videos are spatially and temporally synchronized, we can apply many of the algorithms from Chapters 2 and 3. For example, if one sequence contains live action and the other contains an empty background, we have a strong prior estimate of the alignment required for video matting and inpainting. We can also film one person on the left side of a moving shot, and the same person on the right side of a similar shot, compositing the two videos along a seam to create a "twinning" effect. Alternately, we can replace a stand-in from a live-action plate with a computer-generated character composited over a clean plate.

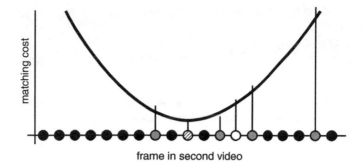

Figure 5.20. Fitting a quadratic function to frame-to-frame matching costs for video matching. The white dot is the current estimate of the matching frame's position in the second video. We evaluate the frame-to-frame matching cost at this estimate, and 1 and 5 frames on either side (gray dots). By fitting a quadratic function to the costs, we obtain a new estimate for the matching frame at the minimizer of the quadratic (striped dot).

5.7   MORPHING

One of the most compelling visual effects created using dense correspondence between an image pair is **morphing**, also known as **image metamorphosis**. Morphing uses an estimated dense correspondence field to create a smooth transformation from one image into another, and was used to great effect in films like *Terminator 2, Indiana Jones and the Last Crusade*, and the video for Michael Jackson's *Black or White*.

Unlike our assumptions for optical flow and stereo, the two images in the morphing problem typically contain different objects (for example, two different faces). Since these images significantly violate the brightness constancy assumption, the dense correspondence is typically estimated from a hand-selected set of feature matches, using methods from Section 5.2. Correspondence fields for morphing applications generally don't take into account occlusions or discontinuities, instead resembling a deformed "rubber sheet." That is, we require each point in the first image to have a correspondence in the second image and vice versa.

We begin with two images, I_1 and I_2, and two dense correspondence fields $(u, v)^{\text{fwd}}$ from I_1 to I_2 and $(u, v)^{\text{bwd}}$ from I_2 to I_1.[21] The morphing problem is to construct a sequence of intermediate images $\{M_t, t \in [0, \Delta t, 2\Delta t, \ldots, 1]$ so that $M_0 = I_1$, $M_1 = I_2$, and the intermediate images create a natural transformation from one image to the other.

A naïve solution to morphing is to simply **cross-dissolve** between the two images, that is, letting

$$M_t(x, y) = (1 - t)I_1(x, y) + tI_2(x, y) \tag{5.60}$$

However, as we can see from Figure 5.21, this approach generates poor results, since corresponding structures in the two images are not aligned. In particular,

---

[21] A consistent $(u, v)^{\text{bwd}}$ can be constructed from a given $(u, v)^{\text{fwd}}$ if we only computed the flow in one direction. However, it is sometimes useful to allow the two fields to be inconsistent (as is the case for the field morphing algorithm discussed shortly).

| t = 0 | t = 0.25 | t = 0.5 | t = 0.75 | t = 1 |

Figure 5.21. Simply cross-dissolving between two original images (far left and right) produces an unrealistic transition between them (intermediate images).

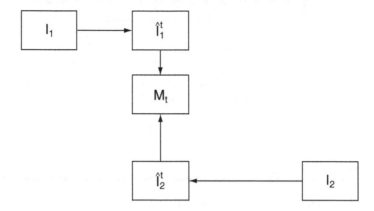

Figure 5.22. The process of image morphing using dense correspondence fields. Intermediate images $\hat{I}_1^t$ and $\hat{I}_2^t$ are created by applying forward and backward optical flow fields to the original images I_1 and I_2, respectively. The morph image M_t is created as a weighted average between the colors of $\hat{I}_1^t$ and $\hat{I}_2^t$. In this sketch, $t \approx \frac{1}{3}$, so the morph image M_t is closer to I_1 both in structure and color.

intermediate images don't look like they contain a single object of the same type as either of the two original images.

The key to an effective morph is to **warp** each image toward the other before performing the cross-dissolve; in this way, the image structures are aligned in each image of the morphing sequence. The process is illustrated in Figure 5.22. Specifically, we apply the following basic algorithm to create each image M_t.

1. Compute intermediate images $\hat{I}_1^t$ and $\hat{I}_2^t$ by warping I_1 and I_2 a fraction of the way along their estimated flow fields:

$$\hat{I}_1^t(x,y) = I_1(x + tu^{\text{fwd}}(x,y), y + tv^{\text{fwd}}(x,y)$$
$$\hat{I}_2^t(x,y) = I_2(x + (1-t)u^{\text{bwd}}(x,y), y + (1-t)v^{\text{bwd}}(x,y)) \tag{5.61}$$

2. Cross-dissolve between the intermediate images to create the morph sequence image $M(t)$:

$$M_t(x,y) = (1-t)\hat{I}_1^t(x,y) + t\hat{I}_2^t(x,y) \tag{5.62}$$

Figure 5.23 illustrates an example with real images. We can see that each intermediate image $\hat{I}_1^t$ is the result of warping the pixels of I_1 the fraction t of the way to their corresponding locations in I_2. Thus, $\hat{I}_1^1$ (the rightmost image in the first row of Figure 5.23) contains the pixel intensities of I_1 at the locations in I_2. A similar argument holds for the intermediate images $\hat{I}_2^t$ in the second row of Figure 5.23. We can

t = 0   t = 0.25   t = 0.5   t = 0.75   t = 1

Figure 5.23. A real example of image morphing using dense correspondence fields. Top row: intermediate images $\hat{I}_1^t$; the original image I_1 corresponds to the leftmost image $\hat{I}_1^0$. Middle row: intermediate images $\hat{I}_2^t$; the original image I_2 corresponds to the rightmost image $\hat{I}_2^1$. Bottom row: final morph sequence created by cross-dissolving between corresponding images in the top and middle rows. The transformation is much more compelling than the simple cross-dissolve in Figure 5.21.

see that the cross-dissolve between corresponding images in the first and second rows of Figure 5.23 yields a realistic morph between both the intensities and image structures.

Morphing algorithms principally differ in their methods for obtaining the dense correspondence fields between the image pair. Early methods used a compatible quadrilateral mesh defined over the images (similar to the optimized-scale-and-stretch grid in Section 3.5.1). Correspondences between points inside mesh quads can be obtained by bilinear interpolation, or more generally using B-splines as discussed earlier in this chapter. The difficulty with this approach comes in attempting to control the mesh to conform well to important image features, resulting in large regions with either too many or too few mesh vertices. An alternate approach is to use one of the scattered data interpolation techniques from Section 5.2; for example, Lee et al. investigated both thin-plate splines [268] and adaptive, nonuniform B-spline interpolating surfaces [269] to define the correspondences for morphing. A unique aspect of the latter approach was the use of "snakes" [230] to automatically snap the user-specified points to image features.

One of the most popular approaches to estimating dense correspondence for morphing is the **field morphing** technique proposed by Beier and Neely [35]. Unlike the methods in Section 5.2, the correspondence is interpolated from a set of several corresponding user-drawn *line segments* on the two images. This allows the animator to have more control over the morph, since the method guarantees that the correspondence between each pair of segments will be maintained in each morphed image — something that a spline interpolation of feature matches cannot guarantee. For example, to morph between two faces, an animator would draw matching lines along the edges of the head, the eyebrows, the lips, and so on, which is more intuitive than trying to establish feature matches in smooth, flat regions.

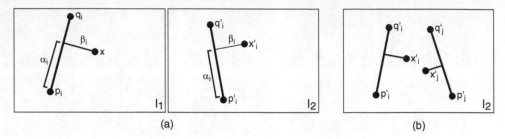

Figure 5.24. (a) Field morphing for a single line pair. α_i is the projection's relative distance from p_i to q_i. β_i is the signed distance to the line segment. (b) When we have more than one line segment pair, each pair generates an estimate for the location $\mathbf{x}'$.

Formally, let's consider a set of oriented line segments $\{(p_i, q_i), i = 1, \ldots, n\}$ in I_1, where p_i and $q_i \in \mathbb{R}^2$ are the starting and ending points of each line segment. The matching line segments in I_2 are given by $\{(p_i', q_i'), i = 1, \ldots, n\}$. Beier and Neely defined the motion vector $(u, v)^{\text{fwd}}$ at a point $\mathbf{x} \in \mathbb{R}^2$ in the first image as a weighted average involving the distance of $\mathbf{x}$ to each line segment in I_1. If $\mathbf{x}$ is very close to one of the segments in I_1, the weight is very high, forcing the correspondence to lie very close to the matching line segment in I_2.

Figure 5.24a illustrates the idea for a point $\mathbf{x}$ in I_1 and a single pair of line segments $\{(p_i, q_i), (p_i', q_i')\}$. We perform a change of coordinates for the point $\mathbf{x}$, so that α_i is the relative distance along the line segment, and β_i is the signed absolute distance perpendicular to the line segment. That is, at p_i, $\alpha_i = 0$ and at q_i, $\alpha_i = 1$. Points whose projection onto the line defined by the segment is on the segment have $0 \leq \alpha_i \leq 1$, while points whose projection is outside the segment have $\alpha_i < 0$ or $\alpha_i > 1$.

The corresponding point $\mathbf{x}_i'$ in I_2 is created by traveling the relative distance α_i along the segment (p_i', q_i') and the signed absolute distance β_i perpendicular to the segment. In this way, a single line segment match generates a dense correspondence field for the entire image. Thus, the flow vector (u_i, v_i) at $\mathbf{x}$ is $\mathbf{x}_i' - \mathbf{x}$.

When we have multiple line segments, as illustrated in Figure 5.24b, we have multiple estimates $\mathbf{x}_i'$ corresponding to each line segment match. The final point $\mathbf{x}'$ is a weighted average of these location estimates, computed as

$$\mathbf{x}' = \sum_{i=1}^{n} w_i \mathbf{x}_i' \bigg/ \sum_{i=1}^{n} w_i \tag{5.63}$$

where Beier and Neely defined the weights as

$$w_i = \left(\frac{\|p_i - q_i\|_2^a}{b + d_i(\mathbf{x})} \right)^c \tag{5.64}$$

Here, $d_i(\mathbf{x})$ is the non-negative distance from the point $\mathbf{x}$ to line segment i in I_1, and a, b, c are user-defined constants. If a is 0, the length of a line segment has no effect on the weight computation; if a is 1 or larger, longer lines have more weight. b is a small number that ensures Equation (5.64) is defined even for points exactly on a line segment. c determines how quickly the influence of a line segment decreases with distance and is usually in the range [1.0, 2.0].

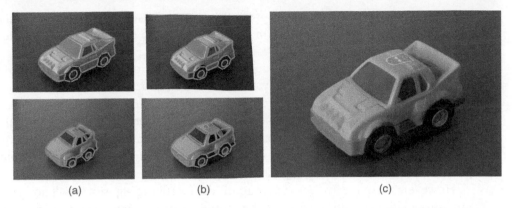

(a)   (b)   (c)

Figure 5.25. (a) User-defined line segment correspondences for the field morphing algorithm. (b) Line segment positions and image warps corresponding to $t = 0.5$. (c) The final morphed image is the average of the images in (b).

To apply field morphing, we first define corresponding line segments for an image pair, and then interpolate corresponding line segment endpoints to determine the intermediate line segment positions in the warped image for each t. We then warp each source image from the original line segments to the intermediate line segments, and cross-dissolve between every pair of warped images. Figure 5.25 illustrates an example of user-defined line segment matches between an image pair and a halfway image created with the induced dense correspondence.

This algorithm is somewhat heuristic, so care must be taken to define "good" pairs of line segments to make a compelling transformation. For example, line segments should not cross, and a segment should span the same apparent region in both images to prevent artifacts that arise from the underlying correspondence field folding back on itself (i.e., being non-diffeomorphic). Typically line segments are added and modified in an iterative process until an acceptable morph is created. Schaefer et al. [422] showed how the as-rigid-as-possible deformation algorithm for interpolating scattered data discussed in Section 5.2.4 can be modified to operate on correspondences between line segments, resulting in more natural deformation fields than Beier and Neely's original algorithm.

Lee et al. [269] noted that the cross-dissolve step in Equation (5.62) can be generalized to allow the two images to warp toward each other at different rates; for example, we could replace t in Equation (5.62) with any function $f(t)$ that monotonically increases from 0 to 1. Even further, we can allow this function to vary spatially, so that different regions of the image move and dissolve at different rates. Wolberg [551] gave a good overview of morphing algorithms and further extensions.

5.8   VIEW SYNTHESIS

Once we have dense correspondence between a pair of images, in certain circumstances we can create new images of the same scene as it would have appeared from different perspectives. This problem is called **view synthesis**, or sometimes **virtual view synthesis** to emphasize that the constructed view was not acquired by any actual camera. View synthesis is a major problem in **image-based rendering**, the general problem of using multiple images of an environment to create realistic new views from different perspectives.

When the original images are close together either in space or time, the view synthesis problem is fundamentally one of interpolation. A common application is changing the frame rate of video, for example from twenty-four frames per second to thirty frames per second. Since adjacent images are very similar, the optical flow vectors are small and easily estimated, and occlusions are unlikely to occur. A morphing/warping algorithm like the one described in the previous section will do a fairly good job of generating the interpolated images.

However, when the images are far apart, the morphing algorithm will not generate interpolated views that look like they could have been generated from an actual camera, even when the correspondence has no errors. Figure 5.26 illustrates an example of the same planar object imaged from two different perspectives. If we apply Equations (5.61)–(5.62) using the correct correspondence fields defined by the underlying projective transformation, we obtain distorted intermediate images that do not match our intuition for a natural interpolation. For example, we expect that straight lines should remain straight in the interpolated images, whereas they clearly bend in Figure 5.26. The fundamental problem is that the morphing algorithm does not guarantee that new intermediate images follow the rules of perspective projection of the underlying scene. We call a view synthesis algorithm that does follow these rules **physically consistent**.

Chen and Williams [88] observed that the morphing algorithm was physically consistent if (1) the image planes corresponding to the source and synthesized views were all parallel with each other, and (2) the source and synthesized camera centers are collinear, corresponding to camera motion parallel to the image planes. This situation is illustrated in Figure 5.27a. They called this special case of the algorithm **view interpolation**. As we can see in Figure 5.27b, the intermediate result from view interpolation is physically valid. That is, these synthesized images look like they were taken with a real camera.

When the images have been taken from cameras that are far apart, we need a method for dealing with **folds and holes** in the view synthesis result, as illustrated in Figure 5.28. Folds are introduced when a pixel in the synthesized view is consistent with multiple correspondences between the two source images. In this case, the pixel can take its intensity from the correspondence with the largest disparity (i.e., the surface closest to the camera). Holes are introduced when a pixel in the synthesized view has no match in one or both of the source images. In this case, we can interpolate the intensities across the hole (e.g., using image inpainting techniques from Section 3.4).

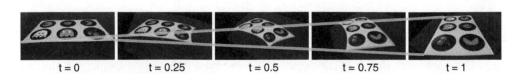

t = 0   t = 0.25   t = 0.5   t = 0.75   t = 1

Figure 5.26. Directly morphing between two very different views of the same object (left and right images) can result in unrealistic intermediate images, even though the supplied correspondence fields contain no errors.

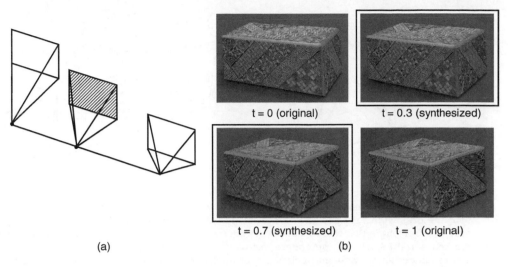

t = 0 (original)   t = 0.3 (synthesized)

t = 0.7 (synthesized)   t = 1 (original)

(a)   (b)

Figure 5.27. (a) The camera configuration for view interpolation. The white image planes represent the original images and the striped image plane represents the synthesized image. The image planes are all parallel to each other and to the baseline. (b) The outlined upper right and lower left images are synthesized from the upper left and lower right images using view interpolation, and are physically consistent with the underlying scene.

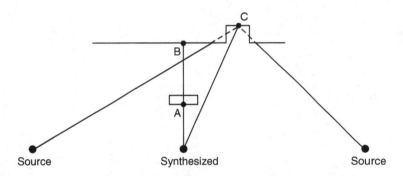

Source   Synthesized   Source

Figure 5.28. Folds and holes can be introduced in the synthesized view based on changes in visibility. Points A and B create a fold, since they both map to the same point in the synthesized view. We select the intensity from A since it has a larger disparity. Point C creates a hole, since it is visible from the synthesized viewpoint but neither source viewpoint.

Seitz and Dyer [434] generalized view interpolation to allow physically consistent view synthesis under the relaxed constraint that the source and synthesized camera centers are collinear, as illustrated in Figure 5.29a. They observed that image planes with arbitrary orientations could be made parallel to each other and to the line connecting the camera centers by applying rectifying projective transformations (called **prewarps**), which we discussed in Section 5.4.3. After rectification, the conditions for view interpolation are met, as illustrated in Figure 5.29b.

We now apply view interpolation to the rectified images and apply a final projective transformation (called a **postwarp**) to the synthesized view to effectively rotate the virtual camera. Seitz and Dyer called this algorithm **view morphing**. Figure 5.30 illustrates an example of view morphing; we can see that the prewarps and postwarps enable view synthesis in situations where the source images are quite different

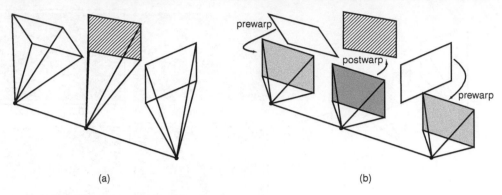

(a)   (b)

Figure 5.29. (a) The camera configuration for view morphing. The white image planes represent the original images and the striped image plane represents the synthesized image. The only requirement is that the virtual camera center lies on the line connecting the source camera centers. (b) Applying appropriate rectifying projective transformations (prewarps) to the source images allows view interpolation to be applied to the intermediate gray image planes. A postwarping projective transformation is used to rotate the virtual camera to the final striped image.

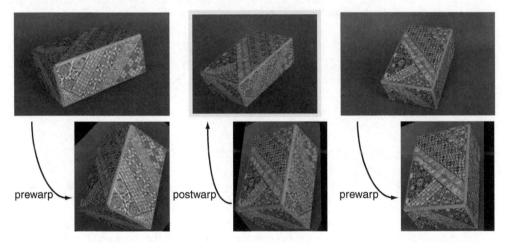

Figure 5.30. An example of view morphing. The original source images at the upper left and upper right are rectified by prewarping projective transformations to the images at the lower left and lower right. These rectified images are interpolated using view interpolation to produce the new synthetic image at the lower center, which is postwarped to produce the synthetic view at the upper center. In this case, the four corners of the top face of the box were used to guide the postwarp.

from each other and from the synthesized view. One way to select the postwarping projective transformation is by linearly interpolating the vertices of a user-specified quadrilateral in each of the source images, since four feature matches define a projective transformation.

Seitz and Dyer observed that the method could also be used to generalize morphing algorithms from the last section; that is, we generate a family of intermediate views $M(t)$ in which $M(0)$ corresponds to the first source image and $M(1)$ to the second source image. When we finely sample t, we obtain an effect of smoothly moving the camera from the position where the first image was taken to the position where the second image was taken. If the images are taken of the same object at the same time, the effect is similar to the "bullet time" effect from *The Matrix*; objects appear frozen in time as the camera moves around them. If the images are actually of different objects from different perspectives, the morphing result seems to simultaneously transform one object into the other while moving the virtual camera. Radke et al. [380] generalized view morphing to create an interpolated virtual video from two source videos, allowing independent temporal manipulation effects and virtual camera motion.

Mahajan et al. [310] noted that the warping and cross-dissolving steps required in morphing and view synthesis tend to blur synthetic views due to repeated pixel resampling and averaging operations (this blurriness is visible in the rectified and synthetic views in Figure 5.30). Instead, inspired by some of the methods we discussed in Chapter 3, they proposed to synthesize sharper virtual images so that each pixel in a synthetic view is taken from exactly one of the source images. Thus, as we morph from one image to the next, the problem is determining a **transition point** for each pixel that specifies which source image should be used for that pixel, and which location in that source image generates the pixel's intensity. The algorithm involves a graph-cut optimization for determining the transition points and Poisson reconstruction to generate the final synthetic view from its gradients.

5.9   INDUSTRY PERSPECTIVES

Marty Ryan, senior software engineer at Rhythm & Hues Studios in El Segundo, CA and Shankar Chatterjee, software developer at Cinesite in Hollywood, CA, discuss the role of optical flow in visual effects.

RJR: What are the most common applications of optical flow in visual effects?

Ryan: The number-one use is for retiming a sequence — speeding it up or slowing it down. The technology is at the point where retiming is fairly routine; it's not just for stunts where they film a slow-speed crash but want it to appear faster. These days, even in non-action films they'll move you forward in time or slow you down. You barely notice it, but the filmmaker often uses it to make a point.

A less glamorous example is that we do a lot of films where we make animals like dogs appear to talk. To make the talking effect, we need to replace the jaw of the dog and estimate the background behind it. Since painting a single clean plate of the background is very labor-intensive, the artist does it for one image, warps it into later frames using the optical flow until it no longer looks good, then paints a new clean plate, warps that one forward, and so on. It's a very low-tech application, but one of those invisible effects that we use a lot.

Chatterjee: We also commonly use optical flow for retiming — one example is *Thirteen Days*, a movie about the Cuban missile crisis. In the very last frames there was a slowdown based on my optical flow algorithm. Optical flow was also used for retiming in the movie *Shanghai Noon*; they wanted to show Jackie Chan's movement in slightly slower than real time, to get the full impact.

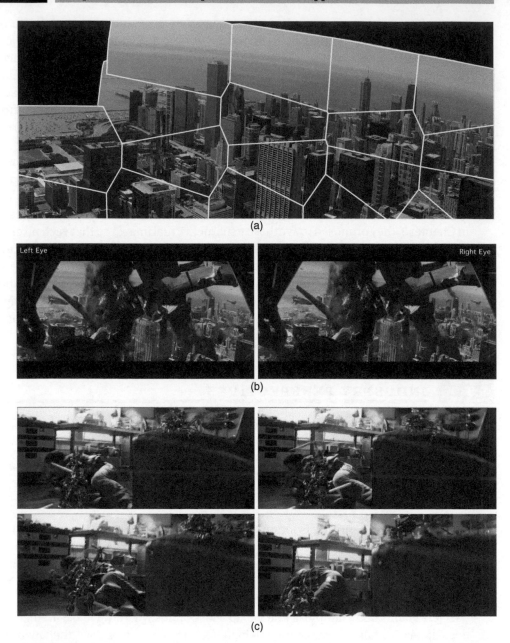

(a)

(b)

(c)

Figure 5.31. (a) In this scene from *Transformers: Dark of the Moon*, parametric transformations are used to register several high-resolution tiles from a rotating camera into a large background plate. (b) Determining accurate stereo correspondence is critical for inserting visual effects into stereo films natively shot in 3D such as *Transformers: Dark of the Moon*. (c) Optical flow is frequently used to retime scenes, such as this fast-moving sequence from *Transformers: Revenge of the Fallen*. *Transformers: Dark of the Moon* ©2011 Paramount Pictures. All Rights Reserved. *Transformers: Revenge of the Fallen* ©2009 DW Studios L.L.C. and Paramount Pictures Corporation. All Rights Reserved.

Before that we used optical flow for a movie called *What Dreams May Come*. We extracted optical flow vectors and used them to "modulate" several scenes. In one scene, the main character slides down a hill into a lake, and the optical flow motion vectors from the clean plate were used to re-render the scene as if he was smearing the surface of a brightly colored oil painting. A related application of optical flow was in a kids' movie called *Clockstoppers*. We estimated the motion vectors from the scene, and used them to create and enhance the motion blur on CGI objects like cars inserted into the scene.

In another movie called *Practical Magic* we used it in a shot where a man's ghost comes up out of the ground. The director wanted mud stuck to him, but when they shot it there was no actual mud. We painted the mud in one keyframe and used the optical flow vectors to track the mud onto him in the rest of the frames. At some point the ghost vanishes into smoke; we used optical flow there as well. We recorded the lighting of a match, reversed the video, and estimated the motion vectors as the full-grown flame shrank to a single spark. We applied those motion vectors to the pixels on the ghost character to create the dissolving effect. We used a similar approach to create the "bamfing" effect of the Nightcrawler character in *X2: X-Men United*, by shooting smoke against a black background, computing the optical flow vectors, and applying them to the character.

RJR: Which optical flow algorithms did you find useful?

Chatterjee: Initially I was working on an optical flow algorithm myself, a modification of Black and Anandan's classic approach. Later I tried Brox et al.'s algorithm and the results were very good, but at the time it was much too slow to handle the 2K-resolution images in digital cinema. That got me interested in looking at Bruhn et al.'s algorithm which was much faster and also gave high-quality results. I made several modifications to the algorithm and implemented it on the Nvidia GPU, where it's near real time. This modified algorithm was recently used to restore the films from the Apollo 11 moon landing long thought lost. You can see a little bit of diffusion effects from optical flow around the edges since they're very high contrast images; the astronaut is in a bright white suit and space is deep black.

Ryan: We were inspired by Black and Anandan's earlier optical flow work, but more recently we've also implemented and had good success with Bruhn et al.'s optical flow algorithms. Adding the gradient consistency assumption really made it successful.

RJR: How does academic research on optical flow differ from the requirements of feature films?

Ryan: There are many reasons why movie frames violate the usual assumptions of optical flow. The biggest difference is the size of the frames. Academic optical flow sequences tend to be a few hundred pixels wide, but we need to track HD plates that are at least 1080p — it's a whole different world. There's often motion blur, which affects heavy movement. Directors love anamorphic lens flare. With a lot of effects-heavy shows, it's very common that action sequences are shot at night, like the big fight sequence that we worked on from *The Incredible Hulk*, to convey a moody, dark feeling. You have very intense bright lights and a lot of murky blacks. There are a lot of tricky things to deal with!

Thad Beier, 3D stereoscopic supervisor at Digital Domain, in Venice, California, was the stereo supervisor on *Transformers: Dark of the Moon*. He discusses the challenges of modern stereo movies.

RJR: What are the different ways stereo movies are created?

Beier: There are two kinds of stereo movies: those that are shot natively in stereo with two cameras like *Avatar*, and movies that are shot "flat" with a single camera and converted to 3D like *Alice in Wonderland. Transformers: Dark of the Moon* is unique in that it's half of each.

The main approach to 3D conversion is based on rotoscoping tools. Regions are segmented into layers, each of which is assigned a depth. They may also add a little bit of shape to each layer — for example, on a face, they might extrude the nose out a little bit. Then the "slivers" of background that were occluded in each eye need to be inpainted and the entire scene is re-rendered. The whole process is extremely labor-intensive. It's a place where computer vision really can pay off. An automatic algorithm doesn't have to solve the whole problem completely; I don't think it should, since there's a lot of artistry involved in creating a good stereo composition.

RJR: What does a stereo rig for a feature film look like?

Beier: It depends on the movie, but typically you have two cameras, such as Sony F35's, mounted at roughly right angles on a rig, viewing the scene through a beam-splitter. Since the cameras and lenses are big and heavy, unfortunately the rig isn't very rigid; if you rotate it slightly, it puts a tremendous amount of torque on the rig and the cameras go out of alignment. There's no time on a busy set to recalibrate the rig, so it has to be fixed in post-production to bring each frame pair back into a perfect stereo alignment. There's a very expensive device on set doing real-time analysis of the videos that will alert you if it sees substantial vertical or rotational disparity, but it doesn't really fix the problem.

The critical parameter for stereo filming is called the **interocular distance**, the equivalent physical separation between the cameras, which is often really small, like three centimeters (it would be more accurate to call this the interaxial distance). This is related to the distance between the viewer's eyes by similar triangles. That is, the ratio between the camera interocular distance and the physical distance to a subject should be the same as the ratio between the viewer's interocular distance and the movie screen. It's important to get this parameter right, because you can't change it in postproduction without messing up the parallax. The only thing you can do after the fact is apply a corner-pin, or projective transformation, to rotate the camera's view. This is important so that when the viewer focuses on far-away points in the background, they don't go walleyed (that is, the gazes of each eye diverge), which is very uncomfortable.

When your eyes see something that's wrong in stereo, it sort of "buzzes," an uncomfortable feeling. I used it to my advantage in one shot in *Transformers: Dark of the Moon*, and I think it's an artistic tool people can use. There's a shot where the camera's dollying in front of the headlights of a car and the lens flare's very different in the two eyes. The result is that it sort of hurts to look right into the headlights, which makes sense!

RJR: What's the typical disparity range for a movie frame?

Beier: In our terminology, objects that appear to lie on the plane of the movie screen have zero disparity. We say that objects "beyond" the screen have positive disparities, and objects "in front of" the screen have negative disparities. For a 2K image, we allow a horizontal disparity range from about negative forty pixels to about positive twenty pixels. The average person can resolve disparity differences of 0.2 pixels or so; that's the minimum stereo difference you can recognize. So our total stereo budget is about $60 \times 5 = 300$ depth levels.

Sometimes you can have an object with ridiculous negative disparity. That's okay if it's going too fast for you to try to focus on it. For example, if it's just particles going past your head, you can sort of feel them going past your head, but you don't try to focus on them and it doesn't become a problem. If it was a big ball going past your head, that would hurt, because you'd try to focus on it and track it as it goes by.

For effects shots with big robots and spaceships, almost everything in the scene has positive disparity. This makes sense; if an object's in front of the screen, first, it hurts to look at, and second, it necessarily looks smaller because it's in the room with us, so it can't be bigger than that. If the object is beyond the screen, it can be as big as you want it to be. In a shot in space, the stars are your interocular distance apart, and appear to be at infinity.

RJR: How does the interocular distance change over the course of a shot?

Beier: There have always been people on the set called focus pullers. While the director of photography or cameraman's looking through the camera, the focus puller is a second person who either has a hand on the camera or a remote control to set the focus. Focus pulling is a big job and good focus pullers are well compensated. These days, there's another person called the convergence puller who has a similar remote control and can adjust the convergence or interocular during the shot.

It turns out that this is very important in scenes where the camera is moving. For example, in one shot in *Transformers: Dark of the Moon* we're on the moon while robots are emerging from its surface. We start out a long way away from everything, and the interocular here is probably half a meter, since these robots are about ten feet tall. Once you we get close to them, the interocular has gone down to maybe one centimeter. If we didn't do that, then these robots would be so in your face that they'd be hugely separated in negative disparity space out in front of the camera. Then, we start to widen the interocular again to give some depth to the scene, otherwise it would look totally flat. If you don't change the interocular throughout a scene like this, then either it always looks flat or it hurts in some places, and you don't get a sense of stereo throughout the shot.

RJR: Do you ever need to touch up the disparity field after it's been acquired by the stereo rig?

Beier: We only do that to fix problems, like if the rigs were badly misaligned. We would never take a live-action element and move it further back. In a few cases, we'll move a CG element to line up with an actor's eyeline so he seems to be looking at it. It would be nice to be able to move stereo elements around after the fact — for example, to bring people in the background forward a bit so they don't all seem to be the same depth — but that's really hard to do since it requires stereo rotoscoping and inpainting. That's one advantage of 3D conversion.

5.10 NOTES AND EXTENSIONS

We generally assumed in this chapter that the dense correspondence field between a pair of images reflects an underlying physical reality — that is, that each pair of corresponding points arises from some single point in the scene. However, dense correspondence doesn't have to be physically meaningful to be useful. For example, in some view synthesis applications, all that really matters is whether the synthesized image is plausible, not whether it's physically consistent with the underlying scene. This is especially true in applications like video coding, where we often just want a good prediction of what an intermediate image will look like.

We focused on dense correspondence in a generic sense, meaning that we assumed no knowledge about the contents of the images. When we know the images come from a certain class, then it would be advisable to use class-specific detection algorithms to obtain better correspondence. For example, if we know the images are close-up views of faces (e.g., for a morphing application), we could apply a customized active appearance model (e.g., [180]) to immediately obtain a meaningful dense correspondence map between them, matching eyes, noses, mouths, and so on.

Outside of visual effects, the medical imaging community is extremely interested in algorithms for **deformable image registration**, which can be viewed as a type of optical flow problem. Generally, the goal is to warp one image to the coordinate system of a second, for example, to compare disease progression in images of of the same patient over time, or to compare similar images of different patients to create an "atlas." The algorithm proposed by Joshi and Miller [228] in Section 5.2.3 is one example of this application. Holden [201] gives a review of deformable image registration techniques for medical image analysis. Medical image registration is often posed using the framework of fluid flow; that is, the image pixels are treated as a viscous fluid that deforms subject to the rules of continuum mechanics. The deformation field is usually obtained by solving a partial differential equation, and the process may be very slow to converge (see, e.g., [94]). A popular method that resembles an iterative, multiscale optical flow algorithm was proposed by Thirion [488]. However, like the methods in Section 5.2, methods for medical image registration are not designed to handle occlusions or discontinuities in the flow fields, and could generally benefit from the modern advances in optical flow and stereo correspondence discussed in the rest of the chapter.

Recent research in both optical flow and stereo correspondence has substantially benefited from high-quality ground-truthed data sets and benchmarks hosted at Middlebury College. Reports by Baker et al. [27] (on optical flow) and Scharstein and Szeliski [425] (on stereo) detail the data generation and testing methodology that is now used as a worldwide benchmark for comparing new flow and stereo algorithms. The high-quality datasets and constantly-updated benchmarks for hundreds of algorithms are available at http://vision.middlebury.edu/flow/ and http://vision.middlebury.edu/stereo/.

Barron et al. [31] proposed an earlier benchmark for optical flow, now superceded by the Middlebury database but responsible for driving much earlier research in the field. Sun et al. [475] investigated the effects of several simple refinements to the classical Horn-Schunck algorithm (such as the choice of robust penalty function, the type of image interpolation, and the use of a median filter in the warping step) to arrive at a set of recommendations and best practices that result in simple, competitive optical flow algorithms. Brown et al. [70] gave a good survey of advances in stereo algorithms, although many of the competitive algorithms discussed in Section 5.5 were proposed after this publication. While we didn't mention it in Section 5.3, the graph-cut stereo methods in Section 5.5.2 can be easily extended to estimate discrete optical flow. In this case, the label at each pixel is multi-valued (i.e., a flow vector (u, v) instead of a disparity d).

Szeliski et al. [485] surveyed methods to efficiently minimize cost functions of the form of Equation (5.50), including the α-expansion and loopy belief propagation methods discussed in Section 5.5, as well as a promising variant of belief propagation called tree-reweighted message passing [525]. They also provided efficient reference implementations for the various algorithms at http://vision.middlebury.edu/MRF/. Felzenszwalb and Zabih [139] recently gave a good survey of dynamic programming and graph-based techniques, with common applications to computer vision.

So far, our discussion of dense correspondence has been motivated almost entirely as a 2D-to-2D matching problem. However, the remainder of the book focuses on 3D considerations, and we will see that disparity is often interpreted as an **inverse depth map**. That is, objects that are closer to the pair of cameras have high disparities and far-away objects have low disparities.[22] Recovering the actual depths from a disparity map requires further physical knowledge about the camera setup, which we discuss in the next chapter. A high-quality optical flow field or disparity map can greatly improve the results of other visual effects algorithms, such as matting, and is at the heart of algorithms for converting monocular films to stereo in post-production. Conversely, an independent estimate of depth (e.g., sparse measurements from a low-resolution range sensor) can definitely improve the results of a dense correspondence algorithm (see Yang et al. [564]).

---

[22] As a simple experiment, hold a finger close to your face and alternate winking your eyes. The relative position of your finger changes substantially compared the the position of a fixed point in the background. If your finger is centered in front of your nose, you will also observe the double nail illusion — that is, a violation of the monotonicity constraint.

While in most of this chapter, we assumed the brightness constancy assumption roughly holds, obtaining dense correspondence between images of the same scene with different exposures is the basis of **high dynamic-range imaging (HDRI)**, used in the visual effects industry to obtain high-quality lighting information about an environment [386]. However, HDRI images are typically acquired from the same camera position, so there is usually little need to compensate for camera motion. Mutual information [543] is a powerful tool for image registration when the brightness constancy assumption is violated but correspondences between images can still be defined; this approach is quite common for aligning medical imagery from different modalities.

As mentioned in Section 5.8, one way to view image-based rendering problems is as interpolating a continuous function from its samples. Formally, each source image provides samples of the **plenoptic function** that defines the scene intensity visible to an observer at every possible location, orientation, time, and light wavelength [2]. To synthesize a new view, we need different samples of the plenoptic function that must be estimated from the given information. For example, instead of the configurations required for view morphing, McMillan and Bishop [322] and Shum and He [446] discussed view synthesis schemes in which the source and synthesized views came from cylindrical panoramas of the scene taken from different locations.

When multiple cameras are available, image-based view synthesis techniques can be applied to generate a wider range of virtual viewpoints (i.e., the virtual camera center can be located anywhere within the convex hull of the source camera centers). For example, Zitnick et al. [581] used an arc of eight cameras for high-quality view synthesis. The lumigraph [175] and light field [274] are approaches that use hundreds or even thousands of closely spaced images of an object for view synthesis. We will return to multicamera methods for 3D acquisition and view synthesis in Section 8.3.

A less flashy but important type of view synthesis is **video stabilization**, the automatic removal of annoying shaky motion from handheld video. For example, Matsushita et al. [315] proposed a video stabilization algorithm that begins with an optical flow field between each pair of adjacent images (defined as an affine transformation plus a local motion field estimated with Lucas-Kanade). A stabilized sequence is created by smoothing the chain of affine transformations to remove high-frequency motions. The resulting images are deblurred, and holes in the synthesized views are filled by inpainting the local motion field. Gleicher and Liu [169] refined this approach with a technique they called re-cinematography, which tries to replace the camera motion with one that follows cinematic conventions, such as a slow, steady pan. In general, video stabilization techniques are improved by reconstructing the camera motion in 3D (e.g., [293, 294]) instead of operating directly on 2D images. The next chapter discusses this matchmoving problem.

Shechtman et al. [440] proposed a generalization of morphing that gradually transforms a source image into a target image, even when the images are so different that a natural correspondence between them is impossible to define (e.g., between a face and an image of clouds). The underlying concept is the bidirectional similarity measure from Section 3.5.3, which encourages each patch in an intermediate image to resemble a patch from either the source or the target, depending on the fraction of the way along the morph.

HOMEWORK PROBLEMS

5.1 Suppose we want to estimate an affine transformation T from a set of feature matches $\{(x_1,y_1),\ldots,(x_n,y_n)\}$ in the first image plane and $\{(x'_1,y'_1),\ldots,(x'_n,y'_n)\}$ in the second image plane. Determine the linear least-squares problem and closed-form solution for the affine parameters that correspond to minimizing

$$\sum_{i=1}^{n}((x'_i,y'_i) - T(x_i,y_i))^2 \tag{5.65}$$

5.2 Determine the 3×3 homogeneous matrix T corresponding to the similarity transform that normalizes the input points $\{(x_1,y_1),\ldots,(x_n,y_n)\}$ for the DLT.

5.3 Show that the h obtained in Step 3 of the DLT corresponds to minimizing $\|Ah\|_2$ subject to the constraint that $\|h\| = 1$. Hint: use Lagrange multipliers.

5.4 Suppose a projective transformation H relates the coordinates (x,y) of I_1 and (x',y') of I_2. Determine the projective transformation $\hat{H}$ that relates the coordinates of the two images after they have been transformed by similarity transformations represented by 3×3 matrices T and T', respectively.

5.5 Show that if only three arbitrary feature matches are supplied to the thin-plate spline interpolation algorithm, solving Equation (5.9) results in an affine transformation (with no nonlinear part).

5.6 A thin-plate spline interpolant $f(x,y)$ is estimated from a set of feature matches
$\{(x_1,y_1),\ldots,(x_n,y_n)\}$ in the first image plane and $\{(x'_1,y'_1),\ldots,(x'_n,y'_n)\}$ in the second image plane using Equation (5.9). We then reverse the roles of the two image planes and estimate a second thin-plate spline interpolant $g(x',y')$. Provide a simple sketch to explain why f and g are not generally inverses of each other. Under what circumstances are f and g inverses of each other?

5.7 Each approach in Section 5.2 produces a forward mapping (i.e., flow field) from the coordinates (x,y) of I_1 to the coordinates (x',y') of I_2. We often want to create a warped image $\hat{I}_1$ that corresponds to rendering the pixel colors of I_1 in the coordinate system of I_2 based on this flow field. Propose a method for coloring the pixels of $\hat{I}_1$, keeping in mind that the forward mapping is not usually invertible in closed form.

5.8 Determine an analogous constraint to the brightness constancy assumption when we want to compute optical flow on color images. How should the Horn-Schunck cost function in Equation (5.21) change when dealing with color images?

5.9 Show that the Taylor expansion of the brightness constancy assumption in Equation (5.16) leads to Equation (5.17).

5.10 Show that Equation (5.17) implies that the component of the flow vector in the direction of the image gradient is given by Equation (5.19).

5.11   Suppose that we assume the optical flow field (u, v) is constant within a window centered at a pixel. Show that summing the Horn-Schunck Euler-Lagrange equations (5.22) over this window is equivalent to solving the Lucas-Kanade equations (5.25) using a box filter corresponding to the window.

5.12   Show that replacing the anisotropic diffusion tensor D in Equation (5.29) with the identity matrix gives the original Horn-Schunck smoothness term.

5.13   Interpret the anisotropic diffusion tensor $D(g)$ in Equation (5.30) when (a) the magnitude of g is 0 and (b) the magnitude of g is much larger than β.

5.14   Show that the Lorentzian robust cost function in Table 5.1 is redescending. Is the generalized Charbonnier cost function redescending for any positive value of β?

5.15   Explain why there are seven degrees of freedom in the nine entries of the fundamental matrix.

5.16   Show why the fundamental matrix constraint in Equation (5.34) leads to the row of the linear system given by Equation (5.40).

5.17   Suppose the fundamental matrix F relates any pair of correspondences (x, y) in I_1 and (x', y') in I_2. Determine the fundamental matrix $\hat{F}$ that relates the correspondences in the two images after they have been transformed by similarity transformations T and T', respectively.

5.18   The basis of the RANSAC method [142] for estimating a projective transformation or fundamental matrix in the presence of outliers is to repeatedly sample sets of points that are minimally sufficient to estimate the parameters, until we are tolerably certain that at least one sample set contains no outliers.

a)   Let the (independent) probability of any point being an outlier be ε, and suppose we want to determine the number of trials N such that, with probability greater than P, at least one random sampling of k points contains no outliers. Show that

$$N = \frac{\log(1 - P)}{\log(1 - (1 - \varepsilon)^k)} \tag{5.66}$$

b)   Compute N for the projective transformation estimation problem where $k = 4$, $P = 0.99$, and $\varepsilon = 0.1$.

5.19   Show why the algorithm in Section 5.4.3 results in a pair of rectified images. That is, show that after applying the given projective transformations, the fundamental matrix is in the form of Equation (5.41).

5.20   Show why any values of a, b, and c in Equation (5.44) preserve the property that (H_1, H_2) is a pair of rectifying projective transformations.

5.21   Determine the disparity map and binary occlusion map with respect to the left-hand image in Figure 5.32 (assuming the background is static).

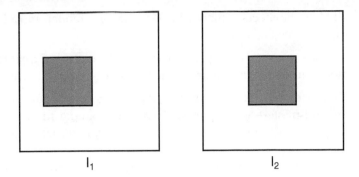

Figure 5.32. The square appears to move five pixels to the right between the left and right images.

5.22 Which generally has a larger disparity: a small object close to the camera, or a large object far from the camera?

5.23 Consider the rows of pixels *A, B,* and *C* in Figure 5.33.
   a) Compute the Birchfield-Tomasi measure between rows *A* and *B* at the highlighted pixels, assuming a 1×1 window.
   b) Compute the Birchfield-Tomasi measure between rows *A* and *C* at the highlighted pixels, assuming a 1×1 window.
   c) Interpret the results. Why do they show that the Birchfield-Tomasi measure is insensitive to differences in sampling of up to half a pixel?

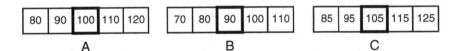

Figure 5.33. Three rows of pixels.

5.24 Construct a simple example in which a winner-take-all strategy for stereo correspondence results in multiple pixels in I_1 matching to the same pixel in I_2.

5.25 Show how four different orderings of the three labeled objects in Figure 5.34 can be obtained by cameras placed below the dotted line.

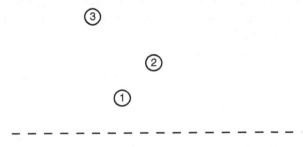

Figure 5.34. An overhead view of three round objects.

5.26   Explain the effects of increasing K in the Potts model, and β in the intensity-adaptive Potts model.

5.27   Provide a counterexample to show that the truncated quadratic function is not a metric (in particular, that it does not satisfy the triangle inequality).

5.28   The grid graph structure common to many computer vision problems (including stereo) is bipartite. That is, we can partition the vertices $\mathcal{V}$ into disjoint sets $\mathcal{V}_1$ and $\mathcal{V}_2$ such that $\mathcal{V} = \mathcal{V}_1 \cup \mathcal{V}_2$ and each edge in $\mathcal{E}$ connects a vertex in $\mathcal{V}_1$ to a vertex in $\mathcal{V}_2$.
   a)   Determine the sets $\mathcal{V}_1$ and $\mathcal{V}_2$ when $\mathcal{E}$ is the usual set of all 4-neighbors.
   b)   Show how the belief propagation algorithm in this case can be sped up by a factor of two, since only half the messages need to be computed in each iteration (see [138]).

5.29   Given a segmented region of roughly constant-intensity pixels, determine the linear least-squares problem to estimate the disparity plane parameters a_i, b_i, c_i in Equation (5.56).

5.30   Compute the parallax (in the sense of Equation (5.59)) for the pair of correspondences $\{(-2, 5), (-9, 7)\}$ and $\{(-1, 4), (-7, 6)\}$.

5.31   Explicitly derive the position of the striped dot in Figure 5.20. That is, show how the quadratic's parameters are obtained using a linear-least-squares problem and determine its minimizer.

5.32   Explicitly determine the affine transformation between image planes induced by a single line segment correspondence $\{(p, q), (p', q')\}$ in field morphing.

5.33   Show that field morphing produces a different dense correspondence field when the order of the input images is switched. That is, create a simple counterexample using two pairs of control lines in which the forward mapping is not the inverse of the backward mapping.

5.34   Describe how to modify the cross-dissolve equation (5.62) so that the top half of an image morphs more quickly to its destination than the bottom half.

5.35   A simple way to show that morphing is not physically consistent is to consider an image of a planar object; thus the dense correspondence is defined by a projective transformation H. Show that the weighted average of correspondences in the first and second images is not a projective transformation of the first image plane, and thus that intermediate images are not physically consistent.

5.36   Determine a two-camera configuration in which view morphing cannot be applied (i.e., when does the rectification process fail?)

6 Matchmoving

Matchmoving, also known as **camera tracking**, is a major aspect of modern visual effects. It's the key underlying process that allows visual effects artists to convincingly insert computer-generated elements and characters into a live-action plate, so that everything appears to "live in" a consistent three-dimensional world. In every modern action movie (and even many non-action movies), the first step after acquiring live footage is to track the camera to enable the addition of spatially accurate visual effects.

The basic problem is to determine, using a given video sequence as input, the three-dimensional location and orientation of the camera at every frame with respect to landmarks in the scene. Depending on the situation, we may have some prior information — such as estimates of the focal length from the camera's lens barrel or labeled landmarks with known 3D coordinates — or the video may come from an entirely unknown camera and environment.

Matchmoving is fundamentally the same as a computer vision problem called **structure from motion**. In fact, several of the main matchmoving software packages for visual effects grew directly out of academic research discussed in this chapter. In turn, structure from motion is closely related to **photogrammetry**, mathematical techniques used by surveyors to estimate the shape of buildings and terrain from multiple images. Many structure from motion techniques "discovered" by computer vision researchers in the 1990s share key steps with photogrammetric techniques developed by cartographers and geodesists[1] in the 1950s or earlier. Finally, structure from motion is closely related to the problem of **simultaneous location and mapping** or **SLAM** from robotics, in which a mobile robot must self-localize by taking measurements of its environment.

In a way, matchmoving ties together the topics discussed so far — matting, compositing, feature tracking, and dense correspondence — as well as the remaining topics in the book, motion capture and three-dimensional data acquisition. That is, the matchmoving process begins with a set of feature points tracked though the video sequence using any of the methods discussed in Chapter 4. We can then apply matting techniques from Chapter 2 to separate foreground and background objects, and compositing techniques from Chapter 3 to insert new elements between the segmented layers. These elements could include computer-generated characters animated with the help of motion capture data, as discussed in Chapter 7.

---

[1] Scientists who study geodesy, or the measurement of different aspects of the earth.

Three-dimensional surveying techniques, which we discuss in Chapter 8, allow us to assign a physically correct scale to the reconstructed scene and camera motion to ensure that all the composited elements are the correct size. Multi-view stereo techniques, also discussed in Chapter 8, can be combined with the methods in this chapter and those in Chapter 5 to create dense 3D reconstructions of objects that can also be used as inserted scene elements.

While the previous chapters in this book emphasized 2D image processing, with little reference to the underlying 3D world from which the images are generated, this chapter, and the rest of the book, focuses on processing 3D information. The fundamental tools we need in this chapter are derived from the pure mathematics of **projective geometry**, since the operation of creating a 2D perspective image of the 3D world is inherently a projective operation. When possible, we try to give a clear geometric or algebraic explanation of the underlying concepts; however, we cannot develop the full theory here. Hartley and Zisserman [188] and Faugeras and Luong [137] recently produced canonical books on the theory of projective geometry as it relates to computer vision, to which we refer the reader for more complete coverage.

The emphasis in this chapter is on recovering the path of the camera in a real-world, physically accurate coordinate system. All of the methods discussed here result in a **sparse** reconstruction of scene points in the environment observed by the cameras; we will show how a camera path can be combined with estimated dense correspondence fields to create dense three-dimensional models of scene objects using multi-view stereo algorithms in Chapter 8.

We begin by revisiting feature matching and tracking, highlighting particular issues related to matchmoving (Section 6.1). Then we discuss the key aspects of perspective image formation, including the way we represent cameras and scene geometry in 3D (Section 6.2). As a first step, we address the problem of calibrating a single, fixed camera in a controlled environment — in particular, the determination of internal parameters using several images of a plane (Section 6.3). We then extend the discussion to a rigidly mounted two-camera rig, as might be used for stereo filming (Section 6.4).

Next, we discuss the key problem in matchmoving, the structure from motion scenario in which we reconstruct the unknown path of a camera as it moves freely through an environment over tens or hundreds of frames (Section 6.5). This process typically includes an initial step where we estimate the geometry of the camera and scene up to an unknown projective transformation, followed by a step in which we upgrade the geometry to a reconstruction in which length ratios and angles are accurate. The results are typically refined by a nonlinear algorithm called **bundle adjustment**. We also discuss several practical issues that arise when processing long video sequences in which the camera may traverse a substantial distance. Finally, we describe modern extensions of matchmoving, including the case of source images sparsely spread over a wide geographical area (Section 6.6).

6.1   FEATURE TRACKING FOR MATCHMOVING

The first step in matchmoving is the detection and tracking of features throughout the image sequence to be processed. Remember that features are regions of an image that can be reliably located in other images of the same environment, and that feature matches ideally result from the image projections of the same 3D scene point.

We can apply any of the detection and matching methods from Chapter 4. If the images are generated by video frames close together in time and space (which is usually the case), we typically select single-scale Harris corners (since a square of pixels is likely to remain a square in an image taken a fraction of a second later) and use a fast matching algorithm like the KLT tracker described in Section 4.1.1.2 and [442]. If the images are taken further apart (which often occurs in hierarchical methods for long sequences, discussed in Section 6.5.1.2), then an invariant detector/descriptor like SIFT will give more reliable matches (but will also be slower). On a closed set or green-screen environment, artificial markers (e.g., gaffer-tape crosses or more advanced markers as discussed in Section 4.5) can be added to the scene to introduce reliably trackable features. Figure 6.1 illustrates tracked features in these various scenarios.

High-quality matchmoving relies on the assumption that matched image features correspond to the same 3D scene point. Therefore, estimating the fundamental matrix (Section 5.4.2) and automatically removing matches inconsistent with the underlying epipolar geometry is very important. Regardless of how the features are obtained, they should generally be visually inspected and edited for correctness, since

Figure 6.1. Tracking features for matchmoving. Top row: When the images are close together, single-scale Harris corners can be easily detected and tracked. Middle row: When the images are further apart, the SIFT detector/descriptor can be used for wider baseline matching. Bottom row: In a green-screen environment, gaffer-tape crosses and artificial markers can be placed on surfaces to aid feature detection and tracking.

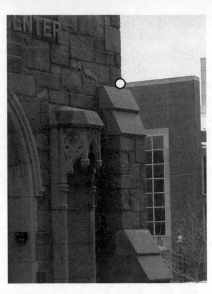

Figure 6.2. A false corner introduced by a coincidence of perspective between two surfaces: one in the foreground and one in the background. From the positions of the chimney and the corner of the background wall in the two images, we can see that the white feature points don't correspond to the same 3D location, even though the pixel neighborhoods are almost identical.

a bad feature track can throw off the rest of the matchmoving process. Furthermore, it's necessary to remove features that may appear mathematically acceptable (i.e., low tracking error and consistent with the epipolar geometry) but nonetheless can cause problems for matchmoving. For example, Figure 6.2 illustrates an example of a mathematically reasonable feature match introduced by a coincidence of perspective. A "corner" has been detected by the visual intersection of two different surfaces: one on the foreground building and one on the background building. As the camera moves, so does the apparent "corner," but it does not correspond to a fixed 3D point. These kinds of **false corners** need to be removed before matchmoving.

In addition, an implicit assumption about the input video in matchmoving is that we're estimating the camera motion with respect to a stationary background. Even though a feature detector may find high-quality matches on foreground objects, these should not be used for matchmoving if they undergo independent motion compared to the larger environment. For examples, features on pedestrians and cars moving down a street should be removed (even if they generate high-quality tracks), leaving only features on the stationary road and buildings. Such situations can also be detected using a robust estimate of the epipolar geometry, but some manual effort may be required to ensure that the right group of matches is used (for example, a large moving foreground object might generate many feature tracks and be mistaken for the "scene"). Finally, features only visible in a few frames (short tracks) are generally not very useful for matchmoving and can be deleted.

While the previous paragraphs addressed the removal of bad or confusing features, we can also *add* new features to the image sequence in several ways. First, the feature detector should always be generating new matches — especially as new parts of the scene come into view at the edges of the image as the camera moves. In natural, highly textured scenes, obtaining a mathematically sufficient number of features to apply the algorithms discussed in this chapter shouldn't be a problem. However, we'll obtain better results if the features are well distributed across the entire image as opposed to being clustered in a small region. One option is to **grow matches** using the estimated epipolar geometry at each frame; that is, we search for feature matches along conjugate epipolar lines using a less stringent criterion for descriptor matching than we might have used when searching over the entire image. In the worst case, it may be necessary to manually add feature tracks in a video sequence in difficult regions to improve the matchmove result. Dobbert's book on the practice of matchmoving [122] discusses several rules of thumb for obtaining suitable feature tracks that produce high-quality results.

6.2   CAMERA PARAMETERS AND IMAGE FORMATION

To proceed, we must establish a mathematical model for how a camera creates an image of a scene. Throughout this and the following chapters, we denote 3D points in the scene by capital letter coordinates (X, Y, Z) and 2D points in an image plane by lowercase coordinates (x, y).

We assume that cameras for visual effects follow the rules of **perspective projection**, resulting in the **pinhole model** illustrated in Figure 6.3a. That is, 3D points in the scene are projected through the **camera center** C onto a 2D **image plane**. The image plane is coincident with a CCD array in a digital camera, or with the physical surface of the film in a film camera.

In a real camera, the camera center lies at the center of the circular shutter or aperture that opens to allow light to fall onto the image plane. The physical distance

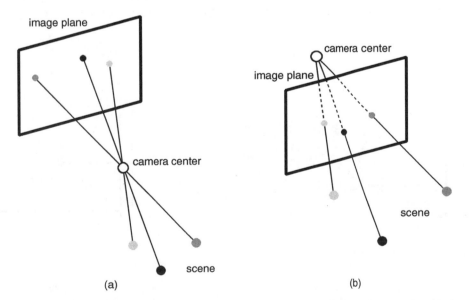

Figure 6.3. The pinhole model of perspective projection. (a) Light rays pass through the camera center and impinge on the image plane (a piece of film or a CCD). (b) For mathematical convenience, we model the image plane as lying between the camera center and the scene.

from the image plane to the camera center is called the **focal length**, denoted by f. From Figure 6.3a we can see that the film/CCD image is "upside down" with respect to the scene because of the way light rays hit the image plane. In computer vision, we usually make the mathematically convenient assumption that the image plane actually lies between the camera center and the scene. As we can see from Figure 6.3b, this results in the same image, but one that is already "right-side up."

6.2.1   Internal Parameters

To create an image, we consider 3D points in the world that are specified in the **camera's coordinate system**, as depicted in Figure 6.4a. The origin of the coordinate system is the camera center C. The image plane is located at a distance f (the focal length) along the positive Z axis and is parallel to the XY plane. The x and y axes of the image plane are parallel to the X and Y axes of the camera coordinate system, and the Z axis of the camera coordinate system (also called the **principal axis**) points outward into the scene. Therefore, any point the camera can "see" has a positive Z-coordinate. Note that our usual Cartesian conventions of x and y mean that the camera coordinate system is left-handed rather than right-handed.

Let's consider a point (X_c, Y_c, Z_c) in the camera coordinate system. Figure 6.4b shows that by reasoning about similar triangles, this point's projection on the physical image plane is given by:

$$\tilde{x} = f\frac{X_c}{Z_c} \qquad \tilde{y} = f\frac{Y_c}{Z_c} \tag{6.1}$$

However, the $\tilde{x}$ and $\tilde{y}$ in Equation (6.1) aren't the same as the pixel coordinates in a digital image, since they're measured in the same physical units as the environment, and thus are likely to be extremely small numbers. For example, a digital camera's CCD is only a few mm wide, so each pixel is physically on the order of 1 μm wide.

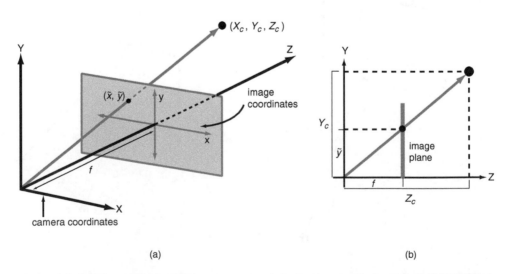

(a)   (b)

Figure 6.4. (a) The camera coordinate system and the image coordinate system. (b) Side view of (a), showing that the projections of scene points onto the image plane can be computed by considering similar triangles.

Also, the origin of the physical image plane is in its center, while we usually index the pixels of an image from the upper left-hand corner. Finally, the physical sensor elements of a CCD may not actually be square, while in digital image processing we assume square pixels.[2] For these reasons, we need to transform the physical image coordinates in Equation (6.1) to determine the pixel coordinates in the digital images we actually obtain, namely:

$$ x = \frac{\tilde{x}}{d_x} + x_0 \qquad y = \frac{\tilde{y}}{d_y} + y_0 \tag{6.2} $$

Here, d_x and d_y are the width and height of a pixel in the physical units used to measure the world (e.g., meters). The quantity d_x/d_y is called the **aspect ratio** of a pixel. The point (x_0, y_0) is the location, in pixel units, corresponding to the ray from the camera center that is perpendicular to the image plane, called the **principal point**. The principal point is usually very near the center of the image, but it may not be exactly centered due to camera imperfections.

The parameters in Equation (6.1) and Equation (6.2) can be neatly encapsulated by the **camera calibration matrix** K:

$$ K = \begin{bmatrix} \alpha_x & 0 & x_0 \\ 0 & \alpha_y & y_0 \\ 0 & 0 & 1 \end{bmatrix} \tag{6.3} $$

where $\alpha_x = f/d_x$ and $\alpha_y = f/d_y$ represent the focal length in units of x and y pixels. The four parameters $(\alpha_x, \alpha_y, x_0, y_0)$ are called the **internal** or **intrinsic parameters** of the camera, since they define the operation of the camera independently of where it is placed in an environment.[3]

We can see that the camera calibration matrix K relates the camera coordinates of a scene point (X_c, Y_c, Z_c) to the homogeneous coordinates of the corresponding pixel (x, y) via the simple equation

$$ \begin{bmatrix} x \\ y \\ 1 \end{bmatrix} \sim K \begin{bmatrix} X_c \\ Y_c \\ Z_c \end{bmatrix} \tag{6.4} $$

The symbol $\sim$ in Equation (6.4) means that the two vectors are equivalent up to a scalar multiple; that is, to obtain actual pixel coordinates on the left side of Equation (6.4), we need to divide the vector on the right side of Equation (6.4) by its third element (corresponding to the perspective projection operation in Equation (6.1)). For example, suppose a camera described by $K = \mathrm{diag}(10, 10, 1)$

---

[2] Most digital cameras today use physically square sensor elements, but this was not always the case.

[3] It is theoretically possible that the sensor elements are not physically rectangles but actually parallelograms, leading to a fifth internal parameter called the **skew** that appears in the (1,2) element of K. We assume that the skew of all cameras considered here is exactly 0, which is realistic for virtually all modern cameras.

observes the scene point $(X_c, Y_c, Z_c) = (100, 200, 400)$. Then applying Equation (6.4) results in the image coordinate $(x, y) = \left(\frac{10 \cdot 100}{400}, \frac{10 \cdot 200}{400} \right) = (2.5, 5)$.

6.2.2   Lens Distortion

Of course, real cameras, especially those used for filmmaking, are much more complicated than pinhole cameras, largely due to complex, multi-component lenses in front of the aperture that gather and focus incoming light. As a result, the image we obtain usually deviates from what Equation (6.4) predicts due to **lens distortion**. This distortion is usually a function of the radial distance from a center point (often near the principal point), as illustrated in Figure 6.5. In the resulting images, a parallel grid either appears to bulge toward the edges (known as barrel distortion) or pinch toward the middle (known as pincushion distortion). In modern, high-quality cameras, barrel distortion is usually much more pronounced than pincushion distortion, and occurs when shooting with wide-angle lenses.

We can't mathematically model lens distortion in the same convenient form as Equation (6.4). Instead, we must interpose a step between Equation (6.1) and Equation (6.2) that expresses the radial distortion in the form

$$\begin{bmatrix} \tilde{x}_{\text{dist}} \\ \tilde{y}_{\text{dist}} \end{bmatrix} = (1 + \kappa_1(\tilde{x}^2 + \tilde{y}^2) + \kappa_2(\tilde{x}^2 + \tilde{y}^2)^2) \begin{bmatrix} \tilde{x} \\ \tilde{y} \end{bmatrix} \tag{6.5}$$

where the κ's are coefficients that control the amount of distortion.[4] Then the affine transformation in Equation (6.2) is applied to the distorted parameters. That is, the observed (distorted) pixel coordinates $(x_{\text{dist}}, y_{\text{dist}})$ are related to the correct

(a)   (b)

Figure 6.5. An example of lens distortion. (a) An ideal image. (b) Barrel distortion observed using a camera with a wide-angle lens. Note how the straight edges of the checkerboard, monitor, desk, and light are bowed outward as a function of distance from the image center.

---

[4] We can add coefficients on higher powers of $(\tilde{x}^2 + \tilde{y}^2)$ for a more accurate model, but one or two terms are often sufficient for a high-quality camera. This formulation also assumes the center of distortion is the principal point, which is usually sufficient.

(undistorted) ones (x, y) by

$$
\begin{bmatrix} x_{\text{dist}} \\ y_{\text{dist}} \end{bmatrix} = \begin{bmatrix} \tilde{x}_{\text{dist}}/d_x \\ \tilde{y}_{\text{dist}}/d_y \end{bmatrix} + \begin{bmatrix} x_0 \\ y_0 \end{bmatrix}
$$

$$
= \begin{bmatrix} x_0 \\ y_0 \end{bmatrix} + (1 + \kappa_1(\tilde{x}^2 + \tilde{y}^2) + \kappa_2(\tilde{x}^2 + \tilde{y}^2)^2) \begin{bmatrix} x - x_0 \\ y - y_0 \end{bmatrix}
$$
(6.6)

This suggests a simple method for estimating the lens distortion coefficients if we know the other internal parameters. We obtain a set of ideal points (x, y) and corresponding observed points $(x_{\text{dist}}, y_{\text{dist}})$; each one generates two equations in the two unknown κ's:

$$
\begin{bmatrix} (x - x_0)(\tilde{x}^2 + \tilde{y}^2) & (x - x_0)(\tilde{x}^2 + \tilde{y}^2)^2 \\ (y - y_0)(\tilde{x}^2 + \tilde{y}^2) & (y - y_0)(\tilde{x}^2 + \tilde{y}^2)^2 \end{bmatrix} \begin{bmatrix} \kappa_1 \\ \kappa_2 \end{bmatrix} = \begin{bmatrix} x_{\text{dist}} - x \\ y_{\text{dist}} - y \end{bmatrix}
$$
(6.7)

When we have a large number of ideal points and corresponding distorted observations, the simultaneous equations given by Equation (6.7) can be solved as a linear least-squares problem. The lens distortion parameters for the image in Figure 6.5 were estimated to be $\kappa_1 = -0.39$, $\kappa_2 = 0.18$.

In Section 6.3.2 we'll discuss methods for estimating the other internal parameters for a camera. In the remainder of the chapter, we assume that the images have already been compensated for any lens distortion, so that the image formation process is well modeled by Equation (6.4).

6.2.3 External Parameters

Expressing points in the camera coordinate system makes it easy to determine their projections. However, for matchmoving we want to determine the locations of such points — as well as the locations and orientations of the cameras — in a **world coordinate system** independent of the cameras. For example, the world coordinate system could be defined with respect to the walls of a movie set or surveyed 3D points in the scene. Therefore, we need to transform points measured in the world coordinate system (X, Y, Z) to the camera coordinate system (X_c, Y_c, Z_c) prior to computing the projection. This transformation is assumed to be a **rigid motion**; that is, a 3D rotation and translation defined by a 3×3 rotation matrix R and 3×1 translation vector t such that

$$
\begin{bmatrix} X_c \\ Y_c \\ Z_c \end{bmatrix} = R \begin{bmatrix} X \\ Y \\ Z \end{bmatrix} + t
$$
(6.8)

The rotation matrix R (a function of 3 parameters, as described in Section 6.5.3.1) and the translation vector t are called the **external** or **extrinsic parameters** of the camera, since they define its position in an environment regardless of its internal functioning.

We now can combine the internal Equation (6.4) with the external Equation (6.8) to obtain a 4×3 **camera matrix** P that contains all the camera parameters:

$$
P = K[R \mid t]
$$
(6.9)

Here, the | notation denotes the horizontal concatenation of matrices that have the same number of rows. The camera matrix P completely determines how a camera obtains its image of a point in the world coordinate system. It operates on the homogeneous coordinate of a 3D point in the world coordinate system by simple multiplication:

$$
\begin{bmatrix} x \\ y \\ 1 \end{bmatrix} \sim K \begin{bmatrix} X_c \\ Y_c \\ Z_c \end{bmatrix}
$$

$$
= K \left(R \begin{bmatrix} X \\ Y \\ Z \end{bmatrix} + t \right) \tag{6.10}
$$

$$
= P \begin{bmatrix} X \\ Y \\ Z \\ 1 \end{bmatrix}
$$

From Equation (6.10), we can see that the camera matrix P is a homogenous quantity, since any multiple of P will produce the same projection relationship. Thus, there are at most eleven degrees of freedom in the twelve entries of P (in fact, using our standard assumptions there are ten degrees of freedom: four for the internal parameters and six for the external parameters). We commonly abbreviate the relationship in Equation (6.10) as

$$
\mathbf{x} \sim P\mathbf{X} \tag{6.11}
$$

where the 3×1 vector $\mathbf{x}$ and the 4×1 vector $\mathbf{X}$ are the homogeneous coordinates of corresponding image and world points, respectively.

Therefore, matchmoving is equivalent to determining the camera matrix P corresponding to each given image. The following sections discuss different circumstances of this general estimation problem.

6.3   SINGLE-CAMERA CALIBRATION

In this section, we discuss the estimation of the parameters of a single camera that is fixed in position. We'll consider two scenarios. In the first, the camera takes a single image of an environment that contains 3D landmarks with known locations in world coordinates. For example, these landmark points may result from an accurate survey of a movie set acquired using a range sensor (see Section 8.1). In this case, we're given both the known 3D world coordinates and corresponding 2D image coordinates, and it's straightforward to estimate the camera matrix using a process called **resectioning**. In Section 6.3.1 we describe resectioning and show how the internal and external parameters of the camera can be recovered from the camera matrix.

The second problem we consider is the estimation of the unknown internal parameters of a camera from several images of a plane — for example, a checkerboard pattern with known dimensions that is shown to the stationary camera in several different orientations. This problem of estimating the internal parameters is often simply called **camera calibration**, and is discussed in Section 6.3.2.[5]

In both cases, the algorithms require that we have some control over the cameras and their environment, which may be a reasonable assumption in a lab setting or on a closed movie set. Section 6.5 addresses algorithms better suited to matchmoving from a video sequence in which no information is available about the imaged environment.

6.3.1   Resectioning

Let's assume we're given a set of 3D points with known world coordinates $\{(X_1, Y_1, Z_1), \ldots, (X_n, Y_n, Z_n)\}$ and their corresponding pixel locations in an image $\{(x_1, y_1), \ldots, (x_n, y_n)\}$. As mentioned earlier, these known 3D locations typically arise from some type of external survey of the environment. The corresponding 2D locations may be hand-picked, or possibly automatically located (e.g., the points could correspond to the centers of unique ARTag markers [140] affixed to the walls of a set). We assume that the 3D points don't all lie on the same plane and that six or more correspondences are available.

The relationship in Equation (6.11) between a 3D point (X_i, Y_i, Z_i), the corresponding 2D pixel (x_i, y_i), and the twelve elements of the camera matrix P is:

$$
\begin{bmatrix} x_i \\ y_i \\ 1 \end{bmatrix} \sim \begin{bmatrix} P_{11} & P_{12} & P_{13} & P_{14} \\ P_{21} & P_{22} & P_{23} & P_{24} \\ P_{31} & P_{32} & P_{33} & P_{34} \end{bmatrix} \begin{bmatrix} X_i \\ Y_i \\ Z_i \\ 1 \end{bmatrix} \tag{6.12}
$$

That is, the vectors on the left-hand side and right-hand side of Equation (6.12) are scalar multiples of each other; thus, their cross-product is zero. This observation leads to two linearly independent equations in the elements of P (see Problem 6.5):

$$
A_i \begin{bmatrix} P_{11} & P_{12} & P_{13} & P_{14} & P_{21} & P_{22} & P_{23} & P_{24} & P_{31} & P_{32} & P_{33} & P_{34} \end{bmatrix}^\top = 0 \tag{6.13}
$$

where

$$
A_i = \begin{bmatrix} 0 & 0 & 0 & 0 & X_i & Y_i & Z_i & 1 & -y_i X_i & -y_i Y_i & -y_i Z_i & -y_i \\ X_i & Y_i & Z_i & 1 & 0 & 0 & 0 & 0 & -x_i X_i & -x_i Y_i & -x_i Z_i & -x_i \end{bmatrix} \tag{6.14}
$$

Collecting these equations for all the correspondences results in a $2n \times 12$ linear system $Ap = 0$. Since the camera matrix is homogeneous, we can minimize $\|Ap\|_2$ subject to the constraint that $\|p\|_2 = 1$ using the Direct Linear Transform described in Section 5.1. Just as described in that section, we normalize the 2D and 3D sets of points prior to solving the estimation problem, and afterward transform the resulting P matrix to relate the original image and world coordinates. We can use the solution as the starting point for minimizing a more geometrically meaningful error (such as the sum of squared reprojection errors in the image plane), but this may not be necessary.

At this point, we have an estimate of the camera matrix P, but often we really want explicit values for the internal parameters K and the external parameters (R, t).

---

[5] However, we slightly abuse this terminology in this chapter, using "calibration" to refer to the process of estimating both internal and external parameters.

These can be easily extracted by considering Equation (6.9). If we denote M as the 3×3 matrix on the left side of P, we can see that $M = KR$; that is, an upper triangular matrix with positive diagonal elements multiplied by a rotation matrix. From linear algebra, we know this factorization is unique and can be easily computed, for example, using the Gram-Schmidt process [173].[6] Once we have factored $M = KR$, we obtain t by multiplying K^{-1} by the last column of P.

6.3.2   Plane-Based Internal Parameter Estimation

A more common approach for obtaining the internal parameters of a stationary camera, which requires no precise measurements of the environment, is to take several pictures of a planar surface in different orientations. For example, we can simply use a **calibration pattern** composed of a checkerboard of black and white squares mounted on a flat board. Alternately, we can display the calibration pattern on a flat-screen monitor, as illustrated in Figure 6.6. The main consideration is that we must be able to associate features (e.g., checkerboard corners) in different images of the plane, so it should be clear where the top left corner of the planar pattern is in any given image.

In practice, the camera is fixed in place and we move the planar surface around in front of it. However, it's mathematically equivalent to view the configuration as a fixed plane in world coordinates that we move the camera around. We define the problem in the latter case. In particular, we assume that the fixed plane lies at $Z = 0$ in world coordinates. Let's rewrite Equation (6.10) in this special case, for a point $(X, Y, 0)$ on the planar surface and its projection (x, y) in the image:

$$\begin{bmatrix} x \\ y \\ 1 \end{bmatrix} \sim K[R \mid t] \begin{bmatrix} X \\ Y \\ 0 \\ 1 \end{bmatrix} \tag{6.15}$$

$$= K[r_1 \ r_2 \ r_3 \ t] \begin{bmatrix} X \\ Y \\ 0 \\ 1 \end{bmatrix} \tag{6.16}$$

$$= K[r_1 \ r_2 \ t] \begin{bmatrix} X \\ Y \\ 1 \end{bmatrix} \tag{6.17}$$

$$\sim H \begin{bmatrix} X \\ Y \\ 1 \end{bmatrix} \tag{6.18}$$

Here, we've denoted the columns of the rotation matrix as r_1, r_2, r_3 in Equation (6.16), and denoted H in Equation (6.18) to be the 3×3 matrix

$$H \sim K[r_1 \ r_2 \ t] \tag{6.19}$$

---

[6] The key linear algebra concept is the **RQ decomposition**, which is a little confusing in this context, since the R stands for an upper (right) triangular matrix and the Q stands for an orthogonal (rotation) matrix.

Image 1   Image 3   Image 5   Image 8

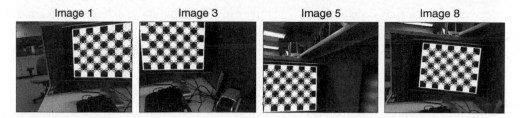

Figure 6.6. Example images used for plane-based internal parameter estimation, with corresponding features at the square corners automatically detected and matched.

In this form, we can see that the relationship between the point on the planar surface, specified by its world coordinates (X, Y), is related to the image coordinate (x, y) through a **projective transformation** H. This stands to reason, since in Section 5.1 we noted that images of a planar surface are related by projective transformations.

For any given position of the camera, we can estimate the projective transformation relating the world planar surface to the image plane by extracting features in each picture of the plane and matching them to world coordinates on the planar surface.[7] The actual physical coordinates of the world points aren't important as long as the relative distances between them are correct. For example, for a checkerboard of squares, we can define the corners of the upper left square to be $(0,0), (0,1), (1,0), (1,1)$, and so forth.

At this point, we've estimated a projective transformation H_i for every view of the planar calibration pattern. Let's see how these projective transformations will help us estimate the internal parameters. Rearranging Equation (6.19), we have:

$$[r_1^i \ r_2^i \ t^i] = \lambda_i K^{-1} H_i$$
$$= \lambda_i K^{-1} [h_1^i \ h_2^i \ h_3^i] \tag{6.20}$$

where we've denoted the columns of H_i as h_1^i, h_2^i, h_3^i. We also introduced a scale factor λ_i to account for the $\sim$ operation. The parameters r_1^i, r_2^i, t^i are columns of the rotation matrix and the translation vector corresponding to the ith position of the camera. Recall that the camera calibration matrix K is fixed for all views.

We know that in a rotation matrix, each column vector is unit norm and that the columns are orthogonal. That is:

$$r_1^{i\top} r_1^i = r_2^{i\top} r_2^i = 1 \qquad r_1^{i\top} r_2^i = 0 \tag{6.21}$$

From Equation (6.20), these constraints turn into constraints on the columns of H_i:

$$h_1^{i\top} (KK^\top)^{-1} h_1^i = h_2^{i\top} (KK^\top)^{-1} h_2^i$$
$$h_1^{i\top} (KK^\top)^{-1} h_2^i = 0 \tag{6.22}$$

We see that Equation (6.22) directly relates the projective transformation for each view to the internal parameters of the camera. If we define the special 3×3 symmetric matrix

$$\omega = (KK^\top)^{-1} \tag{6.23}$$

---

[7] Harris corners will perform well for finding corners of a checkerboard.

we can see that Equation (6.22) is linear in the elements of ω.[8] Since we know the form of the camera calibration matrix in terms of the internal parameters from Equation (6.3), we can verify that

$$
\omega = \begin{bmatrix}
\frac{1}{\alpha_x^2} & 0 & -\frac{x_0}{\alpha_x^2} \\[2mm]
0 & \frac{1}{\alpha_y^2} & -\frac{y_0}{\alpha_y^2} \\[2mm]
-\frac{x_0}{\alpha_x^2} & -\frac{y_0}{\alpha_y^2} & \frac{x_0^2}{\alpha_x^2} + \frac{y_0^2}{\alpha_y^2} + 1
\end{bmatrix} \tag{6.24}
$$

That is, there are five unique parameters $(\omega_{11}, \omega_{13}, \omega_{22}, \omega_{23}, \omega_{33})$ in ω, and each projective transformation H_i puts two linear constraints on them via Equation (6.22). Thus, we need at least three images of the plane in different positions to estimate ω.[9] Since these linear equations are of the form

$$
A_i[\omega_{11},\ \omega_{13},\ \omega_{22},\ \omega_{23},\ \omega_{33}]^\top = 0 \tag{6.25}
$$

we can again use the Direct Linear Transform to estimate the values of ω up to a scalar multiple. Finally, we can recover the actual internal parameters by taking ratios of elements of ω, namely:[10]

$$
\begin{aligned}
x_0 &= -\frac{\omega_{13}}{\omega_{11}} \\[3mm]
y_0 &= -\frac{\omega_{23}}{\omega_{22}} \\[3mm]
\alpha_y &= \left(\frac{\omega_{11}\omega_{22}\omega_{33} - \omega_{22}\omega_{13}^2 - \omega_{11}\omega_{23}^2}{\omega_{11}\omega_{22}^2} \right)^{\frac{1}{2}} \\[3mm]
\alpha_x &= \alpha_y \left(\frac{\omega_{22}}{\omega_{11}} \right)^{\frac{1}{2}}
\end{aligned} \tag{6.26}
$$

This algorithm was proposed by Zhang [575] and independently by Sturm and Maybank [473], who also analyzed planar configurations where the method fails. The solution obtained from the linear estimate can be used as the starting point for subsequent nonlinear estimation of the camera parameters with respect to image reprojection error (see Section 6.5.3). Once the camera calibration matrix K is determined, we can determine the parameters r_1^i, r_2^i, r_3^i, t^i corresponding to the ith position of the camera (see Problem 6.9). If the images of the plane suffer from lens distortion, we can alternate the estimation of the internal parameters using Zhang's algorithm with the estimation of the lens distortion parameters κ using Equation (6.7).

Figure 6.7 shows an example camera calibration result using this approach with nine images of a checkerboard (four of these images are shown in Figure 6.6). In this example, the focal length was computed as 552 pixels (corresponding to 3.1mm for this camera), the principal point was found to be at the center of the image, and the pixels were found to be square $(d_y/d_x = 1)$.

---

[8] For reasons we won't go into here, ω is also called the **image of the absolute conic**. See Section 6.8.
[9] These positions must be non-coplanar to avoid linear dependence of the equations.
[10] These equations can be viewed as the explicit solution of the Cholesky decomposition $\omega^{-1} = KK^\top$.

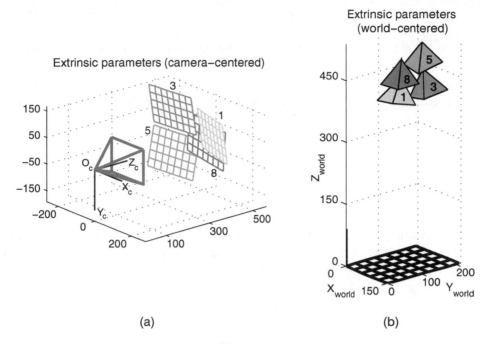

Figure 6.7. Results of camera calibration. (a) The estimated positions of the calibration pattern for the views in Figure 6.6, assuming the camera is in fixed position. (b) Alternately, we can think of the plane being in fixed position and show the estimated positions and orientations of the cameras. The units of the coordinate systems are mm.

6.4   STEREO RIG CALIBRATION

Next, we discuss the calibration of two rigidly mounted cameras, also known as a **stereo rig**. That is, the cameras maintain the same relative orientation and position with respect to each other by being secured together in a fixed housing. Such cameras have recently become popular for filming 3D movies, as described in Section 5.9. The key estimation problem is the determination of the internal parameters of each camera and the relative rotation matrix and translation vector relating the pair. Once we know this information, we can determine the 3D location of a point from its 2D projections in each image using **triangulation**.

As we discussed in Section 5.4.1, the relationship between correspondences for a pair of cameras is entirely encapsulated by the **fundamental matrix,** which defines the epipolar geometry. We can immediately see a problem based on counting degrees of freedom: we have fourteen degrees of freedom for the cameras (four for each camera calibration matrix and six for the relative rotation and translation), but the fundamental matrix only has seven degrees of freedom. Even if we assume that both cameras have exactly the same (unknown) calibration matrix K, we still have extra degrees of freedom. Therefore, while the fundamental matrix for an image pair is unique (up to scale), there are many (substantially) different camera configurations that result in the same fundamental matrix. Therefore, we will inevitably face **ambiguities** in the camera matrices unless we obtain additional information about the cameras or the environment.

In this section, we describe the relationship between the fundamental matrix F and the camera matrices P and P' corresponding to a stereo rig. We assume that the only information available for the estimation problems is a set of feature matches between a single pair of images (one from each camera, taken simultaneously), which can be obtained using any of the methods in Chapter 4. We characterize the ambiguities mentioned previously, and describe how they can be resolved with additional information.

6.4.1   Relating the Fundamental and Camera Matrices

When dealing with a stereo rig, we are predominantly interested in the *relative* rotation matrix and translation vector relating the two cameras, since from point correspondences alone there is no way to determine absolute position with respect to the world coordinates. Therefore, we assume that the first camera is centered at the origin of the world coordinate system and is aligned with the world coordinate axes, and that the second camera matrix is expressed using a rotation and translation with respect to the first camera's coordinate system:

$$P = K[\mathbf{I}_{3\times3} \mid \mathbf{0}_{3\times1}] \qquad P' = K'[R \mid t] \qquad (6.27)$$

Now that we've defined the process of image formation, we can determine the fundamental matrix F relating the two cameras in terms of the camera parameters K, K', R, and t. Since the two camera centers are at $[0,0,0]^\top$ and $-R^\top t$, respectively, we can compute the epipoles by directly applying P' and P to these points:[11]

$$e \sim KR^\top t \qquad e' \sim K't \qquad (6.28)$$

We can show (see Problem 6.10) that the fundamental matrix for the image pair is given by

$$F = [K't]_\times K'RK^{-1} \qquad (6.29)$$

where we used the notation $[\cdot]_\times$ defined in Equation (5.39). This proves a claim we made earlier in Equation (5.38), stating that $F = [e']_\times M$ for some rank-3 matrix M.

When calibrating a stereo rig from feature matches, we first robustly estimate the fundamental matrix (Section 5.4.2), and then extract consistent camera matrices from F.[12] Unfortunately, this is where we run into the **projective ambiguity** referred to earlier. That is, consider a projective transformation of the world coordinate system given by a 4×4 non-singular matrix H. If we consider a camera matrix P and homogeneous world point $\mathbf{X}$, from Equation (6.11) we have the projection $\mathbf{x} \sim P\mathbf{X}$. Now consider an alternate camera matrix $\hat{P} = PH$ and world point $\hat{\mathbf{X}} = H^{-1}\mathbf{X}$; since

$$\hat{P}\hat{\mathbf{X}} = PHH^{-1}\mathbf{X} = P\mathbf{X} \sim \mathbf{x} \qquad (6.30)$$

we get the same projected point on the image. Thus, from image correspondences alone, we have no way to determine whether our estimates of the camera matrices

---

[11] We removed the negative sign from the expression for e in Equation (6.28) since $\sim$ accounts for this scalar multiple.

[12] Zhang [574] and Fitzgibbon [144] described methods for simultaneously estimating lens distortion coefficients and the fundamental matrix from a set of feature matches between an image pair.

are off from the truth by an arbitrary 3D projective transformation.[13] Some of these degrees of freedom are relatively harmless; for example, six of them account for an arbitrary rigid motion of the world coordinate system (which can be removed by fixing the coordinate system of the first camera as in Equation (6.27)). Another degree of freedom corresponds to an unknown scale factor of the world; for example, an image of a given object will look exactly the same as an image of an object that is twice as large and twice as far away. This uncertainty can be resolved if we know the physical length of some line segment in the scene that appears in one of the images (e.g., the height of a table or wall).

However, the class of 3D projective transformations also includes generalizations of the shear and nonlinear distortions corresponding to the last two images in Figure 5.1. These distortions can have a serious effect on the structure of the scene implied by a pair of camera matrices, as illustrated in Figure 6.8c–d. In particular, a general 3D projective transformation can make the underlying true structure almost unrecognizable, since angles and ratios of lengths are no longer preserved.

Without any further information about the cameras or the environment, this is the best we can do for determining the camera matrices from feature matches in a single image pair. A useful general formula for two camera matrices consistent with a given F is

$$P = [\mathbf{I}_{3\times3} \mid \mathbf{0}_{3\times1}] \qquad P' = [[e']_\times F + e'v^\top \mid \lambda e'] \qquad (6.31)$$

where v is any 3×1 vector and λ is any nonzero scalar. This form shows that if we fix P to the canonical form in Equation (6.31), 4 degrees of projective ambiguity remain. Beardsley et al. [34] recommended choosing v so that the left-hand matrix $[e']_\times F + e'v^\top$ is as close to a rotation matrix as possible, resulting in a "quasi-Euclidean" reconstruction.

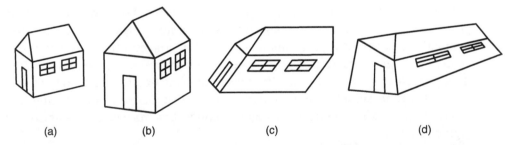

| (a) | (b) | (c) | (d) |

Figure 6.8. Projective ambiguities inherent in the calibration of a stereo rig from feature matches alone. These four scene configurations all differ by a 3D projective transformation and hence can all produce the same image pair. (b) is a similarity transformation (rotation, translation, and scale) of (a), (c) is a 3D shear, and (d) is a general 3D projective transformation. Without further information about the cameras or the environment, there is no way to resolve the ambiguity.

---

[13] Again, we can apply a counting argument: eleven degrees of freedom in each camera matrix (allowing for nonzero skew) minus seven degrees of freedom for the fundamental matrix leaves fifteen degrees of freedom in the 3D projective transformation H.

6.4.2   Recovering Calibrated Cameras

The situation is much improved if we already know the camera calibration matrices K and K'. For example, if we have access to the cameras prior to mounting them on the rig, we can use the plane-based technique described in Section 6.3.2 to independently estimate these internal parameters.

In this case, we consider the camera matrices

$$P = [\mathbf{I}_{3\times3} \mid \mathbf{0}_{3\times1}] \qquad P' = [R \mid t] \tag{6.32}$$

These correspond to transforming the coordinates of the two images by $\hat{\mathbf{x}} = K^{-1}\mathbf{x}$ and $\hat{\mathbf{x}}' = K'^{-1}\mathbf{x}'$, which are called **normalized coordinates**. From Equation (6.29), the fundamental matrix takes the simple form

$$F = [t]_\times R \tag{6.33}$$

and in this situation we refer to it as the **essential matrix**. Longuet-Higgins [300] introduced the essential matrix in a classic paper and proved that the rotation and translation parameters could be uniquely extracted up to a scale ambiguity. In particular, any essential matrix can be decomposed via singular value decomposition as $F = U\text{diag}(1,1,0)V^\top$. Then there are exactly four possibilities for the camera matrix P' in Equation (6.32):

$$P' \in \{[UWV^\top \mid u_3], [UWV^\top \mid -u_3], [UW^\top V^\top \mid u_3], [UW^\top V^\top \mid -u_3]\} \tag{6.34}$$

where u_3 is the last column of U and

$$W = \begin{bmatrix} 0 & -1 & 0 \\ 1 & 0 & 0 \\ 0 & 0 & 1 \end{bmatrix} \tag{6.35}$$

Only one of the four candidates is physically possible (i.e., corresponds to scene points that are in front of both image planes in the stereo rig). This can be tested by **triangulating** one of the feature matches — that is, projecting lines from the camera centers through the corresponding image locations and finding their intersection in three-dimensional space. In practice, the feature matches are noisy, so the two rays will probably not actually intersect. In this case, we estimate the point of intersection as the midpoint of the shortest line segment connecting the two rays, as illustrated in Figure 6.9.[14]

When using noisy feature matches to estimate the relative rotation and translation between a pair of calibrated cameras within a RANSAC approach, the minimal five-point algorithm of Nistér [350] should be used instead of sequentially estimating and factoring F.

---

[14] This method only makes sense when we have calibrated cameras; the midpoint of the segment has no meaning in a projective coordinate frame. In the projective case, the triangulation method described by Hartley and Sturm [189] should be applied. This method is based on minimizing the error between a feature match and the closest pair of conjugate epipolar lines, and involves finding the roots of a sixth-degree polynomial. See also Section 7.2.

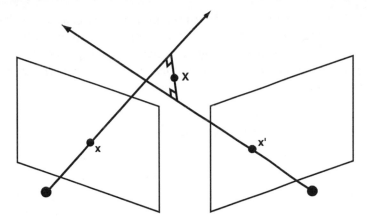

Figure 6.9. Once the camera matrices are estimated, the 3D point corresponding to a given feature match can be estimated by triangulation. The point is chosen as the midpoint of the shortest line segment connecting the two rays.

An alternate approach to the above is to simultaneously recover the internal parameters and the relative rotation/translation for a stereo rig by showing it multiple images of a planar calibration pattern (an extension of Section 6.3.2 described by Malm and Heyden [312]). We can also estimate the camera parameters by observing the changing positions of feature correspondences as the rig is moved freely though a stationary environment ([202, 109]); two stereo views are minimally required for zero-skew cameras. The latter approach is fundamentally related to the algorithms for image sequence calibration that we discuss in more detail in the next section.

6.5   IMAGE SEQUENCE CALIBRATION

We now have the ingredients to discuss the main topic of the chapter, the problem of estimating the varying internal and external parameters of a camera as it moves freely through an environment. This problem of image sequence calibration is the core of the **matchmoving** process required for virtually any visual effects shot that composites 3D computer-generated elements into footage from a moving camera. In computer vision, the process is also called **structure from motion**, since we're estimating the coordinates of 3D points corresponding to image features (i.e., structure) as the camera position is varied (i.e., motion). We assume the camera is always translating between frames, so that any frame pair is related by a fundamental matrix.

Just as in the stereo case, image sequence calibration contains an inherent projective ambiguity analogous to Equation (6.30). Therefore, the first step is usually to estimate a **projective reconstruction** of the cameras and scene points that matches the image feature locations as well as possible. This projective reconstruction is then "upgraded" to what is called a **Euclidean** or **metric reconstruction** that differs from the true configuration by an unknown similarity transformation. Again, Euclidean reconstruction is not possible without some additional assumptions about the camera calibration matrices or the structure of the environment—but in practical scenarios these assumptions are usually easy to make. Once we have a good estimate of a Euclidean reconstruction, all of the camera parameter and scene point estimates are refined using a non-linear estimation step called **bundle adjustment** to make the reconstruction match the image features as well as possible. Finally, we discuss several practical issues for image sequence calibration, which becomes difficult for very long sequences.

6.5.1   Projective Reconstruction

We now formally state the image sequence calibration problem. We detect and track a set of n features across m images from a moving camera. Let the camera matrices corresponding to these images be $\{P_1, \ldots, P_m\}$, and the homogeneous coordinates of the 3D scene points that generated each feature be $\{\mathbf{X}_1, \ldots, \mathbf{X}_n\}$. The homogeneous coordinates of the jth feature in the image from the ith camera are denoted $\mathbf{x}_{ij}$. Since every 3D point may not be observed in each image, we also create a binary variable χ_{ij} that specifies whether the jth point appears in the ith image. That is, if $\chi_{ij} = 1$, we have

$$\mathbf{x}_{ij} \sim P_i \mathbf{X}_j \qquad (6.36)$$

Given the image projections $\{\chi_{ij}, \mathbf{x}_{ij}\}$ as input, we want to determine the unknown camera matrices $\{P_1, \ldots, P_m\}$ and scene points $\{\mathbf{X}_1, \ldots, \mathbf{X}_n\}$. Since we want to find camera matrices and scene points that reproduce the projections we observed, a natural approach is to minimize the sum of squared distances

$$\sum_{i=1}^{m} \sum_{j=1}^{n} \chi_{ij} d(\mathbf{x}_{ij}, P_i \mathbf{X}_j)^2 \qquad (6.37)$$

where d is the Euclidean distance between two points on the image plane (i.e., after we convert from homogeneous to unhomogeneous coordinates).

This minimization problem is generally called **bundle adjustment**, for the reason illustrated in Figure 6.10. That is, we are adjusting the "bundles" of rays emanating from each camera to the scene points in order to bring the estimated projections onto the image planes as close as possible to the observed feature locations. The quantity in Equation (6.37) is also called the **reprojection error**.

We will discuss the numerical solution to this nonlinear problem in Section 6.5.3. However, the first consideration is determining a good initial estimate of the unknown variables so that the bundle adjustment process starting from this initial guess converges to a reasonable answer. We discuss two methods: one based on a factorization approach for all the cameras at once, and one built on sequentially estimating camera matrices, exploiting the knowledge that the images come from a sequence.

6.5.1.1 Projective Factorization

Sturm and Triggs [474, 498] proposed an elegant approach for projective reconstruction based on a **factorization** method.[15] Let's initially assume that all the 3D points are visible in all the images (i.e., $\chi_{ij} = 1$ for all i, j). Then we can collect the projection

---

[15] This approach was inspired by a classic algorithm by Tomasi and Kanade [493], who showed how factorization applied to a simpler method of image formation, orthographic projection.

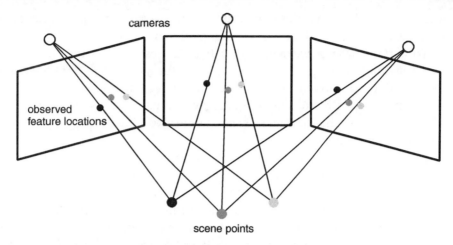

cameras

observed
feature locations

scene points

Figure 6.10. Bundle adjustment for projective reconstruction. We want to adjust the "bundles" of rays emanating from each camera to the scene points in order to bring the estimated projections onto the image plane as close as possible to the observed feature locations. The reprojection error corresponds to the sum of squared distances between every observation and the intersection of the corresponding line and image plane.

equations (6.36) into a large matrix equation:

$$
\begin{bmatrix}
\lambda_{11}\mathbf{x}_{11} & \lambda_{12}\mathbf{x}_{12} & \cdots & \lambda_{1n}\mathbf{x}_{1n} \\
\lambda_{21}\mathbf{x}_{21} & \lambda_{22}\mathbf{x}_{22} & \cdots & \lambda_{2n}\mathbf{x}_{2n} \\
\vdots & \vdots & \ddots & \vdots \\
\lambda_{m1}\mathbf{x}_{m1} & \lambda_{m2}\mathbf{x}_{m2} & \cdots & \lambda_{mn}\mathbf{x}_{mn}
\end{bmatrix}
=
\begin{bmatrix}
P_1 \\
P_2 \\
\vdots \\
P_m
\end{bmatrix}
\begin{bmatrix}
\mathbf{X}_1 & \mathbf{X}_2 & \cdots & \mathbf{X}_n
\end{bmatrix}
\qquad (6.38)
$$

Here, the λ_{ij} are the unknown scalar multiples such that the $\sim$ in Equation (6.36) is an equality: $\lambda_{ij}\mathbf{x}_{ij} = P_i\mathbf{X}_j$. These are called the **projective depths,** and the matrix of feature locations on the left-hand side of Equation (6.38) is called the **measurement matrix**.

Since Equation (6.38) expresses the $3m \times n$ measurement matrix as the product of a $3m \times 4$ matrix containing the cameras $\{P_i\}$ and a $4 \times n$ matrix containing the scene points $\{\mathbf{X}_j\}$, we can see this large matrix has rank at most four. This suggests a natural factorization algorithm based on the SVD. That is, given a guess for the projective depths, we form the measurement matrix on the left-hand side of Equation (6.38) (call it M) and determine the SVD $M = UDV^\top$. U is $3m \times n$, V is $n \times n$, and D is a $n \times n$ diagonal matrix of singular values, which from this reasoning should ideally only have four nonzero elements. Therefore, we define D_4 as the left-hand $n \times 4$ matrix of D. We estimate the $3m \times 4$ matrix of cameras on the right-hand side of Equation (6.38) as UD_4 and the $4 \times n$ matrix of scene points on the right-hand side of Equation (6.38) as the first four rows of $V^\top$.

As for previous algorithms, normalization of the data prior to applying the algorithm is critical to get good results if the data is noisy. A simple approach is to first normalize the feature locations in each image in the usual way (i.e., apply a similarity transformation to each image plane so that the features have zero mean and average distance from the origin of $\sqrt{2}$). Next, we rescale each row of M to have unit norm, and then rescale each column of M to have unit norm. This process can be iterated until the measurement matrix stops changing significantly.

To start the process, we need reasonable initial estimates of the projective depths. One possibility is simply to initialize $\lambda_{ij} = 1$ for all i and j.[16] Then we apply the factorization algorithm to obtain a candidate collection of P's and $\mathbf{X}$'s, and compute the homogeneous reprojections $\hat{\mathbf{x}}_{ij}$. A new estimate of λ_{ij} is obtained as the third element of $\hat{\mathbf{x}}_{ij}$. We then iterate the factorization algorithm until the reprojection error stops changing significantly.

A key problem with the approach is that in practice, all of the 3D points are unlikely to be seen in all of the images. In this case, we eliminate cameras and points until we have a "nucleus" of 3D points that are seen in all of the images from a subset of the cameras. When the factorization algorithm has converged, we can use the resectioning algorithm described in Section 6.3.1 to estimate new camera matrices that see some of the 3D nucleus points based on several of their feature locations. We also use the triangulation algorithm described in Section 6.4.2 to estimate new 3D scene point positions based on feature matches in the camera subset.[17] These processes are sketched in Figure 6.11.

Therefore, the overall projective factorization algorithm is:

1. Determine a subset of scene points and cameras so that the measurement matrix is completely filled.
2. Normalize the set of points in each image by an appropriate translation and scale.
3. Initialize all $\lambda_{ij} = 1$.
4. Form the measurement matrix M.
5. Alternate rescaling the rows of M to have unit norm and the columns of M to have unit norm until M stops changing significantly.
6. Determine the SVD $M = UDV^\top$.

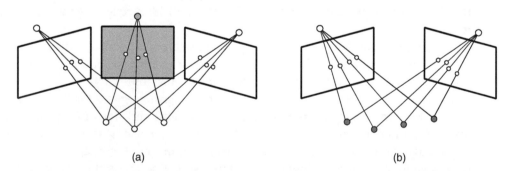

(a)   (b)

Figure 6.11. Interpolating projective camera matrices and scene structure using resectioning and triangulation. (a) If the projective cameras and scene points given by white planes/circles are known, the shaded camera matrix can be computed by resectioning, since the world coordinates and image projections are both known. (b) If the projective cameras and scene points given by white planes/circles are known, the shaded points can be computed by triangulation, since the camera matrices and image projections are both known.

---

[16] Sturm and Triggs also described a more complicated approach to initializing the projective depths based on the estimated fundamental matrices between image pairs.
[17] Since this is only a projective reconstruction, Hartley's algorithm [189] should be used.

7. Let the the $3m \times 4$ matrix of cameras on the right-hand side of Equation (6.38) be UD_4 and the $4 \times n$ matrix of points on the right-hand side of Equation (6.38) be the first four rows of $V^\top$, where D_4 is the left-hand $n \times 4$ matrix of D.
8. Compute the reprojection $\hat{\mathbf{x}}_{ij}$ for each camera and point.
9. If the average reprojection error has converged, stop. Otherwise, let λ_{ij} be the third element of $\hat{\mathbf{x}}_{ij}$ and go to Step 4.
10. Un-normalize the camera matrices and world coordinates.
11. Resection and triangulate the non-nucleus cameras and scene points.

An alternate approach to projective factorization was proposed by Mahamud et al. [311], who noted that the minimization of

$$\sum_{i=1}^{m}\sum_{j=1}^{n}\chi_{ij}\|\lambda_{ij}\mathbf{x}_{ij} - P_i\mathbf{X}_j\|^2 \tag{6.39}$$

is linear in the elements of P if the $\mathbf{X}$'s are known and vice versa. This suggests a natural algorithm of alternating the estimation of one set of quantities while the other is fixed, and has the advantage that not all points must be seen in all images. Along the same lines, Hung and Tang [210] proposed to cycle through updating the cameras, scene points, and inverse projective depths; fixing two of the quantities and estimating the third is a linear least-squares problem. Both algorithms were shown to provably converge.

Clearly, minimizing Equation (6.37) or Equation (6.39) can only result in a reconstruction of the cameras and world points up to a 3D projective transformation, by the same argument as in Equation (6.30). That is, we can replace all the camera matrices and world points by

$$\hat{P}_i = P_i H \qquad \hat{\mathbf{X}}_j = H^{-1}\mathbf{X}_j \tag{6.40}$$

for any 4×4 non-singular matrix H, and still obtain the same measurement matrix. This means that at the end of projective reconstruction, we will most likely have a very strange set of camera matrices and 3D points (e.g., resembling Figure 6.8d), which are not immediately useful. Section 6.5.2 addresses the estimation of an H that upgrades the projective reconstruction to a Euclidean one (e.g., resembling Figure 6.8b).

6.5.1.2 Sequential and Hierarchical Updating

The factorization approach doesn't take advantage of the fact that in matchmoving applications, the images come from a temporal sequence, in which successive images are similar. Projective reconstruction algorithms for long image sequences frequently use a **chaining** approach, in which the projective cameras are successively estimated based on pairs or triples of images, as illustrated in Figure 6.12a.

For example, let's suppose we're given three successive images from a sequence, with a set of feature matches tracked through the triple. From the first two images, we can estimate the fundamental matrix F_{12} from feature matches and obtain a pair of projective cameras P_1 and P_2 in the form of Equation (6.31), as well as the 3D projective points $\mathbf{X}_j$ that correspond to the features. In the third image, we can use the estimated $\mathbf{X}_j$ and their projections $\mathbf{x}_{3j}$ to solve the resectioning problem as described in Section 6.3.1, obtaining an estimate for P_3. It's easy to iterate this process for more

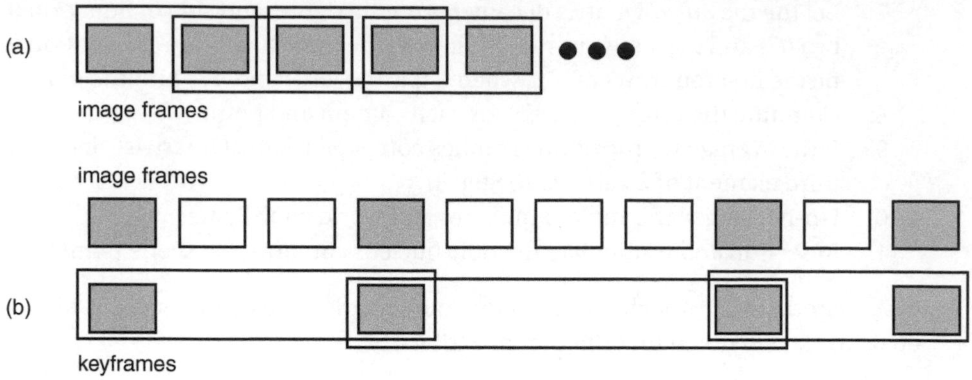

Figure 6.12. (a) Sequential updating of cameras uses overlapping pairs of images to successively estimate projective camera matrices. (b) Hierarchical updating uses a subset of keyframes: images chosen to give wider baselines. Intermediate cameras and scene points can be estimated using resectioning and triangulation. In both cases, triples of images can be used instead, leveraging the trifocal tensor.

images in the sequence. Beardsley et al. [34] described this process in detail, taking into account the problem of maintaining good estimates of the 3D structure used for resectioning as the sequence gets longer and feature matches enter and leave the images.

Avidan and Shashua [22] and Fitzgibbon and Zisserman [145] described methods that "thread together" *triples* of images to estimate the next camera matrix instead of using pairs of images, so that all the cameras are represented in a common projective frame. These methods are based on the **trifocal tensor**, a $3 \times 3 \times 3$ matrix that relates feature correspondences in image triples similarly to how the fundamental matrix relates feature correspondences in image pairs. Methods based on triples of images are often preferred since the trifocal constraint is stronger, making it easier to reject outlier feature matches; also, each triple overlaps the previous one by two images, adding robustness to the solution. Fitzgibbon and Zisserman also described how to enforce a constraint if an image sequence is known to be closed — that is, the first and last camera matrices are the same.

When successive images are very close together spatially (which is not unusual), the decomposition in Equation (6.31) is unstable; that is, the fundamental matrix may be poorly estimated since t is so small in Equation (6.29). In these cases, a global projective transformation may better express the relationship between the two views (since the motion is nearly pure rotation). Torr et al. [495] discussed this problem of **degeneracy** in calibrating image sequences, and proposed methods for "surviving" these situations when they are encountered in practice. The key idea is to incorporate a robust model selection criterion at each frame that decides whether the relationship between an image pair is better modeled by a fundamental matrix or a projective transformation. The same problem occurs when the scene in an image is primarily comprised of a single, dominant plane; Pollefeys et al. [369] extended Torr et al.'s approach to operate on image triples in this situation.

Alternately, we can take **keyframes** from the sequence that are spatially far enough apart to enable robust estimation of F, but not so far apart that feature matching is difficult. The chaining process is therefore hierarchical, rather than sequential, as illustrated in Figure 6.12b. For example, Pollefeys et al. [368] suggested using Torr et al.'s approach to select the next keyframe in a sequence at the point where the epipolar geometry model explains the correspondences better than a projective transformation. Nistér [349] described another example of this idea, using triples of images instead of pairs. The basic approach is to scan through the sequence of images, choosing triples that balance the number of good feature matches with a quality measure of the estimated trifocal tensor. In either case, when the camera moves quickly, the keyframes are taken close together; when the camera moves slowly, we may be able to robustly estimate relationships between keyframes hundreds of frames apart. As in the previous section, after estimating the camera matrices for keyframes, the other camera matrices can be estimated using resectioning (Figure 6.11a), and refined with an overall pass of bundle adjustment (see Section 6.5.3).

6.5.2 Euclidean Reconstruction

Just as for a stereo rig, if we know each camera's calibration matrix K_i, we can undo the projective ambiguity in Equation (6.40). However, in practice this information is difficult to obtain for image sequences in which the camera may be constantly zooming in an unknown way. The process of obtaining a **Euclidean reconstruction** of the cameras and environment using general images (i.e., without a calibration pattern) is also known as **self-** or **auto-calibration**. The idea is to use known properties of the camera calibration matrices K_i (for example, that the skew is 0 and/or the principal point is at the center of the images) to put constraints on the unknown entries of H, the 4×4 matrix in Equation (6.40). Our goal is to determine the entries of H so that

$$\tilde{P}_i = P_i H$$
$$= K_i[R_i \mid t_i] \tag{6.41}$$

where P_i is the result of a projective reconstruction, and $\tilde{P}_i$ is a Euclidean reconstruction where all the K_i's are in the desired form.

Similarly to Equation (6.32), let's assume that the first projective camera matrix has the form

$$P_1 = [\mathbf{I}_{3\times3} \mid \mathbf{0}_{3\times1}] \tag{6.42}$$

which after applying H becomes the Euclidean camera matrix

$$\tilde{P}_1 = K_1[\mathbf{I}_{3\times3} \mid \mathbf{0}_{3\times1}] \tag{6.43}$$

If we split the 4×4 H into submatrices in the form

$$H = \begin{bmatrix} A & b \\ c^\top & d \end{bmatrix} \tag{6.44}$$

where A is 3×3, b and c are 3×1, and d is a scalar, then combining Equations (6.41)–(6.44) gives $A = K_1$ and $b = 0$; since H is nonsingular, we can choose $d = 1$ so that we have the simple form

$$H = \begin{bmatrix} K_1 & 0 \\ c^\top & 1 \end{bmatrix} \tag{6.45}$$

This makes sense; we've removed seven degrees of freedom (a similarity transformation) to fix the first camera, leaving eight degrees of freedom: the unknown five entries of K_1 and the 3×1 vector c, which is related to the 3D projective distortion of the environment.[18] Since K_1 is nonsingular, we can define a vector $v = -K_1^{-\top}c$, so that

$$H = \begin{bmatrix} K_1 & 0 \\ -v^{\top}K_1 & 1 \end{bmatrix} \tag{6.46}$$

Now, if we denote

$$P_i = [A_i | a_i] \tag{6.47}$$

and recall the definition of $\omega_i = (K_i K_i^{\top})^{-1}$ from Equation (6.23), it's straightforward to show (see Problem 6.18) that

$$\begin{aligned} \omega_i^{-1} &= (A_i - a_i v^{\top})\omega_1^{-1}(A_i - a_i v^{\top})^{\top} \\ &= P_i \begin{bmatrix} \omega_1^{-1} & -\omega_1^{-1}v \\ -v^{\top}\omega_1^{-1} & v^{\top}\omega_1^{-1}v \end{bmatrix} P_i^{\top} \\ &\sim P_i Q P_i^{\top} \end{aligned} \tag{6.48}$$

Here, we have introduced a 4×4 symmetric matrix Q that depends only on the elements of the transformation H.[19] The equations in (6.48) are very important, since they relate the projective camera matrices (which we know) to the elements of the projective transformation H and the camera calibration matrices via ω_i.

While we don't know the values of ω_i, at this point we can impose constraints on the form we wish it to take based on our knowledge about the camera calibration matrices K_i. These in turn impose constraints on Q through Equation (6.48).

For example, let's suppose the principal point is known to be $(0,0)$ and the aspect ratio α_y/α_x is known to be 1 — reasonable assumptions for a good camera. In this case, only the focal length f_i of each camera is unknown, and each ω_i has an extremely simple form:

$$\omega_i = \begin{bmatrix} f_i^{-2} & 0 & 0 \\ 0 & f_i^{-2} & 0 \\ 0 & 0 & 1 \end{bmatrix} \tag{6.49}$$

So does the matrix Q:

$$Q = \begin{bmatrix} q_1 & 0 & 0 & q_2 \\ 0 & q_1 & 0 & q_3 \\ 0 & 0 & 1 & q_4 \\ q_2 & q_3 & q_4 & q_5 \end{bmatrix} \tag{6.50}$$

If we denote the rows of P_i as P_i^1, P_i^2, P_i^3 and expand Equation (6.48) in this special situation, we obtain four linear equations in the five unknowns of Q, corresponding

---

[18] It is also related to what is called the **plane at infinity** for the projective reconstruction.
[19] Q is also known as the **absolute dual quadric** [499].

to the four constraints on the form of each ω_i, namely:

$$\omega_i(1,1) = \omega_i(2,2) \qquad \Longrightarrow \qquad P_i^1 Q P_i^{1\,\top} = P_i^2 Q P_i^{2\,\top} \qquad (6.51)$$

$$\omega_i(1,2) = 0 \qquad \Longrightarrow \qquad P_i^1 Q P_i^{2\,\top} = 0 \qquad (6.52)$$

$$\omega_i(1,3) = 0 \qquad \Longrightarrow \qquad P_i^1 Q P_i^{3\,\top} = 0 \qquad (6.53)$$

$$\omega_i(2,3) = 0 \qquad \Longrightarrow \qquad P_i^2 Q P_i^{3\,\top} = 0 \qquad (6.54)$$

Therefore, we need at least three views (i.e., eight equations) to obtain a solution. If we have many views, then we have an overdetermined linear system that can be solved using the same Direct Linear Transform approach we've used for previous problems. We need to make sure that the Q we obtain is rank-3 (using the same approach we used to make sure the estimated fundamental matrix was rank-2 in Section 5.4.2). Once we obtain Q, then the relationships in Equation (6.46) and Equation (6.48) allow us to recover the elements of H, and thus obtain all the cameras in a Euclidean frame via Equation (6.41).[20] Figure 6.13 illustrates a sketch of upgrading a scene containing a wireframe house from a projective reconstruction to a Euclidean reconstruction. That is, we are illustrating the estimated points $\mathbf{X}_j$ before and after applying the 3D projective transformation H^{-1}. We can see that qualitatively, the projective reconstruction is not useful while the Euclidean one is.

The algorithm just discussed was proposed by Pollefeys et al. [366] and is widely used to solve the self-calibration problem, though other methods exist (see Section 6.8). If we know less about the cameras' varying internal parameters (for example, only that the skew is zero), then we can still apply constraints based on Equation (6.48); however, the algorithms are not typically linear. For example, we can directly minimize a nonlinear function of the unknown 3×1 vector v and the

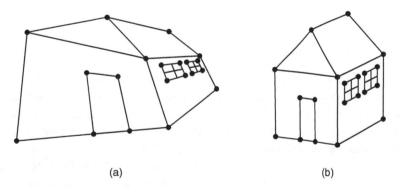

(a)   (b)

Figure 6.13. Upgrading a projective reconstruction of a set of points in (a) to a Euclidean reconstruction in (b). Even though the upgrade is obtained by analyzing the projective camera matrices, it's easier to visualize the effects of the upgrade by looking at the reconstructed scene points.

[20] However, since we are typically solving an overconstrained problem with noisy input camera matrices, the solution we obtain is only approximate and the resulting K_i may not exactly be in the required form. We'll take care of this during bundle adjustment in the next section.

camera calibration parameters in the $\{K_i\}$ given by

$$\sum_{i=1}^{m} \left\| \frac{K_i K_i^\top}{\|K_i K_i^\top\|_F} - \frac{P_i Q P_i^\top}{\|P_i Q P_i^\top\|_F} \right\|_F^2 \tag{6.55}$$

where $\|\cdot\|_F$ is the Frobenius norm.

Later, Pollefeys et al. [368] suggested pre-normalizing the projective camera matrices P_i using

$$P_i = \begin{bmatrix} w+h & 0 & \frac{w}{2} \\ 0 & w+h & \frac{h}{2} \\ 0 & 0 & 1 \end{bmatrix}^{-1} P_i \tag{6.56}$$

prior to self-calibration, where w and h are the width and height of the images. They also recommended weighting Equations (6.51)–(6.54) to reflect reasonable estimates about the cameras' unknown internal parameters. For example, we are usually much more certain that $\omega_i(1,2) = 0$ (i.e., the cameras have zero skew) than we are that the principal points $(\omega_i(1,3), \omega_i(2,3)) = (0,0)$, so Equation (6.52) should have much more weight in the linear system than Equations (6.53)–(6.54).

We should keep in mind that self-calibration from an image sequence fails in certain **critical configurations**, enumerated by Sturm [471, 472]. Unfortunately, some of these critical configurations are not unusual when it comes to video shot for visual effects. For the variable focal length case described earlier, critical configurations include a camera that translates but does not rotate, as well as a camera that moves along an elliptical path, pointing straight ahead (e.g., a camera pointing straight out of a car's windshield as it takes a curve in the road).

As we discuss next, we always follow up a Euclidean reconstruction with the non-linear process of bundle adjustment over all internal and external parameters, so it's not always necessary to obtain a highly accurate Euclidean reconstruction at this stage.

6.5.3   Bundle Adjustment

After upgrading a projective reconstruction to a Euclidean one, we have a good initial estimate of the cameras and structure. However, this reconstruction is typically not ready to use in a high-quality application for two main reasons. First, the various projective and Euclidean reconstruction algorithms don't always minimize an intuitive, geometrically sensible quantity — the natural one being the reprojection error. Second, the Euclidean upgrade step doesn't usually strictly enforce constraints on the camera calibration matrices (such as zero skew) since it's the result of a least-squares problem over noisy data.

We address both of these problems in a final step of **bundle adjustment**, the joint minimization of the sum of reprojection errors

$$\sum_{i=1}^{m} \sum_{j=1}^{n} \chi_{ij} d(\mathbf{x}_{ij}, P_i \mathbf{X}_j)^2 \tag{6.57}$$

over all of the unknown camera matrices $\{P_1, \ldots, P_m\}$ and 3D world points $\{\mathbf{X}_1, \ldots, \mathbf{X}_n\}$, where d is the Euclidean distance between two points on the image plane (i.e., after we convert from homogeneous to unhomogeneous coordinates).[21]

6.5.3.1 Parameterization

A critical aspect is the **minimal parameterization** of the camera matrices to have exactly the number of degrees of freedom we know they should have. For example, in the case of a zero-skew camera, we can explicitly represent each camera matrix P_i using ten numbers as follows.

We parameterize the rotation matrix R_i in terms of a 3×1 vector r^i using the **Rodrigues formula:**[22]

$$R_i = \cos\|r^i\| \mathbf{I}_{3\times3} + \mathrm{sinc}\|r^i\|[r^i]_\times + \frac{1 - \cos\|r^i\|}{\|r^i\|^2} r^i r^{i\top} \tag{6.58}$$

Here, the direction of r^i gives the axis about which the world coordinate system is rotated, and the magnitude of r^i gives the angle of rotation. This is also known as the **axis-angle parameterization** of a rotation matrix.

Then, each P_i is minimally parameterized by ten numbers $(\alpha_x^i, \alpha_y^i, x_0^i, y_0^i, r_1^i, r_2^i, r_3^i, t_1^i, t_2^i, t_3^i)$, using:

$$P_i = K_i[R_i \mid t_i]$$

$$= \begin{bmatrix} \alpha_x^i & 0 & x_0^i \\ 0 & \alpha_y^i & y_0^i \\ 0 & 0 & 1 \end{bmatrix} \left[\cos\|r^i\| \mathbf{I}_{3\times3} + \mathrm{sinc}\|r^i\|[r^i]_\times + \frac{1 - \cos\|r^i\|}{\|r^i\|^2} r^i r^{i\top} \,\middle|\, \begin{array}{c} t_1^i \\ t_2^i \\ t_3^i \end{array} \right] \tag{6.59}$$

We parameterize each 3D point as (X_j, Y_j, Z_j).

However, even if we use this minimal parameterization for each camera and point, there are still seven degrees of freedom in the overall problem due to an arbitrary similarity transformation of the space. These are the degrees of freedom that remain after Euclidean reconstruction; we can't determine the coordinate axes and scale of the world coordinate system without further information about the scene. One possibility is to fix the first camera matrix to $P_1 = K_1[\mathbf{I}_{3\times3} \mid \mathbf{0}_{3\times1}]$ (removing six degrees of freedom) and let the second camera center be at unit distance from the first, parameterizing its heading using two parameters to specify t^2 instead of three (removing the seventh degree of freedom). This process is called fixing a **gauge** for the overall problem. If we don't use a minimal parameterization, there will be **gauge freedoms** in the minimization problem — that is, directions in parameter space where the cost function doesn't change. These can cause numerical problems in the optimization procedure we discuss next.

---

[21] It's also possible to use a distance function that incorporates the underlying uncertainty about each feature measurement; this is called the **Mahalanobis distance**.

[22] Here we use the sinc function, $\mathrm{sinc}\, x = \frac{\sin x}{x}$.

6.5.3.2 Numerical Optimization

At this point, we assume we have an initial estimate for the minimizer to Equation (6.57), parameterized appropriately. In this section, we sketch how to actually solve the bundle adjustment optimization problem numerically. These optimization algorithms are "under the hood" of the software packages visual effects artists use to solve the matchmoving problem. While Appendix A.4 goes into more detail on general nonlinear optimization, we give the main ideas here.

First, we note that Equation (6.57) is the sum of squared functions of the camera parameters and scene points. For the moment, let's denote the vector of parameters to be optimized as θ, and a stacked vector of all the feature point observations as $\mathbf{x}$. For a given estimate of the parameters θ, we compute the reprojections of all the feature points to produce an estimate of $\mathbf{x}$; we denote this estimate as a multi-valued function $\hat{\mathbf{x}} = f(\theta)$. Therefore, we can rewrite Equation (6.57) concisely as:

$$F(\theta) = (\mathbf{x} - f(\theta))^\top (\mathbf{x} - f(\theta)) \tag{6.60}$$

where F is the function we want to minimize. Let's expand the cost function $F(\theta)$ in a Taylor series approximation about some point θ^t:

$$F(\theta) \approx F(\theta^t) + \frac{\partial F}{\partial \theta}(\theta^t)^\top (\theta - \theta^t) + \frac{1}{2}(\theta - \theta^t)^\top \frac{\partial^2 F}{\partial \theta^2}(\theta^t)(\theta - \theta^t) \tag{6.61}$$

The minimizer θ^* of this function is given by setting the gradient of Equation (6.61) to zero:

$$\theta^* = \theta^t - \left[\frac{\partial^2 F}{\partial \theta^2}(\theta^t) \right]^{-1} \frac{\partial F}{\partial \theta}(\theta^t) \tag{6.62}$$

This suggests an iterative process for minimizing F: we start with a good estimate of the minimizer (obtained at the end of Euclidean reconstruction), form the quadratic approximation in Equation (6.61) around this point, and iterate

$$\theta^{t+1} = \theta^t + \left(-\left[\frac{\partial^2 F}{\partial \theta^2}(\theta^t) \right]^{-1} \frac{\partial F}{\partial \theta}(\theta^t) \right) \tag{6.63}$$

We can compute that

$$\frac{\partial F}{\partial \theta}(\theta^t) = J^\top(\theta^t)(\mathbf{x} - f(\theta^t)) \tag{6.64}$$

where J is the **Jacobian** matrix defined by

$$J(\theta^t) = \frac{\partial f}{\partial \theta}(\theta^t) \tag{6.65}$$

That is, the $(j, k)^{th}$ element of J is the partial derivative of the jth reprojection $\hat{\mathbf{x}}_j$ with respect to the kth parameter θ_k. We will return to the structure of this Jacobian matrix in a moment, since it has critical implications for designing a fast bundle adjustment algorithm.

The other important quantity in Equation (6.63) is the matrix of second partial derivatives, also called the **Hessian**. This matrix is impractical (and generally unnecessary) to compute exactly, and optimization algorithms differ in how to approximate it. The **Levenberg-Marquardt** algorithm commonly used for bundle adjustment uses the approximation

$$\frac{\partial^2 F}{\partial \theta^2}(\theta^t) \approx J(\theta^t)^\top J(\theta^t) + \lambda^t \mathbf{I} \tag{6.66}$$

where λ^t is a tuning parameter that varies with each iteration and $\mathbf{I}$ is an appropriately sized identity matrix. The reasoning behind this approximation is described in Appendix A.4.

Therefore, at each Levenberg-Marquardt iteration corresponding to Equation (6.63), we must solve a linear system of the form

$$(J(\theta^t)^\top J(\theta^t) + \lambda^t \mathbf{I})\delta^t = J^\top(\theta^t)(\mathbf{x} - f(\theta^t)) \tag{6.67}$$

where δ^t is the increment we add to θ^t to obtain θ^{t+1}. These are also known as the **normal equations** for the problem.

If we treated Equation (6.67) as a generic linear system, we would waste a lot of computation since the Jacobian matrix J has many zero elements. That is, each reprojection $\hat{\mathbf{x}}_j$ only depends on one camera matrix and one scene point, so all of the derivatives $\frac{\partial f_j}{\partial \theta_k}$ will be zero for θ_k that don't involve the corresponding camera or point. Thus, while there may be hundreds of camera parameters, thousands of scene points, and tens of thousands of feature matches in a realistic bundle adjustment problem, the matrix J is very **sparse**. The matrix $J^\top J$ in Equation (6.67) will also be sparse (but less so). Figure 6.14 illustrates the structure of J and $J^\top J$ for a simple problem, to illustrate the sparsity pattern.

We can exploit this sparsity pattern to more efficiently solve Equation (6.67). From Figure 6.14b, we can see that Equation (6.67) can be written in terms of submatrices

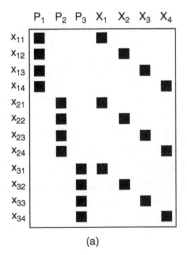

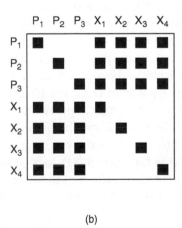

(a)   (b)

Figure 6.14. Suppose we have a bundle adjustment problem in which three cameras observe four points. (a) The structure of the Jacobian J is indicated by dark blocks for nonzero elements and white (empty) blocks for zero elements. The rows index feature observations while the columns index camera and scene parameters. (b) The structure of $J^\top J$ for the same problem. Both matrices are even sparser when all the features aren't seen by all the cameras (which is typical in a real matchmoving problem, see Figure 6.16).

involving the camera parameters and the scene points. That is, it has the form

$$\begin{bmatrix} J_{PP} & J_{PX} \\ J_{PX}^\top & J_{XX} \end{bmatrix} \begin{bmatrix} \delta_P \\ \delta_X \end{bmatrix} = \begin{bmatrix} b_P \\ b_X \end{bmatrix} \tag{6.68}$$

From Figure 6.14b, we know that J_{PP} and J_{XX} are both block-diagonal matrices; that is, each dark square in J_{PP} is a 10×10 matrix involving second derivatives with respect to the parameters of a single camera, while each dark square in J_{XX} is a 3×3 matrix involving second derivatives with respect to the parameters of a single scene point. Since a bundle adjustment problem usually involves many more scene points than cameras, we assume that J_{XX} is larger than J_{PP}.

Now we apply a trick based on the **Schur complement** of J_{XX}; we multiply both sides of Equation (6.68) by

$$\begin{bmatrix} \mathbf{I} & -J_{PX}J_{XX}^{-1} \\ \mathbf{0} & \mathbf{I} \end{bmatrix} \tag{6.69}$$

where $\mathbf{I}$ and $\mathbf{0}$ are appropriately sized identity and zero matrices, respectively. The result is:

$$\begin{bmatrix} J_{PP} - J_{PX}J_{XX}^{-1}J_{PX}^\top & \mathbf{0} \\ J_{PX}^\top & J_{XX} \end{bmatrix} \begin{bmatrix} \delta_P \\ \delta_X \end{bmatrix} = \begin{bmatrix} b_P - J_{PX}J_{XX}^{-1}b_X \\ b_X \end{bmatrix} \tag{6.70}$$

The top half of these equations corresponds to:

$$(J_{PP} - J_{PX}J_{XX}^{-1}J_{PX}^\top)\delta_P = b_P - J_{PX}J_{XX}^{-1}b_X \tag{6.71}$$

which is a relatively small, easily solved linear system for the camera update δ_P. Once we have obtained δ_P, we plug it into the bottom half of Equation (6.70) to obtain:

$$J_{XX}\delta_X = b_X - J_{PX}^\top \delta_P \tag{6.72}$$

which is also easily solved since J_{XX} is block diagonal with small blocks.

This approach is the basis of the sparse Levenberg-Marquardt bundle adjustment algorithm proposed by Lourakis and Argyros [305], which is widely used. However, the same authors [303] also observed that a sparse implementation of Powell's dog-leg algorithm might be an even more efficient optimization algorithm for bundle adjustment. Recently, Agarwal et al. [4] advocated the use of a preconditioned conjugate gradient algorithm for efficiently solving Equation (6.67), instead of using the Schur complement approach. This method is especially useful for the extensions in Section 6.6.2, where the matrix on the left-hand side of Equation (6.71) may be difficult to construct and not sparse. Steedly et al. [468] also discussed related issues for solving Equation (6.71), as well as methods for efficient incremental bundle adjustment as new information becomes available [467]. Triggs et al. [500] discuss further practical optimization issues for bundle adjustment.

6.5.4   An Example Result

Now, we illustrate an example matchmoving result on a real video sequence. Figure 6.15 illustrates several images from the sequence, which was obtained using by moving a handheld camera approximately 180° around a building. The video sequence was 383 frames long.

Figure 6.15. Example images from a video sequence obtained using by moving a handheld camera around a building.

To obtain the input for matchmoving, 19,780 unique features were automatically detected and tracked over the course of the camera motion. Since the camera is moving only slightly between frames, the tracker uses single-scale corners, which are automatically checked to make sure the matches are consistent with the projections of underlying 3D scene points. Figure 6.16 illustrates the presence of a random subset of 200 of the features in each frame; we can see that features constantly enter and leave the camera field of view, and that no single feature lasts very long. On the average, each feature track had a duration of 12 frames, and the maximum duration was 122 frames. An average of 616 tracked features appeared in each frame. Since Figure 6.16 corresponds to the sparsity pattern of the matrix $J_{PX}^{\top}$ in Equation (6.68), we can see that in practice, the matrix $J^{\top}J$ is much sparser than what Figure 6.14b suggests.

Visualizing the estimated camera path with respect to the estimated 3D points is critical for determining whether a matchmoving solution makes sense. Figure 6.17 illustrates a camera tracking result for the video sequence, in which the cameras are represented as red dots and the scene points are represented as blue dots. Each camera's principal axis is indicated by a red line. The camera track was obtained using a combination of the projective reconstruction, metric reconstruction, and sequential updating algorithms described in the previous sections. Even though the reconstructed scene is only sparsely sampled (i.e., we only obtain 3D estimates of points corresponding to tracked features), we get a strong sense of the environment and can be confident that the camera positions are well estimated.

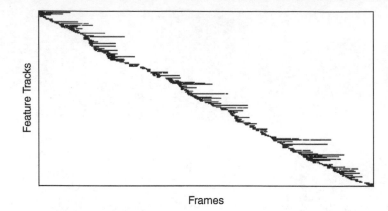

Figure 6.16. A random sample of 200 of the 19,780 features tracked over a 383-frame sequence. A dark box appears in the $(i, j)^{th}$ position if feature i was detected in frame j. We can see that features have various lifetimes and constantly enter and leave the field of view of the moving camera.

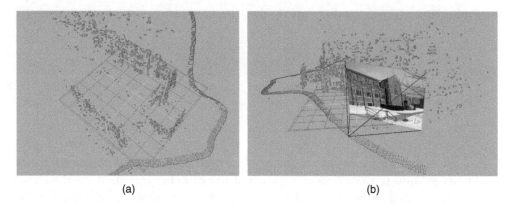

(a)   (b)

Figure 6.17. The camera tracking result obtained for the video sequence. (a) Top view, illustrating the camera track and rough geometry of the building. The ground plane was manually inserted based on the recovered scene points. (b) Side view, including the image and viewpoint for a selected camera.

The quality of camera tracking can also be verified by adding **test objects** into the reconstructed 3D coordinate system. For example, Figure 6.18 illustrates the same frames as Figure 6.15, with added synthetic geometric solids aligned to surfaces in the scene.[23] This is an extremely simple example of adding computer-generated imagery to a real video sequence using matchmoving. In a visual effects company, a match-move expert will typically fit a large number of planar surfaces to the scene to aid 3D animators and compositors further down the pipeline.

---

[23] Note that sometimes the objects "show through" physical surfaces in the scene in this simple picture. The added synthetic objects are simply rendered on top of the original images using the estimated camera perspectives. There is also no attempt to match the lighting of the scene, which is essential for realism.

Figure 6.18. Test objects rendered into the scene are used to verify the quality of a matchmove result. The new objects appear to "stick to" the scene at the correct locations. Feature points tracked through the sequence to obtain the matchmove result are also illustrated as yellow dots.

6.6 EXTENSIONS OF MATCHMOVING

Matchmoving is typically solved off-line (i.e., well after the data is collected) and applied to a sequence of closely spaced images. Here, we briefly discuss extensions in which each constraint is relaxed. First, we address real-time matchmoving, which could be used for adding computer-generated 3D elements to live video from a moving camera. Another application is live pre-visualization of how real video elements interact with computer-generated ones (e.g., augmented reality). The second extension is to structure from motion on large, unordered image datasets that don't come from a video sequence, such as Internet photo collections. We discuss new tools for camera localization by exploiting such large collections.

6.6.1 Real-Time Matchmoving

The sequential techniques for projective reconstruction discussed in Section 6.5.1.2 can be viewed as real-time techniques, in the sense that they are **causal**; that is, they only depend on image frames up to and including the current one. However, we still need to upgrade the projective reconstruction to a Euclidean one, which requires either foreknowledge of the camera calibration matrix at each point in time, or a

Euclidean reconstruction algorithm. In real-time applications, the camera calibration matrix is usually assumed to be known.

Lourakis and Argyros [304] discussed an approach for real-time matchmoving similar to the methods mentioned in Section 6.5.1.2. Instead of using fundamental matrices relating successive image pairs or trifocal tensors relating successive triples, they proposed to track a 3D plane through the video sequence. The plane can be specified as a dominant plane in the image (e.g., a wall or floor), or it can be a virtual plane created as the best fit to the set of feature locations detected in the first image pair. The projective transformation relating the plane's image in the current frame to its image in the first frame is estimated, corresponding to a choice of the free parameters in a camera matrix of the form of Equation (6.31). The cameras' known calibration matrices are then used to upgrade to a Euclidean reconstruction. Mouragnon et al. [340] proposed an algorithm for real-time matchmoving that applies a bundle adjustment only over the parameters of a few of the most recent cameras chosen as keyframes, to maintain computational tractability. Resectioning is applied to obtain camera matrices corresponding to images between keyframes.

The most common application of real-time camera tracking is not in visual effects but in robotics, where the problem is called **simultaneous location and mapping**, or **SLAM**. In this case, the camera is mounted to a mobile robot that tries to self-localize with respect to its environment; the problem is also known as estimating **ego-motion**. If the environment contains distinguishable landmarks with known 3D positions (e.g., ARTags), then the camera's location can be found by resectioning. If the environment is unknown, the robot simultaneously builds a map of its surroundings and its location and heading with respect to the map.

The SLAM problem in robotics differs from the structure from motion problem in computer vision in several important ways:

- The SLAM problem is almost always formulated in a probabilistic way. For example, a SLAM algorithm typically maintains an estimate of the camera's state (i.e., external parameters) as well as the uncertainty in this state (which could be represented by a covariance matrix). This uncertainty estimate comes from a probabilistic model of image formation and often incorporates a prior motion model for the camera (e.g., smooth trajectories are more likely).

- The SLAM problem often (but not always) assumes the camera moves along a plane, reducing the number of degrees of freedom from six external parameters to three (two translation parameters and a rotation angle).

- The SLAM problem is often more focused on accurately reconstructing an environment, which means that recognizing revisited features and closing loops plays a bigger role.

- Features for the SLAM problem often come from nonvisual (e.g., acoustic or range) sensors rather than from images alone. The advantage is that 3D positions of scene points can be directly measured by the robot, instead of obtaining just the heading (direction) to a scene point given by a camera.

Davison et al. [115] described one example of a real-time SLAM algorithm in which the camera can freely move through a 3D environment. They explicitly over-parameterized a calibrated camera by its 3D position, orientation, velocity, and angular velocity, and searched the environment for Shi-Tomasi features that are assumed to lie on planar surfaces. The world coordinate system and its scale are initialized by placing a calibration pattern with known dimensions in front of the camera before it begins to move. The unknown depths of features in the environment are estimated with greater accuracy as the camera views them from different positions. A smoothness prior that the camera moves with constant velocity and angular velocity is imposed to make the camera parameter estimation robust to video segments that contain few features. We discuss probabilistic methods for state estimation in more detail in the context of motion capture in Chapter 7. The book by Thrun et al. [489] is an excellent reference for probabilistic robot localization, though it does not emphasize vision-based SLAM.

While these techniques are promising, a key consideration is **drift** — that is, the accumulation of errors as the sequence gets longer and longer. It's more likely that production-quality real-time matchmoving is accomplished with a special-purpose hardware system, as discussed further in Section 6.8.

6.6.2 Large, Unordered Image Collections

With the advent of large Internet photo collections (e.g., user-contributed photos to Flickr), it has become possible to use structure from motion techniques to reconstruct the accurate 3D structure of a site and the corresponding camera positions using only the images resulting from a simple keyword query. For example, a user can download thousands of images resulting from the query "Statue of Liberty," and automatically obtain a fairly accurate 3D model of the landmark. However, this problem differs from matchmoving in that the input images no longer have a natural order. Additionally, the images may be taken in widely different positions and imaging conditions (e.g., zoom, exposure, weather, illumination), requiring wide baseline matching techniques of the type discussed in Chapter 4. Finally, the sheer number of the images makes bundle adjustment very challenging.

Snavely et al. [462] proposed a well-known system for the 3D exploration of Internet photo collections called **Photo Tourism**, which combined a large-scale structure from motion problem with an intuitive user interface to browse through images and camera positions. The system is especially effective for navigating images of tourist sites that have been acquired by thousands of users from different perspectives and in different viewing conditions. Rather than beginning with a projective reconstruction and upgrading it to a Euclidean one, Photo Tourism directly bundle adjusts over each camera's external parameters and unknown focal length. SIFT feature matches and tracks are estimated across the large image set, and fundamental matrices are estimated for each pair of images that contain a sufficient number of matches. To obtain an initial estimate for the bundle adjustment, the camera parameters for an image pair with a large baseline, a large number of matches, and known focal lengths are estimated. Then overlapping cameras and 3D points are incrementally added to the system using resectioning, triangulation, and bundle adjustment.

Both the feature matching and bundle adjustment steps are extremely time-consuming. Parallel processing, either on a multinode compute cluster [5] or a single PC with multiple GPUs [152], can be used to accelerate feature matching. The main trick is the careful assessment of which pairs of images are worth matching, to obtain clusters of images with similar appearance. Snavely et al. [463] described how to

speed up the bundle adjustment process by selecting a **skeletal set** of images —
that is, a much smaller subset of the large image collection that excludes redundant
images but still results in a complete and accurate scene reconstruction. After bundle adjusting over the skeletal set, the parameters of the cameras not in this set can
be obtained by resectioning. An optional full bundle adjustment over all the camera
parameters and scene points is then much faster than the method described in the
previous paragraph, since the initial estimate is already very good.

6.7   INDUSTRY PERSPECTIVES

Doug Roble, creative director of software, and Som Shankar, integration supervisor of
Digital Domain, in Venice, California discuss the role of matchmoving on a movie set.
In 1999, Doug Roble won a Scientific and Technical Achievement Academy Award for
writing Digital Domain's in-house 3D tracking/scene reconstruction program, called
"Track."

RJR: How do you estimate the lens distortion of a movie camera?

Shankar: To undistort real movie camera lenses on feature films, we shoot a known
square grid with each camera setup and lens, and process those grids to create the
mapping between distorted and ideal coordinates. Sometimes we don't even use a
parametric model for the lens; we just use the nonparametric mapping obtained from
the grid.

Part of the reason is that movie lenses do weird things. Even though two of the
same lenses from the same manufacturer are supposed to have exactly the same
distortion, there are tiny anomalies between those lenses because they're still pieces
of glass. Anamorphic lenses, which stretch a widescreen image vertically to cover
the entire recorded film frame, are even more complicated since they're oval. Even
the lenses on new high-end digital cameras behave very interestingly; the images are
huge but the quality falls off toward the edges since you're not really meant to see
image through those parts of the lenses.

For final movie frames, we never undistort the original images. In our 3D compositing pipeline, we create all of our effects over the "flat," undistorted version of
the plate, and then at the very end use the estimated lens distortion for that shot to
re-distort our 3D elements to match the original plate.

RJR: What kind of surveying do you do on set to help with matchmoving?

Shankar: We're often invited to a built set that will be filmed from different angles
for a whole sequence of shots. Our team goes to the set with a Leica total station (see
Chapter 8) — it's the same kind of device you see surveyors using on roadsides and
construction sites. We survey a sparse set of important locations in the room, such as
corners of objects, and record their 3D coordinates with this very precise device. We
also take a lot of photographs of the set, and then using our in-house software, Track,
we line that survey up to those photographs. It's also becoming much more common
to scan entire sets with LiDAR, which gives us a much denser sampling of 3D points
(see Section 8.1).

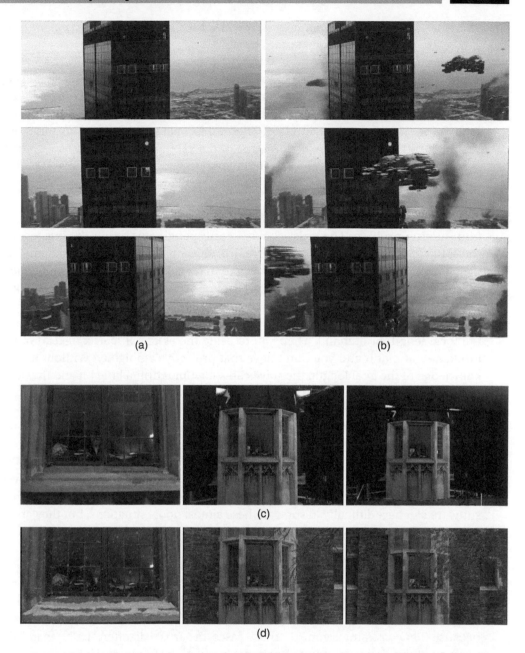

(a)   (b)

(c)

(d)

Figure 6.19. (a,b) Matchmoving is the basic tool for inserting realistic visual effects into background plates. In this example from *Transformers: Dark of the Moon*, spaceships fly around the building and land on its right side. (c,d) Matchmoving is also commonly used for set extension. In this example from *A Beautiful Mind*, only a small piece of the set was built on a soundstage, and the rest of the building was digitally generated. *Transformers: Dark of the Moon* ©2011 Paramount Pictures. All Rights Reserved. *A Beautiful Mind* ©2001 Universal Studios and DW Studios L.L.C. All Rights Reserved. Courtesy of Universal Studios Licensing LLC.

Many companies do pure photogrammetry for set reconstruction — they just take a lot of pictures, and use structure from motion tools to determine 3D points in the scene. You can get a lot done that way, but spatial accuracy is often a problem.

RJR: How do you use resectioning and structure from motion to get the camera track and 3D positions of 2D features in the images?

Roble: An artist starts with the on-set survey and the plates for a given shot. They then manually connect up the 3D points that were surveyed with the corresponding 2D points on the image. We initialize the resectioning problem with the Direct Linear Transform, which gets us really close. Then we formulate a nonlinear cost function based on the weighted reprojection error in the 2D image plane and use gradient descent to find the optimal camera parameters. Using weights on each 2D-3D correspondence gives the artist a little bit more control about where they want the error to end up. That's the essence of Track.

When we don't have an accurate 3D survey, it's basically an iterative structure from motion problem. The artist chooses corresponding points in the images. We can initially estimate the fundamental matrix for each pair of images and then back the camera matrices out. Then we go back to that gradient descent algorithm where we're solving for the rotation and translation parameters of the camera and the depths of the feature points at the same time.

As with all structure from motion algorithms, it works a lot better if you know the focal length beforehand. Then you're using the essential matrix instead of the fundamental matrix and you don't have that projective ambiguity. Without a good knowledge of the focal length, the solve can sometimes drift a little bit and the artist may need to put in more constraints, for example that two 3D lines are known to come together at a right angle.

You can never really tell what the camera is going to be doing. Sometimes the director will say, "This is a nodal move — just camera rotation — so you don't have to worry about the camera track." Then we'll look at it and find out that actually, it's not quite nodal, the camera's moving just a little bit, and that needs to be solved for in order to get CGI elements to stick to the scene. We've found that off-the-shelf software can have difficulty in some of these almost nodal situations, but they aren't a problem for Track as long as we have enough precision in our 3D set survey and 2D point locations.

Another important issue is that, in a feature film, the cameras are often moving like crazy, and points that you're tracking will move in and out of the frame. Since our artists aren't selecting and tracking a ton of points in each frame, when a point leaves the frame, you're basically releasing a constraint, and the camera track will do a wiggle because that constraint is gone. In those cases, the artist will often "hallucinate" the position of the 2D feature point after it moves out of the frame, and lower the weight on that point gradually to prevent that wiggle.

Most smaller visual effects houses use commercial software such as *boujou* to do camera tracking. Michael Capton, 3D supervisor at LOOK Effects in Los Angeles, CA, discusses matchmoving in this context.

RJR: Can you talk about the early days of matchmoving?

Capton: Matchmoving has always been a visual effects problem, anytime you have CG objects. In the early days they shot a lot more plates that were just static, so you didn't have to worry about camera tracking as long as you got the perspective right.

When I first started in the industry, they didn't have these automatic camera tracking programs. You had to do it by hand, starting with the background plate, and just manually put the camera in by eye, trying to match the motion of different features. What now takes a simple program an hour to do would take weeks.

I remember an old commercial I worked on to advertise an SUV. The idea was to show the SUV in place of a lifeboat on a cruise ship, to get across the idea that it was so safe. They shot the *Queen Mary* with a fairly long lens, using a passing shot to make it look like it was traveling through the ocean. That was a really long shot, like 900 frames. It took three or four weeks to do a solid matchmove to put that SUV into the plate and make it not move or shake. I was lucky enough to find a book about the ship that had actual drawings of the rigging that held the lifeboats in place, which helped a lot in figuring out the real shape, size, and dimensions of things.

It was very tedious; you'd position the camera in space in the first frame, rough in the shot and go twenty frames more, and then try to position the camera in space again, and do that over the entire shot. Then you'd go back and fill in the moments in between and the moments in between until the track was good enough. Depending on how bad the camera move is, you might be doing it frame by frame through the whole thing. Often you'd get to a point doing it by eye and then notice that it wasn't working — you were slowly falling off to one side or the camera was doing something it shouldn't have, and you had to throw that out and start again. It was terrible!

Nowadays, you'd be able to run that kind of shot through a piece of commercial software and it would give you, if not an entirely solid track, something good enough that you could tweak a little bit by hand to get the final result. On the other hand, that early tedious experience is beneficial to me, since when the commercial software doesn't work or I need to improve its result, I have that background of being trained to do it by eye. Some other people have only ever known commercial software, and if it doesn't track something they're like, "Well, I can't do anything." No, you can try and do it by eye!

RJR: Can you describe how an artist interacts with a matchmoving program to track a difficult shot?

Capton: These days, it's great that there are a variety of commercial software packages for camera tracking. There's *boujou, PFTrack, SynthEyes*, and several more. I've found that if one program doesn't work on a shot, sometimes I'll take it into another program and for whatever reason that one is able to track it. Another common trick on a difficult shot is reversing it in time and feeding it back into the program — tracking the shot backward. Over the years, you get a sense of the best way to approach a shot. For example, if the shot starts out with a whip pan and ends on something more stable, you know your program may fail since it won't know what feature points to pick until it gets to the very end, so you reverse the shot to start off with solid points. You get accustomed to what the program likes and dislikes and learn to work with it.

It's definitely a million times better than doing it by hand, but as far as the percentage of shots that track well right out of the gate, without any user interaction, it's surprisingly inconsistent. Some shots I think oh, this'll be easy, like a day of my time with an hour of tracking, and it turns out I'll have to tweak the software for a day and a half just to track the shot. And some shots, I think, wow, this is going to be really hard and I send it through the autotracker and it's like click, I'm done. A lot of it has to do with the amount of parallax going on in the shot, how deep the distance is — sometimes if the shot is really shallow the software gets confused.

RJR: Once you get the camera track, are the 3D point locations that were simultaneously estimated useful?

Capton: Sometimes. We worked on the visual effects for the last season of *Lost*. There were a couple of shots in the final episode where a cliffside was supposed to be crumbling and falling away. Based on the camera track we had a good idea of the 3D locations of a sparse set of points on the cliffside. Those enabled us to build a simple 3D model, so we could create small rocks that appeared to bounce off the nooks and crannies of that cliff all the way down. We probably could have done that by eye, but having a sparse point cloud to base it on definitely helped, instead of having to guess how far away the cliff was from the camera. When the autotracker gives you a decent point cloud, it's almost like a poor man's LiDAR scan.

As another example, say we tracked a room and need to create an artificial semi-reflective object in the middle of it. We could use the 3D points from the autotracker to build really simple geometry to mimic the room, project the plate back onto the geometry, and use that to create reflections onto the object. It's kind of a cheat to create a sense of the environment when we don't have any other reference information about the scene.

6.8   NOTES AND EXTENSIONS

Burtch [79] summarized the history of photogrammetry from da Vinci up to the digital age. A brief historical overview also appears at the end of Triggs et al. [500]. In particular, Duane Brown, working for the U.S. Air Force in the 1950s, is widely credited with developing the theory of bundle adjustment [69] as well as many techniques for camera calibration. Kraus's textbook [256] covers modern digital photogrammetric techniques using image and range data.

As mentioned previously, the books by Hartley and Zisserman [188] and Faugeras and Luong [137] are excellent references on the theory of projective geometry as it relates to computer vision. Faugeras and Luong's book [137] is oriented more toward the deep theory of projective geometry, and has several useful tables of invariants at different levels of reconstruction and degrees of freedom in different problems. Hartley and Zisserman's book [188] offers more practical advice for approaching real-world multi-view geometry problems, including many easy to follow algorithms and notes on implementation. All four of the authors have written many landmark articles on issues related to structure from motion, summarized conveniently in these books.

An alternate approach to the plane-based calibration method in Section 6.3.2 is to take a single picture of a **calibration device** containing multiple squares in different orientations. Using the corners of each square to estimate a different projective transformation is mathematically equivalent to imaging a single square in different orientations in different images. However, using a calibration device may be more awkward than simply imaging a single plane in different positions. The camera calibration toolbox provided by Bouguet (http://www.vision.caltech.edu/bouguetj/calib_doc/) is often used to automate the process. Other possibilities for internal parameter estimation include using information about known angles and length ratios in a real scene (e.g., [282]), or reasoning about the vanishing points of parallel lines such as the edges of buildings (e.g., [81, 283]).

As mentioned in Section 6.3.2, the matrix $\omega = (KK^\top)^{-1}$ is also called the **image of the absolute conic**. While our derivation of ω was entirely algebraic, it also has an important geometric interpretation. That is, the set of points in the image plane defined by the second-degree equation $[x, y, 1]\omega[x, y, 1]^\top = 0$ is the projection of a special set of points in the environment called the absolute conic, defined in homogeneous world coordinates by the $[X, Y, Z, W]^\top$ that satisfy $X^2 + Y^2 + Z^2 = 0$ and $W = 0$. This conic lies on the plane at infinity, and is invariant under any similarity transform of the world coordinates. Unfortunately, while they are extremely useful for camera calibration, both the absolute conic and its image are purely imaginary constructs and cannot be visualized. An alternate classical method for camera self-calibration, not discussed here, is based on the **Kruppa equations** (e.g., [308]), which are especially suitable when only two views are available.

In addition to the absolute conic and similar constructs, there are many other important issues in projective geometry that we have omitted in this chapter for space and readability. For example, we only alluded briefly to the **trifocal tensor** [439], an analogue to the fundamental matrix that relates point and line correspondences in triples of views. The concept of an **affine reconstruction** is also frequently used as an intermediate stage when upgrading a projective reconstruction to a Euclidean one. To get a better intuition for these projective geometry concepts, see the books mentioned previously [137, 188].

Unfortunately, the problem of choosing a good gauge for bundle adjustment, as mentioned in Section 6.5.3.1, is tricky. Setting the first camera to the canonical form has the disadvantage of biasing the result; that is, we would get a different solution to the minimization problem if we renumbered the cameras. Another troubling problem is that assessing the quality of a solution to bundle adjustment (for example, understanding how uncertainty in the estimated feature locations propagates to uncertainty in the estimated locations of the 3D points) seems to depend on the gauge. McLauchlan [321] and Morris et al. [337, 338] thoroughly discuss these issues.

Solving the structure from motion problem lies at the core of the matchmoving software used for visual effects production in movies. However, as discussed in Section 6.7, obtaining a good matchmove for difficult sequences is a "black art" and requires an expert's touch. For example, the input video may contain significant motion blur, soft focus, or interlacing, which require preprocessing in the best case and manual feature tracking in the worst case. The matchmover (aided by software) must detect segments with low motion and little parallax that correspond to pure rotations (called **nodal pans**); in this case, it may be necessary to add "helper frames" to the sequence to introduce parallax and add stability to the solution. The match-mover also must incorporate on-set measurements whenever they are available, such as the height of the camera or 3D locations of surveyed points, and be able to assess what information should be collected while a shot is being acquired to simplify the camera tracking solution. The book by Dobbert [122] is an excellent reference on the practical aspects of matchmoving for the visual effects industry.

There are now several software packages for production-quality camera match-moving based on the algorithms discussed in this chapter. These include *boujou* (sold by Vicon), *PFTrack* (sold by The Pixel Farm), *Matchmover* (sold by Autodesk), *SynthEyes* (sold by Andersson Technologies), and the freeware packages *Voodoo* (created at the University of Hannover) and *Bundler* (created at the University of Washington).

It is possible to relax the assumption that the scene observed by the cameras is rigid (i.e., static) in all views. For example, Bregler et al. [66] extended a factorization approach to allow the observed scene points to be an unknown linear combination of unknown basis shapes. The camera pose, basis shapes, and linear coefficients are obtained by successively factoring a measurement matrix similar to Equation (6.38), assuming the camera is orthographic. Torresani et al. [496] proposed a probabilistic approach to the same problem, assuming that shapes are drawn from a Gaussian probability distribution with unknown parameters. These methods are only appropriate when a single deformable object (e.g., a face) dominates the scene. We will address similar issues in more detail in the next chapter.

We mentioned the concepts of image-based video stabilization and re-cinematography in Section 5.10. If we apply matchmoving to an image sequence, we can then smooth the camera path in 3D to remove translational and rotational jitter [296], re-rendering the sequence to make it more pleasing. Camera localization techniques can also help automate **rephotography**, the attempt to exactly duplicate the vantage point of a historical photo in modern day [24], as well as algorithms to automatically infer the order in which historical photos were taken [428].

While we focused exclusively on image-based methods for camera tracking in this chapter, the same problem can also be solved with high precision by several additional means. Welch and Foxlin [542] give a good survey of many different real-time camera tracking systems. These systems can be based on mechanical sensing (e.g., using potentiometers or shaft encoders), inertial sensing (e.g., gyroscopes and accelerometers), acoustic sensing (e.g., ultrasonic ranging), magnetic sensing (common in head-mounted displays), and optical sensing (e.g., active lighting using visible or infrared LEDs). We will discuss several of these technologies in the context of motion capture in the next chapter.

6.9   HOMEWORK PROBLEMS

6.1   Find the values of d_x and d_y in Equation (6.2) for a consumer digital camera.

6.2   Consider a 4096×2160 digital image taken using a camera with principal point at the center (i.e., $x_0 = 2048, y_0 = 1080$) and pixels that are physically 6.7μm square. Suppose the lens distortion parameters for the camera are $\kappa_1 = 10^{-3}, \kappa_2 = 0$. What is the observed (distorted) position of a pixel whose ideal projection is at $(x, y) = (3000, 200)$?

6.3 Show that the world-to-camera coordinate transformation in Equation (6.8) can also be represented in terms of the camera center C by:

$$\begin{bmatrix} X_c \\ Y_c \\ Z_c \end{bmatrix} = R\left(\begin{bmatrix} X \\ Y \\ Z \end{bmatrix} - C \right) \tag{6.73}$$

Hence, show that $t = -RC$.

6.4 Now that we have defined the process of image formation, we can verify the validity of the view interpolation process from Section 5.8. That is, suppose that two cameras are given by

$$P = \begin{bmatrix} f & 0 & 0 & 0 \\ 0 & f & 0 & 0 \\ 0 & 0 & 1 & 0 \end{bmatrix} \qquad P' = \begin{bmatrix} f' & 0 & 0 & -f'C_X \\ 0 & f' & 0 & -f'C_Y \\ 0 & 0 & 1 & 0 \end{bmatrix} \tag{6.74}$$

These correspond to two cameras whose centers are on the world plane $Z = 0$ and whose image planes are parallel to this plane (rectified images are a special case of this situation).

a) If $\mathbf{X} = [X, Y, Z, 1]^\top$ is the homogeneous coordinate of an arbitrary scene point and $\mathbf{x}$ and $\mathbf{x}'$ are the homogeneous coordinates of its projections in the resulting images, show that for any fixed value of $s \in [0, 1]$,

$$(1 - s)\mathbf{x} + s\mathbf{x}' \sim P_s\mathbf{X} \tag{6.75}$$

where P_s is a new camera matrix given by $(1 - s)P + sP'$. That is, linearly interpolating image correspondences produces a physically correct result corresponding to projecting the scene using a new camera.

b) Show that the image plane of P_s is also parallel to $Z = 0$, that the camera is centered at $(sC_X, sC_Y, 0)$, and that it has focal length $(1 - s)f + sf'$. Thus, P_s is "in between" the two original cameras.

6.5 Show that:
a) The cross-product of two 3D vectors in the same direction is 0.
b) The cross-product of the vectors on the left- and right-hand sides of Equation (6.12) produces three linear equations in the elements of P, two of which are given by Equation (6.14).
c) The unused linear equation is linearly dependent on the other two.

6.6 Determine K, R, and t for the camera matrix given by

$$P = \begin{bmatrix} -1.2051 & -1.0028 & -1.9474 & -5 \\ -1.0056 & 0.9363 & 1.1671 & 40 \\ -0.1037 & 0.0583 & -0.9929 & -10 \end{bmatrix} \tag{6.76}$$

6.7 Determine the 2×5 linear system for the elements of ω implied by one planar projective transformation (i.e., determine A_i in Equation (6.25) as a function of the elements of H_i).

6.8 Show how Equation (6.25) can be simplified (that is, the estimation can be taken over fewer parameters) if either:
a) the aspect ratio α_y/α_x is known, or
b) the principal point is known.

6.9   Show how the rotation and translation parameters r_1^i, r_2^i, r_3^i, t^i in Equation (6.20) corresponding to the camera position for each view of the stationary plane can be obtained once the camera is calibrated (i.e., K and H_i are known). What is a possible problem with this technique when dealing with noisy data?

6.10   In this problem, we'll derive the form of the fundamental matrix given in Equation (6.29). Remember that the equation of the epipolar line in the second image for a fixed (x, y) in the first image is given by Equation (5.34):

$$\begin{bmatrix} x' \\ y' \\ 1 \end{bmatrix}^\top \left(F \begin{bmatrix} x \\ y \\ 1 \end{bmatrix} \right) = 0 \qquad (6.77)$$

a)   To determine a line in an image, we must know two points on it. Verify that the parameters of a line ℓ connecting two points in homogeneous coordinates given by $[x, y, 1]^\top$ and $[x', y', 1]^\top$ are given by $\ell = [x, y, 1]^\top \times [x', y', 1]^\top$, where $\times$ denotes the cross product of the vectors.

b)   Verify that for two vectors t and v in $\mathbb{R}^3$, $t \times v = [t]_\times v$, where

$$[t]_\times = \begin{bmatrix} 0 & -t_3 & t_2 \\ t_3 & 0 & -t_1 \\ -t_2 & t_1 & 0 \end{bmatrix} \qquad (6.78)$$

c)   Verify that mathematically, the point in homogeneous world coordinates given by $\begin{bmatrix} K^{-1} \begin{bmatrix} x \\ y \\ 1 \end{bmatrix} \\ 0 \end{bmatrix}$ projects to (x, y) in the first image. This point corresponds to traveling infinitely far along the ray from the first camera center through (x, y) on the image plane.

d)   Show that the homogeneous image coordinates of the projection of this world point in the second image are given by $K'RK^{-1}[x, y, 1]^\top$.

e)   Now we know two points on the epipolar line: the epipole in the second image (since all epipolar lines intersect at the epipole) and the point in (d). Thus, conclude from parts (a) and (b) that

$$F = [K't]_\times K'RK^{-1} \qquad (6.79)$$

6.11   Consider the similarity transformation of world coordinates given by the 4×4 homogeneous matrix

$$H = \begin{bmatrix} R & t \\ 0 & \lambda \end{bmatrix} \qquad (6.80)$$

a)   Determine the effects of this similarity transformation on a camera matrix P and a scene point $\mathbf{X}$ — that is, compute $\hat{P}$ and $\hat{\mathbf{X}}$ in the new coordinate system.

b) Show that the image projections are unchanged by this similarity transformation — that is, that $\mathbf{x} \sim P\mathbf{X} \sim \hat{P}\hat{\mathbf{X}}$. (Note: this is just a special case of Equation (6.30)).

6.12 Assuming a calibrated stereo rig in the canonical form of Equation (6.32), determine the solution to the triangulation problem for a correspondence between the points (x,y) in the first image and (x',y') in the second image implied by Figure 6.9. Hint: the 3D location of the midpoint can be computed as the solution to a simple linear least-squares problem.

6.13 Determine P and P' in the canonical form of Equation (6.31) if the fundamental matrix for an image pair is given by

$$F = \begin{bmatrix} 1.7699 \times 10^{-6} & 1.0889 \times 10^{-5} & -1.6599 \times 10^{-2} \\ -3.3788 \times 10^{-6} & 7.1503 \times 10^{-10} & 8.0432 \times 10^{-4} \\ 1.4372 \times 10^{-2} & -2.9790 \times 10^{-3} & 1 \end{bmatrix} \qquad (6.81)$$

6.14 Determine the transformations that must be applied to the estimated $\{P_i\}$ and $\{\mathbf{X}_j\}$ in the Sturm-Triggs projective factorization algorithm to account for initially normalizing the image feature locations by appropriate similarity transformations T_i.

6.15 Provide a sketch to show that if we only know the fundamental matrices F_{12}, F_{13}, F_{23} relating three views, then knowing the projections $\mathbf{x}_1$ and $\mathbf{x}_2$ of a point $\mathbf{X}$ in the first and second images entirely determines its projection $\mathbf{x}_3$ in the third view. This is one of several three-view properties encapsulated by the **trifocal tensor**.

6.16 Suppose that we estimate the fundmental matrix F_{12} between images 1 and 2 and then use it to determine P_1 and P_2 in canonical form. That is, $P_1 = [\mathbf{I}_{3 \times 3} \mid \mathbf{0}_{3 \times 1}]$ and $P_2 = [A_2 \mid a_2]$. Then we estimate the fundmental matrix F_{23} between images 2 and 3 and then use it to determine P_2 and P_3 in canonical form. That is, $P_2 = [\mathbf{I}_{3 \times 3} \mid \mathbf{0}_{3 \times 1}]$ and $P_3 = [A_3 \mid a_3]$. It might seem like we can obtain P_1, P_2, and P_3 in a consistent projective frame based on

$$P_1 = [\mathbf{I}_{3 \times 3} \mid \mathbf{0}_{3 \times 1}] \qquad P_2 = [A_2 \mid a_2] \qquad P_3 = [A_3 \mid a_3] \begin{bmatrix} A_2 & a_2 \\ \mathbf{0}_{3 \times 1}^\top & 1 \end{bmatrix} \qquad (6.82)$$

and continue onward through the sequence. What's the problem with this approach? (Again, this is an issue that can be addressed with the trifocal tensor; see, e.g., [145].)

6.17 Verify that combining Equations (6.42)–(6.44) results in the form of H given by Equation (6.45).

6.18 Verify the steps of Equation (6.48) that relate ω_i to Q. Hint: first show that $(A_i - a_i v^\top) K_1 = K_i R_i$. Then note that $\omega_i^{-1} = (K_i R_i)(K_i R_i)^\top$ since R_i is a rotation matrix.

6.19 Explicitly determine the first row of the 4×5 linear system for the elements of Q in terms of the elements of P_i corresponding to Equation (6.51).

6.20 Show that the matrix Q in Equation (6.48) is related to the projective-to-Euclidean upgrade matrix H by

$$Q = H \begin{bmatrix} \mathbf{I}_{3\times3} & \mathbf{0}_{3\times1} \\ \mathbf{0}_{3\times1}^{\top} & 0 \end{bmatrix} H^{\top}$$

How can H be recovered once Q is estimated?

6.21 While the Rodrigues formula in Equation (6.58) tells us how to generate R_i given r_i, we also need to know the inverse operation. Show that:

$$R_i r_i = r_i \tag{6.83}$$

$$2\cos(\|r_i\|) = \text{trace}(R) - 1 \tag{6.84}$$

$$2\,\text{sinc}(\|r_i\|)r_i = (R_{32} - R_{23}, R_{13} - R_{31}, R_{21} - R_{12})^{\top} \tag{6.85}$$

That is, Equation (6.83) shows that r_i is an eigenvector of R_i corresponding to a unit eigenvalue, which tells us its direction. The correct magnitude $\|r_i\|$ can be determined from Equations (6.84)–(6.85) using a two-argument arctangent function.

6.22 Show that solving Equation (6.72) is equivalent to solving a series of n independent 3×3 systems, where n is the number of scene points in the bundle adjustment problem.

7 Motion Capture

Motion capture (often abbreviated as **mocap**) is probably the application of computer vision to visual effects most familiar to the average filmgoer. As illustrated in Figure 7.1, motion capture uses several synchronized cameras to track the motion of special **markers** carefully placed on the body of a performer. The images of each marker are triangulated and processed to obtain a time series of 3D positions. These positions are used to infer the time-varying positions and angles of the joints of an underlying skeleton, which can ultimately help animate a digital character that has the same mannerisms as the performer. While the Gollum character from the *Lord of the Rings* trilogy launched motion capture into the public consciousness, the technology already had many years of use in the visual effects industry (e.g., to animate synthetic passengers in wide shots for *Titanic*). Today, motion capture is almost taken for granted as a tool to help map an actor's performance onto a digital character, and has achieved great success in recent films like *Avatar*.[1]

In addition to creating computer-generated characters for feature films, motion capture is pervasive in the video game industry, especially for sports and action games. The distinctive mannerisms of golf and football players, martial artists, and soldiers are recorded by video game developers and strung together in real time by game engines to create dynamic, reactive character animations. In non-entertainment contexts, motion capture is used in orthopedics applications to analyze a patient's joint motion over the course of treatment, and in sports medicine applications to improve an athlete's performance.

Our focus in this chapter is on the computer vision aspects of motion capture, from acquiring the data to fitting it to a 3D skeleton. While we discuss how to string different motion capture sequences together with fluid transitions, we stop short of extensively modifying the motion for production-quality computer animation. The latter problem involves application-specific decisions — both technical and artistic — outside this chapter's scope. Motion capture data is routinely modified by animators, both in small and large part, in order to achieve a director's vision for a computer-generated character or scene. While the popular perception may be that a motion capture actor's performance is mapped directly onto a digital character without modification, this is rarely the case.

---

[1] The end-to-end process from suiting up a performer to animating a character is sometimes called **performance capture**. The term **motion capture** generally refers to the specific technology of 3D marker acquisition, independent of its subsequent use.

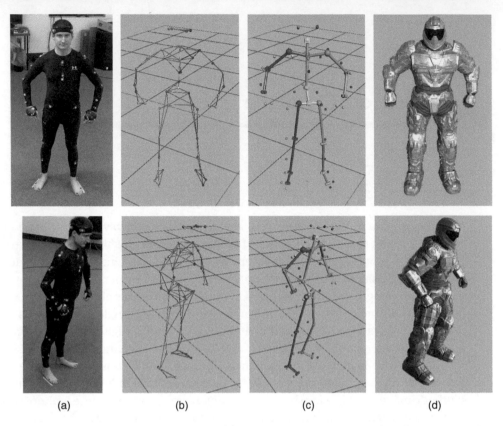

(a)   (b)   (c)   (d)

Figure 7.1. The motion capture problem. (a) A performer wearing a suit of markers is imaged by several calibrated cameras. (b) The markers are detected and triangulated to determine their 3D positions. (c) The markers are fit to a skeleton that can help to drive (d) a 3D animated character.

We begin by describing a typical motion capture environment, including the acquisition hardware and marker configuration for a human body (Section 7.1). We then discuss the processing of the cameras' images to produce 3D time-varying locations of each marker, including simple heuristics for estimating the positions of missing markers (Section 7.2). Next, we describe how to parameterize the **pose** of a human with the relative joint angles of an articulated skeleton (Section 7.3). We address the transformation from the world coordinate system of the 3D markers to the parameters of this skeleton by solving a nonlinear optimization problem based on **inverse kinematics** (Section 7.4).

We often want to stitch separate captured motions together or make minor alterations to a motion while preserving its unique details. We discuss such general problems of **motion editing** in Section 7.5. While the focus of the chapter is on motion capture for the entire human body, we briefly discuss the unique challenges of facial motion capture in Section 7.6.

Finally, we introduce the problem of **markerless motion capture** — that is, the estimation of human pose from natural video, without any special clothing or markers (Section 7.7). This area of computer vision has a massive literature; researchers have been interested in finding humans in images and tracking them through video for decades. However, markerless motion capture (at least for entire bodies) is rarely used for production-quality animation since it is generally less accurate than markered techniques. We give an overall formulation of the problem and review methods based on image silhouettes and visual hulls. This general approach is strongly related to the techniques for 3D data acquisition discussed in more detail in Chapter 8.

7.1   THE MOTION CAPTURE ENVIRONMENT

Today, there are two primary types of production-quality motion capture technology. The first approach is **magnetic**: the performer wears a suit instrumented with small receivers that can accurately determine their three-dimensional position and orientation with respect to an external electromagnetic field. The second approach is **optical**: in this case, the performer's suit is fitted with special markers whose three-dimensional position is inferred by an array of surrounding cameras. While magnetic motion capture systems are relatively inexpensive and each receiver is always "visible," they are sensitive to metal in their environment (commonly found in soundstage walls and computer monitors), which can degrade the tracking output. Earlier magnetic systems also required wires and cables snaking around the performer and a physical attachment to a computer, which can impede natural motion.[2]

In this chapter, we focus exclusively on optical motion capture, exemplified by the industry-standard systems produced by Vicon Motion Systems. The performance to be recorded takes place in a large room containing a defined **capture volume**, a space several meters in each dimension. The capture volume is surrounded by between six and fifty cameras, each of which is circled by a strobe light of infrared LEDs, as illustrated in Figure 7.2. These LEDs strongly illuminate the capture volume with light not visible to the human eye. The cameras are all temporally synchronized with each other and with the strobe lights.

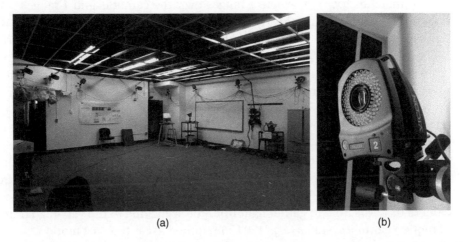

(a)   (b)

Figure 7.2. (a) A typical motion capture volume. (b) A motion capture camera surrounded by infrared LEDs.

---

[2] Other possibilities for motion capture include inertial systems based on gyroscopes and accelerometers, or exoskeletons that directly measure joint angles. Neither are commonly used to collect data for animation and visual effects.

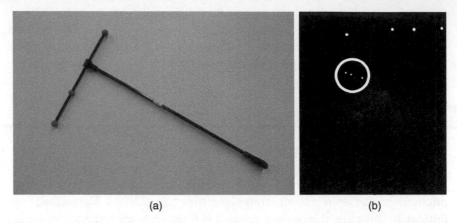

(a)   (b)

Figure 7.3. (a) A calibration device used to precisely spatially calibrate cameras for motion capture. (b) An image of the calibration device (circled) from one of the infrared cameras, showing the highly retro-reflective markers. The other bright spots in the image are the infrared strobe lights from different cameras in the capture volume.

The camera system is precisely spatially calibrated before each capture session using a special device, as illustrated in Figure 7.3a. This device is usually a rigid wand with several markers at measured intervals along its length. As the wand is moved through the capture volume and observed by the surrounding cameras, it generates feature matches across all the images. As illustrated in Figure 7.3b, finding and tracking the markers on the device is an easy image processing problem since under infrared light they appear as bright dots on a dark background. Therefore, in each camera at each point in time, we can uniquely identify several image feature points (which can be disambiguated due to the uneven spacing of the markers). Collecting all the device observations from each camera together gives a set of image feature matches $\{(x_{ij}, y_{ij})\}$ where i ranges over the cameras and j ranges over the unknown 3D device marker locations. This collection of feature matches provides the input for a multicamera calibration problem that can be solved exactly as described in Section 6.5. The known physical distance between the markers is used to recover the scale ambiguity resulting from Euclidean reconstruction. The reconstruction errors obtained with this controlled procedure are very low — less than a millimeter.

The performer wears a tightly fitting body suit with spherical **markers** carefully attached near joints of his or her body. The markers range from five to thirty mm in diameter, and are **retro-reflective**, meaning that they strongly reflect light rays along the vector pointing directly back at the light source.[3] Therefore, the markers are easy to distinguish in each camera's infrared image, since they appear to be extremely bright, as illustrated in Figure 7.4. The retro-reflectivity is also important since each camera has little time to gather light from the scene due to the very high frame rate of motion capture systems (e.g., 120 Hz) required to capture fast motion.[4]

---

[3] This phenomenon is similar to a bicycle reflector or a cat's eye, and is typified by 3M's Scotchlite material.

[4] An alternate optical approach gaining in popularity is the use of active-lighting markers, such as small red LEDs that encode a unique identifier by blinking at high speeds, as in the systems produced by PhaseSpace, Inc.

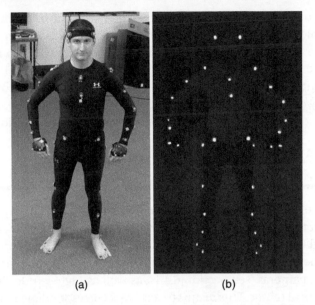

(a)   (b)

Figure 7.4. (a) A visible-spectrum image of markers on a performer. (b) An aligned infrared image, showing that the retro-reflective markers appear as extremely bright dots on a dark background.

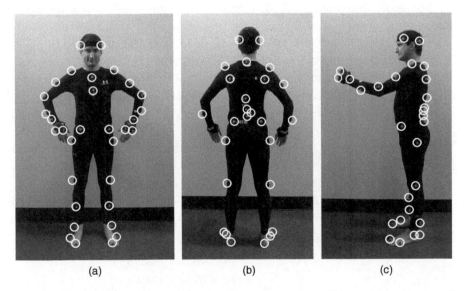

(a)   (b)   (c)

Figure 7.5. An example of marker placement for motion capture. This configuration uses forty-five markers.

The performer's motion capture suit is typically outfitted with between thirty and fifty markers. Motion capture technicians use principles from biomechanics to carefully and repeatably place markers on the performer's joints to give the most useful information about the motion of his or her underlying skeleton. For this reason, the motion capture suit must be tight-fitting, and the markers placed so that they don't slide around the joints. In some cases, markers are directly attached to the skin. Figure 7.5 illustrates a standard configuration for marker placement, designed so that groups of markers work together to define the position and rotation of joints. For example, the four markers on the front and back waist form a quadrilateral that defines the motion of the pelvis. We'll discuss the relationship between the markers and the underlying skeleton in more detail in Section 7.4. It's also common to add additional redundant markers to help the capture system cope with occlusions, or to easily distinguish one performer from another. Menache [323] gives a detailed discussion of marker placement and its biomechanical motivation.

7.2   MARKER ACQUISITION AND CLEANUP

The first problem is to determine the three-dimensional locations of the markers from their projections in the cameras' images. This may seem difficult since all the markers in a typical motion capture setup look exactly the same. However, since the camera array has been precisely calibrated, we can compute the epipolar geometry between any pair of cameras (see Section 6.4.1), as well as higher-order image relationships like the trifocal tensor. This means that correct correspondences are generally easy to obtain, since there are only tens of markers visible in each image and it's unlikely that incorrect matches will be consistent with the epipolar geometry between multiple pairs of images.

Therefore, the problem of 3D marker estimation is one of **triangulation**, as discussed in Section 6.4.2. More precisely, let's assume that a marker is observed at image coordinates (x_i, y_i) in the image from camera i, and that we have M total images of the marker. M is usually less than the total number of cameras in the system due to the substantial self-occlusion of the human body (for example, the sternum marker will not be visible to a camera looking at the back of a performer). Of course, M must be at least two to obtain a triangulation; we deal with the case of missing markers later in this section.

A good initial guess for the marker location is the point in 3D that minimizes the sum of squared distances to each of the M rays from the camera centers through the observed image coordinates, as illustrated in Figure 7.6.

The ray for camera i can be expressed as $C_i' + \lambda V_i$, where V_i is the 3D unit vector pointing from the camera center C_i to the 3D point given by (x_i, y_i) on the image plane, and C_i' is computed as $C_i' = C_i - (C_i^\top V_i) V_i$.[5] Then the point $\mathbf{X}$ that minimizes the distance

$$\sum_{i=1}^{M} \min_{\lambda_i} \|\mathbf{X} - (C_i' + \lambda_i V_i)\|^2 \tag{7.1}$$

is given by

$$\mathbf{X} = \left(\mathbf{I}_{3\times 3} - \frac{1}{M} \sum_{i=1}^{M} V_i V_i^\top \right)^{-1} \left(\frac{1}{M} \sum_{i=1}^{M} C_i' \right) \tag{7.2}$$

This solution can be refined by using it as an initial point for the nonlinear minimization of the sum of squared reprojection errors of $\mathbf{X}$ onto the image planes, as described by Andersson and Betsis [14].

---

[5] C_i' is not the camera center, but a different point on the ray so that $C_i'^\top V_i = 0$.

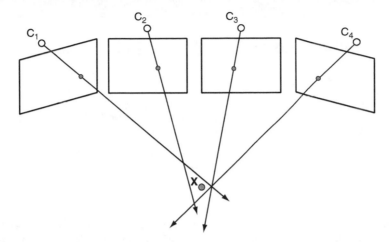

Figure 7.6. Triangulation for motion capture. A good initial guess is the 3D point that minimizes the sum of squared distances to the M rays from each camera.

If the number of cameras that see a certain marker is too small (e.g., due to body self-occlusions) or the images of the markers are of low quality (e.g., due to very fast motion resulting in marker blur), then some of the markers' 3D locations may be noisy, or in the worst case, entirely missing. Raw motion capture data often must be semiautomatically processed after acquisition to ensure that each marker has a complete 3D **trajectory**. The most straightforward approach is to treat the triangulated positions of a particular marker j as samples of a three-dimensional time series, $\mathbf{X}_j(t)$. We can then apply all the tools of one-dimensional signal processing to the X, Y and Z samples. For example, a B-spline can be fit through the 3D sample locations and used to estimate a missing marker, as illustrated in Figure 7.7a.[6] Fitting smooth curves to partial marker trajectories and extrapolating can also help determine whether broken trajectories caused by a long string of missing markers should be merged, as illustrated in Figure 7.7b.

Alternately, Liu and McMillan [295] proposed to leverage a large set of training data and approach filling in missing markers as a learning problem. First, a database of K 3D marker sets is collected; each set is represented as a complete $3N \times 1$ vector corresponding to the N observed 3D marker locations $\{\mathbf{X}_j = (X_j, Y_j, Z_j), j = 1, \ldots, N\}$. **Principal component analysis (PCA)** is applied to this collection of vectors to build a linear model

$$\mathbf{X} = U\beta + \mu \tag{7.3}$$

where U is a $3N \times k$ matrix of orthogonal mode vectors, μ is the $3N \times 1$ average of all the observations, and β is a $k \times 1$ parameter vector that controls the model. Typically k can be chosen much smaller than K since the marker positions contain many correlations induced by the underlying human skeleton.

Now suppose that at a given instant we only observe the first N' markers and need to obtain estimates of the missing $N - N'$ markers. We can split the linear model in

---

[6] Any other form of scattered data interpolation can be applied, as described in Section 5.2.

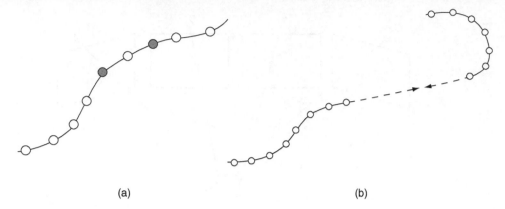

(a)   (b)

Figure 7.7. (a) Interpolation of known marker positions (white dots) can help estimate missing marker positions (gray dots). (b) Extrapolation of partial trajectories can help determine when broken trajectories should be merged.

Equation (7.3) into known and unknown parts:

$$\begin{bmatrix} \mathbf{X_k} \\ \mathbf{X_u} \end{bmatrix} = \begin{bmatrix} U_k \\ U_u \end{bmatrix} \beta + \begin{bmatrix} \mu_k \\ \mu_u \end{bmatrix} \tag{7.4}$$

Solving the top half of Equation (7.4) for β using the known information gives

$$\beta = (U_k^\top U_k)^{-1} U_k^\top (\mathbf{X_k} - \mu_k) \tag{7.5}$$

and plugging this back into the bottom half of Equation (7.4) gives the unknown marker locations as

$$\mathbf{X_u} = U_u (U_k^\top U_k)^{-1} U_k^\top (\mathbf{X_k} - \mu_k) + \mu_u \tag{7.6}$$

Since a global linear model like Equation (7.3) will probably do a poor job of representing the underlying nonlinear relationships in motion capture data, we can replace Equation (7.6) with a weighted combination of linear models, each learned locally on a small segment of simple behavior. Since missing markers are likely only weakly correlated with faraway known markers (e.g., an ankle marker will not help much to estimate a missing wrist marker), better results may be obtained by learning a PCA model only over the missing marker and the markers nearby on the body. However, this approach works best when the markers are spaced very densely on the body (e.g., as described in the experiment by Park and Hodgins [360]). Lou and Chai [302] proposed to incorporate time lags of the vectors into the PCA, as well as a robust estimator to reduce the influence of outliers.

If a marker trajectory contains high-frequency jitter, it can be smoothed, but we must be careful not to remove the nuanced motions that motivate motion capture in the first place; these details are inherently high-frequency. Sharp motions like punches or kicks also contain important high-frequency components whose removal would make the captured motion useless. We should also be aware that a too-low-dimensional PCA basis may abstract away subtle performance details that project onto the higher-order modes.

We can obtain improved solutions to the problems of interpolating missing markers and merging trajectories by leveraging our knowledge of the underlying human skeleton that generates the marker trajectories, instead of treating them as generic signals. We return to the issue in Section 7.4, after defining this skeletal relationship in the next section.

7.3   FORWARD KINEMATICS AND POSE PARAMETERIZATION

While a motion capture system returns the 3D trajectories of each marker, this information is rarely directly useful to an animator. Instead, we prefer to estimate the **pose** of a character, as described by the joint angles of an articulated skeleton of the human body, as pictured in Figure 7.8. The skeleton is made of rigid elements (i.e., bones) connected by joints. Each joint is classified as **spherical**, meaning that it has three degrees of rotational freedom (such as the ball-and-socket joints of the hip and shoulder), or **revolute,** meaning that it has one degree of rotational freedom (such as the hinge joints of the knee and elbow).[7] Together, the skeleton and classification of its joints form a **kinematic model** of the body. A kinematic model is generally much

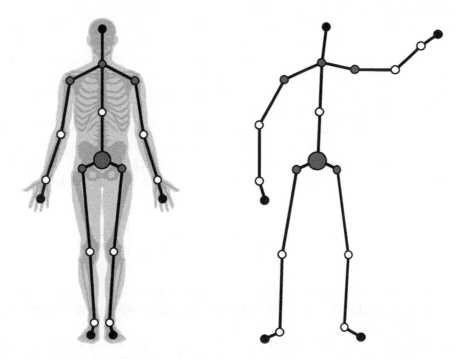

Figure 7.8. A kinematic model of the human body. Spherical joints are indicated as gray circles and revolute joints are indicated as white circles. The root of the kinematic model is shown as the large gray circle. End effectors are shown as black circles.

---

[7] These are in fact highly simplified approximations to the underlying biomechanics of the skeleton. For example, the human shoulder complex is actually composed of three joints, some of which slide as well as rotate, and the wrist and ankle have more degrees of freedom than a simple hinge.

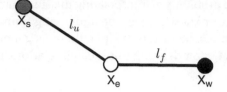

Figure 7.9. A simplified kinematic model of an arm. The shoulder is a spherical joint fixed in place and the elbow is a revolute joint.

more useful to animators, since the skeleton and joints can be mapped onto an animated character. Joints with zero degrees of freedom at the end of each kinematic chain (i.e., the head, hands, and balls of the feet) are called **end effectors**, a term from robotics.

We also need to specify the absolute orientation and position in world coordinates of the **root** of the body, usually chosen as the center of gravity near the pelvis (the large gray circle in Figure 7.8). In total, a kinematic model of the body typically has between thirty and fifty degrees of freedom (i.e., independent parameters), depending on the level of detail. The bone lengths of the skeleton may also be treated as degrees of freedom to be estimated, though they are often estimated once prior to motion capture and treated as constant throughout the session.

We use **forward kinematics** to determine the 3D coordinates of a point on the skeleton given the joint angles of the kinematic model; we can think of this as a change of coordinates. For example, consider the simple model of the human arm in Figure 7.9, which has a spherical joint at the shoulder and a revolute joint at the elbow, specified by rotation matrices R_s and R_e respectively. Suppose the length of the upper arm is given by l_u and the length of the forearm is given by l_f. We assume that the shoulder is fixed in place at the world origin and has a coordinate system aligned with the world coordinate system.

We compute the 3D position of the wrist joint $\mathbf{X}_w$ given values of R_s, R_e, l_u, and l_f by composing two transformations: one to determine the elbow's position based on the shoulder location/rotation and upper arm length, and one to determine the wrist's position based on the elbow location/rotation and forearm length:

$$\mathbf{X}_w = R_s \left(R_e \begin{bmatrix} l_f \\ 0 \\ 0 \end{bmatrix} + \begin{bmatrix} l_u \\ 0 \\ 0 \end{bmatrix} \right) \tag{7.7}$$

That is, if all the angles are 0, the arm points straight along the world x-axis and the wrist is located at $(l_u + l_f, 0, 0)$. If the elbow angle is 0, the arm points straight along the axis specified by the first column of R_s.

Forward kinematics for the full kinematic model of the body are similar; the world coordinates of a point on the skeleton can be determined by following the kinematic chain from the root along the bones to the given point. We simply apply the general formula for a kinematic chain,

$$\begin{bmatrix} R_K^1 & O_K^1 \\ 0 & 1 \end{bmatrix} = \begin{bmatrix} R_2^1 & O_2^1 \\ 0 & 1 \end{bmatrix} \bullet \cdots \bullet \begin{bmatrix} R_K^{K-1} & O_K^{K-1} \\ 0 & 1 \end{bmatrix} \tag{7.8}$$

where R_i^j is the rotation matrix specifying the orientation of the jth coordinate frame with respect to the ith coordinate frame, and O_i^j gives the coordinates of the jth joint in the ith coordinate frame.

A key issue for working with motion capture data is the parameterization of the rotation matrix at each joint. Using three Euler angles (i.e., rotations about the x, y, and z axes) is a poor choice since they are difficult to naturally interpolate and suffer from "gimbal lock," a singularity (loss of a degree of freedom) that results when one of the angles is near a critical value. Instead, pose is typically parameterized using **quaternions** or **twists**.

A **quaternion** represents a rotation with a unit vector in $\mathbb{R}^4$, and is closely related to the axis-angle parameterization discussed in Section 6.5.3.1. In particular, the unit quaternion given by

$$q = \left(\cos \frac{\theta}{2}, \ v_1 \sin \frac{\theta}{2}, \ v_2 \sin \frac{\theta}{2}, \ v_3 \sin \frac{\theta}{2} \right) \tag{7.9}$$

represents a rotation of θ around the unit vector v in $\mathbb{R}^3$. We convert between quaternions and rotation matrices using the **Rodrigues formula** in Equation (6.58) and the equations in Problem 6.21. In a kinematic model, the rotation axis for each joint is defined with respect to a local coordinate system, as discussed earlier. Quaternions were introduced to the animation community by Shoemake [444], though they had been used in mechanical engineering (e.g., spacecraft design) for some time.

The **twist** parameterization combines a rotation and translation (i.e., a rigid motion) into a vector ξ in $\mathbb{R}^6$. It uses the key observation that any rigid motion can be expressed as a rotation around some axis followed by a translation along the same axis (known as Chasles' theorem [342]). This so-called **screw transformation** is illustrated in Figure 7.10.

We break the twist vector into two vectors s and w in $\mathbb{R}^3$, i.e., $\xi = \begin{bmatrix} s \\ w \end{bmatrix}$. The first vector s encodes the direction of the screw axis (given by a unit vector v in $\mathbb{R}^3$) and the amount of rotation around it (given by a scalar ψ) using the axis-angle parameterization. That is, $s = \psi v$. The vector w encodes the origin in space of the screw axis, and the distance along the axis that must be traveled to accomplish the translation. For a translation in world coordinates $t \in \mathbb{R}^3$, the vector w is computed as

$$w = \rho \times v \tag{7.10}$$

where ρ is a point on the axis satisfying $\rho^\top v = 0$, which can be computed as described in Problem 7.5.

The matrices needed for the forward kinematics equation (7.8) can be conveniently represented in terms of the twist vector ξ_i, namely

$$\begin{bmatrix} R_i^{i-1} & O_i^{i-1} \\ 0 & 1 \end{bmatrix} = \exp \left(\begin{bmatrix} \psi_i[v_i]_\times & \psi_i w_i \\ \mathbf{0}^\top & 0 \end{bmatrix} \right) \tag{7.11}$$

$$= \begin{bmatrix} \exp(\psi_i[v_i]_\times) & (\mathbf{I}_{3\times 3} - \exp(\psi_i[v_i]_\times))(v_i \times w_i) + v_i^\top w_i \psi_i v_i \\ \mathbf{0}^\top & 1 \end{bmatrix} \tag{7.12}$$

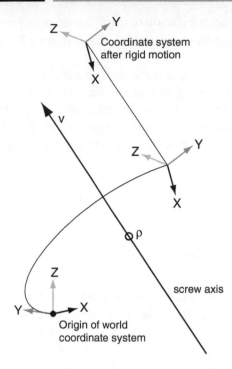

Figure 7.10. Any rigid motion can be expressed as a rotation around some axis followed by a translation along the same axis.

The notation exp in Equations (7.11)–(7.12) denotes the exponential map of a matrix, which can be computed by a matrix Taylor series (see Problem 7.6).[8] In this case, the required exponential map in Equation (7.12) is given by the Rodrigues formula in Equation (6.58) and is simply the matrix rotation corresponding to the axis-angle parameters. Twists were introduced to the animation community by Bregler et al. [67], and are commonly used in robotics applications [342].

Conversion between quaternions, twists, axis-angle representations, and rotation matrices is straightforward (see [526], and Problems 6.21, 7.3, and 7.5). Therefore, we can assume that a kinematic model for the human body is generally represented using six degrees of freedom for the body's root, and some number of "angles" (parameterized by either quaternions or twists) to represent the joints. In total, the number of degrees of freedom in typical parameterizations of the human kinematic model ranges from thirty to fifty.

In the next section, we address the critical problem of the change of coordinates from the Euclidean domain of 3D marker locations to the hierarchy of joints of a kinematic model. This coordinate transformation is more difficult than the forward transformations given earlier; instead we must solve an **inverse kinematics** problem.

7.4   INVERSE KINEMATICS

In motion capture, we're faced with the problem of determining the underlying parameters of a kinematic model from observations of points on (or near) the

---

[8] Hence, Equation (7.8) can be interpreted as a product of exponential maps.

skeleton. Going forward, we'll denote the kinematic model parameters by a vector $\boldsymbol{\theta}$, and the observed skeleton points by a vector $\mathbf{r}$. Let's compactly denote the forward kinematic relationship in Equation (7.8) by

$$\mathbf{r} = f(\boldsymbol{\theta}) \tag{7.13}$$

We'd like to determine $\boldsymbol{\theta}$ from a set of measured values of $\mathbf{r}$; that is, to invert Equation (7.13). Therefore, such problems are termed **inverse kinematics**. Unfortunately, this inversion is problematic for several reasons. First, the relationship in Equation (7.13) is highly nonlinear, involving products of trigonometric functions of the parameters. Second, in some applications, the relationship in Equation (7.13) is many to one; that is, there are more values of $\boldsymbol{\theta}$ than of $\mathbf{r}$. In such cases, the inverse kinematics problem is underdetermined and has many feasible solutions.[9]

In this section, we describe several basic methods for solving the inverse kinematics problem. Algorithms for inverse kinematics were developed in the robotics community many years before their application to motion capture and animation; for example, see Chiaverini et al. [92]. The techniques based on dynamical systems that we discuss in Section 7.7.1 can also be viewed as methods for inverse kinematics.

There's an offset between the markers and the skeleton that we can't ignore (see the left side of Figure 7.8). While some markers can be placed on a performer's suit/skin fairly close to a joint, at places where the motion capture technician can easily feel a bone, other markers are further from the underlying kinematic joint (e.g., those on the shoulders and spine). This relationship can still be taken into account by Equation (7.13); however, we need a model for the relationship between the markers' position on the surface of the skin and the underlying bones. We discuss this issue more in Section 7.4.4.

7.4.1 Inverse Differential Kinematics

We'll generalize Equation (7.13) to be a function of time, since in motion capture we're interested in recovering the kinematic model at every instant of a performer's continuous motion:

$$\mathbf{r}(t) = f(\boldsymbol{\theta}(t)) \tag{7.14}$$

First, we discuss a general approach based on **inverse differential kinematics**, which is based on differentiating Equation (7.14) with respect to time:

$$\begin{aligned}
\frac{d\mathbf{r}(t)}{dt} &= \frac{\partial f(\boldsymbol{\theta})}{\partial \boldsymbol{\theta}}(t)\frac{d\boldsymbol{\theta}}{dt}(t) \\
&= J(t)\frac{d\boldsymbol{\theta}}{dt}(t)
\end{aligned} \tag{7.15}$$

where in Equation (7.15) we introduced the **Jacobian**

$$J(t) = \frac{\partial f(\boldsymbol{\theta})}{\partial \boldsymbol{\theta}}(t) \tag{7.16}$$

---

[9] For example, if the wrist and shoulder positions are fixed, there is still one degree of freedom for the elbow's position — it can rotate in a circle.

If $\mathbf{r} \in \mathbb{R}^N$ and $\boldsymbol{\theta} \in \mathbb{R}^P$, then the Jacobian is $N \times P$; in this section, we assume that $N < P$.[10] This situation occurs in some of the motion editing applications discussed in Section 7.5, and is frequently needed for animation. When we have a large number of motion capture markers, then $N > P$ and the optimization-based methods in the next section are more appropriate.

If we know $\mathbf{r}(t)$ and are solving Equation (7.14) for $\boldsymbol{\theta}(t)$, we therefore expect an infinite number of solutions, since the problem is underconstrained. The general form of this family of solutions is:

$$\frac{d\boldsymbol{\theta}}{dt} = J^\dagger(t)\frac{d\mathbf{r}(t)}{dt} + (\mathbf{I}_{P \times P} - J^\dagger(t)J(t))\frac{d\boldsymbol{\theta}_0}{dt} \tag{7.17}$$

where $J^\dagger(t)$ is the $P \times N$ **pseudoinverse** given by

$$J^\dagger(t) = J(t)^\top (J(t)J(t)^\top)^{-1} \tag{7.18}$$

and $\frac{d\boldsymbol{\theta}_0}{dt}$ is the derivative of some arbitrary trajectory $\boldsymbol{\theta}_0(t)$. That is, the second component of Equation (7.17) is the projection of this trajectory onto the non-empty null space of $J(t)$, which expresses the remaining $P - N$ degrees of freedom in the solution. We can see that choosing $\boldsymbol{\theta}_0(t) = 0$ gives one solution as

$$\frac{d\boldsymbol{\theta}}{dt} = J^\dagger(t)\frac{d\mathbf{r}(t)}{dt} \tag{7.19}$$

which is just the usual least-squares solution in which $\boldsymbol{\theta}(t)$ has minimum norm — that is, it minimizes the cost function

$$C(\boldsymbol{\theta}(t)) = \left\| \frac{d\mathbf{r}(t)}{dt} - J(t)\frac{d\boldsymbol{\theta}(t)}{dt} \right\|^2 \tag{7.20}$$

To reconstruct the actual values of $\boldsymbol{\theta}(t)$ from the recovered derivatives, we just compute

$$\boldsymbol{\theta}(t) = \boldsymbol{\theta}(0) + \int_0^t \frac{d\boldsymbol{\theta}}{dt}(\tau)d\tau \tag{7.21}$$

where $\boldsymbol{\theta}(0)$ is the known starting position of the joints, which can often be estimated by initializing the motion capture in a standard pose (e.g., a "T" pose with arms outstretched).

A related approach that avoids problems with singularities of the Jacobian (that is, when the trajectory passes through or near a region where the Jacobian is not rank N) is to replace the pseudoinverse in Equation (7.18) with a damping factor

$$J^*(t) = J(t)^\top (J(t)J(t)^\top + \lambda^2 \mathbf{I}_{N \times N})^{-1} \tag{7.22}$$

which corresponds to minimizing the damped or **regularized** cost function

$$C_{\text{reg}}(\boldsymbol{\theta}(t)) = \left\| \frac{d\mathbf{r}(t)}{dt} - J(t)\frac{d\boldsymbol{\theta}(t)}{dt} \right\|^2 + \lambda^2 \left\| \frac{d\boldsymbol{\theta}(t)}{dt} \right\|^2 \tag{7.23}$$

Yamane and Nakamura [559] used this approach to compute joint angles for a kinematic model in which some end effectors were fixed ("pinned") and another

---

[10] Recall that we also defined a Jacobian in the context of matchmoving (Section 6.5.3.2), although the Jacobian in that case had $N \gg P$.

was interactively dragged. However, it's important to note that if λ is nonzero, the estimated joint angles will not correspond exactly with the observed marker locations; that is, Equation (7.14) will not be satisfied exactly.

7.4.2 Optimization-Based Inverse Kinematics

Now we discuss the more usual case in which $N > P$ (that is, the markers overconstrain the kinematic model). We want to select trajectories $\theta(t)$ that are as natural as possible while still matching the observed marker positions $\mathbf{r}(t)$ and satisfying any kinematic constraints as well as possible. In this section, we describe different ways to pose this problem that all result in the minimization of a nonlinear objective function $C(\theta(t))$.

Zhao and Badler [577] proposed several building blocks for inverse kinematics cost functions. The simplest is a position goal: for example, we want the 3D position of a point in the kinematic model to be as close as possible to a certain 3D point p:

$$C_{\text{pos}}(\theta(t)) = \|f_p(\theta(t)) - p\|^2 \tag{7.24}$$

where f_p defines the predicted location of p via the forward kinematics in Equation (7.14). Thus, given the trajectories of N 3D motion capture markers $\{\mathbf{X}_j, j = 1, \ldots, N\}$, we can form a cost function that minimizes the sum of squares cost of fitting them to a kinematic model:

$$C_{\text{allpos}}(\theta(t)) = \sum_{j=1}^{N} \|f_j(\theta(t)) - \mathbf{X}_j(t)\|^2 \tag{7.25}$$

where $f_j(\theta(t))$ is the forward kinematics model that determines the position of marker j given the joint parameters.

We might also want to specify vector constraints — for example, that the vector between two observed markers should be parallel to a certain limb in the kinematic model. A corresponding cost function would look like

$$C_{\text{vec}}(\theta(t)) = 1 - \left\| \frac{\mathbf{X}_j(t) - \mathbf{X}_i(t)}{\|\mathbf{X}_j(t) - \mathbf{X}_i(t)\|} \cdot f_{ij}(\theta(t)) \right\| \tag{7.26}$$

where $f_{ij}(\theta(t))$ is a unit vector specifying the direction of the limb relating markers i and j.

A nonlinear cost function can be formed as the weighted sum of such terms and minimized using an algorithm such as the Broyden-Fletcher-Goldfarb-Shanno (BFGS) method [351]. This was one of the earliest inverse kinematics approaches for motion capture [51].

In this framework, we can also impose hard constraints on $\theta(t)$ — for example, to enforce that a joint not exceed the limits of feasible human motion. The expected ranges of motion for performers of different ages and genders can be determined from biomechanical studies (e.g., [465]). If we directly parameterize the vector θ using angles, such limits can be expressed as linear constraints of the form

$$a_i^\top \theta(t) \leq b_i \tag{7.27}$$

The BFGS algorithm can handle such linear constraints, but if we used the quaternion or twist parameterizations, the constraints would be nonlinear, taking the more general form

$$g_i(\boldsymbol{\theta}(t)) \le b_i \qquad (7.28)$$

Problems with nonlinear constraints are generally much harder to solve than those with linear constraints, especially at interactive rates. An alternative is to include the constraints as weighted penalty terms in an unconstrained cost function, e.g., by adding cost function terms of the form

$$C_{\text{constraint}}(\boldsymbol{\theta}(t)) = \max(0, g_i(\boldsymbol{\theta}(t)) - b_i) \qquad (7.29)$$

As with Equation (7.23), the result of minimizing a sum of weighted cost function terms is not guaranteed to strictly satisfy any of the constraints given in each term. That is, the marker positions will generally not agree exactly with the forward kinematics model, and the desired range of motion constraints may not be exactly satisfied. Tolani et al. [491] proposed to mitigate this problem using a hybrid analytical/numerical approach that was able to solve for most of the degrees of freedom of a simplified kinematic chain in closed form.

Figure 7.11 illustrates an example result of optimization-based inverse kinematics, rendering raw motion capture markers alongside the estimated skeletal pose from the same perspective.

In addition to simple, uncoupled limits on the range of motion of each joint that are independent at each point in time, we can incorporate dependencies on joint limits, as discussed by Herda et al. [195]. For example, the range of motion of the knee joint varies depending on the position and orientation of the hip joint. Such dependencies can be characterized by analyzing motion capture training data to

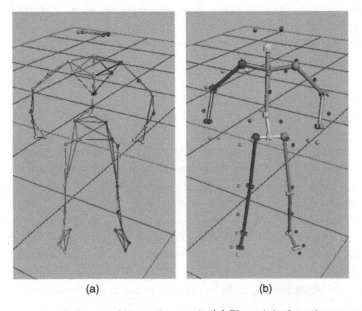

(a)   (b)

Figure 7.11. An example inverse kinematics result. (a) The original motion capture markers, which form the constraints for an optimization-based inverse kinematics problem. Lines are drawn between markers on the same body part to give a sense of the pose. (b) The estimated skeletal pose from the same perspective. We can see that the markers are sometimes quite far from the skeleton.

determine feasible combinations of joint angles. We can also incorporate either hard or soft **dynamical** constraints on the velocities and accelerations of joints, based on biomechanical analysis of how quickly humans can move.

Finally, we can take an alternate approach of fitting the kinematic model to motion capture data using a **physics-based** cost function (e.g., see [584]). That is, we assume that the kinematic model is subjected to forces (e.g., from springs that relate the markers to the skeleton, and from friction with the ground) and its pose corresponds to achieving the most "comfortable" position.

7.4.3 Model-Based Inverse Kinematics

A natural next step is to incorporate learned models for natural human motion, extracted by analyzing training data from previously collected motion capture sessions. That is, we want to find inverse kinematics solutions that are not only biomechanically feasible but also likely for a human to take.

One approach is to build a principal component analysis (PCA) model based on training samples of θ to reduce its dimensionality, and minimize cost functions like those described in the previous section over this smaller set of parameters.[11] For example, Safonova et al. [416] reduced an approximately sixty-dimensional joint parameter vector to about eight dimensions using PCA. Their inverse kinematics cost function was a weighted sum of squared torques, joint accelerations, and PCA coefficient magnitudes.

A more sophisticated approach is to use the training data to build a probability density function that can be used to estimate the likelihood of a given pose, $L(\theta)$. Higher likelihoods mean that the pose is more likely to be taken by a human. Then the general problem is to maximize the likelihood of the probabilistic model given a set of constraints. For example, Grochow et al. [179] proposed to use a nonlinear dimensionality reduction technique called the Scaled Gaussian Process Latent Variable Model. They used the initial portion of a motion capture sequence to learn the "style" of a performer, and used the learned model to estimate poses for the rest of the sequence, even in the presence of missing markers. Urtasun et al. [507] extended this type of approach to include dynamics using a Gaussian Process Dynamical Model. We'll discuss simpler dynamical systems in the context of markerless motion capture (Section 7.7).

The poses estimated by learned-model-based methods seem much more natural to the human eye than those produced by the methods in Section 7.4.1 and 7.4.2. This makes sense since they're trained on a large number of motion capture sessions of real performers instead of simply imposing generic constraints. On the other hand, model-based methods are extremely dependent on the quality and nature of the training data. The methods produce the best results when the training data all has a similar type, such as historical motion capture data of boxers that's applied to solve the inverse kinematics problem for a new boxer. The methods perform more poorly if a general mix of motion capture data is used for input, and they perform badly if the training data doesn't match the online problem at all (for example, if training data

---

[11] The PCA should only be applied to the relative joint angles, and not the position and orientation of the root.

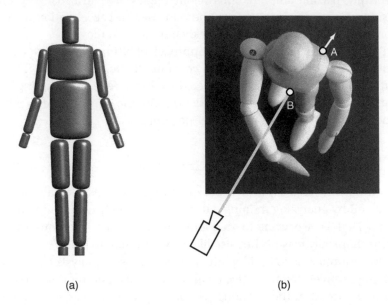

(a)   (b)

Figure 7.12. (a) Attaching tapered cylinders to the skeleton of a kinematic model results in a solid model of the body. (b) The solid model in a given pose can be used to predict which markers will be occluded from a given viewpoint. A marker will not be visible if either its normal points away from the camera (e.g., point A) or a body solid lies between it and the camera (e.g., point B).

from a boxer is used to fit the online behavior of a gymnast). Finally, if our goal is to capture the subtle mannerisms of a skilled performer, a model-based approach may too strongly bias the result toward the library of precaptured motion, smoothing out the subtlety that makes the individual performance unique.

7.4.4   Marker Cleanup with a Kinematic Model

Once we can map a set of 3D marker locations to the joints of kinematic model and vice versa, the kinematic model can be used to predict which markers will be occluded from a given pose and viewpoint. For example, we can put "flesh" on the kinematic skeleton to make a crude body model out of tapered cylinders or ellipsoids, as illustrated in Figure 7.12a.[12] If either the normal vector to the marker points away from the camera or the line connecting the marker and the camera center passes through one of the body solids, the marker will not be visible from the given viewpoint, as illustrated in Figure 7.12b. The solid model can also be used to rule out infeasible configurations in which the limbs inter-penetrate.

Herda et al. [194] showed how a skeleton and body model could be used to predict the location of missing markers. The user associates the detected markers to body parts and joints based on a calibration motion that exercises all the joints. The bone lengths of the skeleton and the distance between markers and underlying joints are then fit to the observed marker trajectories using a least-squares approach. During

---

[12] This can be viewed as a crude **skinning** of the skeleton, that is, a mapping from points on a skeleton to the surface of a 3D character model [29]. We mention more sophisticated body models in Section 7.7 and Chapter 8.

online motion capture, the identities of missing markers can thus be predicted by the body model and filled in with reasonable guesses from inverse kinematics until the markers are reacquired.

A unique consideration for processing motion capture data is the preservation of foot contact with the ground, or **footplants**. Filling in occluded foot markers using the methods described so far can produce a perceptually distracting phenomenon called **footskate**, in which the feet of the resulting kinematic model do not appear to be firmly planted on the ground (or worse, appear to penetrate or hover above the ground in a physically impossible way). Footskate can even result from using inverse kinematics to fit complete motion capture data, since the kinematic model is a simplified version of how the human body actually works. Kovar et al. [254] proposed an algorithm for removing footskate artifacts by allowing small changes to the leg bone lengths in the skeleton. Footplant locations are semiautomatically identified, and an analytic inverse kinematics algorithm is applied to determine the skeletal model most similar to the original data that still satisfies the constraints. This can be viewed as a type of motion editing, which we discuss in the next section.

7.5   MOTION EDITING

The goal of motion capture for visual effects is usually to precisely record a performer's action. However, it's often necessary to modify the recorded motion in a way that preserves the personality of the performance but achieves a space-time goal for animation. We call these **motion editing** problems. For example, we may need to stitch together multiple motions from the same performer captured at different times, such as stringing together separately recorded fighting moves. This is a problem of **motion blending** or **motion interpolation**. We may instead need to extend or alter the path of a performer's walk, since the motion capture volume may not match the environment an animated character must traverse. This is a problem of **motion path editing**.

In this section, we assume that the raw motion capture data has been transformed into a time-varying vector of joint angles by means of an inverse kinematics algorithm, as described in the previous section. That is, a given motion capture clip is represented as $\{\theta(t), t = 1, \ldots, T\}$, where T is the number of frames in the clip.

At the simplest level, we can treat each of the time-varying parameters $\theta_i(t)$ as a one-dimensional signal, and apply any one-dimensional signal processing technique to it, such as filtering. For example, Witkin and Popović [550] discussed motion warping using functions of the form

$$\hat{\theta}_i(t) = a_i(t)\theta_i(t) + b_i(t) \tag{7.30}$$

Another simple application is to change the frame rate of the motion by fitting splines through the samples of the joint angles and resampling.

Bruderlin and Williams [75] applied multiresolution filtering to motion capture signals using a one-dimensional Laplacian pyramid (see Section 3.1.2). This allows the modification of frequency bands for individual joints to alter the corresponding motion. For example, amplifying the middle and high frequencies exaggerates the recorded motion, making it seem more cartoonish.

7.5.1 Motion Interpolation

The most common motion editing problem is **interpolation**; that is, we want to smoothly blend between two given motions $\{\theta(t), t = 1, \ldots, T\}$ and $\{\theta'(t), t = 1, \ldots, T'\}$. For example, as illustrated in Figure 7.13, we may want to blend the end of a walking motion with the beginning of a running motion so that the motion seems to naturally speed up over the transition.

The goal is to stitch the motion capture sequences together without altering them too much. We must consider two important problems. First, we must make sure the motions are spatially aligned, so that the second motion picks up at the location and orientation that the first motion leaves off. Second, and more important, we must make sure that the motions are temporally synchronized so that no artifacts are introduced across the blending interval. For example, the feet in the interpolated motion must appear to make natural contact with the ground.

The synchronization problem is commonly solved using **dynamic time warping**, an application of dynamic programming similar to what we discussed for estimating correspondence along conjugate epipolar lines in Section 5.5.1. Figure 7.14 illustrates the problem. We seek a correspondence between the T frames of the first sequence and the T' frames of the second sequence that minimizes the cost of a path from one corner of the graph to the other.

Formally, the path **P** is defined by a set of frame-to-frame matches $\{(t_1, t_1'), \ldots, (t_L, t_L')\}$ such that $t_1 = t_1' = 1$, $t_L = T$, $t_L' = T'$ and $t_{i-1} \leq t_i$, $t_{i-1}' \leq t_i'$, $i = 2, \ldots L$. That is, the path goes from one corner of the graph to the other and monotonically increases in both directions. The cost of the path is the sum of the costs for associating pairs of frames:

$$C(\mathbf{P}) = \sum_{i=1}^{L} c(\theta(t_i), \theta'(t_i')) \tag{7.31}$$

where $c(\theta(t), \theta'(t'))$ is a distance function between poses. This cost can be minimized using dynamic programming (see Appendix A.1). A simple choice for $c(\theta(t), \theta'(t'))$ is the sum-of-squared distances between corresponding joint angles (not including the root position and orientation). We might give more weight to poses in which a foot

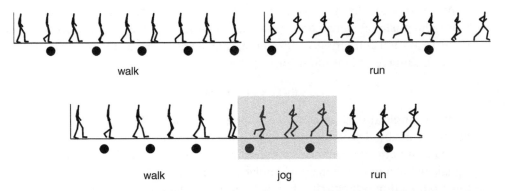

walk   run

walk   jog   run

Figure 7.13. Motion interpolation for stitching sequences together. Dots indicate foot contact with the ground. In this example, a walking motion is blended into a running motion to produce a jog over the transition.

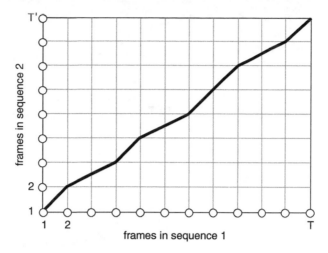

Figure 7.14. Dynamic time warping for estimating correspondence between two motion sequences.

contacts the ground, to ensure that the footplants of the two motions are matched, or more weight to some joints over others (e.g., the shoulder's orientation may be more important than the wrist's). We could also use a surface-to-surface distance function applied to skinned skeletons after the roots have been aligned [252].

Once we have a temporal correspondence between frames over the interval to be blended, we can interpolate between the two sequences, using a weighted average between corresponding frames.[13] We require a weight function w_i that monotonically increases from 0 at $i = 1$ to 1 at $i = L$, so that the motion transitions smoothly from the first motion to the second over the interval.

If we assume that the non-root elements of θ and θ' are parameterized using unit quaternions, then the appropriate interpolation between unit quaternions q and q' is given by **spherical linear interpolation** or **slerp**, defined by

$$\text{slerp}(q, q', w) = \frac{\sin(1 - w)\phi}{\sin\phi} q + \frac{\sin w\phi}{\sin\phi} q' \tag{7.32}$$

where $q \cdot q' = \cos\phi$; that is, ϕ is the angle between the two quaternions on the 3D unit sphere [444].

We also need to know how to place and orient the root at each transition frame. First, we align the second motion with the first as desired (e.g., so that the two motion paths are roughly aligned) by applying the same rigid transformation to the root position and orientation of all the frames of the second motion. Then for each transition frame, the root orientations can be determined given the weight w_i using spherical linear interpolation in the way shown earlier. The root position can be interpolated along a predefined path (e.g., a straight line, a curved line given by the user [361], or

---

[13] This process of warping and cross-dissolving between motions is analogous to the morphing problem we discussed in Section 5.7.

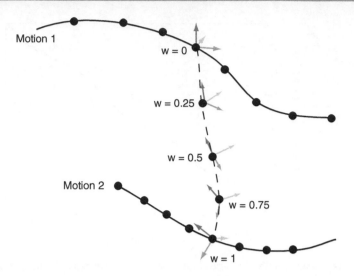

Figure 7.15. Interpolating the root position and orientation for a transition between two motions, for different values of the weight w. In this case, the intermediate positions are created with linear interpolation and the intermediate orientations are created with spherical linear interpolation.

a curved line given by linearly interpolating between the starting and ending velocity vectors [396]). Figure 7.15 illustrates the idea.

The interpolated motion created by this process is aligned to the time indices of the first motion; we can speed up or slow down the motion in the transition region as desired. A natural choice is to remap the interpolated motion to have duration $\frac{1}{2}(T + T')$.

Figure 7.16 illustrates an example of a motion blend using this technique, transitioning from a normal walking motion to a sneaking motion. The result is perceptibly worse without dynamic time warping. For example, in the third frame of Figure 7.16c, both feet are well off the ground, and in the fourth frame the figure is leaning forward on both toes. The figure seems to stutter and glide across the ground, and never makes a satisfactory transition to the crouching posture.

Kovar and Gleicher [252] extended this approach by enforcing that the dynamic time warping path doesn't take too many consecutive horizontal or vertical steps (i.e., mapping the same frame from one sequence onto many frames of the other). They then fit a smooth, strictly increasing spline to the dynamic time warping path, which they called a registration curve. They also generalized the approach to allow the blending of more than two motion sequences. Instead of applying dynamic time warping, Rose et al. [395] modeled the correspondence as a piecewise-linear path defined by annotated keyframe correspondences (e.g., matching points in a walk cycle).

The monotonic function defining the weights w_i could be a simple linear transition, or a function with non-constant slope, e.g., arising from radial basis functions [395], B-splines [266], or the desire for differentiability [254]. In general, when we want to blend between more than two motions, any of the scattered data interpolation techniques from Section 5.2 can be applied.

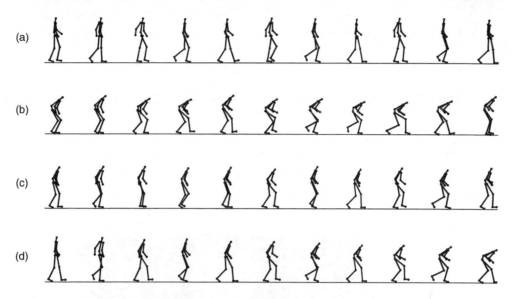

Figure 7.16. Motion interpolation between a walking motion and a sneaking motion. (a) The original walking motion. (b) The original sneaking motion. (c) Interpolation without dynamic time warping. (d) Interpolation with dynamic time warping.

7.5.2   Motion Graphs

The previous section described how to interpolate between two given segments of motion, but these segments must be specified by a user. This section describes how to automate the problem of finding good transition points among a library of many motion capture segments. Once we have this information, we can interactively string together sub-segments of motion capture data that seamlessly satisfy a set of space-time constraints (for example, that the skeleton be in a given pose at a given position at a given time).

The underlying concept is called a **motion graph** [254], and is illustrated in Figure 7.17 for a set of three motions. The idea is to determine a set of vertices (time instants in each subsequence) and a set of edges (viable transitions within or between subsequences) such that transitioning between vertices along edges results in a natural-looking motion.

We already have the ingredients to create the motion graph; good transition points can be identified directly by analyzing local minima of the pose distance function $c(\theta(t), \theta'(t'))$ in Equation (7.31). Examples of such local minima are illustrated in Figure 7.18. We only accept minima whose distances are below a user-specified threshold.

We can then compute the transition between every pair of identified transition points using the interpolation methods of the previous section. Of course, minima that are adjacent to each other within a single sequence don't need to be interpolated since they're already connected by a sub-sequence of original motion capture data. Each edge can be assigned a weight depending on the estimated quality of the transition.

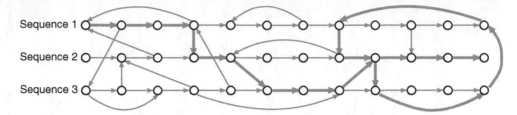

Figure 7.17. An example motion graph for three sequences. The vertices (large dots) are time indices into each subsequence. The edges (directed arrows) indicate viable transitions within or across subsequences. The horizontal edges already exist within the original motion capture data, while the remaining edges must be synthesized by motion interpolation. The thicker edges indicate an example walk on the graph that generates a natural motion.

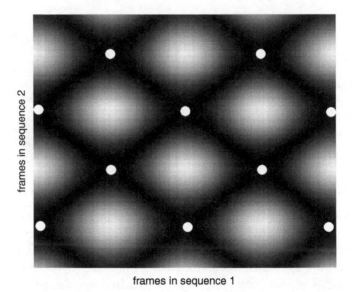

Figure 7.18. Minima of the pose distance function $c(\boldsymbol{\theta}(t), \boldsymbol{\theta}'(t'))$ can be used to identify vertices and edges of the motion graph (white dots).

As illustrated in Figure 7.17, the resulting motion graph can create cycles within the same sequence (for example, between similar footplants in several steps of a walking sequence) as well as create transitions across different sequences. Kovar et al. [254] also described heuristics to prune vertices from the motion graph that are not very well connected such as dead ends (e.g., the last vertex in the second row of Figure 7.17).

After estimating the motion graph for a motion capture database, we can estimate the transitions along edges that best satisfy a higher-level constraint. For example, we may want to create a long sequence in which a character driven by motion capture data travels along a given path the user has traced on the ground. This amounts to estimating a **walk** along the graph defined by a sequence of edges $W = (e_1, e_2, \ldots, e_L)$ that minimizes — or at least has a small value of — a goodness-of-fit function $F(W)$ defined by the user constraints. Kovar et al. [254] described an efficient branch-and-bound technique for finding a graph walk satisfying user-specified path constraints.

Similar approaches to creating and applying motion graphs were described by Lee et al. [265] and Arikan and Forsyth [17].

We can also impose constraints based on motion type, for example, forcing the character to run through a given region by only allowing samples from running motion capture sequences. For this purpose, it may be useful to automatically cluster and annotate a large database of motion capture sequences with descriptions of the performance (e.g., see [18, 253]). Finally, in addition to space-time constraints, we can impose a dynamics-based model for $F(W)$, such as evaluating the total power consumption of a character's muscles [371] or the realism of the recovery from a sharp impact [583].

7.6   FACIAL MOTION CAPTURE

Marker-based motion capture is primarily used to record the full body of a performer. However, it can also be used to focus on a performer's face, for later use in driving the expressions of an animated character. The technology and methods for marker acquisition are basically the same as for full-body motion capture, except that the cameras are closer to the subject and the markers are smaller (i.e., 2–5 mm in diameter). Self-occlusions and marker loss are also less problematic since the facial performance is generally captured head-on by a smaller set of inward-facing cameras. Figure 7.19 illustrates a typical facial motion capture setup.

Facial markers aren't usually related to an underlying skeletal model as in full-body motion capture. Instead, facial markers are commonly related to a taxonomy of expressions called the **Facial Action Coding System (FACS)**, developed by Ekman

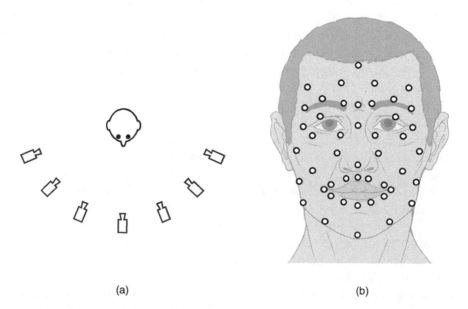

(a)   (b)

Figure 7.19. A sample facial motion capture setup. (a) The camera configuration. (b) The marker configuration.

et al. [129]. FACS decomposes an expression into "action units" related to the activity of facial muscles, which an animator can control to create a character's expression.

Sifakis et al. [448] related facial markers to a highly detailed anatomical model of the head that included bones, muscle, and soft tissue, using a nonlinear optimization similar to the methods in Section 7.4.2. Alternately, the facial markers can be directly related to the vertices of a dense 3D mesh of the head's surface (e.g., [54]), acquired using laser scanning or structured light (both discussed in detail in Chapter 8).

One of the earliest facial motion capture tests was described by Williams [547], who taped dots of retro-reflective Scotchlite material to a performer's face and used the dots' 2D positions to animate a 3D head model obtained using a laser scanner. Guenter et al.'s seminal work [183] described a homemade motion capture framework using 182 fluorescent dots glued to a performer's face that were imaged under ultraviolet illumination. The triangulated 3D dot positions were used to move the vertices of a 3D head mesh obtained using a laser scanner. Lin and Ouhyoung [284] described a unique approach that uses a single video of a scene containing the performer and a pair of mirrors, effectively giving three views of the markers from different perspectives. In several recent films (e.g., *TRON: Legacy*, *Avatar*, and *Rise of the Planet of the Apes*), actors performed on set wearing facial markers whose motion was recorded by a rigid rig of head-mounted cameras, in essence carrying miniature motion-capture studios along with them (see Section 7.8).

On the other hand, marker-based technology is only part of the process of facial capture for visual effects today. In particular, the non-marker-based **MOVA Contour** system is extremely popular and is used to construct highly detailed facial meshes and animation rigs for actors prior to on-set motion capture. With this system, phosphorescent makeup is applied to the performer's entire face. Under normal lighting, the makeup is invisible, but under fluorescent lighting, the makeup glows green and has a mottled texture that generates dense, evenly spaced visual features in the resulting images. The performer is filmed from the front by many cameras, and dense, accurate 3D geometry is computed using multi-view stereo techniques, discussed in Section 8.3. This technology was notably used in *The Curious Case of Benjamin Button*. In related approaches, Furukawa and Ponce [159] painted a subject's face with a visible mottled pattern, and Bickel et al. [44] augmented facial markers with visible paint around a performer's forehead and eyes to track wrinkles.

Facial capture techniques that require no markers or makeup are also a major research focus in the computer vision and graphics communities. Bradley et al. [63] described a system in which the performer's head is surrounded by seven pairs of high-resolution stereo cameras zoomed in to use pores, blemishes, and hair follicles as trackable features. The performer is lit by a bright array of LED lights to provide uniform illumination. The 3D stereo reconstructions (i.e., stereo correspondence followed by triangulation) are merged to create a texture-mapped mesh, and optical flow is used to propagate dense correspondence of the face images throughout each camera's video sequence. This can be viewed as a multi-view stereo algorithm, discussed in detail in Section 8.3. Another major approach is the projection of structured light patterns onto a performer's face, which introduces artificial texture used for multi-view stereo correspondence. This approach is typified by the work of Zhang et al. [570] and Ma et al. [309]. We'll discuss structured light approaches in detail in Section 8.2.

If the goal is simply to record the general shape and pose of the performer's face at each instant, then a lower-resolution approach such as fitting an active appearance model to single-camera video [316] is more appropriate than full motion capture.

7.7 MARKERLESS MOTION CAPTURE

Finally, we discuss **markerless motion capture**, the problem of estimating human pose from images alone, without identifiable markers and preferably without constraints on the performer's clothing or environment. Determining a human's pose in an image and tracking him/her through a video sequence are two of the most studied problems in computer vision, so we can only give a brief overview of this research area here. We'll focus on approaches that have the same goals as markered motion capture — that is, algorithms that estimate an articulated skeleton from a set of images.

To form relationships between the images and the kinematic model, markerless methods generally assume that a solid 3D human model can be created for each pose. As mentioned in Section 7.4.4, this solid model can be composed of ellipsoids or tapered cylinders, or it can be a more detailed model of the human musculature [365]. With the increased availability of full-body 3D scanners (see Section 8.2), it is growing more common to use a detailed triangulated mesh captured from the performer him/herself for the body model. Such a triangulated mesh can be skinned with respect to the underlying kinematic model, or parameterized in a lower-dimensional space based on analyzing training data [12, 15].

First, we describe the general approach common to most markerless motion capture algorithms of formulating pose estimation using a dynamical system. We then review how **silhouettes** and **edges** of the performer extracted from multicamera video can be used as the basis for estimating pose. Finally, we discuss how silhouettes can be backprojected into world coordinates to create **visual hulls**, constraining the estimation problem in 3D rather than 2D.

Markerless motion capture algorithms aren't generally used for production-quality visual effects. The estimated 3D trajectories of points are less accurate, since the underlying 2D correspondences of features in unconstrained video can't be found as accurately and robustly as the highly engineered retro-reflective markers in a conventional motion capture system.[14] Furthermore, the connection between 2D tracked features and the underlying kinematic model is less strict, since street clothes are looser and move more freely than a body suit. Also, the image features are automatically chosen by the algorithm instead of carefully engineered to give maximal information about the skeleton.

In general, markerless systems can produce good estimates for the general pose of a human's limbs in a video sequence, but are unlikely to yield the fine-detail,

---

[14] Markered motion capture systems can triangulate 3D markers to sub-millimeter accuracy. In contrast, markerless motion capture systems often use markered motion capture as a ground-truth reference and the best algorithms usually report 3D errors from these measurements of around three centimeters.

individual nuances of joint motion (especially around wrists and feet, or in cases of rapid motion) that are essential for an animator [168].[15] The techniques in this section lead into the more general algorithms for 3D data acquisition discussed in Chapter 8.

7.7.1   The Dynamical System Model

Most markerless techniques use a **dynamical system** model, in which we want to estimate the underlying **state** of a system based on a sequence of **observations**. For motion capture, we define the state $\theta(t)$ as a random variable specifying the underlying pose of the human (for example, a parameterization of the root position and joint angles of a kinematic model). The state can't be directly observed, but instead must be inferred based on a series of observations up to the current time, $\{\mathbf{r}(1),\ldots,\mathbf{r}(t)\}$. In motion capture, these observations are features extracted from images from a set of synchronized cameras surrounding a performer.

The relationships between successive states and between the states and observations are described by probabilistic models, respectively defined by the **state transition probability**

$$p(\theta(t)\mid\theta(1),\ldots,\theta(t-1)) \tag{7.33}$$

and the **observation likelihood**

$$p(\mathbf{r}(1),\ldots,\mathbf{r}(t)\mid\theta(1),\ldots,\theta(t)) \tag{7.34}$$

These are usually simplified using the **Markov property** and the assumption that the current observation only depends on the current state to

$$p(\theta(t)\mid\theta(1),\ldots,\theta(t-1)) = p(\theta(t)\mid\theta(t-1))$$

$$p(\mathbf{r}(1),\ldots,\mathbf{r}(t)\mid\theta(1),\ldots,\theta(t)) = \prod_{i=1}^{t} p(\mathbf{r}(i)\mid\theta(i)) \tag{7.35}$$

We therefore take a Bayesian approach, searching for the maximum (or multiple modes) of a **posterior** probability distribution

$$p(\theta(t)\mid\mathbf{r}(1),\ldots,\mathbf{r}(t)) \propto p(\mathbf{r}(t)\mid\theta(t))\,p(\theta(t)\mid\mathbf{r}(1),\ldots,\mathbf{r}(t-1))$$

$$\propto p(\mathbf{r}(t)\mid\theta(t))\int p(\theta(t)\mid\theta(t-1))\,p(\theta(t-1)\mid \tag{7.36}$$

$$p(\theta(t-1)\mid\mathbf{r}(1),\ldots,\mathbf{r}(t-1))\,d\theta(t-1)$$

Therefore, we can recursively update the posterior density based on its previous estimate and our models for the state transition and observation likelihoods. Markerless motion capture approaches differ in how the observation $\mathbf{r}(t)$ is extracted from the current image and related to the state, how the various probability densities are represented, and how the posterior is used to obtain the current state estimate.

---

[15] To be fair, many algorithms in this section aren't designed for highly accurate motion capture but for robust human detection, pose estimation, and tracking in video sequences, where the results are sufficient.

When the probability densities in Equation (7.35) are modeled using Gaussian distributions, the computation of the posterior reduces to the **Kalman filter**, a well-known signal processing algorithm [165]. However, in the motion capture problem, both densities are poorly modeled by Gaussians (in particular, they are multimodal) and a more appropriate approach is **particle filtering** [212]. In particle filtering, the posterior density is represented as a set of samples $\{s_k\}$ of the distribution, each with a probability $\{\pi_k\}$. This allows us to easily extract a single estimate of the current state (either by selecting the sample with the highest probability or by computing a weighted average of the samples based on their probabilities) or to retain multiple hypotheses about the current state (given by the top modes of the sample set).

However, since the state space for human pose is very large (that is, the vector $\theta(t)$ is usually at least thirty-dimensional), a standard particle filter would require an intractable number of samples to accurately represent the posterior density. Deutscher and Reid [119] proposed a modified particle filter for pose estimation that borrows ideas from simulated annealing and genetic algorithms to successively refine the estimate of the posterior with a viable number of samples. An alternate approach proposed by Sminchisescu and Triggs [457] focuses the samples in regions with high uncertainty.

Another way to deal with the large state space is to reduce its dimensionality. For example, a specific action such as walking has fewer degrees of freedom than a generic pose, which can be revealed by analyzing a training dataset using principal component analysis [447] or a more sophisticated latent variable model (see Section 7.4.3).

Modeling the state transition likelihood $p(\theta(t) \mid \theta(t-1))$ in Equation (7.36) is similar to the methods discussed in Section 7.4.3. For example, we can use single-frame and dynamical constraints based on biomechanical training data, in addition to incorporating character- or activity-specific learned models. In the rest of this section, we briefly overview typical features for markerless motion capture, which are used to form the observation likelihood $p(\mathbf{r}(t) \mid \theta(t))$ in Equation (7.36).

7.7.2   Silhouettes and Edges

Conventional motion capture systems use a large number of cameras to triangulate the observed images of the markers. In contrast, markerless systems often use a smaller number of cameras (as few as one), using features extracted in the set of images at each instant as the basis for pose estimation. When multiple cameras are involved, they must be calibrated using methods similar to those in Section 7.1.

First, we illustrate why the markerless problem is hard. Figure 7.20 illustrates several inherent difficulties with estimating pose from a single image. First, we face the challenging problem of isolating the human figure from a non-ideal background, a natural image matting problem of the type discussed in Chapter 2. This can be mitigated by using as simple of a background as possible, but markerless methods rarely go so far as to use a green screen.

Assuming we've accurately segmented the human from the background, several challenges remain. Foremost, in the absence of carefully placed markers and tight-fitting clothing, the positions of joints are much more difficult to infer from an image. For example, in Figure 7.20 the torso and arms all have the same texture and are

Figure 7.20. Estimating human pose from a single image (a) is a difficult computer vision problem. Even if the human can be automatically segmented from the image as in (b), loose clothing, confounding textures, and kinematic ambiguities mean that many degrees of freedom are estimated poorly.

(a)   (b)

difficult to individually segment, and the right knee has a bulge of fabric far from the actual joint. Image edges can help separate an image of a human into body parts for a bottom-up segmentation, but edges can also be confounding (e.g., a striped shirt).

We also face kinematic ambiguities. For example, in Figure 7.20 the left arm is foreshortened and the position of the left elbow joint is unclear; the right wrist and hand are completely obscured. Even with high-resolution cameras, it's also difficult to resolve rotations of the arm bones around their axes; for example, the orientation of the left hand in Figure 7.20 is difficult to guess. Sminchisescu and Triggs [457] estimated that up to a third of the underlying degrees of freedom in a kinematic model are usually not observable from a given viewpoint due to self-occlusions and rotational ambiguities. The poses of hands and feet are especially difficult to determine, which is why markerless systems frequently don't include degrees of freedom for the wrist and ankle joints.

Many markerless algorithms discard the original image entirely in favor of a **silhouette** of the human, estimated using background subtraction (i.e., matting; see Chapter 2). This exacerbates the problems illustrated in Figure 7.20, and introduces new ones. In Figure 7.21a-b, we can see that it's impossible to disambiguate the right limbs of the body from the left limbs by looking at the silhouette, leading to major ambiguities in interpretation. It's also difficult to resolve depth ambiguities (e.g., whether a foreshortened arm is pointed toward the camera or away from it). More generally, we can see that two very different poses can have similar silhouettes. Consequently, small changes in a silhouette can correspond to large changes in pose (e.g., an arm at the side (Figure 7.21a) versus an arm pointing outward (Figure 7.21c)). Therefore, several silhouettes from different perspectives are required to obtain a highly accurate pose estimate.

Figure 7.22 illustrates that some uncertainties can be mitigated if we also use **edge information** inside the silhouette. For example, the location of an arm crossed in front of the body might be better estimated if the boundary between the forearm and torso can be found with an edge detector.

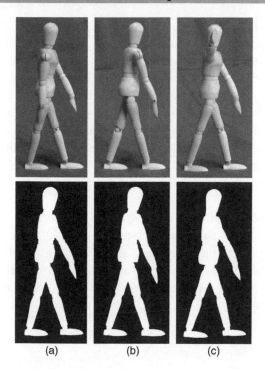

Figure 7.21. Three different poses and their corresponding silhouettes. We can see that major left/right and depth ambiguities are introduced when we only consider the silhouette from a given view, and that different poses can have similar silhouettes.

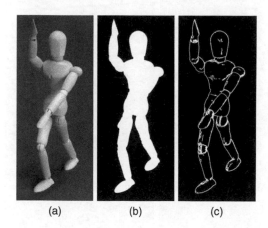

Figure 7.22. (a) Original image. (b) Silhouette. (c) Edges detected inside the silhouette. The edges clarify the position of the left arm, which was difficult to determine from the silhouette.

We describe a basic approach to computing the observation likelihood $p(\mathbf{r}(t) \mid \boldsymbol{\theta}(t))$ when $\mathbf{r}(t)$ consists of the binary silhouettes $\{S_i(t)\}$ and edge maps $\{E_i(t)\}$ from multiple images, $i = 1, \ldots, M$. A given value of $\boldsymbol{\theta}(t)$ is used to generate a solid human model in a certain pose. Since the cameras are calibrated, we can project this pose into each camera's view to obtain M silhouette images of the model $\{\hat{S}_i(t)\}$ and M edge maps of the model $\{\hat{E}_i(t)\}$. The observation likelihood is therefore related to how well the corresponding silhouette and edge images match, as illustrated in Figure 7.23.

For example, we could use

$$p(\mathbf{r}(t) \mid \boldsymbol{\theta}(t)) \propto \exp - \left(\lambda_1 \sum_{i=1}^{M} D_s(S_i(t), \hat{S}_i(t)) + \lambda_2 \sum_{i=1}^{M} D_e(E_i(t), \hat{E}_i(t)) \right) \qquad (7.37)$$

where λ_1, λ_2 are weights and D_s and D_e are distance functions between binary silhouette images and edge maps, respectively. A natural choice for D_s is the **Hamming distance** — that is, the number of pixels that have different labels in the two binary images. A common variant called the **chamfer distance**, suggested in this context by Gavrila and Davis [164], penalizes pixels in one image that are further from the silhouette in the other image more severely. We can also construct a weighted average of the pixels seen in one silhouette but not the other [449]. Ren et al. [388] proposed to learn an effective D_s based on a database of labeled poses; the distance function was composed of computationally efficient rectangular binary filters. We could also create D_s based on the correspondence between estimated matching points on the silhouettes.

The edge distance function D_e can be defined similarly to D_s; for example, we can count the number of edge pixels in $\hat{E}_i(t)$ that are observed in $E_i(t)$ [119]. We can see from Figure 7.23c that there are likely to be many edges in the real image not in the model, but most of the model edges should appear in the image if the model is correctly posed. The edge pixels can also be weighted by their gradient magnitude and orientation as a measure of importance [236].

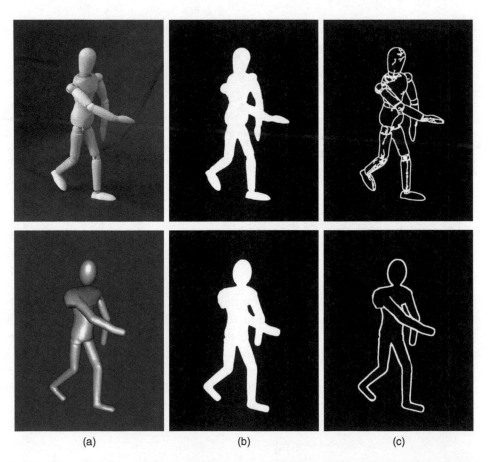

(a)   (b)   (c)

Figure 7.23. Silhouettes and edge maps for observed images (top) are compared to predicted silhouettes and edge maps corresponding to a candidate model position (bottom).

If we have a strong appearance model for the performer — for example, a model for the expected color of each body part [447] — this information can also be incorporated into $p(\mathbf{r}(t) \mid \theta(t))$. Shaheen et al. [438] compared the performance of markerless motion capture algorithms as the choices of image features and optimization approaches were varied.

Instead of explicitly specifying a generative model from a pose to image features, Agarwal and Triggs [3] used nonlinear regression on training data to directly predict pose as a function of an image silhouette. Sigal et al. [450] used belief propagation on a graphical model of body part relationships to estimate pose from an observation likelihood model.

7.7.3 Backprojections and Visual Hulls

A cost function like Equation (7.37) operates entirely in the domain of the M camera images. An alternate use of silhouettes is to project them into 3D space to constrain the location of the solid model. As Figure 7.24 illustrates, the rim of each silhouette back-projects into a region of 3D space. The edges of the correctly posed solid model must be tangent to each of the back-projected silhouette regions (which we can compute because the cameras are calibrated). That is, we can define $D_s(S_i(t), \hat{S}_i(t))$ in Equation (7.37) as the sum of distances between the 3D ray through each point on the ith silhouette to the closest point on the 3D body model (the short, thick lines in Figure 7.24a). Rosenhahn and Brox [397] and Gall et al. [161] described examples of this approach when the kinematic model is parameterized by twists.

The intersection of the backprojected silhouette volumes in 3D space corresponding to all of the available cameras is called the **visual hull** [263]. That is, the visual hull consists of the voxels inside all of the silhouettes from each camera perspective. As the number of cameras and the diversity of the set of perspectives grows, the visual hull becomes a more accurate estimate of the 3D space occupied by the solid body. The general concept is illustrated in Figure 7.25, and Figure 7.26 shows a real example involving an articulated human body. Generating the visual hull is also known as the **shape-from-silhouette** problem. Similar techniques are discussed in Section 8.3.1.

Generally, a visual hull approximation is fairly coarse (i.e., blocky) since subdivision of the capture volume into small voxels requires a substantial amount of memory. Also, a large number of cameras may be required to carve away voxels consistent with all the silhouettes but nevertheless incorrect (e.g., the protrusions from the chest in Figure 7.26b). The visual hull is always an overestimate of the occupied space, and cannot detect concavities.

Several markerless methods operate entirely in 3D by matching the solid body model to the visual hull or by matching the respective surfaces. The observation likelihood has the general form

$$p(\mathbf{r}(t) \mid \theta(t)) \propto \exp(D_v(V(t), \hat{V}(t))) \tag{7.38}$$

where $V(t)$ is the visual hull at time t and $\hat{V}(t)$ is the solid model corresponding to pose $\theta(t)$. D_v is a distance function defined over sets of voxels in 3D. Mikić et al. [324] described an early approach in which ellipsoids representing limbs were fit to the visual hull and their centroids and endpoints were used to fit a kinematic model parameterized with twists. Cheung et al. [91] described a similar hierarchical

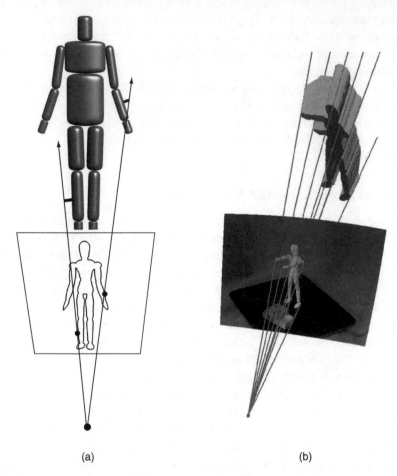

(a)   (b)

Figure 7.24. (a) The solid human model should be tangent to the 3D region created by back-projecting each observed silhouette. A distance function can be constructed as the sum of distances (short, thick lines) between rays from the camera center through points on the silhouette and the closest points on the 3D model. (b) An example backprojected silhouette region for a real image.

approach of fitting body parts of the kinematic model to the visual hull. Kehl and Van Gool [236] computed D_v as a weighted sum of squared distances between points on the model and the closest points on the visual hull. Corazza et al. [105] used a variant of the Iterative Closest Points (ICP) algorithm (see Section 8.4.2), commonly used for registering 3D point sets, to compute D_v. Vlasic et al. [520] took a slightly different approach of first fitting a kinematic skeleton directly inside the visual hull in each frame, and then refining a high-quality mesh model $\hat{V}(t)$ based on the skeletal poses and a skinned model.

7.7.4   Direct Depth Sensing

A final possibility for markerless motion capture is the use of sensors that directly recover the **depth** or distance to each point in the scene, using either time-of-flight or structured light technology. We'll discuss such systems extensively in Chapter 8. In

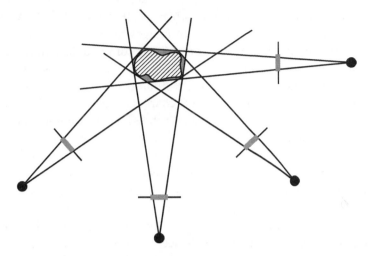

Figure 7.25. Four cameras observe the striped object. The visual hull is the shaded region formed by intersecting the backprojected silhouettes (gray lines on the image planes). The visual hull is always larger than the actual object.

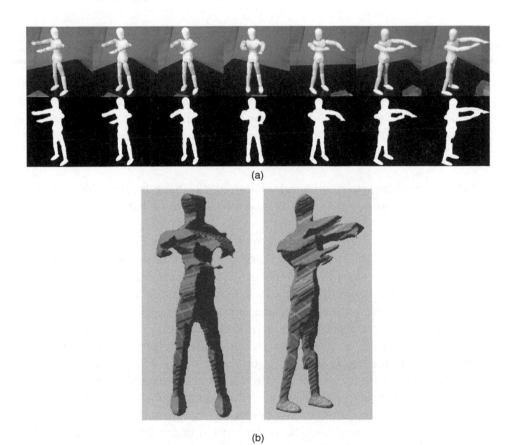

(a)

(b)

Figure 7.26. (a) Images of a mannequin acquired by seven calibrated cameras, and the corresponding automatically extracted silhouettes. (b) The resulting visual hull from a frontal and side view. The coarse 3D approximation is reasonable, but more cameras would be required to carve away the extraneous voxels.

the context of motion capture, Ganapathi et al. [162] fit a full-body skinned kinematic model to a stream of monocular depth images from a time-of-flight sensor in real time. Since the sensor observations are directly comparable to the model surface, the observation likelihood is relatively straightforward and is based on the noise model for the sensor. However, the proposed inference algorithm produced errors with respect to conventional motion capture markers that were still fairly high.

A more familiar consumer technology is the **Kinect** sensor introduced by Microsoft in 2010 as a new game-controlling interface for the Xbox 360, which uses a infrared structured-light-based sensor to produce a stream of monocular depth images. As described by Shotton et al. [445], hundreds of thousands of training images (both motion-captured and synthetic) were used to build a finely tuned classifier that maps each depth image to a set of candidate joint locations. The offline learning process is incredibly computationally intensive, but the resulting online classifier is extremely fast and can be hard coded into the device. The system is impressive for its ability to robustly succeed across a wide range of body types and environmental conditions in real time, though the goal is general pose estimation and not highly accurate motion capture (the depth sensor only has an accuracy of a few centimeters).

7.8   INDUSTRY PERSPECTIVES

Senior software engineers Nick Apostoloff and Geoff Wedig from Digital Domain in Venice, California discuss the role of body and facial motion capture in visual effects. Digital Domain is particularly well known for creating photo-realistic digital doubles using facial motion capture, as in the movies *The Curious Case of Benjamin Button* and *TRON: Legacy*.

RJR: The popular perception is that motion capture directly drives the performance of an animated character. Can you comment on how accurate this perception is?

Apostoloff: For early all-digital characters, like Gollum in the *Lord of the Rings* trilogy, mocap was completely used as reference material for the animators; it didn't directly drive the character at all. Today, we're getting much closer to applying mocap directly to animation. No company ever shows you how far you actually get, but I think we're at the point where, toward the end of a production, you get seventy to eighty percent of the character motion from mocap. In some cases, the animator's just touching up data you get back from the mocap. In other cases, there's lots of art direction that happens after the actual shoot. It's common that the actor will do something the director's not happy with looking at the data after the capture session, so they'll have to reanimate a lot of that. You might only use timing information from the mocap — for example, making sure the jaw moves at the right time — but they're going to animate a lot on top of that. There are certain things like eyes that they do from scratch all the time, just because eyelines change whenever a person moves around in a scene. We don't even bother capturing that here at the moment.

It also comes back to the complexity of the animation rig and the mapping from the motion capture data onto the animation controls. For *TRON: Legacy*, both the rig and the motion capture were modeled as two different linear systems, so that mapping

(a)

(b)

Figure 7.27. Motion capture was used extensively to help create the lifelike apes in *Rise of the Planet of the Apes*. In this example, actor Andy Serkis performs on a full-scale set of the Golden Gate Bridge, wearing a state-of-the-art body suit instrumented with infrared LED markers that were imaged by forty motion capture cameras. He also wears a facial motion-capture rig comprised of a head-mounted camera and green facial marker dots. The arm prosthetics allow Serkis to more accurately simulate an ape's proportions and gait. *Rise of the Planet of the Apes* ©2011 Twentieth Century Fox. All rights reserved.

was very easy. But the actual solution for the final geometry might not have looked as good as what you get from complex rigs that contain a lot of nonlinear functions like skin sliding. The more complex the animation rig, the better the final result looks, but it makes the job of mapping the mocap data onto the rig harder.

Wedig: In terms of facial motion capture, for the most part we were never aiming for a 100 percent solution of directly mapping mocap data onto a final animated character. Our goal is to produce a tool that gets rid of the boring work and the things that annoyed the animators on previous shows. The animator spends so long on a shot, and probably eighty to ninety percent of that time is just getting to the point where it's fun, where the animator is working on all the subtleties, emotional cues, and micro-expressions of the character. That's where we want our animators focused; we don't want them focused on how the jaw moves or whether the character's making a pucker with their lips.

RJR: Can you comment on the amount of cleanup that mocap data requires these days? What are the common types of errors and ways to fix them?

Apostoloff: In terms of body mocap, it's fairly straightforward. The capture system often works at about 120Hz, so you have a lot of temporal information in there that you can use to clean up missing markers.

   We often use what we call a "rigid fill" to fill in gaps in marker trajectories. That is, if a marker appears in one frame but not the next, we solve a least-squares problem to align nearby known markers in both frames with a rigid transformation. Then we can fill in the missing marker in the current frame by applying the rigid transformation to its position in the previous frame. People will also use splines to bridge gaps in trajectories or to remove noise from individual trajectories.

   For facial motion capture, we've developed several more advanced algorithms. Prior to going into production, we put the actors into a separate capture volume and have them go over a set of facial poses that try to cover the entire gamut of what they can do in terms of facial deformation. These include a mix of visemes, facial action coding units, and emotional ranges. These facial poses are recorded using the MOVA Contour system. We remove the head motions and use those to build a an actor-specific statistical model of what their face does when it deforms, which we put into a Bayesian framework to estimate missing markers when they occur. The prior term is built from the captured training data, and the data likelihood term involves what you get back from the mocap. We use simple Gaussian models for the face and it works well, but we'd need a different approach for the body since there's more articulated motion.

Wedig: Another approach we use is to build a face model as a linear combination of selected shapes from the training process. We then can project mocap data onto this model, with a bias toward having large contributions from a small set of shapes. The animator can then use the shapes "activated" in a given frame as a basis for subsequent animation.

RJR: What kinds of problems arise when mapping mocap data onto an animated character with a different body size and shape?

Apostoloff: A big problem is scale differences between the actors and characters. If you have a constant scale change among all of your actors and the characters — say you've got actors playing giants and you're going to scale all of them four times — they usually behave well in the same environment. But say you have one actor who's being scaled by a factor of 1.2 to make their character bigger and you have another actor who's being scaled by a factor of 0.8 to make their character smaller. You can record them together on the motion capture stage, for example approaching each other and shaking hands. But when you put them into the virtual environment and scale everything, they no longer meet up and connect at the same point. This is a huge issue in mocap.

In particular, you may record an actor on the motion capture stage walking across the room and interacting with different props. If you scale an actor's mocap data down to make a smaller character, they don't actually make it to the other side of the room! You have to introduce extra gait or strides somewhere for them to make it across. That's a fairly big problem and the process for fixing it is usually quite manual. Often you capture a lot of generic background motion of actors so you can then insert these bits into scenes to fix them. I don't think people often use things like automatic gait generation to fix these kinds of issues, since that involves a different simulation pipeline that's difficult to insert into a production.

RJR: Can you describe your system for facial motion capture?

Wedig: We have a head-mounted camera system that uses four grayscale cameras on carbon fiber rods that sit around the jaw line. You get very good pictures of the mouth and jaw area. If we were to put the cameras higher up, they would interact with the actor's eye line, which some actors find very distracting. By putting the cameras in a flat sort of curve around the bottom of the head we can be sure that any part of the face is seen by at least two cameras. We use the images from the four cameras to individually track dots on the actor's face, which are placed in a specific pseudo-random pattern developed over several years. Initially the dots are applied by hand, and afterward we use a plastic mask with holes drilled in it to try to get some consistency across shots. We can't put the dots very close to the actor's lips because they get messed up when they eat or wipe their face.

Matching the marker set on a given shot with our canonical marker set is still a problem we have to write a lot of code to address. Another big issue is stabilization. No matter how good the carbon fiber rods are, they're going to bounce. They bounce when the actor breathes, when they walk, or when they move their head. Filtering the unwanted motion is very difficult.

Finally, we map the motion of the dots onto the actor-specific face model created from training data described earlier.

RJR: Has markerless motion capture made any inroads into visual effects production?

Apostoloff: It's used sometimes in the film industry, mostly for body double work. You can get a very high-resolution dense mesh from that kind of setup. If you're going to have a character that looks very similar to your actor, and you want to capture all the nuanced performance of your actor without doing a lot of animation on top of that, it's great.

For example, you may want some high-profile actors to appear to fall out of a plane and perform some stunts, but you don't actually want to throw your high-profile actors out of the plane. Instead, you might take them to one of those free-fall, vertical wind tunnel places and capture a bunch of footage from twenty different cameras around them, reconstruct the volume around them, and insert it into a new scene like a blue-screen kind of effect. That kind of voxel-carving effect was used for a sequence in *Quantum of Solace*. While the reconstructed geometry may not be great, you'd be amazed at how believable it looks if you've got great texture. While it wasn't for a feature film, the video game *L.A. Noire* used a kind of facial markerless mocap for a digital body double effect. They captured high-resolution textured geometry of people and just streamed it directly into the game to get some amazing results.

On the other hand, markerless mocap isn't a viable technique for replacing traditional mocap on a large film production at this point in time. What you can get from a traditional motion capture system like a Vicon is incredibly accurate, and the retargeting to different characters works very well. It's a seamless pipeline and there are real-time systems that can do live pre-visualization of the animated characters on set in the virtual production environment, which is very useful for the directors.

While markerless systems are incredibly convenient, because you don't have to dress somebody up in a ridiculous outfit, what you get back from such systems is often quite jerky and noisy. Also, you're usually restricted in the size of the volume that you can film the actors in. If you want to shoot a scene with twenty different actors doing a dance sequence you can't do that with markerless mocap.

One of the biggest issues is that we need to have a system that we can use for animation after we process the mocap data. If your character looks a lot different from your actor, it's not often clear how you would use the high-resolution mesh data from markerless motion capture to animate a character. Taking traditional mocap data and mapping it to a complicated network of animation controls is already a really hard problem! We haven't reached the point where we can map the data across from motion capture into animation accurately enough to worry about that little bit of information that we lose from not having a complete mesh.

7.9   NOTES AND EXTENSIONS

Motion capture is related to the classical perceptual experiments described by Johansson in the 1970s [223]. Markers were attached to the joints of a performer wearing tight clothing (i.e., a primitive motion capture suit). The performer was filmed by a static camera while acting out different motions in a studio, and the resulting video was processed so that only the markers were visible in each frame. Untrained observers watching the videos could immediately identify the motions as a human walking, climbing, dancing, and so on, even when less than ten markers were used. This remarkable human ability to recognize human motion from very little information suggests that the sparse input of marker motion is sufficient to capture a recognizable, individual performance.

The book by Menache [323] gives an excellent first-hand account of the history and filmmaking applications of motion capture, as well as practical advice for setting up a motion capture session and processing the resulting data files. Moeslund and colleagues [331, 332] and Poppe [372] surveyed and categorized the literature on markerless motion capture. In particular, [332] gives an exhaustive taxonomy of vision-based pose estimation through 2006.

Today, a large amount of motion capture data is freely available to researchers and animators. In particular, the Carnegie Mellon University motion capture database (http://mocap.cs.cmu.edu) is an excellent resource containing thousands of sequences from more than 100 performers in motion capture suits. The captured activities range widely, including walking, dancing, swordfighting, doing household chores, and mimicking animals. The data is available in many formats, and useful tools for interacting with it are provided. The newer HumanEva datasets, also made available by CMU [449], have a smaller range of activities, but include multi-view video sequences synchronized with motion capture trajectories from markers placed on normal clothing. These datasets are valuable for developing markerless techniques and have become benchmarks for the computer vision community.

In this chapter, we focused on motion capture technology using infrared lighting and retro-reflective markers, but the same algorithms for marker triangulation and processing apply to any markers (e.g., table tennis balls or ARTags), provided that they can easily be detected and tracked in video. For example, the Imocap system designed by Industrial Light and Magic uses white balls and binary patterns fastened to a gray bodysuit to allow performances to be captured in natural environments instead of on a motion capture stage. This technology was notably used in the *Pirates of the Caribbean* and *Iron Man* movies. Also, facial motion capture markers are often directly drawn or painted on the skin. Prototype technologies for new motion capture sensors include tiny ultrasound microphones coupled with miniature gyroscopes and accelerometers [519] and lightweight photosensitive tags that respond to coded optical transmitters [382]. These new technologies carry the promise of accurate motion capture in real-world outdoor environments instead of carefully controlled indoor stages.

We assumed that the kinematic models for humans were known; however, it's also possible to learn these models and their relationship to motion capture markers (e.g., [394, 241]). Ross et al. [399] even showed how the kinematic models for unusual objects (e.g., giraffes or construction cranes) could be estimated from tracked 2D features alone. Such methods might be useful in situations where we have no good prior model for the kinematic skeleton (e.g., motion capture of an unusual animal like a kangaroo).

Yan and Pollefeys [560] extended factorization techniques for structure from motion to estimate an underlying articulated skeleton from tracked features. Indeed, the calibration and triangulation problems in motion capture are closely related to aspects of the matchmoving problem we discussed in Chapter 6, and familiar techniques for structure from motion can be extended to markerless motion capture to allow for moving cameras. For example, Liebowitz and Carlsson [281] extended metric reconstruction in the case where the scene points lie on a dynamic articulated skeleton whose bone lengths are known. Hasler et al. [190] automated the synchronization of the cameras and improved the feature detection and body model.

Brand and Hertzmann [65] discussed how a database of performances of the same action (e.g., walking) by different performers could be used to separate the style of a motion from its content and estimate style parameters for each performer. This approach enabled previously recorded activities to be rendered in the style of a different performer, as well as the generation of new styles not in the database. Liu et al. [290] estimated biomechanical aspects of a performer's style (e.g., relative preferences for using joints and muscles), assuming that the recorded motion capture data optimizes a personal physics-based cost function.

The more extensively component motions are edited, the greater the risk the synthesized motion appears unnatural to human eyes. Ren et al. [387] designed a classifier trained on a database of both natural and unnatural motions that could predict whether a new motion had a natural appearance. The classifier is based on a hierarchical decomposition of the body into limbs and joints, so that the source of an unnatural motion can be automatically pinpointed. In addition to motion editing, this approach could also be used to detect errors in raw motion capture data and to determine markers and intervals that need to be fixed. Safonova and Hodgins [415] proposed an algorithm that analyzed the physical correctness of a motion sequence, taking into account linear and angular momentum and ground contact, which can improve the appearance of interpolated motions.

Cooper et al. [104] applied an adaptive learning algorithm to direct the sequence of actions that a motion capture performer should execute in order to efficiently build a good library of clips for motion editing and synthesis. Kim et al. [239] discussed the extension of motion editing to enable multiple characters to interact in a task (e.g., carrying objects in a relay).

The main goal of full-body motion capture is to record the geometric aspects of a performance. However, many applications of facial motion capture require not only the recording of facial geometry but also high-resolution facial appearance — for example, to make an entirely convincing digital double. Alexander et al. [11] gives an interesting overview of the evolution of photorealistic actors in feature films. They used the Light Stage at the University of Southern California to acquire the detailed facial geometry and reflectance of a performer, producing an incredibly lifelike facial animation rig.

We generally assumed that motion capture data is processed for production well after it is acquired. However, in a live setting, we may need to use motion capture data to drive an animated character in real time, which is sometimes called **computer puppetry**. This process is now commonly used on motion capture stages to allow a director to crudely visualize the mapping of an actor's performance onto an animated character in real time, notably for movies like *Avatar*.

The main problem is delivering fast, reliable inverse kinematics results to drive a rigged character at interactive rates. Shin et al. [443] described one such algorithm, which makes instantaneous choices about which end-effector motions are most important to preserve in the inverse kinematics, and leverages analytic solutions for speed. Chai and Hodgins [85] showed how a performer wearing only a few markers attached to normal clothing could drive an animated character in real time. The low-dimensional input is used to quickly search a database of high-quality motion capture subsequences that are seamlessly strung together and played back in real time.

While we only discussed motion capture for full bodies and faces, biomechanical engineers often use markered systems to study hands (e.g., [64]) for understanding dexterity and grasping. These can be augmented with force-feedback sensors to study how fingers interact with objects they contact [257]. Park and Hodgins [360] used about 350 markers finely spaced over a performer's body to collect accurate data about the motion of skin, muscle, and flesh (e.g., bulging, stretching, jiggling). Feature films such as the *Lord of the Rings* trilogy have even incorporated motion capture data from horses; of course, this requires an entirely different kinematic model. Rosenhahn et al. [398] studied markerless motion capture of athletes interacting with machines (e.g., bicycles and snowboards), which makes the kinematic skeleton more complicated (i.e., since the legs are now connected by the machine into a closed chain).

7.10   HOMEWORK PROBLEMS

7.1   a)   Show that if P, C_i, and V_i are fixed, then the inner term of Equation (7.1) for one camera

$$\|P - (C_i' + \lambda_i V_i)\|^2 \tag{7.39}$$

is minimized by $\lambda_i = V_i^\top P$. Show that the minimum distance of the point to the ray is thus

$$P^\top P - 2C_i'^\top P + C_i'^\top C_i' - (V_i^\top P)^2 \tag{7.40}$$

Recall that by definition V_i is unit length and $V_i^\top C_i' = 0$.

     b)   Verify Equation (7.2) by differentiating Equation (7.1) with respect to P and using the results of (a).

7.2   Compute the number of degrees of freedom for the human kinematic model illustrated in Figure 7.8 (including the root).

7.3   Derive the forward and inverse conversion formulas between a rotation represented as a unit quaternion $q \in \mathbb{R}^4$ and as an axis-angle vector $r \in \mathbb{R}^3$.

7.4   Compute the position of the wrist with respect to the shoulder's coordinate system using a forward kinematics model for the arm illustrated in Figure 7.9. Assume that the upper arm is 28 cm long and the forearm is 25 cm long, and that the quaternions specifying the shoulder and elbow rotations are $q_s = [0.1089, 0.3969, -0.6842, -0.6021]$ and $q_e = [0.3410, 0.2708, 0.4564, -0.7760]$ respectively.

7.5   Here, we prove that if a three-dimensional rigid motion is specified by a rotation matrix R (corresponding to a rotation ψ around a unit vector v) and a translation vector t, then the vector $\rho \in \mathbb{R}^3$ needed in Equation (7.10) to form the twist representation is given by

$$\rho = \frac{(\mathbf{I}_{3\times3} - R^\top)t}{2(1 - \cos\psi)} \tag{7.41}$$

a) By equating the rigid motion $RX + t$ with the equivalent screw transformation $R(\mathbf{X} - \rho) + dv + \rho$ (where d is the linear displacement along the screw axis), show that $t = (\mathbf{I}_{3\times3} - R)\rho + dv$.

b) Show that $(\mathbf{I}_{3\times3} - R^\top)t = (2\mathbf{I}_{3\times3} - R - R^\top)\rho$.

c) Use the Rodrigues formula and the fact that $\rho^\top v = 0$ to show that $(2\mathbf{I}_{3\times3} - R - R^\top)\rho = 2(1 - \cos\psi)\rho$, proving Equation (7.41).

7.6 The exponential map of a 3×3 matrix is defined by a matrix Taylor series:

$$\exp(M) = \mathbf{I}_{3\times3} + M + \frac{1}{2}M^2 + \frac{1}{6}M^3 + \cdots$$

$$= \sum_{k=0}^{\infty} \frac{1}{k!}M^k \tag{7.42}$$

In Equation (7.12) we have the special case of $\exp[v]_\times$, where $[v]_\times$ is the skew-symmetric matrix defined in Equation (5.39).

a) Show that $[v]_\times^2 = vv^\top - \|v\|^2\mathbf{I}_{3\times3}$ and $[v]_\times^3 = -\|v\|^2[v]_\times$.

b) By considering the first 6 terms of the exponential Taylor series, conclude that

$$\exp[v]_\times = \cos\|v\|\mathbf{I}_{3\times3} + \text{sinc}\|v\|[v]_\times + \frac{1 - \cos\|v\|}{\|v\|^2}vv^\top \tag{7.43}$$

thus proving the Rodrigues formula.

7.7 Show how to modify Equation (7.26) when the angle between the vectors $\mathbf{X}_j(t) - \mathbf{X}_i(t)$ and $f_{ij}(\boldsymbol{\theta}(t))$ should be as close as possible to a given angle ϕ.

7.8 Show how the constraint that a specific joint angle remain in the limits $\theta_l \leq \theta_i(t) \leq \theta_u$ can be expressed in the form of Equation (7.27) (assuming the joint is directly parameterized with angles, not quaternions or twists).

7.9 Show how to formulate limits on (a) joint velocity and (b) joint acceleration as soft constraints in an inverse kinematics cost function. Be sure to specify whether your limits are in 3D space or joint angle space.

7.10 Give specific examples of (a) a linear low-pass and (b) a nonlinear noise-removing filter that can be applied independently to each joint parameter channel $\theta_i(t)$.

7.11 Explain why simply linearly interpolating quaternions is incorrect.

7.12 Using spherical linear interpolation, compute the rotation matrix that is one-third of the way from

$$R_1 = \begin{bmatrix} -0.4129 & 0.8744 & 0.2547 \\ -0.6783 & -0.1086 & -0.7267 \\ -0.6077 & -0.4729 & 0.6380 \end{bmatrix} \quad \text{to}$$

$$R_2 = \begin{bmatrix} -0.6101 & 0.5428 & 0.5772 \\ -0.4169 & 0.3996 & -0.8164 \\ -0.6738 & -0.7387 & -0.0175 \end{bmatrix}$$

You'll need to convert from rotation matrices to quaternions and back.

7.13 Sketch how a mirror-based facial motion capture setup as mentioned in Section 7.6 (sketched in Figure 7.28) effectively creates multiple virtual cameras. How can such a system be calibrated?

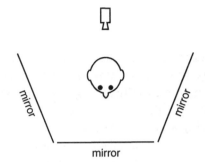

Figure 7.28. A camera positioned above the performer's head views images of the face reflected in three mirrors (one parallel to the image plane, two at angles).

7.14 Provide sketches to show that (a) the visual hull cannot resolve concavities and (b) the visual hull can be substantially larger than the actual object.

7.15 Sketch an eighth perspective of the human in Figure 7.26 that would carve away the voxels protruding from the chest area.

8 Three-Dimensional Data Acquisition

A key responsibility of a visual effects supervisor on a movie set is to collect three-dimensional measurements of structures, since the set may be broken down quickly after filming is complete. These measurements are critical for guiding the later insertion of 3D computer-generated elements. In this chapter, we focus on the most common tools and techniques for acquiring accurate 3D data.

Visual effects personnel use several of the same tools as professional surveyors to acquire 3D measurements. For example, to acquire accurate distances to a small set of 3D points, they may use a **total station**. The user centers the scene point to be measured in the crosshairs of a telescope-like sight, and the two spherical angles defining the heading are electronically measured with high accuracy.[1] Then an electronic distance measuring device uses the time of flight of an infrared or microwave beam that reflects off of the scene point to accurately determine the distance to the target. However, acquiring more than a few 3D distance measurements in this way is tedious and time-consuming.

It's recently become common to automatically survey entire filming locations using laser range-finding techniques, which we discuss in Section 8.1. The result is a cloud of hundreds of thousands of 3D points visible along lines of sight emanating from the laser scanner. These techniques, collectively called **Light Detection and Ranging** or **LiDAR**, are highly accurate and allow the scanning of objects tens to hundreds of meters away.

For closer-range three-dimensional acquisition, the key technology is **structured light**, which we describe in Section 8.2. A stripe or pattern of visible light is projected onto the surface of an object, and the deformation of this pattern as seen by a nearby camera provides sufficient information to determine the shape of the object's surface. Structured light is commonly used for scanning actors' bodies and faces, as well as movie props and models. A variety of patterns can be used for structured light, from a single plane of laser light that casts a sharp stripe on the object to an array of colored stripes projected from an off-the-shelf LCD or DLP projector. High-speed projector-camera systems can even allow us to recover the real-time 3D motion of a performer's face.

While highly accurate, LiDAR and structured light have the disadvantage that they are **active** techniques — that is, visible light is projected into the scene. This can be disorienting, especially for an actor suffering brightly colored, changing patterns of

---

[1] This part of the device is called a **theodolite** or **transit**.

light projected onto his or her face. An up-and-coming alternative from traditional computer vision is the passive technique of **multi-view stereo (MVS)**. Multi-view stereo algorithms combine the natural images from a large set of calibrated cameras with dense correspondence estimation to create a 3D dataset, typically represented as a texture-mapped mesh or a set of colored voxels (Section 8.3). While MVS techniques are about an order of magnitude less accurate than active lighting methods, they can still produce convincing, high-resolution 3D data.

Finally, we discuss common algorithms required for registering 3D datasets, since several scans from different locations may be required to see all sides of an object to build a complete model (Section 8.4). As in the 2D case, we detect, describe, and match features, and use these as the basis for automatically registering two scans of the same scene from different perspectives. We then address the fusion of a large number of scans into a single coordinate system and data representation.

8.1   LIGHT DETECTION AND RANGING (LIDAR)

We can think about a LiDAR scanner[2] as an advanced version of the "laser measuring tape" that can be found in a hardware store. The basic principles are similar: a laser pulse or beam is emitted from a device, reflects off a point in the scene, and returns to the device. The time of flight of the pulse or the phase modulation of the beam is used to recover the distance to the object, based on a computation involving the speed of light. While the hardware store laser measuring tape requires the user to manually orient the laser beam, a LiDAR scanner contains a motor and rapidly spinning mirror that work together to sweep the laser spot across the scene in a grid pattern.

Figure 8.1 depicts two 3D scanners based on the main methodologies for LIDAR data acquisition. The first scanner, in Figure 8.1a, uses a time-of-flight-based sensor and can measure distances of hundreds of meters, while the second scanner, in Figure 8.1b, is a phase-based system with a maximum range of about eighty meters. Despite the long distances involved, both types of scanners are accurate to within a few millimeters. An added advantage is that the distance to each point is measured directly, as opposed to inferred using a vision-based method like multi-view stereo. For these reasons, laser scanning is considered the gold standard for 3D data acquisition. We'll discuss the physical principles behind both scanners shortly.

As illustrated in Figure 8.2, LiDAR data is usually collected in a spherical coordinate system. For every azimuth and elevation angle (θ, ϕ), the scanner returns a distance $d(\theta, \phi)$, measured in physical units like meters, to the first point in the scene encountered along the specified ray.[3] For given intervals of θ and ϕ, the $d(\theta, \phi)$ values can be interpreted as a **range** or **depth image**, which can be manipulated using standard image processing algorithms.[4] Well before their application to visual effects, LiDAR

---

[2] In military applications, the acronym LADAR (LAser Detection And Ranging) is often used instead.

[3] Some LiDAR scanners report multiple distance returns per ray, which can occur due to transparent, reflective, or quickly moving surfaces in the scene.

[4] Scanners also frequently report the **return intensity** at each ray, which is related to the reflectance, material properties, and orientation of the corresponding surface. This return intensity image can also be processed like a normal digital image.

Figure 8.1. (a) A time-of-flight-based LiDAR scanner. (b) A phase-based LiDAR scanner.

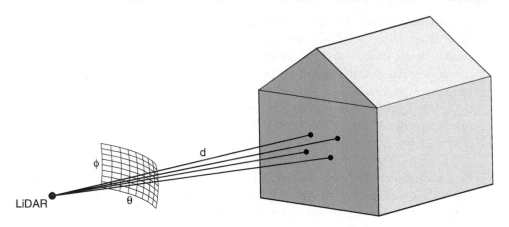

Figure 8.2. The principle of LiDAR scanning.

scanners were mounted in airplanes and used to generate high-quality terrain maps for military and geospatial applications.

Figure 8.3 illustrates an example LiDAR scan of a large building. We can appreciate the millimeter accuracy of the scan, even though the scanner was approximately fifty meters away from the sixty-meter-wide building. Since the scanner's laser can't penetrate solid objects, LiDAR scans have characteristic "shadows" of missing data produced by occluding foreground objects, which can be seen in Figure 8.3a. These shadows can be filled in with data from scans from different perspectives once they have been registered to a common coordinate system, as described in Section 8.4.2.

While the 3D data acquired from a LiDAR scanner is generally of very high quality, it's important to note that some materials are problematic for laser-ranging technologies. Highly reflective surfaces such as glass generally result in missing or incorrect distance measurements, since the laser beam can easily bounce off the object and hit another surface in the scene. Depending on the type of glass, the laser beam may

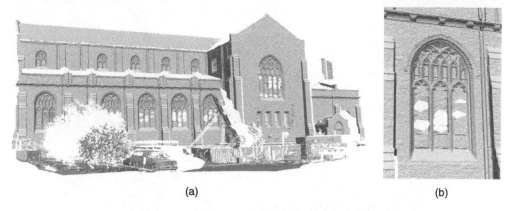

(a)   (b)

Figure 8.3. (a) An example LiDAR scan of a large building. This scan contains approximately 600,000 points and the building face is approximately 60m across. Note the characteristic "shadows" on the building due to occlusions by the tree and truck in the foreground, and missing returns in several of the windows. (b) A detail of the scan.

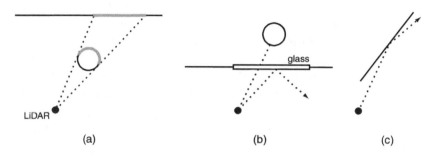

(a)   (b)   (c)

Figure 8.4. Characteristic problems with LiDAR scanning. (a) Missing data (thick gray lines) due to occlusion (back side of circular object) and "shadows" (hidden area of rear wall). (b) False or missing returns from rays directed at glass surfaces. (c) Grazing-angle errors from surfaces nearly parallel to the incident ray.

also pass directly through it, returning the distance to an object on the other side. Also, dark or highly absorptive surfaces may be difficult to scan since an insufficient amount of light is reflected back to the scanner. Finally, surfaces nearly parallel to the laser beam often produce poor-quality distance measurements, since most of the light is reflected away from the scanner; these are called "grazing-angle" errors. Figure 8.4 illustrates these characteristic problems with LiDAR scanning.[5]

Therefore, the best-case scenario for LiDAR scanning is a scene containing bright, matte surfaces that are all roughly perpendicular to the laser beam. Man-made structures like buildings typically scan well (except for the windows, as can be seen in Figure 8.3b). Accurately scanning a difficult object like a shiny car typically requires it to be treated with an even coat of matte white spray-on powder beforehand.

---

[5] There are many smaller issues as well. For example, the spread of the laser spot over a long distance can affect the accuracy of the return, as well as the interaction between the color of the laser and the color of the scene surface. That is, a green laser may be very accurate for a faraway white surface but give an inaccurate or missing return for a red surface at the same distance.

Figure 8.5. A co-registered color camera can be used to texture-map the points in a LiDAR scan, making it more understandable.

While LiDAR scanners are designed only to return distance measurements, many systems include an integrated RGB camera whose pixels are precisely aligned with the (θ, ϕ) rays. This allows the raw 3D points to be texture mapped with color for a more pleasing and understandable rendering, as illustrated in Figure 8.5. Furthermore, the color information can be extremely useful when registering multiple LiDAR scans, as discussed in Section 8.4. If a LiDAR sensor doesn't come with a co-registered camera, a rigidly mounted auxiliary RGB camera can be calibrated against the LiDAR sensor based on the resectioning algorithms discussed in Section 6.3.1 and an appropriate calibration target.

8.1.1   Pulse-Based LiDAR

Pulse-based LiDAR systems are based on a simple idea, as illustrated in Figure 8.6. A laser pulse is emitted along the given ray into space; it bounces off a surface in the scene and the scanner measures the elapsed time t for the round trip. The pulse traveled a distance $2d$ in this time, and we use the constant speed of light c to compute d from the **time of flight** t:

$$d = \frac{1}{2}ct \tag{8.1}$$

To reduce noise in the measurement, the times of flight of several pulses sent in quick succession are often averaged. The lasers in pulse-based systems are generally eye safe and have wavelengths of 500-1000nm (i.e., green, red, or, infrared light). On a clear day, pulse-based LiDAR can receive returns from over a kilometer away (though this is rarely necessary for visual effects applications).

Suppose we want to ensure that the distance measurements are accurate to within $\pm$5mm; today's pulse-based LiDAR systems can achieve or exceed this accuracy. Equation (8.1) implies stringent tolerances on the receiver electronics, since they must be able to resolve time differences of 33 picoseconds or less. Furthermore, the returned pulse may be very weak since its energy falls off with the inverse fourth power of distance [216]. Pulse-based LiDAR systems are often somewhat expensive for these reasons. The process of scanning a large scene with fine resolution in θ and

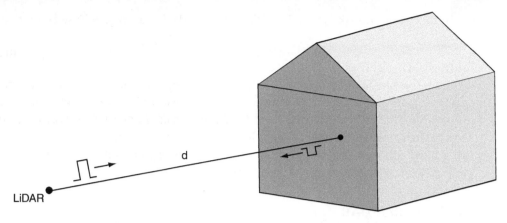

Figure 8.6. The time of flight of a laser pulse can be used to infer the distance to an object in the scene.

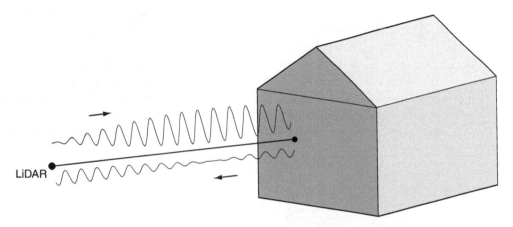

Figure 8.7. The phase shift of a sinusoidally-modulated continuous laser waveform can be used to infer the distance to an object in the scene.

ϕ can take tens of minutes with a pulse-based system — time that's precious on a busy movie set, and raises the likelihood of significant changes occurring in the scene during the scan.

8.1.2 Phase-Based LiDAR

A faster alternative technology that's even more accurate than pulse-based LiDAR but has a smaller operating range is **phase-based LiDAR**. Instead of using the time of flight of a pulse, phase-based systems use the amplitude modulation of a continuous-waveform laser, as illustrated in Figure 8.7. A sinusoidal laser waveform is emitted along the given ray into space; it bounces off a surface in the scene and the scanner measures the phase shift ψ between the transmitted and received signals over the round trip.

This phase shift is related to the time of flight t and the frequency of the modulating sinusoid in radians ω by

$$\psi = \omega t \tag{8.2}$$

Combining Equation (8.1) with Equation (8.2) yields the key phase-based equation

$$d = \frac{c\psi}{2\omega} \qquad (8.3)$$

Since the phase difference can only be measured modulo 2π, this introduces a constraint on the maximum range that can be measured before introducing **range ambiguity**. That is, we require that $0 < \psi < 2\pi$, which in practice imposes a maximum range of forty to eighty meters, depending on the modulation frequency [42].[6] On the other hand, phase-based systems are quite a bit faster than pulse-based systems, a great advantage when time is of the essence.

8.1.3   Flash LiDAR

Flash LiDAR is the name given to a technology used for obtaining low-resolution, close-range depth maps in real time. However, the name is a bit confusing since there's no laser that scans across the scene point by point. Instead, the scene is bathed in spatially uniform, temporally modulated infrared light, and a CMOS sensor computes depth measurements over all the pixels of a small (e.g., 176×144) array simultaneously. Such devices are also called **time-of-flight cameras**. This name is also somewhat confusing, since pulse-based LiDAR directly (and more accurately) measures time of flight to compute distances. Figure 8.8 depicts a flash LiDAR device.

Flash LiDAR data acquisition uses the same principles as the LiDAR technologies discussed earlier. Some systems use a pulse (often the pulses are a bit wider than

Figure 8.8. A flash LiDAR device, also known as a time-of-flight camera. The CMOS sensor in the middle (the silver circle) is surrounded by a bank of infrared LEDs that illuminate the scene.

---

[6] It's possible to design algorithms to resolve this ambiguity using phase unwrapping techniques, if we put constraints on the extent or spatial gradient of objects in the scene. Alternately, multiple modulating frequencies can be used with the downside of increasing scanning time.

in Section 8.1.1, resulting in a shorter-range system) while others are phase-based, using four samples of the incident waveform to estimate the phase (see Problem 8.7).

The main advantage of a flash LiDAR system is its speed; short-range depth images can be generated in real time at thirty frames per second or higher. Flash LiDAR devices are also relatively inexpensive and much easier to set up and use than pulse- or phase-based LiDAR systems. On the other hand, there are several disadvantages to current flash LiDAR systems in addition to the low resolution. In particular, the measurement accuracy is quite a bit worse than either of the LiDAR technologies discussed previously or the structured light and multi-view stereo methods discussed next (i.e., errors on the order of centimeters rather than millimeters). Furthermore, the sensors may work poorly outdoors or at very close range, and typically exhibit a systematic distance error [244]. Computer vision researchers have recently made progress in applying super-resolution techniques to flash LiDAR, combining multiple successive images from a moving sensor to improve the quality of each frame [110]. There are also several visual effects applications, such as projecting image-based environment lighting onto a 3D object, where high accuracy in the 3D measurements isn't critical and the speed of collection is more important.

8.2   STRUCTURED LIGHT SCANNING

The best method for acquiring three-dimensional measurements of a small object — such as a movie prop or an actor's head — is **structured light scanning**. For every major visual effects movie, the principal actors' bodies and heads are scanned before or during production using the types of scanners pictured in Figure 8.9. The resulting 3D scans are used to build digital stunt doubles for actors, to aid in creating realistic

(a)   (b)

Figure 8.9. (a) A body scanner based on structured light. The performer stands on the middle platform as four structured-light scanners move up and down the surrounding gantry. (b) A head scanner based on structured light. The performer sits in the chair as the gantry moves around his or her head.

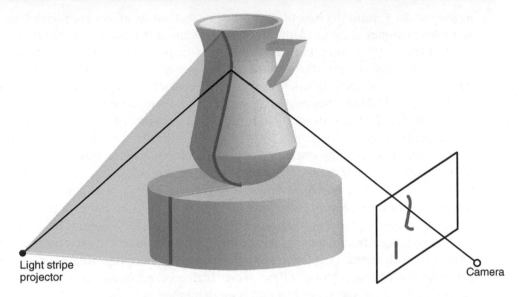

Figure 8.10. The principle of structured light scanning. The object is illuminated with a plane of light that intersects the surface of the object as a deformed stripe, which is observed by an offset camera. The projector and camera are accurately calibrated so that 3D locations can be recovered by triangulation.

aging transformations, or to provide a starting point for morphing into a computer-generated creature.

The basic principle of structured light scanning is illustrated in Figure 8.10. The object to be scanned is illuminated with a vertical plane of light that intersects the surface of the object as a deformed **stripe**. This light plane can be created with a visible-spectrum laser that passes through a cylindrical lens, a slide projector, or an off-the-shelf LCD or DLP projector.

The stripe has kinks where the surface normal changes, and discontinuities where it falls on two physically separated surfaces. The stripe is observed from a nearby camera that has been accurately calibrated with respect to the projector; the camera's image of the stripe allows us to reconstruct its 3D profile using triangulation. Often, the camera is fitted with a special lens, filter, or polarizer to attenuate interference from ambient light conditions and accentuate the color of the laser stripe.

Sweeping the light plane across the object allows its entire surface to be digitized. A well-calibrated structured light system is extremely accurate, with errors of less than a millimeter for tabletop-scanning scenarios. Structured light scans obtained as an object is rotated in front of a fixed projector-camera system can be registered and fused into a complete 360° model of an object.

We first describe how to calibrate a structured light system consisting of a projector and a camera, and how to use triangulation to obtain accurate 3D measurements (Section 8.2.1). We then extend the single-stripe approach to **time-multiplexing** methods, in which multiple stripe patterns are projected onto a static object to obtain a scan much more quickly than sweeping the stripe across the object (Section 8.2.2). We next explore **color stripe coding** methods, in which a more complex projected pattern of light effectively casts multiple finely spaced stripes on the surface at once, enabling so-called **one-shot scanning** (Section 8.2.3). Finally, we discuss structured light systems targeted at capturing dynamic scenes in real time using **fringe projection** (Section 8.2.4).

8.2.1   Calibration

The earliest range scanners used a visible-spectrum laser passing through a cylindrical lens to cast a strong, bright stripe on the object to be scanned, and this technique is still used today (e.g., for the scanners pictured in Figure 8.9). The key problem is to determine the geometric relationship between each plane of laser light and the camera's image plane, as illustrated in Figure 8.11. As we'll see, this process is very much like calibrating two cameras, except that one of the cameras is replaced by a laser.

As we know from Sections 5.1 and 6.3.2, the relationship between the coordinates of two 3D planes is given by a 2D **projective transformation**. We assume that the plane of laser light has world coordinates given by (X, Y, Z) with $Z = 0$, so that the coordinates of the plane are given by (X, Y) and we have

$$\begin{bmatrix} X \\ Y \\ 1 \end{bmatrix} \sim \begin{bmatrix} h_{11} & h_{12} & h_{13} \\ h_{21} & h_{22} & h_{23} \\ h_{31} & h_{32} & h_{33} \end{bmatrix} \begin{bmatrix} x \\ y \\ 1 \end{bmatrix} \tag{8.4}$$

where the image plane coordinates of the camera are given by (x, y). Here, we've represented the 2D quantities as homogeneous coordinates and the projective transformation as a 3×3 matrix H defined up to scale.

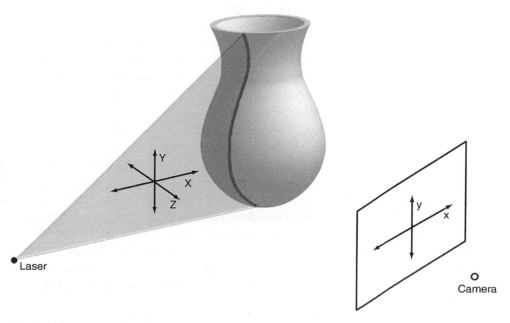

Figure 8.11. The image plane of the camera (with coordinates (x, y)) and the plane of laser light (with coordinates (X, Y)). The two 2D coordinate systems are related by a projective transformation.

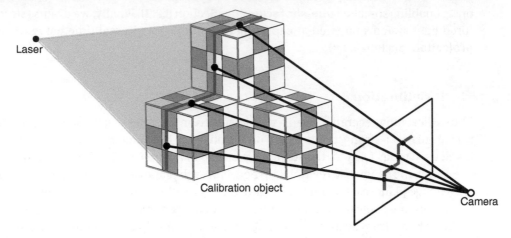

Figure 8.12. An object with known 3D geometry can be used to calibrate a light plane with respect to an image plane. The black 3D dots on different surfaces of the calibration object are all coplanar since they lie on the laser plane.

There are several ways to obtain the correspondences between the image plane and the light plane that we need to estimate the parameters of the projective transformation, all of which require a calibration object with known 3D geometry. Typically we exploit the knowledge that a given image point lies on a known world plane [385] or world line [86], or matches exactly with a known world point [211].

A straightforward approach uses a calibration object made up of cubes with checkerboard faces of known dimensions, as illustrated in Figure 8.12. With the laser turned off, the checkerboards supply the information required to calibrate the camera using the plane-based method of Section 6.3.2 or the resectioning method of Section 6.3.1. With the laser turned on, the light plane intersects multiple planes in the image whose equations are known. By intersecting rays from the now calibrated camera's center with these planes, we obtain a set of co-planar points, to which we can fit a 3D plane (at least three points are required on two different surfaces). Once we have the equation of the plane in 3D, we can change coordinates to obtain the projective transformation in Equation (8.4).[7]

Now we have a direct mapping given by Equation (8.4) between any point in the image plane and 3D world coordinates, but only for a single position of the light plane (i.e., a single stripe on the object). To scan the entire object, the laser stripe projector and camera (which are rigidly mounted to each other) usually move along a precisely controlled linear (e.g., Figure 8.9a) or circular (e.g., Figure 8.9b) path, such that the world coordinate transformation between any two positions of the scanner head is known. Alternately, the projector/camera rig stays in place while a precisely computer-controlled stage translates the object through the light plane. Handheld laser stripe scanners (e.g., the Polhemus FastSCAN) use a magnetic sensor to localize the scanner head in space (using similar technology to magnetic motion capture systems).

---

[7] Or, we can simply leave the (X, Y, Z) values in the same world coordinate system in which the planes were defined.

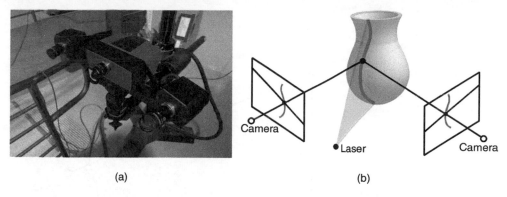

(a) (b)

Figure 8.13. (a) A 3D acquisition rig containing two calibrated cameras (left and right) and a structured light projector (center). (b) The intersection of the laser stripe's projection and an epipolar line in the left image plane generates a unique correspondence in the right image plane, which can be triangulated to determine a 3D point on the object's surface.

Precise calibration of such laser-stripe systems is critical; vendors of commercial systems usually offer precisely machined calibration objects of known geometry to aid in recalibration. An easier approach that doesn't require precise calibration between the image and light planes is to use two rigidly mounted cameras (i.e., a stereo rig), as illustrated in Figure 8.13a. In this case, we first calibrate the stereo rig as described in Section 6.4. Then an uncalibrated, roughly vertical laser stripe is swept across the surface. Each position of the stripe results in a pair of images from the two cameras. The intersection of the stripe with each pair of conjugate epipolar lines produces an image correspondence. Since the stereo rig is calibrated, the rays through each pair of corresponding points can be triangulated to obtain a 3D point, as illustrated in Figure 8.13b. In this case, the laser stripe simply provides a way to obtain an unambiguous correspondence along each pair of conjugate epipolar lines.[8]

In the previous discussion, we assumed that the center of the laser stripe could be accurately determined in the camera image (for example, by fitting a Gaussian distribution to the stripe's profile and finding the peak). However, this approach can be problematic when the stripe hits a corner in the scene or straddles a reflectance discontinuity on the object. Curless and Levoy [111] showed that the triangulation could be made even more precise using **space-time analysis** — that is, by observing the evolution of the stripe's image as it moves across the object. Figure 8.14 illustrates the idea; as the stripe passes across the indicated point on the object, the returned laser intensity at the camera rises, then falls. By finding the peak of a Gaussian function fit to this space-time curve, the exact time at which the stripe hits the point can be estimated.

Finally, we note that much computer vision research uses an LCD or DLP projector to create stripes and patterns instead of a laser. In this case, the calibration process is very similar to the plane-based camera calibration method described in Section 6.3.2. First we calibrate the camera as usual by showing it several images of a moving checkerboard. The projector can also be thought of as a camera that always "sees"

---

[8] Davis and Chen [113] describe how a single camera and a system of mirrors can be used to avoid the need for a second camera.

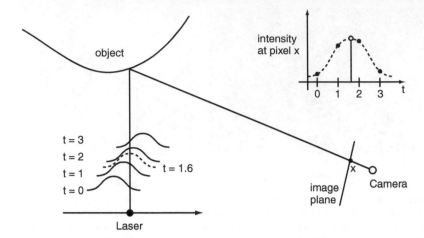

Figure 8.14. Space-time analysis for better triangulation. The observed intensity at pixel **x** as a laser stripe sweeps across the surface of an object is modeled as a Gaussian function (dotted line, top right). The mean of the Gaussian gives an estimate of the time at which the laser stripe is centered directly on the corresponding point on the 3D object.

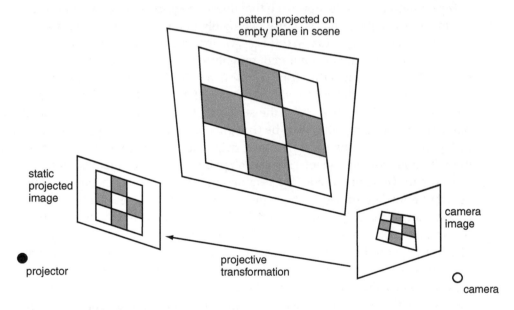

Figure 8.15. Calibrating an LCD or DLP projector by observing the projections of a checkerboard on a blank plane.

the image it projects, as illustrated in Figure 8.15. Thus, we can compute the internal and external parameters of the projector using a clever approach: we *project* a static image of a checkerboard or a grid onto an empty white plane that is moved around the scene [240].

For each position of the plane, the camera views a skewed checkerboard, and we compute the projective transformation H_i mapping the skewed camera image to the rectilinear projected image. By collecting the projector-to-camera correspondences for all the positions of the plane, we can easily estimate the fundamental matrix and epipolar geometry relating the projector and camera (see Section 5.4.2). The camera matrix for the projector P_{proj} is related to the fundamental matrix through the relationships in Section 6.4 and the projective transformations $\{H_i\}$ through the relationships in Section 6.3.2. A method similar to the plane-based calibration of Section 6.3.2 can then be applied to the set of $\{H_i\}$ to estimate P_{proj} [381, 125].[9] Once we have these external and internal parameters, the triangulation process is the same as in Section 6.4.

8.2.2 Time-Multiplexing Methods

In order to scan a stationary object using N stripes, it seems like we'd need to project N separate planes of laser light. One possibility is to project multiple light planes at once; unfortunately, as Figure 8.16 illustrates, determining which stripe is which can be a difficult, ambiguous problem in the presence of complex scene geometry. Stripes may be missing, and they may even switch orders. Therefore, we need some way to uniquely identify a stripe from its appearance.

This section describes a solution to the problem based on projecting a series of binary patterns onto the object with a slide or LCD/DLP projector, as illustrated in Figure 8.17. That is, at each instant, a point on the object is either illuminated (corresponding to bit 1) or not illuminated (corresponding to bit 0). The temporal pattern of zeros and ones at a pixel forms a binary codeword that uniquely identifies the index of the projected stripe. The number of stripes we can generate is limited by the width resolution of the projector as well as the narrowest stripe width that the nearby camera can accurately resolve. Since the codeword is created by flashing different intensity patterns over time, these are called **time-multiplexing** methods.

Figure 8.17 illustrates the most basic approach using simple binary codewords. The patterns go from low frequency to high frequency; if we use M patterns, then 2^M unique stripes can be resolved. Therefore, we have a side benefit that to obtain K stripes, we only need to project $\log_2 K$ patterns.

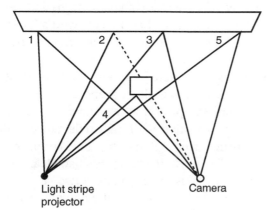

Figure 8.16. Simultaneously projecting multiple planes of laser light onto an object can lead to ambiguity in stripe identification. In this top view, the stripes are projected left to right in the order 1-2-3-4-5, but the camera sees the stripes in the order 1-4-3-5.

Light stripe projector

Camera

---

[9] An alternate approach is to project a checkerboard image onto a physical checkerboard in the scene. Since the camera is calibrated, the positions of the 3D points corresponding to the corners of the projected checkerboard can be computed, and we can apply resectioning (Section 6.3.1) to estimate P_{proj} [414].

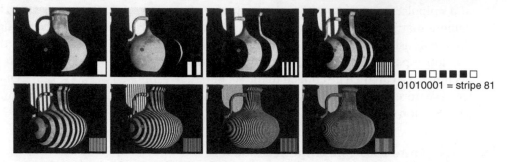

■□■□■■■□
01010001 = stripe 81

Figure 8.17. Projecting M binary patterns (inset at the lower right of each image) onto an object allows 2^M on/off patterns to be generated, effectively coding the index of the light plane. In this example, we use eight binary patterns, allowing 256 stripes to be uniquely indexed. The on/off patterns at the indicated point show that it corresponds to stripe 81 in the finest-resolution pattern.

Figure 8.18. This slightly different set of binary patterns is based on Gray codes. The codewords for each pair of adjacent stripes only differ in one bit.

It's much more common to use a slightly different set of binary patterns illustrated in Figure 8.18 based on **Gray codes**. The advantage is that the codewords for each pair of adjacent stripes only differ in one bit, making it easier to accurately determine where the stripe transition occurs.[10]

Determining whether a scene point is illuminated or not illuminated at a given instant is harder than it may sound. For example, a scene point with low reflectance under bright illumination from the projector may have a comparable intensity in the camera's image to a scene point with high reflectance under no projection illumination. Therefore, using a single global threshold to make the illuminated/non-illuminated decision for all pixels in the image is a bad idea.

One possibility, as illustrated in Figure 8.19a, is to first acquire two calibration images: one in which the projector is on for all pixels (i.e., an all-white pattern) and one in which the scene is not illuminated by the projector at all (i.e, an all-black pattern). The average of these calibration images gives a *spatially adaptive* threshold

---

[10] Another way to think about this is that we're using the same 2^M codewords, but just changing their left-to-right order in the projected image.

(a)   (b)

Figure 8.19. (a) Two images in which the projector is fully on and totally off allow the determination of a per-pixel threshold. In this case the (on,off) intensities at the (darker) red pixel are (137, 3) and at the (brighter) green pixel are (226, 18), leading to per-pixel thresholds of 70 and 122, respectively. (b) Alternately, each binary pattern and its inverse can be projected, and we interpret a 1 if the pattern at a pixel is brighter than its inverse.

Figure 8.20. Hall-Holt and Rusinkiewicz's proposed patterns for stripe boundary coding.

that we can use to determine the on/off state for each pixel in the subsequent binary patterns.

Alternately, Scharstein and Szeliski [426] suggested projecting each binary pattern followed by its inverse, as illustrated in Figure 8.19b. The codeword bit is assigned as 1 if the pixel's intensity is brighter in the original pattern compared to the inverse pattern, and 0 in the opposite case. They claimed this approach was more reliable than using all-on and all-off images; on the other hand, it requires projecting twice as many patterns. Regardless of the approach, scanning objects that are shiny or contain surfaces with very different reflectances can be difficult. As with LiDAR scanning, the best-case scenario is a matte object with uniform reflectance.

Hall-Holt and Rusinkiewicz [185] advocated the use of **stripe boundary codes**. That is, instead of trying to detect the *center* of each stripe to use in triangulation, they proposed to detect the *boundary* between stripes, which can be more accurately located. Thus the changing pattern of on/off illumination of the stripes on each side of the boundary generates the codeword. In particular, they proposed the set of four patterns illustrated in Figure 8.20; each pattern contains 111 stripes, and each of the 110 quadruples of on-off patterns across the stripe boundaries occurs only once.[11]

Clearly, we can reduce the number of projected patterns required to define a codeword if we allow the patterns to have more than two states. One possibility is to allow grayscale values in the projections, and another is to allow colored stripes. In either case, if each stripe in a pattern can be in one of N states, then N^M unique stripes can be coded with M patterns. Horn and Kiryati [204] explored the grayscale approach, using Hilbert space-filling curves to produce well-separated codewords for a user-specified number of patterns or stripes. However, the more gray-level states

---

[11] Note that we can't directly resolve a boundary when the illumination is constant across it (e.g., white-white). However, the sequence is designed so that the patterns both before and after such an occurrence have a visible illumination change, which localizes the boundary.

are allowed, the more difficult it is to correctly resolve the state, especially in the presence of nonuniform-reflectance objects.

Caspi et al. [83] studied the problem of colored stripes in more detail. They carefully modeled the relationship between the projected color, the surface reflectance, and the camera's color response for each scene point, resulting in a set of color patterns adapted to the environment to be scanned. The model can be written as

$$C_{cam} = A\,D\,P(C_{proj}) + C_0 \tag{8.5}$$

where C_{cam} is the observed RGB color at a camera pixel, C_{proj} is the color instruction given to the projector, and C_0 is the observed color with no projector illumination. The constant 3×3 matrix A defines the coupling, or cross-talk, between the color channels of the projector and the camera, and the pixel-dependent diagonal matrix D is related to the corresponding scene point's reflectance. The projection operator P accounts for the difference between the instruction given to the projector and the actual projected color. All of the parameters of the model can be estimated prior to scanning using a simple colorimetric calibration process. Given this model, the goal is to choose scene-adapted color patterns that can be maximally discriminated by the camera. The result is a generalized Gray code that uses a different number of levels for each color channel and was shown to improve on binary Gray codes. In the next section, we discuss color-stripe methods in more detail.

8.2.3   Color-Stripe Coding Methods

Clearly, to get a high-quality (many-stripe) scan of an object using the methods in the previous section, we need to project quite a few patterns onto it. This is fine for stationary objects like movie props, but it presents a problem for moving objects. For example, even if an actor is asked to stay very still, their subtle head movements may lead to substantial variations over the course of ten or more projected patterns, resulting in unusable 3D data. There is thus much research interest in **one-shot** methods that effectively acquire many stripes simultaneously using a single pattern. These methods typically use a static projected image of colored vertical bars, designed so that no local neighborhood of bar-to-bar transitions is repeated across the width of the image. Therefore, instead of using a time-multiplexed pattern of illumination to uniquely identify the stripes as in the previous section, here we exploit the knowledge that the spatial neighborhood of a given stripe is unique by construction.

The key concept underlying many modern one-shot techniques is a special type of numerical pattern called a **de Bruijn sequence**. A de Bruijn sequence of order k using an alphabet of N symbols is a cyclic sequence of length N^k of symbols from the alphabet that contains each possible length-k subsequence exactly once. For example, the sequence

0001002000301101201302102202303103203311112113122123132133222323333

is a de Bruijn sequence of order 3 over an alphabet of four symbols. We can verify that every possible length-3 subsequence occurs exactly once.

Figure 8.21. Zhang et al.'s color stripe pattern created using a de Bruijn sequence of order 3 over five symbols.

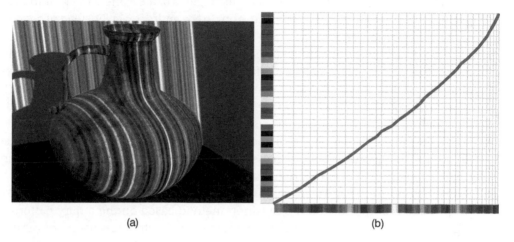

(a)   (b)

Figure 8.22. (a) An image of an object illuminated using the stripe pattern in Figure 8.21. (b) Recovering the correspondence between the projected and observed color patterns using dynamic programming.

Zhang et al. [568] proposed a good example of a color-stripe technique based on de Bruijn sequences. Their goal was to select a color stripe pattern such that every stripe differed from its neighbor in at least one color channel, and that each subsequence of three stripe transitions was unique. They thus used a de Bruijn sequence of order 3 over five symbols to create the 125-stripe pattern illustrated in Figure 8.21.[12]

Zhang et al. also used Caspi et al.'s color model in Equation (8.5) to preprocess the camera colors to be better correlated with the color instructions to the projector. Finally, they used dynamic programming (Appendix A.1) to correlate the observed stripe pattern along a scanline with the known projected pattern. As illustrated in Figure 8.22, dynamic programming works well to obtain this correspondence when the stripes don't change positions (i.e., the surface is sufficiently smooth). In cases where the order of stripes is non-monotonic, Zhang et al. applied multiple passes of dynamic programming to recover each "piece" of the correspondence, removing the rows and columns of the dynamic programming graph corresponding to already found pieces. The cost function for the dynamic program is based on a model of consistency between two candidate color transitions. Finally, Zhang et al. incorporated

---

[12] In this application, $N = 5$, not 8, since Zhang et al. did not allow adjacent stripes to be the same color, and ruled out neighbors in which the red and green channels changed at the same time.

Curless and Levoy's space-time analysis to improve stripe localization by smoothing the color stripe pattern and shifting it across the object's surface (this is only applicable to static scenes).[13]

Several researchers have extended the basic idea proposed earlier. Je et al. [217] analyzed the problem of color selection for the stripes and suggested that patterns that used only red, green, and blue were most reliable. Pagès et al. [359] proposed a hybrid color stripe pattern that contains both color edges and a square-wave pattern of intensity; employing multiple intensity levels allows fewer colors to be used. Schmalz and Angelopoulou [429] described a fast method for decoding the stripe index based on aggregating similarly colored regions of the camera image into superpixels and applying a graph-based algorithm to the entire image (instead of decoding each scanline independently).

In general, correctly identifying stripe colors and color transitions is difficult when the scene to be scanned is also colorful. For example, a red stripe falling on a green object surface and a green stripe falling on a red object surface may both present the same dark color in the camera image. Thus, as with the other methods discussed so far, a neutral-colored, matte surface is the best-case scenario.

It's important to note that an algorithm that computes 3D point locations based on a one-shot approach is not necessarily real time. Indeed, Zhang et al.'s original one-shot algorithm had a reported running time of a minute per frame (later reduced to five seconds per frame using a modern processor [429]). Rusinkiewicz et al. [410] proposed a real-time 3D data acquisition method based on the binary patterns in Figure 8.20 that operated at sixty frames per second with a latency of four frames. In order to allow object motion during scanning, they tracked the stripe boundaries across the frames to maintain the correct correspondence of points on the object surface. Koninckx and Van Gool [250] achieved real-time scanning at around twenty frames per second using a one-shot technique. They used a pattern composed of periodic black and white stripes, cut diagonally by a series of colored lines. The intersections of the diagonal lines with the bars provide uniquely identifiable points for triangulation; the stripe labels are refined with a graph-cut algorithm. An interesting feature of this approach is that the vertical stripe frequency and the color and slope of the diagonal lines are adapted to the current scene over time, instead of always using the same pattern. Algorithms from the last class of structured-light approaches we discuss, fringe-based methods, are also well suited to real-time acquisition.

8.2.4   Fringe Projection Methods

The stripe-based methods we've discussed so far implicitly assume that the projected pattern looks like a step function in color space. The final class of methods we discuss is based on the projection of a continuous sinusoidal pattern of intensity, also known as a **fringe pattern**. This pattern is swept across the scene in discrete steps of phase, so such methods are also known as **phase-shifting methods**.

---

[13] We discuss similar phase shifting techniques in the next section.

Figure 8.23. The three phase-shifted images used in the fringe projection algorithm.

Huang et al. [206] described the basic approach of projecting three sinusoidal images with frequency ω separated by $\frac{2\pi}{3}$ in phase:

$$I_R(x,y) = \frac{1}{2}\left(1 + \cos\left(\omega x - \frac{2\pi}{3}\right)\right)$$

$$I_G(x,y) = \frac{1}{2}\left(1 + \cos\left(\omega x\right)\right) \tag{8.6}$$

$$I_B(x,y) = \frac{1}{2}\left(1 + \cos\left(\omega x + \frac{2\pi}{3}\right)\right)$$

The images have been scaled in intensity to take up the full [0, 1] range, and are illustrated in Figure 8.23.

Huang et al. made the clever observation that these fringe patterns could be projected at extremely high speed (i.e., 240 frames per second) by modifying a single-chip DLP projector. A DLP projector modulates the white light from a projector bulb into grayscale intensities using a digital micromirror device (DMD), an array of tiny mirrors that rapidly flip back and forth. RGB colors are created at each pixel by placing a rapidly spinning "color wheel" between the bulb and the DMD. If the color wheel is removed, then sending a static RGB image to the projector results in moving grayscale fringes projected at high speed onto an object. This trick has been adopted by many researchers in the projector-camera community.

The DLP projector is synchronized with a high-speed digital camera. Therefore, a sequence of three successive images captured by the camera will be given by

$$I_1(x,y) = A(x,y) + B(x,y)\ \cos\left(\psi(x,y) - \frac{2\pi}{3}\right)$$

$$I_2(x,y) = A(x,y) + B(x,y)\ \cos\left(\psi(x,y)\right) \tag{8.7}$$

$$I_3(x,y) = A(x,y) + B(x,y)\ \cos\left(\psi(x,y) + \frac{2\pi}{3}\right)$$

where $A(x,y)$ is the per-pixel average intensity of the three images, $B(x,y)$ is the per-pixel amplitude of the observed sinusoid, and $\psi(x,y)$ is the observed phase map. We can recover this phase map at each pixel by combining the three observed intensities:

$$\psi(x,y) = \arctan\left(\sqrt{3}\frac{I_1(x,y) - I_3(x,y)}{2I_2(x,y) - I_1(x,y) - I_3(x,y)}\right) \tag{8.8}$$

While $\psi(x,y)$ is only recovered modulo 2π, if the surface is sufficiently smooth, the phase can be unwrapped into a continuous function. This uniquely identifies the column of the projected image, allowing the usual triangulation method to be used to obtain the 3D location of each point.

This general approach has been extended in various ways to improve the speed of image acquisition and processing. For example, Zhang and Huang [571] replaced the calculation in Equation (8.8) with one that depends simply on intensity ratios, and Zhang and Yau [572] used two fringe images and a flat (projector-fully-on) image to mitigate measurement errors and increase processing speed. Weise et al. [540] noted that moving objects inevitably generate "ripple" artifacts in 3D since the assumption that the same pixel location in all three images in Equation (8.7) corresponds to the same scene point is incorrect. They proposed a method to estimate and compensate for the underlying motion to remove the artifacts.

Phase unwrapping is a major challenge for fringe-projection methods, and there is a vast literature on methods to solve the problem (e.g., see [166]). Luckily, in applications where real-time performance is required (e.g., real-time 3D measurement of facial expressions), the surface generally changes sufficiently smoothly (except in problematic regions like facial hair).

8.3   MULTI-VIEW STEREO

The final technology we'll discuss for obtaining detailed 3D measurements of an object or scene is **multi-view stereo (MVS)**. This term covers a large class of methods with the common theme that only a set of source images $\{I_1, \ldots, I_M\}$ from calibrated cameras is used as the basis for the 3D estimation problem. In contrast to LiDAR and structured light methods, multi-view stereo algorithms are **passive**, meaning that the sensing technology doesn't interfere at all with the scene.

We can think of multi-view stereo as a combination of the material in Chapters 5 and 6. That is, first a set of cameras (typically ten or more) is accurately calibrated, either using a calibration device or by matching features in a natural scene. Then, region correspondence techniques are adapted from the stereo literature to obtain dense correspondences between pairs of images and across sets of images. Since the cameras are calibrated, triangulating these correspondences leads to 3D measurements of scene points.

In this section we overview four general approaches to multi-view stereo. The first set of **volumetric** methods represents the scene as a finely sampled set of colored voxels, and selects a set of voxels whose shape and color is consistent with all the images. The second set of **surface deformation** methods evolves a mesh or level-set function to enclose the final set of 3D points using partial-differential-equation-based techniques. The third set of **patch-based** methods generates small 3D planar patches in the scene by triangulating multi-image feature matches, and grows these patches in 3D to account for as much of the scene as possible. Finally, the fourth set of **depth map fusion** methods begins with dense depth maps obtained from stereo pairs and tries to incrementally fuse them into a unified set of 3D points.[14]

Seitz et al. [433] gave an important overview of the multi-view stereo literature as of 2006, and contributed a carefully ground-truthed evaluation benchmark used by most modern multi-view stereo researchers. This benchmark[15] catalyzed multi-view stereo research in the same way that the previous Middlebury benchmarks

---

[14] Algorithms that only produce a sparse, irregular set of 3D points (e.g., the recovered 3D points produced by a matchmoving algorithm) are not considered to be multi-view stereo algorithms.

[15] Datasets and continually-updated results are available at http://vision.middlebury.edu/mview/.

accelerated research in stereo and optical flow. The two main evaluation datasets are based on roughly constant-reflectance models approximately ten centimeters on a side, captured from a hundreds of viewpoints distributed on a hemisphere (see Figure 8.27a). Strecha et al. [470] later contributed a benchmarking dataset for large-scale multi-view stereo algorithms, using high-resolution images of buildings many meters on a side.

It's important to note that while modern multi-view stereo results are qualitatively quite impressive, and quantitatively (i.e., sub-millimeter) accurate for small objects, purely image-based techniques are not yet ready to replace LiDAR systems for highly accurate, large-scale 3D data acquisition. For example, Strecha et al. [470] estimated that for large outdoor scenes, only forty to sixty percent of the 3D points for a top MVS algorithm applied to high-resolution images were within three standard deviations of the noise level of a LiDAR scanner, while ten to thirty percent of the ground truth measurements were missing or wildly inaccurate in the MVS result. For this reason, multi-view stereo papers typically use LiDAR or structured light results as the ground truth for their algorithm comparisons. Multi-view stereo algorithms can also be quite computationally expensive and hence slow, another drawback compared to near-real-time structured light systems.

8.3.1 Volumetric Methods

Volumetric methods for 3D data acquisition share similarities with the problem of finding the visual hull from silhouettes of an object, as discussed in Section 7.7.3. As in the visual hull problem, we require a set of accurately calibrated cameras, and represent 3D space as a set of occupied voxels. The finer the voxelization of the space is, the more accurate the 3D reconstruction will be. However, in the multi-view stereo problem, we also use the colors of the pixels inside the object silhouette — not only to color the voxels on the resulting 3D surface but also to remove voxels inconsistent with the observed color in some source image. Therefore, the result of a volumetric multi-view stereo method is usually a subset of the visual hull with colors associated to each surface voxel, so that rendering the voxels from the point of view of each camera should produce a similar image to what was actually acquired.

The basic **voxel coloring** idea originated in a paper by Seitz and Dyer [435]. In this approach, a plane of voxels is swept through space along the direction of increasing distance from the cameras. A special camera configuration — for example, that no scene point is contained within the convex hull of the camera centers — is required. Each voxel in the current plane is projected to the images, and the colors of the corresponding image pixels are evaluated for consistency. If the colors are all sufficiently similar (e.g., the standard deviation of the set of color measurements is sufficiently small), the voxel is called **photo-consistent**, kept and colored; otherwise, it is removed.[16] The photo-consistency idea is illustrated in Figure 8.24. Voxels along lines of sight "behind" (i.e., in a depth plane after) a colored voxel are not considered in subsequent steps.

---

[16] This method, and multi-view stereo methods in general, perform best on Lambertian surfaces, as opposed to specular or translucent ones. Of course, the same is true for LiDAR and structured light methods.

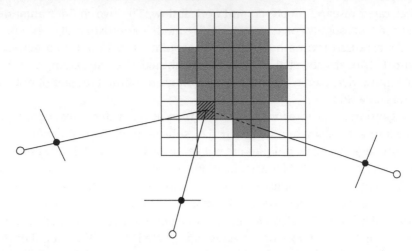

Figure 8.24. A top view of one plane of voxels and three cameras with associated image planes. Gray voxels are occupied, and white voxels are empty. A voxel is photo-consistent if its color closely matches the color of all the pixels in the images in which it is visible. In this example, the color of the striped voxel only needs to agree with the colors of the pixels in the left and middle cameras, since it is occluded from the perspective of the right camera.

Kutulakos and Seitz [258] later proposed the seminal **space carving** approach, which formalized the concept of the **photo hull**, the largest set of colored voxels that is photo-consistent with the input images. The space carving algorithm provably achieves the photo hull by iteratively removing voxels from an initial volume (e.g., the visual hull), either one by one or along a set of orthogonal sweeping planes. While there are no restrictions on the camera configuration, many sweep iterations may be required to reach the photo hull.

Kolmogorov and Zabih [247] proposed an algorithm that can handle the same camera configurations as voxel coloring, but has the advantages that spatial coherence between the source image pixels is enforced, and that irreversible incremental decisions about voxel removal are avoided. They posed the problem as a labeling problem over the pixels in all the source images, where the label corresponded to a discretized depth from a reference camera. The problem of finding an optimal labeling is posed as a graph-cut problem in which the data term is related to voxel photo-consistency and the smoothness term encourages neighboring pixels to have similar depths. An additional visibility term is required to encode the notion that voxels are opaque. The multi-label graph-cut problem is solved using α-expansion.

Vogiatzis et al. [522] investigated a different graph-cut approach for more realistic multi-view stereo problems. Instead of using multiple labels, they posed a two-label problem in which each voxel was classified as part of the object or not.[17] The smoothness term in the problem is related to the photo-consistency of neighboring voxels, while the data term encourages the volume to expand (to avoid incomplete reconstructions). Voxels outside the visual hull can be automatically ruled out if image silhouettes are available. Once the voxels are selected with either graph-cut approach,

---

[17] In a sense, this is a 3D generalization of the matting problem.

they can be colored (e.g., using the average color of the corresponding pixels in the images in which they are visible).

An interesting feature of volumetric approaches is that neither sparse nor dense correspondences between the images are typically required, unlike some of the other algorithms in this section. However, the general problem with volumetric approaches is that their accuracy is limited by the size of the voxel grid. Even at tabletop scale, the grid needs to be hundreds of voxels on a side to achieve sub-millimeter accuracy, and the resulting space carving or graph-cut methods are computationally demanding, both in terms of speed and required memory. Also, as with voxel carving, a reasonably large number (tens to hundreds) of calibrated images may be required to get an acceptable result.

8.3.2   Surface Deformation Methods

The next class of methods is based on evolving a 3D surface to wrap tightly around the region in 3D containing an object, which can be viewed as a generalization of active contours or "snakes" for image segmentation [230]. The surface can be represented either explicitly as a **triangle mesh**, or implicitly as the **zero-level set** of a 3D functional. The triangle mesh approach is appealing in that the vertex coordinates don't need to be discretized, and the mesh representation is immediately useful for subsequent tasks. On the other hand, maintaining the correct topology of the mesh can be difficult, especially for scenes containing multiple objects or objects containing holes. The level-set approach gracefully handles the changing topology of the underlying surface, but has similar problems with resolution and memory requirements as volumetric methods since a voxel grid is required.

The algorithm by Hernández and Schmitt [131] is a good representative of triangle-mesh-deformation methods. First, the visual hull is estimated and fit with a triangulated mesh[18], which serves as the initial 3D surface S. The **energy** of a candidate surface is defined as

$$E(S) = E_{\text{texture}}(S) + E_{\text{silhouette}}(S) + E_{\text{internal}}(S) \qquad (8.9)$$

In Equation (8.9), the E_{texture} term is based on the consistency of each surface point with the projections in the resulting images, measured using the normalized cross-correlation of windows around the projected correspondences. That is, for vectors of image intensities u and v taken from square windows surrounding a correspondence in a pair of images, we compute

$$NCC(u, v) = \sum_{i=1}^{n} \frac{1}{s_u s_v} (u_i - \mu_u)(v_i - \mu_v) \qquad (8.10)$$

where μ_u and s_u are the mean and standard deviation of the elements of u. The normalized cross-correlation is robust to affine changes in intensity between the windows. The $E_{\text{silhouette}}$ term forces the surface to project to the silhouettes in the source images, and the E_{internal} term acts to smooth the surface by decreasing its surface area. The overall energy function is minimized by evolving the vertices of the

---

[18] See Section 8.4.3 for more information on fitting a mesh to 3D points.

triangle mesh in the negative direction of the gradient of Equation (8.9) according to a partial differential equation.

The algorithm by Pons et al. [370] represents the evolving surface using a level-set function instead of a triangulated mesh. That is, the desired set of 3D points S is implicitly defined as those points that satisfy $f(S) = 0$ for some function $f : \mathbb{R}^3 \to \mathbb{R}$. The values of the function f on a voxel grid are iteratively updated until convergence according to a partial differential equation, and S is subsequently extracted using an isosurfacing algorithm (see more in Section 8.4.3). The theory of how to evolve f when we really want to minimize a cost function on S is discussed in Sethian [436].

An important aspect of Pons et al.'s approach is their cost function, which is based on **reprojection**, as illustrated in Figure 8.25. For a set of M source images $\{I_1, \ldots, I_M\}$, and a neighborhood relation on the images $\mathcal{N}$, this reprojection function can be stated simply as

$$E(S) = \sum_{i=1}^{M} \sum_{j \in \mathcal{N}(i)} E_{ij}(S) \tag{8.11}$$

where E_{ij} represents the dissimilarity between image I_i and its reprojection on the image plane of I_j, via the surface S. This approach contrasts with methods that simply compute the normalized cross-correlation of square windows of pixels, not taking into account the deformation of the patch induced by the shape of the surface. This is important since a patch that projects to a square region in one image may project to a skinny, lopsided region in another, or be partially occluded by another piece of the surface.

Hiep et al. [198] addressed the challenges of applying surface deformation methods to large-scale multi-view stereo problems, using the benchmark datasets of Strecha et al. [470]. They matched and triangulated DoG and Harris features across the image set, producing a dense set of 3D points that they turned into a mesh using Delaunay

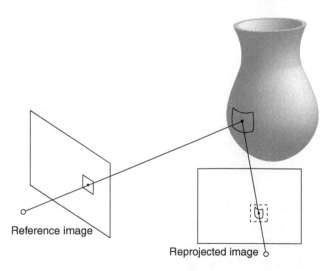

Reference image

Reprojected image

Figure 8.25. A square patch in the left image is reprojected onto the right image via an estimated 3D surface, resulting in the non-square black-outlined area. A square patch in the right image (dotted outline) centered at the projection would not correctly represent the correspondence between the two images.

triangulation. This mesh is then evolved and adapted using a regularized partial differential equation.

Surface deformation methods generally have a bias toward computing surfaces with minimal surface area or bending energy, which can have the effect of smoothing away sharp details. On the other hand, the continuity of the mesh/level-set enables the 3D reconstruction to span flat, untextured regions on the underlying surface that are challenging for the methods we discuss next. Thus, surface deformation results typically don't contain missing regions.

8.3.3 Patch-Based Methods

The multi-view stereo methods discussed so far are well suited to a single object in an uncluttered scene (e.g., a small statue rotated on a turntable in front of a camera), especially in situations where silhouettes can be extracted to estimate the visual hull. However, such techniques don't scale well to reconstructing 3D environments (e.g., movie sets) that contain many disconnected surfaces at different depths, as well as clutter like fences and trees. We now turn to **patch-based methods**, which impose no assumptions about the structure of the scene and are much better suited for these types of problems. The scene is modeled as a collection of small 3D planar patches initially created by triangulating feature matches and then grown to cover surfaces of the scene based on the evidence from surrounding pixels in the source images.

Here, we overview the **patch-based multi-view stereo (PMVS)** algorithm of Furukawa and Ponce [160], one of the best-known and top-performing multi-view stereo algorithms.[19] A patch p is defined as a 3D rectangle with center $c(p)$ and unit normal vector $n(p)$, sized to project to a small (e.g., 5×5 pixel) window in a specified reference image. The goal is to generate a large number of such patches that cover the scene as well as possible and are consistent with the source images.

We begin by detecting DoG and Harris features in each source image, as discussed in Chapter 4. To ensure uniform coverage, a coarse grid is overlaid on each image and the strongest four features are selected in each grid square. For each feature in a given image, the corresponding epipolar lines in other images are searched for a high-quality match, in order of increasing distance from the camera that acquired the reference image. If a good match is found, a patch p is generated with initial center computed by triangulating the feature match, and initial normal given by the unit vector pointing toward the reference camera. The set of images in which p is visible, denoted $V(p)$, is initialized as those images for which the angle between the patch normal and viewing angle is sufficiently small.

We impose a regular grid on p, project it to all the images in $V(p)$, and score each image based on the normalized cross-correlation of the intensities at the projected locations, as illustrated in Figure 8.26a. Then images that match poorly are removed from $V(p)$, and the patch is assigned an overall score based on the average normalized cross-correlation of the remaining samples. Finally, the center and normal of each patch are simply optimized by minimizing this overall score function with respect to these parameters.

[19] A publicly available implementation is available at http://grail.cs.washington.edu/software/pmvs/.

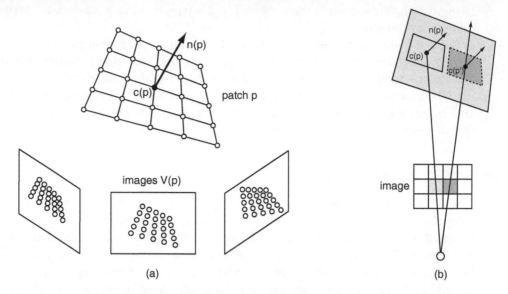

Figure 8.26. (a) To compute a 3D patch's score in PMVS, we sample it on a regular grid in 3D, project these samples to points in each image in which the patch might be visible, and compute the normalized cross-correlation of blocks of intensities around the projected locations. (b) If a cell of the coarse image grid (dark gray) has no corresponding patch, we hypothesize a the center of a new patch p' by intersecting the viewing ray through the cell with the plane corresponding to a nearby patch p from an adjacent cell (light gray).

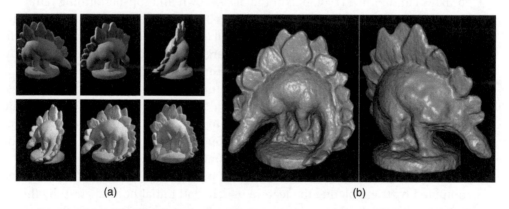

Figure 8.27. (a) Six of sixteen input images for a multi-view stereo algorithm. (b) Two views of the 3D result of PMVS (after creating a triangle mesh from the estimated points).

The next step is to expand the patches generated for high-quality feature matches into regions where no good features were found. This is accomplished by finding a cell of the coarse grid in some image that has no corresponding patch but has a neighbor cell with a well-estimated patch p. We simply create a new patch p' for the patchless cell, estimating $c(p')$ as the intersection of the viewing ray with the plane containing the neighbor's 3D patch, and initializing $n(p') = n(p)$ and $V(p') = V(p)$. The process of refining the patch parameters then continues as shown previously. If the fit is poor (e.g., p' is not visible in enough images, or straddles a depth discontinuity in the scene) the new patch is rejected.

The result of PMVS is a dense collection of small 3D patches with associated normals. This collection can optionally be turned into a triangulated mesh, for example using the Poisson surface reconstruction method discussed in Section 8.4.3. The resulting 3D reconstructions can obtain sub-millimeter accuracy on tabletop-sized objects, and centimeter accuracy on large-scale scans. Figure 8.27 illustrates an example result on one of Seitz et al.'s benchmarking datasets.

One drawback of patch-based methods is that they may contain holes, especially in places where texture information in the images is unreliable. This may require a 3D-inpainting-like method to fill in holes and obtain a complete model. The algorithms can also be quite slow (e.g., hours of running time). Nonetheless, patch-based methods are quite appealing due to their generality; a patch-based multi-view stereo approach was used by Goesele et al. [171] to generate high-quality models of landmarks and large-scale building interiors/exteriors solely using community photo collections (e.g., by keyword searching for "Trevi Fountain" on Flickr).

8.3.4 Depth Map Fusion

Since algorithms for creating disparity maps from stereo images (which correspond to depth maps when the cameras are calibrated) are now fairly mature (see Section 5.5), it makes sense to leverage such techniques when we have more than two source images. The increased number of images has the additional benefit of decreasing noise in the depth estimates and removing errors and outliers that might be difficult to detect in each stereo pair independently.

Goesele et al. [170] presented a simple but highly effective multi-view stereo algorithm based on depth map fusion. Each of the source images is considered in turn as a reference image, and a set of spatially nearby cameras is chosen as its neighborhood. For each pixel p in the reference view, a ray is backprojected into the scene, and a candidate depth $d(p)$ is considered, as illustrated in Figure 8.28.

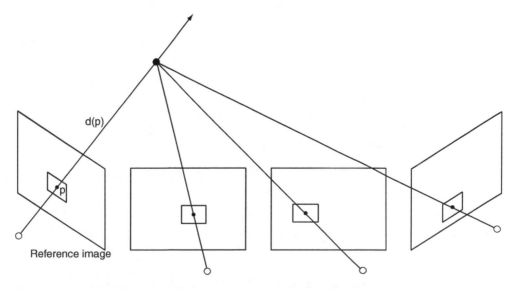

Figure 8.28. A depth $d(p)$ is evaluated for a pixel p in the reference view by considering the normalized cross-correlation of windows around the projected image locations.

Normalized cross-correlations are computed between a window of pixels around p in the reference image and the windows in the neighborhood images implied by the hypothesized depth $d(p)$. If the candidate depth is correct, we expect all of the normalized cross-correlation values to be high; thus, the depth is accepted if these values are above a threshold for enough of the neighborhood images. On the other hand, if all depths are incorrect or some depth is correct but several images contain specularities or occlusions, no $d(p)$ is estimated at p. Points that are assigned depths are also given confidences in the depth estimates based on the average normalized cross-correlation values of the neighbors that contributed. The higher the values, and the more neighbors that agreed, the higher the confidence in the depth estimate. The multiple depth maps are then merged using Curless and Levoy's VRIP algorithm, discussed in detail in Section 8.4.3. As with patch-based methods, the resulting 3D reconstructions may contain holes in low-confidence regions, which can be smoothly interpolated if desired.

In contrast to the methods discussed in Section 5.5, depth map computation for multi-view stereo pairs is usually fairly unsophisticated, often using simple normalized cross-correlation instead of a more geometrically or photometrically natural measure. The rationale is that the merging algorithm should take care of outlier rejection, especially when there is substantial redundancy in the source images. On the other hand, when there are few source images, some per-pair outlier rejection prior to depth map fusion can obtain better results (e.g., see Campbell et al. [80]). Another approach is to evaluate normalized cross-correlations between a square window in the reference image and rectangular windows of different widths in the neighborhood images, to account for perspective distortion [62].

8.3.5   Space-Time Stereo

Finally, we briefly describe **space-time stereo** approaches, which are a hybrid between multi-view stereo and structured lighting algorithms. The basic observation is that stereo algorithms perform poorly in regions with little texture; thus, a projector is used to introduce artificial texture into the scene in the form of a high-frequency pattern. This texture gives the stereo algorithms something to "grab onto." The main difference from structured light techniques is that the projector is not calibrated; the pattern is only used to introduce texture, as opposed to coding the precise horizontal position of a stripe.

The space-time stereo concept was proposed at about the same time by Zhang et al. [569] and Davis et al. [114]. We begin with a normal window-based stereo matching cost function between two rectified images I_1 and I_2,

$$C(x_0, y_0, d) = \sum_{(x,y) \in \mathcal{W}} e(I_2(x - d, y), I_1(x, y)) \tag{8.12}$$

where $\mathcal{W}$ is a window centered at the pixel of interest (x_0, y_0), d is a candidate disparity, and e is some pixel-to-pixel cost function (e.g., the absolute or squared distance). The key idea is to extend Equation (8.12) to a space-time-window-based matching function

$$C(x_0, y_0, t_0, d) = \sum_{t \in \mathcal{T}} \sum_{(x,y) \in \mathcal{W}} e(I_2(x - d, y, t), I_1(x, y, t)) \tag{8.13}$$

where T is a temporal window of frames centered at the current time instant t_0. The basic observation is that the spatio-temporal profile centered at a pixel is more discriminative than the spatial neighborhood alone, which is the same concept that underlies the space-time analysis of structured light patterns illustrated in Figure 8.14. The number of frames in T and they way they are chosen is up to the user, and could depend on the speed of motion in the scene; in the same way, the size of the window W depends on the image resolution and amount of scene texture.

The advantage of the space-time framework is that it's well suited to dynamic scenes, since accurate correspondences may be difficult to intuit on a frame-by-frame basis. Zhang et al. accounted for surfaces that are non-fronto-parallel and/or moving using a linear prediction of each pixel's changing disparity (i.e., the spatio-temporal windows are "slanted" along all three axes, not rectangular solids). They later introduced further constraints to enforce spatio-temporal consistency in the estimates by formulating the optimization globally [570].

Since the projector isn't calibrated against the cameras and the pattern isn't coded, any pattern with high-frequency spatial detail will do. Zhang et al. [569] used shuffled Gray codes and binary checkerboards, while Davis et al. [114] used random patterns of binary vertical stripes and even a simple flashlight. Both groups based the cost function C in Equation (8.13) simply on the sum of squared differences.

8.4   REGISTERING 3D DATASETS

3D data acquired using LiDAR or structured light from a single point of view suffers from the shadowing problem illustrated in Figure 8.3. That is, we only get a depth estimate at a given pixel for the corresponding scene surface closest to the camera. Therefore, we commonly move the scanner around the scene to acquire scans from viewpoints that fill in the gaps and make the 3D model more complete.

In this section, we address two key problems associated with this process. The first is how to align multiple 3D datasets into the same coordinate system. We take a similar approach to the problem of 2D image alignment: features in each scan are detected, matched, and used as the basis for estimating a parametric transformation between each scan pair. However, in 3D we need different methods for feature detection and registration, as we discuss in Sections 8.4.1 and 8.4.2.

Once we have a method for aligning scans, the second problem is how to create a usable triangular mesh from the resulting collection of points. Algorithms for these problems of multiscan fusion and meshing are overviewed in Section 8.4.3. Throughout this section, we motivate the algorithms using data acquired from LiDAR scanners, but the same methods apply to point clouds created from structured light or multi-view stereo.

8.4.1   Feature Detection and Matching

The goal of feature detection and matching in 3D is the same as in 2D: to find regions of a scan that can be reliably, unambiguously matched with scans of the same scene from different perspectives. These feature matches can subsequently be used to initialize or aid in registration, as described in the next section. However, the nature of 3D data requires us to rethink the criteria for what makes a "good" feature. Figure 8.29a,

(a)   (b)

Figure 8.29. (a) 3D data is fundamentally represented as a point cloud. (b) The point cloud inherits a mesh from the order of scanning.

a close-up of the LiDAR data from Figure 8.3, illustrates the problem. Instead of having a uniform grid of pixels with associated intensities, we have a nonuniform collection of data points that all look the same.[20]

However, the 3D point cloud is not totally unstructured; the way in which the data is acquired usually imposes a mesh. For example, a LiDAR scan inherits a natural triangulation based on connecting the measurements from adjacent (θ, ϕ) bins, as illustrated in Figure 8.29b. Usually we apply a heuristic to ensure that the triangles don't span depth discontinuities; for example, we can remove mesh edges that are longer than some multiple of the median edge length. Such a triangulation also allows us to compute an estimate of the normal $n(p)$ at each point p in the point cloud. The easiest ways to compute the normal are to take the average normal of all the mesh triangles that meet at the vertex, or to use the normal to a plane fit to the points in p's local neighborhood.

The two most common methods for feature description in this type of point cloud data are **spin images** and **shape contexts**. Both methods are based on computing histograms of points lying within 3D bins in the neighborhood of a selected point, but differ in the structure of the bins.

Spin images, proposed by Johnson and Hebert [224], consider a cylindrical volume centered around the selected point, with the cylinder's axis aligned with the point's estimated normal, as illustrated in Figure 8.30a. The cylinder is partitioned into uniformly spaced bins along the radial and normal directions, with a bin size roughly equal to the distance between scan points. The number of bins is generally chosen so that each model point falls in some bin. We then create an "image" $h(i,j)$ as the number of points falling in the $(i,j)^{th}$ bin, where i corresponds to the radial direction and j to the normal direction. Only entries that have similar normals to the center point contribute to each histogram bin, to avoid contributions from points on the other side of the model. Examples of spin images at various points on an example mesh are illustrated in Figure 8.30b-c.

If we observe the same 3D object in a different orientation, the spin images at corresponding points will agree, making them an attractive basis for feature description.

---

[20] If an RGB camera image is also available, feature detection and matching is more reliable, as we discuss shortly. While the intensity-of-return image from the LiDAR scanner could theoretically be used for feature detection, this is rare in practice.

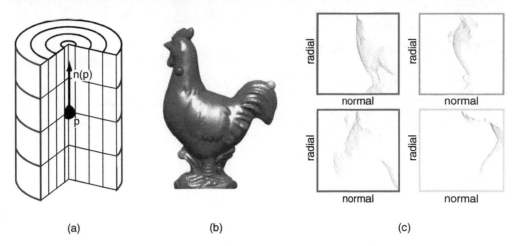

(a)   (b)   (c)

Figure 8.30. (a) The cylindrical bins used to create a spin image. (b) Several points on a mesh. (c) The corresponding spin images. A darker value indicates that more points are in the corresponding bin.

Note that the cylinder can "spin" around the normal vector while still generating the same descriptor (hence the name), avoiding the need to estimate a coordinate orientation on the tangent plane at the point. The similarity between two spin images can be simply measured using either their normalized cross-correlation or their Euclidean distance. Johnson and Hebert also recommended using principal component analysis to reduce the dimensionality of spin images prior to comparison. Another option is to use a multiresolution approach to construct a hierarchy of spin images at each point with different bin sizes [121].

Shape contexts were originally proposed by Belongie et al. [38] for 2D shapes and extended to 3D point clouds by Frome et al. [155]. As illustrated in Figure 8.31, a 3D shape context also creates a histogram using bins centered around the selected point, but the bins are sections of a sphere. The partitions are uniformly spaced in the azimuth angle and normal direction, and logarithmically spaced in the radial direction. Since the bins now have different volumes, larger bins and those with more points are weighted less. As with spin images, the "up" direction of the sphere is defined by the estimated normal at the selected point. Due to the difficulty in establishing a reliable orientation on the tangent plane, one 3D shape context is compared to another by fixing one descriptor and evaluating its minimal Euclidean distance over the descriptors generated by several possible rotations around the normal of the other point.

However, neither approach specifies a method for reliably, repeatably choosing the 3D points around which the descriptors are based. In practice, a set of feature points from one scan is chosen randomly and compared to all the descriptors from the points in the other scan. While this approach works moderately well for small, complete, uncluttered 3D models of single objects, it can lead to slow or poor-quality matching for large, complex scenes.

As we mentioned earlier, LiDAR scanners are often augmented with RGB cameras that can associate each 3D point with a color. Actually, the associated image is usually

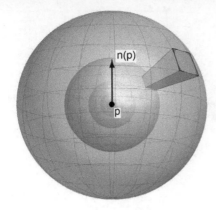

Figure 8.31. The spherical bins used to create a 3D shape context.

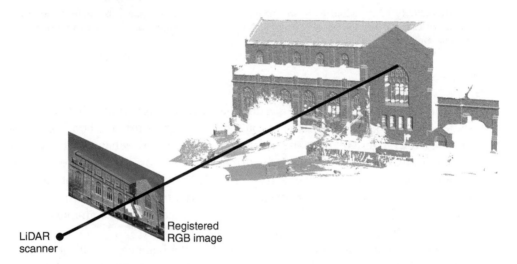

Figure 8.32. Frequently, a LiDAR scanner is augmented with an RGB camera image calibrated to be in the same coordinate system.

higher resolution than the laser scan, so it's more accurate to say that we know where the image plane is in the scanner's coordinate system, as illustrated in Figure 8.32. This additional color and texture information allows us to leverage the techniques described in Chapter 4 to create feature detectors and descriptors better suited to large, complex scenes.

One effective approach, as proposed by Smith et al. [460], is to detect DoG features in the co-registered RGB images as described in Section 4.1.4. Next, each detected feature location can be backprojected from the scanner's perspective into the scene, until the ray penetrates the scan mesh, as illustrated in Figure 8.33. A square planar patch is constructed in 3D whose normal agrees with the normal at the backprojected point and whose orientation is defined with respect to the dominant gradient of the image feature (Section 4.2.1). A 4×4 grid superimposed on this 3D patch is reprojected onto the image plane, and these non-square bins are used to construct a SIFT descriptor (Section 4.2.3). The advantage of these **back-projected SIFT features** is that they exploit both image and range information

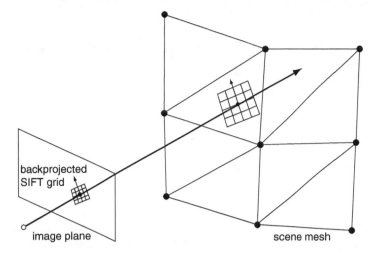

Figure 8.33. Back-projected SIFT features for 3D data, as proposed by Smith et al. [460].

in the feature detection and descriptor construction. For example, features that seem appealing based on the image evidence alone can be ruled out if they straddle a depth discontinuity in 3D.

Smith et al. later observed that the full invariance of SIFT detection and description isn't necessary for 3D data, since distance measurements produced by LiDAR already have a physically meaningful scale. That is, even if we view the same object from different perspectives in two scans, there is no ambiguity about the object's scale (unlike two images at different perspectives). This insight led to the development of **physical scale keypoints** [459], which are computed at a predefined set of physical scales in 3D. Unlike back-projected SIFT features, the keypoint detection and description takes place directly on the 3D mesh, aided by the backprojected texture from the co-registered images. An analogue of the LoG detection operator is applied to the textured mesh, downweighting points whose normals disagree with the normal of the point under consideration. A SIFT-like descriptor is computed on the tangent plane to the detected feature, and descriptors are considered for matching only at the same physical scale. The overall process eliminates many false matches and has the additional benefit of allowing the correct detection and matching of features near physical discontinuities.

8.4.2 Pairwise Registration

Since LiDAR points are measured in a highly accurate physical coordinate system, any two scans of the same environment are related by a 3D rigid motion, that is, a rotation matrix R and a translation vector t, each described by three parameters. In some sense, this is an easier problem than image registration. Only six parameters suffice to describe the relationship between any two 3D scans, no matter how complex, while images are only rarely related by simple parametric transformations. On the other hand, untextured 3D scans are typically much less "feature-rich" than images, which makes the problem more challenging.

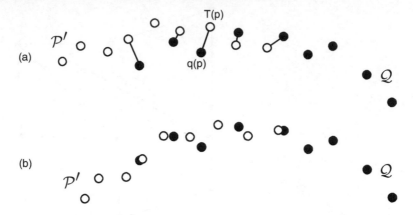

Figure 8.34. The basic Iterative Closest Points (ICP) algorithm alternates between two steps to align two 3D point sets $\mathcal{P}$ and $\mathcal{Q}$. (a) For a fixed candidate transformation T, the closest point $q(p) \in \mathcal{Q}$ to each point in $T(p) \in \mathcal{P}'$ is determined. (b) A new rigid motion T is computed that minimizes the sum of distances between the estimated correspondences.

In this section, we review the **Iterative Closest Points (ICP)** algorithm, the most commonly used method for 3D scan registration. This fundamental approach to registration was discovered and described roughly simultaneously by several research groups, including Besl and McKay [41], Chen and Medioni [89], and Zhang [573]. The basic idea is simple: given two unordered sets of 3D points $\mathcal{P}$ and $\mathcal{Q}$ to be registered and an initial rigid motion T, we alternate between two steps, as illustrated in Figure 8.34:

1. Transform the points in $\mathcal{P}$ by T to obtain a new set of points $\mathcal{P}' = T(\mathcal{P})$. For each $p \in \mathcal{P}$, compute the closest point $q(p) \in \mathcal{Q}$, i.e.,

$$q(p) = \arg\min_{q \in \mathcal{Q}} \| T(p) - q \|_2 \qquad (8.14)$$

2. Estimate the rigid motion T that minimizes the sum of errors

$$E(T) = \sum_{p \in \mathcal{P}} e(T(p), q(p)) \qquad (8.15)$$

where $e(p, q)$ is a suitable error function between pairs of 3D points. That is, we alternate between fixing the transformation and estimating the correspondence, and vice versa. The algorithm stops when $E(T)$ falls below a user-specified threshold. Besl and McKay proved that when $e(p, q)$ in Equation (8.15) is the squared Euclidean distance $\|p - q\|_2^2$, then the ICP algorithm converges monotonically to a local minimum of the cost function $E(T)$.

We must address two additional issues. First, how can we obtain a good initialization T before starting the ICP iterations? This is where the feature detection and matching results from the previous section come in. Any three feature matches in 3D (e.g., obtained using spin images or shape contexts) define a rigid transformation T. Furthermore, if co-registered RGB images are available, matching a single pair of back-projected SIFT or physical scale keypoints between two different scans gives an immediate estimate of the 3D rigid motion relating them, since each descriptor is associated with a full coordinate frame.

The second issue is how to minimize the sum-of-distances function in Equation (8.15). When $e(p,q)$ in Equation (8.15) is the squared Euclidean distance, we can apply a classic result by Umeyama [504]. Suppose the two ordered point sets are denoted by $\{(p_i, q_i), i = 1, \ldots, N\}$. We define μ_p and μ_q to be the mean values of the sets $\{p_i\}$ and $\{q_i\}$ respectively, and compute the 3×3 covariance matrix

$$\Sigma = \frac{1}{N} \sum_{i=1}^{N} (q_i - \mu_q)(p_i - \mu_p)^\top \tag{8.16}$$

Let the singular value decomposition of Σ be given by $UDV^\top$, where the entries of D decrease along the diagonal. Then the rigid motion (R, t) that minimizes

$$\frac{1}{N} \sum_{i=1}^{N} \|q_i - (Rp_i + t)\|_2^2 \tag{8.17}$$

is given in closed form by

$$R = USV^\top \tag{8.18}$$

$$t = \mu_q - R\mu_p \tag{8.19}$$

where $S = \mathbf{I}_{3 \times 3}$ if $\det \Sigma \geq 0$ and $S = \mathrm{diag}(1, 1, -1)$ otherwise.

While the ICP algorithm underlies almost every 3D registration algorithm, researchers have suggested various modifications to improve its convergence, make it more robust to outliers, and make it more generally applicable to large-scale, cluttered scans in which many points in one set may have no valid correspondences in the other set. Rusinkiewicz and Levoy [411] gave an excellent overview of proposed variants to the basic algorithm described previously. We briefly mention some of the most effective refinements here.

- Instead of using all the points from $\mathcal{P}$ in the closest-point and distance-minimization steps, only use a subset of the points (e.g., chosen randomly in space, at the locations of detected features, or so that the normal vectors' angles are widely distributed).
- Choose the "closest" point $q(p)$ not simply as the point that minimizes the Euclidean distance, but as the closest point whose normal vector is within a specified angle of the normal at $T(p)$.
- Don't allow points near the boundary of scans to participate in matching, to prevent many points in one scan being matched to the same point in the other. This is especially important when the scans represent partial views of a larger scene.
- Instead of using the Euclidean distance in the distance-minimization step, use the **point-to-plane** distance illustrated in Figure 8.35. The error function in Equation (8.15) is

$$e(T(p), q(p)) = ((T(p) - q(p))^\top \eta_{q(p)})^2 \tag{8.20}$$

Figure 8.35. The point-to-plane distance for ICP is the square of the length of the dotted line for each pair of matching points. The gray line indicates a plane through each destination point using its estimated normal.

where $\eta_{q(p)}$ is the estimated unit normal vector at $q(p)$. While this step has been shown to provide much faster convergence in practice, it no longer permits a simple closed-form solution to minimizing Equation (8.15), and the convergence proof of Besl and McKay doesn't hold.

- Instead of treating every pair of points equally in Equation (8.15), weight the pairs differently. For example, Smith et al. [460] recommended weighting feature points in proportion to their quality of match and using a robust cost function related to those discussed in Section 5.3.3.3 to downweight points with large alignment errors.

An additional refinement proposed by Smith et al. [460] is to incrementally expand the regions of $\mathcal{P}$ and $\mathcal{Q}$ allowed to participate in the minimization, starting from a very narrow 3D window around an initial feature location and expanding the window outward where there is sufficient evidence that the current estimate T is valid. This is a variant of the dual-bootstrap ICP algorithm proposed by Yang et al. [562] for 2D images.

Aligning a large number of 3D scans into the same coordinate system frequently leverages pairwise scan registrations. Pulli [378] proposed an approach that begins by aligning neighboring scans with point-to-plane ICP and forming a graph in which the vertices correspond to scans and an edge connects two vertices if a high-quality (i.e., low error) rigid motion has been estimated between them. We record not only the rigid motion T_{ij} along the edge between scans i and j, but also uniformly subsampled sets of the points in scans i and j in their area of overlap. We also compute the estimated point positions $T_{ij}(p)$ for each subsample point p in scan i and $T_{ij}^{-1}(q)$ for each subsample point q in scan j. A multi-view registration cost function is then formed as the sum of squared distances between each point and its predicted positions according to the pairwise transformations from its neighbors in the graph. Pulli's algorithm incrementally adds scans into the registered set in order of the number of neighbors each scan has (i.e., its degree in the graph), solving a linear least-squares problem at each step.

Rusinkiewicz and Levoy [410] combined several of these improvements to create an ICP algorithm that ran in real time for the incremental registration of structured-light scans of tabletop-sized models. While we typically want to register scans taken with the same modality (e.g., LiDAR to LiDAR), algorithms like ICP can also be used to register data from different modalities. For example, Zhao et al. [578] discussed the use of ICP for registering LiDAR data with a point cloud generated using multi-view stereo on a video sequence.

Finally, we note that variations of ICP can handle the problem of registering a textured LiDAR scan to a camera image taken at a substantially different viewpoint. For example, Yang et al. [561] proposed an algorithm that begins by applying 2D ICP to the camera image and the scanner's co-located RGB image, and then upgrades the problem to a 2D-3D registration when the correspondences are no longer well modeled by a projective transformation. We can think of this as a resectioning problem (Section 6.3.1) in which the 2D-3D correspondences are iteratively discovered.

8.4.3   Multiscan Fusion

After registration, we have two or more scans in the same coordinate system. While each set of 3D points may have its own triangular mesh inherited from the scanning process, we now address the problem of obtaining a single, uniformly sampled mesh representing the entire collection of registered data.

One problem is that in areas where two scans overlap, we have a large number of redundant points and triangles, as illustrated in Figure 8.36a. Turk and Levoy [501] introduced an early **mesh zippering** approach to address this issue. First, triangles at the edge of each mesh are iteratively removed until the meshes only slightly overlap (Figure 8.36b), and new triangles are introduced to bridge the two scans (Figure 8.36c-d). Each vertex of the mesh is then allowed to move along its estimated normal to minimize its average distance to the original meshes.

One of the most commonly used scan fusion algorithms is the **Volumetric Range Image Processing (VRIP)** algorithm proposed by Curless and Levoy [112]. This method is volumetric, dividing the environment into equally sized voxels and computing the value of a function $f : \mathbb{R}^3 \to \mathbb{R}$ at each voxel. The final merged surface S is implicitly defined by those points that satisfy $f(S) = 0$, i.e., the zero-level set.

We first describe how to form the function $f(\mathbf{X})$ for each voxel $\mathbf{X}$. Each of M registered range scans is assumed to be triangulated, and the ith scan is associated with a signed distance function $d_i(\mathbf{X})$ and a weight function $w_i(\mathbf{X})$.

The signed distance function $d_i(\mathbf{X})$ is computed with respect to lines of sight from scanner i. Points on the triangular mesh have $d_i(\mathbf{X}) = 0$, points in front of the mesh

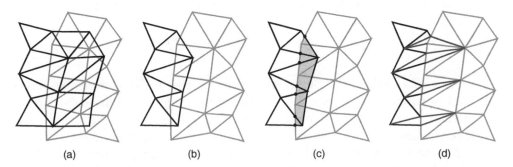

(a)   (b)   (c)   (d)

Figure 8.36. (a) Many redundant points and triangles exist where two registered 3D scans overlap. (b) Overlapping triangles from the edges of the black mesh are removed. (c) New points are introduced at intersections between the black and gray meshes. Shaded parts of the black mesh will be removed. (d) A new triangulation is formed.

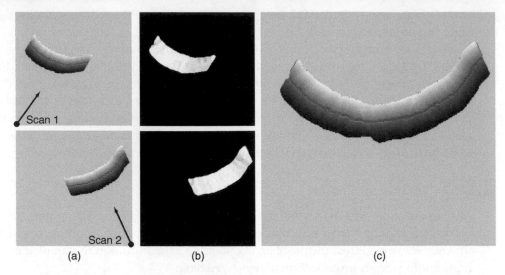

(a)   (b)   (c)

Figure 8.37. (a) Signed distance functions to the triangle meshes (in red) for two range scans taken from different perspectives. The figure represents a 2D slice through 3D space. Gray indicates a distance near 0; black indicates a large negative distance and white a large positive distance. The tan background indicates that the distance function isn't computed because it's too far from the surface. (b) Corresponding weight functions. Black indicates zero weight while white indicates a large weight. (c) The weighted sum of signed distance functions after fusion; red indicates the VRIP isosurface.

have $d_i(\mathbf{X}) < 0$, and points behind the mesh have $d_i(\mathbf{X}) > 0$. The weight function is roughly constant near the triangular mesh along scanner lines of sight, and falls off quickly on either side of the mesh. It can also increase with the angle between the scanner line of sight and the surface normal, or with our confidence in the measurement. The basic idea is that the weight expresses the neighborhood in which a scanner data point plays a role in the fusion. Examples of these functions are illustrated in Figure 8.37a-b for one plane of voxels that intersects the range data. Since the weights are only nonzero very close to the original 3D samples, we only need to store the weights and distance functions at a relatively small fraction of voxels in the volumetric grid; Curless and Levoy used a run-length-encoded volume to efficiently store the necessary information.

We simply compute $f(\mathbf{X})$ as a weighted sum of the component signed distance functions:

$$f(\mathbf{X}) = \frac{\sum_{i=1}^{M} w_i(\mathbf{X}) d_i(\mathbf{X})}{\sum_{i=1}^{M} w_i(\mathbf{X})} \qquad (8.21)$$

An example result of merging is illustrated in Figure 8.37c. The triangulated zero-level isosurface can be efficiently extracted using the **marching cubes** algorithm originally proposed by Lorensen and Cline [301] or one of its modern variants (see Newman and Yi [348] for a good survey). The isosurface has the additional advantage of interpolating across small holes or surface discontinuities in the original data.

A related approach is to view the fusion problem as one of scattered data interpolation, using similar methods to what we discussed in Section 5.2.1. We denote the collection of all range points from all the contributing scans as $\{\mathbf{X}_j, j = 1, \ldots, n\}$. As earlier, we create a function $f(\mathbf{X})$ defined in 3D space, and think of the original range

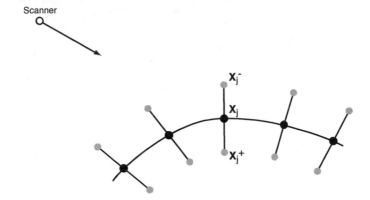

Figure 8.38. 3D sample points (black dots) and normal constraints (gray dots) for constructing an interpolating implicit function.

points as samples at which $f(\mathbf{X}_j) = 0$. We want to extract a "reasonable" interpolating 3D surface that passes through these points. We must provide additional constraints to prevent $f(\mathbf{X}) = 0$ for all $\mathbf{X}$ from being a viable solution; these come in the form of normal constraints, as illustrated in Figure 8.38. For example, we can travel a short distance along the estimated normal in both directions at each point, generating a point in front of the surface $\mathbf{X}_j^-$ and a point behind the surface $\mathbf{X}_j^+$. Then we assign the values $f(\mathbf{X}_j^-) = -1$ and $f(\mathbf{X}_j^+) = 1$.[21] For notational convenience, we denote all 3D points where the function f is constrained — either by an original range sample or by a normal constraint — as $\{\mathbf{X}_j, j = 1, \ldots, N\}$.

Similarly to Section 5.2.1, we postulate a functional form for f that's a combination of an affine term and a sum of radial basis functions centered at each point where we have constrained its value:

$$f(\mathbf{X}) = \sum_{j=1}^{N} w_j \phi(r_j) + a^\top \mathbf{X} + b \tag{8.22}$$

where $a \in \mathbb{R}^3$, $b \in \mathbb{R}$, and $r_j = \|\mathbf{X} - \mathbf{X}_j\|_2$. In 3D applications, we use the function $\phi(r) = r$ or $\phi(r) = r^3$, both of which produce a smooth interpolation of the data. The weights on the basis functions and the affine coefficients can be computed by solving a linear system:

$$\left[\begin{array}{cccc|cc} 0 & \phi(r_{12}) & \cdots & \phi(r_{1N}) & \mathbf{X}_1^\top & 1 \\ \phi(r_{21}) & 0 & \cdots & \phi(r_{2N}) & \mathbf{X}_2^\top & 1 \\ \vdots & \vdots & \ddots & \vdots & \vdots & \vdots \\ \phi(r_{N1}) & \phi(r_{N2}) & \cdots & 0 & \mathbf{X}_N^\top & 1 \\ \hline \mathbf{X}_1 & \mathbf{X}_2 & \cdots & \mathbf{X}_N & 0 & 0 \\ 1 & 1 & \cdots & 1 & 0 & 0 \end{array}\right] \left[\begin{array}{c} w_1 \\ w_2 \\ \vdots \\ w_N \\ \hline a \\ b \end{array}\right] = \left[\begin{array}{c} f(\mathbf{X}_1) \\ f(\mathbf{X}_2) \\ \vdots \\ f(\mathbf{X}_N) \\ \hline 0 \\ 0 \end{array}\right] \tag{8.23}$$

---

[21] In practice, we may not need to provide two normal constraints for every range point, especially if the normal estimate is not reliable at the point.

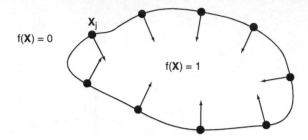

Figure 8.39. The setup for Poisson surface reconstruction. 3D sample points (black dots) are viewed as locations where the gradient is large and points inward.

where $r_{ij} = \|\mathbf{X}_i - \mathbf{X}_j\|_2$. Now we can compute $f(\mathbf{X})$ at any 3D location we like, and apply the same marching-cubes technique to obtain the isosurface. This approach 3D to surface interpolation was proposed by Turk and O'Brien [502], though it can be traced back to the thin-plate spline techniques of Bookstein [53] and earlier.

However, for scans with more than a few thousand data points, forming and solving the linear system in Equation (8.23) quickly becomes computationally intractable. Carr el al. [82] showed how such techniques could be made feasible using fast multipole methods, which use near-field and far-field approximations to compute the radial basis functions efficiently. Such approaches also allow the specification of a desired fitting accuracy, which is useful for merging multiple LiDAR scans that may not overlap exactly after registration. They showed how merged LiDAR datasets containing hundreds of thousands of points could be well approximated with a triangular mesh in a matter of minutes.

On the other hand, radial basis function approaches may smooth over sharp features in the data that we want to preserve, introduce pieces of surface far from the original data points, and perform badly in the presence of outliers or poorly sampled data. More recent approaches to surface reconstruction (e.g.,[353, 245]) address these problems.

Finally, we mention one of the most effective 3D data fusion techniques, **Poisson surface reconstruction**, proposed by Kazhdan et al. [232]. Like the previous techniques, we compute a function $f(\mathbf{X})$ defined on $\mathbb{R}^3$; however, this function has a very different interpretation, as sketched in Figure 8.39. We define $f(\mathbf{X}) = 0$ for points outside the surface to be reconstructed, and $f(\mathbf{X}) = 1$ for points inside the surface to be reconstructed. Therefore, the gradient of the function is identically zero, except for points $\mathbf{X}$ on the surface, at which the gradient is very large (theoretically infinite). The observed range data points $\{\mathbf{X}_j, j = 1, \ldots, n\}$ are viewed as samples where the gradient is known; that is, its norm is large and it points inward along the estimated normal.

This problem, in which we have samples of the gradient of a function at several points and want to reconstruct the function everywhere, naturally lends itself to Poisson reconstruction techniques, as we described for image editing in Section 3.2. The approach proposed by Kazhdan et al. has several advantages: it's relatively robust to sparse or noisy gradient samples, it generates surfaces that stick closely to the original data without requiring normal constraints, and it allows the use of a multiresolution (octree) data structure to represent the result instead of requiring a discretization of the entire volume. Many multiscan fusion algorithms use Poisson surface reconstruction thanks to Kazhdan et al.'s publicly available implementation.[22]

8.5   INDUSTRY PERSPECTIVES

Gentle Giant Studios, in Burbank, California, provides large object, vehicle, and set scanning for nearly every blockbuster Hollywood movie, and has scanned the faces and bodies of thousands of actors and performers. Steve Chapman, Gentle Giant's vice president of technology, discusses the role of LiDAR, structured light, and multi-view stereo in visual effects.

RJR: How has the use of LiDAR for large-scale scanning of movie sets changed over the years?

Chapman: In the 1990s we used a slow triangulation-based LiDAR scanner. At that point, time-of-flight systems from Cyrax were the size of a dishwasher, so we found a system developed for the French nuclear power department that was designed to attach to a radio-controlled robot. Things are quite different now, and speed of capture has been a primary motivation for obtaining newer gear. LiDAR doesn't work well for smaller subjects, though we'll occasionally use it "in a pinch" for cars or medium-sized objects.

You're usually limited on time when you're working on a movie set. Often there's a time window where the main film unit has just "wrapped" filming and you have a short amount of time before they come back to shoot more scenes. On the other hand, you might come in at the end of a shoot, when they're about to destroy a set and build another set in the same place as soon as you finish the scan. There are people standing around looking at their watches grumbling, "When is this LiDAR thing going to finish?"

Now that we have phase-based systems, we can scan anything from a human body to a building, and the process is quick enough that we can hop around and collect a more comprehensive dataset than we could with older time-of-flight systems. We can scan an entire soundstage from one viewpoint in just a few minutes and get more data than a time-of-flight LiDAR would collect in hours. Because the phase-based system can read objects at a much closer range than a time-of-flight device, we can start do things like scan behind small set pieces, and we can simply set up dozens of scan locations where in the past we'd have only scanned from a handful of viewpoints.

RJR: What kinds of things will a movie production do with LiDAR data once you deliver it to them?

Chapman: Early on, few movie crews knew what to do with the data. Now, everyone from set designers, pre-visualization departments, set extension painters, camera trackers, particle effects artists, and character placement animators are clamoring for

[22] http://www.cs.jhu.edu/~misha/Code/PoissonRecon/

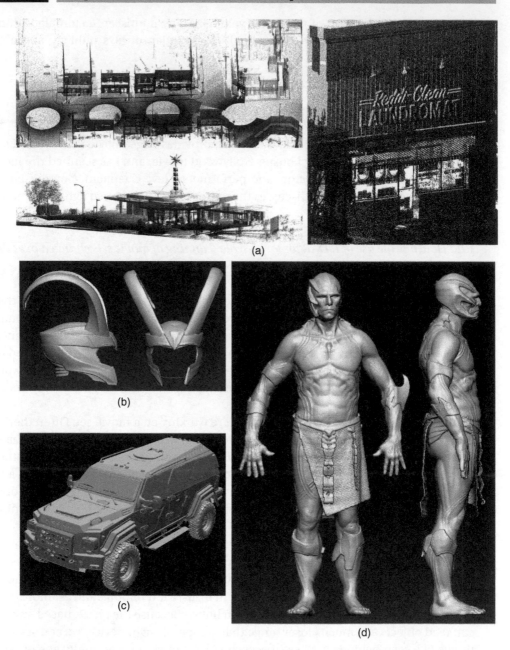

Figure 8.40. (a) An entire small town outdoor set created for *Thor* containing many buildings was LiDAR-scanned from multiple locations. (b) A structured-light scan of a prop helmet for *Thor*. (c) A phase-based LiDAR scan of an armored military vehicle for *Fast Five*. (d) A laser-stripe scan of actor Darren Kendrick in the Sentry Frost Giant makeup and costume for *Thor*. *Thor* images appear courtesy of Marvel Studios, TM & ©2011 Marvel and Subs. www.marvel.com. *Fast Five* courtesy of Universal Studios Licensing LLC.

the data. For example, in the movie *2012*, Sony constructed a five-story door of a huge ship, but the entire remaining vessel had to be 3D modeled and composited to match film of the actors standing on this door set. The visual effects designers at ImageWorks knew that the LiDAR data we took of this model would precisely match the camera footage. They used the LiDAR geometry for several purposes: to help with camera tracking, to extend the set to cover the whole frame, and to add animated water and atmospheric elements that realistically interacted with the real-world geometry of the film set.

For the movie *Zookeeper*, we scanned an entire real zoo in Boston so that ImageWorks animators could plant the feet of photorealistic digital animals that interacted with the filmed surroundings. A giraffe might go under and around a tree because the animators have the model of the real tree in 3D and the data of the ground that it needs to step on — it interacts with the actors and environment seamlessly.

Visual effects companies might also use LiDAR data to make a complete textured digital duplicate of the same set. For example, in *The Matrix Revolutions*, there's an underground "rave" scene featuring football-field-sized gate mechanisms. They only built and LiDAR scanned one gate, and used the resulting data as a template to model and texture all the other gates around the digital set. This required the processing of the raw LiDAR point cloud into a clean polygonal model that can be easily manipulated in 3D animation software such as Maya.

RJR: How about laser stripe systems for scanning bodies and props?

Chapman: It's interesting that the concept behind laser stripe scanning was used in Renaissance times. An artist would make a maquette of a sculpture that was to be carved from a huge piece of marble. Then they would lower that maquette into milk or ink in order to study the waterline and analyze how the contour appeared, before cutting the unforgiving stone. What's happening now is that the waterline is a laser stripe, and digital cameras and computers take the place of the artist's eyes and memory. Laser stripe scanners offer instant feedback so that a visual effects supervisor leaves the set confident that the 3D model is complete and accurate, and that the animation supervisor will have the expression and muscle movement reference he or she will need to recreate an actor's performance.

Laser-stripe technology is the oldest and simplest approach, and most of the equipment we've used for decades has been based on it. The body scanner we use (Figure 8.9a) uses four calibrated light stripes and cameras that move down the sides of a person in unison; it takes about twenty seconds to do a complete pass. This usually gets about ninety percent of the geometry, but there's always going to be something occluding the cameras that we must "get hands on" in a software package like Zbrush and touch up. With any scanning process, there seems to be a point where you can easily capture a majority of the object or environment in a reasonable amount of time. Then it becomes a tremendous effort to chase down the rest of the shape that was hidden from the scanner behind occlusions. It takes some practice to know when to make the effort to move the scanner to get more viewpoints, and when the time might be better spent moving on to the next set piece on the long checklist of things to scan. The scanning service vendor needs to have both the equipment to capture data as well as the talent to process whatever is finally obtained into something suitable for use by the next person in the production pipeline. This might mean anything from simple hole filling to recreating a fabric texture and underlying surface curvature to make a seamless model. Since Gentle Giant started out as a traditional clay sculpting studio, we have artists who have made the move to 3D and can easily handle any digital cosmetic surgery needed when scanning organic subjects.

A decade ago, it wasn't commonplace to scan actors, but the production companies that make the movies have now realized how important this is to their vendors. They might have a scene where the film production company has not yet hired a visual effects vendor, even though filming is already occurring. The visual effects supervisors know that the vendor is likely to need 3D reference several months later, so they'll ask us to go ahead and scan anything and everything on set. Maybe they'll need it and maybe they won't, but it's neither feasible to rebuild a set nor get an actor who's already filming another movie to come back and get in makeup and costume for a texture shoot or 3D scan.

Once acquired, the scan data is often used by toy companies for action figure design and by video game companies for movie tie-in games. Actors often voice concern about the data being used to later animate them and make them "sell vacuum cleaners" after they die, but they probably aren't aware of the inevitability of purely image-based 3D reconstruction algorithms that will make the whole issue moot. It's conceivable that at some point in the near future, 3D information can be extracted from even the earliest motion picture footage.

RJR: Do you also use patterns of structured light?

Chapman: Structured light systems can also work well for head and body scanning, but they're riskier to use in practice compared to laser-stripe systems due to the complexity of the underlying image processing. Often, an actor is only available for a few short minutes and may even called back to the set in the middle of a 3D scan. As one A-list actor put it after a few seconds of delay in starting the body scanning on the set of a blockbuster, "Let's go, gentlemen!" As a result, many visual effects supervisors will lean toward using laser-stripe systems for actor scanning simply because they know they're much less prone to failure compared to structured light devices.

Trying to project structured light onto larger objects is extremely difficult since you can't get a projector bright enough and you can't get the camera far enough away to make the algorithms work. There are also limitations you run into with the vibration of the mounting systems and the resolution of the cameras. We have a structured light system that could theoretically scan a jumbo jet, but realistically that's a job much more suited to LiDAR.

We still use structured light for scanning our smallest subjects because it excels at capturing fine details that laser "blooming" obliterates. For example, we used structured light to capture a small pirate coin at sufficient detail for it to be projected three stories high in the opening credits of a film. Real-time performance capture scanning once required structured light solutions, but stereo matching has evolved to replace that need, with the added benefit of not blinding the actor with a projector pattern.

One common issue with structured light is that if you're scanning a human subject and they are moving, as inevitably happens, you see a sort of a "cheese grater" effect, where some parts of the surface will be further out or in than other parts, and you see bands going across the data. Systems that tie the projector timing into the camera's frame acquisition timing help alleviate, but not entirely eliminate, this artifact.

RJR: Have multi-view stereo techniques made an impact in 3D data acquisition for visual effects yet?

Chapman: We've been exploring the photogrammetric solution for quite some time and think that it's trending toward the point that it's likely going to replace most of the other processes very soon. However, in movies there are a lot of black sets, costumes, and shiny things for aesthetic reasons — Batman's outfit or *TRON*'s sets, for example. If you try to use multi-view stereo to capture that you might end up with just the edges of objects. We've attempted to aid the algorithms by projecting a pattern onto the object so it's sort of a mix of structured light and multi-view stereo. We often have to quickly improvise with materials on set, like powdering a sarcophagus in order to read the reflective gold, taping lines onto a shiny helicopter, or even kicking up some dirt onto a black waxed pickup truck.

If we need to do something even grander than we could handle with time-of-flight LiDAR, we'd likely use a photo modeling technique, but today the results are often simply not yet good enough to deliver as-is to a visual effects company. We have to do a lot of work to make it presentable. I used one such tool — PhotoSynth — on a project where we needed to model the Statue of Liberty. We didn't have the time or money to do the job in person, and even if we did, getting permission to scan it would have been very difficult for security reasons. We used PhotoSynth to get the essential proportions of the statue, and discovered roughly where and how big things needed to be, but we still needed a sculptor to go in and recreate the accurate likeness underneath.

On a movie set, we definitely take as much video footage and supplemental photography as we can and catalog it for reference, since we never know when we'll scan something and find that somebody moved it the next day or even destroyed it. We have terabytes of photos that were once intended solely for reference but that now might be reprocessed through multi-view stereo software to derive new information.

RJR: What techniques do you use for registering multiple scans?

Chapman: When we started doing LiDAR in the 1990s, we needed to place registration spheres all over the set, similar to little magnetic pool balls. We would find the centers of the spheres in the data and use them to do a three-point alignment, and then do a best-fit registration automatically from that. It took a lot of time to climb around the set and place these targets, which resulted in being able to take fewer scans.

Since then, commercial software has evolved so that we can quickly pick three points in one scan, pick roughly the same points in another scan, and the software will automatically register them. Currently we use custom software to greatly reduce the data for registration purposes. We usually scan one pass at the farthest possible distance from the scene to act as a key alignment pass, to which all of the other scan passes will be aligned. We often devote a single LiDAR scanner solely to perform this "master" scan while we use other scanners to do the remaining multiple viewpoints.

After registering all the scans, the data is divided into sub-objects such as lampposts, trees, and cars, which are polygonized and reduced in point density to fit the standard requirements of visual effects data processing pipelines. Some skill and practice is needed to know what data will be needed to accurately recreate each object while discarding redundant information.

8.6   NOTES AND EXTENSIONS

In the days before laser range finding, the main way to acquire highly accurate 3D data was by means of a coordinate measuring machine (CMM), a bulky system in which a user pressed a pen-like probe against the surface of an object to record (X, Y, Z) locations.

Outside of visual effects, one of the most striking applications of 3D data acquisition was Levoy et al.'s Digital Michelangelo Project [275]. Piecewise scans of ten Michelangelo statues were painstakingly acquired using a custom laser stripe scanner and registered into highly detailed and textured models for use in art history and preservation. This project highlighted the many practical challenges of scanning priceless objects on a tight timeline. LiDAR technology is frequently used for cultural heritage applications in architecture (e.g., [13]) and archaeology (e.g., http://cyark.org/). In construction applications, LiDAR is important for quality assurance that an as-built building conforms to an original blueprint [207]. Finally, many of the autonomous vehicles in the recent DARPA Grand Challenges (http://archive.darpa.mil/grandchallenge/) used LiDAR for real-time terrain mapping.

Since the data in laser-stripe scanning is usually acquired as a temporal sequence of stripes, keeping track of this sequence can help with filling in missing data or fixing poor returns. That is, a human in the loop can fix or recreate a bad stripe by interpolating the 3D contours acquired just before and after it. This approach was taken for human body scanning in the *Star Wars* prequels and the early *Harry Potter* movies.

An early classic paper by Bouguet and Perona [56] described a clever structured-light-inspired system in which images of the shadow of a pencil moving across objects on a desk acted as the "stripe" for producing 3D measurements. They obtained surprisingly good, sub-millimeter-accuracy results for small objects with this simple technique. Fisher et al. [143] presented a similar idea using a special striped wand that also had to be visible in the camera image. Boyer and Kak [57] were among the first researchers to propose a one-shot, color-stripe-based structured light technique using an empirically derived pattern of red, green, blue, and white stripes. They used a region-growing approach to expand the list of identified stripes from a set of reliable seeds.

Salvi et al. [419, 418] gave excellent overviews of the state of the art in structured light pattern design. They discussed several techniques not mentioned here, in particular the class of methods based on extending the idea of locally unique color subsequences to two-dimensional patterns. For example, the scene can be projected with a pattern of colored dots, such that each 3×3 neighborhood of dots does not repeat anywhere in the pattern. Such patterns are called **pseudorandom** or **M-arrays**, and a good example of their application was described by Morano et al. [334]. One advantage of using 2D pseudorandom arrays is that the correspondence problem is relatively unambiguous. A related idea proposed by Salvi et al. [417] is to use a grid generated by a (red, green, blue) de Bruijn sequence for the horizontal lines and a (cyan, magenta, yellow) de Bruijn sequence for the vertical lines. The intersections of the grid thus uniquely encode a location in the projected image. However, these 2D approaches generally have lower spatial resolution in the image plane than the other methods discussed in Section 8.2. Lanman et al. [262] described a clever approach for 360° structured light scanning of small objects using an array of mirrors to surround the object with light and enable viewing it from all sides with a single camera.

Koppal et al. [251] noted that a high-speed DLP projector could be reverse engineered to determine the dithering pattern it uses to display a grayscale intensity — that is, the on/off flipping each micromirror uses to modulate the light from the always-on projector bulb. They exploited this dithering pattern as a means of creating coded structured light for a very high-speed camera. Other extensions to structured light include modifications for underwater scanning, in which the water significantly scatters the light beam [345] or for scanning difficult refractive objects (e.g., a crystal goblet) by immersing them in a fluorescent liquid [209].

While most structured light methods operate in the visible spectrum, Früh and Zakhor [157] suggest using infrared light instead, which is likely to be much less perceptually distracting for a human being scanned. Since there is no natural sense of "color" in the infrared spectrum, they used a pattern of vertical stripes along with a periodically sweeping horizontal line that cuts across the stripes to disambiguate the stripe index. The **Microsoft Kinect** also uses a proprietary structured light approach in the infrared spectrum to generate real-time depth maps. A pseudorandom pattern of infrared dots is projected into the scene, which plays the same role as a coded light stripe pattern since the local dot neighborhoods are unique.

The proprietary **MOVA Contour** system used in the visual effects community for markerless facial motion capture also works in the nonvisual spectrum. Phosphorescent makeup is applied to a performer that is invisible under white light but phosphoresces as a blotchy, mottled pattern under fluorescent light. The two types of light are toggled rapidly and the visible and fluorescent images are separated by multiple high-speed video cameras surrounding the performer. A proprietary multi-view stereo technique fuses the depth maps obtained from the fluorescent images.

In 1996, Debevec et al. presented the Façade system for 3D modeling and rendering of architectural scenes [117], a great example of research from the academic community that had a major impact on visual effects production in Hollywood. This image-based modeling approach has been used in many movies including the *Matrix* and *Transformers* series. A user sketches edges on a small set of wide-baseline photographs of a piece of architecture, and interactively specifies how the edges match to block primitives of a 3D model. The user can specify how blocks are related (for example, that a roof must sit squarely on its base) as well as symmetries in the model (for example, that a clock tower has four identical sides). The 3D model then highly constrains a structure from motion problem in which the parameters of the architectural model and the camera locations are estimated. To create a new view of the piece of architecture, the 3D model is texture-mapped with an appropriate set of input images, which can produce a visually compelling result even when the underlying model is fairly simple. If the model needs to be refined, a higher-quality depth map can be estimated for each image by stereo matching based on reprojecting via the model, similar to Figure 8.25. This approach can be viewed as an early multi-view stereo algorithm in which the 3D points are constrained to lie on geometric primitives interactively created by the user.

Two notable early multi-view stereo algorithms were proposed by Okutomi and Kanade [354] and Collins [100]. Another approach to multi-view stereo not discussed here is **photometric stereo**, in which the 3D shape of a shiny object (e.g., a ceramic statue) is estimated by acquiring multiple images of it under different illumination conditions (e.g., [196, 521]). The changing intensity patterns provide clues about the normal vector at each surface point. Nehab et al. [347] observed that normals estimated from triangulation-based scanners could be improved by combining the data with the output of photometric stereo techniques.

Two exciting avenues of research have recently been enabled by the confluence of commercial 3D scanning technology, ample processing power and storage, and massive internet photography databases. In one direction, the thousands of images resulting from a keyword search on Flickr or Google Images can be viewed as the input to a large multi-view stereo problem. Snavely et al. [464] described how to calibrate the cameras underlying such a collection based on correspondence estimation and structure from motion, and how to then apply multi-view stereo techniques to obtain a dense 3D reconstruction of the scene. In contrast to conventional multi-view stereo techniques, this type of approach simply discards entire images that are of low quality or for which the camera calibration is uncertain; indeed, a key component of these large-scale algorithms is the careful choice of image sets that are likely to be productive.

Another exciting direction is **city-scale scanning**, using a vehicle equipped with some combination of cameras, laser rangefinders, and GPS/inertial navigation units to help with its localization. Pollefeys et al. [367] described an impressive system that generates textured 3D mesh reconstructions in real time using a vehicle mounted with eight cameras. They used an incremental depth map fusion algorithm to process tens of thousands of video frames into a single, consistent, and detailed 3D model. Alternately, Früh and Zakhor [158] designed a vehicle equipped with a camera and two laser rangefinders. One rangefinder acquired vertical 3D strips of building facades, which were registered using images from the camera and horizontal 3D data from the second rangefinder. The 3D datasets estimated from the vehicle were then refined (e.g., to remove drift) based on registration to an aerial map of the scanned area. This system registered thousands of images and 3D strips to produce an accurate textured model of streets around the Berkeley campus. Subsequent work addressed the problem of inpainting façade geometry and texture in LiDAR "shadows" caused by foreground occlusions [156]. For large holes, a patch-based inpainting approach inspired by the techniques in Section 3.4.2 might be more appropriate (e.g., [124]).

Finally, we mention that once 3D data has been acquired by any of the means discussed in this chapter, several image understanding techniques can be applied to it.[23] For example, Verma et al. [513] discussed how to detect and model buildings

---

[23] "Image understanding" is used in a broad sense here; automatic analysis and understanding of 3D data typically falls under the umbrella of computer vision, even if there weren't any conventional images actually involved in the data collection.

from aerial LiDAR data, while Dick et al. [120] addressed how to fit architectural primitives (walls, roofs, columns) to image sets taken at ground level. Golovinskiy et al. [172] trained a system to recognize objects like lampposts, traffic lights, and fire hydrants in large-scale LiDAR datasets, while Vasile and Marino [511] addressed the detection of military ground vehicles from foliage-penetrating aerial LiDAR. Kim et al. [238] discussed how salient regions could be automatically detected in co-registered camera and laser scans of an outdoor scene. Huber et al. [208] proposed an algorithm for part-based 3D object classification (e.g, types of vehicles) based on spin images. More generally, Chen and Stamos [87] discussed how to segment range images of urban scenes into planar and smooth pieces, which can be of later use in registration and object detection.

8.7   HOMEWORK PROBLEMS

8.1   A LiDAR scanner reports that a point at azimuth 60° and elevation 20° is located 100m away. Convert this measurement into an (X, Y, Z) Cartesian coordinate system in which the scanner is located at (0,0,0).

8.2   Compute the time resolution required, in picoseconds, for a pulse-based LiDAR's receiver electronics if we want the system to have ±2mm accuracy.

8.3   Compute the distance to a scene point for which 500 nanoseconds was recorded for the time-of-flight of a LiDAR pulse.

8.4   Prove the relationship between the phase shift ψ and the time of flight t in Equation (8.2).

8.5   Show that the restriction on the range ambiguity in a phase-based LiDAR scanner, $0 < \psi < 2\pi$, imposes a maximum range of $\pi c/\omega$, where c is the speed of light and ω is the frequency of the modulating sinusoid in radians.

8.6   A phase-based LiDAR with carrier frequency 1.3×10^7 radians/sec is used to scan a scene. Compute the distance to a scene point for which a $\pi/3$ radian phase shift was recorded.

8.7   Some flash LiDAR systems estimate the phase of an amplitude-modulated signal using four samples. Suppose the transmitted signal is $f(t) = \cos(\omega t)$ and the received signal is $g(t) = A\cos(\omega t + \psi) + B$, where A is the attenuated amplitude of the signal and B is a constant offset. Show that the phase shift ψ can be recovered as

$$\psi = \arctan \frac{g_3 - g_1}{g_0 - g_2} \qquad (8.24)$$

where $g_i = g\left(\frac{i\pi}{2\omega}\right)$.

8.8   We can interpret the triangulation process for a stripe-based structured light sensor as the intersection of a 3D line (corresponding to the ray from the camera center through the observed image coordinates (x, y) on the stripe) with a 3D plane $aX + bY + cZ + d = 0$ (corresponding to the light plane from the laser). Determine a closed-form formula for this line-plane intersection as the solution of a 3×3 linear system. (Hint: write the line as the intersection of two planes corresponding to the locations along the x and y axes.)

8.9   The k-bit Gray code G_k for $k \geq 1$ is a sequence of 2^k binary codewords $\{G_k(1), \ldots, G_k(2^k)\}$ constructed recursively as follows. First, we initialize G_0 as the empty set, $\{\emptyset\}$. Then G_k is built from G_{k-1} as:

$$G_k = \{0G_{k-1}(1), \ldots, 0G_{k-1}(2^{k-1}), 1G_{k-1}(2^{k-1}), \ldots, 1G_{k-1}(1))\} \qquad (8.25)$$

That is, the first 2^{k-1} codewords are the same as G_{k-1} with a 0 prefix, and the second 2^{k-1} codewords are the codewords of G_{k-1} in reverse order with a 1 prefix.

a)   Construct G_4.

b)   Prove that each of the 2^k possible binary codewords appears exactly once in G_k.

c)   Prove that each pair of adjacent entries of G_k (i.e., $G_k(i)$ and $G_k(i+1)$) differs in exactly one bit (including the cyclic pair $G_k(2^k)$ and $G_k(1)$).

8.10   How many patterns would be needed to resolve 600 unique vertical stripe indices using patterns of red, green, blue, and white stripes?

8.11   In Figure 8.19 we assumed the on/off decision was based on the grayscale intensity of the two images at a given pixel. Generalize the decision criterion in the case where a color and its RGB complement are projected onto a colorful scene surface.

8.12   Construct a stripe boundary code similar to Figure 8.20 of two patterns containing thirteen stripes each, such that (a) each of the twelve pairs of on-off transitions occurs exactly once, (b) no stripe is continuously on or off for more than two time units, and (c) at least one stripe changes at every time step.

8.13   Determine a de Bruijn sequence of order 3 over an alphabet of three symbols.

8.14   Verify the three-image phase recovery Equation (8.8).

8.15   This problem is meant to suggest some of the issues that can occur when a scene is changing as it is being scanned. Consider the scenario illustrated in Figure 8.41. A fixed-stripe laser scanner is mounted on a vehicle, pointed at a right angle to the direction of motion. Suppose the scanner vehicle moves forward at a constant rate of ten meters per second, and the laser acquires a vertical stripe of range data every 0.25 seconds. We assume that the scanner knows where to correctly place the range samples it acquires in 3D space (e.g., using an inertial measurement unit).

a)   The scanner vehicle passes a 3m long pickup truck with the profile sketched in Figure 8.41 traveling at nine meters per second. How many stripes from the scanner will hit the truck, and where will the resulting range samples be in 3D? What will be the apparent length and direction of the truck?

b)   What if the scanner vehicle is passed by a truck traveling at twelve meters per second?

c) What if both the scanner vehicle and the truck travel at ten meters per second?

Note that these phenomena can be viewed as a type of spatial aliasing.

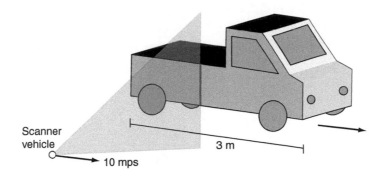

Scanner
vehicle

3 m

10 mps

Figure 8.41. A laser stripe scanner mounted on a vehicle (white dot) moves forward at 10 mps while the truck moves forward at a different speed.

8.16 Following Figure 8.25, sketch examples in which a patch that projects to a square region in one image
   a) projects to a skinny region in another image
   b) projects to a wide region in another image
   c) is partially occluded in another image by another piece of the scene.

8.17 Show that the normalized cross-correlation is unchanged if the values of one vector in Equation (8.10) are subjected to an affine transformation $\hat{u}_i = au_i + b, i = 1, \ldots, n$.

8.18 Provide a sketch to show why the image pairs (i, j) and (j, i) produce different contributions to the cost function in Equation (8.11).

8.19 Mathematically formalize these two descriptions of how to compute a unit normal at a 3D point p of a triangular mesh:
   a) Compute the normal of a plane fit to all the points within a radius r of p using principal component analysis.
   b) Compute a weighted average of the normals to all the triangles that have p as a vertex, where the weight for each triangle is proportional to its area.

8.20 If the radii of a spin image descriptor are given by the increasing sequence $\{r_i\}$ and the levels of the normal bins are given by the increasing sequence $\{z_j\}$, then compute the volume of the $(i, j)^{th}$ bin.

8.21 Determine the 3D transformation defined by 3 point matches in 3D given by
$\{(X_i, Y_i, Z_i), (X_i', Y_i', Z_i'), i = 1, \ldots, 3\}$. Why are 2 matches insufficient?

8.22 Reformulate the VRIP fusion Equation (8.21) so that it can be computed incrementally by merging the component scans one at a time. Does the incremental result depend on the order of merging?

A Optimization Algorithms for Computer Vision

A.1 DYNAMIC PROGRAMMING

We discussed dynamic programming in several contexts: finding the lowest-cost seam in seam carving (Section 3.5), computing the best correspondence between a pair of conjugate epipolar lines (Section 5.5), and aligning two motion capture sequences (Section 7.5). Here we give a brief description of how to set up and solve these types of dynamic programming problems.

We can think of each problem as assigning each of M nodes one of N labels. For example, if we want to carve a vertical seam in an image, the nodes index the rows, and the labels specify the column of the pixel to remove from each row. In the stereo correspondence problem, the nodes index the pixels of one epipolar line, and the labels specify the pixels of the other epipolar line (or the corresponding disparities).

Our goal is to find the labeling $L = (L(1), \ldots, L(M))$ with the lowest cost, where the cost function is of the form

$$C(L) = \sum_{i=1}^{M} E_{\text{data}}^{i}(L(i)) + \sum_{i=1}^{M-1} E_{\text{smoothness}}^{i,i+1}(L(i), L(i+1)) \qquad (\text{A.1})$$

where $E_{\text{data}}^{i}(k)$ represents the cost of assigning label k to node i (the data term) and $E_{\text{smoothness}}^{i,i+1}(k,l)$ represents the cost of assigning labels k and l to adjacent nodes i and $i+1$ (the smoothness term). The data term usually involves the intensities of image pixels (for example, in seam carving, it's related to the gradient at the pixel corresponding to the label). The smoothness term reflects constraints or assumptions about how similar adjacent labels should be. For example, in seam carving, a vertical seam must separate the image into left and right parts; thus, the label at node i is constrained to be within the range $\{L_{i-1} - 1, L_{i-1}, L_{i-1} + 1\}$. Similarly, in the stereo correspondence problem, we usually impose the monotonicity constraint that $L_i > L_{i-1}$, and may further weight the allowable disparities at each pixel, for example by assigning higher costs to larger disparities. We can think of a labeling as a **path** through a graph of $M \times N$ vertices, as illustrated in Figure A.1.

To find the minimum-cost labeling, we apply a recursive algorithm, building tables of incrementally optimal costs and corresponding minimizers. That is, we fill in the entries of two $M \times N$ matrices. Each entry of the first matrix, $S(i,k)$, is defined as the minimum cost of the path that begins in row 1 and ends at vertex (i,k) of the graph. Each entry of the second matrix, $R(i,k)$, is defined as the index of the node in row $i-1$ of the graph that resulted in the cost $S(i,k)$ (which we can think of as the "predecessor" of that node).

Formally, we apply the following algorithm:

1. Initialize $S(1,k) = E_{\text{data}}^1(k)$ for $k = 1,\ldots,N$. That is, the first row is initialized with the data costs of assigning $L(1) = 1,\ldots,L(1) = N$. Initialize $R(1,k) = 0$ (these entries are arbitrary and won't be used).
2. For $i = 2,\ldots,M$, iterate the following step:
3. Compute $S(i,k)$ and $R(i,k)$ as:

$$S(i,k) = E_{\text{data}}^i(k) + \min_l(S(i-1,l) + E_{\text{smoothness}}^{i-1,i}(l,k))$$

$$R(i,k) = \arg\min_l(S(i-1,l) + E_{\text{smoothness}}(l,k)) \tag{A.2}$$

That is, $S(i,k)$ is the lowest cost that can be achieved considering the allowable predecessors in the previous row of the matrix, and $R(i,k)$ is the index of the predecessor in row $i-1$ that achieves this cost. The notion of allowability depends on the application, as illustrated in Figure A.1.

4. The matrix has thus been filled in from the first row to the last. In the stereo correspondence case (or more generally when we require the path to end at the corner of the matrix), we fix $L_M = N$. In the seam carving case (or more generally when the path can end at any point in the last row of the image), we fix $L_M = N^*$, where

$$N^* = \arg\min_k S(M,k) \tag{A.3}$$

5. We finally extract the minimal cost path by backtracking from row M. That is, for $i = M-1:-1:1$, we compute

$$L_i = R(i+i, L_{i+1}) \tag{A.4}$$

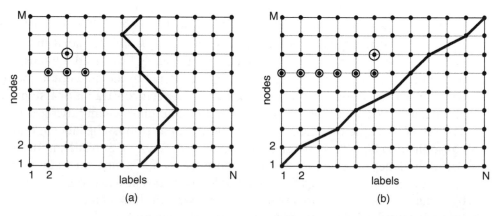

(a)   (b)

Figure A.1. Paths for dynamic programming problems. (a) A path for a seam carving problem must connect the top and bottom edges; adjacent labels can differ by at most 1. (b) A path for a stereo correspondence problem must have non-decreasing labels and connect the lower left corner to the upper right corner. The smaller circled pixels in each case indicate the allowable predecessors of the large circled pixel (each of which may have a different weight specified by the smoothness term).

Dynamic programming is highly efficient, finding the optimal solution in polynomial time compared to the worst-case exponential-time problem of evaluating all possible paths. Many well-known signal processing algorithms in addition to those we discussed are forms of dynamic programming, including the Viterbi algorithm for decoding convolutional codes in communication theory and the Baum-Welch algorithm for maximum likelihood estimation of unknown parameters in a Hidden Markov Model. For more information on the general algorithm, see Cormen et al. [106]. An excellent overview of applications of dynamic programming to computer vision is given by Felzenszwalb and Zabih [139].

A.2   BELIEF PROPAGATION

We can think of Equation (A.1) as a special case of a **Gibbs energy**

$$E(L) = \sum_{i \in \mathcal{V}} E_{\text{data}}^{i}(L(i)) + \sum_{(i,j) \in \mathcal{E}} E_{\text{smoothness}}^{i,j}(L(i), L(j)) \tag{A.5}$$

where $\mathcal{V}$ is a set of nodes and $\mathcal{E}$ is a set of undirected edges along which we want to enforce smoothness. When these edges form a one-dimensional chain, we can find the labeling $\{L(i), i \in \mathcal{V}\}$ that minimizes Equation (A.5) in polynomial time using dynamic programming. However, when the edge set $\mathcal{E}$ contains cycles, dynamic programming no longer applies, and there is no higher-dimensional analogy.

In particular, we frequently want to minimize Equation (A.5) when $\mathcal{V}$ is the set of pixels in an image, and $\mathcal{E}$ is the set of all adjacent pixels (for example, 4-neighbors). The resulting graph is planar and contains a large number of cycles. Unfortunately, there is no efficient algorithm that provably finds the minimal labeling in this situation. However, the algorithm called **loopy belief propagation** has found great practical success in the computer vision community for approximately minimizing Equation (A.5) despite its lack of formal guarantees on convergence or exact optimality. For example, we discussed loopy belief propagation's application to matting problems in Section 2.5 and to stereo correspondence in Section 5.5.

Minimizing a function like Equation (A.5) often arises from a **maximum a posteriori (MAP)** estimation problem on a Markov Random Field, in which we want to find the labeling that maximizes the probability density function[1] given by

$$p(L) = \frac{1}{Z} \prod_{i \in \mathcal{V}} \phi_i(L(i)) \prod_{(i,j) \in \mathcal{E}} \psi_{ij}(L(i), L(j)) \tag{A.6}$$

where $\phi_i(k)$ is called the **evidence potential function**, $\psi_{ij}(k, l)$ is called the **compatibility potential function**, and Z is a normalization constant so the probability density function sums to 1. Comparing Equation (A.5) to Equation (A.6), we can see that the data/smoothness terms and evidence/compatibility potential functions can easily be related by

$$E_{\text{data}}^{i}(k) = -\log \phi_i(k)$$
$$E_{\text{smoothness}}^{i,j}(k, l) = -\log \psi_{ij}(k, l) \tag{A.7}$$

---

[1] Technically, this is a probability mass function since the label set is discrete.

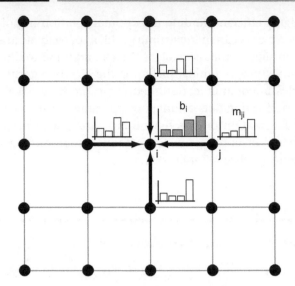

Figure A.2. One iteration of belief propagation. Node i collects incoming messages m_{ji} from its neighbors $\{j \mid (i,j) \in \mathcal{E}\}$, which are used to update its belief b_i about its label.

In loopy belief propagation, each node maintains an evolving **belief** about its labeling — that is, a probability distribution function over the possible labels, denoted at node i as $\{b_i(k), k = 1, \ldots, N\}$. The beliefs are iteratively updated by means of **messages** passed along edges, denoted $\{m_{ji}, (i,j) \in \mathcal{E}\}$, that convey neighboring nodes' current opinions about the belief at node i. The idea is sketched in Figure A.2.

The beliefs and messages are initialized as uniform distributions and iteratively updated according to the following rules:

$$b_i(L(i)) \leftarrow \frac{1}{Z_B} \phi_i(L(i)) \prod_{j \mid (i,j) \in \mathcal{E}} m_{ji}(L(i)) \tag{A.8}$$

$$m_{ij}(L(j)) \leftarrow \frac{1}{Z_M} \max_{L(i)} \left(\phi_i(L(i)) \psi_{ij}(L(i), L(j)) \prod_{h \mid (i,h) \in \mathcal{E}, h \neq j} m_{hi}(L(i)) \right) \tag{A.9}$$

This is called the **max-product algorithm**. Z_B in Equation (A.8) and Z_M in Equation (A.9) are normalization constants so that the belief and message distributions sum to one. The messages are updated a specified number of times or until the beliefs stop changing significantly. The final label at node i is the one that maximizes $b_i(L(i))$ at convergence. The stereo algorithm given in Section 5.5.3 gives a version of the max-product algorithm that operates on the data/smoothness terms of Equation (A.5) (i.e., log likelihoods) instead of the potential functions.

If we replace Equation (A.9) by

$$m_{ij}(L(j)) \leftarrow \frac{1}{Z_M} \sum_{i=1}^{N} \phi_i(L(i)) \psi_{ij}(L(i), L(j)) \prod_{h \mid (i,h) \in \mathcal{E}, h \neq j} m_{hi}(L(i)) \tag{A.10}$$

we obtain the **sum-product algorithm**, which results in estimates of the marginal posterior at each node as opposed to the joint MAP estimate. Both algorithms are widely used in computer vision problems (with the max-product algorithm slightly more common).

The original message-passing algorithm was proposed by Pearl [362]. Detailed descriptions of loopy belief propagation in computer vision were given by Freeman et al. [154] and Yedidia et al. [566]. Szeliski et al. [485] compared the performance of loopy belief propagation with graph cuts using α-expansion (see the next section) and several of their variants on a benchmark dataset of computer vision problems. They also provided a freely available implementation using a common problem specification (see http://vision.middlebury.edu/MRF).

Felzenszwalb and Huttenlocher [138] described several simple modifications to the basic loopy belief propagation algorithm that dramatically speed up its convergence for the graphs and cost functions typically encountered in computer vision applications like stereo.

A.3   GRAPH CUTS AND α-EXPANSION

The main alternative to loopy belief propagation for minimizing energies of the form of Equation (A.5) is the use of **graph cuts**. We introduced graph cuts in Section 2.8 in the context of hard segmentation of an image; in this case, there are only two labels (i.e., a pixel is either part of the foreground or part of the background). We also discussed graph cuts with binary labels in Section 3.3 for finding good compositing seams and in Section 3.5 for seam carving.

The main advantage of graph cuts in these two-label situations is that efficient algorithms exist to globally minimize the Gibbs energy in the special case when the smoothness term satisfies a **Potts model**,[2] namely

$$
\begin{aligned}
E^{i,j}_{\text{smoothness}}(L(i), L(j)) &= 0 && \text{if } L(i) = L(j) \\
E^{i,j}_{\text{smoothness}}(L(i), L(j)) &= V_{ij} && \text{if } L(i) \neq L(j)
\end{aligned}
\tag{A.11}
$$

Section 2.8.1 describes how to map a Gibbs energy in this form onto a graph with weighted edges. To review, we begin with the set of nodes $\mathcal{V}$ used to define the Gibbs energy function, and add two special **terminal nodes** that we call the source $\mathbb{S}$ and the sink $\mathbb{T}$. We assume the source is associated with label 0 and the sink is associated with label 1.[3] We also augment the set of edges $\mathcal{E}$ used to define the Gibbs energy function, adding edges $e_{i\mathbb{S}}$ and $e_{i\mathbb{T}}$ between each regular node and each of the two terminals. We put a nonnegative weight w_{ij} on each edge e_{ij}. The weights on each edge are related to the data and smoothness terms of Equation (A.5) by:

$$
\begin{aligned}
w_{i\mathbb{S}} &= E_{\text{data}}(L(i) = 1) \\
w_{i\mathbb{T}} &= E_{\text{data}}(L(i) = 0) \\
w_{ij} &= V_{ij}
\end{aligned}
\tag{A.12}
$$

---

[2] More generally, Kolmogorov and Zabih [248] proved that a binary Gibbs energy function can be minimized using graph cuts if and only if $E^{i,j}_{\text{smoothness}}(0,0) + E^{i,j}_{\text{smoothness}}(1,1) \leq E^{i,j}_{\text{smoothness}}(0,1) + E^{i,j}_{\text{smoothness}}(1,0)$ for each (i,j). See that paper for details on how to handle non-Potts models.

[3] This is a minor change from the previous section, where we assumed the labels were indexed starting from 1.

That is, if node i should have label 0, we want $E_{\text{data}}(L(i) = 0)$ to be low and $E_{\text{data}}(L(i) = 1)$ to be high. Thus we want the weight of the edge attaching node i to the source (label 0) to be high and the weight of the edge attaching node i to the sink (label 1) to be low, so that the edge to the sink is cut and node i remains attached to the source.

In this section, we briefly describe how to compute the **minimum cut** on such a graph — that is, a subset of edges C such that if we remove these edges from $\mathcal{E}$, there is no path from $\mathbb{S}$ to $\mathbb{T}$ in the resulting subgraph, and the subset C minimizes the cost

$$|C| = \sum_{(i,j) \in C} w_{ij} \tag{A.13}$$

The key concept is to transform the minimum cut problem to a **maximum flow** problem on the graph. That is, we think of the edge weights as capacities for transporting material (e.g., water), and want to determine the maximum amount of material that can be flowed from the source to the sink along the edges.[4] After computing the maximum flow, the set of edges at full capacity corresponds to the minimum cut (and the cost of this cut corresponds to the maximum amount of material that can be flowed).

Computing the maximum flow is a well-studied problem in combinatorial optimization, and one of the main approaches is called the **Ford-Fulkerson** method, which at a high level operates as follows:

1. Initialize the flow along each edge e_{ij} to 0.
2. While there is still a path p from $\mathbb{S}$ to $\mathbb{T}$ along which we can push more flow, add more flow along p until one of its edges is at capacity.

The main issue is how to efficiently find good paths in Step 2 to reach the maximum flow as quickly as possible. Cormen et al. [106] describe various classical approaches, including the Edmonds-Karp algorithm, in which the augmenting path is the shortest path from $\mathbb{S}$ to $\mathbb{T}$ in the residual network (i.e., a graph in which an edge appears if it has unused capacity). From the perspective of computer vision problems, in which the graphs have a typical, regularly connected structure, the most important contribution was made by Boykov and Kolmogorov [60]. They used a pair of search trees emanating from the source and the sink that explore non-saturated edges to find augmenting paths, and efficiently reuse these trees in each step. Their algorithm has superior performance on computer vision problems such as image segmentation and stereo compared to the leading maximum-flow algorithms. Many computer vision researchers use Kolmogorov's publicly available maximum-flow/minimum-cut implementation (http://vision.csd.uwo.ca/code/), which was also incorporated into Szeliski et al.'s common interface for minimizing energies over Markov Random Fields (see the previous section).

Many Gibbs energy problems require more than two labels at a node, and the algorithm used previously can't be directly applied. For example, in Section 5.5.2 we discussed the problem of stereo correspondence, in which the labels correspond

---

[4] Maximum flow problems generally require the graph to be directed, not undirected; this is addressed by creating a directed graph that has two opposing directed edges $i \rightarrow j$ and $j \rightarrow i$ in place of every edge (i,j) in the original undirected graph. Each directed edge is given the same weight as the original undirected edge.

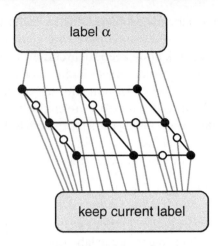

label α

keep current label

Figure A.3. The binary-label graph for one step of α-expansion. The source node is identified with the action "label α," while the sink node is identified with "keep current label." The black dots are nodes of the original problem, while the white dots are auxiliary nodes introduced between nodes that currently have different labels.

to several possible disparities. We can tackle such problems by decomposing them into a sequence of binary-label graph cut problems, using the α-**expansion** algorithm proposed by Boykov et al. [61].[5]

The key idea is to solve a series of minimum-cut subproblems on graphs of the type illustrated in Figure A.3, each starting with an initial labeling. In each problem, a certain label value $\alpha \in \{1, \dots, N\}$ is fixed. We build a new graph containing all the nodes and edges of the original problem. In this graph, the source node $\mathbb{S}$ is identified with the action "label α," while the sink node $\mathbb{T}$ is identified with "keep current label." We also must add an **auxiliary node** a_{ij} between every pair of nodes i and j whose current labels $L(i)$ and $L(j)$ disagree. These auxiliary nodes are only connected to the sink.

Boykov et al. [61] defined the weights on the edges for the α-expansion subproblem as follows:

$$
\begin{aligned}
w_{i\mathbb{T}} &= \infty & &\text{if } L(i) = \alpha \\
w_{i\mathbb{T}} &= E_{\text{data}}(L(i) = \text{current label}) & &\text{if } L(i) \neq \alpha \\
w_{i\mathbb{S}} &= E_{\text{data}}(L(i) = \alpha) & &\text{all } i \in \mathcal{V} \\
w_{i\,a_{ij}} &= E_{\text{smoothness}}^{i,j}(L(i), \alpha) & &\text{if } (i,j) \in \mathcal{E}, L(i) \neq L(j) \qquad \text{(A.15)} \\
w_{a_{ij}\,j} &= E_{\text{smoothness}}^{i,j}(\alpha, L(j)) & &\text{if } (i,j) \in \mathcal{E}, L(i) \neq L(j) \\
w_{a_{ij}\,\mathbb{T}} &= E_{\text{smoothness}}^{i,j}(L(i), L(j)) & &\text{if } (i,j) \in \mathcal{E}, L(i) \neq L(j) \\
w_{ij} &= E_{\text{smoothness}}^{i,j}(L(i), \alpha) & &\text{if } (i,j) \in \mathcal{E}, L(i) = L(j)
\end{aligned}
$$

---

[5] As previously, we require some conditions on the $E_{\text{smoothness}}$ term; specifically that it is a metric. That is, for any labels $L(i), L(j), L(h)$,

$$
\begin{aligned}
E_{\text{smoothness}}^{i,j}(L(i), L(j)) &= 0 \iff L(i) = L(j) \\
E_{\text{smoothness}}^{i,j}(L(i), L(j)) &= E_{\text{smoothness}}^{i,j}(L(j), L(i)) \geq 0 \qquad \text{(A.14)} \\
E_{\text{smoothness}}^{i,j}(L(i), L(j)) &\leq E_{\text{smoothness}}^{i,h}(L(i), L(h)) + E_{\text{smoothness}}^{h,j}(L(h), L(j))
\end{aligned}
$$

However, unlike our interpretation in the binary labeling problem, after we compute the minimum cut, all of the nodes *separated from* the source node are given the label α, and all of the nodes *separated from* the sink node keep their current label. This is a little counterintuitive and opposite our interpretation earlier in this section and in Chapter 2, but we maintain this notation to be consistent with the original formulation. We can see that since all the nodes already labeled α are connected to the sink node with infinite weight, the only outcome of solving the subproblem is that some nodes not currently labeled α change their label to α.

For the overall algorithm with N labels, we iterate the following steps:

1. Initialize the labeling L with random labels at each node.
2. For $i = 1, \ldots, N$
   a) Solve the α-expansion subproblem with $\alpha = i$. Finding the minimum cut for this binary labeling problem produces a candidate labeling L'.
   b) If $E(L') < E(L)$, replace L with L'.
3. If a cycle through all N labels has produced no improvement in the cost function, stop and return the converged labels L. Otherwise, go to step 2.

While the overall solution to the multi-label problem resulting from α-expansion doesn't enjoy the global optimality guarantee that we have for the binary-label problem, it still has several desirable properties. First, it provably converges in a finite number of iterations, and convergence is relatively fast since a large number of spatially distant pixels can change their label simultaneously in each subproblem. Second, Boykov et al. proved that the cost of the labeling at convergence is within a known factor of the global minimum cost. In particular, for the multi-label Potts model, the cost of the converged labeling is at most twice the global minimum cost. This is an excellent result considering that finding the global minimum of the multi-label problem is known to be NP-hard.

A.4 NEWTON METHODS FOR NONLINEAR SUM-OF-SQUARES OPTIMIZATION

Many computer vision optimization problems can be formulated as the minimization of the sum of squared terms that depend nonlinearly on the parameters to be estimated. For example, the projective transformation estimation problem in Section 5.1, the bundle adjustment problem in Section 6.5.3, and the inverse kinematics problem in Section 7.4.2 can all be cast in this form. In this section, we briefly review **Newton methods** for this type of optimization problem, leading up to the Levenberg-Marquardt algorithm frequently used in computer vision problems.

We assume the functional we want to minimize has the form

$$F(\boldsymbol{\theta}) = (\mathbf{x} - f(\boldsymbol{\theta}))^\top (\mathbf{x} - f(\boldsymbol{\theta})) \tag{A.16}$$

where $\boldsymbol{\theta} \in \mathbb{R}^M$ is the vector of parameters we want to estimate and $\mathbf{x} \in \mathbb{R}^N$ is a given vector of measurements. The function f maps a choice of the parameters $\boldsymbol{\theta}$ to a vector in $\mathbb{R}^N$; we interpret the minimization of Equation (A.16) as trying to bring the model of the system specified by f as close as possible to the actual observed measurements $\mathbf{x}$.

The necessary conditions for θ^* to minimize Equation (A.16) are

$$\frac{\partial F}{\partial \theta}(\theta^*) = \begin{bmatrix} \frac{\partial F}{\partial \theta_1} \\ \vdots \\ \frac{\partial F}{\partial \theta_M} \end{bmatrix} (\theta^*) = 0 \tag{A.17}$$

$$\frac{\partial^2 F}{\partial \theta^2}(\theta^*) = \begin{bmatrix} \frac{\partial^2 F}{\partial \theta_1^2} & \cdots & \frac{\partial^2 F}{\partial \theta_1 \partial \theta_M} \\ \vdots & \ddots & \vdots \\ \frac{\partial^2 F}{\partial \theta_1 \partial \theta_M} & \cdots & \frac{\partial^2 F}{\partial \theta_M^2} \end{bmatrix} (\theta^*) > 0 \tag{A.18}$$

The notation in Equation (A.18) is shorthand for the positive definiteness of the matrix $\frac{\partial^2 F}{\partial \theta^2}(\theta^*)$, which is called the **Hessian**.

The condition in Equation (A.17) can be written:

$$\frac{\partial F}{\partial \theta}(\theta^*) = -2(\mathbf{x} - f(\theta^*))^\top \frac{\partial f}{\partial \theta}(\theta^*) = 0 \tag{A.19}$$

or equivalently,

$$\frac{\partial f}{\partial \theta}^\top (\theta^*)(\mathbf{x} - f(\theta^*)) = 0 \tag{A.20}$$

Note that $\frac{\partial f}{\partial \theta}$ is a $N \times M$ matrix. When f is a linear function of the parameters θ given by $f(\theta) = A\theta$, where $A \in \mathbb{R}^{N \times M}$ doesn't depend on θ, then Equation (A.20) is a linear equation in θ^*, the solution of which is:

$$\theta^* = (F^\top F)^{-1} F^\top \mathbf{x} \tag{A.21}$$

However, in general, Equation (A.20) is a nonlinear system of equations in θ that must be solved by numerical means.

Let's expand the cost function $F(\theta)$ in a Taylor series approximation about some point θ^t:

$$F(\theta) \approx F(\theta^t) + \frac{\partial F}{\partial \theta}(\theta^t)^\top (\theta - \theta^t) + \frac{1}{2}(\theta - \theta^t)^\top \frac{\partial^2 F}{\partial \theta^2}(\theta^t)(\theta - \theta^t) \tag{A.22}$$

We can compute the Hessian matrix of second derivatives in Equation (A.22) as:

$$\frac{\partial^2 F}{\partial \theta^2}(\theta^t) = -2\left[\sum_{k=1}^{N}(\mathbf{x}_k - f(\mathbf{x}_k; \theta))\frac{\partial^2 f(\mathbf{x}_k; \theta)}{\partial \theta^2}(\theta^t)\right] + 2\frac{\partial f}{\partial \theta}(\theta^t)^\top \frac{\partial f}{\partial \theta}(\theta^t)$$

$$= -2\left[\sum_{k=1}^{N}(\mathbf{x}_k - f(\mathbf{x}_k; \theta))\frac{\partial^2 f(\mathbf{x}_k; \theta)}{\partial \theta^2}(\theta^t)\right] + 2J(\theta^t)^\top J(\theta^t) \tag{A.23}$$

where J is the **Jacobian** matrix defined by

$$J(\theta^t) = \frac{\partial f}{\partial \theta}(\theta^t) \tag{A.24}$$

That is, the $(j, k)^{th}$ element of J is the partial derivative of the jth model prediction $\hat{\mathbf{x}}_j$ with respect to the kth parameter θ_k.

The minimizer of this function, which we'll denote θ^{t+1}, is given by setting the gradient of Equation (A.22) to zero:

$$\theta^{t+1} = \theta^t - \left[\frac{\partial^2 F}{\partial \theta^2}(\theta^t) \right]^{-1} \frac{\partial F}{\partial \theta}(\theta^t) \tag{A.25}$$

When we add a step size parameter to Equation (A.25), and substitute the expansion in Equation (A.23), we obtain:

$$\theta^{t+1} = \theta^t + \rho \left[J(\theta^t)^\top J(\theta^t) - \sum_{k=1}^{N} (\mathbf{x}_k - f(\mathbf{x}_k; \theta)) \frac{\partial^2 f(\mathbf{x}_k; \theta)}{\partial \theta^2}(\theta^t) \right]^{-1} J(\theta^t)^\top [\mathbf{x} - f(\theta^t)] \tag{A.26}$$

Under certain conditions, if θ^t is a good estimate of the minimizer θ^*, the parameters θ^{t+1} produced by Equation (A.26) are an incrementally better estimate of θ^*. The new estimate can then replace the old (i.e., incrementing t by 1) and Equation (A.26) reapplied. The iterations terminate when the term $J(\theta^t)^\top (\mathbf{x} - f(\theta^t))$ in Equation (A.26) becomes vanishingly small (which is the condition in Equation (A.20)). The iteration suggested by Equation (A.26) is called the **Newton-Raphson method**.

The convergence of the algorithm is governed by the choice of the step size parameter ρ. One possibility is to choose $\rho = 1$, corresponding to explicitly minimizing the quadratic approximation at each iteration, but in practice we can choose $\rho < 1$ to simply reduce the cost function in the direction of the vector on the right-hand side of Equation (A.26).

A simplification of Equation (A.26) is obtained by dropping the second term in the inverted matrix, producing the update equation

$$\theta^{t+1} = \theta^t + \rho \left[J(\theta^t)^\top J(\theta^t) \right]^{-1} J(\theta^t)^\top (\mathbf{x} - f(\theta^t)) \tag{A.27}$$

This simplified iteration is known as **Gauss's method** or the **Gauss-Newton method**.

A third algorithm is obtained by assuming that the inverted matrix in Equation (A.26) is equal to the identity; that is,

$$\theta^{t+1} = \theta^t + \rho J(\theta^t)^\top (\mathbf{x} - f(\theta^t)) \tag{A.28}$$

The iteration suggested by Equation (A.28) is the well-known **steepest descent method**. The descent direction $J(\theta^t)^\top (\mathbf{x} - f(\theta^t))$ is simply the gradient of the function F.

Finally, the **Levenberg-Marquardt method** is obtained as a cross between the Gauss-Newton and steepest descent methods. The Levenberg-Marquardt iteration is based on the recursion:

$$\theta^{t+1} = \theta^t + \rho \left[J(\theta^t)^\top J(\theta^t) + \lambda^t \mathbf{I}_{N \times N} \right]^{-1} J(\theta^t)^\top (\mathbf{x} - f(\theta^t)) \tag{A.29}$$

When $\lambda^t = 0$, the Levenberg-Marquardt iteration is the same as a Gauss-Newton iteration. As $\lambda^t \to \infty$, the Levenberg-Marquardt iteration tends to a step along the gradient. Careful tuning of the parameter λ^t as the algorithm progresses generally leads to a quicker convergence rate than either of the two sub-methods. The idea is to encourage the Gauss-Newton method to be globally convergent by ensuring that the approximated Hessian is positive definite. This falls into a more general class of techniques called **trust region methods**.

More details about these algorithms (e.g. choice of step size, termination criteria, search directions, pitfalls) can be found in numerical optimization textbooks (e.g., [118, 351]). Implementations of the algorithms in pseudocode can be found in Press et al. [374].

As discussed in Section 6.5.3.2, the structure of the Jacobian matrix has critical implications for designing a fast numerical optimization algorithm. In particular, if $J(\theta^t)$ is sparse (that is, each element of f only depends on a few elements of θ), the computations should be arranged so that needless multiplications and additions of elements known to be 0 are avoided.

B Figure Acknowledgments

All figures were created by the author and/or contain the author's original images, with the following exceptions:

- Figures 2.4, 2.14 and 2.16: images and trimaps courtesy Christoph Rhemann, from www.alphamatting.com.
- Figure 2.26: *Source Code* courtesy of Summit Entertainment, LLC. Images provided by Oblique FX. *Iron Man 2* images appear courtesy of Marvel Studios, TM & ©2010 Marvel and Subs. www.marvel.com.
- Figure 3.33: image courtesy Jacob Becker.
- Figure 3.38: adidas, the 3-Stripes mark and the *Impossible is Nothing* mark are registered trademarks of the adidas Group used with permission. The name, image and likeness of Muhammad Ali are provided courtesy of Muhammad Ali Enterprises LLC. *Transformers: Dark of the Moon* ©2011 Paramount Pictures. All Rights Reserved. *The Mummy: Tomb of the Dragon Emperor* courtesy of Universal Studios Licensing LLC. Images provided by Digital Domain.
- Figure 4.22: QR Code is a registered trademark of Denso Wave Incorporated, Japan. ARToolKit markers from Kato et al. [231]. ARTags from Fiala [140].
- Figure 4.23: *Thor* images appear courtesy of Marvel Studios, TM & ©2011 Marvel and Subs. www.marvel.com. *Transformers: Revenge of the Fallen* ©2009 DW Studios L.L.C. and Paramount Pictures Corporation. All Rights Reserved. *Transformers: Revenge of the Fallen* images provided by Digital Domain.
- Figure 5.9: Table image, layers, and flow field from Liu et al. [288].
- Figure 5.18: Tsukuba images from Nakamura et al. [344] and stereo result from the Middlebury benchmark at http://vision.middlebury.edu/stereo/.
- Figure 5.31: *Transformers: Dark of the Moon* ©2011 Paramount Pictures. All Rights Reserved. *Transformers: Revenge of the Fallen* ©2009 DW Studios L.L.C. and Paramount Pictures Corporation. All Rights Reserved. Images provided by Digital Domain.
- Figures 6.5 and 6.6: source images courtesy Ziyan Wu.
- Figure 6.19: *Transformers: Dark of the Moon* ©2011 Paramount Pictures. All Rights Reserved. *A Beautiful Mind* ©2001 Universal Studios and DW Studios L.L.C. All Rights Reserved. Courtesy of Universal Studios Licensing LLC. Images provided by Digital Domain.
- Figure 7.1d: XSuit character and posing courtesy of Noah Schnapp.

- Figure 7.8: underlying skeleton image and Figure 7.19 underlying face image by Patrick J. Lynch, illustrator, and C. Carl Jaffe MD, cardiologist, Yale University Center for Advanced Instructional Media. Creative Commons Attribution 2.5 generic license.
- Figure 7.27: *Rise of the Planet of the Apes* ©2011 Twentieth Century Fox. All rights reserved.
- Figure 8.3 and elsewhere in Chapter 8: building scan provided by David Doria.
- Figure 8.27: multi-view stereo dataset images and PMVS result from the Middlebury benchmark at `http://vision.middlebury.edu/mview/`.
- Figure 8.30b: chicken mesh from A. Mian et al., `http://www.csse.uwa.edu.au/~ajmal/3Dmodeling.html`.
- Figure 8.40: *Thor* images appear courtesy of Marvel Studios, TM & ©2011 Marvel and Subs. www.marvel.com. *Fast Five* courtesy of Universal Studios Licensing LLC. Images provided by Gentle Giant Studios.

The algorithmic results in several figures were created using original or modified versions of publicly available executables and source code from various researchers. The researchers, webpages, and corresponding figures are listed in this section. Thanks to the researchers for making their code available.

- Closed-form matting, A. Levin, `http://www.wisdom.weizmann.ac.il/~levina/matting.tar.gz` (Figures 2.2, 2.13, and 2.22)
- Spectral matting, A. Levin, `http://www.vision.huji.ac.il/SpectralMatting/` (Figures 2.14 and 2.16)
- Graph-cut segmentation implementation, P. Wang, `https://mywebspace.wisc.edu/pwang6/personal/` (Figure 2.20)

- Laplacian pyramid toolbox, M. Do, `http://www.mathworks.com/matlabcentral/fileexchange/9868` (Figures 3.4, 3.5, and 3.7)
- Graph-cut compositing, A. Agarwala et al., `http://grail.cs.washington.edu/projects/photomontage/release/` (Figures 3.15 and 3.16)
- PDE-based inpainting, W. Yung and A. J. Ahankar, `http://www.boopidy.com/aj/cs/inpainting/` (Figures 3.18 and 3.19)
- Patch-based inpainting implementation, S. Bhat, `http://www.cc.gatech.edu/~sooraj/inpainting/` (Figure 3.22)
- Itti's saliency measure, D. Walther, `http://saliencytoolbox.net/` (Figure 3.25)
- Optimized scale-and-stretch resizing, Y. Wang et al., `http://graphics.csie.ncku.edu.tw/Image_Resizing/` (Figure 3.26)
- Forward and backward seam carving, M. Rubinstein, `http://people.csail.mit.edu/mrub/code.html` (Figures 3.27, 3.28, 3.29, 3.30, and 3.33)
- PatchMatch implementation, A. Adams et al., `http://code.google.com/p/imagestack/` (Figure 3.36)

- Affine feature detectors and descriptors, K. Mikolajczyk, `http://www.robots.ox.ac.uk/~vgg/research/affine/` (Figures 4.5, 4.6, and 4.12)

- Laplacian- and Difference-of-Gaussian detectors, W.-L. Zhao, `http://www.cs.cityu.edu.hk/~wzhao2/lip-vireo.htm` (Figures 4.6 and 4.10)
- Matlab SIFT implementation, A. Vedaldi and B. Fulkerson, `http://www.vlfeat.org` (Figures 4.17 and 4.18)
- QR code generator, J. Delport, `http://createqrcode.appspot.com/` (Figure 4.22)
- ARToolkit markers, M. Billinghurst et al., `http://www.hitl.washington.edu/artoolkit/download/` (Figure 4.22)
- ARTag markers, M. Fiala, `http://www.artag.net/` (Figure 4.22)

- Horn-Schunck optical flow, D. Sun et al., `http://www.cs.brown.edu/~dqsun/code/flow_code.zip` (Figure 5.5)
- Human-assisted motion estimation, C. Liu et al., `http://people.csail.mit.edu/celiu/motionAnnotation/` (Figure 5.9)
- Fundamental matrix estimation, P. Kovesi, `http://www.csse.uwa.edu.au/~pk/research/matlabfns/` (Figure 5.12)
- Rectification, M. Dailey, `http://se.cs.ait.ac.th/cvwiki/matlab:tutorial:rectification` (Figure 5.14)
- Graph-cut stereo, R. Szeliski et al., `http://vision.middlebury.edu/MRF/code/` (Figure 5.18)
- Robust homography estimation, D. Capel et al., `http://www.robots.ox.ac.uk/~vgg/hzbook/code/` (Figure 5.30)

- Camera calibration, J.-Y. Bouguet, `http://www.vision.caltech.edu/bouguetj/calib_doc/` (Figures 6.5 and 6.7)
- Matchmoving results created using the *boujou* matchmoving software by 2d3 (now sold by Vicon) (Figures 6.17 and 6.18)

- Matlab motion capture toolbox, N. Lawrence, `http://www.cs.man.ac.uk/~neill/mocap/` (Figure 7.13)
- Visual hull examples based on voxel carving code, B. Tordoff, `http://www.mathworks.com/matlabcentral/fileexchange/26160-carving-a-dinosaur` (Figures 7.24b and 7.26)

- Normal estimation and spin image code, A. Mian et al., `http://www.csse.uwa.edu.au/~ajmal/code.html` (Figure 8.30c)

Bibliography

[1] A. Abdel-Hakim and A. Farag. CSIFT: A SIFT descriptor with color invariant characteristics. In *IEEE Computer Society Conference on Computer Vision and Pattern Recognition (CVPR)*, 2006.

[2] E. Adelson and J. Bergen. The plenoptic function and the elements of early vision. In M. S. Landy and J. A. Movshon, editors, *Computational Models of Visual Processing*, chapter 1. MIT Press, 1991.

[3] A. Agarwal and B. Triggs. Recovering 3D human pose from monocular images. *IEEE Transactions on Pattern Analysis and Machine Intelligence*, 28(1):44–58, Jan. 2006.

[4] S. Agarwal, N. Snavely, S. M. Seitz, and R. Szeliski. Bundle adjustment in the large. In *European Conference on Computer Vision (ECCV)*, 2010.

[5] S. Agarwal, N. Snavely, I. Simon, S. Seitz, and R. Szeliski. Building Rome in a day. In *IEEE International Conference on Computer Vision (ICCV)*, 2009.

[6] A. Agarwala. Efficient gradient-domain compositing using quadtrees. In *ACM SIGGRAPH (ACM Transactions on Graphics)*, 2007.

[7] A. Agarwala, M. Dontcheva, M. Agrawala, S. Drucker, A. Colburn, B. Curless, D. Salesin, and M. Cohen. Interactive digital photomontage. In *ACM SIGGRAPH (ACM Transactions on Graphics)*, 2004.

[8] A. Agarwala, A. Hertzmann, D. Salesin, and S. Seitz. Keyframe-based tracking for rotoscoping and animation. In *ACM SIGGRAPH (ACM Transactions on Graphics)*, 2004.

[9] A. Agarwala, K. C. Zheng, C. Pal, M. Agrawala, M. Cohen, B. Curless, D. Salesin, and R. Szeliski. Panoramic video textures. In *ACM SIGGRAPH (ACM Transactions on Graphics)*, 2005.

[10] A. Agrawal, R. Raskar, S. K. Nayar, and Y. Li. Removing photography artifacts using gradient projection and flash-exposure sampling. In *ACM SIGGRAPH (ACM Transactions on Graphics)*, 2005.

[11] O. Alexander, M. Rogers, W. Lambeth, M. Chiang, and P. Debevec. The Digital Emily project: photoreal facial modeling and animation. In *ACM SIGGRAPH Courses*, 2009.

[12] B. Allen, B. Curless, and Z. Popović. The space of human body shapes: reconstruction and parameterization from range scans. In *ACM SIGGRAPH (ACM Transactions on Graphics)*, 2003.

[13] P. K. Allen, A. Troccoli, B. Smith, I. Stamos, and S. Murray. The Beauvais Cathedral project. In *Workshop on Applications of Computer Vision in Archeology*, 2003.

[14] M. Andersson and D. Betsis. Point reconstruction from noisy images. *Journal of Mathematical Imaging and Vision*, 5(1):77–90, Jan. 1995.

[15] D. Anguelov, P. Srinivasan, D. Koller, S. Thrun, J. Rodgers, and J. Davis. SCAPE: shape completion and animation of people. In *ACM SIGGRAPH (ACM Transactions on Graphics)*, 2005.

[16] N. Apostoloff and A. Fitzgibbon. Bayesian video matting using learnt image priors. In *IEEE Computer Society Conference on Computer Vision and Pattern Recognition (CVPR)*, 2004.

[17] O. Arikan and D. A. Forsyth. Interactive motion generation from examples. In *ACM SIGGRAPH (ACM Transactions on Graphics)*, 2002.

[18] O. Arikan, D. A. Forsyth, and J. F. O'Brien. Motion synthesis from annotations. In *ACM SIGGRAPH (ACM Transactions on Graphics)*, 2003.

[19] S. Arya, D. M. Mount, N. S. Netanyahu, R. Silverman, and A. Y. Wu. An optimal algorithm for approximate nearest neighbor searching in fixed dimensions. *Journal of the ACM*, 45(6):891–923, Nov. 1998.

[20] M. Ashikhmin. Synthesizing natural textures. In *Symposium on Interactive 3D Graphics*, 2001.

[21] S. Avidan and A. Shamir. Seam carving for content-aware image resizing. In *ACM SIGGRAPH (ACM Transactions on Graphics)*, 2007.

[22] S. Avidan and A. Shashua. Threading fundamental matrices. In *European Conference on Computer Vision (ECCV)*, 1998.

[23] S. Ayer and H. Sawhney. Layered representation of motion video using robust maximum-likelihood estimation of mixture models and MDL encoding. In *IEEE International Conference on Computer Vision (ICCV)*, 1995.

[24] S. Bae, A. Agarwala, and F. Durand. Computational rephotography. *ACM Transactions on Graphics*, 29(3):1–15, June 2010.

[25] X. Bai and G. Sapiro. Geodesic matting: A framework for fast interactive image and video segmentation and matting. *International Journal of Computer Vision*, 82(2):113–32, Apr. 2009.

[26] X. Bai, J. Wang, D. Simons, and G. Sapiro. Video SnapCut: robust video object cutout using localized classifiers. In *ACM SIGGRAPH (ACM Transactions on Graphics)*, 2009.

[27] S. Baker, D. Scharstein, J. Lewis, S. Roth, M. Black, and R. Szeliski. A database and evaluation methodology for optical flow. *International Journal of Computer Vision*, 92(1):1–31, Mar. 2011.

[28] Y. Bando, B. Chen, and T. Nishita. Extracting depth and matte using a color-filtered aperture. In *ACM SIGGRAPH Asia (ACM Transactions on Graphics)*, 2008.

[29] I. Baran and J. Popović. Automatic rigging and animation of 3D characters. In *ACM SIGGRAPH (ACM Transactions on Graphics)*, 2007.

[30] C. Barnes, E. Shechtman, A. Finkelstein, and D. B. Goldman. PatchMatch: a randomized correspondence algorithm for structural image editing. In *ACM SIGGRAPH (ACM Transactions on Graphics)*, 2009.

[31] J. L. Barron, D. J. Fleet, and S. S. Beauchemin. Performance of optical flow techniques. *International Journal of Computer Vision*, 12(1):43–77, Feb. 1994.

[32] A. Baumberg. Reliable feature matching across widely separated views. In *IEEE Computer Society Conference on Computer Vision and Pattern Recognition (CVPR)*, 2000.

[33] H. Bay, T. Tuytelaars, and L. Van Gool. SURF: Speeded up robust features. In *European Conference on Computer Vision (ECCV)*, 2006.

[34] P. Beardsley, A. Zisserman, and D. Murray. Sequential updating of projective and affine structure from motion. *International Journal of Computer Vision*, 23(3):235–59, June 1997.

[35] T. Beier and S. Neely. Feature-based image metamorphosis. In *ACM SIGGRAPH (ACM Transactions on Graphics)*, 1992.

[36] J. Beis and D. Lowe. Shape indexing using approximate nearest-neighbour search in high-dimensional spaces. In *IEEE Computer Society Conference on Computer Vision and Pattern Recognition (CVPR)*, 1997.

[37] P. N. Belhumeur. A Bayesian approach to binocular steropsis. *International Journal of Computer Vision*, 19(3):237–60, Aug. 1996.

[38] S. Belongie, J. Malik, and J. Puzicha. Shape matching and object recognition using shape contexts. *IEEE Transactions on Pattern Analysis and Machine Intelligence*, 24(4):509–22, Apr. 2002.

[39] J. Bergen, P. Anandan, K. Hanna, and R. Hingorani. Hierarchical model-based motion estimation. In *European Conference on Computer Vision (ECCV)*, 1992.

[40] M. Bertalmio, G. Sapiro, V. Caselles, and C. Ballester. Image inpainting. In *ACM SIGGRAPH (ACM Transactions on Graphics)*, 2000.

[41] P. Besl and H. McKay. A method for registration of 3-D shapes. *IEEE Transactions on Pattern Analysis and Machine Intelligence*, 14(2):239–56, Feb. 1992.

[42] P. J. Besl. Active, optical range imaging sensors. *Machine Vision and Applications*, 1(2):127–52, June 1988.

[43] P. Bhat, C. L. Zitnick, M. Cohen, and B. Curless. GradientShop: A gradient-domain optimization framework for image and video filtering. *ACM Transactions on Graphics*, 29(2):1–14, Mar. 2010.

[44] B. Bickel, M. Botsch, R. Angst, W. Matusik, M. Otaduy, H. Pfister, and M. Gross. Multiscale capture of facial geometry and motion. In *ACM SIGGRAPH (ACM Transactions on Graphics)*, 2007.

[45] J. Bilmes. A gentle tutorial of the EM algorithm and its application to parameter estimation for Gaussian mixture and hidden Markov models. Technical Report TR-97-021, University of California, Berkeley, 1997.

[46] S. Birchfield and C. Tomasi. A pixel dissimilarity measure that is insensitive to image sampling. *IEEE Transactions on Pattern Analysis and Machine Intelligence*, 20(4):401–6, Apr. 1998.

[47] M. Black and A. Jepson. Estimating optical flow in segmented images using variable-order parametric models with local deformations. *IEEE Transactions on Pattern Analysis and Machine Intelligence*, 18(10):972–86, Oct. 1996.

[48] M. J. Black and P. Anandan. The robust estimation of multiple motions: Parametric and piecewise-smooth flow fields. *Computer Vision and Image Understanding*, 63(1):75–104, Jan. 1996.

[49] A. Blake, C. Rother, M. Brown, P. Pérez, and P. Torr. Interactive image segmentation using an adaptive GMMRF model. In *European Conference on Computer Vision (ECCV)*, 2004.

[50] M. Bleyer, C. Rother, and P. Kohli. Surface stereo with soft segmentation. In *IEEE Computer Society Conference on Computer Vision and Pattern Recognition (CVPR)*, 2010.

[51] B. Bodenheimer, C. Rose, S. Rosenthal, and J. Pella. The process of motion capture: Dealing with the data. In *Eurographics Workshop on Computer Animation and Simulation*, 1997.

[52] J. Bolz, I. Farmer, E. Grinspun, and P. Schröoder. Sparse matrix solvers on the GPU: conjugate gradients and multigrid. In *ACM SIGGRAPH (ACM Transactions on Graphics)*, 2003.

[53] F. Bookstein. Principal warps: thin-plate splines and the decomposition of deformations. *IEEE Transactions on Pattern Analysis and Machine Intelligence*, 11(6):567–85, June 1989.

[54] G. Borshukov, J. Montgomery, and W. Werner. Playable universal capture: compression and real-time sequencing of image-based facial animation. In *ACM SIGGRAPH Courses*, 2006.

[55] J. Bouguet. Pyramidal implementation of the Lucas-Kanade feature tracker: description of the algorithm. Technical report, Intel Corporation, 1999.

[56] J.-Y. Bouguet and P. Perona. 3D photography on your desk. In *IEEE International Conference on Computer Vision (ICCV)*, 1998.

[57] K. L. Boyer and A. C. Kak. Color-encoded structured light for rapid active ranging. *IEEE Transactions on Pattern Analysis and Machine Intelligence*, PAMI-9(1):14–28, Jan. 1987.

[58] Y. Boykov and D. Huttenlocher. Adaptive Bayesian recognition in tracking rigid objects. In *IEEE Computer Society Conference on Computer Vision and Pattern Recognition (CVPR)*, 2000.

[59] Y. Boykov and M. Jolly. Interactive graph cuts for optimal boundary and region segmentation of objects in N-D images. In *IEEE International Conference on Computer Vision (ICCV)*, 2001.

[60] Y. Boykov and V. Kolmogorov. An experimental comparison of min-cut/max-flow algorithms for energy minimization in vision. *IEEE Transactions on Pattern Analysis and Machine Intelligence*, 26(9):1124–37, Sept. 2004.

[61] Y. Boykov, O. Veksler, and R. Zabih. Fast approximate energy minimization via graph cuts. *IEEE Transactions on Pattern Analysis and Machine Intelligence*, 23(11):1222–39, Nov. 2001.

[62] D. Bradley, T. Boubekeur, and W. Heidrich. Accurate multi-view reconstruction using robust binocular stereo and surface meshing. In *IEEE Computer Society Conference on Computer Vision and Pattern Recognition (CVPR)*, 2008.

[63] D. Bradley, W. Heidrich, T. Popa, and A. Sheffer. High resolution passive facial performance capture. In *ACM SIGGRAPH (ACM Transactions on Graphics)*, 2010.

[64] P. Braido and X. Zhang. Quantitative analysis of finger motion coordination in hand manipulative and gestic acts. *Human Movement Science*, 22(6):661–78, Apr. 2004.

[65] M. Brand and A. Hertzmann. Style machines. In *ACM SIGGRAPH (ACM Transactions on Graphics)*, 2000.

[66] C. Bregler, A. Hertzmann, and H. Biermann. Recovering non-rigid 3D shape from image streams. In *IEEE Computer Society Conference on Computer Vision and Pattern Recognition (CVPR)*, 2000.

[67] C. Bregler, J. Malik, and K. Pullen. Twist based acquisition and tracking of animal and human kinematics. *International Journal of Computer Vision*, 56(3):179–94, Feb. 2004.

[68] R. Brinkmann. *The Art and Science of Digital Compositing*. Morgan Kaufmann, 2nd edition, 2008.

[69] D. Brown. The bundle adjustment - progress and prospects. *International Archives of the Photogrammetry, Remote Sensing and Spatial Information Sciences*, 21(3):1–33, 1976.

[70] M. Brown, D. Burschka, and G. Hager. Advances in computational stereo. *IEEE Transactions on Pattern Analysis and Machine Intelligence*, 25(8):993–1008, Aug. 2003.

[71] M. Brown, G. Hua, and S. Winder. Discriminative learning of local image descriptors. *IEEE Transactions on Pattern Analysis and Machine Intelligence*, 33(1):43–57, Jan. 2011.

[72] M. Brown and D. Lowe. Automatic panoramic image stitching using invariant features. *International Journal of Computer Vision*, 74(1):59–73, Aug. 2007.

[73] T. Brox, C. Bregler, and J. Malik. Large displacement optical flow. In *IEEE Computer Society Conference on Computer Vision and Pattern Recognition (CVPR)*, 2009.

[74] T. Brox, A. Bruhn, N. Papenberg, and J. Weickert. High accuracy optical flow estimation based on a theory for warping. In *European Conference on Computer Vision (ECCV)*, 2004.

[75] A. Bruderlin and L. Williams. Motion signal processing. In *ACM SIGGRAPH (ACM Transactions on Graphics)*, 1995.

[76] A. Bruhn, J. Weickert, and C. Schnörr. Lucas/Kanade meets Horn/Schunck: Combining local and global optic flow methods. *International Journal of Computer Vision*, 61(3):211–31, Feb. 2005.

[77] G. J. Burghouts and J.-M. Geusebroek. Performance evaluation of local colour invariants. *Computer Vision and Image Understanding*, 113(1):48–62, Jan. 2009.

[78] P. J. Burt and E. H. Adelson. A multiresolution spline with application to image mosaics. *ACM Transactions on Graphics*, 2(4):217–36, Oct. 1983.

[79] R. Burtch. History of photogrammetry. Technical report, The Center for Photogrammetric Training, Ferris State University, 2008.

[80] N. Campbell, G. Vogiatzis, C. Hernández, and R. Cipolla. Using multiple hypotheses to improve depth-maps for multi-view stereo. In *European Conference on Computer Vision (ECCV)*, 2008.

[81] B. Caprile and V. Torre. Using vanishing points for camera calibration. *International Journal of Computer Vision*, 4(2):127–39, Mar. 1990.

[82] J. C. Carr, R. K. Beatson, J. B. Cherrie, T. J. Mitchell, W. R. Fright, B. C. McCallum, and T. R. Evans. Reconstruction and representation of 3D objects with radial basis functions. In *ACM SIGGRAPH (ACM Transactions on Graphics)*, 2001.

[83] D. Caspi, N. Kiryati, and J. Shamir. Range imaging with adaptive color structured light. *IEEE Transactions on Pattern Analysis and Machine Intelligence*, 20(5):470–80, May 1998.

[84] Y. Caspi and M. Irani. Spatio-temporal alignment of sequences. *IEEE Transactions on Pattern Analysis and Machine Intelligence*, 24(11):1409–24, Nov. 2002.

[85] J. Chai and J. K. Hodgins. Performance animation from low-dimensional control signals. In *ACM SIGGRAPH (ACM Transactions on Graphics)*, 2005.

[86] C. Chen and A. Kak. Modeling and calibration of a structured light scanner for 3-D robot vision. In *IEEE International Conference on Robotics and Automation*, 1987.

[87] C. Chen and I. Stamos. Range image segmentation for modeling and object detection in urban scenes. In *International Conference on 3-D Digital Imaging and Modeling (3DIM)*, 2007.

[88] S. E. Chen and L. Williams. View interpolation for image synthesis. In *ACM SIGGRAPH (ACM Transactions on Graphics)*, 1993.

[89] Y. Chen and G. Medioni. Object modeling by registration of multiple range images. In *IEEE International Conference on Robotics and Automation*, 1991.

[90] M.-M. Cheng, F.-L. Zhang, N. J. Mitra, X. Huang, and S.-M. Hu. Repfinder: finding approximately repeated scene elements for image editing. In *ACM SIGGRAPH (ACM Transactions on Graphics)*, 2010.

[91] K. Cheung, S. Baker, and T. Kanade. Shape-from-silhouette of articulated objects and its use for human body kinematics estimation and motion capture. In *IEEE Computer Society Conference on Computer Vision and Pattern Recognition (CVPR)*, 2003.

[92] S. Chiaverini, G. Oriolo, and I. D. Walker. Kinematically redundant manipulators. In B. Siciliano and O. Khatib, editors, *Springer Handbook of Robotics*, pages 245–68. Springer, 2008.

[93] T. S. Cho, M. Butman, S. Avidan, and W. Freeman. The patch transform and its applications to image editing. In *IEEE Computer Society Conference on Computer Vision and Pattern Recognition (CVPR)*, 2008.

[94] G. Christensen, R. Rabbitt, and M. Miller. Deformable templates using large deformation kinematics. *IEEE Transactions on Image Processing*, 5(10):1435–47, Oct. 1996.

[95] H.-K. Chu, W.-H. Hsu, N. J. Mitra, D. Cohen-Or, T.-T. Wong, and T.-Y. Lee. Camouflage images. In *ACM SIGGRAPH (ACM Transactions on Graphics)*, 2010.

[96] Y. Chuang, A. Agarwala, B. Curless, D. Salesin, and R. Szeliski. Video matting of complex scenes. In *ACM SIGGRAPH (ACM Transactions on Graphics)*, 2002.

[97] Y. Chuang, D. Goldman, B. Curless, D. Salesin, and R. Szeliski. Shadow matting and compositing. In *ACM SIGGRAPH (ACM Transactions on Graphics)*, 2003.

[98] Y. Chuang, D. Zongker, J. Hindorff, B. Curless, D. Salesin, and R. Szeliski. Environment matting extensions: Towards higher accuracy and real-time capture. In *ACM SIGGRAPH (ACM Transactions on Graphics)*, 2000.

[99] Y.-Y. Chuang, B. Curless, D. Salesin, and R. Szeliski. A Bayesian approach to digital matting. In *IEEE Computer Society Conference on Computer Vision and Pattern Recognition (CVPR)*, 2001.

[100] R. Collins. A space-sweep approach to true multi-image matching. In *IEEE Computer Society Conference on Computer Vision and Pattern Recognition (CVPR)*, 1996.

[101] R. Collins, Y. Liu, and M. Leordeanu. Online selection of discriminative tracking features. *IEEE Transactions on Pattern Analysis and Machine Intelligence*, 27(10):1631–43, Oct. 2005.

[102] D. Comaniciu and P. Meer. Mean shift: a robust approach toward feature space analysis. *IEEE Transactions on Pattern Analysis and Machine Intelligence*, 24(5):603–19, May 2002.

[103] D. Comaniciu, V. Ramesh, and P. Meer. Kernel-based object tracking. *IEEE Transactions on Pattern Analysis and Machine Intelligence*, 25(5):564–77, May 2003.

[104] S. Cooper, A. Hertzmann, and Z. Popović. Active learning for real-time motion controllers. In *ACM SIGGRAPH (ACM Transactions on Graphics)*, 2007.

[105] S. Corazza, L. Mündermann, E. Gambaretto, G. Ferrigno, and T. Andriacchi. Markerless motion capture through visual hull, articulated ICP and subject specific model generation. *International Journal of Computer Vision*, 87(1):156–69, Mar. 2010.

[106] T. Cormen, C. Leiserson, R. Rivest, and C. Stein. *Introduction to Algorithms*. MIT Press, 3rd edition, 2009.

[107] A. Criminisi, G. Cross, A. Blake, and V. Kolmogorov. Bilayer segmentation of live video. In *IEEE Computer Society Conference on Computer Vision and Pattern Recognition (CVPR)*, 2006.

[108] A. Criminisi, P. Pérez, and K. Toyama. Region filling and object removal by exemplar-based image inpainting. *IEEE Transactions on Image Processing*, 13(9):1200–12, Sept. 2004.

[109] G. Csurka, D. Demirdjian, A. Ruf, and R. Horaud. Closed-form solutions for the Euclidean calibration of a stereo rig. In *European Conference on Computer Vision (ECCV)*, 1998.

[110] Y. Cui, S. Schuon, D. Chan, S. Thrun, and C. Theobalt. 3D shape scanning with a time-of-flight camera. In *IEEE Computer Society Conference on Computer Vision and Pattern Recognition (CVPR)*, 2010.

[111] B. Curless and M. Levoy. Better optical triangulation through spacetime analysis. In *IEEE International Conference on Computer Vision (ICCV)*, 1995.

[112] B. Curless and M. Levoy. A volumetric method for building complex models from range images. In *ACM SIGGRAPH (ACM Transactions on Graphics)*, 1996.

[113] J. Davis and X. Chen. A laser range scanner designed for minimum calibration complexity. In *International Conference on 3-D Digital Imaging and Modeling (3DIM)*, 2001.

[114] J. Davis, D. Nehab, R. Ramamoorthi, and S. Rusinkiewicz. Spacetime stereo: a unifying framework for depth from triangulation. *IEEE Transactions on Pattern Analysis and Machine Intelligence*, 27(2):296–302, Feb. 2005.

[115] A. Davison, I. Reid, N. Molton, and O. Stasse. MonoSLAM: Real-time single camera SLAM. *IEEE Transactions on Pattern Analysis and Machine Intelligence*, 29(6):1052–67, June 2007.

[116] P. Debevec, A. Wenger, C. Tchou, A. Gardner, J. Waese, and T. Hawkins. A lighting reproduction approach to live-action compositing. In *ACM SIGGRAPH (ACM Transactions on Graphics)*, 2002.

[117] P. E. Debevec, C. J. Taylor, and J. Malik. Modeling and rendering architecture from photographs: a hybrid geometry- and image-based approach. In *ACM SIGGRAPH (ACM Transactions on Graphics)*, 1996.

[118] J. Dennis, Jr. and R. Schnabel. *Numerical Methods for Unconstrained Optimization and Nonlinear Equations*. Society for Industrial and Applied Mathematics, 1996.

[119] J. Deutscher and I. Reid. Articulated body motion capture by stochastic search. *International Journal of Computer Vision*, 61(2):185–205, Feb. 2005.

[120] A. Dick, P. Torr, and R. Cipolla. Modelling and interpretation of architecture from several images. *International Journal of Computer Vision*, 60(2):111–34, Nov. 2004.

[121] H. Dinh and S. Kropac. Multi-resolution spin-images. In *IEEE Computer Society Conference on Computer Vision and Pattern Recognition (CVPR)*, 2006.

[122] T. Dobbert. *Matchmoving: the Invisible Art of Camera Tracking*. Sybex, 2005.

[123] W. Dong, N. Zhou, J.-C. Paul, and X. Zhang. Optimized image resizing using seam carving and scaling. In *ACM SIGGRAPH Asia (ACM Transactions on Graphics)*, 2009.

[124] D. Doria and R. J. Radke. Filling large holes in LiDAR data by inpainting depth gradients. In *Workshop on Point Cloud Processing in Computer Vision (PCP2012)*, 2012.

[125] J. Draréni, S. Roy, and P. Sturm. Methods for geometrical video projector calibration. *Machine Vision and Applications*, 23(1):79–89, Jan. 2012.

[126] I. Drori, D. Cohen-Or, and H. Yeshurun. Fragment-based image completion. In *ACM SIGGRAPH (ACM Transactions on Graphics)*, 2003.

[127] Y. Dufournaud, C. Schmid, and R. Horaud. Matching images with different resolutions. In *IEEE Computer Society Conference on Computer Vision and Pattern Recognition (CVPR)*, 2000.

[128] A. A. Efros and W. T. Freeman. Image quilting for texture synthesis and transfer. In *ACM SIGGRAPH (ACM Transactions on Graphics)*, 2001.

[129] P. Ekman, W. V. Friesen, and J. C. Hager. *Facial Action Coding System: The Manual*. A Human Face, 2002.

[130] J. H. Elder and R. M. Goldberg. Image editing in the contour domain. *IEEE Transactions on Pattern Analysis and Machine Intelligence*, 23(3):291–6, Mar. 2001.

[131] C. H. Esteban and F. Schmitt. Silhouette and stereo fusion for 3D object modeling. *Computer Vision and Image Understanding*, 96(3):367–92, Dec. 2004.

[132] Z. Farbman, G. Hoffer, Y. Lipman, D. Cohen-Or, and D. Lischinski. Coordinates for instant image cloning. In *ACM SIGGRAPH (ACM Transactions on Graphics)*, 2009.

[133] H. Farid. Image forgery detection. *IEEE Signal Processing Magazine*, 26(2):16–25, Mar. 2009.

[134] H. Farid. Seeing is not believing. *IEEE Spectrum*, 46(8):44–51, Aug. 2009.

[135] G. Farin. *Curves and Surfaces for CAGD: A Practical Guide*. Morgan Kaufmann, 5th edition, 2001.

[136] R. Fattal, D. Lischinski, and M. Werman. Gradient domain high dynamic range compression. In *ACM SIGGRAPH (ACM Transactions on Graphics)*, 2002.

[137] O. Faugeras and Q.-T. Luong. *The Geometry of Multiple Images: The Laws That Govern the Formation of Multiple Images of a Scene and Some of Their Applications*. MIT Press, 2004.

[138] P. Felzenszwalb and D. Huttenlocher. Efficient belief propagation for early vision. In *IEEE Computer Society Conference on Computer Vision and Pattern Recognition (CVPR)*, 2004.

[139] P. Felzenszwalb and R. Zabih. Dynamic programming and graph algorithms in computer vision. *IEEE Transactions on Pattern Analysis and Machine Intelligence*, 33(4):721–40, Apr. 2011.

[140] M. Fiala. Designing highly reliable fiducial markers. *IEEE Transactions on Pattern Analysis and Machine Intelligence*, 32(7):1317–24, July 2010.

[141] G. Finlayson, S. Hordley, C. Lu, and M. Drew. On the removal of shadows from images. *IEEE Transactions on Pattern Analysis and Machine Intelligence*, 28(1):59–68, Jan. 2006.

[142] M. A. Fischler and R. C. Bolles. Random sample consensus: a paradigm for model fitting with applications to image analysis and automated cartography. *Communications of the ACM*, 24(6):381–95, June 1981.

[143] R. Fisher, A. Ashbrook, C. Robertson, and N. Werghi. A low-cost range finder using a visually located, structured light source. In *International Conference on 3-D Digital Imaging and Modeling (3DIM)*, 1999.

[144] A. Fitzgibbon. Simultaneous linear estimation of multiple view geometry and lens distortion. In *IEEE Computer Society Conference on Computer Vision and Pattern Recognition (CVPR)*, 2001.

[145] A. Fitzgibbon and A. Zisserman. Automatic camera recovery for closed or open image sequences. In *European Conference on Computer Vision (ECCV)*, 1998.

[146] M. Floater. Mean value coordinates. *Computer Aided Geometric Design*, 20(1):19–27, Mar. 2003.

[147] J. Flusser. On the independence of rotation moment invariants. *Pattern Recognition*, 33(9):1405–10, Sept. 2000.

[148] P.-E. Forssén. Maximally stable colour regions for recognition and matching. In *IEEE Computer Society Conference on Computer Vision and Pattern Recognition (CVPR)*, 2007.

[149] P.-E. Forssén and D. Lowe. Shape descriptors for maximally stable extremal regions. In *IEEE International Conference on Computer Vision (ICCV)*, 2007.

[150] W. Förstner. A feature based correspondence algorithm for image matching. *International Archives of Photogrammetry and Remote Sensing*, 26(3):150–66, 1986.

[151] J. Foster. *The Green Screen Handbook: Real-World Production Techniques*. Sybex, 2010.

[152] J.-M. Frahm, P. Fite-Georgel, D. Gallup, T. Johnson, R. Raguram, C. Wu, Y.-H. Jen, E. Dunn, B. Clipp, S. Lazebnik, and M. Pollefeys. Building Rome on a cloudless day. In *European Conference on Computer Vision (ECCV)*, 2010.

[153] W. Freeman and E. Adelson. The design and use of steerable filters. *IEEE Transactions on Pattern Analysis and Machine Intelligence*, 13(9):891–906, Sept. 1991.

[154] W. T. Freeman, E. C. Pasztor, and O. T. Carmichael. Learning low-level vision. *International Journal of Computer Vision*, 40(1):25–47, Oct. 2000.

[155] A. Frome, D. Huber, R. Kolluri, T. Bülow, and J. Malik. Recognizing objects in range data using regional point descriptors. In *European Conference on Computer Vision (ECCV)*, 2004.

[156] C. Frueh, S. Jain, and A. Zakhor. Data processing algorithms for generating textured 3D building facade meshes from laser scans and camera images. *International Journal of Computer Vision*, 61(2):159–84, Feb. 2005.

[157] C. Frueh and A. Zakhor. Capturing 2 1/2 D depth and texture of time-varying scenes using structured infrared light. In *International Conference on 3-D Digital Imaging and Modeling (3DIM)*, 2005.

[158] C. Früh and A. Zakhor. An automated method for large-scale, ground-based city model acquisition. *International Journal of Computer Vision*, 60(1):5–24, Oct. 2004.

[159] Y. Furukawa and J. Ponce. Dense 3D motion capture for human faces. In *IEEE Computer Society Conference on Computer Vision and Pattern Recognition (CVPR)*, 2009.

[160] Y. Furukawa and J. Ponce. Accurate, dense, and robust multiview stereopsis. *IEEE Transactions on Pattern Analysis and Machine Intelligence*, 32(8):1362–76, Aug. 2010.

[161] J. Gall, C. Stoll, E. de Aguiar, C. Theobalt, B. Rosenhahn, and H.-P. Seidel. Motion capture using joint skeleton tracking and surface estimation. In *IEEE Computer Society Conference on Computer Vision and Pattern Recognition (CVPR)*, 2009.

[162] V. Ganapathi, C. Plagemann, D. Koller, and S. Thrun. Real time motion capture using a single time-of-flight camera. In *IEEE Computer Society Conference on Computer Vision and Pattern Recognition (CVPR)*, 2010.

[163] E. Gastal and M. Oliveira. Shared sampling for real-time alpha matting. In *Eurographics*, 2010.

[164] D. Gavrila and L. Davis. 3-D model-based tracking of humans in action: a multiview approach. In *IEEE Computer Society Conference on Computer Vision and Pattern Recognition (CVPR)*, 1996.

[165] A. Gelb. *Applied Optimal Estimation*. MIT Press, 1974.

[166] D. C. Ghiglia and M. D. Pritt. *Two-Dimensional Phase Unwrapping: Theory, Algorithms, and Software*. Wiley-Interscience, 1998.

[167] J. Gibson. *The Perception of the Visual World*. Riverside Press, 1950.

[168] M. Gleicher and N. Ferrier. Evaluating video-based motion capture. In *Computer Animation*, 2002.

[169] M. L. Gleicher and F. Liu. Re-cinematography: Improving the camerawork of casual video. *ACM Transactions on Multimedia Computing, Communications and Applications*, 5(1):1–28, October 2008.

[170] M. Goesele, B. Curless, and S. Seitz. Multi-view stereo revisited. In *IEEE Computer Society Conference on Computer Vision and Pattern Recognition (CVPR)*, 2006.

[171] M. Goesele, N. Snavely, B. Curless, H. Hoppe, and S. Seitz. Multi-view stereo for community photo collections. In *IEEE International Conference on Computer Vision (ICCV)*, 2007.

[172] A. Golovinskiy, V. Kim, and T. Funkhouser. Shape-based recognition of 3D point clouds in urban environments. In *IEEE International Conference on Computer Vision (ICCV)*, 2009.

[173] G. H. Golub and C. F. Van Loan. *Matrix Computations*. Johns Hopkins, 3rd edition, 1996.

[174] A. A. Gooch, S. C. Olsen, J. Tumblin, and B. Gooch. Color2Gray: salience-preserving color removal. In *ACM SIGGRAPH (ACM Transactions on Graphics)*, 2005.

[175] S. J. Gortler, R. Grzeszczuk, R. Szeliski, and M. F. Cohen. The lumigraph. In *ACM SIGGRAPH (ACM Transactions on Graphics)*, 1996.

[176] L. Grady. Random walks for image segmentation. *IEEE Transactions on Pattern Analysis and Machine Intelligence*, 28(11):1768–83, Nov. 2006.

[177] L. Grady. A lattice-preserving multigrid method for solving the inhomogeneous Poisson equations used in image analysis. In *European Conference on Computer Vision (ECCV)*, 2008.

[178] L. Grady, T. Schiwietz, S. Aharon, and R. Westermann. Random walks for interactive alpha-matting. In *IASTED International Conference on Visualization, Imaging and Image Processing*, 2005.

[179] K. Grochow, S. L. Martin, A. Hertzmann, and Z. Popović. Style-based inverse kinematics. In *ACM SIGGRAPH (ACM Transactions on Graphics)*, 2004.

[180] R. Gross, I. Matthews, and S. Baker. Active appearance models with occlusion. *Image and Vision Computing*, 24(1):593–604, June 2006.

[181] A. Grundhöfer and O. Bimber. VirtualStudio2Go: digital video composition for real environments. In *ACM SIGGRAPH Asia (ACM Transactions on Graphics)*, 2008.

[182] Y. Guan, W. Chen, X. Liang, Z. Ding, and Q. Peng. Easy matting – a stroke based approach for continuous image matting. In *Eurographics*, 2006.

[183] B. Guenter, C. Grimm, D. Wood, H. Malvar, and F. Pighin. Making faces. In *ACM SIGGRAPH (ACM Transactions on Graphics)*, 1998.

[184] G. Hager and P. Belhumeur. Real-time tracking of image regions with changes in geometry and illumination. In *IEEE Computer Society Conference on Computer Vision and Pattern Recognition (CVPR)*, 1996.

[185] O. Hall-Holt and S. Rusinkiewicz. Stripe boundary codes for real-time structured-light range scanning of moving objects. In *IEEE International Conference on Computer Vision (ICCV)*, 2001.

[186] C. Harris and M. Stephens. A combined corner and edge detector. In *Alvey Vision Conference*, 1988.

[187] R. Hartley. Theory and practice of projective rectification. *International Journal of Computer Vision*, 35(2):115–27, Nov. 1999.

[188] R. Hartley and A. Zisserman. *Multiple View Geometry in Computer Vision*. Cambridge University Press, 2nd edition, 2004.

[189] R. I. Hartley and P. Sturm. Triangulation. *Computer Vision and Image Understanding*, 68(2):146–57, Nov. 1997.

[190] N. Hasler, B. Rosenhahn, T. Thormahlen, M. Wand, J. Gall, and H.-P. Seidel. Markerless motion capture with unsynchronized moving cameras. In *IEEE Computer Society Conference on Computer Vision and Pattern Recognition (CVPR)*, 2009.

[191] J. Hays and A. A. Efros. Scene completion using millions of photographs. In *ACM SIGGRAPH (ACM Transactions on Graphics)*, 2007.

[192] K. He, J. Sun, and X. Tang. Fast matting using large kernel matting Laplacian matrices. In *IEEE Computer Society Conference on Computer Vision and Pattern Recognition (CVPR)*, 2010.

[193] X. He and P. Niyogi. Locality preserving projections. In *Advances in Neural Information Processing Systems*, 2003.

[194] L. Herda, P. Fua, R. Plänkers, R. Boulic, and D. Thalmann. Using skeleton-based tracking to increase the reliability of optical motion capture. *Human Movement Science*, 20(3):313–41, June 2001.

[195] L. Herda, R. Urtasun, and P. Fua. Hierarchical implicit surface joint limits to constrain video-based motion capture. In *European Conference on Computer Vision (ECCV)*, 2004.

[196] C. Hernandez, G. Vogiatzis, and R. Cipolla. Multiview photometric stereo. *IEEE Transactions on Pattern Analysis and Machine Intelligence*, 30(3):548–54, Mar. 2008.

[197] A. Hertzmann, C. E. Jacobs, N. Oliver, B. Curless, and D. H. Salesin. Image analogies. In *ACM SIGGRAPH (ACM Transactions on Graphics)*, 2001.

[198] V. Hiep, R. Keriven, P. Labatut, and J.-P. Pons. Towards high-resolution large-scale multi-view stereo. In *IEEE Computer Society Conference on Computer Vision and Pattern Recognition (CVPR)*, 2009.

[199] P. Hillman, J. Hannah, and D. Renshaw. Semi-automatic foreground/background segmentation of motion picture images and image sequences. *IEE Proceedings on Vision, Image, and Signal Processing*, 152(4):387–97, Aug. 2005.

[200] H. Hirschmüller and D. Scharstein. Evaluation of stereo matching costs on images with radiometric differences. *IEEE Transactions on Pattern Analysis and Machine Intelligence*, 31(9):1582–99, Sept. 2009.

[201] M. Holden. A review of geometric transformations for nonrigid body registration. *IEEE Transactions on Medical Imaging*, 27(1):111–28, Jan. 2008.

[202] R. Horaud and G. Csurka. Self-calibration and Euclidean reconstruction using motions of a stereo rig. In *IEEE Computer Society Conference on Computer Vision and Pattern Recognition (CVPR)*, 1998.

[203] B. K. Horn and B. G. Schunck. Determining optical flow. *Artificial Intelligence*, 17(1-3):185–203, Aug. 1981.

[204] E. Horn and N. Kiryati. Toward optimal structured light patterns. In *International Conference on 3-D Digital Imaging and Modeling (3DIM)*, 1997.

[205] M.-K. Hu. Visual pattern recognition by moment invariants. *IRE Transactions on Information Theory*, 8(2):179–87, Feb. 1962.

[206] P. S. Huang, C. Zhang, and F.-P. Chiang. High-speed 3-D shape measurement based on digital fringe projection. *Optical Engineering*, 42(1):163–8, Jan. 2003.

[207] D. Huber, B. Akinci, P. Tang, A. Adan, B. Okorn, and X. Xiong. Using laser scanners for modeling and analysis in architecture, engineering, and construction. In *Conference on Information Sciences and Systems (CISS)*, 2010.

[208] D. Huber, A. Kapuria, R. Donamukkala, and M. Hebert. Parts-based 3D object classification. In *IEEE Computer Society Conference on Computer Vision and Pattern Recognition (CVPR)*, 2004.

[209] M. B. Hullin, M. Fuchs, I. Ihrke, H.-P. Seidel, and H. P. A. Lensch. Fluorescent immersion range scanning. In *ACM SIGGRAPH (ACM Transactions on Graphics)*, 2008.

[210] Y. Hung and W. Tang. Projective reconstruction from multiple views with minimization of 2D reprojection error. *International Journal of Computer Vision*, 66(3):305–17, Mar. 2006.

[211] D. Huynh. Calibration of a structured light system: a projective approach. In *IEEE Computer Society Conference on Computer Vision and Pattern Recognition (CVPR)*, 1997.

[212] M. Isard and A. Blake. CONDENSATION - conditional density propagation for visual tracking. *International Journal of Computer Vision*, 29(1):5–28, Aug. 1998.

[213] F. Isgrò and E. Trucco. Projective rectification without epipolar geometry. In *IEEE Computer Society Conference on Computer Vision and Pattern Recognition (CVPR)*, 1999.

[214] H. Ishikawa and D. Geiger. Occlusions, discontinuities, and epipolar lines in stereo. In *European Conference on Computer Vision (ECCV)*, 1998.

[215] L. Itti, C. Koch, and E. Niebur. A model of saliency-based visual attention for rapid scene analysis. *IEEE Transactions on Pattern Analysis and Machine Intelligence*, 20(11):1254–9, Nov. 1998.

[216] R. A. Jarvis. A perspective on range finding techniques for computer vision. *IEEE Transactions on Pattern Analysis and Machine Intelligence*, PAMI-5(2):122–39, Mar. 1983.

[217] C. Je, S. Lee, and R.-H. Park. High-contrast color-stripe pattern for rapid structured-light range imaging. In *European Conference on Computer Vision (ECCV)*, 2004.

[218] S. Jeschke, D. Cline, and P. Wonka. A GPU Laplacian solver for diffusion curves and Poisson image editing. In *ACM SIGGRAPH Asia (ACM Transactions on Graphics)*, 2009.

[219] J. Jia, J. Sun, C. Tang, and H. Shum. Drag-and-drop pasting. In *ACM SIGGRAPH (ACM Transactions on Graphics)*, 2006.

[220] J. Jia, Y.-W. Tai, T.-P. Wu, and C.-K. Tang. Video repairing under variable illumination using cyclic motions. *IEEE Transactions on Pattern Analysis and Machine Intelligence*, 28(5):832–39, May 2006.

[221] J. Jia and C. Tang. Inference of segmented color and texture description by tensor voting. *IEEE Transactions on Pattern Analysis and Machine Intelligence*, 26(6):771–86, June 2004.

[222] H. Jin, P. Favaro, and S. Soatto. Real-time feature tracking and outlier rejection with changes in illumination. In *IEEE International Conference on Computer Vision (ICCV)*, 2002.

[223] G. Johansson. Visual perception of biological motion and a model for its analysis. *Attention, Perception, and Psychophysics*, 14(2):201–11, June 1973.

[224] A. Johnson and M. Hebert. Using spin images for efficient object recognition in cluttered 3D scenes. *IEEE Transactions on Pattern Analysis and Machine Intelligence*, 21(5):433–49, May 2002.

[225] M. Johnson, G. Brostow, J. Shotton, O. Arandjelovic, V. Kwatra, and R. Cipolla. Semantic photo synthesis. In *Eurographics*, 2006.

[226] N. Joshi, W. Matusik, and S. Avidan. Natural video matting using camera arrays. In *ACM SIGGRAPH (ACM Transactions on Graphics)*, 2006.

[227] N. Joshi, W. Matusik, S. Avidan, H. Pfister, and W. Freeman. Exploring defocus matting: Nonparametric acceleration, super-resolution, and off-center matting. *IEEE Computer Graphics and Applications*, 27(2):43–52, March–April 2007.

[228] S. Joshi and M. Miller. Landmark matching via large deformation diffeomorphisms. *IEEE Transactions on Image Processing*, 9(8):1357–70, Aug. 2000.

[229] T. Kadir, A. Zisserman, and M. Brady. An affine invariant salient region detector. In *European Conference on Computer Vision (ECCV)*, 2004.

[230] M. Kass, A. Witkin, and D. Terzopoulos. Snakes: Active contour models. *International Journal of Computer Vision*, 1(4):321–31, Jan. 1988.

[231] H. Kato and M. Billinghurst. Marker tracking and HMD calibration for a video-based augmented reality conferencing system. In *IEEE and ACM International Workshop on Augmented Reality*, 1999.

[232] M. Kazhdan, M. Bolitho, and H. Hoppe. Poisson surface reconstruction. In *Eurographics Symposium on Geometry Processing*, 2006.

[233] M. Kazhdan and H. Hoppe. Streaming multigrid for gradient-domain operations on large images. In *ACM SIGGRAPH (ACM Transactions on Graphics)*, 2008.

[234] Q. Ke and T. Kanade. A robust subspace approach to layer extraction. In *Workshop on Motion and Video Computing*, 2002.

[235] Y. Ke and R. Sukthankar. PCA-SIFT: a more distinctive representation for local image descriptors. In *IEEE Computer Society Conference on Computer Vision and Pattern Recognition (CVPR)*, 2004.

[236] R. Kehl and L. V. Gool. Markerless tracking of complex human motions from multiple views. *Computer Vision and Image Understanding*, 104(2-3):190–209, Nov. 2006.

[237] C. Kenney, M. Zuliani, and B. Manjunath. An axiomatic approach to corner detection. In *IEEE Computer Society Conference on Computer Vision and Pattern Recognition (CVPR)*, 2005.

[238] G. Kim, D. Huber, and M. Hebert. Segmentation of salient regions in outdoor scenes using imagery and 3-D data. In *IEEE Computer Society Workshop on Applications of Computer Vision*, 2008.

[239] M. Kim, K. Hyun, J. Kim, and J. Lee. Synchronized multi-character motion editing. In *ACM SIGGRAPH (ACM Transactions on Graphics)*, 2009.

[240] M. Kimura, M. Mochimaru, and T. Kanade. Projector calibration using arbitrary planes and calibrated camera. In *IEEE Computer Society Conference on Computer Vision and Pattern Recognition (CVPR)*, 2007.

[241] A. Kirk, J. O'Brien, and D. Forsyth. Skeletal parameter estimation from optical motion capture data. In *IEEE Computer Society Conference on Computer Vision and Pattern Recognition (CVPR)*, 2005.

[242] A. Klaus, M. Sormann, and K. Karner. Segment-based stereo matching using belief propagation and a self-adapting dissimilarity measure. In *International Conference on Pattern Recognition (ICPR)*, 2006.

[243] A. Kokaram, B. Collis, and S. Robinson. Automated rig removal with Bayesian motion interpolation. *IEE Proceedings on Vision, Image and Signal Processing*, 152(4):407–14, Aug. 2005.

[244] A. Kolb, E. Barth, R. Koch, and R. Larsen. Time-of-flight cameras in computer graphics. In *Eurographics*, 2010.

[245] R. Kolluri, J. R. Shewchuk, and J. F. O'Brien. Spectral surface reconstruction from noisy point clouds. In *Eurographics Symposium on Geometry Processing*, 2004.

[246] V. Kolmogorov and R. Zabih. Computing visual correspondence with occlusions using graph cuts. In *IEEE International Conference on Computer Vision (ICCV)*, 2001.

[247] V. Kolmogorov and R. Zabih. Multi-camera scene reconstruction via graph cuts. In *European Conference on Computer Vision (ECCV)*, 2002.

[248] V. Kolmogorov and R. Zabin. What energy functions can be minimized via graph cuts? *IEEE Transactions on Pattern Analysis and Machine Intelligence*, 26(2):147–59, Feb. 2004.

[249] N. Komodakis and G. Tziritas. Image completion using efficient belief propagation via priority scheduling and dynamic pruning. *IEEE Transactions on Image Processing*, 16(11):2649–61, Nov. 2007.

[250] T. Koninckx and L. Van Gool. Real-time range acquisition by adaptive structured light. *IEEE Transactions on Pattern Analysis and Machine Intelligence*, 28(3):432–45, Mar. 2006.

[251] S. Koppal, S. Yamazaki, and S. Narasimhan. Exploiting DLP illumination dithering for reconstruction and photography of high-speed scenes. *International Journal of Computer Vision*, 96(1):125–44, Jan. 2012.

[252] L. Kovar and M. Gleicher. Flexible automatic motion blending with registration curves. In *ACM SIGGRAPH/Eurographics Symposium on Computer Animation*, 2003.

[253] L. Kovar and M. Gleicher. Automated extraction and parameterization of motions in large data sets. In *ACM SIGGRAPH (ACM Transactions on Graphics)*, 2004.

[254] L. Kovar, M. Gleicher, and F. Pighin. Motion graphs. In *ACM SIGGRAPH (ACM Transactions on Graphics)*, 2002.

[255] P. Krähenbühl, M. Lang, A. Hornung, and M. Gross. A system for retargeting of streaming video. In *ACM SIGGRAPH Asia (ACM Transactions on Graphics)*, 2009.

[256] K. Kraus. *Photogrammetry: Geometry from Images and Laser Scans.* de Gruyter, 2007.

[257] P. G. Kry and D. K. Pai. Interaction capture and synthesis. In *ACM SIGGRAPH (ACM Transactions on Graphics)*, 2006.

[258] K. N. Kutulakos and S. M. Seitz. A theory of shape by space carving. *International Journal of Computer Vision*, 38(3):199–218, July 2000.

[259] V. Kwatra, A. Schödl, I. Essa, G. Turk, and A. Bobick. Graphcut textures: image and video synthesis using graph cuts. In *ACM SIGGRAPH (ACM Transactions on Graphics)*, 2003.

[260] J.-F. Lalonde and A. Efros. Using color compatibility for assessing image realism. In *IEEE International Conference on Computer Vision (ICCV)*, 2007.

[261] J.-F. Lalonde, D. Hoiem, A. A. Efros, C. Rother, J. Winn, and A. Criminisi. Photo clip art. In *ACM SIGGRAPH (ACM Transactions on Graphics)*, 2007.

[262] D. Lanman, D. Crispell, and G. Taubin. Surround structured lighting: 3-D scanning with orthographic illumination. *Computer Vision and Image Understanding*, 113(11):1107–17, Nov. 2009.

[263] A. Laurentini. The visual hull concept for silhouette-based image understanding. *IEEE Transactions on Pattern Analysis and Machine Intelligence*, 16(2):150–62, Feb. 1994.

[264] S. Lazebnik, C. Schmid, and J. Ponce. A sparse texture representation using local affine regions. *IEEE Transactions on Pattern Analysis and Machine Intelligence*, 27(8):1265–78, Aug. 2005.

[265] J. Lee, J. Chai, P. S. A. Reitsma, J. K. Hodgins, and N. S. Pollard. Interactive control of avatars animated with human motion data. In *ACM SIGGRAPH (ACM Transactions on Graphics)*, 2002.

[266] J. Lee and S. Y. Shin. A hierarchical approach to interactive motion editing for human-like figures. In *ACM SIGGRAPH (ACM Transactions on Graphics)*, 1999.

[267] S. Lee, G. Wolberg, and S. Y. Shin. Scattered data interpolation with multilevel B-splines. *IEEE Transactions on Visualization and Computer Graphics*, 3(3):228–44, July 1997.

[268] S.-Y. Lee, K.-Y. Chwa, J. Hahn, and S. Y. Shin. Image morphing using deformation techniques. *The Journal of Visualization and Computer Animation*, 7(1):3–23, 1996.

[269] S.-Y. Lee, K.-Y. Chwa, S. Y. Shin, and G. Wolberg. Image metamorphosis using snakes and free-form deformations. In *ACM SIGGRAPH (ACM Transactions on Graphics)*, 1995.

[270] V. Lepetit and P. Fua. Keypoint recognition using randomized trees. *IEEE Transactions on Pattern Analysis and Machine Intelligence*, 28(9):1465–79, Sept. 2006.

[271] A. Levin, D. Lischinski, and Y. Weiss. A closed-form solution to natural image matting. *IEEE Transactions on Pattern Analysis and Machine Intelligence*, 30(2):228–42, Feb. 2008.

[272] A. Levin, A. Rav-Acha, and D. Lischinski. Spectral matting. *IEEE Transactions on Pattern Analysis and Machine Intelligence*, 30(10):1699–1712, Oct. 2008.

[273] A. Levin, A. Zomet, and Y. Weiss. Learning how to inpaint from global image statistics. In *IEEE International Conference on Computer Vision (ICCV)*, 2003.

[274] M. Levoy and P. Hanrahan. Light field rendering. In *ACM SIGGRAPH (ACM Transactions on Graphics)*, 1996.

[275] M. Levoy, K. Pulli, B. Curless, S. Rusinkiewicz, D. Koller, L. Pereira, M. Ginzton, S. Anderson, J. Davis, J. Ginsberg, J. Shade, and D. Fulk. The digital Michelangelo project: 3D scanning of large statues. In *ACM SIGGRAPH (ACM Transactions on Graphics)*, 2000.

[276] J. Lewis. Fast template matching. In *Vision Interface*, 1995.

[277] H. Li, B. S. Manjunath, and S. K. Mitra. Multisensor image fusion using the wavelet transform. *Graphical Models and Image Processing*, 57(3):235–45, May 1995.

[278] Y. Li, L. Sharan, and E. H. Adelson. Compressing and companding high dynamic range images with subband architectures. In *ACM SIGGRAPH (ACM Transactions on Graphics)*, 2005.

[279] Y. Li, J. Sun, and H. Shum. Video object cut and paste. In *ACM SIGGRAPH (ACM Transactions on Graphics)*, 2005.

[280] Y. Li, J. Sun, C. Tang, and H. Shum. Lazy snapping. In *ACM SIGGRAPH (ACM Transactions on Graphics)*, 2004.

[281] D. Liebowitz and S. Carlsson. Uncalibrated motion capture exploiting articulated structure constraints. *International Journal of Computer Vision*, 51(3):171–87, Feb. 2003.

[282] D. Liebowitz and A. Zisserman. Metric rectification for perspective images of planes. In *IEEE Computer Society Conference on Computer Vision and Pattern Recognition (CVPR)*, 1998.

[283] D. Liebowitz and A. Zisserman. Combining scene and auto-calibration constraints. In *IEEE International Conference on Computer Vision (ICCV)*, 1999.

[284] I.-C. Lin and M. Ouhyoung. Mirror MoCap: Automatic and efficient capture of dense 3D facial motion parameters from video. *The Visual Computer*, 21(6):355–72, July 2005.

[285] T. Lindeberg. Detecting salient blob-like image structures and their scales with a scale-space primal sketch: A method for focus-of-attention. *International Journal of Computer Vision*, 11(3):283–318, Dec. 1993.

[286] T. Lindeberg. Feature detection with automatic scale selection. *International Journal of Computer Vision*, 30(2):79–116, Nov. 1998.

[287] T. Lindeberg and J. Gårding. Shape-adapted smoothing in estimation of 3-D shape cues from affine deformations of local 2-D brightness structure. *Image and Vision Computing*, 15(6):415–34, June 1997.

[288] C. Liu, W. Freeman, E. Adelson, and Y. Weiss. Human-assisted motion annotation. In *IEEE Computer Society Conference on Computer Vision and Pattern Recognition (CVPR)*, 2008.

[289] C. Liu, J. Yuen, and A. Torralba. SIFT flow: Dense correspondence across scenes and its applications. *IEEE Transactions on Pattern Analysis and Machine Intelligence*, 33(5):978–94, May 2011.

[290] C. K. Liu, A. Hertzmann, and Z. Popović. Learning physics-based motion style with nonlinear inverse optimization. In *ACM SIGGRAPH (ACM Transactions on Graphics)*, 2005.

[291] F. Liu and M. Gleicher. Automatic image retargeting with fisheye-view warping. In *ACM Symposium on User Interface Software and Technology*, 2005.

[292] F. Liu and M. Gleicher. Video retargeting: automating pan and scan. In *ACM International Conference on Multimedia*, 2006.

[293] F. Liu, M. Gleicher, H. Jin, and A. Agarwala. Content-preserving warps for 3D video stabilization. In *ACM SIGGRAPH (ACM Transactions on Graphics)*, 2009.

[294] F. Liu, M. Gleicher, J. Wang, H. Jin, and A. Agarwala. Subspace video stabilization. *ACM Transactions on Graphics*, 30(1):4:1–4:10, Feb. 2011.

[295] G. Liu and L. McMillan. Estimation of missing markers in human motion capture. *The Visual Computer*, 22(9):721–8, Sept. 2006.

[296] J. Liu, J. Sun, and H. Shum. Paint selection. In *ACM SIGGRAPH (ACM Transactions on Graphics)*, 2009.

[297] L. Liu, R. Chen, L. Wolf, and D. Cohen-Or. Optimizing photo composition. In *Eurographics*, 2010.

[298] W.-Y. Lo, J. V. Baar, C. Knaus, M. Zwicker, and M. Gross. Stereoscopic 3D copy and paste. In *ACM SIGGRAPH Asia (ACM Transactions on Graphics)*, 2010.

[299] H. Lombaert, Y. Sun, L. Grady, and C. Xu. A multilevel banded graph cuts method for fast image segmentation. In *IEEE International Conference on Computer Vision (ICCV)*, 2005.

[300] H. C. Longuet-Higgins. A computer algorithm for reconstructing a scene from two projections. *Nature*, 293:133–5, Sept. 1981.

[301] W. E. Lorensen and H. E. Cline. Marching cubes: A high resolution 3D surface construction algorithm. In *ACM SIGGRAPH (ACM Transactions on Graphics)*, 1987.

[302] H. Lou and J. Chai. Example-based human motion denoising. *IEEE Transactions on Visualization and Computer Graphics*, 16(5):870–9, Sept. 2010.

[303] M. Lourakis and A. Argyros. Is Levenberg-Marquardt the most efficient optimization algorithm for implementing bundle adjustment? In *IEEE International Conference on Computer Vision (ICCV)*, 2005.

[304] M. I. Lourakis and A. A. Argyros. Efficient, causal camera tracking in unprepared environments. *Computer Vision and Image Understanding*, 99(2):259–90, Aug. 2005.

[305] M. I. A. Lourakis and A. A. Argyros. SBA: a software package for generic sparse bundle adjustment. *ACM Transactions on Mathematical Software*, 36(1):2:1–2:30, Mar. 2009.

[306] D. G. Lowe. Distinctive image features from scale-invariant keypoints. *International Journal of Computer Vision*, 60(2):91–110, Nov. 2004.

[307] B. D. Lucas and T. Kanade. An iterative image registration technique with an application to stereo vision. In *Imaging Understanding Workshop*, 1981.

[308] Q.-T. Luong and O. Faugeras. Self-calibration of a moving camera from point correspondences and fundamental matrices. *International Journal of Computer Vision*, 22(3):261–89, Mar. 1997.

[309] W.-C. Ma, A. Jones, J.-Y. Chiang, T. Hawkins, S. Frederiksen, P. Peers, M. Vukovic, M. Ouhyoung, and P. Debevec. Facial performance synthesis using deformation-driven polynomial displacement maps. In *ACM SIGGRAPH Asia (ACM Transactions on Graphics)*, 2008.

[310] D. Mahajan, F. Huang, W. Matusik, R. Ramamoorthi, and P. Belhumeur. Moving gradients: a path-based method for plausible image interpolation. In *ACM SIGGRAPH (ACM Transactions on Graphics)*, 2009.

[311] S. Mahamud, M. Hebert, Y. Omori, and J. Ponce. Provably-convergent iterative methods for projective structure from motion. In *IEEE Computer Society Conference on Computer Vision and Pattern Recognition (CVPR)*, 2001.

[312] H. Malm and A. Heyden. Stereo head calibration from a planar object. In *IEEE Computer Society Conference on Computer Vision and Pattern Recognition (CVPR)*, 2001.

[313] A. Mansfield, P. Gehler, L. Van Gool, and C. Rother. Scene carving: Scene consistent image retargeting. In *European Conference on Computer Vision (ECCV)*, 2010.

[314] J. Matas, O. Chum, M. Urban, and T. Pajdla. Robust wide-baseline stereo from maximally stable extremal regions. *Image and Vision Computing*, 22(10):761–7, 2004.

[315] Y. Matsushita, E. Ofek, W. Ge, X. Tang, and H.-Y. Shum. Full-frame video stabilization with motion inpainting. *IEEE Transactions on Pattern Analysis and Machine Intelligence*, 28(7):1150–63, July 2006.

[316] I. Matthews and S. Baker. Active appearance models revisited. *International Journal of Computer Vision*, 60(2):135–64, Nov. 2004.

[317] S. Maybank. *Theory of Reconstruction from Image Motion*. Springer-Verlag, 1993.

[318] J. McCann and N. S. Pollard. Real-time gradient-domain painting. In *ACM SIGGRAPH (ACM Transactions on Graphics)*, 2008.

[319] M. McGuire, W. Matusik, H. Pfister, J. Hughes, and F. Durand. Defocus video matting. In *ACM SIGGRAPH (ACM Transactions on Graphics)*, 2005.

[320] M. McGuire, W. Matusik, and W. Yerazunis. Practical, real-time studio matting using dual imagers. In *Eurographics Symposium on Rendering*, 2006.

[321] P. McLauchlan. Gauge independence in optimization algorithms for 3D vision. In B. Triggs, A. Zisserman, and R. Szeliski, editors, *Vision Algorithms: Theory and Practice*, pages 183–99. Springer, 2000.

[322] L. McMillan and G. Bishop. Plenoptic modeling: an image-based rendering system. In *ACM SIGGRAPH (ACM Transactions on Graphics)*, 1995.

[323] A. Menache. *Understanding Motion Capture for Computer Animation*. Morgan Kaufmann, 2nd edition, 2011.

[324] I. Mikić, M. Trivedi, E. Hunter, and P. Cosman. Human body model acquisition and tracking using voxel data. *International Journal of Computer Vision*, 53(3):199–223, July 2003.

[325] K. Mikolajczyk and C. Schmid. Indexing based on scale invariant interest points. In *IEEE International Conference on Computer Vision (ICCV)*, 2001.

[326] K. Mikolajczyk and C. Schmid. An affine invariant interest point detector. In *European Conference on Computer Vision (ECCV)*, 2002.

[327] K. Mikolajczyk and C. Schmid. Scale and affine invariant interest point detectors. *International Journal of Computer Vision*, 60(1):63–86, Oct. 2004.

[328] K. Mikolajczyk and C. Schmid. A performance evaluation of local descriptors. *IEEE Transactions on Pattern Analysis and Machine Intelligence*, 27(10):1615–30, Oct. 2005.

[329] K. Mikolajczyk, T. Tuytelaars, C. Schmid, A. Zisserman, J. Matas, F. Schaffalitzky, T. Kadir, and L. Van Gool. A comparison of affine region detectors. *International Journal of Computer Vision*, 65(1):43–72, Nov. 2005.

[330] F. Mindru, T. Tuytelaars, L. Van Gool, and T. Moons. Moment invariants for recognition under changing viewpoint and illumination. *Computer Vision and Image Understanding*, 94(1-3):3–27, Apr.–Jun. 2004.

[331] T. B. Moeslund and E. Granum. A survey of computer vision-based human motion capture. *Computer Vision and Image Understanding*, 81(3):231–68, Mar. 2001.

[332] T. B. Moeslund, A. Hilton, and V. Krüger. A survey of advances in vision-based human motion capture and analysis. *Computer Vision and Image Understanding*, 104(2-3):90–126, Nov. 2006.

[333] P. Montesinos, V. Gouet, R. Deriche, and D. Pelé. Matching color uncalibrated images using differential invariants. *Image and Vision Computing*, 18(9):659–71, June 2000.

[334] R. Morano, C. Ozturk, R. Conn, S. Dubin, S. Zietz, and J. Nissano. Structured light using pseudorandom codes. *IEEE Transactions on Pattern Analysis and Machine Intelligence*, 20(3):322–7, Mar. 1998.

[335] H. Moravec. Obstacle avoidance and navigation in the real world by a seeing robot rover. Technical Report CMU-RI-TR-3, Carnegie Mellon University, 1980.

[336] P. Moreels and P. Perona. Evaluation of features detectors and descriptors based on 3D objects. *International Journal of Computer Vision*, 73(3):263–84, July 2007.

[337] D. Morris, K. Kanatani, and T. Kanade. Uncertainty modeling for optimal structure from motion. In B. Triggs, A. Zisserman, and R. Szeliski, editors, *Vision Algorithms: Theory and Practice*, pages 315–45. Springer, 2000.

[338] D. Morris, K. Kanatani, and T. Kanade. Gauge fixing for accurate 3D estimation. In *IEEE Computer Society Conference on Computer Vision and Pattern Recognition (CVPR)*, 2001.

[339] E. Mortensen and W. Barrett. Interactive segmentation with intelligent scissors. *Graphical Models and Image Processing*, 60(5):349–84, Sept. 1998.

[340] E. Mouragnon, M. Lhuillier, M. Dhome, F. Dekeyser, and P. Sayd. Generic and real-time structure from motion using local bundle adjustment. *Image and Vision Computing*, 27(8):1178–93, July 2009.

[341] K. Murphy, Y. Weiss, and M. Jordan. Loopy belief propagation for approximate inference: An empirical study. In *Uncertainty in AI*, 1999.

[342] R. M. Murray, Z. Li, and S. S. Sastry. *A Mathematical Introduction to Robotic Manipulation*. CRC Press, 1994.

[343] H.-H. Nagel and W. Enkelmann. An investigation of smoothness constraints for the estimation of displacement vector fields from image sequences. *IEEE Transactions on Pattern Analysis and Machine Intelligence*, PAMI-8(5):565–93, Sept. 1986.

[344] Y. Nakamura, T. Matsuura, K. Satoh, and Y. Ohta. Occlusion detectable stereo-occlusion patterns in camera matrix. In *IEEE Computer Society Conference on Computer Vision and Pattern Recognition (CVPR)*, 1996.

[345] S. Narasimhan, S. Nayar, B. Sun, and S. Koppal. Structured light in scattering media. In *IEEE Computer Society Conference on Computer Vision and Pattern Recognition (CVPR)*, 2005.

[346] S. Negahdaripour. Revised definition of optical flow: integration of radiometric and geometric cues for dynamic scene analysis. *IEEE Transactions on Pattern Analysis and Machine Intelligence*, 20(9):961–79, Sept. 1998.

[347] D. Nehab, S. Rusinkiewicz, J. Davis, and R. Ramamoorthi. Efficiently combining positions and normals for precise 3D geometry. In *ACM SIGGRAPH (ACM Transactions on Graphics)*, 2005.

[348] T. S. Newman and H. Yi. A survey of the marching cubes algorithm. *Computers & Graphics*, 30(5):854–79, Oct. 2006.

[349] D. Nistér. Reconstruction from uncalibrated sequences with a hierarchy of trifocal tensors. In *European Conference on Computer Vision (ECCV)*, 2000.

[350] D. Nistér. An efficient solution to the five-point relative pose problem. *IEEE Transactions on Pattern Analysis and Machine Intelligence*, 26(6):756–70, June 2004.

[351] J. Nocedal and S. Wright. *Numerical Optimization*. Springer Verlag, 1999.

[352] Y. Ohta and T. Kanade. Stereo by intra- and inter-scanline search using dynamic programming. *IEEE Transactions on Pattern Analysis and Machine Intelligence*, 7(2):139–54, Mar. 1985.

[353] Y. Ohtake, A. Belyaev, M. Alexa, G. Turk, and H.-P. Seidel. Multi-level partition of unity implicits. In *ACM SIGGRAPH (ACM Transactions on Graphics)*, 2003.

[354] M. Okutomi and T. Kanade. A multiple-baseline stereo. *IEEE Transactions on Pattern Analysis and Machine Intelligence*, 15(4):353–63, Apr. 1993.

[355] I. Omer and M. Werman. Color lines: Image specific color representation. In *IEEE Computer Society Conference on Computer Vision and Pattern Recognition (CVPR)*, 2004.

[356] M. Orchard and C. Bouman. Color quantization of images. *IEEE Transactions on Signal Processing*, 39(12):2677–90, Dec. 1991.

[357] A. Orzan, A. Bousseau, H. Winnemöller, P. Barla, J. Thollot, and D. Salesin. Diffusion curves: a vector representation for smooth-shaded images. In *ACM SIGGRAPH (ACM Transactions on Graphics)*, 2008.

[358] M. Özuysal, M. Calonder, V. Lepetit, and P. Fua. Fast keypoint recognition using random ferns. *IEEE Transactions on Pattern Analysis and Machine Intelligence*, 32(3):448–61, Mar. 2010.

[359] J. Pagès, J. Salvi, C. Collewet, and J. Forest. Optimised De Bruijn patterns for one-shot shape acquisition. *Image and Vision Computing*, 23(8):707–20, Aug. 2005.

[360] S. I. Park and J. K. Hodgins. Capturing and animating skin deformation in human motion. In *ACM SIGGRAPH (ACM Transactions on Graphics)*, 2006.

[361] S. I. Park, H. J. Shin, and S. Y. Shin. On-line locomotion generation based on motion blending. In *ACM SIGGRAPH/Eurographics Symposium on Computer Animation*, 2002.

[362] J. Pearl. *Probabilistic Reasoning in Intelligent Systems: Networks of Plausible Inference*. Morgan Kaufmann, 1988.

[363] P. Pérez, A. Blake, and M. Gangnet. Jetstream: Probabilistic contour extraction with particles. In *IEEE International Conference on Computer Vision (ICCV)*, 2001.

[364] P. Pérez, M. Gangnet, and A. Blake. Poisson image editing. In *ACM SIGGRAPH (ACM Transactions on Graphics)*, 2003.

[365] R. Plankers and P. Fua. Articulated soft objects for multiview shape and motion capture. *IEEE Transactions on Pattern Analysis and Machine Intelligence*, 25(9):1182–7, Sept. 2003.

[366] M. Pollefeys, R. Koch, and L. Van Gool. Self-calibration and metric reconstruction in spite of varying and unknown intrinsic camera parameters. *International Journal of Computer Vision*, 32(1):7–25, Aug. 1999.

[367] M. Pollefeys, D. Nistér, J.-M. Frahm, A. Akbarzadeh, P. Mordohai, B. Clipp, C. Engels, D. Gallup, S.-J. Kim, P. Merrell, C. Salmi, S. Sinha, B. Talton, L. Wang, Q. Yang, H. Stewénius, R. Yang, G. Welch, and H. Towles. Detailed real-time urban 3D reconstruction from video. *International Journal of Computer Vision*, 78(2):143–67, July 2008.

[368] M. Pollefeys, L. Van Gool, M. Vergauwen, F. Verbiest, K. Cornelis, J. Tops, and R. Koch. Visual modeling with a hand-held camera. *International Journal of Computer Vision*, 59(3):207–32, Sept. 2004.

[369] M. Pollefeys, F. Verbiest, and L. Van Gool. Surviving dominant planes in uncalibrated structure and motion recovery. In *European Conference on Computer Vision (ECCV)*, 2002.

[370] J.-P. Pons, R. Keriven, and O. Faugeras. Multi-view stereo reconstruction and scene flow estimation with a global image-based matching score. *International Journal of Computer Vision*, 72(2):179–93, June 2007.

[371] Z. Popović and A. Witkin. Physically based motion transformation. In *ACM SIGGRAPH (ACM Transactions on Graphics)*, 1999.

[372] R. Poppe. Vision-based human motion analysis: An overview. *Computer Vision and Image Understanding*, 108(1-2):4–18, Oct. 2007.

[373] T. Porter and T. Duff. Compositing digital images. In *ACM SIGGRAPH (ACM Transactions on Graphics)*, 1984.

[374] W. Press, B. Flannery, S. Teukolsky, W. Vetterling, et al. *Numerical Recipes*. Cambridge University Press, 2007.

[375] D. Price. *The Pixar Touch*. Vintage, 2009.

[376] Y. Pritch, E. Kav-Venaki, and S. Peleg. Shift-map image editing. In *IEEE International Conference on Computer Vision (ICCV)*, 2009.

[377] A. Protiere and G. Sapiro. Interactive image segmentation via adaptive weighted distances. *IEEE Transactions on Image Processing*, 16(4):1046–57, Apr. 2007.

[378] K. Pulli. Multiview registration for large data sets. In *International Conference on 3-D Digital Imaging and Modeling (3DIM)*, 1999.

[379] R. Radke, S. Andra, O. Al-Kofahi, and B. Roysam. Image change detection algorithms: a systematic survey. *IEEE Transactions on Image Processing*, 14(3):294–307, Mar. 2005.

[380] R. Radke, P. Ramadge, S. Kulkarni, and T. Echigo. Efficiently synthesizing virtual video. *IEEE Transactions on Circuits and Systems for Video Technology*, 13(4):325–37, Apr. 2003.

[381] R. Raskar and P. Beardsley. A self-correcting projector. In *IEEE Computer Society Conference on Computer Vision and Pattern Recognition (CVPR)*, 2001.

[382] R. Raskar, H. Nii, B. deDecker, Y. Hashimoto, J. Summet, D. Moore, Y. Zhao, J. Westhues, P. Dietz, J. Barnwell, S. Nayar, M. Inami, P. Bekaert, M. Noland, V. Branzoi, and E. Bruns. Prakash: lighting aware motion capture using photosensing markers and multiplexed illuminators. In *ACM SIGGRAPH (ACM Transactions on Graphics)*, 2007.

[383] A. Rav-Acha, P. Kohli, C. Rother, and A. Fitzgibbon. Unwrap mosaics: a new representation for video editing. In *ACM SIGGRAPH (ACM Transactions on Graphics)*, 2008.

[384] A. Rav-Acha, Y. Pritch, D. Lischinski, and S. Peleg. Dynamosaicing: Mosaicing of dynamic scenes. *IEEE Transactions on Pattern Analysis and Machine Intelligence*, 29(10):1789–1801, Oct. 2007.

[385] I. D. Reid. Projective calibration of a laser-stripe range finder. *Image and Vision Computing*, 14(9):659–66, Oct. 1996.

[386] E. Reinhard, G. Ward, S. Pattanaik, and P. Debevec. *High Dynamic Range Imaging: Acquisition, Display, and Image-Based Lighting*. Morgan Kaufmann, 2005.

[387] L. Ren, A. Patrick, A. A. Efros, J. K. Hodgins, and J. M. Rehg. A data-driven approach to quantifying natural human motion. In *ACM SIGGRAPH (ACM Transactions on Graphics)*, 2005.

[388] L. Ren, G. Shakhnarovich, J. K. Hodgins, H. Pfister, and P. Viola. Learning silhouette features for control of human motion. *ACM Transactions on Graphics*, 24(4):1303–31, Oct. 2005.

[389] C. Rhemann, C. Rother, and M. Gelautz. Improving color modeling for alpha matting. In *British Machine Vision Conference (BMVC)*, 2008.

[390] C. Rhemann, C. Rother, P. Kohli, and M. Gelautz. A spatially varying PSF-based prior for alpha matting. In *IEEE Computer Society Conference on Computer Vision and Pattern Recognition (CVPR)*, 2010.

[391] C. Rhemann, C. Rother, A. Rav-Acha, and T. Sharp. High resolution matting via interactive trimap segmentation. In *IEEE Computer Society Conference on Computer Vision and Pattern Recognition (CVPR)*, 2008.

[392] C. Rhemann, C. Rother, J. Wang, M. Gelautz, P. Kohli, and P. Rott. A perceptually motivated online benchmark for image matting. In *IEEE Computer Society Conference on Computer Vision and Pattern Recognition (CVPR)*, 2009.

[393] R. Rickitt. *Special Effects: The History and Technique*. Billboard Books, 2nd edition, 2007.

[394] M. Ringer and J. Lasenby. A procedure for automatically estimating model parameters in optical motion capture. *Image and Vision Computing*, 22(10):843–50, Sept. 2004.

[395] C. Rose, M. Cohen, and B. Bodenheimer. Verbs and adverbs: multidimensional motion interpolation. *IEEE Computer Graphics and Applications*, 18(5):32–40, Sept. 1998.

[396] C. Rose, B. Guenter, B. Bodenheimer, and M. F. Cohen. Efficient generation of motion transitions using spacetime constraints. In *ACM SIGGRAPH (ACM Transactions on Graphics)*, 1996.

[397] B. Rosenhahn and T. Brox. Scaled motion dynamics for markerless motion capture. In *IEEE Computer Society Conference on Computer Vision and Pattern Recognition (CVPR)*, 2007.

[398] B. Rosenhahn, C. Schmaltz, T. Brox, J. Weickert, D. Cremers, and H.-P. Seidel. Markerless motion capture of man-machine interaction. In *IEEE Computer Society Conference on Computer Vision and Pattern Recognition (CVPR)*, 2008.

[399] D. Ross, D. Tarlow, and R. Zemel. Learning articulated structure and motion. *International Journal of Computer Vision*, 88(2):214–37, June 2010.

[400] E. Rosten and T. Drummond. Fusing points and lines for high performance tracking. In *IEEE International Conference on Computer Vision (ICCV)*, 2005.

[401] E. Rosten and T. Drummond. Machine learning for high-speed corner detection. In *European Conference on Computer Vision (ECCV)*, 2006.

[402] E. Rosten, R. Porter, and T. Drummond. FASTER and better: A machine learning approach to corner detection. *IEEE Transactions on Pattern Analysis and Machine Intelligence*, 32(1):105–19, Jan. 2010.

[403] S. Roth and M. Black. On the spatial statistics of optical flow. *International Journal of Computer Vision*, 74(1):33–50, Aug. 2007.

[404] C. Rother, L. Bordeaux, Y. Hamadi, and A. Blake. Autocollage. In *ACM SIGGRAPH (ACM Transactions on Graphics)*, 2006.

[405] C. Rother, V. Kolmogorov, and A. Blake. GrabCut: Interactive foreground extraction using iterated graph cuts. In *ACM SIGGRAPH (ACM Transactions on Graphics)*, 2004.

[406] S. Roy and I. Cox. A maximum-flow formulation of the N-camera stereo correspondence problem. In *IEEE International Conference on Computer Vision (ICCV)*, 1998.

[407] M. Rubinstein, D. Gutierrez, O. Sorkine, and A. Shamir. A comparative study of image retargeting. In *ACM SIGGRAPH Asia (ACM Transactions on Graphics)*, 2010.

[408] M. Rubinstein, A. Shamir, and S. Avidan. Improved seam carving for video retargeting. In *ACM SIGGRAPH (ACM Transactions on Graphics)*, 2008.

[409] M. Rubinstein, A. Shamir, and S. Avidan. Multi-operator media retargeting. In *ACM SIGGRAPH (ACM Transactions on Graphics)*, 2009.

[410] S. Rusinkiewicz, O. Hall-Holt, and M. Levoy. Real-time 3D model acquisition. In *ACM SIGGRAPH (ACM Transactions on Graphics)*, 2002.

[411] S. Rusinkiewicz and M. Levoy. Efficient variants of the ICP algorithm. In *International Conference on 3-D Digital Imaging and Modeling (3DIM)*, 2001.

[412] M. Ruzon and C. Tomasi. Alpha estimation in natural images. In *IEEE Computer Society Conference on Computer Vision and Pattern Recognition (CVPR)*, 2000.

[413] Y. Saad. *Iterative Methods for Sparse Linear Systems*. Society for Industrial and Applied Mathematics, 2003.

[414] F. Sadlo, T. Weyrich, R. Peikert, and M. Gross. A practical structured light acquisition system for point-based geometry and texture. In *Eurographics/IEEE VGTC Symposium on Point-Based Graphics*, 2005.

[415] A. Safonova and J. K. Hodgins. Analyzing the physical correctness of interpolated human motion. In *ACM SIGGRAPH/Eurographics Symposium on Computer Animation*, 2005.

[416] A. Safonova, J. K. Hodgins, and N. S. Pollard. Synthesizing physically realistic human motion in low-dimensional, behavior-specific spaces. In *ACM SIGGRAPH (ACM Transactions on Graphics)*, 2004.

[417] J. Salvi, J. Batlle, and E. Mouaddib. A robust-coded pattern projection for dynamic 3D scene measurement. *Pattern Recognition Letters*, 19(11):1055–65, Sept. 1998.

[418] J. Salvi, S. Fernandez, T. Pribanic, and X. Llado. A state of the art in structured light patterns for surface profilometry. *Pattern Recognition*, 43(8):2666–80, Aug. 2010.

[419] J. Salvi, J. Pagès, and J. Batlle. Pattern codification strategies in structured light systems. *Pattern Recognition*, 37(4):827–49, Apr. 2004.

[420] P. Sand and S. Teller. Video matching. In *ACM SIGGRAPH (ACM Transactions on Graphics)*, 2004.

[421] H. S. Sawhney, Y. Guo, K. Hanna, R. Kumar, S. Adkins, and S. Zhou. Hybrid stereo camera: an IBR approach for synthesis of very high resolution stereoscopic image sequences. In *ACM SIGGRAPH (ACM Transactions on Graphics)*, 2001.

[422] S. Schaefer, T. McPhail, and J. Warren. Image deformation using moving least squares. In *ACM SIGGRAPH (ACM Transactions on Graphics)*, 2006.

[423] F. Schaffalitzky and A. Zisserman. Multi-view matching for unordered image sets, or "How do I organize my holiday snaps?". In *European Conference on Computer Vision (ECCV)*, 2002.

[424] F. Schaffalitzky and A. Zisserman. Automated location matching in movies. *Computer Vision and Image Understanding*, 92(2-3):236–64, Nov. 2003.

[425] D. Scharstein and R. Szeliski. A taxonomy and evaluation of dense two-frame stereo correspondence algorithms. *International Journal of Computer Vision*, 47(1):7–42, Apr. 2002.

[426] D. Scharstein and R. Szeliski. High-accuracy stereo depth maps using structured light. In *IEEE Computer Society Conference on Computer Vision and Pattern Recognition (CVPR)*, 2003.

[427] H. Schey. *Div, Grad, Curl, and All That: An Informal Text on Vector Calculus*. W.W. Norton and Company, 2005.

[428] G. Schindler, F. Dellaert, and S. B. Kang. Inferring temporal order of images from 3D structure. In *IEEE Computer Society Conference on Computer Vision and Pattern Recognition (CVPR)*, 2007.

[429] C. Schmalz and E. Angelopoulou. A graph-based approach for robust single-shot structured light. In *IEEE International Workshop on Projector-Camera Systems (PROCAMS)*, 2010.

[430] C. Schmid and R. Mohr. Local grayvalue invariants for image retrieval. *IEEE Transactions on Pattern Analysis and Machine Intelligence*, 19(5):530–5, May 1997.

[431] C. Schmid, R. Mohr, and C. Bauckhage. Evaluation of interest point detectors. *International Journal of Computer Vision*, 37(2):151–72, June 2000.

[432] S. Se, D. Lowe, and J. Little. Vision-based mobile robot localization and mapping using scale-invariant features. In *IEEE International Conference on Robotics and Automation*, 2001.

[433] S. Seitz, B. Curless, J. Diebel, D. Scharstein, and R. Szeliski. A comparison and evaluation of multi-view stereo reconstruction algorithms. In *IEEE Computer Society Conference on Computer Vision and Pattern Recognition (CVPR)*, 2006.

[434] S. M. Seitz and C. R. Dyer. View morphing. In *ACM SIGGRAPH (ACM Transactions on Graphics)*, 1996.

[435] S. M. Seitz and C. R. Dyer. Photorealistic scene reconstruction by voxel coloring. *International Journal of Computer Vision*, 35(2):151–73, Nov. 1999.

[436] J. A. Sethian. *Level Set Methods and Fast Marching Methods: Evolving Interfaces in Computational Geometry, Fluid Mechanics, Computer Vision, and Materials Science*. Cambridge University Press, 1999.

[437] V. Setlur, S. Takagi, R. Raskar, M. Gleicher, and B. Gooch. Automatic image retargeting. In *International Conference on Mobile and Ubiquitous Multimedia*, 2005.

[438] M. Shaheen, J. Gall, R. Strzodka, L. Van Gool, and H.-P. Seidel. A comparison of 3d model-based tracking approaches for human motion capture in uncontrolled environments. In *IEEE Computer Society Workshop on Applications of Computer Vision*, 2009.

[439] A. Shashua. Algebraic functions for recognition. *IEEE Transactions on Pattern Analysis and Machine Intelligence*, 17(8):779–89, Aug. 1995.

[440] E. Shechtman, A. Rav-Acha, M. Irani, and S. Seitz. Regenerative morphing. In *IEEE Computer Society Conference on Computer Vision and Pattern Recognition (CVPR)*, 2010.

[441] J. Shi and J. Malik. Normalized cuts and image segmentation. *IEEE Transactions on Pattern Analysis and Machine Intelligence*, 22(8):888–905, Aug. 2000.

[442] J. Shi and C. Tomasi. Good features to track. In *IEEE Computer Society Conference on Computer Vision and Pattern Recognition (CVPR)*, 1994.

[443] H. J. Shin, J. Lee, S. Y. Shin, and M. Gleicher. Computer puppetry: An importance-based approach. *ACM Transactions on Graphics*, 20(2):67–94, Apr. 2001.

[444] K. Shoemake. Animating rotation with quaternion curves. In *ACM SIGGRAPH (ACM Transactions on Graphics)*, 1985.

[445] J. Shotton, A. Fitzgibbon, M. Cook, T. Sharp, M. Finocchio, R. Moore, A. Kipman, and A. Blake. Real-time human pose recognition in parts from a single depth image. In *IEEE Computer Society Conference on Computer Vision and Pattern Recognition (CVPR)*, 2011.

[446] H.-Y. Shum and L.-W. He. Rendering with concentric mosaics. In *ACM SIGGRAPH (ACM Transactions on Graphics)*, 1999.

[447] H. Sidenbladh, M. Black, and D. Fleet. Stochastic tracking of 3D human figures using 2D image motion. In *European Conference on Computer Vision (ECCV)*, 2000.

[448] E. Sifakis, I. Neverov, and R. Fedkiw. Automatic determination of facial muscle activations from sparse motion capture marker data. In *ACM SIGGRAPH (ACM Transactions on Graphics)*, 2005.

[449] L. Sigal, A. Balan, and M. Black. HumanEva: Synchronized video and motion capture dataset and baseline algorithm for evaluation of articulated human motion. *International Journal of Computer Vision*, 87(1):4–27, Mar. 2010.

[450] L. Sigal, S. Bhatia, S. Roth, M. Black, and M. Isard. Tracking loose-limbed people. In *IEEE Computer Society Conference on Computer Vision and Pattern Recognition (CVPR)*, 2004.

[451] D. Simakov, Y. Caspi, E. Shechtman, and M. Irani. Summarizing visual data using bidirectional similarity. In *IEEE Computer Society Conference on Computer Vision and Pattern Recognition (CVPR)*, 2008.

[452] T. Simchony, R. Chellappa, and M. Shao. Direct analytical methods for solving Poisson equations in computer vision problems. *IEEE Transactions on Pattern Analysis and Machine Intelligence*, 12(5):435–46, May 1990.

[453] E. Simoncelli and W. Freeman. The steerable pyramid: A flexible architecture for multiscale derivative computation. In *IEEE International Conference on Image Processing (ICIP)*, 1995.

[454] D. Singaraju, C. Rother, and C. Rhemann. New appearance models for natural image matting. In *IEEE Computer Society Conference on Computer Vision and Pattern Recognition (CVPR)*, 2009.

[455] S. Sinha, J.-M. Frahm, M. Pollefeys, and Y. Genc. Feature tracking and matching in video using programmable graphics hardware. *Machine Vision and Applications*, 2007.

[456] J. Sivic and A. Zisserman. Video Google: a text retrieval approach to object matching in videos. In *IEEE International Conference on Computer Vision (ICCV)*, 2003.

[457] C. Sminchisescu and B. Triggs. Estimating articulated human motion with covariance scaled sampling. *International Journal of Robotics Research*, 22(6):371–91, June 2003.

[458] A. Smith and J. Blinn. Blue screen matting. In *ACM SIGGRAPH (ACM Transactions on Graphics)*, 1996.

[459] E. Smith, R. J. Radke, and C. Stewart. Physical scale keypoints: Matching and registration for combined intensity/range images. *International Journal of Computer Vision*, 97(1):2–17, Mar. 2012.

[460] E. R. Smith, B. J. King, C. V. Stewart, and R. J. Radke. Registration of combined range-intensity scans: Initialization through verification. *Computer Vision and Image Understanding*, 110(2):226–44, May 2008.

[461] S. M. Smith and J. M. Brady. SUSAN— a new approach to low level image processing. *International Journal of Computer Vision*, 23(1):45–78, May 1997.

[462] N. Snavely, S. Seitz, and R. Szeliski. Modeling the world from internet photo collections. *International Journal of Computer Vision*, 80(2):189–210, Nov. 2008.

[463] N. Snavely, S. Seitz, and R. Szeliski. Skeletal graphs for efficient structure from motion. In *IEEE Computer Society Conference on Computer Vision and Pattern Recognition (CVPR)*, 2008.

[464] N. Snavely, I. Simon, M. Goesele, R. Szeliski, and S. Seitz. Scene reconstruction and visualization from community photo collections. *Proceedings of the IEEE*, 98(8):1370–90, Aug. 2010.

[465] J. M. Soucie, C. Wang, A. Forsyth, S. Funk, M. Denny, K. E. Roach, and D. Boone. Range of motion measurements: reference values and a database for comparison studies. *Haemophilia*, 17(3):500–7, May 2011.

[466] D. Stavens and S. Thrun. Unsupervised learning of invariant features using video. In *IEEE Computer Society Conference on Computer Vision and Pattern Recognition (CVPR)*, 2010.

[467] D. Steedly and I. Essa. Propagation of innovative information in non-linear least-squares structure from motion. In *IEEE International Conference on Computer Vision (ICCV)*, 2001.

[468] D. Steedly, I. Essa, and F. Dellaert. Spectral partitioning for structure from motion. In *IEEE International Conference on Computer Vision (ICCV)*, 2003.

[469] G. Strang. *Introduction to Linear Algebra*. Wellesley Cambridge Press, 4th edition, 2009.

[470] C. Strecha, W. von Hansen, L. Van Gool, P. Fua, and U. Thoennessen. On benchmarking camera calibration and multi-view stereo for high resolution imagery. In *IEEE Computer Society Conference on Computer Vision and Pattern Recognition (CVPR)*, 2008.

[471] P. Sturm. Critical motion sequences for monocular self-calibration and uncalibrated Euclidean reconstruction. In *IEEE Computer Society Conference on Computer Vision and Pattern Recognition (CVPR)*, 1997.

[472] P. Sturm. Critical motion sequences for the self-calibration of cameras and stereo systems with variable focal length. In *British Machine Vision Conference (BMVC)*, 1999.

[473] P. Sturm and S. Maybank. On plane-based camera calibration: A general algorithm, singularities, applications. In *IEEE Computer Society Conference on Computer Vision and Pattern Recognition (CVPR)*, 1999.

[474] P. Sturm and B. Triggs. A factorization based algorithm for multi-image projective structure and motion. In *European Conference on Computer Vision (ECCV)*, 1996.

[475] D. Sun, S. Roth, and M. Black. Secrets of optical flow estimation and their principles. In *IEEE Computer Society Conference on Computer Vision and Pattern Recognition (CVPR)*, 2010.

[476] D. Sun, S. Roth, J. Lewis, and M. Black. Learning optical flow. In *European Conference on Computer Vision (ECCV)*, 2008.

[477] D. Sun, E. Sudderth, and M. Black. Layered image motion with explicit occlusions, temporal consistency, and depth ordering. In *Conference on Neural Information Processing Systems*, 2010.

[478] J. Sun, J. Jia, C. Tang, and H. Shum. Poisson matting. In *ACM SIGGRAPH (ACM Transactions on Graphics)*, 2004.

[479] J. Sun, Y. Li, S. Kang, and H. Shum. Flash matting. In *ACM SIGGRAPH (ACM Transactions on Graphics)*, 2006.

[480] J. Sun, Y. Li, S. Kang, and H.-Y. Shum. Symmetric stereo matching for occlusion handling. In *IEEE Computer Society Conference on Computer Vision and Pattern Recognition (CVPR)*, 2005.

[481] J. Sun, L. Yuan, J. Jia, and H.-Y. Shum. Image completion with structure propagation. In *ACM SIGGRAPH (ACM Transactions on Graphics)*, 2005.

[482] J. Sun, N.-N. Zheng, and H.-Y. Shum. Stereo matching using belief propagation. *IEEE Transactions on Pattern Analysis and Machine Intelligence*, 25(7):787–800, July 2003.

[483] K. Sunkavalli, M. K. Johnson, W. Matusik, and H. Pfister. Multi-scale image harmonization. In *ACM SIGGRAPH (ACM Transactions on Graphics)*, 2010.

[484] R. Szeliski. Locally adapted hierarchical basis preconditioning. In *ACM SIGGRAPH (ACM Transactions on Graphics)*, 2006.

[485] R. Szeliski, R. Zabih, D. Scharstein, O. Veksler, V. Kolmogorov, A. Agarwala, M. Tappen, and C. Rother. A comparative study of energy minimization methods for Markov Random

Fields with smoothness-based priors. *IEEE Transactions on Pattern Analysis and Machine Intelligence*, 30(6):1068–80, June 2008.

[486] H. Tao, H. Sawhney, and R. Kumar. A global matching framework for stereo computation. In *IEEE International Conference on Computer Vision (ICCV)*, 2001.

[487] D. Tell and S. Carlsson. Wide baseline point matching using affine invariants computed from intensity profiles. In *European Conference on Computer Vision (ECCV)*, 2000.

[488] J.-P. Thirion. Image matching as a diffusion process: an analogy with Maxwell's demons. *Medical Image Analysis*, 2(3):243–60, Sept. 1998.

[489] S. Thrun, W. Burgard, and D. Fox. *Probabilistic Robotics*. MIT Press, 2005.

[490] E. Tola, V. Lepetit, and P. Fua. DAISY: An efficient dense descriptor applied to wide-baseline stereo. *IEEE Transactions on Pattern Analysis and Machine Intelligence*, 32(5):815–30, May 2010.

[491] D. Tolani, A. Goswami, and N. I. Badler. Real-time inverse kinematics techniques for anthropomorphic limbs. *Graphical Models*, 62(5):353–88, Sept. 2000.

[492] C. Tomasi and T. Kanade. Detection and tracking of point features. Technical Report CMU-CS-91-132, Carnegie Mellon University, 1991.

[493] C. Tomasi and T. Kanade. Shape and motion from image streams under orthography: a factorization method. *International Journal of Computer Vision*, 9(2):137–54, Nov. 1992.

[494] T. Tommasini, A. Fusiello, E. Trucco, and V. Roberto. Making good features track better. In *IEEE Computer Society Conference on Computer Vision and Pattern Recognition (CVPR)*, 1998.

[495] P. H. Torr, A. W. Fitzgibbon, and A. Zisserman. The problem of degeneracy in structure and motion recovery from uncalibrated image sequences. *International Journal of Computer Vision*, 32(1):27–44, Aug. 1999.

[496] L. Torresani, A. Hertzmann, and C. Bregler. Learning non-rigid 3D shape from 2D motion. In *Conference on Neural Information Processing Systems*, 2004.

[497] M. Trajković and M. Hedley. Fast corner detection. *Image and Vision Computing*, 16(2):75–87, 1998.

[498] B. Triggs. Factorization methods for projective structure and motion. In *IEEE Computer Society Conference on Computer Vision and Pattern Recognition (CVPR)*, 1996.

[499] B. Triggs. Autocalibration and the absolute quadric. In *IEEE Computer Society Conference on Computer Vision and Pattern Recognition (CVPR)*, 1997.

[500] B. Triggs, P. McLauchlan, R. Hartley, and A. Fitzgibbon. Bundle adjustment — a modern synthesis. In B. Triggs, A. Zisserman, and R. Szeliski, editors, *Vision Algorithms: Theory and Practice*, pages 153–77. Springer, 2000.

[501] G. Turk and M. Levoy. Zippered polygon meshes from range images. In *ACM SIGGRAPH (ACM Transactions on Graphics)*, 1994.

[502] G. Turk and J. F. O'Brien. Shape transformation using variational implicit functions. In *ACM SIGGRAPH (ACM Transactions on Graphics)*, 1999.

[503] T. Tuytelaars and L. Van Gool. Matching widely separated views based on affine invariant regions. *International Journal of Computer Vision*, 59(1):61–85, Aug. 2004.

[504] S. Umeyama. Least-squares estimation of transformation parameters between two point patterns. *IEEE Transactions on Pattern Analysis and Machine Intelligence*, 13(4):376–80, Apr. 1991.

[505] R. Unnikrishnan and M. Hebert. Extracting scale and illuminant invariant regions through color. In *British Machine Vision Conference (BMVC)*, 2006.

[506] S. Uras, F. Girosi, A. Verri, and V. Torre. A computational approach to motion perception. *Biological Cybernetics*, 60(2):79–87, Dec. 1988.

[507] R. Urtasun, D. Fleet, and P. Fua. 3D people tracking with Gaussian process dynamical models. In *IEEE Computer Society Conference on Computer Vision and Pattern Recognition (CVPR)*, 2006.

[508] K. van de Sande, T. Gevers, and C. Snoek. Evaluating color descriptors for object and scene recognition. *IEEE Transactions on Pattern Analysis and Machine Intelligence*, 32(9):1582–96, Sept. 2010.

[509] J. van de Weijer and C. Schmid. Coloring local feature extraction. In *European Conference on Computer Vision (ECCV)*, 2006.

[510] L. Van Gool, T. Moons, and D. Ungureanu. Affine / photometric invariants for planar intensity patterns. In *European Conference on Computer Vision (ECCV)*, 1996.

[511] A. Vasile and R. Marino. Pose-independent automatic target detection and recognition using 3D laser radar imagery. *Lincoln Laboratory Journal*, 15(1):61–78, 2005.

[512] M. V. Venkatesh, S. S. Cheung, and J. Zhao. Efficient object-based video inpainting. *Pattern Recognition Letters*, 30(2):168–79, 2009.

[513] V. Verma, R. Kumar, and S. Hsu. 3D building detection and modeling from aerial LIDAR data. In *IEEE Computer Society Conference on Computer Vision and Pattern Recognition (CVPR)*, 2006.

[514] L. Vincent and P. Soille. Watersheds in digital spaces: an efficient algorithm based on immersion simulations. *IEEE Transactions on Pattern Analysis and Machine Intelligence*, 13(6):583–98, June 1991.

[515] V. Vineet and P. Narayanan. CUDA cuts: Fast graph cuts on the GPU. In *CVPR Workshop on Visual Computer Vision on GPUs*, 2008.

[516] P. Viola and M. J. Jones. Robust real-time face detection. *International Journal of Computer Vision*, 57(2):137–54, May 2004.

[517] P. Vlahos. Composite photography utilizing sodium vapor illumination, 1963. US Patent 3,095,304.

[518] P. Vlahos. Electronic composite photography, 1971. US Patent 3,595,987.

[519] D. Vlasic, R. Adelsberger, G. Vannucci, J. Barnwell, M. Gross, W. Matusik, and J. Popović. Practical motion capture in everyday surroundings. In *ACM SIGGRAPH (ACM Transactions on Graphics)*, 2007.

[520] D. Vlasic, I. Baran, W. Matusik, and J. Popović. Articulated mesh animation from multi-view silhouettes. In *ACM SIGGRAPH (ACM Transactions on Graphics)*, 2008.

[521] D. Vlasic, P. Peers, I. Baran, P. Debevec, J. Popović, S. Rusinkiewicz, and W. Matusik. Dynamic shape capture using multi-view photometric stereo. In *ACM SIGGRAPH Asia (ACM Transactions on Graphics)*, 2009.

[522] G. Vogiatzis, C. Hernandez, P. Torr, and R. Cipolla. Multiview stereo via volumetric graph-cuts and occlusion robust photo-consistency. *IEEE Transactions on Pattern Analysis and Machine Intelligence*, 29(12):2241–6, Dec. 2007.

[523] D. Wagner, G. Reitmayr, A. Mulloni, T. Drummond, and D. Schmalstieg. Real-time detection and tracking for augmented reality on mobile phones. *IEEE Transactions on Visualization and Computer Graphics*, 16(3):355–68, May 2010.

[524] D. Wagner and D. Schmalstieg. ARToolKitPlus for pose tracking on mobile devices. In *Computer Vision Winter Workshop*, 2007.

[525] M. Wainwright, T. Jaakkola, and A. Willsky. MAP estimation via agreement on trees: message-passing and linear programming. *IEEE Transactions on Information Theory*, 51(11):3697–717, Nov. 2005.

[526] K. Waldron and J. Schmiedeler. Kinematics. In B. Siciliano and O. Khatib, editors, *Springer Handbook of Robotics*, pages 9–33. Springer, 2008.

[527] H. Wang, R. Raskar, and N. Ahuja. Seamless video editing. In *International Conference on Pattern Recognition (ICPR)*, 2004.

[528] J. Wang and E. Adelson. Representing moving images with layers. *IEEE Transactions on Image Processing*, 3(5):625–38, Sept. 1994.

[529] J. Wang, M. Agrawala, and M. Cohen. Soft scissors: an interactive tool for realtime high quality matting. In *ACM SIGGRAPH (ACM Transactions on Graphics)*, 2007.

[530] J. Wang, P. Bhat, R. Colburn, M. Agrawala, and M. Cohen. Interactive video cutout. In *ACM SIGGRAPH (ACM Transactions on Graphics)*, 2005.

[531] J. Wang and M. Cohen. An iterative optimization approach for unified image segmentation and matting. In *IEEE International Conference on Computer Vision (ICCV)*, 2005.

[532] J. Wang and M. Cohen. Optimized color sampling for robust matting. In *IEEE Computer Society Conference on Computer Vision and Pattern Recognition (CVPR)*, 2007.

[533] J. Wang and M. Cohen. Simultaneous matting and compositing. In *IEEE Computer Society Conference on Computer Vision and Pattern Recognition (CVPR)*, 2007.

[534] Y.-S. Wang, H. Fu, O. Sorkine, T.-Y. Lee, and H.-P. Seidel. Motion-aware temporal coherence for video resizing. In *ACM SIGGRAPH Asia (ACM Transactions on Graphics)*, 2009.

[535] Y.-S. Wang, H.-C. Lin, O. Sorkine, and T.-Y. Lee. Motion-based video retargeting with optimized crop-and-warp. In *ACM SIGGRAPH (ACM Transactions on Graphics)*, 2010.

[536] Y.-S. Wang, C.-L. Tai, O. Sorkine, and T.-Y. Lee. Optimized scale-and-stretch for image resizing. In *ACM SIGGRAPH Asia (ACM Transactions on Graphics)*, 2008.

[537] Z.-F. Wang and Z.-G. Zheng. A region based stereo matching algorithm using cooperative optimization. In *IEEE Computer Society Conference on Computer Vision and Pattern Recognition (CVPR)*, 2008.

[538] A. Wedel, T. Pock, C. Zach, H. Bischof, and D. Cremers. An improved algorithm for TV-L_1 optical flow. In *Statistical and Geometrical Approaches to Visual Motion Analysis*, 2009.

[539] L.-Y. Wei and M. Levoy. Fast texture synthesis using tree-structured vector quantization. In *ACM SIGGRAPH (ACM Transactions on Graphics)*, 2000.

[540] T. Weise, B. Leibe, and L. Van Gool. Fast 3D scanning with automatic motion compensation. In *IEEE Computer Society Conference on Computer Vision and Pattern Recognition (CVPR)*, 2007.

[541] Y. Weiss. Smoothness in layers: Motion segmentation using nonparametric mixture estimation. In *IEEE Computer Society Conference on Computer Vision and Pattern Recognition (CVPR)*, 1997.

[542] G. Welch and E. Foxlin. Motion tracking: no silver bullet, but a respectable arsenal. *IEEE Computer Graphics and Applications*, 22(6):24–38, Nov. 2002.

[543] W. Wells III, P. Viola, H. Atsumi, S. Nakajima, and R. Kikinis. Multi-modal volume registration by maximization of mutual information. *Medical Image Analysis*, 1(1):35–51, Mar. 1996.

[544] Y. Wexler, A. Fitzgibbon, and A. Zisserman. Bayesian estimation of layers from multiple images. In *European Conference on Computer Vision (ECCV)*, 2002.

[545] Y. Wexler, A. Fitzgibbon, and A. Zisserman. Image-based environment matting. In *Eurographics Workshop on Rendering*, 2002.

[546] Y. Wexler, E. Shechtman, and M. Irani. Space-time completion of video. *IEEE Transactions on Pattern Analysis and Machine Intelligence*, 29(3):463–76, Mar. 2007.

[547] L. Williams. Performance-driven facial animation. In *ACM SIGGRAPH (ACM Transactions on Graphics)*, 1990.

[548] S. Winder and M. Brown. Learning local image descriptors. In *IEEE Computer Society Conference on Computer Vision and Pattern Recognition (CVPR)*, 2007.

[549] S. Winder, G. Hua, and M. Brown. Picking the best DAISY. In *IEEE Computer Society Conference on Computer Vision and Pattern Recognition (CVPR)*, 2009.

[550] A. Witkin and Z. Popović. Motion warping. In *ACM SIGGRAPH (ACM Transactions on Graphics)*, 1995.

[551] G. Wolberg. Image morphing: a survey. *The Visual Computer*, 14(8):360–72, Dec. 1998.

[552] L. Wolf, M. Guttmann, and D. Cohen-Or. Non-homogeneous content-driven video-retargeting. In *IEEE International Conference on Computer Vision (ICCV)*, 2007.

[553] S. Wright. *Digital Compositing for Film and Video*. Focal Press, 3rd edition, 2010.

[554] H. Wu, R. Chellappa, A. Sankaranarayanan, and S. Zhou. Robust visual tracking using the time-reversibility constraint. In *IEEE International Conference on Computer Vision (ICCV)*, 2007.

[555] T. Wu, C. Tang, M. Brown, and H. Shum. Natural shadow matting. *ACM Transactions on Graphics*, 26(2), June 2007.

[556] J. Xiao, H. Cheng, H. Sawhney, C. Rao, and M. Isnardi. Bilateral filtering-based optical flow estimation with occlusion detection. In *European Conference on Computer Vision (ECCV)*, 2006.

[557] L. Xu and J. Jia. Stereo matching: An outlier confidence approach. In *European Conference on Computer Vision (ECCV)*, 2008.

[558] L. Xu, J. Jia, and Y. Matsushita. Motion detail preserving optical flow estimation. In *IEEE Computer Society Conference on Computer Vision and Pattern Recognition (CVPR)*, 2010.

[559] K. Yamane and Y. Nakamura. Natural motion animation through constraining and deconstraining at will. *IEEE Transactions on Visualization and Computer Graphics*, 9(3):352–60, July 2003.

[560] J. Yan and M. Pollefeys. A factorization-based approach for articulated nonrigid shape, motion and kinematic chain recovery from video. *IEEE Transactions on Pattern Analysis and Machine Intelligence*, 30(5):865–77, May 2008.

[561] G. Yang, J. Becker, and C. Stewart. Estimating the location of a camera with respect to a 3D model. In *International Conference on 3-D Digital Imaging and Modeling (3DIM)*, 2007.

[562] G. Yang, C. Stewart, M. Sofka, and C.-L. Tsai. Registration of challenging image pairs: Initialization, estimation, and decision. *IEEE Transactions on Pattern Analysis and Machine Intelligence*, 29(11):1973–89, Nov. 2007.

[563] Q. Yang, L. Wang, R. Yang, H. Stewenius, and D. Nister. Stereo matching with color-weighted correlation, hierarchical belief propagation, and occlusion handling. *IEEE Transactions on Pattern Analysis and Machine Intelligence*, 31(3):492–504, Mar. 2009.

[564] Q. Yang, R. Yang, J. Davis, and D. Nister. Spatial-depth super resolution for range images. In *IEEE Computer Society Conference on Computer Vision and Pattern Recognition (CVPR)*, 2007.

[565] L. Yatziv, A. Bartesaghi, and G. Sapiro. O(N) implementation of the fast marching algorithm. *Journal of Computational Physics*, 212(2):393–9, Mar. 2006.

[566] J. Yedidia, W. Freeman, and Y. Weiss. Understanding belief propagation and its generalizations. In G. Lakemeyer and B. Nebel, editors, *Exploring Artificial Intelligence in the New Millennium*, pages 239–70. Elsevier, 2003.

[567] R. Zabih and J. Woodfill. Non-parametric local transforms for computing visual correspondence. In *European Conference on Computer Vision (ECCV)*, 1994.

[568] L. Zhang, B. Curless, and S. Seitz. Rapid shape acquisition using color structured light and multi-pass dynamic programming. In *International Symposium on 3D Data Processing Visualization and Transmission (3DPVT)*, 2002.

[569] L. Zhang, B. Curless, and S. Seitz. Spacetime stereo: shape recovery for dynamic scenes. In *IEEE Computer Society Conference on Computer Vision and Pattern Recognition (CVPR)*, 2003.

[570] L. Zhang, N. Snavely, B. Curless, and S. M. Seitz. Spacetime faces: high resolution capture for modeling and animation. In *ACM SIGGRAPH (ACM Transactions on Graphics)*, 2004.

[571] S. Zhang and P. S. Huang. High-resolution, real-time three-dimensional shape measurement. *Optical Engineering*, 45(12):123601–1:8, Dec. 2006.

[572] S. Zhang and S.-T. Yau. High-speed three-dimensional shape measurement system using a modified two-plus-one phase-shifting algorithm. *Optical Engineering*, 46(11):113603:1–6, Nov. 2007.

[573] Z. Zhang. Iterative point matching for registration of free-form curves and surfaces. *International Journal of Computer Vision*, 13(2):119–52, Oct. 1994.

[574] Z. Zhang. On the epipolar geometry between two images with lens distortion. In *International Conference on Pattern Recognition (ICPR)*, 1996.

[575] Z. Zhang. A flexible new technique for camera calibration. Technical Report MSR-TR-98-71, Microsoft Research, 1998.

[576] Z. Zhang, R. Deriche, O. Faugeras, and Q.-T. Luong. A robust technique for matching two uncalibrated images through the recovery of the unknown epipolar geometry. *Artificial Intelligence*, 78(1-2):87–119, Oct. 1995.

[577] J. Zhao and N. I. Badler. Inverse kinematics positioning using nonlinear programming for highly articulated figures. *ACM Transactions on Graphics*, 13(4):313–36, Oct. 1994.

[578] W. Zhao, D. Nister, and S. Hsu. Alignment of continuous video onto 3D point clouds. *IEEE Transactions on Pattern Analysis and Machine Intelligence*, 27(8):1305–18, Aug. 2005.

[579] Y. Zheng and C. Kambhamettu. Learning based digital matting. In *IEEE International Conference on Computer Vision (ICCV)*, 2009.

[580] J. Zhu, M. Liao, R. Yang, and Z. Pan. Joint depth and alpha matte optimization via fusion of stereo and time-of-flight sensor. In *IEEE Computer Society Conference on Computer Vision and Pattern Recognition (CVPR)*, 2009.

[581] C. L. Zitnick, S. B. Kang, M. Uyttendaele, S. Winder, and R. Szeliski. High-quality video view interpolation using a layered representation. In *ACM SIGGRAPH (ACM Transactions on Graphics)*, 2004.

[582] D. Zongker, D. Werner, B. Curless, and D. Salesin. Environment matting and compositing. In *ACM SIGGRAPH (ACM Transactions on Graphics)*, 1999.

[583] V. B. Zordan, A. Majkowska, B. Chiu, and M. Fast. Dynamic response for motion capture animation. In *ACM SIGGRAPH (ACM Transactions on Graphics)*, 2005.

[584] V. B. Zordan and N. C. Van Der Horst. Mapping optical motion capture data to skeletal motion using a physical model. In *ACM SIGGRAPH/Eurographics Symposium on Computer Animation*, 2003.

Index